# ETHICS
# IN THE
# WORLD OF
# BUSINESS

# PHILOSOPHY AND SOCIETY

*General Editor:* Marshall Cohen

# ETHICS
# IN THE
# WORLD OF
# BUSINESS

David Braybrooke

ROWMAN & ALLANHELD
Totowa, N.J.

In some of the legal cases reported in this book—where the cases have not yet become prominently discussed—names have been changed to spare people and firms unnecessary embarrassment. Occasionally, individual names have been changed elsewhere for the same reason. In all cases the names supplied are fictitious; they are, in fact, except for "Edmonton Pierce-Arrow & Hupmobile Ltd.," all taken from the works of Dickens. Any coincidence with the names of real people or real firms is entirely unintended.

Copyright © 1983 by Rowman & Allanheld

First published in the United States 1983 by
Rowman & Allanheld,
81 Adams Drive, Totowa, New Jersey 07512.

**Library of Congress Cataloging in Publication Data**

Braybrooke, David.
  Ethics in the world of business.

  (Philosophy and society)
  Bibliography: p.
  Includes index.
  1. Business ethics. I. Title. II. Series.
HF5387.B72  1983    174'.4    82-18547
ISBN 0-8476-7069-4
ISBN 0-8476-7107-0 (pbk.)

Printed in the United States of America

*To*
*Margaret Eva Odell*
*who, besides helping me put this book together,*
*helped me come back to it again and again*

# Preface:
# Guide to Table of Contents

This book is concerned with ethics and not just "business ethics," some special department of ethics in which a minimal code is laid down for businessmen and women. Business is a world—a context, an ordered whole—in which much the same ethical issues come up as in other contexts. People strive to behave decently in it. Yet they frequently deceive each other, and are as frequently deceived; they practice oppression in various forms, or are subjected to it; they miss opportunities for increasing the happiness of many, and sometimes carry on in ways bound to worsen other people's lives (perhaps even their own). Such issues invite moral judgments parallel to judgments called for in other contexts, and founded on the same general moral principles. Moreover, those judgments and principles touch us all. We may not all be "in business"; we may be otherwise employed; but, inevitably, we all play parts in the world of business, as consumers and citizens if not as entrepreneurs or employees. Moreover, we can play those parts scrupulously or unscrupulously. Ethics has questions to raise, not just about how businesses deal with us, but also about how we deal with business, and how we deal with each other in business connections.

Sometimes we deal with each other in the absence of firms; and although firms are now so prominent a feature of the world of business as to seem inescapable, in fact a good deal of business is carried on without them. We trade among ourselves or, individually, deal with individual plumbers and painters. One way of dividing the contents of this book would be into materials on business without firms, on the one hand, and materials on business with firms present, on the other. If the contents had been divided in this way, a very short first part on business without firms (Chapter 1 in the Contents) would have preceded a very long part on ethics in a world of firms (the present Parts II, III, IV, V and VI taken together, embracing

Chapters 3 through Chapter 20), with the philosophical readings in Chapter 2 serving as an intermediate second part, and a few small parts left over at the end. This division would have struck some people as bizarre. Yet the disproportionately large space accorded by it to business with firms would have reflected the disproportionate importance and frequency of issues involving firms.

In the end, I have been brought to rely mainly on another principle of division, and to concede more to people's expectations of a division into equal parts. Part I is concerned with the actions of natural persons, whether in their dealings with each other or in their dealings with firms. The next five more or less equal parts—Parts II through VI—deal with various aspects of *the actions of firms.* The repetition of that phrase in one part title after another helps to make manifest the disproportionate importance of issues involving firms. The division into several parts meets the demand for symmetry. At the same time it makes a significant beginning at making visible the variety of aspects under which the actions of firms invite moral judgment.

How firms deal with consumers is distinguished from how they deal with employees; how they deal with stockholders and other firms, from the cumulative impact of their activities; and all of these things, from how they deal with governments. The chapter headings falling in each of these five parts and the lists of topics taken up in each chapter have further lessons to teach about the variety of issues, as does the variety of materials and sources (barely visible in the Contents, but immediately apparent to anyone who leafs through the book). Nor does the variety end there. To be added is the variety taken up in other parts of the book. Even then one can hardly think that the whole range of issues has been represented.

Is the variety that is represented already too luxuriant to be managed? I doubt whether any comprehensive scheme of moral principles exists that will resolve all the issues tidily. Certainly I do not pretend to supply such a scheme. I do supply a simple basis for coping with the issues that I raise, a framework lightly constructed from a few familiar moral notions; proximately, deception, oppression (more correctly, abuses of power), and adverse cumulative effects; ultimately (but not so far away even so), happiness and public agreement, with justice figuring at both the proximate and the ultimate levels, and thus serving to link them. In accordance with what I call "the triplet principle"—namely, that on every moral issue we can find clear cases of doing wrong and clear cases of doing what is at least all right, as well as cases hard to determine one way or the other—the framework suffices to produce firm moral judgments in many cases and, besides, to make some headway in the hard cases with sorting out unobjectionable ingredients from objectionable ones, which can be eliminated or offset.

The notions involved in this framework, and the connections between them, are brought forth and explained bit by bit, characteristically after cases that I have found in class to demand their introduction, rather than beforehand, without specific cases having already been presented to the reader. Anyone reading the book who wishes to obtain beforehand—before considering any cases at all, or part way into the book, before moving on to further cases—a complete view of the framework can do so by reading the passages designated "Comment" (sometimes, "Introductory Comment") and Chapter 22 in Part VIII. (The titles and designations of these passages are underscored in the Contents.)

Clearly, a good deal of ethics, as well as the greater part of ethical theory (reasoning about the foundations of ethics), is left out of the framework. Although I sketch the place of the framework in the perspective of ethical theory at the end of the book, I do not offer there or anywhere else a systematic account of utilitarianism, or contract theory, or any other attempt to deal systematically with the problems of ethical theory. I hope, in fact, the framework is something that the adherents of different ethical systems can all accept as part of the core of ethics that they each try in their different ways to accommodate. It could not be this if it tried to settle any theoretical issues.

With the help of this framework, applied to the variety of materials and issues to be found in this book, the reader can gain practice asking moral questions—relevant and important questions—about actions in business, and can gain practice, too, finding answers to those questions. With such practice, long enough continued, people will become habituated to asking questions about actions now too often taken for granted: "Is this deception?" "Is it oppression?" "Is it one more contribution to a cumulative effect adverse to happiness?" At the same time, people will become accustomed to good and evil in business taking many different forms, some of them very subtle. Yet they will have grounds, and will persist in having grounds, for expecting that in many instances determinate guidance about how to act better, rather than worse, can be found in simple and straightforward terms.

# Contents

*The passages in which my own account of basic ethical notions is given are designated by underscoring. The titles of various pedagogical devices are bracketed.

PART EIGHT    THE ISSUES REVIEWED AND A LOOK AT LARGER ISSUES

# ETHICS
# IN THE
# WORLD OF
# BUSINESS

# PART ONE
## *The Actions of Natural Persons*

# CHAPTER 1

# *Business Without Firms*

*Introductory Comment:*

## HONEST DEALING OR SHARP PRACTICE

Nowadays in the world of business, most of the actions and practices that give rise to ethical issues involve firms. People make most of their purchases not from other people, taking them one by one, or even from individual shopkeepers, but from stores large enough, or service organizations large enough, to be reckoned firms, and these in their turn are supplied by firms often even larger. People rarely find themselves employed by single persons. They find themselves employed by firms, and we expect firms to be incorporated businesses of substantial size. Formerly, it was quite the other way around: incorporated businesses were rare and firms were for the most part quite small, carried on by single proprietors or by a few owners in partnership.

Even now, however, people do business with each other, in the absence of firms, often enough for us all to be familiar with such business. Even now, without reference to firms, they hire each other to perform various services: gardening; a bit of carpentry around the house; carting away some rubbish. The issues about buying and selling (exchange) and about the employment relationship that arise even when firms are not in the picture are therefore still current issues.

They are issues in which, when things go wrong, deception or abuses of power characteristically figure. One person deceives another or exercises power over another in an objectionable way. Such actions by natural persons are possibilities in each of the six cases that follow, among them one case on the employment relationship. Yet they are not merely cases in which natural persons rather than legal persons—firms—are alone involved. They are, unlike the case from the past that follows in the selection from Dickens, so much a part of familiar everyday life that you yourself have surely been involved in cases like one or another of them, perhaps in cases like each of them. So the right or the wrong that is done is right or wrong that you may have done or thought of doing, or maybe have had done you.

## FOUR CASES IN WHICH YOU MIGHT BE INVOLVED

SELLING YOUR CAR

*[There's nothing wrong with selling a car (if it's your own car, or somebody has authorized you to sell it). Something may go wrong, however, with the way you go about selling it.]*

*First time.* You are trying to sell your car to raise money for pressing university expenses. A couple of weeks ago, an automobile mechanic whom you trust told you that the engine was going to break down any time and would then have to be replaced at a minimum cost of $700 including labor. For the time being, however, it runs quite well, and it's exceptionally clean inside and out. After a turn around the block, a man offers you $1,000, which he points out is a couple of hundred more than the going price for a 1975 Dynamic Motors Scatback. You accept the offer without mentioning the problem with the engine.

*Second time.* The buyer's check bounces and you get the Scatback back. You now have a temporary job after class and to get to and fro you decide to keep the car and drive it for awhile. Although the engine keeps on running, you notice that the car has developed an unsettling and apparently incurable habit of losing its left rear wheel on right turns. Not very often, mind you—just once in, say, a hundred times. (My father once had a car like that.) After weeks during which no prospective buyers turned up, another man appears and shows some interest. You accompany him on a test drive and contrive to have him make left turns only. He seems pleased and offers you $800 (by certified check). You're very strapped, in spite of your job. Do you tell him about the wheel?

## *Note on Preparing Agendas*

In using these materials I have found it an effective technique to meet, before any given assignment is discussed in class, with a couple of students appointed to think up questions about the material assigned. Pair by pair, the students have invariably taken this task very seriously; together we have worked out the specific agendas for successive classes; and each discussion has begun with some students present who are committed to the agenda and who now put the questions to the other members of the class. I shall not supply such agendas for the cases, invented or not, that follow, or for the extracts from philosophical writings. To do so would impair the interest that readers—teachers and students—using this book in class might take in generating questions of their own. By exception, and as an example, I give the agenda that students and I worked out for a discussion held on "Selling Your Car":

1. Originally, you sold the car without mentioning the bad engine. Is there any special reason why you didn't consider moral questions then, instead of waiting, apparently, until the point about the wheel came up?
2. The buyer may have problems with the engine before he has problems with the wheel anyway. Would there be no objection to your not telling him about the wheel if you told him about the engine?
3. Is there any way in which the bad check cancels out the omission on your part to mention the bad engine?
4. Should it be the sole responsibility of the buyer to find out if there is anything wrong with the car before he buys?

TICKET-SCALPING

*[Here is a case that comes with a bad name. Is the bad name entirely warranted?]*

*First time.* Months ago, thinking you'd treat your favorite cousin, just your own age and very sexy, coming for an annual visit, you bought tickets for *Plaza Suite* at the Neptune Theater. It turns out that the cousin can't come, and meanwhile you've got interested in someone else, who prefers bowling. On the evening of the performance, you go to turn in your tickets, hoping for a refund. As you approach the box office, you see people being turned away. One of them walks by you to rejoin his companion and tells her with chagrin, "I might have known—it's a smash hit. Sold out for the rest of the week. I know you've been counting on it. So have I! And tonight's my last night in town for a while. I'd give $20 apiece for tickets, but where could I get them?" You step up and offer to sell your tickets at the price mentioned. You paid $6 each for them, and you need a pair of bowling shoes.

*Second time.* You speculate that a rerun of *Arms and the Man* is going to be sold out, too. Months ahead of a certain performance, you buy half a dozen tickets at the box-office price, $6. When the time comes, you sell them all, at $22 each, to people who have turned up at the box office hoping that some other people would not be using tickets bought earlier.

MORE BARGAINING POWER

*[Ticket-scalping is an attractive venture for the person with tickets, only if she cares significantly less to have the tickets than the money, and other people care significantly less to have the money than the tickets. She has, in respect at least to holdings of money, greater bargaining power. Yet eager as the people buying the tickets may be to get them, it is hardly vital to them that they do so; and thus the bargaining power that the scalper has over them is limited: it goes no further than to make inroads into the discretionary part of their budgets. What would you make of someone's having and exerting greater bargaining power? If the power was exerted upon you, would you protest, and what sorts of ideas would you appeal to if you did?]*

The fall term at the university is about to begin. You were not lucky enough to get a room in a university residence; and you were unable to get to town earlier to look for a room off-campus. There just don't seem to be any rooms off-campus—you've looked for three days and found absolutely nothing. Today you run across a classmate who has been living with his family a few blocks from the university, but who has nevertheless rented a room for the year on the other side of the campus. He has, of course, been attracted by the notion of living more independently. Yet it turns out that he doesn't feel much pressure to move out from under the family roof. He gets along quite well with his family; he's used to the comforts that he enjoys with them; he has convenient access to his father's car. You, on the other hand, will have to drop out of the university if you can't find a place to live, soon. Already, staying at a motel has used up a horrifyingly large sum. Talking things over with you, your classmate sizes up the situation. Then he offers to move back with his family and sublet to you the room that he found—looking about months earlier, when few students were about. He asks, however, that you pay him a one-time premium of $300 over the regular rent. You can just manage the premium if you give up entertainment entirely and observe five meatless days every week.

THE HANDYMAN'S PROCRASTINATION

*[You may have been inclined to protest in the last case, but perhaps protesting was easy—your own interest and notions about ethics marched hand in hand. But suppose you are on the receiving end of the protests: What reasons do you have, if any, for taking them into account?]*

You have worked through the summer as a handyman and are continuing to do a few odd jobs in the fall while taking classes. A man named Wrayburn (some sort of lawyer or government official, you're not sure what, but quite prosperous, judging from the house that he lives in) hired you in August to do a number of jobs—repair a fence; insert a piece of wood to cover a gap between his new brick steps and the clapboard running under his front door; replace a pane in one of the basement windows; fix the hinges on the basement windows, which slope out from the house; cover the gap between those windows and their frames with waterproof stripping. You and he agree on a sum of $200 for the whole set of jobs. By the end of August, you have done all of them except the last: on one window the waterproof stripping split as you tacked it down, and you haven't put any stripping on the other window at all. You'll have to make a special visit to the lumberyard to get more (and better) stripping, which won't be convenient just now, since you have jobs to do elsewhere. Yet you need the $200 to pay the first installment of your tuition. You tell Mr. Wrayburn this and point out that you're all but finished. You say that it will take you ten or fifteen minutes to put down the waterproof stripping once you've had a chance to get materials. He gives you a check for $200 and you use it with other funds to pay the installment of tuition. Some weeks pass by. You're busy, and you don't get around to the waterproof stripping. More weeks pass; it's the end of October and still the job hasn't been done. Wrayburn phones and reminds you pleasantly about it; he mentions that he is concerned to have the stripping put down before the snow comes. You say, "No problem, Gene; I'll do it this weekend." But something comes up—a bigger job at the other end of the city. Wrayburn calls again at the end of November, in the evening. It has been raining heavily during the previous couple of weeks. He points out, however, that the prediction for the next day, Saturday, is for fair weather. "Won't you please do it tomorrow," he asks, "while you have a good chance? You know I want to be sure of having the stripping in place before it begins snowing." You think privately that this fellow is becoming somewhat of a bore, but you assure him again, "No problem." Actually you have a job out of town and so Saturday passes without your getting to Wrayburn's waterproof stripping. It begins raining again. Then the weather turns colder and snows. Two weeks into December, you hear from Wrayburn again; this time he phones you at 7:30 Saturday morning, waking you up. He says, "Look, the stripping still hasn't been done. The snow has started, but the first lot has melted away. Today will be dry, a good day to work. Can't you fit in half an hour sometime today and get the job done?" You think he's being pretty insistent about a pretty small thing, but you say, "No problem, Gene." He says, "I've heard that before. Can I count on you today?" You say, "No problem." Well, what does the man think he's doing, putting you under so much pressure? You have a number of other things to do, and the stripping doesn't turn out to be one of them.

*Comment:*

## MASTER AND SERVANTS

In the past, people were usually employed by single persons rather than by large firms, and might well be employed for their whole working lives by the same persons (or by their heirs)—landowners, or the individual capitalists that Marx continually had in view in his mid-19th-century picture of the market economy. So employed, people were persistently dependent on the persons who employed them, and were bound to be deferential toward them. In traditional language—the language in which the common law treated the relationship—they were servants, who had those masters.

The inequality of power, and the abuses of unequal power, to be found in the relationship have not disappeared from the modern world. Even single persons now typically go through the form of incorporating their businesses. In substance, however, there are still quite a number of individual capitalists offering employment, so the issues associated with the employment relationship when it holds between persons, in the absence of firms, are still substantially alive. Moreover, as we shall see, there are parallels to the inequality and the abuses when the employer in the relationship is a sizeable firm—a large enterprise owned by many stockholders and run as a sort of private bureaucracy not by the owners, but by professionalized managers.

It seems sensible, however, to represent the employment relationship, when the employers in question are not firms of such sorts, as something anachronistic to a degree, by a selection that is clearly anachronistic. The selection I have chosen is the greater part of a chapter from *Dombey and Son*, by Dickens. It is, I think, reasonably balanced: the power that reposes in Mr. Dombey fosters servility in his employees and induces vanity in him, and it obviously can be used with great indifference to the impact that it makes on the lives of others. On the other hand, as it happens, the power is not used with anything like savage oppression; and in one connection it is shown used with some kindness, or at least with mercy.

## DICKENS, "MR. DOMBEY AND HIS EMPLOYEES"*

Mr. Dombey's offices were in a court where there was an old-established stall of choice fruit at the corner: where perambulating merchants, of both

*Charles Dickens, *Dombey and Son*, chapter 13: "Shipping Intelligence and Office Business" (1846–48).

sexes, offered for sale at any time between the hours of ten and five, slippers, pocket-books, sponges, dogs' collars, and Windsor soap, . . .

When Mr. Dombey appeared, the dealers in those wares fell off respectfully. The principal slipper and dogs' collar man—who considered himself a public character, and whose portrait was screwed on to an artist's door in Cheapside—threw up his forefinger to the brim of his hat as Mr. Dombey went by. The ticket-porter, if he were not absent on a job, always ran officiously before to open Mr. Dombey's office door as wide as possible, and hold it open, with his hat off, while he entered.

The clerks within were not a whit behind-hand in their demonstrations of respect. A solemn hush prevailed, as Mr. Dombey passed through the outer office. The wit of the Counting-House became in a moment as mute, as the row of leathern fire-buckets hanging up behind him. Such vapid and flat daylight as filtered through the ground-glass windows and skylights, leaving a black sediment upon the panes, showed the books and papers, and the figures bending over them, enveloped in a studious gloom, and as much abstracted in appearance, from the world without, as if they were assembled at the bottom of the sea; while a mouldy little strong room in the obscure perspective, where a shady lamp was always burning, might have represented the cavern of some ocean-monster, looking on with a red eye at these mysteries of the deep.

When Perch the messenger, whose place was on a little bracket, like a timepiece, saw Mr. Dombey come in—or rather when he felt that he was coming, for he had usually an instinctive sense of his approach—he hurried into Mr. Dombey's room, stirred the fire, quarried fresh coals from the bowels of the coal-box, hung the newspaper to air upon the fender, put the chair ready, and the screen in its place, and was round upon his heel on the instant of Mr. Dombey's entrance, to take his great-coat and hat, and hang them up. Then Perch took the newspaper, and gave it a turn or two in his hands before the fire, and laid it, deferentially, at Mr. Dombey's elbow. And so little objection had Perch to doing deferential in the last degree, that if he might have laid himself at Mr. Dombey's feet, or might have called him by some such title as used to be bestowed upon the Caliph Haroun Alraschid, he would have been all the better pleased.

As this honour would have been an innovation and an experiment, Perch was fain to content himself by expressing as well as he could, in his manner, You are the light of my Eyes. You are the Breath of my Soul. You are the commander of the Faithful Perch! With this imperfect happiness to cheer him, he would shut the door softly, walk away on tiptoe, and leave his great chief to be stared at, through a dome-shaped window in the leads, by ugly chimney-pots and backs of houses, and especially by the bold window of a hair-cutting saloon on a first floor, where a waxen effigy, bald as a Mussulman in the morning, and covered after eleven o'clock in the day, with luxuriant hair and whiskers in the latest Christian fashion, showed him the wrong side of its head for ever.

Between Mr. Dombey and the common world, as it was accessible through the medium of the outer office—to which Mr. Dombey's presence in his own room may be said to have struck like damp, or cold air—there were two degrees of descent. Mr. Carker in his own office was the first step; Mr. Morfin, in *his* own office, was the second. Each of these gentlemen occupied a little chamber like a bath-room, opening from the passage outside Mr. Dombey's door. Mr. Carker, as Grand Vizier, inhabited the room that was nearest to the Sultan. Mr. Morfin, as an officer of inferior state, inhabited the room that was nearest to the clerks . . .

Mr. Carker was a gentleman thirty-eight or forty years old, of a florid complexion, and with two unbroken rows of glistening teeth, whose regularity and whiteness were quite distressing. It was impossible to escape the observation of them, for he showed them whenever he spoke; and bore so wide a smile upon his countenance (a smile, however, very rarely, indeed, extending beyond his mouth), that there was something in it like the snarl of a cat. He affected a stiff white cravat, after the example of his principal, and was always closely buttoned up and tightly dressed. His manner towards Mr. Dombey was deeply conceived and perfectly expressed. He was familiar with him, in the very extremity of his sense of the distance between them. 'Mr. Dombey, to a man in your position from a man in mine, there is no show of subservience compatible with the transaction of business between us, that I should think sufficient. I frankly tell you, Sir, I give it up altogether. I feel that I could not satisfy my own mind; and Heaven knows, Mr. Dombey, you can afford to dispense with the endeavour.' If he had carried these words about with him, printed on a placard, and had constantly offered it to Mr. Dombey's perusal on the breast of his coat, he could not have been more explicit than he was.

This was Carker the Manager. Mr. Carker the Junior, Walter's friend, was his brother; two or three years older than he, but widely removed in station. The younger brother's post was on the top of the official ladder; the elder brother's at the bottom. The elder brother never gained a stave, or raised his foot to mount one. Young men passed above his head, and rose and rose; but he was always at the bottom. He was quite resigned to occupy that low condition: never complained of it: and certainly never hoped to escape from it.

'How do you do this morning?' said Mr. Carker the Manager, entering Mr. Dombey's room soon after his arrival one day: with a bundle of papers in his hand.

'How do you do, Carker?' said Mr. Dombey, rising from his chair, and standing with his back to the fire. 'Have you anything there for me?'

'I don't know that I need trouble you,' returned Carker, turning over the papers in his hand. 'You have a committee to-day at three, you know.'

'And one at three, three-quarters,' added Mr. Dombey.

'Catch you forgetting anything!' exclaimed Carker, still turning over his papers. 'If Mr. Paul inherits your money, he'll be a troublesome customer in the house. One of you is enough.'

'You have an accurate memory of your own,' said Mr. Dombey.

'Oh! *I!*' returned the manager. 'It's the only capital of a man like *me.*'

Mr. Dombey did not look less pompous or at all displeased, as he stood leaning against the chimneypiece, surveying his (of course unconscious) clerk, from head to foot. The stiffness and nicety of Mr. Carker's dress, and a certain arrogance of manner, either natural to him or imitated from a pattern not far off, gave great additional effect to his humility. He seemed a man who would contend against the power that vanquished him, if he could, but who was utterly borne down by the greatness and superiority of Mr. Dombey.

'Is Morfin here?' asked Mr. Dombey after a short pause, during which Mr. Carker had been fluttering his papers, and muttering little abstracts of their contents to himself.

'Morfin's here,' he answered, looking up with his widest and most sudden smile; 'humming musical recollections—of his last night's quartette party, I suppose—through the walls between us and driving me half mad. I wish he'd make a bonfire of his violoncello, and burn his music-books in it.'

'You respect nobody, Carker, I think,' said Mr. Dombey.

'No?' inquired Carker, with another wide and most feline show of his teeth. 'Well! Not many people, I believe. I wouldn't answer perhaps,' he murmured, as if he were only thinking it, 'for more than one.'

A dangerous quality, if real; and a not less dangerous one, if feigned. But Mr. Dombey hardly seemed to think so, as he still stood with his back to the fire, drawn up to his full height, and looking at his head-clerk with a dignified composure, in which there seemed to lurk a stronger latent sense of power than usual.

'Talking of Morfin,' resumed Mr. Carker, taking out one paper from the rest, 'he reports a junior dead in the agency at Barbados, and proposes to reserve a passage in the Son and Heir—she'll sail in a month or so—for the successor. You don't care who goes, I suppose? We have nobody of that sort here.'

Mr. Dombey shook his head with supreme indifference.

'It's no very precious appointment,' observed Mr. Carker, taking up a pen, with which to endorse a memorandum on the back of the paper. 'I hope he may bestow it on some orphan nephew of a musical friend. It may perhaps stop *his* fiddle-playing, if he has a gift that way. Who's that? Come in!"

'I beg your pardon, Mr. Carker. I didn't know you were here, Sir,' answered Walter, appearing with some letters in his hand, unopened, and newly arrived. 'Mr. Carker the Junior, Sir—'

At the mention of this name, Mr. Carker the Manager was, or affected to be, touched to the quick with shame and humiliation. He cast his eyes full on Mr. Dombey with an altered and apologetic look, abased them on the ground, and remained for a moment without speaking.

'I thought, Sir,' he said suddenly and angrily, turning to Walter, 'that you had been before requested not to drag Mr. Carker the Junior into your conversation.'

'I beg your pardon,' returned Walter. 'I was only going to say that Mr.

Carker the Junior had told me he believed you were gone out, or I should not have knocked at the door when you were engaged with Mr. Dombey. These are letters for Mr. Dombey, Sir.'

'Very well, Sir,' returned Mr. Carker the Manager, plucking them sharply from his hand. 'Go about your business.'

But in taking them with so little ceremony, Mr. Carker dropped one on the floor, and did not see what he had done; neither did Mr. Dombey observe the letter lying near his feet. Walter hesitated for a moment, thinking that one or other of them would notice it; but finding that neither did, he stopped, came back, picked it up, and laid it himself on Mr. Dombey's desk. . . . Mr. Dombey, having his attention silently called to this letter [addressed in his daughter's handwriting] by Walter, started, and looked fiercely at him, as if he believed that he had purposely selected it from all the rest.

'You can leave the room, Sir!' said Mr. Dombey, haughtily.

He crushed the letter in his hand; and having watched Walter out at the door, put it in his pocket without breaking the seal.

'You want somebody to send to the West Indies, you were saying,' observed Mr. Dombey, hurriedly.

'Yes,' replied Carker.

'Send young Gay.'

'Good, very good indeed. Nothing easier,' said Mr. Carker, without any show of surprise, and taking up the pen to re-endorse the letter, as coolly as he had done before. " 'Send young Gay.' "

'Call him back,' said Mr. Dombey.

Mr. Carker was quick to do so, and Walter was quick to return.

'Gay,' said Mr. Dombey, turning a little to look at him over his shoulder. 'Here is a—'

'An opening,' said Mr. Carker, with his mouth stretched to the utmost.

'In the West Indies. At Barbados. I am going to send you,' said Mr. Dombey, scorning to embellish the bare truth, 'to fill a junior situation in the counting-house at Barbados. Let your uncle know from me, that I have chosen you to go to the West Indies.'

Walter's breath was so completely taken away by his astonishment, that he could hardly find enough for the repetition of the words 'West Indies.'

'Somebody must go,' said Mr. Dombey, 'and you are young and healthy, and your uncle's circumstances are not good. Tell your uncle that you are appointed. You will not go yet. There will be an interval of a month—or two perhaps.'

'Shall I remain there, Sir?' inquired Walter.

'Will you remain there, Sir!' repeated Mr. Dombey, turning a little more round towards him. 'What do you mean? What does he mean, Carker?'

'Live there, Sir,' faltered Walter.

'Certainly,' returned Mr. Dombey.

Walter bowed.

'That's all,' said Mr. Dombey, resuming his letters. 'You will explain to him in good time about the usual outfit and so forth, Carker, of course. He needn't wait, Carker.'

'You needn't wait, Gay,' observed Mr. Carker: bare to the gums.

'Unless,' said Mr. Dombey, stopping in his reading without looking off the letter, and seeming to listen. 'Unless he has anything to say.'

'No, Sir,' returned Walter, agitated and confused, and almost stunned, as an infinite variety of pictures presented themselves to his mind; among which . . . his uncle bemoaning his loss in the little back parlour, held [a] prominent [place]. 'I hardly know—I—I am much obliged, Sir.'

'He needn't wait, Carker,' said Mr. Dombey.

And as Mr. Carker again echoed the words, and also collected his papers as if he were going away too, Walter felt that his lingering any longer would be an unpardonable intrusion—especially as he had nothing to say—and therefore walked out quite confounded. . . . [Emerging from Mr. Dombey's office, Mr. Carker the Manager calls into his own office Walter and Mr. Carker the Junior, and professes, in view of some disgrace attaching to the latter, to be greatly embarrassed to have Walter mention Mr. Carker the Junior's name in Mr. Dombey's presence. Mr. Carker the Manager prolongs his reproaches at painful length even before dismissing Walter.]

Walter passed out at the door, and was about to close it after him, when, hearing the voice of the brothers again, and also the mention of his own name, he stood irresolutely, with his hand upon the lock, and the door ajar, uncertain whether to return or go away. In this position he could not help overhearing what followed.

'Think of me more leniently, if you can, James,' said John Carker, 'when I tell you I have had—how could I help having, with my history, written here'—striking himself upon the breast—'my whole heart awakened by my observation of that boy, Walter Gay. I saw in him when he first came here, almost my other self.'

'Your other self!' repeated the Manager, disdainfully.

'Not as I am, but as I was when I first came here too; as sanguine, giddy, youthful, inexperienced; flushed with the same restless and adventurous fancies; and full of the same qualities, fraught with the same capacity of leading on to good or evil.'

'I hope not,' said his brother, with some hidden and sarcastic meaning in his tone.

'You strike me sharply; and your hand is steady, and your thrust is very deep,' returned the other, speaking (or so as Walter thought) as if some cruel weapon actually stabbed him as he spoke. 'I imagined all this when he was a boy. I believed it. It was truth to me. I saw him walking on the edge of an unseen gulf where so many others walk with equal gaiety, and from which—'

'The old excuse,' interrupted his brother, as he stirred the fire. 'So many. Go on. Say, so many fall.'

'From which ONE traveller fell,' returned the other, 'who set forward, on his way, a boy like him, and missed his footing more and more, and slipped a little and a little lower, and went on stumbling still, until he fell headlong and found himself below a shattered man. Think what I suffered, when I watched that boy.'

'You have only yourself to thank for it,' returned the brother.

'Only myself,' he assented with a sigh. 'I don't seek to divide the blame or shame.'

'You *have* divided the shame,' James Carker muttered through his teeth. And through so many and such close teeth, he could mutter well.

'Ah, James,' returned his brother, speaking for the first time in an accent of reproach, and seeming, by the sound of his voice, to have covered his face with his hands, 'I have been, since then, a useful foil to you. You have trodden on me freely in your climbing up. Don't spurn me with your heel!'

A silence ensued. After a time, Mr. Carker the Manager was heard rustling among his papers, as if he had resolved to bring the interview to a conclusion. At the same time his brother withdrew nearer to the door.

'That's all,' he said. 'I watched him with such trembling and such fear, as was some little punishment to me, until he passed the place where I first fell; and then, though I had been his father, I believe I never could have thanked God more devoutly. I didn't dare to warn him, and advise him; but if I had seen direct cause, I would have shown him my example. I was afraid to be seen speaking with him, lest it should be thought I did him harm, and tempted him to evil, and corrupted him: or lest I really should. There may be such contagion in me; I don't know. Piece out my history, in connexion with young Walter Gay, and what he has made me feel; and think of me more leniently, James, if you can.'

With these words he came out to where Walter was standing. He turned a little paler when he saw him there, and paler yet when Walter caught him by the hand, and said in a whisper:

'Mr. Carker, pray let me thank you! Let me say how much I feel for you! How sorry I am, to have been the unhappy cause of all this! How I almost look upon you now as my protector and guardian! How very, very much, I feel obliged to you and pity you!' said Walter, squeezing both his hands, and hardly knowing, in his agitation, what he did or said.

Mr. Morfin's room being close at hand and empty, and the door wide open, they moved thither by one accord: the passage being seldom free from some one passing to or fro. When they were there, and Walter saw in Mr. Carker's face some traces of the emotions within, he almost felt as if he had never seen the face before; it was so greatly changed.

'Walter,' he said, laying his hand on his shoulder. 'I am far removed from you, and may I ever be. Do you know what I am?'

'What you are!' appeared to hang on Walter's lips, as he regarded him attentively.

'It was begun,' said Carker, 'before my twenty-first birthday—led up to, long before, but not begun till near that time. I had robbed them when I came of age. I robbed them afterwards. Before my twenty-second birthday, it was all found out; and then, Walter, from all men's society, I died.'

Again his last few words hung trembling upon Walter's lips, but he could neither utter them, nor any of his own.

'The House was very good to me. May Heaven reward the old man for his forbearance! This one, too, his son, who was then newly in the firm, where I had held great trust! I was called into that room which is now his—I have never entered it since—and came out, what you know me. For many years I sat in my present seat, alone as now, but then a known and recognised example to the rest. They were all merciful to me, and I lived. Time has altered that part of my poor expiation; and I think, except the three heads of the House, there is no one here who knows my story rightly. Before the little boy grows up, and has it told to him, my corner may be vacant. I would rather that it might be so! This is the only change to me since that day, when I left all youth, and hope, and good men's company, behind me in that room. God bless you, Walter! Keep you, and all dear to you, in honesty, or strike them dead!'

Some recollection of his trembling from head to foot, as if with excessive cold, and of his bursting into tears, was all that Walter could add to this, when he tried to recall exactly what had passed between them.

When Walter saw him next, he was bending over his desk in his old silent, drooping, humbled way. Then, observing him at his work, and feeling how resolved he evidently was that no further intercourse should arise between them, and thinking again and again on all he had seen and heard that morning in so short a time, in connexion with the history of both the Carkers, Walter could hardly believe that he was under orders for the West Indies, and would soon be lost to Uncle Sol . . . and to all he loved, and liked, and looked for, in his daily life.

But it was true, and the news had already penetrated to the outer office; for while he sat with a heavy heart, pondering on these things, and resting his head upon his arm, Perch the messenger, descending from his mahogany bracket, and jogging his elbow, begged his pardon, but wished to say in his ear, Did he think he could arrange to send home to England a jar of preserved Ginger, cheap, for Mrs. Perch's own eating, in the course of her recovery from her next confinement?

\*    \*    \*

*Comment:*

# DECEPTION AND OPPRESSION;
## THE TRIPLET PRINCIPLE

A variety of ethical issues arise in discussing business without firms. They, or close counterparts, will arise again as we discuss business with firms present. I shall comment on them, in several rounds, more extensively in such successive round, as we go on. For now, I limit myself to pointing out that two dimensions of moral concern have already clearly manifested themselves.

One has to do with deception. We can readily imagine a range of cases, at one end of which no sort of deception is present at all: one person is full and frank with another, anticipates any point on which the other might be expected to be misled, and continues discussion until every misunderstanding has been eliminated. Sometimes this is easy: I am selling you an avocado, and I let you see for yourself that the skin is intact, and feel for yourself that the avocado is ripe, but not too ripe. At the other end of the range, there will be cases in which the deception is flagrant and multiple: I am selling you a car, and everything that I tell you about it, or get you to believe, is untrue. It is not mine to sell; it has not passed inspection; it was not lovingly treated by a single previous owner, a little old lady, or by me; it has not traveled less than 25,000 miles; it does not have a reliable engine; and so forth. In between there will be cases in which it is not so clear whether deception is involved—maybe people misled themselves, unreasonably—or whether, if it is, it is deliberate and blamable. (There may also be, in between, rare cases—especially rare in business—in which deception clearly occurs, but it is not condemned, because only by deception can a greater evil be prevented. A classic example is deceiving a would-be assassin as to the whereabouts of his proposed victim.)

The other dimension that has already come to light has to do with oppression. At one end of the range of cases, one person has illegitimate power over another and uses it ruthlessly to extract every possible benefit for himself; the other person loses out all along the line in time, money, goods, and life-chances. A sweatshop owner who employs an illegal immigrant and holds over her the threat of denouncing her to the authorities might offer an example. At the other end of the range, the person with the power has it legitimately—she is the ship's captain and he signed on voluntarily as a member of the crew; and she uses the power scrupulously, indeed with delicate consideration, so that the other person is not only not injured but actually advances in skills and in capacity for happiness.

Can we arrange in the same dimension cases in which two persons have equal power and use it maybe to help each other, maybe to harm? We can if we place at one end cases where people clearly intend each to help the other, unselfishly, as well as cases where unequal power is used in a praiseworthy way; and place at the other end, along with cases of oppression, cases where each, with utter selfishness, is trying to outreach the other and do him harm, which is how Marx looked upon exchange. Then cases where people, without intending benefit or harm, benefit each other incidentally while they seek benefits for themselves—which is how others look upon exchange—could be placed somewhere beyond the middle, on the good side, as something unobjectionable.

This would be a little awkward, because we might want to hold that cases of fair exchange were not just unobjectionable, but things to be praised as good all around. We would not perhaps want to put them at the very extreme of goodness, where the relationship between the persons concerned, given the distribution of power, was as good as it could be. Yet the degree of uncertainty about just where to place such cases may well indicate that the idea of the two dimensions is here being asked to do too much work. Even without the complication of having to accommodate both unequal and equal power, the second dimension described may be over-loaded, since one has to take into account the good and evil of intentions as well as the good and evil of consequences, and it is important in ethics to distinguish between these things.

Nevertheless, the idea of the two dimensions does suffice to do the work that I want from it. Besides identifying two important subjects of moral concern, it illustrates the hypothesis that on every such subject we can find polar cases in which they are clearly behaving badly. We may also expect to encounter cases in which the behavior is clearly unobjectionable, even if it is not especially to be praised or encouraged. Among the in-between cases that will be found on any dimension, a number of cases will remain, that lie, as it were, on the evil side of unobjectionable: these we find it hard to make up our minds about, because there are arguments pulling both ways. Some arguments would make out the behavior in them to be unobjectionable, or even outright laudable; other arguments would make out the behavior to be evil to some degree.

Some people thinking about ethics give such disproportionate amounts of attention to these controversial cases that they evidently clean forget the polar cases (and the clearly unobjectionable ones). They end up despairing of ever reaching agreement on ethical questions. They incline to say, "It's all a matter of opinion" or "It's all relative." Throwing up their hands, they ask, "Is there any right opinion? Who's to say?" In fact, there is widespread agreement on many points in ethics, and not only on what judgment to offer about the clear cases, but on principles as well. The agreement extends across cultures and across epochs. A man invites his brother to dinner and serves up parts of his brother's sons as the main meat dish. The ancient Greeks, contemplating this action, which led to a lot of further trouble for the reigning dynasty in Mycenae, including the assassination of Agamemnon, were just as sure as we are—and aren't we perfectly sure?—that this was an evil deed—an atrocity. The clear cases that we might encounter in business, whether of good or of evil, are, thank goodness, likely to be less poignant, but there is going to be just as much solid agreement on them by people who understand what they amount to. They must be borne in mind as touchstones for assessing principles, and as clues that may help to resolve some at least of the controversial cases.

# CHAPTER 2

# Philosophical Discussions of Exchange and Competition

---

*Introductory Comment:*

---

## IS BUSINESS MORAL OR IMMORAL AT BOTTOM?

---

The cases brought up for discussion in the preceding chapter may have made more vivid, for a moment, the impression that things can go very wrong with exchanges, whether they are of transitory goods like tickets, or of the labor of a lifetime. We hardly needed the cases, however, to create this impression. Normally, the impression consorts comfortably enough with an assumption on our part that most of the time exchanges go perfectly well, or at least well enough for both parties to any given exchange to be better off, and think themselves better off, as a result.

I think this assumption is well founded: most exchanges are unobjectionable and most are mutually beneficial—otherwise they would not be freely entered into. Yet it does not follow that the practice of exchanging goods—a fundamental feature of business as we know it—is in every respect ideal. We might well not want to organize society, and our lives, so that everything that we do is done with a view to making the most profitable exchanges open to us. Marx, in the passage that follows as the first of the four readings in this chapter, argues vehemently that we should not organize any part of our social lives this way. Like many religious thinkers from Old Testament times to the present day, he thinks that it is infinitely preferable to have people devote themselves to meeting other people's needs, acting out of love for them rather than from any expectation of gain. One may wish to consider whether he (and they) do not underestimate the difficulties of carrying out this principle in a very populous society producing myriad different goods. That, however, is a different thing from rejecting the principle as foolish and unattractive; and in fact the principle has enough hold over so many people that it persistently accounts for part at least of the residual ambivalence and uneasiness that many people feel about business.

Another source of that residual uneasiness lies, I expect, in ambivalent feelings about competition. On the one hand, people are inclined to think that competition is such a good thing in business that the more of it the better. Doesn't competition force people to do their best, to be a productive and efficient as they can be? To offer the best goods and services that they are capable of, on pain of losing out in business if they don't? We commonly think that competition is good for character, too; people do not make the most of themselves unless they are compelled to strive for excellence. Both because of what they are doing for themselves and because of what they are doing for others, people take pride in meeting "the competition," and the more pride, the more rigorous the competition happens to be.

On the other hand, we sense that some very valuable things—like love and friendship, as well as peace of mind and quiet leisure—are liable to be sacrificed under the pressure of competition. Moreover, we have lots of reason to suspect that competition does not work out in the real world to all the good things promised in its name by economic theory. In the second selection in this chapter, Frank H. Knight makes explicit a great number of ways in which competition as we find it practiced in business falls short of realizing these good things, and as well of even better things that it is not suited to pursuing.

Do Marx and Knight between them entirely discredit both exchange and competition? If they did, we might have to conclude that business was at bottom irremediably immoral, although it would be far from clear how we were to do better without it. It might, even in being morally doubtful, be better in practice than the alternatives. In fact, we do not have to take a view even this negative. Marx's and Knight's criticisms are not the last word on the subject. Their criticisms are substantially offset by the observations to be found regarding exchange in the third selection by W. D. Lamont; and regarding competition, in the fourth selection by Georg Simmel. Business—like government, the family, and the historical performance of the Christian religion—is much too many-sided to lend itself readily to any simple judgment as good or evil.

# KARL MARX, "FREE HUMAN PRODUCTION"*

*[In the following passage, from Marx's notebooks of 1844, he expresses more clearly than anywhere else the moral grounds for his uncompromising, lifelong hostility to an economy in which what people produce and consume is governed by a market rather than by planning. Under planning, as he conceived it, people would affirm their responsibility for the welfare of the community by prescribing what parts each is to play in a concerted effort. The effort, moreover, would be designed to guarantee meeting everyone's needs.]*

It is the basic presupposition of private property that man *produces* only in order to *own*. The purpose of production is to *own*. It not only has such a *useful* purpose; it also has a *selfish* purpose. Man only produces in order to *own* something for himself. The object of his production is the objectification of his *immediate*, selfish *Need*. Man—in his wild, barbaric condition—determines his production by the *extent* of his immediate need whose content is the *immediately* produced object itself.

In that condition man produces *no more* than he immediately needs. The *limit of his need* is the *limit of his production*. Demand and supply coincide. Production is *determined* by need. Either no exchange takes place or the exchange is reduced to the exchange of man's labor for the *product of his labor, and this exchange is the latent form (the germ)* of real exchange.

As soon as exchange occurs, there is an overproduction beyond the immediate boundary of ownership. But this overproduction does not exceed selfish need. Rather it is only an *indirect* way of satisfying a need which finds its objectification in the production of another person. Production has become a *source of income*, labor for profit. While formerly need determined the extent of production, now production, or rather the *owning of the product*, determines how far needs can be satisfied.

I have produced for myself and not for you, just as you have produced for yourself and not for me. The result of my production as such has as little direct connection with you as the result of your production has with me, that is, our production is not production of man for man as man, not *socialized* production. No one is gratified by the product of another. Our mutual production means nothing for us as human beings. Our exchange, therefore, cannot be the mediating movement in which it would be acknowledged that my product means anything for you because it is an *objectification* of your being, your need. *Human nature* is not the bond of our production for each other. Exchange can only set in *motion* and confirm the *relationship* which each of us has to his own product and to the production of the other person. Each of us sees in his product only his *own* objectified self-

*Excerpts from *Writings of the Young Marx on Philosophy and Society* by Loyd D. Easton and Kurt H. Guddat. Reprinted by permission of Doubleday & Company, Inc.

interest and in the product of another person, *another* self-interest which is independent, alien, and objectified.

As a human being, however, you do have a human relation to my product; you *want* my product. It is the object of your desire and your will. But your want, desire, and will for my product are impotent. In other words, your *human* nature, necessarily and intimately related to my human production, is not your *power*, not your sharing in this production, because the *power* of human nature is not acknowledged in my production. Rather it is the *bond* which makes you dependent upon me because it makes you dependent on my product. It is far from being the *means* of giving you *power* over my production; rather it is the *means* of giving me power over you.

When I produce *more* than I can consume, I subtly *reckon* with your need. I produce only the *semblance* of a surplus of the object. In truth I produce a *different* object, the object of your production which I plan to exchange for this surplus, an exchange already accomplished in thought. My *social* relationship with you and my labor for your want is just plain *deception* and our mutual redintegration is *deception* just as well. Mutual pillaging is its base. Its background is the intent to pillage, to defraud. Since our exchange is selfish on your side as well as mine and since every self-interest attempts to surpass that of another person, we necessarily attempt to defraud each other. The power I give my object over yours, however, requires your *acknowledgement* to become real. Our mutual acknowledgement of the mutual power of our objects is a battle and the one with more insight, energy, power, and cleverness is the winner. If my physical strength suffices, I pillage you directly. If there is no physical power, we mutually dissemble and the more adroit comes out on top. It makes no difference for the *entire* relationship who the winner is, for the *ideal* and *intended* victory takes place on both sides; in his own judgment each of the two has overcome the other.

On both sides exchange necessarily requires the *object* of mutual production and mutual ownership. The ideal relationship to the mutual objects of our production is our mutual need. But the *real* and *truly effective* relationship is only the mutually *exclusive ownership* of mutual production. It is your *object*, the *equivalent* of my object, that gives your want for my object, *value*, *dignity*, and *efficacy* for me. Our mutual product, therefore, is the *means*, the *intermediary*, the *instrument*, the *acknowledged power* of our mutual needs. Your *demand* and the *equivalent* of *your property* are terms which for me are *synonymous* and equally valid, and your demand is effective only when it has an effect on me. Without this effect your demand is merely an unsatisfied effort on your part and without consequence for me. You have no relationship to my object as a human being because I *myself* have no human relation to it. But the *means* is the *real power* over an object, and we mutually regard our product as the *power* each one has over the other and over himself. In other words, our own product is turned against us. It appeared to be our property, but actually we are its property. We ourselves are excluded from *true* property because our *property* excludes the other human being.

Our objects in their relation to one another constitute the only intelligible language we use with one another. We would not understand a human language, and it would remain without effect. On the one hand, it would be felt and spoken as a plea, as begging, and as *humiliation* and hence uttered with shame and with a feeling of supplication; on the other hand, it would be heard and rejected as *effrontery* or *madness*. We are so much mutually alienated from human nature that the direct language of this nature is an *injury to human dignity* for us, while the alienated language of objective values appears as justified, self-confident, and self-accepted human dignity.

To be sure, from your point of view your product is an *instrument*, a *means* for the appropriation of my product and for the satisfaction of your need. But from my point of view it is the *goal* of our exchange. I regard you as a means and instrument for the production of this object, that is, my goal, and much more so than I regard you as related to my object. But (1) each of us actually *does* what the other thinks he is doing. You actually made yourself the means, the instrument, and the producer of *your* own object in order to appropriate mine; (2) for you, your own object is only the *sensuous shell* and *concealed form* of my object; its production *means* and *expressly* is the *acquisition* of my object. You indeed become the *means* and *instrument* of your object; your greed is the *slave* of this object, and you performed slavish services so that the object is never again a remission of your greed. This mutual servitude to the object is actually manifested to us at the beginning of its development as the relationship of *lordship* and *slavery*, and is only the crude and *frank* expression of our *essential* relationship.

Our *mutual* value is the *value* of our mutual objects for us. Man himself, therefore, is mutually *valueless* for us.

Suppose we had produced things as human beings: in his production each of us would have *twice affirmed* himself and the other. (1) In my *production*, I would have objectified my *individuality* and its *particularity*, and in the course of the activity I would have enjoyed an individual *life*; in viewing the object I would have experienced the individual joy of knowing my personality as an *objective, sensuously perceptible*, and *indubitable* power. (2) In your satisfaction and your use of my product I would have had the *direct* and conscious satisfaction that my work satisfied a *human* need, that it objectified *human* nature, and that it created an object appropriate to the need of another *human* being. (3) I would have been the *mediator* between you and the species and you would have experienced me as a redintegration of your own nature and a necessary part of your self; I would have been affirmed in your thought as well as your love. (4) In my individual life I would have directly created your life; in my individual activity I would have immediately *confirmed* and *realized* my true *human* and *social* nature.

Our productions would be so many mirrors reflecting our nature.

What happens so far as I am concerned would also apply to you.

Let us summarize the various factors in the supposition above:

My labor would be a *free manifestation of life* and an *enjoyment* of *life*. Under the presupposition of private property it is an *externalization of life* because I work *in order to live* and provide for myself the *means* of living. Working *is not living*.

Furthermore, in my labor the *particularity* of my individuality would be affirmed because my *individual* life is affirmed. Labor then would be *true, active property*. Under the presupposition of private property my individuality is externalized to the point where I *hate* this *activity* and where it is a *torment* for me. Rather it is then only the *semblance* of an activity, only a *forced* activity, imposed upon me only by *external* and accidental necessity and not by an *internal* and *determined* necessity.

My labor can appear in my object only according to its nature; it cannot appear as something *different* from itself. My labor, therefore, is manifested as the objective, sensuous, perceptible, and indubitable expression of my *self-loss* and my *powerlessness*.

\*　　\*　　\*

# FRANK H. KNIGHT, "THE ETHICS OF COMPETITION" [in part]\*

*[Marx (like Adam Smith before him) was a philosopher by training who made himself into an economist as well. Frank H. Knight, long a great star at the University of Chicago, was an economist who became, as well, a philosopher. He sets forth the case against competition. Parts of the familiar case on the other side can be gathered by reversing items in his catalogue of its unlovely aspects, a catalogue more minutely detailed and convincing than anything that can be found elsewhere on the subject. Naturally enough, however, the full strength of the case for competition cannot be gathered from a list of its failings; one cannot even infer the extent to which Knight himself, in spite of the failings, subscribed to the case for competition. Given the distribution of wealth, given the assortment of goods that is to be produced, and given the technology available, a competitive market economy may do better than a plan in assigning agents and resources to their most productive uses, and simultaneously better in producing the goods in quantities and prices adapted to the preferences expressed by consumers. (The best way of carrying on planning, in fact, my be to simulate a competitive market economy in some respects.) The theory on which these claims rest does not comment on the distribution of wealth and it does not extend entirely comfortably to the introduction of new goods or of changes in technology. One can readily see how, however, if people are free to innovate in these respects, that some will be led to do so, in hopes of extraordinary profits; and then how competitors—some of them perhaps newcomers attracted to the field by the profits that the pioneers are realizing—will bring out the new goods and adopt the new techniques. The result, if all goes well, will be to reduce prices to a competitive minimum and to reduce profits to the normal rate. With or without innovation,*

\*Excerpts from an essay originally published in *The Quarterly Journal of Economics* 37 (1923): 579–624, and later reprinted in a book by Knight, *Ethics of Competition and Other Essays* (London: George Allen & Unwin, and New York: John Wiley & Sons, 1935). Reprinted by permission.

*competition operates to discipline producers (the point that Adam Smith,
1723-90, set most store by): it limits, sometimes drastically, the extent to
which they can push up prices, reduce the quality of their goods, or fatten
on profits at the consumers' expense. Yet there is a lot to be said against it.]*

[IS COMPETITION AS WE KNOW IT AN IDEAL WAY OF
SATISFYING WANTS?]

A clear formulation of the postulates of theoretical individualism will bring
out the contrast with practical *laissez-faire*, and will go far to discredit the
latter as a policy. In the present paper the attempt to state the presupposi-
tions of a competitive system cannot be carried beyond a bare outline; it will
be developed with reference to our special purpose of showing that in the
conditions of real life no possible social order based upon a *laissez-faire* policy
can justify the familiar ethical conclusions of apologetic economics.

1. In the first place, an individualistic competitive system must be made
up of freely contracting individuals. As a matter of fact, a rather small
fraction of the population of any modern national enter into contracts on
their own responsibility. Our "individualism" is really "familism"; all
minors, the aged, and numerous persons in other classes, including for
practical purposes the majority of adult women, have their status-determin-
ing bargains made for them by other persons. The family is still the unit in
production and consumption. It is hardly necessary to point out that all
arguments for free contract are nullified or actually reversed whenever one
person contracts on behalf of another.

2. Moreover, the freest individual, the unencumbered male in the prime
of life, is in no real sense an ultimate unit or social datum. He is in large
measure a product of the economic system, which is a fundamental part of
the cultural environment that has formed his desires and needs, given him
whatever marketable productive capacities he has, and which largely controls his opportunities. Social organization through free contract implies
that the contracting units know what they want and are guided by their
desires, that is, that they are "perfectly rational," which would be equivalent to saying that they are accurate mechanisms of desire-satisfaction. In
fact, human activity is largely impulsive, a relatively unthinking and unde-
termined response to stimulus and suggestion. Moreover, there is truth in
the allegation that unregulated competition places a premium on deceit and
corruption. In any case, where the family is the social unit, the inheritance
of wealth, culture, educational advantages, and economic opportunities
tend toward the progressive increase of inequality, with bad results for
personality at both ends of the scale. It is plainly contrary in fact to treat the
individual as a *datum*, and it must be conceded that the lines along which a
competitive economic order tends to form character are often far from being
ethically ideal.

3. It is universally recognized that effective competition calls for "fluid-
ity," the perfect divisibility and mobility of all goods and services entering

into exchange. The limited extent to which this assumption fits the facts of life sets limits to the "tendency" of actual competition, which in many cases nullify the principle. Here, as in the case of other assumptions, it is illegitimate to draw practical conclusions from a "tendency," however real, without taking account of contradictory tendencies also, and getting the facts as to their relative strength. One of the dangers of reasoning from simplified premises is the likelihood that the abstract factors may be overlooked in drawing conclusions and formulating policies based thereon.

4. One of the most important prerequisites to perfect competition is complete knowledge on the part of every competing individual of the exchange opportunities open to him. A "perfect market" would involve perfect, instantaneous, and costless intercommunication among all the traders. This condition is really approximated quite closely in the case of a few commodities dealt in on the organized exchanges; but the market for most consumption goods is very crude in its workings. As regards the productive services, abstract pecuniary capital does indeed flow through a highly developed market; but the market for labour, land, and real capital, and their uses, leaves wide margins for "bargaining power" and accidental aberrations. Both the organization of production and the distribution of the product diverge correspondingly from the theoretically ideal results.

5. Competition further requires that every actual or potential buyer of every saleable good or service shall know accurately its properties and powers to satisfy his wants. In the case of productive goods this means knowledge of their technical significance. In an industrial civilization as complex as that of the modern world it is clear that the divergencies from this "tendency" must often be more important than the tendency. Indirect knowledge is available to offset direct ignorance in many subtle ways, and yet no individual can know enough to act very closely according to the ideal of perfect intelligence. Moreover, perfect competition does not stop at requiring knowledge of things as they are; the competitor must foresee them as they will be, often a very considerable distance in the future, and the limitations of foreknowledge are of course more sweeping than those of knowledge.

6. The results of intelligent action are the purposes to which it is directed, and will be ethically ideal only if these ends are true values. Under individualism this means that the wants of individuals must be ideal, as well as their knowledge perfect. We have commented enough on the fact that the social order largely forms as well as gratifies the wants of its members, and the natural consequence that it must be judged ethically rather by the wants which it generates, the type of character which it forms in its people, than by its efficiency in satisfying wants as they exist at any given time.

7. Another sweeping limitation to the actual workings of free competition arises from the fact that men do not have free access to such imperfect markets as exist. No error is more egregious than that of confounding freedom with free competition, as is not infrequently done. As elementary theory itself shows, the members of any economic group can always make more by combining than they can by competing. Under freedom all that

would stand in the way of a universal drift toward monopoly is the fortunate limitations of human nature, which prevent the necessary organization from being feasible or make its costs larger than the monopoly gains which it might secure. But universal monopoly is self-contradictory, and against any such tendency social action is the only recourse. The workings of competition educate men progressively for monopoly, which is being achieved not merely by the "capitalist" producers of more and more commodities, but by labour in many fields, and in many branches of agriculture, while the producers of even the fundamental crops are already aspiring to the goal.

8.  The individualistic competitive organization of want-satisfying activity presupposes that wants and the means of satisfying them are individual, that is, that wants attach to things and services which gratify the wants of the person consuming them without affecting other persons. As a matter of fact, what is desired is more largely a matter of human relations than goods and services as such; we want things because other people have them, or cannot have them, as the case may be. Then, too, the appurtenances of civilized life can be furnished to an individual only by providing them for the community, and we want to live in a civilized community as well as to live in a civilized way ourselves. With rare exceptions exchanges or contracts between individuals affect for good and for ill persons not represented in the bargain itself, and for these the bargain is not "free." Social action is necessary to promote the exchanges which diffuse benefits on others for which the parties cannot collect payment in the market, and to suppress those which diffuse evils for which the contracting parties do not have to pay. A typical illustration is the improvement or use of property in ways which add value to or subtract value from neighbouring property. In a developed social order hardly any "free exchange" between individuals is devoid of either good or bad results for outsiders.

9.  An exchange system cannot work at all according to "theory" without a scientific unit for measuring values. Society has to take over or carefully control activities which have to do with the circulating medium. With the use of credit highly developed, the control of banking and currency involves a large measure of control over all business, but really free banking would soon reduce all exchange relations to chaos.

10.  An economic organization must employ its available productive power in part to provide for current needs of society and in part to provide for future growth. If this second function is to be performed intelligently through individual intitiative under competitive organization, each member of the system must make a correct comparison and choice between his own present wants and future social requirements. The weakness of competitive individualism in this field is well recognized, since manifestly progress is essentially a social fact. In an individualistic system provision for progress depends upon the interest of present individuals in future individuals— engendered to an uncertain extent and with uncertain consequences on the form of progress by the family system—or upon their interest in progress itself or some form of it as an ideal value, or upon some accidental

connection which makes progress a by-product of activities directed toward other ends. None of these, nor all together, produce results invulnerable to criticism; but the problems of social action in the same field are likewise so difficult and the ideal of progress itself so vague that it is impossible in short compass to say anything of value about the relation of different forms of social organization to the solution of the problem. It is a fact that social interference has gone further in this field than in that of controlling current production and consumption, as witness especially the social provision for education and scientific research.

11. All human planning and execution involve uncertainty, and a rational social order can be realized through individual action only if all persons have a rational attitude toward risk and chance. But the general human attitude is proverbially irrational, and much social limitation of individual freedom is called for. Not only is it necessary to prohibit gambling, but provision has to be made for placing control of resources and the direction of wealth-production in the hands of persons reasonably fit and competent to take responsibility; and the freedom of these individuals to take chances has to be further restricted by general regulations. Thus no society has in fact ever treated productive resources as private property in any strict sense. It seems likely, however, that a socialistic society would err rather on the side of overconservatism than on that of recklessness.

12. The last heading in this list of reasons why individualism and competition cannot bring about an ideal utilization of social resources will be the ethics of distribution. In a competitive system distribution is effected by a marketing process, the evaluation of productive services, and is of course subject to all the limitations of marketing in general, as enumerated in the last half-dozen pages. But that is not the main point. It is a common assumption—for which the exponents of the "productive theory" are partly responsible—that productive contribution is an ethical measure of desert. This has improperly tended to bring the theory itself, as a causal explanation of what happens in distribution, into disrepute; because those who are misled into accepting the standard, but cannot approve the result realized, react by attacking the theory. An examination of the question will readily show that productive contribution can have little or no ethical significance from the standpoint of absolute ethics. (The question of practicability, it must be kept in mind, is eliminated by the boundaries set for this discussion; we are dealing with ideals and not inquiring whether or in what respects the possibilities of the real world may be harmonious with our moral cravings.) The examination of productivity as a standard of desert must again be handled in outline.

(a) In the first place, as already noted, there is only a "general tendency" to impute to each productive agency its true product. The factor of ignorance is especially important here, since correct imputation would require perfect technological knowledge and foresight. Human beings do not live on averages, and it is only to a very limited extent that a system of free exchange can make it possible for one to live this year on what he may (or may not) earn next year. To a still more limited extent, if at all, can the particular individual whom the tendency passes over live, through free exchange, on the compensating extra share of a more favoured person.

(b) The tendency to place each productive agency in the position where it will make the greatest contribution is far less effective even than the force which adjusts remuneration to actual contribution. A social system which sets artists to shining shoes and pays them what they are worth in that occupation is no less open to condemnation than one that sets them to work at their art and pays them what they would be worth as boot-blacks.

(c) The product or contribution is always measured in terms of price, which does not correspond closely with ethical value or human significance. The money value of a product is a matter of the "demand," which in turn reflects the tastes and purchasing power of the buying public and the availability of substitute commodities. All these factors are largely created and controlled by the workings of the economic system itself, as already pointed out. Hence their results can have in themselves no ethical significance as standards for judging the system. On the contrary, the system must be judged by the conformity to ethical standards of these facts of demand rather than by the conformity to demand of the actual production and distribution of goods. And the final results diverge notoriously from the ethical standards actually held. No one contends that a bottle of old wine is ethically worth as much as a barrel of flour, or a fantastic evening wrap for some potentate's mistress as much as a substantial dwelling-house, though such relative prices are not unusual. Ethically, the whole process of valuation is literally a "vicious" circle, since price flows from demand and demand from prices.

(d) The income does not go to "factors," but to their owners, and can in no case have more ethical justification than has the fact of ownership. The ownership of personal or material productive capacity is based upon a complex mixture of inheritance, luck, and effort, probably in that order of relative importance. What is the ideal distribution from the standpoint of absolute ethics may be disputed, but of the three considerations named none but the effort can have ethical validity. From the standpoint of absolute ethics most persons will probably agree that inherited capacity represents an obligation to the world rather than a claim upon it. The significance of luck will be discussed below in connection with the conception of business as a game. We must contend that there is a fallacy in the common position which distinguishes between the ethical significance of the income from labour and that from other factors. Labour in the economic sense may represent either a sacrifice or a source of enjoyment, and the capacity to labour productively derives from the same three sources as property ownership, namely, inheritance, luck, and effort of acquisition, and with no obvious general difference from the case of property in their relative importance.

(e) The value of any service or product varies from zero to an indefinite magnitude, according to the demand. It is hard to see that even when the demand is ethical, possession of the capacity to furnish services which are in demand, rather than other capacities, constitutes an ethical claim to a superior share of the social dividend, except to the extent that the capacity is itself the product of conscientious effort.

(f) The value of a productive service varies from zero to indefinite magnitude, according to its scarcity. The most vital ministrations become valueless if offered in superabundance, and the most trivial performance becomes exceedingly valuable if sufficiently unique and rare, as when a human monstrosity satisfied an economic demand by letting people look at him. It is hard to see how it is more meritorious merely to be different from other people than it is to be like them—except again, possibly, if the capacity has been cultivated by an effort which others refused to put forth.

(g) Finally, it may be pointed out that modern society does accept and honour the claim of the entirely helpless to a tolerable human existence, and that there is no difference in principle between this recognition in the extreme case and admitting that differences in degree of competence form no valid basis for discriminatory treatment in distribution. But, after all, does anyone really contend that "competence," as measured by the price system, corresponds to ethical merit? Is it not obvious that "incompetence" follows just as surely if not quite so commonly from being too good for the world as from being blameworthy in character?

Thus the competitive system, viewed simply as a want-satisfying mechanism, falls far short of our highest ideals. To the theoretical tendencies of perfect competition must be opposed just as fundamental limitations and counter-tendencies, of which careful scrutiny discloses a rather lengthy list. Its standards of value for the guidance of the use of resources in production are the prices of goods, which diverge widely from accepted ethical values; and if the existing order were more purely competitive, if social control were reduced in scope, it seems clear that the divergence would be enormously wider still. Moreover, untrammelled individualism would probably tend to lower standards progressively rather than to raise them. "Giving the public what it wants" usually means corrupting popular taste. The system is also inefficient in utilizing resources to produce the values which it sets up, as brought out with startling force by the report on Waste in Industry, by a Committee of the Confederated Engineering Societies. It distributes the produce of industry on the basis of power, which is ethical only in so far as right and might are one. It is a confessed failure in the field of promoting many forms of social progress, and its functions in this regard are being progressively taken over by other social agencies. Left to itself, such a system "collapses" at frequent intervals through dilution of its value unit and through other causes which produce violent oscillation instead of the equilibrium of theory.

It is expressly excluded from the field of the present paper to pass any practical judgment upon the competitive system in comparison with any possible alternative. But in view of the negative tone of the discussion, it seems fair to remark that many of these problems are exceedingly difficult and that many of the evils and causes of trouble are inherent in all large-scale organizations as such, irrespective of its form. It must be said also that radical critics of competition as a general basis of the economic order generally underestimate egregiously the danger of doing vastly worse. Finally, let us repeat that practically there is no question of the exclusive use or entire abolition of any of the fundamental methods of social organization, individualistic or socialistic. Economic and other activities will always be organized in all the possible ways, and the problem is to find the right proportions between individualism and socialism and the various varieties of each, and to use each in its proper place.

[IS COMPETITION IN BUSINESS A GOOD COMPETITIVE GAME?]

The problem of an ethical standard or ideal in terms of which to judge the economic order is of a different and far more difficult sort when we leave the field of more or less comparable burdens and quantities of goods, to consider power and prestige as ends. In a competitive game it is absurd to speak of equality as an ideal, a fact which much radical discussion overlooks. Some of the criticisms brought against existing society amount to condemning a foot-race as unfair because someone has come out ahead. We must bear in mind, too, that the system is a want-satisfying agency at the same time that it is a competitive game, and that the two functions are inseparable, while the two sets of ideals are different. For efficiency in the production of goods a large concentration of authority is necessary. But this concentration violates the principle of equality of opportunity in the game; and when power of control carries with it the right to consume product accordingly, as it actually does, the result is flagrant inequality in this respect also. There appears to be a deep-seated conflict between liberty and equality on the one hand and efficiency on the other. There is little comfort for democratic, equalitarian idealism in the study of evolutionary biology, in which the highly centralized or "cephalized" forms have always come out ahead. Yet apparently human society is different in some degree at least, for there appears to be a tendency for autocracies, aristocracies, and systems approaching a caste organization to be beaten out in history by the apparently less efficient "democracy," though democracies have not in practice approached closely to the equalitarian ideal. . . .

An attempt to formulate accurately the conditions of a fair and interesting game leads into difficult problems. . . . A few general statements may be made with some confidence in regard to the difference between a good competitive game and a poor one. In the first place, there are three elements which affect the question of who is to win and thus contribute to the interest: these are ability to play, effort, and luck. It is also significant that the ability to play brought to the game on any particular occasion is, like all human capacity, a compound of innate endowment and "education" acquired from the previous expenditure of effort in play or practice, or perhaps in some closely related activity of either a recreative or a serious character. A good game must test the capacity of the players, and to do this it must compel them to exert effort. At the same time, it must involve more than a purely objective measure of capacity (assuming maximum effort). The result must be unpredictable: if there is no element of luck in it there is no game. There is no game in lifting weights, after one once knows how much can be lifted, even though the result measures capacity. Where "records" are made, the interest centres in the unpredictable fluctuations in the powers of men (or horses, etc.) from one trial to another.

A good game calls for some reasonable, though far from definite, proportion among the three elements, capacity, effort, and luck—except that apparently most human beings are susceptible to fascination by pure chance, in spite of the obvious fact that a competitive game of pure chance involves a logical contradiction. Certainly there is general agreement that games of skill are "superior" to games of chance. Effort is called forth by interest, and intelligent interest is dependent on the fact that effort makes some difference in the result. But effort is futile or superfluous if there is too great a difference in the abilities of the players, and the game is spoiled. Even the hunter who considers himself a sportsman always gives his quarry a chance. Finally, it will no doubt be admitted that some games are "higher class" than others, depending presumably on the human qualities necessary to play them successfully and to enjoy them. The actual ranking of games would, it is true, raise the same problems of value standards which beset the path to objectivity in all fields of artistic criticism; and here also we should have to appeal to a general consensus and perhaps admit within limits the equal validity of opposing judgments.

No doubt different judges would disagree in their ranking of business as a competitive game, but the principles sketched above suggest some shortcomings. Its outcome is a very inaccurate test of real ability, for the terms on which different individuals enter the contest are too unequal. The luck element moreover is so large—far larger than fairly successful participants in the game will ever admit—that capacity and effort may count for nothing. And this luck element works cumulatively, as in gambling games generally. The effects of luck in the first hand or round, instead of tending to be evened up in accord with the law of large numbers in the further progress of the game, confer on the player who makes an initial success a differential advantage in succeeding hands or rounds, and so on indefinitely. Any particular individual may be eliminated by the results of his first venture, or placed in a position where it is extraordinarily difficult to get back into the game.

Again, differences in the capacity to play the business game are inordinately great from one person to another. But as the game is organized, the weak contestants are thrown into competition with the strong in one grand mêlée; there is no classification of the participants or distribution of handicaps such as is always recognized to be necessary to sportsmanship where unevenly matched contestants are to meet. In fact the situation is worse still; there are handicaps, but, as we have seen, they are distributed to the advantage of the strong rather than the weak. We must believe that business ability is to some extent hereditary, and social institutions add to inherited personal superiority the advantages of superior training, preferred conditions of entrance into the game, and even an advance distribution of the prize money.

The distribution of prizes diverges from the highest level of sportsmanship in another way. In a competition where the powers of the contestants are known to be unequal but the inequalities are not well enough determined to permit the classification of the players or an equalization of chances by means of handicaps, it is possible to sustain interest by offering a larger number of prizes less unequal in value. This method brings about an automatic classification of the contestants by the progress of the game iteself. But in the business game the tendency is to multiply inequalities of performance in the inequality of distribution of the stakes. Let us suppose that we are organizing a footrace among a thousand men taken at random from the general population. At one extreme they might be all lined up on a mark and made to race for a single first prize; at the other, the prize money might be distributed equally, irrespective of the results of the race. From the standpoint of sport, the one proceeding would be as absurd as the other. If the critics of competition tend to make a fetish of equality, the system itself does undoubtedly go very far to the opposite extreme.

Admitting that business success tends in the large to go with business ability, we must face the question of the abstract merit of such capacity as a human trait, and hence of business as a game. It can hardly be denied that there is a preponderance of cultivated opinion against it. Successful business men have not become proverbial for the qualities that the best minds and most sensitive spirits of the race agree in calling noble. Business as it is and has been does not commonly display a very high order of sportsmanship, not to mention the question which will be raised presently as to whether sportsmanship itself is the highest human ideal. As to the human qualities developed by business activity and requisite to enjoyment of and successful participation in it, there is no objective measure and no opinion will be accepted as free from "prejudice" by those who disagree with it. We shall dismiss the subject by quoting a statement from Ruskin, which can hardly be waived aside as valueless or unrepresentative. "In a community regulated by laws of demand and supply, but protected from open violence," he says, "the persons who become rich are, generally speaking, industrious, resolute, proud, covetous, prompt, methodical, sensible, unimaginative, insensitive, and ignorant. The persons who remain poor are the entirely foolish, the entirely wise, the idle, the reckless, the humble, the thoughtful, the dull, the imaginative, the sensitive, the well-informed, the improvident, the irregularly and impulsively wicked, the clumsy knave, the open thief, the entirely merciful, just, and godly person."

However favourable an opinion one may hold of the business game, he must be very illiberal not to concede that others have a right to a different view and that large numbers of admirable people do not like the game at all. It is then justifiable at least to regard as unfortunate the dominance of the business game over life, the virtual identification of social living with it, to the extent that has come to pass in the modern world. In a social order where all values are reduced to the money measure in the degree that this is true of modern industrial nations, a considerable fraction of the most noble and sensitive characters will lead unhappy and even futile lives. Everyone is compelled to play the economic game and be judged by his success in playing it, whatever his field of activity or type of interest, and has to squeeze in as a side line any other competition, or non-competitive activity, which may have for him a greater intrinsic appeal. . . .

[IS EVEN A GOOD COMPETITIVE GAME A GOOD WAY OF LIFE?]

We must treat still more inadequately our third main question, which from the point of view of pure ethics is the most important of all—the question of the ethics of competition as such. Is emulation as a motive ethically good or base? Is success in any sort of *contest*, as such, a noble objective? Are there no values which are real in a higher sense than the fact that people have agreed to strive after them and to measure success in life by the result of their striving? . . . It is in fact much easier to argue that the introduction of the contest motive into economic life has made it more efficient than that it has made it more pleasurable! Candid observations of industrial operatives at work, and of their frenzied, pathetic quest for recreation when off duty, alike fail to give the impression of particularly happy existence. As already observed, economic production has been made a fascinating sport *for the leaders*, but this had been accomplished by reducing it to mechnical drudgery for the rank and file. In the large is the competitive urge a lure, or is it rather a goad? Is it positive or negative, especially when we recall that for the masses the competition is in the field of consumption, with production regarded purely as a means? From the standpoint of pleasure, does the normal human being prefer a continuous, unquestioning, and almost deadly competition, or the less strenuous atmosphere of activity undertaken for ends that seem intrinsically worth while, with a larger admixture of the spectator attitude of appreciation? . . .

Competition may form an added source of pleasure in activity, especially to the winner or, in the progress of the game, to those who stand some chance to win. But it is more likely to become a goad, especially when participation in the contest is compulsory. There is a fairly established consensus that happiness depends more on spiritual resourcefulness, and a joyous appreciation of the costless things of life, especially affection for one's fellow creatures, than it does on material satisfaction. A strong argument for co-operation, if it would work, would be its tendency to teach people to like each other in a more positive sense than can ever be bred by participation in a contest—certainly in a contest in which the means of life, or of a decent life, are felt to be at stake. The dominance of salesmanship in the business world, as well as the spirit of economic rivalry, must also tend to work against the appreciation of the "free goods." . . .

We appear to search in vain for any really ethical basis for competition as a basis for an ideal type of human relation, or as a motive to action. It fails to harmonize either with the Pagan ideal of society as a community of friends or the Christian ideal of spiritual fellowship. Its only justification is that it is effective in getting things done; but any candid answer to the question, "what things," compels the admission that they leave much to be desired.

Whether for good or bad, its aesthetic ideals are not such as command the approval of the most competent judges, and as for spirituality, commercialism is in a fair way to make that term incomprehensible to living men. The motive itself has been generally condemned by the best spirits of the race. In academic life, for example, though every (American) institution feels itself compelled to use credit, marks, and honours, they are virtually never defended as intrinsically worthy incentives to effort.

Whether it is possible to bring about improvement by substituting some other basis of social organization for competitive individualism is a question beyond the scope of this paper. Its purpose has been merely to bring out fundamental weaknesses of competition from the standpoint of purely ideal standards, and so to establish bases for comparison with any other possible system. Summarizing the argument, it was first emphasized by way of introduction that any judgment passed upon a social order is a value judgment and presupposes a common measure and standard of values, which must be made as clear and explicit as possible if the judgment is to be intelligent. Efficiency is a value category and social efficiency an ethical one. Now the standards which underlie a competitive system, according to orthodox economic theory, are the actual desires of the individual members of society. Competition is supposed to effect a comparison of these, and to organize the resources of society in such a way as to satisfy them to the greatest possible extent in order of magnitude—that is, it is supposed to "tend" to do so. The first main task of the paper was therefore to enumerate the more fundamental and obvious limitations on this tendency, or counter-tendencies which are in many cases quite as important as the tendency itself. Economic theory must isolate the ideal tendencies with which it can deal most readily; but no practical conclusions as to the real beneficence of the system can be drawn until the actual relative importance of the tendencies recognized by the general theory—which in endeavouring to explain always seems to justify—are measured in comparison with divergent tendencies and these taken into account.

In the second division of the paper it was pointed out that the competitive economic life has value implications on the production side, the most notable of which is its appeal as a competitive game. An examination from this point of view reveals notable shortcomings of business considered purely as a game. There is also a certain ethical repugnance attached to having the livelihood of the masses of the people made a pawn in such a sport, however fascinating the sport may be to its leaders.

Finally, we have called in question from the standpoint of ideal ethics the predominance of the institution of sport, or action motivated by rivalry, and in particular have contrasted it with the Pagan ethics of beauty or perfection and the Christian ideal of spirituality.

\*     \*     \*

## *Paper-Organizing Game:*
## *Good and Bad Sides of Competitiveness*

The object of the game is to put the following questions into a perspicuous order, which will form the overall plan or skeleton for your paper. I have found that having a class meet to play the game together often results in a lively and useful session.

1. Does striving to win become a bad thing when one strives to win always or to win so big as to drive others out of the game (out of business)?

2. Is not competition sometimes mutually stimulating to the competitors?

3. Are not the benefits of competition to be ascribed in part to competitiveness?

4. Where do such considerations as bringing out one's talents, training oneself to the highest pitch of skill, making the most of opportunities to exhibit excellence fit in?

5. What are the benefits of competition, in quantity of goods, variety, quality, and prices?

6. Is preoccupation with winning the same as competitiveness?

7. Do the benefits of competition go hand in hand with some drawbacks, for example, preoccupation with material comforts in the public, in the competitors, preoccupation with winning?

8. Have the moral limits of competition been reached when competitors are driven out with no alternative to turn to?

9. Are winning and striving to win sometimes good things, even among friends and lovers, and within families?

10. What is the difference between competitiveness and competition? Which has more to do with character than with action?

11. What is done among friends and lovers and within families about competitions in which someone always wins?

12. Are there benefits of competition for competitors as well as for the public? What are they?

# W. D. LAMONT, "THE ECONOMIC RELATION AND THE IDEA OF GOOD"*

*[Marx thinks of people in the market as selfishly pursuing their own ends by taking advantage of other people's needs. Is the behavior in question necessarily selfish, however? Must it be thought of as taking advantage? Lamont gives a different view of these matters from Marx's.]*

The economic relation is but one of many relations in which men stand to each other within the total social order. It cannot, as we have just seen, exist alone. It can however be distinguished from other relations; and perhaps its nature will become sufficiently clear if we distinguish it from two others which we may call the 'fellowship' and the 'juridical' relation, respectively.

*The Fellowship Relation:* The name given to this relation does not matter so long as we understand the kind of relation which is meant. It is the relation in which individuals stand to each other when they are pursuing a genuinely common good. A common good is an end which is pursued by a number of persons in collaboration, each pursuing it, not only because he himself wants it to be realised, but also because he knows that those collaborating with him want it to be realised. Thus, if A thinks x good, and pursues it quite irrespective of whether B thinks it good, there is obviously no common good. Or if A thinks it good, and at the same time thinks that its realisation would be good for B, we cannot say that is necessarily a conception of common good operating. Thus, if A thinks x good for A and for B, and pursues it because of this; and if B thinks x good for B and for A, and pursues it because of this; we are not necessarily dealing with a common good x. Before we can say that we are dealing with a common good, in the proper sense of the term, A must think x good for A and B, B must think x good for B and A, A must know that B thinks so, B must know that A thinks so, and the knowledge that both desire the realisation of x must be part of the motive which determines each of them to pursue it. Possibly a simple but adequate illustration of the fellowship relation, when individuals are pursuing a common good, may be found in a choir. Smith and White are both members, tenor and bass. In this respect they regard themselves (and not merely their vocal organs) as 'instruments for the realisation of a common purpose' or a common good which is the making of grave, sweet melody. As members of the fellowship they are not thinking of a right-duty relationship in which they stand to each other (although there is this relationship also), but of making their respective contributions to a common end for the production of which they have a joint responsibility.

*From W. D. Lamont, *The Value Judgement* (Edinburgh: The University of Edinburgh Press, 1955), pages 36–40. Reprinted by permission.

*The Juridical Relation:* Smith and White are also neighbours living in adjoining houses. Smith has a passion for fruit. White has a small orchard, some of the best fruit-trees growing temptingly near the wall dividing the two properties. But Smith respects the property rights of White and refrains from touching the apples and plums. He limits the pursuit of the ends he considers good out of respect to White's rights, i.e. from a sense of duty. However, some time earlier Smith and White have made an agreement—an economic agreement, as they both consider it—that, when the fruit is ready, White will sell Smith $x$ stone of apples at $y$ shillings the stone. When the crop is ready for market, White finds that the prevailing conditions show that his bargain with Smith was a bad one from the economic point of view. He could have got more than double the price in the open market. But the contract has vested a certain right in Smith, and White does not hesitate about fulfilling his obligation. He carries out what is in fact a bad bargain for him, one which he would never have made had he been able to anticipate what the conditions would be. Here Smith and White are standing in juridical relations with each other, thinking in terms of their mutual rights and duties—White's real rights as owner of the orchard, and Smith's personal rights against White in consequence of the contract.

*The Economic Relation:* The economist, as such, is not interested in either the fellowship or the juridical relationship between White and Smith. It is true that the economic relation presupposes the existence of juridical relationships at least; and it is true that, when a business deal is put through, it establishes a new juridical relation which we call the right and obligation arising from contract. But the subject-matter of economics is the process of making the business deal, and not the juridical relations which it presupposes or those in which it results.

The economic relation is of the following kind: Let us say that Smith is anxious to found a Home for destitute children. White is not interested; he has got his own preoccupations, being anxious to send an orphaned nephew to the university to take a medical degree, a project in which Smith is politely interested, but in which he feels no call to render assistance. Smith and White may, nevertheless, co-operate in the realisation of each other's ends. White is a builder; and, in the ordinary course of business, he submits a tender and secures the contract for the building of Smith's Home. In return, he is paid a sum of money by Smith; and this money actually makes it possible for him to send his nephew to the university. Smith and White here stand in an economic relationship. They are not interested in each other's ends (the ends relevant to this relationship); they do not (in this respect) have any rights and duties until they have made the economic agreement; and yet they do assist each other in essential ways to realise each other's ends (the building of the Home and the education of the nephew). They help each other by exchanging services and money on a business footing.

What is the bearing of this account of the economic relation on the question of 'egoism'? What is certainly true is that each party to the economic exchange is actuated by the motive of maximum gain for himself, not for the other party. But by 'gain' we mean a realisation of what he personally considers to be good. Maximum gain is the greatest possible realisation in the circumstances of some end or ends which is or are part of the content of his total personal conception of good. But, quite obviously, many of the things which a person considers good are not pursued for selfish or egoistic reasons. We cannot—as some of the older economists supposed—adopt a theory of egoism, hedonistic or otherwise. The fact that the economic relation presupposes the existence of juridical relations makes egoism quite untenable as a psychological theory for the economist to assume. What the economist is really assuming is not that the parties to the exchange are egoists, but that they are each engaged in the pursuit of a total conception of good, utilising scarce resources, and that the particular end each is at the moment pursuing is not also an end to the other. The total conception of good, as entertained by Smith, will include all sorts of ends, some of them common ends which he shares with White, some common ends which he shares with other persons, and some of his ends will be best stated in terms of the performance of personal or social obligations. But, in anyone's total conception of good, there will always be some end which is not also an end to (i.e., not also a common end with) another person who is yet in a position to help the former. When there is a mutual 'uninterestedness' along with a mutual ability to assist, and when such assistance can be geared to the promotion of the ends which are not common ends to the two parties in question, and when there is no existing obligation to render such assistance, that is when the economic relation is likely to arise.

Thus, in the case supposed, Smith's desire to found the Home is anything but egoistic; and the same may be said of White's desire to send his nephew to the university. Both of the ends are 'other regarding'; and we may assume that the former is a common good cherished by Smith and some others including the children who will benefit, and that the latter is a common good cherished by White and his nephew. The point is simply that the building of the Home and the nephew's education are not common goods to Smith and White. Of course Smith may have 'ulterior motives'; he may be angling for public approbation and a title. White may also have the 'ulterior motive' of retiring and living on his nephew's earnings. But such egoistic motives, if they exist at all, will have to be established by the appropriate evidence. That the motives are egoistic could not be deduced from the fact that Smith and White are, in this case, bargaining for gain as against each other; nor, if we could establish ulterior motives, would it help us in the least to understand the transaction between Smith and White. All we need assume is that each is conserving scarce resources in the pursuit of a total conception of good, and that neither will 'waste' resources on the production of an end not included in his conception of the good.

To put the general point as concisely as possible:

When $A$ is pursuing an end $x$ (which may in fact be a common good for $A$, $C$, and $D$), and $B$ is pursuing and end $y$ (which may in fact be a common good for $B$, $C$, and $D$), and neither $x$ nor $y$ is a common good to $A$ and $B$, and neither $A$ nor $B$ has a duty to assist in the production of $y$ or $x$ respectively; and when, nevertheless, $A$ and $B$ do render each other assistance such as to make possible the attainment of $x$ and $y$; then here we have the establishment of the economic relation. It is not egoism, but the absence of common good in the relevant respect, which is assumed.

*   *   *

## GEORG SIMMEL, "THE SOCIALIZING AND CIVILIZING FUNCTION OF COMPETITION"*

*[The following passage from the German philosopher and sociologist Simmel may be counterpoised against Knight's bleak view of competition. Simmel finds something good to say about it that Knight does not say (though Knight might agree, accommodating what Simmel says under the contribution that competition makes—so far as it makes one—to efficiency in meeting people's wants). There is a more dramatic opposition between Simmel and Marx: Marx's model of exchange involves two people; exchange looks surprisingly different when one shifts to Simmel's model, in which there are three people.]*

. . . The aim for which competition occurs within a society is presumably always the favor of one or more third persons. Each of the competing parties there tries to come as close to that third one as possible. Usually, the poisonous, divisive, destructive effects of competition are stressed, and for the rest it is merely admitted that it creates certain values as its product. But in addition, it has, after all this immense sociating effect. Competition compels the wooer, who has a co-wooer, and often in this way alone comes to be a wooer properly speaking, to go out to the wooed, come close to him, establish ties with him, find his strengths and weaknesses and adjust to them, find all bridges, or cast new ones, which might connect the competitor's own being and doing with his.

To be sure, this often happens at the price of the competitor's own dignity and of the objective value of his product. Competition, above all competition among the makers of the highest intellectual products, makes those who are destined to guide the mass subordinate themselves to it. In order to permit the effective exercise of their function as teachers, party leaders, artists, or journalists, they must obey the instincts or moods of the mass once the mass can choose among them, which it can because of their competition. As far as *content* is concerned, this certainly makes for a reversal of the hierarchy of social life-values; but this does not detract from the *formal* significance of competition for the synthesis of society. Innumerable times, it achieves what usually only love can do: the divination of the

*Reprinted by permission of Macmillan Publishing Co., Inc., from *Conflict: The Web of Group Affiliation* by Georg Simmel, trans. by Kurt H. Wolf and Reinhard Bendix, pages 61–64. Copyright 1955 by The Free Press.

innermost wishes of the other, even before he himself becomes aware of them. Antagonistic tension with his competitor sharpens the businessman's sensitivity to the tendencies of the public, even to the point of clairvoyance, in respect to future changes in the public's tastes, fashions, interests—not only the businessman's, but also the journalist's, artist's, bookseller's, parliamentarian's. Modern competition is described as the fight of all against all, but at the same time it is the fight of all *for* all. Nobody will deny the tragedy of social elements working against one another, instead of for; of the squandering of innumerable forces in the struggle against the competitor—forces which could be used for positive achievements; or, finally, of the discarding of the positive and valuable achievement, unused and unrewarded, as soon as a more valuable or at least a more appealing one competes with it.

But all these liabilities of competition in the social balance sheet must only be added to the immense synthetic force of the fact that, in society, competition is competition for man, a wrestling for applause and effort, exemption and devotion of all kinds, a wrestling of the few for the many, as well as of the many for the few. In short, it is a web of a thousand sociological threads by means of conscious concentration on the will and feeling and thinking of fellowmen, of the adaptation of the producers to the consumers, of the delicately multiplied possibilities of gaining favor and connection. Once the narrow and naïve solidarity of primitive social conditions yielded to decentralization (which was bound to have been the immediate result of the quantitative enlargement of the group), man's effort toward man, his adaptation to the other, seems possibly only at the price of competition, that is, of the simultaneous fight *against* a fellowman *for* a third one—*against* whom, for that matter, he may well compete in some other relationship *for* the former. Given the breadth and individualization of society, many kinds of interest, which eventually hold the group together throughout its members, seem to come alive and stay alive only when the urgency and requirements of the competitive struggle force them upon the individual.

The socializing power of competition shows itself not only in these coarser, so-to-speak public, cases. We find two parties competing for a third in numberless combinations of family and love relationships, of social small talk and discussions over convictions, of friendship and satisfactions of one's vanity; sometimes, of course, only in allusions, beginnings which are dropped, side phenomena and partial phenomena of an over-all process. Wherever it occurs, however, the antagonism of the competitors is paralleled by some offering, coaxing, promising, imposing, which sets each of them in relation to the third party. For the victor in particular, this relation often attains an intensity which it would not have without the excitement by the chances of competition and without the peculiar, continuous comparison of his own achievement with the achievement of the other, which is possibly only through competition. The more liberalism penetrates not only economic and political conditions but also those of the family, sociability, the church, friendship, stratification, and general social intercourse—that is, the less these conditions are pre-determined and regulated by broad, historical norms and the more they are left to shifting forces or to an unstable equilibrium which must be attained from case to case—the more will their shape depend on continual competitions. And the result of these competitions will in turn depend in most cases upon the interest, love, hope which the competitors know to arouse in different degrees in these or those third parties, the centers of the competitive movements.

Man's most valuable object is man, directly and indirectly. Indirectly, because in him are stored the energies of sub-human nature, as in the animal we eat or make work for us, are stored those of the vegetable kingdom; and in plants, those of sun and earth, air and water. Man is the most condensed, most fruitfully exploitable phenomenon; and the necessity of psychologically winning him over grows in the measure in which slavery, that is, his mechanical appropriation, weakens. The fight against man, which was a fight for him and his enslavement, thus changes into the more complex phenomenon of competition. To be sure, in it too, a man fights another man, but *for* a third one. And the winning over of that third one can be achieved in a thousand ways only through the sociological means of persuasion or conviction, surpassing or underselling, suggestion or threat, in short, through psychological connection. But just as often, this winning over also means in its effect such a psychological connection, the founding of a relationship—from the momentary relation established by a purchase in a store to marriage. As the intensity and condensation of life-contents increases culturally, the struggle for the most condensed of all goods, the human soul, must take on ever larger proportions and must multiply and deepen interactions which bring men together and which are both the means and the ends of that struggle.

\*     \*     \*

# CHAPTER 3

# *Persons Dealing with Firms*

*Introductory Comment:*

## MORAL RULES; THE LAW; PUBLIC AGREEMENT

Only a few of the ethical issues that arise in the world of business have come up so far, although the ones that have, and the subjects of moral concern they involve, are of great importance. We shall now undertake a much more comprehensive survey. Besides seeing how the picture is complicated by there being ethical issues to cope with, which often intersect, we shall have continually in view the complication of there being firms to deal with besides people. We might wish to have firms brought under the same ethics as people, but certain difficulties stand in the way of doing this; and we have still to settle just what parts of ethics apply in the world of business.

Whether we're dealing with persons or dealing with firms, how are we to cope with subjects of moral concern like deception or oppression? One conception of how we're to cope—the conception that has long prevailed in Western ethics—is that we are to consider ourselves bound to act by rules. Some rules specify what is to count as deception and when deception is to be avoided (perhaps always). Others specify various uses of power, prohibiting some, such as oppression, prescribing others, and permitting the rest. Where are these rules to be found, however? They can hardly all be just rules that we thing up on the spur of the moment, or any of them just rules that we one by one choose to lay down as policies for ourselves. The maxim "Whenever I find keeping a promise or contract burdensome, I shall ignore it" lays down such a policy, but it is hardly a morally defensible one. Not only is it indefensible; we could not succeed in acting upon it if we made it public, for who then would accept our promises?

Many moral rules are embodied in the law, which deals with deception, for example, under many heads, fraud being one of the broadest. The fact that we can find moral rules in law implies that we need never be wildly uncertain about where to find some examples. The examples to be found there also show us what sorts of rules we should (at least for the most part) be looking for—not rules that have no exceptions, or rules that spell out in advance what all the exceptions are going to be, but rules that will apply normally, allowing for adjustments in unanticipated circumstances. Normally, you are to have your bill rung up and to pay the cashier before you leave the restaurant, but you won't have to if a fire breaks out just as you get ready to leave, or if you're attacked by a mad dog. (Then you come back to pay later.) Furthermore, you may be excused if the cashier is away from her post and you see the last bus for home just stopping outside, provided you leave the bill and enough money to cover it by the register. These exceptions do not overturn the rule; they just show what sort of rule—a typical sort—it is. No attempt is made in the law to specify all the exceptions in advance, when a rule is laid down (although some important exceptions may be anticipated in its formulation). It would be absurd to try. The same thing holds for moral rules.

Nevertheless, we should hesitate to accept any standing body of laws as a complete and satisfactory embodiment of ethics, for at least two reasons. It is sometimes not clear how a particular law is to apply to a given case. When this is so, judges may draw upon moral ideas not expressed in the law as a source of arguments for resolving the case. It is also sometimes questionable whether a particular law is morally acceptable. Indeed, many laws known to history, like the laws that in the United States used to uphold slavery, invite outright condemnation. Ethics and moral rules are drawn upon to determine whether particular laws are good or evil.

One might conceive of having all the moral rules that were needed for such a determination themselves enacted into law. Then the moral assessment of a particular law would be the same thing, in effect, as determining whether one law was consistent with other ones, morally more fundamental. As a matter of fact, however, the bodies of law that we actually find enacted by governments and upheld in the courts do not embrace all the important points of ethics. For example, it is an important point in ethics that people should help others who are in distress; it is another important point that people should be kind to each other. So far as I know, however, no current government (with the possible exception of Vatican City) has laws that require these things generally; and it is a contingent matter whether a government has a law requiring either of them in any particular application. France has a law requiring people to help others who are in physical danger, when they can do so without undue danger to themselves; Canada and the United States do not (except in Quebec and Vermont).

At most we might hold that every important moral rule currently needed ought to have been enacted and would have been enacted under ideal circumstances for law making. What would these circumstances have been? The beginnings of an answer: the circumstances should not be so ideal, in respect either to the character of the persons involved or to the external causes operating upon them, that the issues with which we are concerned would not arise in them. It may suffice to imagine circumstances like our own, with people as reasonable as most people we know and with as much good will, but more fully informed, more equal in say as to what is to be done, and more systematically required to justify their opinions and actions. When choosing rules, in such circumstances, every person would be impelled to take into account every other person's interests and to deal with those interests on an equal footing. Rules that favored some people rather than others would be rejected; they could not be defended by any person to every other person simultaneously. They would not meet the test proposed by Bentham (1748–1832) of being in principle capable of being justified "by a person addressing himself to the community" (*Introduction to the Principles of Morals and Legislation* [London: 1789–1823], chapter 2, footnote 7). Nor would they meet the test proposed by Kant (1724–1804) of being rules that could be legislated by rational agents as rules which everyone could rationally follow (see his *Critique of Practical Reason and Other Writings in Moral Philosophy*, translated by Lewis White Beck [Chicago: University of Chicago Press, 1949]).

## *Comment:*

# PERSONS NATURAL AND UNNATURAL

It is indispensable, of course, that one understand what other people's interests amount to before one can take them into account; and one may expect moral agents to understand and appreciate each other's interests better the more the agents resemble one another. Moreover, if the agents are all of the same kind, this will help a great deal to keep the rules simple while they yet apply to every agent with the same effect, as the agents turn and turn about act upon each other or are acted upon. James S. Coleman, in an interesting discussion of the difficulties that firms and people have in dealing with each other (*Power and the Structure of Society* [New York: Norton, 1974], especially chapter 4), argues that one of the great difficulties of arriving at a satisfactory system of rules, once firms are brought into the picture, is that firms are not agents of the same kind as natural persons. They do not have the same interests, nor do they pursue their interests in the same way.

Economists disagree about whether firms continually seek to maximize profits. Firms may forego greater profits in the short run to have greater profits in the long run. They may even act more with the aim of having a longer run—staying in business as long as possible—than with the aim of assuring themselves of having the greatest amount of profits from their whole time in business. Or they may aim simply to have as much profit as they got last year and more besides. Given any of these aims, however, their interests are much more concentrated than the interests of natural persons. In every transaction, making money, as a condition of staying in business, is directly or indirectly the uppermost consideration.

Natural persons, by contrast, have all sorts of interests to be pursued outside business. They may not want to be in business at all, much less stay in it indefinitely. Moreover, in business, as well as out of it, their interests are not concentrated on making money. For example, they want to make friends, even in business, and keep them; they want sympathy and heart-felt approval from their friends. Are these selfish interests? If they are, they can hardly be disentangled from unselfish ones, since the people who have them want also to serve their friends and may enjoy doing kindnesses for them even more than they enjoy having kindnesses returned.

Firms do not have interests rooted like these in feeling. There is, more-over, a dramatic difference between firms and natural persons in respect to fellow-feeling. One thing we might wish to postulate in describing the ideal circumstances for making laws or rules—it may be indispensable to generat-ing more than a minimal body of moral rules—is that the actors' good will extends to feeling for each other, rejoicing in each other's moments of happiness, feeling compassion for each other's misfortunes. Firms, how-ever, do not feel anything (whatever their advertising and publicity may pretend); and, on Coleman's showing, natural persons, when they act for firms, are systematically induced to act with less than natural feeling. They are not so involved as when they are acting for themselves; and insofar as they are involved, they are likely to be more concerned with their position and prospects in the firm than with treating fairly and adequately the interests of individual natural persons who are struggling for the firm's attention.

Firms, including giant firms, have become very familiar presences in modern societies. Yet people still feel more comfortable—more familiar with what is at stake on both sides, and with how to act for mutual benefits—dealing with other people, other natural persons. Coleman points out that as customers they like dealing with small shopkeepers and will often even pay a premium in higher prices to do so; and that as workers they are less militant in small workshops than they are in huge factories. On the other hand—in revenge, as the French say—firms seem to be set up better to deal with firms than they are with natural persons. They give each other more favorable rates and more attentive service.

When persons do turn to dealing with firms, their moral consciousness tends to thin out. Many do not feel that "ripping off" the telephone company is a serious form of moral delinquency, although reflection and argument may well show otherwise. They are inclined to be amused, even to applaud, when they see someone score a point against a firm. Since firms, for their part, are often inflexible and inconsiderate of individual persons' particular needs, it often seems that the firm somehow deserves to be punished. On the firms' side, policies are often adopted that involve deception (for example, in misleading advertising) or oppression (in the treatment of workers or in legal action against customers) or other evils that natural persons would feel ashamed to practice upon other persons face to face.

This behavior—on both sides—may have as much to do with there being no settled moral rules to follow as with there being rules that are commonly flouted. The received morality, developed to deal with relations between persons, may expect people to give consideration to each other in ways that are not appropriate in relations between firms or between firms and persons. Do we then have to work out another morality for these relations? Perhaps so. Yet we shall not want to sacrifice more than we have to of the safeguards for personal interests furnished in received morality. Moreover, we may well want to invoke the same general principles that lie behind received morality. Firms are institutions organized by human beings, and like other institutions may be required to serve in the end the interests of all the human beings who are affected by the presence and the conduct of the institutions.

# SEVEN MORE CASES IN WHICH YOU MIGHT BE INVOLVED

*[You can hardly have escaped having had some business dealings with other people. Unless you have led an extraordinarily sheltered life, you are even less likely, in society as it is today, to have never dealt with firms. Whether you have always dealt with them perfectly correctly from a moral point of view depends upon issues that arise in the following seven cases.]*

### THE GREAT MIXED NUTS CAPER

*[Experience shows that in answering an anonymous quiz about the following case and its three versions, students offer extremely varied reactions.]*

You are one of the most devoted consumers of dry-roasted mixed nuts in the city. A jar of them usually costs almost twice as much as a jar of dry-roasted peanuts, the current price of which is $1.19.

*Version 1.* You take a jar of mixed nuts from the shelf and find that the price sticker reads "$1.19." Evidently the stockboy has mistaken the jar for a jar of peanuts; indeed, he has mistaken some two dozen jars for jars of peanuts, which stand next on the shelf.

*Version 2.* You bring a jar of mixed nuts, with an appropriate price sticker ($2.29) to the check-out. The cashier, mistaking it for a jar of peanuts, rings up, you notice, "$1.19."

*Version 3.* You did not notice when you took the jar of mixed nuts from the shelf that it had no price sticker. The cashier asks you whether you remember the price.

*[I interpolate a comment before going on to the four next cases.]*

## Comment:

## TRADERS' MORALITY

One thing that I expect will have emerged from the discussion of this case is that the rules to govern it do not seem to have been fully fixed for us in our society. (This does not mean that every subject of moral concern that it touches upon is in flux in every possible way.) For one thing, it's not quite clear when the price demanded is set by the supermarket (or the supermarket chain). Is it set when the stockboy puts the price sticker on, or when the check-out girl rings a price up?

Once we know what is to count as setting the price, we have the beginning of formulation of a rule for dealing with the supermarket—the beginning of the "Whenever . . ." or the "Given that . . ." part of the rule. It is only the beginning, however. It does not tell us whether we are to go on and fill out the rule so as to say, "Pay whatever price is thus set"; or to allow, in filling out the rule, that when the supermarket has made a mistake in setting the price, we should refrain from taking advantage of the firm, and even, helpfully, call one of its employees' (say, the check-out girl's) attention to the mistake. These two ways of filling out the rule reflect two very different approaches to dealing with the supermarket, each of which could be argued to be guided by morally defensible rules—rules that persons would adopt in ideal circumstances as being at least consistent with protecting and advancing the interests of everybody.

One approach is that of what we might call "traders' morality." According to traders' morality, every party to a transaction—in the mixed nuts case, you on the one hand, the supermarket chain on the other—looks out for his or her own interest. In particular, everyone is responsible for anticipating and correcting his or her own mistakes. Force and fraud are ruled out. However, if one party makes a mistake in favor of the other—setting a lower price than was intended, for example—the other is free to take full advantage of the lapse. One could argue, morally, that everyone's interests will be taken care of well enough, even best of all, under this system. Everyone will have an incentive to be specially alert to losses and benefits, and a lot of trouble and confusion will be avoided if the other parties just act on lapses and don't have to discuss how the lapses are to be rectified.

Yet does this not seem a very minimal sort of morality? It does not encourage people to help others; it has no room for compassion or neighborliness. Given the corporate character of a supermarket chain, it may be hard to imagine how to treat it as a friend or neighbor. However, we might—surely many of us would—treat very differently a corner grocer who made a mistake in setting a price. People who would cheerfully take advantage of the lapse by the supermarket chain would be disinclined to take similar advantage of "Aunt Sally" Smith at the corner store and would be very embarrassed if they were caught doing so. Is the supermarket chain entirely unworthy of benefiting from neighbors' morality? Would we be content to have it practice traders' morality on us, taking advantage of our mistakes?

### TEMPTATIONS IN COLLECTING INSURANCE

*[The following double case may make it clearer why it is difficult for natural persons to practice neighbors' morality with corporations. It is not just size and impersonality; the corporations offer people a limited number of alternatives, none of which may match a given person's needs. The person typically has no chance to negotiate for something that does match. The firms' scale of operations tends to make them (as Coleman pointed out) inflexible in matters of detail. Is it unreasonable then for people to take matters into their own hands, and in effect to adapt the alternatives to suit themselves and their situations? This may not be quite right either. It may not look right at all, if you reflect that you have agreed to a contract with the insurance company that excludes coverage of certain sorts. Does it make any difference that you may reasonably suppose that the company expects certain liberties to be taken with its contracts, and therefore charges a higher premium as a precaution?]*

*One.* You are a master gardener and landscape contractor, justly proud of your reputation for doing good work and standing by it. Tools worth more than $850 are stolen one night from your truck while it is parked in your driveway. You have a homeowner's policy that covers you against theft of personal belongings, and you can recover $400 under this policy if the tools are counted as personal belongings. As you well know, however, the company puts business equipment in a different category; if it discovers that the tools were used by you in your business, it will not pay a cent.

*Two.* You visit an artist's studio while you are out on a drive with your girl(boy)friend. She(he) is very much taken with a framed watercolor landscape, and in a burst of affection and enthusiasm, you buy it for (her)(him) for $150. You put the picture in the car and drive on. An hour or so later, while you stop for lunch at a village café, the car is broken into, and the picture is stolen. You have an insurance policy protecting you against theft of your personal belongings; your girl(boy)friend does not.

COMPETING FOR A SUMMER JOB

*[Evidently we can think of connections—parts of the world of business—in which traders' morality may work out to an economic optimum for everybody, considering the confusion and waste motion that it spares us. Does the same sort of reasoning justify letting other people shift for themselves in competing for employment? The following case also raises—again—the question whether a different approach would be appropriate if we were dealing not with a firm, but with a natural person. Can a small proprietor who has built up the business herself, and who will have to work side by side with the new employee every day, be excused for practicing discrimination to an extent that a big firm wouldn't be allowed to?]*

You and another student (whom you know fairly well without being buddies) have both applied for a summer job in the local office of Universal Turing Machines. You are finalists among the applicants—the only two people on the final short list. Summer jobs are scarce this year and this is a good job, but only one of you is going to get it. During your interview, the office manager seems very concerned to know whether you smoke grass. It turns out that he is an uncompromising opponent of the use of drugs hard or soft. You blandly and convincingly deny anything of the sort. So does your rival. You hear in the next few days, however—before either of you has been offered the job—that somebody on the regular staff told the manager that your rival is a heavy user of hash. You know this to be false: the rival smokes up a great deal less often than you do. Yet you say nothing to the manager and take the job when he offers it to you.

CAN A FELLOW-EMPLOYEE COUNT ON FRIENDSHIP?

*[The same questions about rivalry between persons and the unequal power than the firm has over them in deciding for or against employment arise again once people have been employed. Moreover, rivalry in seeking jobs and rivalry in keeping them can both be pushed to the point of sacrificing friendships. In the following case, the friends are not exactly rivals in keeping a job; one is going to lose employment anyway. The question is whether the other shall consult self-interest rather than friendship in doing what is required to stay on. There is something further involved: not the firm's power, nor the fact of adaptation to the firm's demands, but the extent to which the adaptation is sometimes carried as being employed on the firm's conditions becomes a habitual expectation.]*

You and your roommate (who is also your best friend) have for three summers running had jobs with with Amalgamated Pop and Consolidated

Tonic, the leading local bottler of soft drinks. You now rank as management trainees, you at the head office, your friend in the sales force assigned to the northern district. In fact, your friend has been acting head of the sales force there this summer. Things have not been going well. Sales in the district, compared to last summer, are down by two-thirds. You're convinced that it's not your friend's fault. On the contrary, sales could have been kept up if the head office had agreed to your friend's suggestion that Amalgamated Pop match the rebates which a rival firm has been offering shopkeepers in the district. Moreover, your friend has been imaginative and energetic in checking the decline in sales so far as it could be checked without rebates: the Amalgamated Pop Golliwog has put in an appearance at every bingo game, clambake, and garage sale in the district during the past two months. Yet you also know that the executives in the head office have fastened the blame on your friend. Visitors from the head office have complained about your friend's being out of the district office more often than not when they dropped in; they have disliked his somewhat casual attire; they have found his records and reports a bit sloppy. You have been asked to write an analysis of the trouble in the northern district. You know that any attempt on your part to absolve your friend will be unwelcome. The head office is determined to fire the friend, halfway through the summer. You are expected to portray your friend as slack and incompetent. You know that if you don't, your own promising future with Amalgamated Pop will fizzle out. What do you do? Will it make a difference to what you do that your friend will never see your analysis, or know who wrote it?

## LOOKING OUT FOR YOURSELF OR LOOKING OUT FOR MASSEY-FERGUSON

*[You have surely been a customer of various firms; you have very likely been an employee of one firm or another, and if you haven't you surely have friends who have. It is less likely that you have been a stockholder—partly because only a small fraction of the population in any country directly own stock in any firm (though quite a large proportion may have an indirect interest in stockownership, through pension funds and other institutions). It is less likely also because you may not yet have got far enough along in life and business to acquire any stock. Yet some people do become stockholders very young, thanks in most cases to gifts or inheritances, so you can easily imagine being a stockholder even if you haven't yet become one. In this and the following case, you will have a chance to consider how stockholders are to act toward firms in which they own stock. Are they to make as much money out of the connection as possible? Or, considering that a firm is a social institution that they may affect to some degree for good or ill (at least if enough of them act in the same way), do they have some obligation to try to affect it for the better? We shall consider first a case that raises the issue of whether there is any obligation to help the firm continue in being, considering that the good of a lot of other people beside the stockholders may depend on its continuing. This sort of issue will make different demands on*

stockholders depending on the amount of stock they hold. In the case at hand, it is assumed that you are only one of many stockholders, each of whom owns only a small amount of stock in the firm. This complicates the issue—in a way typical of many that arise in ethics, whether in the world of business or elsewhere—by making it seem rational, at least in a narrow sense, to act in your own interest without regard for what other people might do. If you can get away without helping out, it may seem rational for you to avoid going to even the least amount of trouble to help out. Yet many people would consider that it is morally worthwhile to go to some trouble, and rather contemptible to shirk any part in helping out.]

Your Uncle Harry has left you a small bundle of stock. It includes 100 shares in Massey-Ferguson, a multinational manufacturer of farm machinery that is currently having a very bad time. Past management raised capital by borrowing rather than by issuing stock, to such an extent that the firm's ratio of borrowed capital to equity capital is extraordinarily high. Several years of poor sales—due to a slump in the market for grain and high interest rates—have made it increasingly difficult for Massey-Ferguson to service its debt-load (high interest rates don't help here, either). The banks have become less and less patient. So Massey-Ferguson, a mainstay of industry in many places, with dozens of plants and thousands of employees, now teeters on the edge of bankruptcy. A new management has come in. It is energetically trying to effect economies; at the same time it is trying to refinance the firm. As part of its refinancing scheme, it hopes to sell new stock. You realize that if you and other present stockholders sell out now, the stock will go down in price, jeopardizing the chances of the firm's raising enough money to survive. On the other hand, the issuance of new shares will dilute ownership and probably drive down the price of the stock anyway. There is, furthermore, no guarantee that, even if the firm raises all the money it plans to, the firm will become profitable again. Would it be quixotic of you to refrain from selling on the ground that refraining would help the firm?

[I interpolate another comment before going on to the remaining two cases.]

## Comment:

# HUMAN WELFARE, HAPPINESS, AND RIGHTS

In the case just preceding, the good of people dependent on the firm, apart from the stockholders—the good of the employees and of the townspeople with whom the employees traded—was a consideration that operated independently of any rights that they had. The rights—certainly the legal rights—were all on the side of the stockholders, who were free to sell out if they pleased. On the other side, as things stand in the world of business, no rights were at stake, but simply the happiness or welfare of the people affected. The happiness of the people affected is the consideration chiefly insisted upon by the leading philosophers in the utilitarian school of ethics, among them Bentham. Their position is called "utilitarian" because they hold that actions and policies must be justified ultimately by being useful, or having utility, in contributing to happiness.

They would have done better to represent themselves as maintaining the ethics of human welfare. In fact, the particular matters that come up under human welfare—for example, how many people have jobs, or other means of obtaining the income to meet their needs—are just the matters that in practical applications utilitarianism has been most concerned with. Bentham talked about measuring happiness and outlined a calculus for doing so. Yet nobody has ever seriously tried to use such a calculus. It has been very rare for censuses to be taken, or in lieu of censuses sample surveys, to discover what proportions of people are happy (or say they are happy) as against the proportions unhappy.

Applied ethics and social policy have been preoccupied instead with particular matters of welfare: jobs, housing, sanitation, diet. These can, of course, be taken as conditions of happiness, in the sense that if they are provided for, the chances of people's being happy are greater. So it has been consistent of utilitarians to aim at providing for them in the first instance. However, they have a greater moral importance than the first instance alone confers upon them, as mere means to happiness. Utilitarians would have avoided a lot of objections if they had seen more clearly that our basic obligations to other people attach to their welfare rather than to their happiness. A common objection to utilitarianism is that it calls, gratuitously, for some people to forego some pleasure if other people obtain a more than equal increement of pleasure as a result. The objection does not hold against calling upon some people to forego some pleasure in order to keep other people from starving.

This is not to say that happiness has no claim to moral attention. The utilitarians' Greatest Happiness Principle, if it is understood as calling, first, for meeting the needs of everybody affected (under certain constraints like letting people manage their own lives) and, second, for doing what can be done (again under certain constraints) to make people happy who are not happy now, remains an impressive candidate for serving as the one fundamental principle of ethics. (Notice that I do not speak of "the greatest happiness of the greatest number"; that is a notion which breaks down as soon as we consider the possibility of raising a few people to a higher level of happiness instead of raising many to a level somewhat less high.)

Beside human welfare and happiness, ethics is concerned with rights. Some rights may originate—or be justified—as devices to protect the welfare of the people to whom they are ascribed, and enable them to meet their needs; or as devices for advancing their happiness. Other rights, however, represent constraints upon the Greatest Happiness Principle—for example, the right to have effects on oneself considered along with effects on others; the right to have the effects weighed on the same basis; the right to continue as a living member of the community. At first sight, justice has more to do with respecting rights, especially these rights, than it does with happiness. I shall try to explain later how justice and happiness are related.

For the moment, as we contemplate the following case, it may suffice to recognize that on the side of the people affected by what the stockholders do there are, as there were not in the case just preceding, rights as well as welfare and happiness to consider. They are the rights to have the same chances of employment as other people, and the same conditions of work; and the rights to have access on an equal basis to all public facilities. These, of course, have been rights of much agitated domestic concern in the United States and Canada in the past thirty years or so. Stockholders, demanding that their firms respect these rights at home (and thereby at least take into account the welfare and happiness of the people whose rights they are), are acting simultaneously as public-spirited citizens. When the stockholders demand the same things when the firms operate abroad, we may look upon them as acting as citizens of the world.

STOCKHOLDER AND CITIZEN OF THE WORLD

In the bundle that Uncle Harry left you, there are also 100 shares of the Worldwide Typewriter and Adding Machine Company, which has a branch in South Africa. The call for the annual general meeting, which you have just received, reveals that a church-oriented group of stockholders has put forward a motion condemning the racial discrimination sanctioned—indeed, prescribed—by law in South Africa and urging Worldwide to suspend operations there while the discrimination continues. Management (as corporation managements typically do in such cases) asks you to vote, or to give your proxy for voting, against the motion. It argues that Worldwide's operations are helping to improve conditions in South Africa by giving blacks employment and paying them better wages than local employers would. How do you vote? Would you vote differently if you were a stockholder in a big bank that was being urged to stop lending money to the government of South Africa?

CITIZEN AND EMPLOYEE

*[As a citizen, you have reasons for wanting firms to refrain from injuring fellow-citizens; to respect the law when the law is a good one; and to cooperate in legal ways to change the law when the law is a bad one. We have just seen that these reasons may create problems for people who are stockholders as well as citizens. They may create problems for people who are both citizens and employees. In the following case, the issue has to do with a matter of special importance to citizens: to have a government tolerably free from undue influence by special interests. Having such a*

*government is the purpose of regulating campaign contributions. Which does a stockholder—or an employee, here an employee—put first, civic duty or economic interest?]*

Your summer job as a management trainee with Albatross Airlines, a big transcontinental carrier, leads by chance to your discovering that the company has made an illegal contribution of $55,000 in corporate funds to the campaign of a candidate for president of the United States. The contribution was paid into the Swiss bank account of a Lebanese agent of the company as a "special commission" for selling "used aircraft to Middle East Airlines." Thus laundered, it was turned over by the agent to the candidate's finance committee. There is no sign that any investigator for the government has knowledge of the contribution. You have hitherto been a conscientious citizen. You turned out, during the spring term, to applaud a congressman who denounced the influence that large firms often acquired through political contributions. You even signed a petition supporting a bill that the congressman introduced to have campaign contributions regulated more closely. On the other hand, you're looking forward to a career with Albatross Airlines. Do you "blow the whistle" on the $55,000 contribution by giving information about it to the police or to the press?

## *Comment:*

# A WORKING BASIS FOR ETHICAL DISCUSSION

Piece by piece, in previous comments I have supplied, by way of reminders, enough of the main pieces of ethics to assemble a working basis for discussing the issues that have come up so far. I have also supplied, chiefly in my comment on moral rules arrived at in ideal circumstances and in my comment on the Greatest Happiness Principle, some clues as to how the pieces fit into a general view of ethics, and hence how they may be used together as an approximation to such a general view.

With only a little supplementation, the same working basis will serve for discussing the diverse illustrative materials that follow in this book. There are many more particular issues to treat in these materials; and at least one leading subject of moral concern to add to those already remarked on, deception and oppression. At a few points during the survey of these materials I shall interpolate comments in which I introduce some further ideas that have an important place in a general view of ethics. However, for the most part I shall confine myself, during the survey, to explaining how each item fits into the tableau of issues presented in my outline. Only occasionally will this explanation amount to an extended comment about what the item reveals, and this comment may have to do with the appropriate analogies for understanding competition, or with impacts on culture, rather than with systematically completing the work of giving a general view of ethics.

I shall wait to complete that work—so far as I try to complete it in this book—until after the survey is over. I shall wait until then, too, to do what I try to do to resolve the conflict between traders' morality and neighbors' morality. Even then, I propose to do no more than offer one consistent general view of ethics, and one scheme of resolution consistent with it. I mean to leave open, as much as possible, the opportunity for people using this book to adopt other views, both particular and general. I do not mean to suggest—I reject the suggestion—that there is no difference between true views and false views. Discussion of the cases just presented will, I hope, have renewed faith in the triplet principle—that on any subject of moral concern, sometimes it is clear that everything is all right, and sometimes it is clear that something is drastically wrong, even if sometimes, again, arguments pull both ways, and one must expect to encounter a diversity of particular views.

Ethics is a rich and complex subject—as it is bound to be, considering the variety of human circumstances and the variety of possible responses to them—and there are, I suppose, a number of equally convincing ways of developing general views of it, although the results should be capable of being harmonized. The cases assembled in this book are sufficiently diverse to represent at least approximately the richness and complexity of ethics as a whole; and I offer them, arranged in a tableau, rather than my comments as the main source of stimulus to developing a view of ethics.

Let me nevertheless say a few more words about moral rules and the Greatest Happiness Principle.

First, Kant's test for rules is doubly an artifice: we do not normally formulate the maxims—the policies—under which we propose to act; nor do we ask systematically whether such maxims can be generalized. It might be an improvement in some respects if we did these things; in other respects—flexibility, the capacity to balance between marginal improvements on different lines—we might do worse. In any case, we don't carry things that far. The notion of rules, when rules explicit in the laws are not in question, represents our actual practices in moral discussion no further than to indicate that we do check, or can be asked to check, the consistency of what we do in one case with what we do in another ("If you do A when the situation is S, why don't you do A when the situation seems much the same, S-prime?"). We also, the notion of rules indicates, check the consistency of what we do with what we expect others to do when they are similarly placed, especially when they are placed so as to be able to act upon us in the same way.

Second, the relation between rules and the Greatest Happiness Principle is this: when we do (as in the law) have explicit rules in view, they should be consistent with the Greatest Happiness Principle, and so should any approximations to rules that are at issue when the rules are not explicit. If they are not consistent, they should be changed. Some philosophers think that rules other than the Greatest Happiness Principle are only a convenience, which spares us the trouble of actually working out what that principle prescribes in the case of any particular action. I think they are assuming, unrealistically, that we could always, given enough trouble, provide ourselves with the information required to apply the Principle directly. They may even be mistaken in thinking that full information would always enable us to resort to the principle directly. We need not decide this issue here. (It can serve as an example of a problem, beyond the scope of this book, to be taken up in advanced ethical theory.) For our purposes, it will suffice to recognize that the Greatest Happiness Principle is itself an explicit rule, which, carefully enough formulated to mention various constraints, will pass Kant's test.

It is a more basic rule, closer to the heart of morality, than any other, except the rule in which Kant's test is expressed. With that rule it is in a relation of mutual dependence: it supplies considerations without which Kant's test remains too formal to have convincing applications in real-world morality; on the other hand, it can be required to pass Kant's test itself, and given suitable constraints, it does so. The Greatest Happiness Principle is also, along with Kant's test, a more general rule than any other, since it applies to every situation whatever. If it does not apply directly, it applies indirectly, by selecting a rule (or something like a rule, the approximation of a rule) that does apply directly.

# PART TWO

# The Actions of Firms: Firms Dealing with the Consuming Public

# CHAPTER **4**

# *Sales Tactics*

*Introductory Comment:*

## LEGAL JUDGMENTS AND MORAL ONES

Only now do we begin focusing upon what might have seemed at first sight to embrace the whole field of ethics in business. We have spent a surprisingly long time considering one person dealing with another, or persons dealing with—acting upon—firms. Only now does the focus shift to how firms behave, whether acting upon people or otherwise. (Typically, remember, as I am using the term, firms are incorporated businesses, some of them very large and complex organizations.) However, this focus on firms is the focus that we shall keep for most of the rest of the book, so its importance will not be slighted.

The variety of illustrative materials to be brought forward in this chapter and succeeding ones will often include rulings of courts and by quasi-judicial bodies; sometimes statutes are mentioned or represented by excerpts. These materials give some idea of what the law is on certain points, and simultaneously some idea of what people have cared enough about morally to make into law. This legal information, however, is entirely incidental to the purpose for which these materials are gathered here. I have not even systematically made sure of the final disposition of the cases at issue, whether after appeal to a higher court (where one exists) or after being remanded for a new trial (which does not always occur, since the parties may at that point settle out of court). For the most part, the cases do represent current precedents; but exactly how the precedents apply to further cases requires more legal knowledge than this book contains or pretends to.

The materials are presented for ethical discussion. The legal examples are especially useful in this connection because in them we find judges and others reasoning out issues more carefully and more explicitly than we normally do in everyday life. Moreover, the issues are entirely authentic ones, which have come up in the real world of business. The reasoning runs, at least part of the way, along lines on which moral reasoning and legal reasoning might coincide.

This is not to say that the moral reasoning is correct; it may sometimes be reasoning that you will find quite misguided. Nor is the law, in the statutes and precedents relevant to the case or in what the judges make of them, necessarily morally good law, however firmly established. How courts decide issues is one thing; how the issues ought to be decided, if the laws were good ones, is another. Laws sometimes actively promote bad things; even more often, they fall short of reaching all outrageous instances of deception, oppression, and other evils. Some people in business (and elsewhere) profess to think they are being sufficiently ethical if they stay within the law. Nothing in ethics is more doubtful, as we have already seen and will see again many times over.

*[Knavery is often more interesting—it is more scandalous than exemplary good conduct. Certainly it comes before the courts more often. The items that I bring up under "sales tactics" are in number disproportionately knavish. Yet the triplet principle is not to be forgotten: the last item but one is an in-between case; and the last item offers a code of good conduct. Good conduct is further alluded to in my comments; and what it amounts to can always be inferred, at least in outline, from an instance of knavery, as its opposite.]*

## THE QUEEN v. EDMONTON PIERCE-ARROW & HUPMOBILE LTD.*

*District Court, Northern Alberta, Judicial District of Edmonton, 1974*

LEGG, D. C. J.:—Edmonton Pierce-Arrow & Hupmobile Ltd is charged with two counts of fraud . . . through its used-car sales manager, Daniel Doyce, [it] purchased some 26 automobiles in Ontario and shipped them to Alberta. After the vehicles were unloaded, but before being placed on the used-car sales lot, the odometers of some of these vehicles were turned back so that

*Excerpt from *Dominion Law Reports* (49 DLR 3rd, pp. 131–37). Copyright 1975 by Canada Law Book Ltd., 240 Edward St., Aurora, Ontario L4G 3S9, and reprinted by their permission. Except for the judge's name, names are changed throughout.

the odometer reading showed that the vehicle had been driven a substantially smaller number of miles than it had in fact been driven.

The vehicles which are the subject-matter of the two counts of fraud in the indictment were two of the vehicles purchased in Ontario on which the odometers were turned back.

The odometers were altered by a third party on the instructions of the used-car sales manager, Doyce, and when the vehicles were offered for sale the odometer reading was incorrect.

With regard to count number one, I find that Mr. & Mrs. Gargery were defrauded of the sum of $2,495. Mr. Gargery was interested in purchasing a vehicle with a correct odometer reading in the 30,000-mile bracket. He located a 1970 Torino with an odometer reading of 39,000 miles plus, which he purchased for $2,495 by trading in a vehicle for which he received credit of $895 and by paying cash of $1,600.

He testified that he was not interested in purchasing a vehicle with mileage in excess of 50,000 miles, which was the correct number of miles the 1970 Torino had been driven, and would not have purchased the vehicle had he known the correct mileage. He had asked the salesman if the mileage of 39,000 miles plus was correct, and the salesman replied that it was.

The Gargerys were induced to purchase the vehicle by the false and deceitful statements of the salesman, and by the fact that the vehicle was offered for inspection by them with an incorrect odometer reading. . . .

I am also satisifed that Mr. Lillyvick was defrauded of the sum of $2,595, as set out in count number two, when he purchased a 1971 Ford Custom 500 showing a mileage of 32,000 miles plus. The evidence disclosed that the vehicle had been driven in excess of 62,000 miles. Lillyvick testified that he would not have purchased the vehicle with that number of miles on it.

Lillyvick testified that he had heard that if an odometer is turned back it is impossible to get the numbers on the odometer lined up evenly. He noted that the numbers on the odometer on the vehicle in question were uneven, and this prompted him to inquire if the odometer reading for the vehicle was correct. The salesman made some comments which Lillyvick describes as being made somewhat in jest, but in any event he was satisfied by the salesman's comment that the odometer reading was correct.

The main issue in this trial is whether the accused corporation can be held criminally liable for the act of its used-car sales manager if such act is done within the scope of his authority. . . .

In the case at bar the used-car sales manager, Doyce, was not an officer or director of the accused company. He operated two used-car lots for the accused, which was [sic] situated close to, but did not form part of the main offices of the accused. His responsiblities were to buy used cars, clean them up, do minor reconditioning on them, fix the sales price, arrange advertising and promotion, demonstrate them to, and make sales to the public. In these duties he was assisted by a sales and other staff consisting of 12 people. He approved all sales made by the salesmen.

In the corporation structure he was responsible to Mr. Strong, the general sales manager who in turn was responsible to Mr. Wilding, the president of the accused, or to Mr. Tackleton, the secretary-treasurer and comptroller of the accused. Doyce was not a signing officer of the corporate accused, nor was he authorized to sign cheques of the accused company. However, he did approve all invoices for payment relating to the used-car segment of the accused business, and these were processed through the comptroller and cheques were prepared and placed on Mr. Wilding's desk for signature. The signing officers for the corporate accused were Mr. Wilding and Mr. Tackleton or either of them together with Mr. Chivery, the business manager of the accused.

Once the invoices were approved for payment by Doyce they were processed and paid. Mr. Wilding testified that he signed cheques on the basis of a summary presented to him with the cheques and that he had no personal knowledge of what they were for. He estimated that he signed 7,500 to 8,000 cheques annually in this fashion.

I mention this because, while Doyce did not have power to sign cheques, he had authorization to incur debts against the company which were paid by the company once he gave his approval. In my opinion the distinction between the two is very narrow.

Specifically, when the used-car stock was low, Doyce suggested that some cars be purchased from eastern Canada, and he was authorized to make the purchases and did in fact purchase the vehicles to a value in excess of $48,000. In doing so he selected the vehicles, signed all the necessary documentation, arranged shipping, and did all things necessary to acquire title to the vehicles in the name of the accused company. After the vehicles were placed on the sales lots he fixed the sales price and advertised some of them in the *Edmonton Journal*. All these acts were within the scope of Doyce's authority as used-car sales manager.

In my opinion, Doyce was not a lesser employee. I find that it was the policy of the accused corporation to delegate to him "the sole active and directing will" of the corporation in all matters relating to the used-car operation of the company, and as such he was its directing mind and will. His actions and intent were those of the accused itself and his conduct renders the company criminally liable. . . .

I accept the evidence of Mr. Wilding that he had no personal knowledge of the circumstances which led to these charges being laid and that he had circulated written instructions to all segments of his company not to alter odometers on the vehicles. However, this is not, in my opinion, a defence in light of the findings I have made.

Edmonton Pierce-Arrow & Hupmobile Ltd. is guilty on both counts in the indictment.

*[One should not think that only active measures of deception like turning back the odometer constitute fraudulent sales tactics. Bearing upon the earlier automobile case, the sale of the Scatback, courts have held that the failure to mention material facts as to the drawbacks of what is being offered for sale amounts to fraud. In a case from 1911, a man and wife named Sterns sued a man named Weikel who had sold them a house without telling them*

*that in the cellar was a pit collecting sewage from a neighboring building. The Kentucky Court of Appeals held that "a man must be presumed to intend the necessary consequences of his own voluntary act. The voluntary doing of an act which necessarily results in injury to another, where the party knows the facts and had reason to know that the injury will result, will sustain an action for fraud. . . . It is not necessary that a misrepresentation in words be made . . . [Weikel] knew the pit full of sewage was in the cellar, and a reasonable man situated as he was must have known that such a pit, with a pipe running into it carrying in water and more sewage every day . . . would render that house unfit for a residence. To sell such a house without disclosing the situation, when the purchaser would have no means of knowing the facts from the pit being covered up . . . was to practice a fraud upon him."*

## Anonymous Quiz: *Are There Any Nice Guys in Business?*

At this point, it should be interesting for a class using this book to collect its opinions on a question that must already have come up often in the discussion.

1.  Imagine a used-car dealer, when he realizes the customer is too inexperienced to recognize what a lemon he is being offered, and yet needs a car badly, with little to spend on one, relenting and shifting the customer to a reasonably reliable automobile.
2.  Imagine a house-owner, discovering that his carpenter badly underestimated the costs of a repair and stands to lose money in return for three days' hard work, offering to renegotiate the price of the work. the work.

For each of these cases, say whether you think the action is

A.  Crazy?
B.  Quite extraordinary in human relations of any kind, though not crazy?
C.  Neither crazy nor extraordinary in other sorts of human relations, but absent from normal business practice?

*The next item comes from one of a number of lawsuits concerning commercial dance studios. Not all of the suits have gone the same way, but the judgment reproduced here indicates that not even flattery is always a permissible sales tactic.]*

# SNEVELLICCI* v. ARTHUR MURRAY, INC.

*District Court of Appeals of Florida, 1968.*

PIERCE, Judge. This is an appeal by Sally Snevellicci, plaintiff below, from a final order dismissing with prejudice, for failure to state a cause of action, her . . . complaint.

Plaintiff Mrs. Sally Snevellicci, a widow of 51 years and without family, had a yen to be "an accomplished dancer" with the hopes of finding "new interest in life." So on February 10, 1961, a dubious fate, with the assist of a motivated acquaintance, procured [sic] her to attend a "dance party" at Davenport's "School of Dancing" where she whiled away the pleasant hours, sometimes in a private room, absorbing [Davenport's] accomplished sales technique, during which her grace and poise were elaborated upon and her rosy future as "an excellent dancer" was painted for her in vivid and glowing colors. As an incident to this interlude, [Davenport] sold her eight half-hour dance lessons to be utilized within one calendar month therefrom, for the sum of $14.50 cash in hand paid, obviously a baited "come-on."

Thus she embarked upon an almost endless pursuit of the terpsichorean art during which, over a period of less than sixteen months, she was sold fourteen "dance courses" totaling in the aggregate 2302 hours of dancing lessons for a total cash outlay of $31,090.45, all at [Davenport's] dance emporium. All of these fourteen courses were evidenced by execution of a written "Enrollment Agreement—Arthur Murray's School of Dancing" with the addendum in heavy black print, "No one will be informed that you are taking dancing lessons. Your relations with us are held in strict confidence," setting forth the number of "dancing lessons" and the "lessons in rhythm sessions" currently sold to her from time to time, and always of course accompanied by payment of cash of the realm.

These dance lesson contracts and the monetary consideration therefor of over $31,000 were procured from her by means and methods of Davenport and his associates which went beyond the unsavory, yet legally permissible, perimeter of "sales puffing" and intruded well into the forbidden area of undue influence, the suggestion of falsehood, the suppression of truth, and the free exercise of rational judgment, if what plaintiff alleged in her complaint was true. From the time of her first contact with the dancing school in February 1961, she was influenced unwittingly by a constant and continuous barrage of flattery, false praise, excessive compliments, and panegyric encomiums, to such extent that it would be not only inequitable, but unconscionable, for a Court exercising inherent chancery power to allow such contracts to stand.

*A fictitious name.

She was incessantly subjected to overreaching blandishment and cajolery. She was assured she had "grace and poise"; that she was "rapidly improving and developing in her dancing skill"; that the additional lessons would "make her a beautiful dancer, capable of dancing with the most accomplished dancers"; that she was "rapidly progressing in the development of her dancing skill and gracefulness", etc., etc. She was given "dance aptitute tests" for the ostensible purpose of "determining" the number of remaining hours instructions needed by her from time to time. . . .

In fact she did not develop in her dancing ability, she had no "dance aptitude," and in fact had difficulty in "hearing the musical beat." The complaint alleged that such representations to her "were in fact false and known by the defendant to be false and contrary to the plaintiff's true ability, the truth of plaintiff's ability being fully known to the defendants, but withheld from the plaintiff for the sole and specific intent to deceive and defraud the plaintiff and to induce her in the purchasing of additional hours of dance lessons." It was averred that the lessons were sold to her "in total disregard to the true physical, rhythm, and mental ability of the plaintiff." In other words, while she first exulted that she was entering the "spring of her life," she finally was awakened to the fact there was "spring" neither in her life nor in her feet.

The complaint prayed that the Court decree the dance contracts to be null and void and to be canceled, that an accounting be had, and judgment entered against the defendants "for that portion of the $31,090.45 not charged against specific hours of instruction given to the plaintiff." The Court held the complaint not to state a cause of action and dismissed it with prejudice. We disagree and reverse.

The material allegations of the complaint must, of course, be accepted as true for the purpose of testing its legal sufficiency. Defendants contend that contracts can only be rescinded for fraud or misrepresentation as to a material fact, rather than an opinion, prediction or expectation, and that the statements and representations set forth at length in the complaint were in the category of "trade puffing," within its legal orbit.

It is true that "generally a misrepresentation, to be actionable, must be one of fact rather than of opinion." . . . But this rule has significant qualifications, applicable here. It does not apply where there is a fiduciary relationship between the parties, or where there has been some artifice or trick employed by the representor, or where the parties do not in general deal at "arm's length" as we understand the phrase, or where the representee does not have equal opportunity to become apprised of the truth or falsity of the fact represented. . . .

It could be reasonably supposed here that defendants had "superior knowledge" as to whether plaintiff had "dance potential" and as to whether she was noticeably improving in the art of terpsichore. . . .

Even in contractural situations where a party to a transaction owes no duty to disclose facts within his knowledge or to answer inquires respecting such facts, the law is if he undertakes to do so he must disclose the *whole truth*.

We repeat that where parties are dealing on a contractual basis at arm's length with no inequities or inherently unfair practices employed, the Courts will in general "leave the parties where they find themselves." But in the case sub judice . . . from the showing made in her complaint, plaintiff is entitled to her day in Court.

*   *   *

## Comment:

# EASY STAGES

---

[Snevellicci] v. Arthur Murray Inc. illustrates, among other things, the sales tactic of "easy stages," which is worth discussing to bring to light some subtler objections to salesmanship.

One of the entries in a spring sales catalogue from Simpsons-Sears (the Canadian branch of Sears Roebuck) suggests, "Save $120 on our most powerful CRAFTSMAN air compressor: $799.99." Wouldn't it break their salesmen's hearts to have to say, "$800; and if you buy it on time at 20 percent interest, repaying over a two-year period, you're really contemplating an outlay of $960"? Yet the style of the entry is comparatively straightforward. It is common practice to offer an encyclopedia, an automobile, or a new roof at so much (some easily digestible figure) *down*. Perhaps one adds "24 months to pay." The idea, of course, is to divert prospects' attention from the full cost of the merchandise in question and thereby improve the chances that they will consider they can afford to buy it.

This is, as I say, common practice—so common that it is taken for granted on both sides, which somewhat mitigates the deception. However, looked at closely, is it not clearly a dishonest practice, which succeeds only insofar as the customers are effectively distracted and to some degree deceived about the full cost? One may hypothesize that some sales would be lost if instead the cost had been frankly stated. Moreover, it will not suffice, for strict honesty, for the salesman(person) to come clean sometime or other before the deal is concluded—perhaps only when the prospects, who by now have quite rearranged their assumptions about the gratifications awaiting them in the immediate future, have their pens in the air, poised to sign the contract. For deception is involved when the prospects are sucked in by easy stages.

Are such tactics in accord even with traders' morality? When the notion of traders' morality was introduced it was conceived of as ruling out force and outright fraud (for example, not delivering the goods specified), but as licensing both sides of a transaction to take advantage of the other's mistakes. It was up to the supermarket to set the price on mixed nuts, perhaps by what the sticker said, perhaps by what the cashier rang up (the indeterminacy here represents a real indeterminacy in our practices). It was up to the customers to make sure that they did not hand over more money than was asked for. (People are perhaps much less willing to abide by traders' morality in the second way.) So conceived, traders' morality does not necessarily license any attempt on either side to deceive or mislead the other. Should we, to match common practice in business, accept some sorts of deceptions, among them the deceptions involved in "easy stages"? Or should we abandon such practices? There is a rather strong argument for doing the latter and—concurrently—defining traders' morality to exclude all forms of deception. It just isn't true that everybody is on guard. Once again, we must consider that unless the deceptions sometimes work, leading people to give up money that with a clearer view of their situation they would not, there would be no point in practicing the deceptions.

Is there no room left for salesmanship? Surely there is a good deal of room. Even if salespersons were required to show prospects a card on which the products in hand were compared point by point with rival products, it would be possible for the salespersons to stress the advantages to be gained from the points on which their products were generally favored or specially suited the prospects' circumstances. Even if the full costs had to be made clear at the beginning, it would be possible sometimes to argue that the costs were lower than the costs of rival products; and the benefits more attractive than those of alternative ways in which the prospects might spend the money. If it were not possible to talk up the product in at least one of these ways, to at least some prospective customers, should the product be on the market at all? Moreover, just keeping track of particular customers and of their needs, and periodically suggesting to them that they may relish certain features of new models or new products, is an approach to sales that succeeds without deception and even provides a certain service to the customers. It has worked well for car salesmen.

I think that we can leave some room for salespersons to try to change people's preferences, so long as such attempts are open and aboveboard. An open and aboveboard attempt is to allow the prospect to use the product for a trial period. "Easy stages," even in those cases where it does involve a change of preferences, is not open and aboveboard; it is devious. Just before signing, the customers, having worked out how the encyclopedia will fit into their family lives, may really want the encyclopedia; but they were led to wanting it through deception.

## CODE OF ETHICS OF THE CANADIAN DIRECT MAIL/MARKETING ASSOCIATION*

---

*[On every hand in North America there are businesses eagerly soliciting mail orders for merchandise of limitless variety. These businesses, of course, face a problem about overcoming the inertia of their prospective*

---

*Reproduced by permission of the Canadian Direct Mail/Marketing Association.

customers. They have to make the offers so tempting that people will actually take them up. One might think, however, that they have every advantage in making the pictures and descriptions of their merchandise as flattering as possible. In most cases, the customers would be in no position beforehand to compare the pictures and descriptions with the goods themselves.

Unfortunately, many of those customers have been tempted before, and disappointed. So the mail order merchants have another problem of overcoming suspicions that the goods will not turn out, after they arrive, to match the expectations aroused by the pictures and descriptions. One way of dealing with this problem is to exercise ingenuity in putting the terms on which the goods are offered. The customers are invited to take part in a contest; or in a regional trial preceding general distribution; or in an advertising test. Sometimes the customers may become confused about whether they are buying anything; they may have the impression that they are performing some sort of community service and assisting in the advancement of science and technology.

There is, of course, a simpler way of dealing with these problems. That is to remove any cause for the customers' being dissatisifed, which implies telling the truth about the merchandise, offering it on straightforward terms, and offering relief for disappointment. It was not *caveat emptor* that big mail order houses like Sears, Roebuck depended on to build up their businesses; it was "Satisfaction—Or Your Money Back." It is not *caveat emptor* that smaller mail order businesses invoke, if they want repeated orders from the same customers; it is ethics. They want themselves known for professing ethical standards; and for abiding by them. They may organize, as in the following instance, specifically to make their adherence to ethics visible and thereby gain public confidence.]

Members of the Canadian Direct Mail/Marketing Association are expected to subscribe to and abide by the following standards. Members who use direct marketing media, who create direct mail/marketing advertisements and who are suppliers of the industry, are required to adhere to them both in fact and in spirit.

To attain the essence of the objectives of CDMMA all members shall attempt to bring about a harmonious and productive business atmosphere within the framework of free enterprise. No one shall knowingly transgress the legal or moral rights of any individual or group of individuals.

1. When goods or services are offered, copy must be completely clear and honest. An offer must be set out in such a way that it can be easily understood by the reader.
2. Photography or artwork, when used, must accurately illustrate the actual product.
3. When price comparisons are used, they must be factual and verifiable.
4. When testimonals are used they must be from bona fide users of the products or services offered, and in the possession of the seller or readily accessible.

5. When the word "guarantee" or any synonym is used, the terms of the guarantee must be clearly stated.

6. When a bonus item is offered conditional on the purchase of another item, the conditions must be stated in easily legible type.

7. Merchandise must not be shipped by sellers or their agencies without authority from the customer. In the case of "negative option" sales operations in provinces where they are permitted—(that is where the customer receives merchandise unless he instructs the seller that he does not wish to receive it)—this fact must be clearly stated in the original offer.

8. When merchandise is offered "on approval" and an advance payment has been received, a refund statement must clearly indicate whether or not mailing, shipping or handling charges are included. Refunds must be made promptly within a maximum time period of 30 days from receipt of request.

9. Mailings that promote material that can be construed as pornographic, salacious, vulgar, indecent or offensive are unacceptable to and will not be countenanced by the Canadian Direct Mail/Marketing Association.

10. Should a person request that his name be removed from a mailing list owned by a member, every conscientious effort must be made to comply. Any person making such a request should be advised of the Mail Preference Service offered by the CDMMA.

11. If there is delay in shipping goods, the customer must be advised in writing within 30 days of receipt of order, provided a proper method of communication is possible. Subject to acceptance of an unpaid order, goods offered from stock must be shipped within 30 days of receipt of order or the time limit as stated in the original offer. Any substitution of the original offer must be of a higher quality or approved by the customer before shipment.

12. When contests or prizes are used to promote the sale of merchandise, the rules of the contest must be clearly stated. All aspects of the contest must adhere precisely to constraints outlined in Section 37.2 of the Combines Investigation Act, effective January 1, 1976. Further, in addition to complying with paragraphs (a) (b) and (c) of Section 37.2, a contest must be lawful under the provisions of the Criminal Code, other federal or provincial statutes, and local by-laws.

13. The procedure for payment and collection should be so applied as to avoid undue inconvenience to the customer, making *inter alia* due allowance for postal delays.

14. Where direct marketers use a Post Office Box as a reference for customer response, a street address must also be included in the advertisement.

15. Whenever a seller uses a different name than that with which he is either registered or prominently known, he must identify the parent company.

\* \* \*

*Comment:*

# IS IT FUTILE—QUIXOTIC—TO TRY TO DO BETTER THAN OTHERS ARE DOING?

A number of occasions have come up already for critical reassessment, from a moral point of view, of practices commonly taken for granted in business. More will follow to the same effect. How readily, however, will critical thinking about these matters translate into improvements on common practices? Will people act better, mindful of the reassessment?

The thought must have occurred to you several times—it is a thought that haunts the subject—that firms or people who take it upon themselves, as individuals, to refrain from questionable practices are going to pay for doing so. Their out-of-pocket costs are likely to be greater, and they are likely to be treated to the spectacle of their rivals walking off with the business. Nice guys finish last, don't they? And, more self-critical than Don Quixote, when they do, they may find it hard not to agree with their rivals that they were suckers to be nice.

There is no way of dispelling this difficulty entirely. Sometimes, as Job lamented, the wicked prosper. Sometimes virtue requires sacrifices that are never requited. On the other hand, against one proverb we can weigh another: honesty pays, at least in the sense that there is often a coincidence between what honest—virtuous—dealing requires and what is in one's long-run business interest. A reputation for honest dealing is an important business asset, and such a reputation is hard to maintain unless it is well founded. People and firms also find it an advantage to have a reputation for respecting the public interest, and this, too, is harder to keep up if their practice in fact runs the other way.

It seems clear that the proverb "Nice guys finish last" does not give reliable comprehensive guidance to people or firms that mean to stay in business for some time. Nor is it a good general argument for getting away with anything that you can get away with. Could you use it, in a high-crime district when the police are elsewhere, to justify mugging the next person to come down the street? You might be quite correct in thinking that if you don't mug him, in all probability someone else will and will make off with gains that you are relinquishing. Similarly, you might be quite correct in thinking that if you don't misrepresent the products you are selling, competitors will. You may have competitors ready to do all sorts of things that you, as a matter of scruples and self-respect, could not bring yourself to do. If what they do does not settle what you should do here, why should it settle that issue when your feelings leave the issue open—for you— to some degree, not being so strong as to stop you from wondering what to do? Your feelings, when they are strong, can be represented as amounting to attachment to certain moral rules, and these may be carried over to settle the cases where your feelings are not so strong.

People have interests that are not confined to success in business. They have an interest in living in a society that, abiding by various moral rules, is morally congenial to them, and congenial in ways that are generally attractive. In such a society, mutual trust and mutual aid will flourish as well as mutual forbearance. If business practices conflict with these things, they sacrifice good things that people cannot expect to make up for entirely by succeeding with the questionable practices. Even if they do not, in their own view, lose as much or more by the sacrifices as they gain by the practices, it is some consolation for them that refraining from the practices assists in maintaining a congenial society, with benefits for them apart from business.

Yet in a really desperate situation, it may be ruinous for you to try to do better than the prevailing practice, and it may be futile; by yourself, you cannot make any visible difference to the practice and its consequences, even in setting an example. Even in that case, you may still have some options. You can retreat to another line of business. You can agitate for reform of the practice (finding yourself in alliance with the victims). Sometimes that will mean demanding regulation by the government. Sometimes it will mean starting up some private organization for self-regulation (like the Canadian Direct Mail/Marketing Association, at whose self-regulating code we just looked).

Moreover, it is easy to pretend that situations are desperate when in fact they are not. People commonly describe themselves as facing ruthless and relentless competition, when in fact—even when their competitors are unscrupulous—they have enough room to do various good actions without risking immediate ruin. Pending a general reform of the practice, you can refrain from taking any initiative to worsen it; you can even take some initiative to mitigate its objectionable features. Being a little franker with the customers—leaving the odometers untouched, for example—is a beginning. It may become common as a consequence of a number of uncoordinated initiatives; and, once common, be built on in further small, uncoordinated improvements. In this way, the practice and along with it accepted ideas about how the practice may be carried on can shift over time. Can you justify taking no part in this process?

A firm might argue that if by taking part it forfeits any of the profits that it might otherwise make, it will be acting contrary to the demands of its stockholders. Those demands themselves might, however, be modified if the stockholders became aware of the objections to the practice. If they were not modified, they would still not justify leaving objectionable practice unimproved by even the smallest initiative. Only when greater profits are to be had from a policy that is morally defensible is the firm's responsibility to obtain for its stockholders the maximum return on their investment justifiably a decisive consideration.

# CHAPTER 5

# *Honesty in Advertising*

---

*Introductory Comment:*

## THE MANY VARIETIES OF DECEPTION

---

Several of the items brought up in the last chapter had as much to do with honesty in advertising as with sales tactics. Several of the items that I shall now bring up could have been considered under sales tactics rather than under advertising. One might try for a distinction by saying that the deceptions involved, or alleged, would be sales tactics, not advertising, when they turn up in what merchants and salespeople tell individual prospects face to face. They would be advertising, not sales tactics, when they are broadcast to the public. However, advertising, when it mentions special terms ("six months to pay"; "10% off with coupon"), seems to be an ingredient in sales tactics. In any case, it sets up the scene on which sales tactics are directed at particular people. Consider, further, that what a salesperson says on the spot may be something that she repeats time and again: "If you're looking for convenient attachments, this is the kitchen processor to buy."

More important than any distinction between sales tactics and advertising is the variety of deceptions that may be practiced. It is a variety that must be increasing daily—hourly. The more obvious forms—outright falsehood, irresponsible exaggeration; breath-taking omission—do not fall out of use, and admit themselves of infinite variation. If the obvious forms are some-times stopped from operating, human ingenuity is quite capable of invent-ing something less obvious. Think of what can be done merely with arrangements of information, and with timing! Think of "easy stages"! In a case below, the deception operates through a refund offer, which is itself strictly in good faith, in the sense that one can hardly doubt the store would make good on the offer if it ever had to.

One cannot cover—one can hardly suggest—the whole range of possible deceptions in two chapters. The most that one can do is provide a diverse enough set of examples to make the point that, although again and again deception is the subject of moral concern in them, the issue of what constitutes deception changes so much from one example to another as to present a problem of recognition. In real life, one has to be more than ordinarily alert in many instances to suspect deception—which makes it easier to succumb to, and easier to practice with a comfortable conscience.

The materials offered in this chapter, diverse again in origin, length, and import, are diverse, too, in the possibilities for deception that they represent. The possibilities are not always realized in the actual cases set forth. Some of the cases may be said, to invoke the triplet principle once more, to be clear cases of being wrong; others, clear cases of being all right at least, perhaps sometimes more. One, I think, is a clear case of being wrong, perversely denied to be such by the court whose judgment is quoted. The courts themselves sometimes to the wrong thing.

So do regulatory commissions. We begin, however, with a case in which the commission was upheld. Cardozo's opinion transforms the humdrum subject of lumber. The opinion is lucid, broad in historical vision, firm on the central points to be made about misrepresentation, rich in implications about the relations of competition and regulation to the public interest.

# FEDERAL TRADE COMMISSION v. ALGOMA CO.

*Supreme Court of the United States, 1933*

Mr. JUSTICE CARDOZO delivered the opinion of the Court.

In May 1929, the Federal Trade Commission filed and served complaints against a group of fifty manufacturers on the Pacific Coast charging "unfair competition in interstate commerce."

The practice complained of as unfair and enjoined by the Commission is the use by the respondents of the words "California white pine" to describe lumber, logs or other forest products made from the pine species known as *Pinus ponderosa*. The findings as to this use and its effect upon the public are full and circumstantial. They are too long to be paraphrased conveniently within the limits of an opinion. We must be content with an imperfect summary.

The respondents are engaged in the manufacture and sale of lumber and timber products which they ship from California and Oregon to customers in other states and foreign lands. Much of what they sell comes from the species of tree that is known among botanists as *Pinus ponderosa*. The respondents sell it under the name of "California white pine," and under that name, or at times "white pine" simply, it goes to the consumer. In truth it is not a white pine, whether the tests to be applied are those of botanical science or of commercial practice and understanding.

Pine trees, the genus "Pinus," have for a long time been divided by botanists, foresters and the public generally into two groups, the white pine and the yellow. The white pine group includes, by common consent, the northern white pine *(Pinus strobus)*, the sugar pine and the Idaho white pine. It is much sought after by reason of its durability under exposure to weather and moisture, the proportion of its heartwood as contrasted with its sapwood content, as well as other qualities. For these reasons it commands a high price as compared with pines of other species. The yellow pine group is less durable, harder, heavier, more subject to shrinkage and warping, darker in color, more resinous, and more difficult to work. It includes the long leaf yellow pine *(Pinus palustris)*, grown in the southern states, and the *Pinus ponderosa*, a far softer wood, which is grown in the Pacific coast states, and in Arizona and New Mexico, as well as in the "inland empire" (eastern Washington, Oregon, Idaho, and western Montana).

Of the varieties of white pine, the northern or *Pinus strobus* has been known better and longer than the others. It is described sometimes as northern white pine, sometimes as white pine simply, sometimes with the addition of its local origin, as Maine white pine, Michigan, Wisconsin, Minnesota, Canadian, New Brunswick. It is native to the northeastern states and to the Great Lakes region, as far west as Minnesota. It is found also in Canada and along the Appalachian highlands. It was almost the only building material for the settlers of New England, and so great is its durability that many ancient buildings made from it in the seventeenth and eighteenth centuries survive in good condition. The sugar pine is native to the upland regions of California, southern Oregon and parts of Nevada. The Idaho white pine grows in the mountainous sections of Idaho, Washington and Oregon and in parts of British Columbia. The white pine species "still holds an exalted reputation among the consuming public" and "in general esteem is the highest type of lumber as respects the excellences desired in soft wood material." "It is coming more and more to be a specialty wood, largely devoted to special purposes, as it becomes scarcer and higher in price. It is in great demand."

About 1880 the *Pinus ponderosa*, though botanically a yellow pine, began to be described as a white pine when sold in the local markets of California, New Mexico, and Arizona, the description being generally accompanied by a reference to the state of origin, as "California white pine," etc. By 1886, sales under this description had spread to Nevada and Utah, with occasional shipments farther east. About 1900, they entered the middle western states, and about 1915 had made their way into New England, though only to a small extent. The pines from the "inland empire" traveled east more slowly, and when they did were described as western white pine, a term now generally abandoned. The progress of the newcomers, both from the coast and from the "inland empire," was not wholly a march of triumph. In their movement to the central and eastern markets they came into competition more and more with the genuine white pine, with which those markets had been long familiar. Mutterings of discontent were heard. In 1924, partly as a result of complaints and official investigations, many of the producers, notably those of the "inland empire," as well as some producers in California and Arizona, voluntarily gave up the use of the adjective "white" in connection with their product, and adopted the description "pondosa pines," pondosa being a corruption or abbreviation of the ponderosa of the botanists. "Pondosa pine is the term employed for ponderosa by the representatives of producers of slightly more than half of the ponderosa marketed." The respondents and others, however, declined to make a change. During the next five years California white pine and its equivalents became an even more important factor in the lumber markets of the country. Accumulating complaints led to an inquiry by the Commission, which had its fruit in this proceeding.

The confusion and abuses growing out of these interlocking names have been developed in the findings. Many retail dealers receiving orders for white pine deliver California white pine, not knowing that it differs from the lumber ordered. Many knowing the difference deliver the inferior product because they can buy it cheaper. Still others, well informed and honest, deliver the genuine article, thus placing themselves at a disadvantage in the race of competition with the unscrupulous and the ignorant. Trade has thus been diverted from dealers in white pine to dealers in *Pinus ponderosa* masquerading as white pine. Trade has also been diverted from dealers in *Pinus ponderosa* under the name pinus pondosa to dealers in *Pinus ponderosa* under the more attractive label. The diversion of trade from dealers of one class to dealers of another is not the only mischief. Consumers, architects and retailers have also been misled. They have given orders for the respondents' product, supposing it to be white pine and to have the qualities associated with lumber of that species. They have accepted deliveries under the empire of that belief. True indeed it is that the woods sold by the respondents, though not a genuine white pine, are nearer to that species in mechanical properties than they are to the kinds of yellow pine indigenous to the south. The fact that for many purposes they are half way between the white species and the yellow makes the practice of substitution easier than it would be if the difference were plain. Misrepresentation and confusion flourish in such a soil. From these findings and others the Commission was brought to the conclusion that the respondents compete unfairly in transacting business as they do, and that in the interest of the public their methods should be changed.

"The findings of the Commission as to facts, if supported by testimony, shall be conclusive." 15 U.S.C. §45. The Court of Appeals, though professing adherence to this mandate, honored it, we think, with lip service only. In form the court determined that the finding of unfair competition had no support whatever. In fact what the court did was to make its own appraisal of the testimony, picking and choosing for itself among uncertain and conflicting inferences. Statute and decision forbid that exercise of power.

*First.* The argument is made that unfair competition is disproved by the "simplified practice recommendations" of the Bureau of Standards when read in conjunction with the testimony as to the comparative utility of the genuine white pine and *Pinus ponderosa.*

The Court of Appeals concedes that the recommendations of the Bureau will not avail, without more, to control the action of the Commission. . . . The view was expressed, however, that alone they are in a high degree persuasive, and that in conjunction with other evidence they are even controlling. In particular that result was thought to follow in this case because the substituted wood, in the judgment of the court, is so nearly equal in utility that buyers are not injured, even though misled.

Such a holding misconceives the significance of the Government's endeavor to simplify commercial practice. It misconceives even more essentially the significance of the subsitution of one article for another without notice to the buyer.

(a) The Bureau of Standards is a branch of the Department of Commerce. At its instance representatives of manufacturers, sellers, and users of lumber, as well as architects, engineers and others, met in conference at various times between 1922 and 1928 in an endeavor to simplify methods of business in the lumber industry. Following these conferences the Bureau in 1929 issued a report entitled "Lumber, Simplified Practice Recommendations." Many subjects that were considered are without relation to this case. The report dealt with standards of size, of inspection, of structural material, and other cognate themes. One of its subdivisions, however, enumerates the standard commercial names for lumber of many types. Sixteen names of pines are stated in the list, and among them is the name "California white pine" with its botanical equivalent, *Pinus ponderosa.*

The recommendations of the Bureau of Standards for the simplification of commercial practice are wholly advisory. Dealers may conform or diverge as they prefer. The Bureau has defined its own function in one of its reports. The Purpose and Application of Simplified Practice, National Bureau of Standards, Department of Commerce, July 1, 1931, pp. 2, 7, 10, 17. "Simplified practice is a method of eliminating superfluous variety through the voluntary action of industrial groups." "The Department of Commerce has no regulatory powers" with reference to the subject and hence "it is highly desirable that this recommendation be kept distinct from any plan or method of governmental regulation or control." There is nothing to show that in making up the list of names the Bureau made any investigation of the relation between *Pinus ponderosa* and the white pines of the east. Certainly it had no such wealth of information on the subject as was gathered by the Commission in the course of this elaborate inquiry. There is nothing to show to what extent its advice has been accepted by the industry. The record does show that the recommendation does not accord with the practice of other governmental agencies. For example, the United States Forest Service in its publications and forest signs describes the ponderosa species as western yellow pine. In such circumstances the action of the Bureau was at most a bit of evidence to be weighed by the Commission along with much besides. It had no such significance as to discredit in any appreciable degree a conclusion founded upon evidence otherwise sufficient. The powers and function of the two agencies of government are essentially diverse. The aim of the one is to simplify business by substituting uniformity of methods for wasteful diversity, and in the achievement of these ends to rely upon cooperative action. The aim of the other is to make the process of competition fair. There are times when a description is deceptive from the very fact of its simplicity.

(b) The wood dealt in by the respondents is not substantially as good as the genuine white pine, nor would sales under the wrong name be fitting if it were.

The ruling of the court below as to this is infected by a twofold error. The first is one of fact. The supposed equivalence is unreal. The second is one of law. If the equivalence existed, the practice would still be wrong.

The Commission found as a fact that the genuine white pine is superior for many reasons to *Pinus ponderosa*, and notably because of its greater durability. The court held the view that the difference in durability had not been proved so clearly as to lay a basis for the orders, and this, it seems, upon the ground that though the superiority exists, the evidence fails to disclose its precise degree. "What the testimony appears to establish is that Northern white pine has relatively a greater durability for exterior use without establishing any comparative degree of such durability." . . .

Court and counsel for the respondents lean heavily at this point upon the testimony of the Director of the United States Forest Products Laboratory at Madison, Wisconsin, and his assistant, Mr. Hunt. The Director testified that he did not know the comparative durability of the pines and would refer any inquirer to specialists, of whom Mr. Hunt was one. The testimony of Mr. Hunt is that there have been no tests in a strict sense, but that the comparison between the white pines and *Pinus ponderosa* has been based upon observation and opinion. He continues: "The general experience with the use of the white pines, during the two hundred years since they began to be used, indicated that those pines had moderately high durability. The general experience with *Pinus ponderosa* indicated that that wood had low durability in contact with the ground or any place favoring the growth of decay. That is a matter of common knowledge." Inquirers at the Laboratory were accordingly advised that "the heartwood of the white pine has more decay resistance, will give longer service under conditions favoring decay than the heartwood of pinus ponderosa," and "the mill run of the white pine probably would average higher in durability under decay-producing conditions."

This testimony, even if it stood alone, would tend to sustain rather than to discredit the findings by the Commission that the genuine white pines are materially superior to the woods that the respondents are selling as a substitute. It is fortified, however, by evidence from many other sources. To be sure there is contradiction which we have no thought to disparage. For present purposes we assume the credibility of those who spoke for the complainants. Wholesalers, retailers, manufacturers, lumber graders, laboratory experts and others bore witness to the comparative merits of the woods, stating their own experience as well as common opinion among their fellows in the industry. If all this may be ignored in the face of the findings of the Commission, it can only be by turning the court into an administrative body which is to try the case anew.

What has been written has been aimed at the position that *Pinus ponderosa* is as good or almost as good as the white pines of the east. We have yet to make it plain that the substitution would be unfair though equivalence were shown. This can best be done in considering another argument which challenges the finding of the Commission that there has been misunderstanding on the part of buyers. To this we now turn.

*Second.* The argument is made that retailers and consumers are not shown to have been confused as to the character of the lumber supplied by the respondents, and that even if there was confusion there is no evidence of prejudice.

Both as to the fact of confusion and its consequences the evidence is ample. Retailers order "white pine" from manufacturers and take what is sent to them, passing it on to their customers. At times they do this knowing or suspecting that they are supplying California white pine instead of the genuine article, and supplying a wood that is inferior, at least for the outer parts of buildings. Its comparative cheapness creates the motive for the preference. At times they act in good faith without knowledge of the difference between the California pines and others. Architects are thus misled, and so are builders and consumers. There is a suggestion by the court that for all that appears the retailers, buying the wood cheaper, may have lowered their own price, and thus passed on to the consumer the benefit of the saving. The inference is a fair one that this is not always done, and perhaps not even generally. If they lower the price at all, there is no reason to believe that they do so to an amount equivalent to the saving to themselves.

But saving to the consumer, though it be made out, does not obliterate the prejudice. Fair competition is not attained by balancing a gain in money against a misrepresentation of the thing supplied. The courts must set their faces against a conception of business standards so corrupting in its tendency. The consumer is prejudiced if upon giving an order for one thing, he is supplied with something else. In such matters, the public is entitled to get what it chooses, though the choice may be dictated by caprice or by fashion or perhaps by ignorance. Nor is the prejudice only to the consumer. Dealers and manufacturers are prejudiced when orders that would have come to them if the lumber had been rightly named, are diverted to others whose methods are less scrupulous. "A method inherently unfair does not cease to be so because those competed against have become aware of the wrongful practice." . . . The careless and the unscrupulous must rise to the standards of the scrupulous and diligent. The Commission was not organized to drag the standards down.

*Third*. The argument is made that the name for the respondents' lumber was adopted more than thirty years ago without fraudulent design, and that a continuation of the use is not unfair competition, though confusion may have developed when the business, spreading eastward, attained national dimensions.

The Commission made no finding as to the motives animating the respondents in the choice of the contested name. The respondents say it was chosen to distinguish their variety of yellow pine from the harder yellow pines native to the southern states. We may assume that this is so. The fact remains, however, that the pines were not white either botanically or commercially, though the opportunity for confusion may have been comparatively slight when the sales were restricted to customers in local markets, buying for home consumption. Complaints, if there were any, must have been few and inarticulate at a time when there was no supervisory body to hold business to its duty. According to the law as then adjudged, many competitive practices that today may be suppressed . . . were not actionable wrongs, the damage to the complainants being classified often as collateral and remote . . . The Federal Trade Commission was not organized till 1914, its jurisdiction then as now confined to interstate and foreign commerce. Silence up to that time is not even a faint token that the misapplied name had the approval of the industry. It may well have meant no more than this, that the evil was not great, or that there was no champion at hand to put an end to the abuse. Even silence thereafter will not operate as an estoppel against the community at large, whatever its effects upon individuals asserting the infringement of proprietary interests. . . . There is no bar through lapse of time to a proceeding in the public interest to set an industry in order by removing the occasion for deception or mistake, unless submission has gone so far that the occasion for misunderstanding, or for any so widespread as to be worthy of correction, is already at an end. Competition may then be fair irrespective of its origin. This will happen, for illustration, when by common acceptation the description, once misused, has acquired a secondary meaning as firmly anchored as the first one. Till then, with every new transaction, there is a repetition of the wrong.

The evidence here falls short of establishing two meanings with equal titles to legitimacy by force of common acceptation. On the contrary, revolt against the pretender, far from diminishing, has become increasingly acute. With the spread of business eastward, the lumber dealers who sold pines from the states of the Pacific Coast were involved in keen competition with dealers in lumber from the pines of the East and Middle West. In the wake of competition came confusion and deception, the volume mounting to its peak in the four or five years before the Commission resolved to act. Then, if not before, misbranding of the pines was something more than a venial wrong. The respondents, though at fault from the beginning, had been allowed to go their way without obstruction while the mischief was not a crying one. They were not at liberty to enlarge the area of their business without adjusting their methods to the needs of new conditions. An analogy may be found in the decisions on the law of trademarks, where the principle is applied that a name legitimate in one territory may generate confusion when carried into another, and must then be given up. . . . More than half the members of the industry have disowned the misleading name by voluntary action and are trading under a new one. The respondents who hold out are not relieved by innocence of motive from a duty to conform. Competition may be unfair within the meaning of this statute and within the scope of the discretionary powers conferred on the Commission, though the practice condemned does not amount to fraud as understood in courts of law. Indeed there is a kind of fraud, as courts of equity have long perceived, in clinging to a benefit which is the product of misrepresentation, however innocently made. . . . That is the respondents' plight today, no matter what their motives may have been when they began. They must extricate themselves from it by purging their business methods of a capacity to deceive.

*Fourth.* Finally, the argument is made that the restraining orders are not necessary to protect the public interest . . . but to the contrary that the public interest will be promoted by increasing the demand for *Pinus ponderosa*, though it be sold with a misleading label, and thus abating the destruction of the pine forests of the East.

The conservation of our forests is a good of large importance, but the end will have to be attained by methods other than a license to do business unfairly.

The finding of unfair competition being supported by the testimony, the Commission did not abuse its discretion in reaching the conclusion that no change of the name short of the excision of the word "white" would give adequate protection.

The judgment is

*Reversed.*

\* \* \*

# S. BUCHSBAUM & CO. v. FEDERAL TRADE COMMISSION

*[Here is a case that goes just the other way, in the legal ruling quoted, from the ponderosa pine case. Is it sufficiently different to be a clear case of being all right?]*

United States Circuit Court of Appeals, Seventh Circuit, 1947

SPARKS, Circuit Judge.

The articles manufactured and sold by petitioner are numerous and include such things as suspenders, rain coats, garters, belts, shampoo capes, watch straps and the like. They are made and sold at a much cheaper price than articles made of that kind of glass in which silica is an essential ingredient. Petitioner's products are made of plastics and are quite pliable, tensile, durable and transparent, and fully serve the purposes for which they are manufactured and marketed to the general public.

Illustrative of the use by the general public of plastic glass is "shatter-proof glass" which has been used many years and still is in constant use. It is a laminated glass consisting of two layers of silica glass with a layer of plastic glass between them. Each layer is perfectly transparent. The three layers are indistinguishable and appear to the eye as one glass. The middle plastic layer is the element that prevents the other layers from shattering when broken, and as a unit it is known and recognized generally as "shatter-proof glass."

Petitioner's products are made from plastic material such as used in the middle layer of the "shatter-proof glass," and it advertises and sells its products as "Elasti-Glass" products. Certain competitors of petitioner manufacture their products from the same elements used in making the upper and lower layers of the "shatter-proof glass." At any rate they use no plastics, and they therefore contend that petitioner should not be permitted to advertise or sell its products under the name "Elasti-Glass," or any other name containing the word "glass."

The Commission, in proof that the word "glass" as understood by the public means common glass, such as that found in window panes, tumblers and bottles, submitted the testimony of 10 witnesses,—two housewives, a junior college student, a laundry employee, two hospital employees, an assistant of the local office of a life insurance company, an employee of the National Association of Dyers and Cleaners, a local operating manager of the National Better Business Bureau, and a writer of non-fiction articles which had appeared in such magazines as *Coronet, Cosmopolitan*, the *Reader's Digest*, and the *Saturday Evening Post*. All save one, after reading petitioner's advertisements of "Elasti-Glass," thought that petitioner had discovered and was using a new process by which it was able to change the nature of and to make pliable the glass which is found in window panes and the like, although there was nothing in such advertisements which intimated any such thing. The manager of the National Better Business Bureau was not in any manner deluded or confused by such advertisements, for he said the Bureau differentiates between vinyon and glass fiber, and that the latter is made of real fiber glass and that the former is the trade name of vinyl plastic yarn contained in "Elasti-Glass" neckties. In making this differentiation the Bureau evidently gave no consideration whatever to the definitions of the word "glass" as contained in the American dictionaries, or the Oxford (English) dictionary, as we shall later show.

The writer of non-fiction articles assumed that "Elasti-Glass" products were made of window pane glass which caused her to characterize them as "fiber glass" in an article written by her for *Cosmopolitan*. She was not an employee of petitioner, nor was she authorized by it to make such statement. She received but one criticism concerning that characterization, and it developed later that it came from a person considerably interested in defeating petitioner's contention before the Commission and here. This witness said that she was neither a chemist nor an expert on glass; that all she knew about the subject was her general public understanding of what glass is, and she supposed she did not know whether "synthetic resin materials are not glass."

This record does not disclose that any witness for the respondent, except this lady, ever consulted any dictionary before testifying, as to the meaning of the word "glass." She consulted the Oxford, while dressing, just before she left her home to testify. Of course, neither the Oxford nor any of the many American dictionaries which we have consulted limit the definitions of the word "glass" to that made from silica, or to that from which window panes or goblets are usually made. True, the latter are perhaps the most usual forms in which we see glass, but each dictionary defines the word as any substance that resembles glass. The word is not derived from any element or combination of elements from which any kind of glass is made. From all sources available to us it is clear that the word glass derives from the appearance of the product after it is made. No one denies that the resemblance of the substance of petitioner's products to that of articles made from common window glass or tumblers or that of shatter-proof glass is perfect, and not one dissatisfied customer of petitioner's products has voiced an objection or complaint with respect to them.

The complaint filed by the Federal Trade Commission alleges in substance that petitioner operates a factory wherein are manufactured the various articles above referred to, and allied merchandise, made from "Vinylite," an *organic* material of *glass-like appearance* which it advertises, sells and distributes in interstate commerce in the United States (our emphasis throughout); that "Vinylite" is the registered trademark of a chemically manufactured, plasticized resinous material *resembling glass*, purchased by petitioner, in the form of pliable, clear or colored, transparent or translucent, semi-elastic sheets, which after further processing petitioner converts into the various articles of men's accessories above referred to, as made of "Elasti-Glass," the trade name so used by it. Petitioner in advertising sometimes refers to its products as a form of glass.

The complaint further alleges that processes for the fabrication of *inorganic glass* into similar materials have been developed at considerable expense by various members of the glass industry, and that many of such articles made from inorganic glass materials have already been manufactured and, amidst wide publicity, have been and are being marketed to the public, "long accustomed to the worth and use of glass."

The Commission further alleges that articles made of Vinylite "contain no glass whatsover, for . . . Vinylite is not a glass but rather . . . a product made by the heating and mixing of petroleum or coal and salt with a special catalytic agent and chemicals to induce the formation of certain gases and distillates, which in cooling results in the synthetic resin product known as Vinylite." Hence, they say, the acts and practices of petitioner, as enumerated, are all to the prejudice and injury of the public and constitute unfair and deceptive acts and practices in commerce within the intent and meaning of the Federal Trade Commission Act. . .

[1] We find nothing in that Act which discloses any intention on the part of Congress to prevent any citizen from selling and transporting in interstate commerce any article useful and beneficial to the public, made by him under a descriptive name as recognized and approved by our American lexicographers since the birth of our Nation, or which at this time is recognized and approved by them. We find in this record no evidence of any injury to any dissatisifed customer, indeed, there are no dissatisifed customers so far as this record discloses. It is intimated that the injury will occur to those who have been "long accustomed to the worth and use of glass." If this class of customers would consult their lexicons and inform the merchants as to the kind of glass they desire they will never be misled. Certainly they can not be misled or injured by petitioner's advertisements.

[2] The Commission contends that actual deception of purchasers need not be shown in its proceedings, and that representations which have a "capacity" to deceive may be proscribed. This is quite true. . . . However, even though there be no proof of actual deception required, there must be a showing that the acts and practices sought to be proscribed are detrimental to the public interest in order to satisfy the statutory requirement that the proceeding be in the public interest. . . . Here the Commission made no finding that the deception, if any, had ever resulted in or had any tendency to result in detriment to the purchasing public. We find nothing in the findings to support the conclusion that the acts and practices are "all to the prejudice and injury of the public."

It is quite evident that this proceeding was actuated by the manufacturers of such glass as contained in window panes, tumblers and the like. The trouble arises in trying to compete with petitioner in the sale of the same articles made of "Elasti-Glass" by petitioner. Thus far, it appears from the record, the competition has not been successful for such manufacturers, because of the cheaper prices of petitioner's products.

[3] The findings and conclusion of the Commission that petitioner has been guilty of false and prejudical statements and unfair and deceptive acts which have injured or will injure the public are not supported by substantial evidence.

The order of the Board is set aside.

\*     \*     \*

# BARGAIN PRICE OFFERS IN
# OECD COUNTRIES*

The price of goods and services is one of the most important factors in determining the consumer's buying decisions. Clear and conspicuous indication of the selling price is therefore a basic element for enabling him to make a rational choice in the market place. Furthermore, price competition, though its importance may vary slightly in different markets, is the decisive element in a market economy. Thus, a clear presentation of the price is in the interest both of the consumer and manufacturers and traders in a competitively organised market system.

There is only a small step from merely indicating the selling price to supplementing this indication by comments stressing that the price of an item is particularly advantageous, e.g., cheaper than somewhere else, cheaper than it used to be or cheaper than comparable articles. In addition, regardless of whether this view is justified or not, many consumers tend to conclude from the price that it is an indication of the quality. Therefore, since display of the price is particularly effective in attracting the consumer's interest, the use of the price indication as a promotional device is, understandably, a common feature in retail marketing in Member Countries.

Bargain offer claims, "essentially an indication that a trader's selling price is less than some other price or some notional assessment of worth or value," . . . are therefore based on amplifying the attractiveness of a selling price. Consumer policy problems in this field arise mainly out of the fact that due to varying degrees of knowledge on the part of the public as to the real and regular market price and whether such a price exists, a substantial portion of the public may be misled by these offers. Price awareness of consumers, with regard to all markets and all products, even including frequently purchased staples, is often not highly developed. The opportunity of gaining sufficient knowledge of the average prices charged through consumer magazines, comparative surveys, etc., is certainly not widely enough available to avoid exploitation of the consumer's ignorance.

Thus, bargain offer claims can be viewed in three different ways: they can be considered as a desirable promotional activity which helps to stimulate competition and directly saves the consumer's money. Secondly, where these claims are false or misleading, they become an unfair practice providing misleading price information which is detrimental to both competitors and consumers. Finally, the question may arise whether certain types of bargain offers can be undesirable "per se" due to their capacity to confuse and mislead consumers.

*Excerpts from *Bargain Price Offers and Similar Marketing Practices* (Paris, 1979). Copyright 1979 by The Organisation for Economic Co-Operation and Development and reprinted with their permission.

. . . Surveys undertaken in Norway, Sweden, Denmark and Finland clearly indicated that even where the price comparison highlighting the bargain offer was genuine and truthful, only few consumers were actually aware of what the comparison was related to.

. . . Bargain offer claims are a common practice. . . . The major types and the related abuses vary only slightly from country to country. According to the basic patterns used to convey the idea of a bargain, a general distinction can be made between the main types of bargain offers:

a) with price comparison referring to another higher price such as:
   —recommended price;
   —own former price;
   —price of another named trader;
   —price of other unnamed traders;
   —"normal" price;
   —future price (e.g. when a new product is introduced);
   —"worth and value" claims;
   —price reductions "up to" a certain limit;
b) without direct price comparison but with implied reference to the bargain character of the offer:
   —"factory" or "wholesale prices";
   —"special sales," "clearance sales," etc.;
   —bargain offers based on claimed unusual circumstances, e.g., "special purchases," "manufacturer's close down," etc.

All these types of practices can be encountered. . . . It would be impossible to list them in the order of their economic importance. As with many other promotional practices, they must be frequently changed in order to remain attractive for consumers. However, several countries indicate that the reference price most frequently found is the "recommended" selling price. Such is the case in Finland, Germany, the Netherlands, the United Kingdom and the United States. Thus, in the United Kingdom, such abbreviations as "MRP" or "Man. rec. price" (for manufacturer's recommended price), "RRP" (recommended retail price) are frequently used by traders to describe the higher price referred to in bargain offer claims. The wording of course varies widely and leaves much room for the trader's inventiveness in advertising.

The risk of misleading consumers with regard to bargain price offers is relatively great, both with regard to the offers using reference prices and with regard to the so-called implied bargain offer claims. In the one case the misrepresentation concerns the reference price as such, which may not be understood, or may be difficult to confirm or check and indeed may be entirely the product of the seller's imagination. In the second case, the trader's status or the claimed special circumstances may be misrepresented. Two issues which are closely related to this problem shall not be further discussed in this context because they raise much wider questions. The first problem linked with the misrepresentation of the price is that of misrepresentation of the quality in cases where the price indicated refers—more or less expressly—to a similar and not to an identical product. Here the bargain offer idea is extended to the comparison of quality which, even more than price comparison, may be based on a subjective judgement. However, this practice related to the problem of misrepresentation in general. A second issue not dealt with, though in practice also closely related to bargain offer claims, is bait and switch selling, i.e., the announcing of bargains where no adequate stock is available combined with an attempt to persuade the customer to purchase a different product or service. In order to gain an illustrative overview of the various possiblities of abuse, the main types of bargain offers in the narrow sense are examined in more detail below.

a)   BARGAIN OFFERS WITH PRICE COMPARISON

*Comparison with recommended prices.* Recommended resale prices can be set by manufacturers or wholesalers. They are generally defended by supporters as a means of facilitating the calculation of retail prices for the small trader. They also provide manufacturers with the possibility of indicating the approximate price and value of an item in their media advertising. However, recommended prices can provide producers with an opportunity to fix them at unduly high levels in order to provide retailers with an additional promotional tool, i.e., the permanent possibility of announcing bargain offers, even where the recommended price is rarely charged. The consumer who tends to accept the recommended price as at least an indication of the value or quality of the goods or services thus finds himself in a market situation where serious price competition is replaced by a race for higher reductions, and retailers may even pressurise manufacturers to set high recommended prices in order to enable them to increase the size of the "savings" claimed.

*Comparison with own former price.* The main danger with this commonly used type of bargain offer (e.g., "X" pens were $10, now only $7.50) lies in the fact that it can hardly be checked whether, how long and to what extent this price was really practised. Thus, a retailer may expressly advertise an extremely high price for a few days, knowing that he will sell none or very few of the articles involved at this inflated price and then offer a considerable reduction, which brings the offer down to a normal price level, but uses the bargain offer claim as the major sales argument. Additionally, the former price may not have been charged or advertised in the recent past but may refer to prices offered a considerable time before.

*Comparison with the price of another named trader.* Comparisons with prices charged by another trader who is identified by name are relatively rare. In some countries, such comparisons are prevented by law, and in others traders may avoid them for fear that the other trader may change his price and thus render the comparison false. For the consumer, however, truthful comparisons of this kind provide a useful means of ascertaining the range of competing prices currently being charged.

*Comparison with the prices of other unnamed traders.* In this type of price comparison the trader or traders charging the higher price remain unidentified. These comparisons are in widespread use in some countries (e.g., "price elsewhere . . ." or similar formulations). The danger for the consumer is that, even if the reference price is indeed charged by another trader or traders, this price may be unrepresentative of the price generally charged in the geographical area in which the consumer is likely to make his purchase.

*Comparison with a "normal price".* This too is a type of bargain offer where the possibility to deceive consumers is based on an extremely vague and undefined reference price. Thus, it is difficult to find out what the term "normal price" and similar formulations are intended to convey. It may or may not be the price in a certain geographical area, or the price charged normally by the trader making the claim or the recommended price.

*Comparison with a future price.* Such comparison is occasionally used when a new product is introduced or when there is old stock to be cleared before the arrival of new stock at higher prices. Claims of this kind seem to be relatively rare. However, it has happened that the future price changes, which have been referred to, have not taken place or have taken place only to a limited extent. This makes the former offer misleading, since it may have incorrectly influenced the timing of the consumer's purchase.

*"Worth and value" claims.* "Worth and value" claims basically involve the same risks as the above practices. Such offers as "comparable retail value . . . ; my price . . ." are often based on a subjective evaluation of the market situation and would only be valid where the higher figure given was being generally charged in an area which is relevant for the consumer. Similar claims which are in frequent and widespread use are those simply based on the seller's opinion as to the item's value ("e.g., my selling price, 20, worth 36") although the bargain is represented as being carefully quantified.

*Bargain offers based on price reductions "up to" a certain limit.* Claims setting out price reductions "up to" a certain limit are generally used when advertising price reductions across a range of goods. Where the goods are reduced by varying rates, it is more convenient to specify one figure rather than several, identifying the extent of the price reduction across the goods. Generally, however, the figure chosen is the maximum reduction available. Alternative methods of presenting reductions, such as specifying the minimum reductions, e.g., from 10 percent off, or the range of reductions, e.g., from 10 to 50 percent off, are not considered to have the same promotional attractiveness. There is often no indication as to what proportion of the goods the reduction applies, and no indication as to what reduction is available on the rest of the goods. The consumer then is often given an unrepresentative indication of the extent of the price reductions across the range of the items offered.

b)   BARGAIN OFFERS WITHOUT PRICE COMPARISON (IMPLIED BARGAIN PRICE
     OFFER CLAIMS)

The so-called implied bargain offer claims encountered in Member Countries basically suffer from the same deficiencies as the aforementioned ones with direct double pricing; comparison with a fictitious, artificial or undefined selling price is replaced by an appeal to the consumer's desire to take advantage of special circumstances enabling or forcing the seller to offer lower prices. For the various types of bargain offers the major possible abuses implied are the following:

*"Factory" or "wholesale" prices.* The indication of "factory" or "wholesale" prices often misleads consumers into believing that the prices are those available at the factory or to wholesalers. However, there can be no doubt that there is a cost of distribution, even if these may vary between producers as a result of different operational procedures. This additional cost is passed on to the consumer, although it is suggested to the consumer that this is not the case.

*Special sales, clearance sales, etc.* In certain cases such special devices which incite consumers to make a quick buying decision are in fact a promotional device used on a regular or even on a permanent basis. The "special" sales go on, maybe with short interruptions; the stock is not limited but is continuously renewed; and in some cases articles are specifically manufactured for "all year" special sales.

*Bargain offers based on claimed unusual circumstances.* The special stocks available in connection with such special circumstances (special purchases, manufacturer's sell out, etc., reconstruction of the sales premises, etc.) are sometimes very limited and mixed up with other items. Thus, the bargain offer frequently serves as a basis for "bait and switch" offers.

. . . The question arises whether and to what extent the concept of monitoring bargain price offers on the basis of evaluating whether they are genuine and truthful is sufficient to protect and promote both the consumer's interest and fair competition. Leaving aside the question of the resources necessary to carry out a satisfactory supervision of malpractices, the problem involved is, with regard to some bargain offers, whether the consumer or even a more sophisticated surveyor of the market scene would be in a position to tell, in a reasonable time, whether certain types of such offers are "genuine and truthful" or not.

The approach which seems to emerge from recent developments is that of questioning the usefulness of certain types of bargain offers per se. Certain types of bargain offer claims do not provide the necessary information to allow the consumer to be certain that by responding to the offer, the best price is obtained. Worth and value claims are the typical example for this type of bargain offer. In addition, surveys in several Member Countries show that recommended resale prices are often used with the aim of providing an additional promotional tool by retailers, instead of reflecting the general price level.

[Yet] if consumers are given accurate information on prices, then the ability to compare between competing products is facilitated and the competitive market economy operates by allowing the consumer to allocate his preferences effectively to his own benefit and to that of ethical traders. If these conditions are to operate, then price is a subject about which there should be no misinformation, and consumers should not be distracted in choosing what, when and where to buy, by bargain offer claims which are either untrue, incomprehensible or unrelated to market prices.

Consequently, the Committee supports the following principles with regard to bargain offer claims:

a) the claim must be truthful;

b) it must give sufficient relevant information to allow an assessment of the nature of the bargain, including details of the actual selling price, the nature and, in most cases the level of the higher price from which a reduction is claimed;

c) the information given in the bargain offer claim should be capable of reasonably easy and accurate verification, ultimately by authorities if need be;

d) claims should be relevant to the consumer's purchasing decisions in the sense that the reference price used in the comparison should be one which has actually been charged by a source of supply that represents a realistic alternative source for the consumer;

e) the merchandise offered on bargain terms should be available in a quantity capable of satisfying a reasonably foreseeable demand.

*    *    *

## $250 TO ACAPULCO?

*[The following advertisement appeared in Halifax newspapers early in 1981. Bearing upon one of a number of features worth discussing is the fact that Halifax is 507 miles by air east of Montreal.]*

# travel service

service • experience • reliability

# Great News Atlantic Canada!
# Take-off $250
# and fly to per couple
# SERAPHINA'S ACAPULCO

On any February or March departure to Acapulco from Montreal Seraphina will take $250 off per couple towards the cost of air transportation, plus provide one complimentary over-night hotel room at the Chateau de l'Aeroport at Montreal!

SUNDAY DEPARTURES:
1 week from $669 per person.
2 weeks from $869 per person.
Space is limited—call today for further information and reservations.

\*   \*   \*

## PEOPLE v.
## LE WINTER'S RADIO STORES, INC.

*[Le Winter's Radio Stores, Incorporated, was charged with misleading advertising. They had displayed a refrigerator and on it a sign, "1938 Norge $119.50," in large letters and in smaller letters, "10 yr. warranty, 3 yr. to pay"; in smaller letters, too, the word "from" was placed in front of the large*

*numerals. It was charged that in fact Le Winter's was not ready to sell the refrigerator at the price given on the sign; at that price only a smaller refrigerator was offered. Le Winter's was convicted, but appealed.]*

*Supreme Court of New York, Appellate Division, Second Department, 1939*

Argued before LAZANSKY, P. J., and HAGGARTY, CARSWELL, JOHN-STON, and ADEL, J. J.

MEMORANDUM BY THE COURT.

. . . Reversed on the law, information dismissed and fine remitted. The card or advertisement and the matter thereon is not violative of section 421 of the Penal Law. While it had the effect of luring a customer into the store, it did not have the effect of causing a customer to part with value or enter into an obligation in connection with the purchase of a commodity, as a consequence of any deceit within the meaning of the statute. The sign did not indicate that the particular refrigerator upon which it was placed could be purchased for the figure stated on the sign.

\* \* \*

# THE GROCERY CHAIN THAT WILL NOT BE UNDERSOLD

Retail businesses, claiming that they "will not be undersold," sometimes make standing offers to match the prices of their competitors, given proof that the competitors are charging lower prices for the same goods. A food chain in the United States recently set forth such an offer in print on its grocery bags. There it undertook to "insure" its customers against higher prices. It suggested that customers do their weekly shopping in one of the stores in the chain. If, having bought 25 or more items, any customer could find some other chain that was currently charging less for the whole set of goods taken together, and supplied proof of this along with proof of her purchases at the chain making the offer, she would get a refund of 10 percent of what she had paid the chain. One has no reason to doubt that the chain would pay up when required to. Yet is the offer as open and generous as it looks?

## DISCO DRUGS*

---

*[Supermarkets aren't the only aggressive businesses in Southern California. According to Consumer Reports (1978), after the Los Angeles City Attorney brought in a complaint about an earlier advertisement, Disco Drugs consented to a judgment requiring it to run the following ad for a week in the same daily newspaper that carried the ad complained of.]*

DISCO DRUGS
INFORMATION FOR
CONSUMERS

DO YOU KNOW?

It is unlawful

. . . if an advertisement creates a misleading impression to the average consumer, even if "careful" inspection may show that the words and sentences may be literally true

. . . if an advertisement is capable of two meanings, one of which would leave a false impression.

In May 1976, Disco drugs in Pacific Palisades advertised in this paper. The ad was a "Notice to Malibu Residents" which in part, stated:

> "Are you having trouble getting your
> prescriptions filled in Malibu? . . . Disco
> Drugs is closest to you . . . only a short
> distance away."

An average consumer could reasonably believe that the May, 1976, ad meant that Disco Drugs was closer to Malibu residents than other competing drugstores. There are at least six (6) other drugstores closer to Malibu than Disco Drugs.

**THAT IS WHY DISCO DRUGS WAS ORDERED TO PRINT THIS AD!**

\*     \*     \*

# THE QUEEN v. COLGATE-PALMOLIVE LTD.*

*[It would be easy to fill this book and several others with cases of questionable advertising, increasingly bizarre, perhaps increasingly funny. I shall produce some further examples of advertising under a later heading, where in question will be not just honesty, but the impact on reason and culture in society as a whole. On honesty in advertising, I stop with a case involving nationwide advertising and TV. The company charged in the case was exonerated, but the judgment indicates quite clearly the grounds on which in other cases charges would be sustained.]*

*Judicial District of Ottawa-Carleton, 1977*

MARIN, Co. Ct. J. (orally):

The indictment against the company defendant is that: The said COLGATE-PALMOLIVE LIMITED, amalgamated under articles of amalgmation as CKR Incorporated, stands charged that on or about the 28th day of February, 1973, at the City of Ottawa, in the said Judicial District, it did unlawfully, to promote the sale of Ajax Cleanser, by means of printing on containers of Ajax Cleanser displayed on premises occupied by the Lisgar I.G.A. store at 231 Bank Street, in the City of Ottawa, cause to be published an advertisement containing a statement to wit:

"CLEANS BETTER THAN ANY LEADING CLEANSER"

which statement purported to be a statement of fact, but was untrue, deceptive or misleading and did thereby commit an indictable offence contrary to the provisions of Section 37(1) of the Combines Investigation Act, R.S.C. 1970, Chapter C-23, as amended. AND FURTHER THAT, the said COLGATE-PALMOLIVE LIMITED, amalgamated under articles of amalgamation as CKR Incorporated, further stands charged that on or about the 28th day of February, 1973, at the City of Ottawa, in the said Judicial District, it did unlawfully, to promote the sale of Ajax Cleanser, cause to be published by means of a broadcast over television station CFCF-TV, a television station broadcasting to the City of Ottawa, an advertisement containing a statement, to wit:

"CLEANS BETTER THAN ANY LEADING CLEANSER"

which statement purported to be a statement of fact, but was untrue, deceptive or misleading and did thereby commit an indictable offence contrary to the provisions of Section 37(1) of the Combines Investigation Act, R.S.C. 1970, Chapter C-23, as amended.

The corporation is, amongst other endeavors, in the production of a variety of cleaners, cleansers and detergents and is, according to its charter, committed to operate within Canada; the company has extensive research facilities in Ontario where it has some 13 employees and where research is done on a number of cleansers.

On or about February 28, 1973, one James Albert Walker, an investigator with Consumer and Corporate Affairs, now Chief of the Policy Planning and Program Development Division, made several purchases of a variety of cleaners in the City of Ottawa. These included Ajax, Comet and Super Dutch cleansers. Mr. Walker was originally examining the cleansers with respect to their respective claims as to quantities offered but his attention was drawn to the superiority claims appearing on the labels of some of the cleansers above described. The cleansers were received as exs. 3, 4 and 5 respectively. Mr. Walker also at or about that date, attended the C.R.T.C. (Canadian Radio and Television Commission) at its premises in Ottawa to view a television commercial claiming the superiority of Ajax over other leading cleansers. The film clip of the television commercial, entitled "BLOWTORCH," was viewed by the Court and has been received as an exhibit in this matter.

The "BLOWTORCH" commercial, as it was commonly known within the trade, was viewed within the City of Ottawa by cablevision subscribers and includes, amongst other claims, a claim of superiority of the product Ajax which compelled CBC to refuse to air the same commercial on its affiliate stations.

On or about February 20, 1973, Mr. Walker wrote to the manufacturers of the products, referred to above, asking for views and comments with respect to their respective products, also requesting comparisons and the nature of stains used and an outline of the chemical constituents of the cleansers. The letter to Colgate-Palmolive was filed as ex. 8 to this trial.

In his letter of February 20th to Colgate-Palmolive, the defendant corporation, Mr. Walker stated as follows:

> A complaint concerning a television commercial for Ajax Cleanser has come to the attention of the Director of Investigation and Research for consideration under the misleading advertising provisions of the Combines Investigation Act.

Paragraph 2 of the said letter reads in part:

> We have received information that seems to suggest that there may not be any significant differences in the capabilities of the "leading brand" cleansers, including Ajax, to remove most ordinary sink stains.

Much has been said about the character of that letter since, while Mr. Walker seems to suggest that a consumer complaint has been received, it was in fact not so. Mr. Walker initiated the complaint with his supervisor, and to that extent, the first reference to the complaint in the letter can be said to be somewhat misleading.

It can also be suggested that Mr. Walker had, neither personally, nor did anyone on his behalf have evidence at that time to suggest that there were no significant differences between the leading brands. It is noted for the record that the tests did not commence until much later on and were certainly inconclusive for a period of time thereafter.

The maufacturers of Comet and Super Dutch responded to the letter of Mr. Walker but the defendant corporation chose to issue an invitation to Mr. Walker to witness testing in their laboratory in order to gather the information requested in the letter of February 20, 1973. It is significant that the two other companies, in supplying the data requested, outlined the tests which they had performed on their own product and other information requested.

The defendant corporation was in due course visited by Mr. Walker and, subsequently, had their premises subjected to an extensive search for documentation under the relevant provisions of the *Combines Investigation Act*, R.S.C. 1970, c. C-23. The visit at the laboratory by Mr. Walker consisted of a number of carefully organized experiments by Colgate-Palmolive and watched by the witnesses. First, porcelain plates were acquired for purposes of testing and, in the presence of Mr. Walker, a variety of tests were conducted. The best that can be said as to the conclusions drawn from these tests must be extracted from the transcript. Under cross-examination, Mr. Walker was asked:

Q. Were the results the same as we saw?
A. Ajax was superior to Comet in those circumstances.
Q. And you saw that with your eyes?
A. Oh, yes.
Q. And it wasn't difficult to see?
A. No.
Q. You didn't need . . . you didn't use a reflectometer?
A. There was a difference that was noticeable to the eye.
Q. So in those circumstances, as far as you you, Mr. Walker, are concerned, Ajax cleaned better than Comet which was the other product?
A. Used in that way and on that stain, yes, and I think Mr. Ferguson's tests further substantiated that.
Q. I want to know about your reaction. Did Mr. Fell agree with you or do you know that?
A. Yes, he agreed with me on that point.

Nonetheless, on the strength of what had been observed and on the information available, the Department of Consumer and Corporate Affairs concluded that Colgate-Palmolive ought to be prosecuted; in the words of Mr. Walker, the Department concluded that "it had the strongest case against Colgate-Palmolive." It was at that juncture that documents were seized pursuant to s. 10 of the Act.

It was within a few days of the testing that Mr. Walker was directed to Mr. Ferguson of the Department of Public Works with respect to independent tests to be performed. It needs to be understood that there were no independent guidelines set up to carry out testing of cleansers in 1973; Mr. Walker had to informally approach the National Research Council, Health and Welfare, his own Department and Public Works before he was finally able to be directed to Mr. Ferguson who had some experience in the field of evaluation of cleansers.

Mr. Ferguson, in his testing of cleansers, was given some rather specific tests which ought to be performed and, in my view, it is also of importance that the parameters of the testing suggested by Mr. Walker to Mr. Ferguson were those used by the major competitors of Ajax in the testing of their own product within their own facilities.

At the trial, Mr. Casson gave extensive testimony with respect to the Colgate-Palmolive testing procedures. Mr. Casson is a professional chemist holding degrees in chemistry and is a fellow of the Royal Institute of Chemistry. In addition, he has taken a course in industrial research management at Harvard University. At the time, he was in charge of 13 persons of whom five hold honours degrees from Canadian universities, four are senior non-professional people and the others have post-graduate recognition. The laboratory operations cost the accused defendant $300,000 a year in direct costs and the facilities are those which were used for the testing of the product Ajax.

Mr. Casson's testimony is succinct; the tests which he and his fellow chemists carried out on the cleanser are varied and the criteria for testing a cleanser is suggested to be wide enough to encompass not only the bleaching and cleansing action of the cleanser, but also its detergency and abrasive power. The company has always assumed that a cleanser will be used under dynamic conditions and that anyone using the cleanser will use it with a scouring effect; it may be useful to inject at this point that there are basically two methods in using a cleanser—the static and the dynamic method, the latter having been described and the former being one where the user would allow the chemical compound to be sprinkled and remain static for a period of up to 60 seconds before attempting to use it for cleansing.

Mr. Casson suggests that a modern cleanser in his view must bleach and must also contain a portion of detergent.

This witness outlined in great detail how in early 1971, Comet had attained parity in bleach speed with Ajax and henceforth the defendant's advertising campaign to the effect that Ajax outbleached Comet was altered as a result of the conclusions mentioned. It is in light of these developments with Comet that in 1971, and for some months in 1972, steps were undertaken by the laboratory at Colgate-Palmolive to revitalize and reconstitute Ajax by increasing some of its cleansing ability. The formula for Ajax was altered and the silex content increased. It was then that the company defendant undertook to test its product with a variety of stains, including crusted-on, dried-on stains and other chemically produced stains. The chemical content of Ajax is referred to in the testimony of Casson and, in my view, need not be exhaustively examined here except to suggest that the bleaching components were increased and the sodium-bromide portions were also increased; in the view of Casson, a view which has not been detracted from throughout this trial, at that time it had attained superiority over Comet.

The laboratory testing consisted of a number of strokes applied in a dynamic test to remove dirt or stain and it is suggested that stains could be removed with fewer strokes with Ajax when compared with Comet. During the course of testing, the defendant corporation employed an instrument called a digital reflectometer which indicates the degree of cleanliness after scouring; in addition, the company also employed some 20 or 30 women expressing opinions as to the degree of cleanliness of pre-selected strips cleaned by various cleansers during dynamic tests. The superiority claim, according to Casson, was only used after the experimentation I have described above, experimentation which he has described in great detail throughout. Mr. Casson was well aware that Comet's claim with respect to superiority in its earlier commercial was predicated on the fact that Comet was superior in a static test which required a one-minute delay period and he became convinced that Ajax used under dynamic conditions was superior. He was also equally convinced that most users of a cleanser do so under dynamic conditions.

After the product was revitalized, Mr. Casson then had the opportunity of assisting the commercial advertising firm at his own corporation in the preparation of a claim of superiority to be shown on television commercial clips.

As a chemist with 32 years' experience, Mr. Casson's testimony was impressive and, as is the case with respect to all professional witnesses called in this case, the question of credibility does not enter into my mind since they all approached their performance and their work with a high degree of professionalism. While the methods in some cases were superior, depending on the qualification of the chemist, I can truthfully say that they were witnesses whose credibility is beyond attack.

Mr. Casson's testimony was followed by the testimony of Mr. Ferguson, a chemist employed with the Department of Public Works. Mr. Ferguson has been employed with the Research and Development Laboratory of the Canada Department of Public Works since 1955, and he is now a group head in the engineering chemistry section.

The cleanser was handed to him by Mr. Walker and, as I have alluded to in my earlier comments, the method of testing was prescribed for him. It bears repeating that the method of testing suggested by Walker was inspired from the correspondence and information already received from the manufacturers of Comet and Super Dutch.

In addition to the instructions, Mr. Ferguson was provided with enamel testing plates by the same company which produces the porcelain testing plates for Colgate-Palmolive. The witness Ferguson attempted what, in my view, may be described as an exhaustive series of tests and it is regrettable that the plates in the ensuing four years between the testing and the trial have been allowed to yellow and deteriorate. It is difficult by visual or other examination to determine the efficacy of the tests because of the long period of time which has elapsed between the testing and the hearing of this matter.

While Mr. Ferguson's testing was exhaustive within the methods prescribed by Walker, it is not unfair to suggest that in retrospect it seems that Mr. Ferguson would have preferred to develop his own testing method. Ferguson's testimony was honest and straightforward. In his testimony, in answer to a question by the Crown prosecutor, he stated:

> [I]n retrospect, I think our test procedures were quite good as far as they went. They were probably not the final answer in the field. One of the conclusions that I drew was that different people, using different test parameters, might very well rank all these products in a different order than I did.

When asked to give a conclusion to his testing, the following was his reply:

> All these products are considered to be good quality cleansers. It is difficult to make an overall comparative evaluation because of the different effects found with various stains and cleaning procedures. Ajax seems to have the most rapid bleaching action and to be the most efficient cleanser on iron/tannin type stains; if some time is allowed for a certain amount of action to occur, Comet appears to be the most efficient on grease-covered stains and on aluminum stains; Dutch has perhaps slightly more abrasive action than the others and, if given sufficient time, will eventually get more bleaching agent into action.

His overall conclusion is not altogether different from the conclusion of Mr. Casson, namely, that in any dynamic test, Ajax may be superior while in a static test, Comet may have an advantage.

While many of the witnesses were called to testify, I do not wish to exhaustively review each witness's evidence except to suggest that I was fairly unimpressed with the witness [Redlaw], whose professionalism and approach to testing hardly compares with that of Moeser who, incidentally, was also employed with Procter & Gamble, the manufacturer of Comet.

Moeser outlined what was obvious from the beginning of this case, that a cleanser should have abrasive qualities and it must bleach and disinfect. He does not dispute that in a scouring test, Ajax would have the lead, while in a static test, Comet may very well be superior. It is obvious that the method of use of a cleanser can never be effectively tested on the public unless exhaustive market surveys are conducted with respect to how users of cleansers attempt to remove stains, namely, whether the cleanser is used in dynamic or static action. It can, nevertheless, be suggested that surely the public must understand the difference between a cleaner and a cleanser and that, while the unwary and unsuspecting public must be protected, it certainly cannot be deemed that the public is altogether ignorant, unthinking and credulous. To suggest that would be to do violence to one's concept of public appreciation.

During the course of submissions by counsel for the Crown and counsel for the defendant, I have made brief reference to a very basic question in this matter, namely, the discretion of the Crown to prosecute in cases of superiority claims where the evidence may be marginal. While it is true that s. 39 [rep. & sub. 1974-75-76, c. 76, s. 18(1)] creates a regulatory offence in the sense that *mens rea* is not required, thereby giving relief to the Crown from having to make proof of intent, it must nevertheless be ascertained before a prosecution is initiated that the claim of a potential defendant could have had an effect on the public mind, which effect can be proved to be "untrue, misleading and deceptive" within the meaning of the *Combines Investigation Act*.

To do otherwise would be to unnecessarily place the citizens and corporations of this country at the mercy of Government and at the mercy of law enforcers and administrators. I have no suggestion to make as to how administrative discretion must be used with respect to prosecutions in cases of claims of superiority, but most certainly it must always be fairly exercised and there is no substitute for what we need—namely, a mixture of law and discretion which we know as justice—before prosecutions of strict liability offences can be undertaken.

Criminal liability without fault could potentially lead criminal law into disrepute and disrespect; certainly, the avenue of prosecution must only be used in cases where there is cogent evidence of violation of the statute and where the business practices of corporations involved are well below acceptable standards of care and honesty; where the degree of care and the standards exercised are such that conclusions may be subjective or inconsistent, most certainly prosecutorial discretion ought not to be exercised merely to test the effective enforcement of the law.

In the matter before me, it is obvious that the defendant corporation had not only undertaken a great number of tests but that subjectively those in charge of the laboratory had concluded that their product was superior, a conclusion which has not been disproved. It was not suggested that the witness giving such testimony was either improper or incorrect. The challenge to the claim of superiority of Ajax insofar as it comes from the mouth of the employees of a competitor is not suspect solely because of that fact, but, in my view, its source may affect the weight I should ascribe to it.

I have examined very carefully the evidence of Mr. Ferguson and I cannot find that it contradicts the chemist of the defendant corporation; indeed, his conclusion above stated must reinforce the position of the defendant's chemist, and there is no amount of eloquence that can possibly suggest that the Crown's case is not wedded to the opinion of these two chemists.

To suggest that a case has been made on behalf of the Crown from the frail testimony and very superficial testing of the chemist from Procter & Gamble, Mr. [Redlaw], would be to underestimate the ability of free enterprise. Mr. [Redlaw]'s attempt at showing the product Comet was at least equal if not superior to Ajax lacked proper testing methods. It lacked the proper use of instruments and has, in my view, a very limited amount of professionalism when compared to the laboratory testing of chemists from Ajax. Likewise, the testimony of Moeser, while impressive, falls quite short of suggesting that Ajax may not be slightly superior than the product Comet. In fact, the witness Moeser under cross-examination did concede that he may have made a minor but nonetheless difficult error in his own process of experimentation.

To say that the defendant has not raised a reasonable doubt would be to avoid a logical conclusion which is inescapable in this case. While the legislation should and indeed must be enforced, it is, in my view, incumbent upon the Government of Canada to enforce it in such a way that claims of superiority are challenged upon evidence and testing which it can carry out without the dependence of competitors of the brand being attacked or challenged. It is not uncommon in the criminal process to rely on the evidence of an accomplice to secure conviction. I in no way suggest any similarity with respect to the matter before me but strongly disapprove of testing methods which rely so heavily on competitors of one's product; I even raise a basic question as to whether or not the Crown came to Court with clean hands.

In the case before me, it became obvious that one of the products, namely, Dutch, was certainly not living up to its claim and yet no prosecution was undertaken. It also became painfully clear that the defendant corporation attempted to co-operate in every possible way with Consumer and Corporate Affairs, but despite this obvious co-operation which is so necessary, it was singled out for the purpose of prosecution. The awesome power of the State to compel a corporation to come to Court and divulge its tests and lay naked its experiments is necessary, but, in my view, ought to be used with a great deal of scruple. I, therefore, refuse to convict the accused corporation of the offences charged since the evidence, in my opinion, not only fell below the standard in a criminal trial, but I would hazard to say that not even a *prima facie* case had been made out.

I am extremely grateful to both counsel for their competence, assistance and advocacy in this difficult matter.

*Accused acquitted.*

\* \* \*

# THE CONSUMERS' CONTRIBUTION TO MISUNDERSTANDING

The American Association of Advertising Agencies' Educational Foundation reported in 1980 that more than 90 percent of television viewers "misunderstand some part of what they see, no matter what kind of broadcast they are watching." Moreover, they normally misunderstand between a quarter and a third of the telecast "whether it is an entertainment-news program, commercial advertisement, or public service announcement." The psychologist who directed the study, Jacob Jacoby, a professor at Purdue, commented, "Public policy makers should not automatically assume that an advertisement is itself misleading simply because there is evidence that viewers misunderstand part of it."*

How far does this information go to excuse various advertising practices?

*Quotations from *The Misconception of Televised Communications*, a pamphlet published by the AAAA Educational Foundation, New York, and drawn on with its permission.

# CHAPTER 6

# The Character of Products

*Introductory Comment:*

## EFFECTIVENESS, RELIABILITY, AND DURABILITY

In the chapters on "Sales Tactics" and "Honesty in Advertising," we have been considering how firms represent or misrepresent their products to consumers. The products themselves may be good or bad, however represented. Even if no claims were made for them, except that they were goods of this or that specific kind, consumers are entitled to expect that they will be effective to some degree, reliable, durable, and safe.

Cigarettes have various bad effects on health and the environment arising from their repeated consumption by great numbers of people. Those effects and the questions that they raise will be treated later. Here, if we were to bring up cigarettes as an example, we would be concerned only to know such things as whether they should be firmly filled with tobacco, burn a reasonable length of time, and refrain from exploding.

Products are different things from the packages that they come in; but packages raise the same issues, so we may understand the "character of products" as embracing the character of packages, too. In fact, one of the most vivid cases that I have to offer has to do with the safety of packages.

The items on safety, whether they have to do with packages or not, outshine the items on effectiveness, reliability, and durability. These, as a little reflection will confirm, are four distinct properties of goods. Products often fail in respect to all the last three properties together, however; and, very often, even in respect to all four. They each raise much the same issues for the ethical conduct of business as any of the others, and the issues are raised far more vividly when safety is in question. I shall confine myself to offering, under effectiveness, reliability, and durability, one case, which involves safety as well and would never have been brought to court if it had not, a quiz, and a general comment on the self-respect of producers. Then I shall bring up a number of cases under safety.

I might mention that I would have liked to supply, under "durability," an example of a forthright statement championing "planned obsolescence," but I have not come across one. There are, regrettably, limits to which the idea can be applied to hammers.

# DUNHAM v.
# VAUGHAN & BUSHNELL MFG. CO.

*Supreme Court of Illinois, 1969*

SCHAEFER, Justice.

A jury in the circuit court of Macoupin County returned a verdict in the sum of $50,000 in favor of the plaintiff, Benjamin E. Dunham, and against the defendants, Vaughan & Bushnell Mfg. Co. and Belknap Hardware and Mfg. Co. Judgment was entered on the verdict and the Appellate Court for the Fourth Judicial District affirmed. . . . We allowed the defendants' petition for leave to appeal.

The injury that gave rise to this action occurred while the plaintiff was fitting a pin into a clevis to connect his tractor to a manure spreader. He had made the connection on one side, using a hammer to insert the pin. To insert the second pin he lay on his right side underneath the tractor and used the hammer extended about two and one-half feet above his head. The hammer moved through an arc which he described as about 8 inches. He testified that as he undertook to "tap" the pin into the clevis a chip from the beveled edge of the hammer, known as the chamfer, broke off and struck him in the right eye. He lost the sight of that eye.

The hammer in question is a claw hammer of the best grade manufactured by the defendant Vaughan & Bushnell Mfg. Co. It bore the "Blue-Grass" trademark of its distributor, the other defendant, Belknap Hardware and Manufacturing Co. The plaintiff had received the hammer from a retailer, Heyen Implement Company, located near his home. He received it as a replacement for another "Blue-Grass" hammer, the handle of which had been broken. Before the accident occurred the plaintiff had used the hammer for approximately 11 months in connection with his farming and custom machine work. He had used it in repairing a corn crib and had also used it in working upon his farming implements and machinery.

Each party offered the testimony of an expert metallurgist. Neither expert found any flaws due to the forging of the hammer, or any metallurgical defects due to the process of manufacture. The experts agreed that the hammer was made of steel with a carbon content of "1080." The plaintiff's expert testified that such a hammer was more likely to chip or shear than one made of steel with a lower carbon content of "1040," which would not be as hard. The defendant's expert disagreed; it was his opinion that a hammer made of harder steel, with the higher carbon content, would be less likely to chip or shear than one made of steel with a lower carbon content. Both experts testified that use of a hammer produced a condition described as "work hardening" or "metal failure," which made a hammer more likely to chip or shear.

The defendants apparently suggest that the plaintiff should not have used a claw hammer to tap the pin into the clevis because the mushroom head of the pin was made of steel of a "Rockwell" test hardness of C57, which was harder than the head of the hammer, which tested Rockwell C52. But as the appellate court pointed out, the specifications of the General Service Administration used by all Federal agencies, call for a Rockwell "C" hardness of 50–60 in carpenter's claw hammers and a Rockwell "C" hardness of 50–57 for machinist's ball-peen hammers. Those specifications also require that sample carpenters' claw hammers and sample ball-peen hammers be subjected to identical tests, by striking them against another hammer and against a steel bar, to determine that tendency to "chip, crack or spall." The specifications thus negate the defendant's suggestion that the plaintiff should have used a ball-peen hammer, rather than the hammer in question, in tapping the pin into the clevis.

The basic theory of the defendant in this court is that the requirements of strict liability, as announced in Suvada vs. White Motor Co., . . . were not established, because the testimony of the experts showed that the hammer contained no defect. *Suvada* required a plaintiff to prove that his injury resulted from a condition of the product which was unreasonably dangerous, and which existed at the time the product left the manufacturer's control. But the requirement that the defect must have existed when the product left the manufacturer's control does not mean that the defect must manifest itself at once. The defective "minimum brake linkage bracket," with which the court was concerned in ruling upon the legal sufficiency of the complaint in *Suvada*, was alleged to have been installed in the tractor not later than March of 1957; it did not break until June of 1960.

Although the definitions of the term "defect" in the context of products liability law use varying language, all of them rest upon the common premise that those products are defective which are dangerous because they fail to perform in the manner reasonably to be expected in light of their nature and intended function. So, Chief Justice Traynor has suggested that a product is defective if it fails to match the average quality of like products. . . . The Restatement emphasizes the viewpoint of the consumer and concludes that a defect is a condition not contemplated by the ultimate consumer which would be unreasonably dangerous to him. . . . Dean Prosser said that "the product is to be regarded as defective if it is not safe for such a use that can be expected to be made of it, and no warning is given." . . . Dean Wade has suggested that apart from the existence of a defect, "the test for imposing strict liability is whether the product is unreasonably dangerous, to use the words of the Restatement. Somewhat preferable is the expression 'not reasonably safe.' " . . .

The evidence in this case, including both the General Services Administration specifications and tests and the testimony of the experts as to "work hardening" or "metal failure," shows that hammers have a propensity to chip which increases with continued use. From that evidence it would appear that a new hammer would not be expected to chip, while at some point in its life the possibility of chipping might become a reasonable expectation, and a part of the hammer's likely performance. The problems arise in the middle range, as Chief Justice Traynor has illustrated: "If an automobile part normally lasts five years, but the one in question proves defective after six months of normal use, there would be enough deviation to serve as a basis for holding the manufacturer liable for any resulting harm. What if the part lasts four of the normal five years, however, and then proves defective? For how long should a manufacturer be responsible for his product?" . . .

The answers to these questions are properly supplied by a jury, and on the record that is before us this case presents only the narrow question whether there is sufficient evidence to justify the jury's conclusion that the hammer was defective. The record shows that it was represented as one of "best quality" and was not put to a use which was regarded as extraordinary in the experience of the community. The jury could properly have concluded that, considering the length and type of its use, the hammer failed to perform in the manner that would reasonably have been expected, and that this failure caused the plaintiff's injury.

\* \* \*

## Anonymous Quiz on Reliability and Misrepresentation

One year I asked my class to answer the following quiz. I think I'll make it a regular practice.

*Do not put your name on the paper.*
Fountain pens, flashlights, and automobiles are all products that have been strenuously advertised on the point of reliability. Keep them in mind as examples in answering the following questions; but do not feel restricted to them as examples.

1. Reliability is somewhat difficult to distinguish from effectiveness, durability, and even safety (consider, besides automobiles, smoke-fire alarms). Why? How would you distinguish it after all?
2. Is the consumer entitled to take a certain degree of reliability for granted (so that goods not reliable to that degree should be returnable for full reimbursement)?

3. If you advertised a product, stressing its reliability, is the consumer entitled to expect that it will be reliable to a significantly greater degree than (a) products generally (b) rival products?

4. Competing firms are putting out cheaply made products that are not as reliable as yours. You cannot make a reliable product and meet their price. Do you put out an unreliable one? How would you make sure, if so, that the consumer is not misled?

5. Suppose that you are operating in a sector of the market where you cannot hope to attract repeated sales under your brand name. You can treat each sale as a one-time affair, with no effects on future sales. Will you even so make sure that your product is reliable?

6. Would you regard a system of testing by the government, with results as to reliability expressed as numerical probabilities and included by law in your labelling, as an unwarranted intrusion into free enterprise? Explain your answer.

*Comment:*

## SELF-RESPECT

The answers that the class gave to the anonymous quiz seemed to me very revealing of their moral convictions, and led to the following comment on my part.

In the returns of the anonymous questionnaire on reliability and misrepresentation, the policy of meeting competition from cheaper goods by putting out a less reliable product of your own was unanimously rejected. There was near-unanimity, too, in rejecting the idea of putting out an unreliable product for sale in a one-time market where you could not expect to build up a following, though several people did not fully adopt the assumption about no following, and one person said that the quality of the good could be signaled by an appropriate price. In one return, the reason given for sticking with reliability in the face of competition from cheaper goods was the attraction of "a target market." Most returns, however, on both of the issues referred to, explained the attachment to reliability by reference to something close to self-respect. The basic idea was that one could hardly take pride in what one was doing—or, reflecting on one's life, in what one had done with it—if one had been occupied in making and selling inferior goods.

How far does self-respect extend? And what is its moral significance? Less than half the class filled out the questionnaire and returned it. One may suspect that those who did were, unrepresentatively, more conscientious than the rest of the class. The class as a whole, consisting of people who have bothered to give ethics in business extended consideration, may be unrepresentative both of university students in general and of university students headed toward careers in commerce. About a third of the class in fact consists of B.A. students, not commerce students. Still, in discussion and in past exercises, the class as a whole has not been divided in such proportions on moral views (or anything else) as to prevent us from hypothesizing, on the basis of the returns, that a substantial proportion of people who will be pursuing careers in commerce will be reluctant to engage in any practices that jeopardize their self-respect, and that trading in unreliable goods is one such practice.

Obviously, the moral significance of self-respect rests in large part on just such consequences. It is good to have people care about self-respect, because if they do they will refrain from doing bad things. But how do people come to care about self-respect? Is it simply a matter of having been trained not to respect oneself unless one has other people's respect, and not to respect other people unless they do beneficial things?

Certainly it is difficult to imagine anyone having self-respect who does not believe at least that he or she deserves the respect of others; and the opinion that one deserves the respect of others is not easy to maintain in the face of what is in fact widespread disrespect. Moreover, when people honor someone, the honor is given, in part at least, perhaps exclusively, for benefits (including exemplary achievements) conferred. Consider how you would fill out a statement beginning "I honor him for . . ." Could you put "swindling," or "piracy," or "having his own way"?

Yet, though honor always implies respect, and is an especially gratifying manifestation of respect, perhaps respect does not always imply honor. Do not people in fact respect successful pirates and bandits? The respect gained by men on horseback—chevaliers, in other words predatory oppressors—in our past history is not even yet entirely extinct. Or think of our lingering respect for the Viking raiders. Even swindlers can obtain some respect if they operate on a sufficiently large scale and bring off their coups in the face of great difficulties.

Even these variant forms of respect, however, and the forms of self-respect that may be founded on them, seem to exclude trading in unreliable goods. Partly this is because if one goes in for making or selling goods piecemeal to the public as a line of work one in effect gives up being a bandit, or even a swindler with large-scale schemes. One is running a different sort of race. But partly it is because such trading is a mean—ignoble—way of acting. It does not require any sort of courage or astuteness. The large-scale swindler must display both. So must the bandit, who in addition must display them openly and publicly, for he—or she—will not gain much respect from sneak attacks on defenseless people. Even the swindler, to gain respect, must operate in circumstances where there is a fair chance of being detected. We can regard this chance as an approximation to the openness and publicity assumed in ideal circumstances for choosing moral rules.

Openness and publicity go at least part of the way toward meeting the requirement, characteristic of ethics, that rules and practices and actions can stand being made public. That is to say, they could be acknowledged without provoking outrage and indignation—or if they did, it could be shown in public debate that the outrage and indignation were unwarranted. Self-respect founded on morally upright conduct meets this requirement fully. Public debate in which everyone's interest was fully expressed would condemn, in particular, making and selling unreliable goods. It would bring out the extent to which those who supplied reliable goods deserved honor. Moreover, against the benefits that they conferred with such goods one would not inevitably have to offset some harm that they did by their activities, as one would in the case of the bandit or the swindler. Respect and hence self-respect have a firmer as well as a more attractive foundation if they can be vindicated in this way.

## Comment:

# SAFETY

Every reason for making sure that the goods which a firm supplies are up to standard as regards effectiveness, durability, and reliability applies to making sure that they are safe, too. They will not be suitable for the uses for which they are bought if they are substantially less than normally safe, compared to other goods of the same kind or designed for the same uses. But safety brings more dramatic reasons into consideration as well. At stake with it are people's very lives, as well as their health and their bodies, and hence their basic prospects of having decently happy lives. One could hardly broach a topic that reached more swiftly and surely into the center of ethics.

Excitement about the topic should not, however, be allowed to distort the moral judgments that one makes about it. In particular, awful as the weight of responsibility may sometimes be on the supplier of unsafe goods, one must beware of ascribing all the responsibility, or even the preponderant responsibility, to the supplier in case after case. Some products—dynamite; pocket-knives—are inherently dangerous; others—automobiles—can hardly be used without bringing people into dangerous situations; still others are dangerous when they are used in abnormal ways—an orange-crate set on end to serve as a stepping-stool. Almost anything, in sufficient quantity, can be dangerous if it is spilled or dislodged overhead. In all these cases, the responsibility for precautions is shared between the firm that supplies the good and the person who in the end uses it; and often it is the precautions that the user takes or fails to take which are decisive for safety.

These cases, however, all have in common the feature that the user (if he is a normal user, an adult with relevant experience) could reasonably be expected to anticipate the dangers involved. In other cases, the user is in no position to anticipate the dangers. There the decisive responsibility shifts to the firm supplying the good.

Generations of law students in the British Commonwealth have found the first item amusing, and I hope you will, too. Things become abruptly less amusing with subsequent items.

# DONOGHUE (or McALISTER) v. STEVENSON*

---

*[In the United Kingdom, the final court of appeal is the House of Lords, where cases are heard by committees of jurists made lords specially for the purpose.]*

*House of Lords, 1932*

LORD THANKERTON—In this action the appellant claims reparation from the respondent in respect of illness and other injurious effects resulting from the presence of a decomposed snail in a bottle of ginger-beer, which is alleged to have been manufactured by the respondent, and which was partially consumed by her, it having been ordered by a friend on her behalf in a café in Paisley.

The action is based on negligence, and the only question in this appeal is whether, taking the appellant's averments *pro veritate*, they disclose a case relevant in law, so as to entitle her to have them remitted for proof. The Lord Ordinary allowed a proof, but, on a reclaiming note for the respondent, the Second Division of the Court of Session recalled the Lord Ordinary's interlocutor and dismissed the action . . .

The appellant's case is that the bottle was sealed with a metal cap and was made of dark opaque glass, which not only excluded access to the contents before consumption if the contents were to retain their aerated condition, but also excluded the possibility of visual examination of the contents from outside; and that on the side of the bottle there was pasted a label containing the name and address of the respondent, who was the manufacturer. She states that the shopkeeper who supplied the ginger-beer opened it and poured some of its contents into a tumbler, which contained some ice cream, and that she drank some of the contents of the tumbler; that her friend then lifted the bottle and was pouring the remainder of the contents into the tumbler when a snail, which had been, unknown to her, her friend, or the shopkeeper, in the bottle, and was in a state of decomposition, floated out of the bottle.

The duties which the appellant accuses the respondent of having ne-

---

*Excerpts from *All England Law Reports,* reprinted by their permission.

glected may be summarised as follows: (a) that the ginger-beer was manufactured by the respondent or his servants to be sold as an article of drink to members of the public (including the appellant), and that, accordingly, it was his duty to exercise the greatest care in order that snails should not get into the bottles, render the ginger-beer dangerous and harmful, and be sold with the ginger-beer; (b) a duty to provide a system of working his business which would not allow snails to get into sealed bottles, and, in particular, would not allow the bottles when washed to stand in places to which snails had access; (c) a duty to provide an efficient system of inspection, which would prevent snails from getting into the sealed bottles; and (d) a duty to provide clear bottles, so as to facilitate the said system of inspection.

There can be no doubt, in my opinion, that equally in the law of Scotland and of England it lies upon the party claiming redress in such a case to show that there was some relation of duty between her and the defender which required the defender to exercise due and reasonable care for her safety. It is not at all necessary that there should be any direct contract between them, because the action is not based upon contract but upon negligence; but it is necessary for the pursuer in such an action to show there was a duty owed to her by the defender, because a man cannot be charged with negligence if he has no obligation to exercise diligence. . . . The question in each case is whether the pursuer has established, or, in the stage of the present appeal, has relevantly averred, such facts as involve the existence of such a relation of duty.

We are not dealing here with a case of what is called an article per se dangerous or one which was known by the defender to be dangerous, in which cases a special duty of protection or adequate warning is placed upon the person who uses or distributes it. The present case is that of a manufacturer and a consumer, with whom he has no contractual relation, of an article which the manufacturer did not know to be dangerous; and, unless the consumer can establish a special relationship with the manufacturer, it is clear, in my opinion, that neither the law of Scotland nor the law of England will hold that the manufacturer has any duty towards the consumer to exercise diligence. In such a case the remedy of the consumer, if any, will lie against the intervening party from whom he has procured the article. I am aware that the American courts, in the decisions referred to by my noble and learned friend LORD MACMILLAN, have taken a view more favourable to the consumer.

The special circumstances, from which the appellant claims that such a relationship of duty should be inferred, may, I think, be stated thus, namely, that the respondent, in placing his manufactured article of drink upon the market, has intentionally so excluded interference with, or examination of, the article by any intermediate handler of the goods between himself and the consumer that he has, of his own accord, brought himself into direct relationship with the consumer, with the result that the consumer is entitled to rely upon the exercise of diligence by the manufacturer to secure that the article shall not be harmful to the consumer. If that contention be sound, the consumer, on her showing that the article has reached her intact, and that she has been injured by the harmful nature of the article owing to the failure of the manufacturer to take reasonable care in its preparation before its enclosure in the sealed vessel, will be entitled to reparation from the manufacturer.

In my opinion, the existence of a legal duty in such circumstances is in conformity with the principles of both the law of Scotland and the law of England. The English cases demonstrate how impossible it is finally to catalogue, amid the ever-varying types of human relationships, those relationships in which a duty to exercise care arises apart from contract, and each of these cases relates to its own set of circumstances, out of which it was claimed that the duty had arisen. In none of these cases were the circumstances identical with the present case as regards that which I regard as the essential element in this case, namely, the manufacturer's own action in bringing himself into direct relationship with the party injured. I have had the privilege of considering the discussion of these authorities by my noble and learned friend LORD ATKIN in the judgment which he has just delivered, and I so entirely agree with it that I cannot usefully add anything to it.

An interesting illustration of similar circumstances is to be found in *Gordon v. McHardy* (31), in which the pursuer sought to recover damages from a retail grocer on account of the death of his son by ptomaine poisoning, caused by eating tinned salmon purchased from the defender. The pursuer averred that the tin, when sold, was dented, but he did not suggest that the grocer had cut through the metal and allowed air to get in, or had otherwise caused injury to the contents. The action was held irrelevant, the LORD JUSTICE CLERK remarking, "I do not see how the defender could have examined the tin of salmon which he is alleged to have sold without destroying the very condition which the manufacturer had established in order to preserve the contents, the tin not being intended to be opened until immediately before use." Apparently in that case the manufacturers' label was off the tin when sold, and they had not been identified. I should be sorry to think that the meticulous care of the manufacturer to exclude interference or inspection by the grocer in that case should relieve the grocer of any responsibility to the consumer without any corresponding assumption of duty by the manufacturer.

I am of opinion that the contention of the appellant is sound and that she has relevantly averred a relationship of duty as between the respondent and herself, as also that her averments of the respondent's neglect of that duty are relevant.

The cases of *Mullen* and *McGowan* (16), which the learned judges of the Second Division followed in the present case, related to facts similar in every respect except that the foreign matter was a decomposed mouse. In these cases the same court—LORD HUNTER dissenting—held that the manufacturer owed no duty to the consumer. The view of the majority was that the English authorities excluded the existence of such a duty, but LORD ORMIDALE (1929 S.C. at p. 471) would otherwise have been prepared to come to a contrary conclusion. LORD HUNTER's opinion seems to be in conformity with the view which I have expressed above. My conclusion rests upon the facts averred in this case, and would apparently also have applied in the cases of *Mullen* and *McGowan* (16), in which, however, there had been a proof before answer, and there was also a question as to whether the pursuers had proved their averments. I am, therefore, of opinion that the appeal should be allowed and the case should be remitted for proof, as the pursuer did not ask for an issue.

LORD BUCKMASTER—In my view, . . . the authorities are against the appellant's contention, and apart from authority it is difficult to see how any common law proposition can be formulated to support her claim.

The principle contended for must be this—that the manufacturer, or, indeed, the repairer, of any article, apart entirely from contract, owes a duty to any person by whom the article is lawfully used to see that it has been carefully constructed. . . . the duty, if it exists, must extend to every person who, in lawful circumstances, uses the article made. There can be no special duty attaching to the manufacture of food, apart from those implied by contract or imposed by statute. If such a duty exists it seems to me it must cover the construction of every article, and I cannot see any reason why it should not apply to the construction of a house. If one step, why not fifty? Yet if a house be, as it sometimes is, negligently built, and in consequence of that negligence the ceiling falls and injures the occupier or anyone else, no action against the builder exists according to the English law, although I believe such a right did exist according to the laws of Babylon. Were such a principle known and recognised, it seems to me impossible, having regard to the numerous cases that must have arisen to persons injured by its disregard, that with the exception of *George v. Skivington* (5) no case directly involving the principle has ever succeeded in the courts, and were it well known and accepted much of the discussion of the earlier cases would have been waste of time.

In *Mullen v. Barr & Co., McGowan v. Barr & Co.* (16), a case indistinguishable from the present, except upon the ground that a mouse is not a snail, and necessarily adopted by the Second Division in their judgment, LORD ANDERSON says this (1929 S.C. at p. 479):

> In a case like the present, where the goods of the defenders are widely distributed throughout Scotland, it would seem little short of outrageous to make them responsible to members of the public for the condition of the contents of every bottle which issues from their works. It is obvious that, if such responsibility attached to the defenders, they might be called on to meet claims of damages which they could not possibly investigate or answer.

In agreeing, as I do, with the judgment of LORD ANDERSON, I desire to add that I find it hard to dissent from the emphatic nature of the language with which his judgment is clothed. I am of opinion that this appeal should be dismissed, and I beg to move your Lordships accordingly.

LORD MACMILLAN—. . . Where, as in cases like the present, so much depends upon the avenue of approach to the question it is very easy to take the wrong turning. If you begin with the sale by the manufacturer to the retail dealer, then the consumer who purchases from the retailer is at once seen to be a stranger to the contract between the retailer and the manufacturer and so disentitled to sue upon it. There is no contractual relation between the manufacturer and the consumer, and thus the plaintiff if he is to succeed is driven to try to bring himself within one or other of the exceptional cases where the strictness of the rule that none but a party to a contract can found on a breach of that contract has been mitigated in the public interest, as it has been in the case of a person who issues a chattel which is inherently dangerous or which he knows to be in a dangerous condition. If, on the other hand, you disregard the fact that the circumstances of the case at one stage include the existence of a contract of sale between the manufacturer and the retailer and approach the question by asking whether there is evidence of carelessness on the part of the manufacturer and whether he owed a duty to be careful in a question with the party who has been injured in consequence of his want of care, the circumstance that the injured party was not a party to the incidental contract of sale becomes irrelevant and his title to sue the manufacturer is unaffected by that circumstance. The appellant in the present instance asks that her case be approached as a case of delict, not as a case of breach of contract. She does not require to invoke the exceptional cases in which a person not a party to a contract has been held to be entitled to complain of some defect in the subject-matter of the contract which has caused him harm. The exceptional case of things dangerous in themselves or known to be in a dangerous condition has been regarded as constituting a peculiar category outside the ordinary law both of contract and of tort. I may observe that it seems to me inaccurate to describe the case of dangerous things as an exception to the principle that no one but a party to a contract can sue on that contract. I rather regard this type of case as a special instance of negligence where the law exacts a degree of diligence so stringent as to amount practically to a guarantee of safety.

[In] the American case of Thomas v. Winchester . . . a chemist carelessly issued, in response to an order for extract of dandelion, a bottle containing belladonna which he labelled "extract of dandelion," with the consequence that a third party who took a dose from the bottle suffered severely. The chemist was held responsible. This case is quoted by LORD DUNEDIN in giving the judgment of the Privy Council in *Dominion Natural Gas Co. v. Collins* (6) as an instance of liability to third parties, and I think it was a sound decision.

In the American courts the law has advanced considerably in the development of the principle exemplified in *Thomas v. Winchester* (14). In one of the latest cases in the United States, *McPherson v. Buick Motor Co.* (15), the plaintiff, who had purchased from a retailer a motor car, manufactured by the defendant company, was injured in consequence of a defect in the construction of the car and was held entitled to recover damages from the manufacturer. CARDOZO, J., the very eminent Chief Judge of the New York Court of Appeals, and now an associate justice of the United States Supreme Court, thus stated the law:

There is no claim that the defendant knew of the defect and willfully concealed it. . . . The charge is one not of fraud but of negligence. The question to be determined is whether the defendant owed a duty of care and vigilance to anyone but the immediate purchaser. . . . The principle of Thomas v. Winchester (14) is not limited to poisons, explosives, and things of like nature, to things which in their normal operation are implements of destruction. If the nature of a thing is such that it is reasonably certain to place life and limb in peril when negligently made, it is then a thing of danger. Its nature gives warning of the consequences to be expected. If to the element of danger there is added knowledge that the thing will be used by persons other than the purchaser, and used without new tests, then, irrespective of contract, the manufacturer of this thing of danger is under a duty to make it carefully. That is as far as we are required to go for the decision of this case. There must be knowledge of a danger. . . . There must also be knowledge that in the usual course of events the danger will be shared by others than the buyer. Such knowledge may often be inferred from the nature of the transaction. . . . The dealer was indeed the one person of whom it might be said with some approach to certainty that by him the car would not be used. Yet the defendant would have us say that he was the one person whom it [the defendant company] was under a legal duty to protect. The law does not lead us to so inconsequent a conclusion.

The law takes no cognizance of carelessness in the abstract. It concerns itself with carelessness only where there is a duty to take care and where failure in that duty has caused damage. In such circumstances carelessness assumes the legal quality of negligence and entails the consequences in law of negligence. What then are the circumstances which gave rise to this duty to take care? In the daily contacts of social and business life human beings are thrown into or place themselves in an infinite variety of relationships with their fellows, and the law can refer only to the standards of the reasonable man in order to determine whether any particular relationship gives rise to a duty to take care as between those who stand in that relationship to each other. The grounds of action may be as various and manifold as human errancy, and the conception of legal responsibility may develop in adaptation to altering social conditions and standards. The criterion of judgment must adjust and adapt itself to the changing circumstances of life. The categories of negligence are never closed. The cardinal principle of liability is that the party complained of should owe to the party complaining a duty to take care and that the party complaining should be able to prove that he has suffered damage in consequence of a breach of that duty. Where there is room for diversity of view is in determining what circumstances will establish such a relationship between the parties as to give rise on the one side to a duty to take care and on the other side to a right to have care taken.

To descend from these generalities to the circumstances of the present case, I do not think that any reasonable man or any twelve reasonable men would hesitate to hold that if the appellant establishes her allegations the respondent has exhibited carelessness in the conduct of his business. For a manufacturer of aerated water to store his empty bottles in a place where snails can get access to them and to fill his bottles without taking any adequate precautions by inspection or otherwise to ensure that they contain no deleterious foreign matter may reasonably be characterised as carelessness without applying too exacting a standard. But, as I have pointed out, it is not enough to prove the respondent to be careless in his process of manufacture. The question is: Does he owe a duty to take care, and to whom does he owe that duty? I have no hesitation in affirming that a person who for gain engages in the business of manufacturing articles of food and drink intended for consumption by members of the public in the form in which he issues them is under a duty to take care in the manufacture of these articles. That duty, in my opinion, he owes to those whom he intends to consume his products. He manufactures his commodities for human consumption; he intends and contemplates that they shall be consumed. By reason of that very fact he places himself in a relationship with all the potential consumers of his commodities, and that relationship, which he assumes and desires for his own ends, imposes upon him a duty to take care to avoid injuring them. He owes them a duty not to convert by his own carelessness an article which he issues to them as wholesome and innocent into an article which is dangerous to life and health.

It is sometimes said that liability can arise only where a reasonable man would have foreseen and could have avoided the consequences of his act or omission. In the present case the respondent, when he manufactured his ginger-beer, had directly in contemplation that it would be consumed by members of the public. Can it be said that he could not be expected as a reasonable man to foresee that if he conducted his process of manufacture carelessly he might injure those whom he expected and desired to consume his ginger-beer? The possibility of injury so arising seems to me in no sense so remote as to excuse him from foreseeing it. Suppose that a baker through carelessness allows a large quantity of arsenic to be mixed with a batch of his bread, with the result that those who subsequently eat it are poisoned, could he be heard to say that he owed no duty to the consumers of his bread to take care that it was free from poison, and that, as he did not know that any poison had got into it, his only liability was for breach of warranty under his contract of sale to those who actually bought the poisoned bread from him? Observe that I have said "through carelessness" and thus excluded the case of a pure accident such as may happen where every care is taken. I cannot believe, and I do not believe, that neither in the law of England nor in the law of Scotland is there redress for such a case. The state of facts I have figured might well give rise to a criminal charge, and the civil consequences of such carelessness can scarcely be less wide than its criminal consequences. Yet the principle of the decision appealed from is that the manufacturer of food products intended by him for human consumption does not owe to the consumers whom he has in view any duty of care, not even the duty to take care that he does not poison them.

The burden of proof must always be upon the injured party to establish that the defect which caused the injury was present in the article when it left the hands of the party whom he sues, that the defect was occasioned by the carelessness of that party, and that the circumstances are such as to cast upon the defender a duty to take care not to injure the pursuer. There is no presumption of negligence in such a case as the present, nor is there any justification for applying the maxim *res ipsa loquitur.* Negligence must be both averred and proved. The appellant accepts this burden of proof and, in my opinion, she is entitled to have an opportunity of discharging it if she can. I am, accordingly, of opinion that this appeal should be allowed, the judgment of the Second Division of the Court of Session reversed, and the judgment of the Lord Ordinary restored.

*　　*　　*

## JACQUELINE SWARTZ, "POP BOTTLES: THE EXPLOSION OF DAVID BARHAM"*

Once a week, Professor David Barham watches the University glass-blower make test tubes.

"I'd love to get into *artistic* glass blowing, but you really have to devote your life to it," he says. Barham loves glass, and the flowing forms it can be moulded into, but the closest he gets to creating soaring Steuben-like designs is when he shows his first year students how glass can be shaped and composed. "Look at this one, it's 100 years old," he says, holding an amber hand-made apothecary's jar. He finds beauty even in industrial glass.

Gazing out of the large windows of his bottled-filled office, Barham muses that he could probably eke out a living as an artist/artisan. At home in the quiet suburban milieu he has chosen, he carves wood, makes cabinets and fashions semi-precious stones into jewelry. "I don't like to work in just one area. That's why I like the University: here I have variety, teaching, research, working with industry."

A chemical engineer, he teaches glass and ceramics technology and chemistry, and does research in several different areas. He is involved in developing a mineral-wool insulation from blast furnace slag, a tape that will keep pipes warm and a plastic coating for glass bottles.

During his 14 years at the U of T, his first job after getting his PhD in ceramics silicate technology from the Imperial College of Science and Technology, University of London, he has acted as a consultant to the glass industry. Which is why he was contacted last April by a lawyer to testify as an expert against the Pepsi-Cola company. A three-year-old boy, Matthew McNair, had been playing on the kitchen floor when a 1.5-litre bottle exploded in his face, permanently blinding him in one eye.

"It took a long time to get that boy out of my mind. Even now I could almost sit down and cry." Barham went out and bought 25 bottles of Pepsi-Cola in the 1.5-litre size and gently tipped them over. When the third one exploded on the first tip he tried the test on other bottles—7-Up, Canada

*From *Graduate* (the University of Toronto Alumni Magazine), January-February 1980. Copyright 1980 by the University of Toronto. Reprinted by permission of the editor of *Graduate.*

Dry, Wilson's Ginger Ale, Schweppes and Coca-Cola. Only Coke did not explode in the first few tips.

Barham, who had never been active in any political or consumer movement, reported the results of his tip tests to the Hazardous Products Division of the federal Department of Consumer and Corporate Affairs and to the Canadian Soft Drink Association. Within a week, the two parties had met and the government began its own tests.

When Barham asked that the bottles be taken off the shelves, he was told by the federal agency that it would be six to nine months before even a public announcement could be made about the problem.

Barham, angry, called the CBC. Two nights later he appeared on "The National."

"I felt nervous, but then I still get nervous when I stand up in front of a class." Barham is not a crusader but "somebody had to say something, especially in the year of the child." He became that somebody and soon he was contacted by other television stations, newspapers and radio. He was the media scientist of the summer.

Not hard to understand, he's a reporter's dream: witty, forthright, and energetic.

When the publicity started, and he was in the newspapers and on television, he and his wife were both upset. "I don't enjoy the limelight," Barham says.

But his main fear was of what he called character assassination. "Just the innuendo that I was seeking publicity could have hurt me." For that reason, he refused all payment for media appearances and found himself $150 out of pocket from the 200 bottles of pop he bought.

While Barham's report resounded in newspaper editorials to "ban the bottle," there was no response from the soft drink industry which, by June, had to contend with the government's report.

The first effect of the government's test was a stern warning to the soft drink industry that most 1.5-litre pop bottles would explode simply by falling over on a hard surface. To Barham, this was not enough. He was angry not only because the bottles remained on the shelves but because he felt the government was soft on 750-ml bottles which, he found in a June test, exploded half of the time.

Barham demonstrates this in his lab. He places a 750-ml bottle of root beer in a Plexiglas cabinet with a hole in it. He gently tips the bottle over and with a loud "pop" it shatters, showering the cabinet with broken glass. "How would you like to be hit with this?" he asks, picking up an ominously jagged shard swimming in a shallow bath of fizzing root beer. "When you hear 100 bottles a day go off you go home shell-shocked," he says, mopping up the mess.

While Barham blames the government, his ire is directed at the soft drink companies. "They're selling products, not safety," he says, adding with incredulity that he had never given much thought to large corporations putting profits before people.

Cynical is the last word you would use to describe Barham, who only now, looking back, can admit that he did in fact take on a billion dollar industry. And he won. In August, after receiving over 50 complaints from people who were injured by exploding pop bottles, the government banned 1.5-litre bottles of carbonated beverages. That's 20 percent of the industry's sales.

Canadian Soft Drink Association statistics indicate that only one in eight million bottles explodes. Barham puts it another way. "They have 22 billion pop bottles on the shelves each year. If you divide that by eight million, you're looking at close to ten incidents a day."

One reason why no one made a fuss before, he says, is that most people were not aware that bottles exploded regularly. They thought it was a freak accident when it did happen. When people did notify a soft drink company they were offered a couple of free cases or told that legal action could be long and costly and most cases were settled out of court. Quietly. One settlement, Barham says, was conditional on the plaintiff not publicizing the matter.

"Glass will be glass—that's what one soft drink executive said!" The point is that the industry is failing to warn the public of the dangers of carbonated drinks in glass bottles. "They say that more people are injured in bed. Next thing you know they'll be saying that the number of people injured in bed with pop bottles is even less."

Barham's lively grin fades when he talks about such callousness.

"When I think of that little three-year-old boy going through life with one eye—and eye injuries are horribly common—I'm not sure I could live with myself if that happened to my kid."

While the ban has prohibited 1.5-litre bottles, there are still some around, he says, adding that we should also treat 750-ml bottles as dangerous. But by far the greatest danger is from the 40-ounce bottles of Coca-Cola. These, slightly smaller than the 1.5-litre size, haven't been banned and Barham says they explode on the tip test every single time.

Last July, Coke came out with an ad which, making no mention of the 40-ounce bottle, proclaimed that its squat 1.5-litre bottle was relatively safe. "Recent tests by Dr. Barham of the University of Toronto and The Product Safety Laboratory of the Federal Department of Consumer and Corporate Affairs have demonstrated that it is stronger, less likely to shatter and explode."

When Barham saw the ad he did explode—"and I didn't have to be tipped over." Consumer and Corporate Affairs told the Coca-Cola company to cease and desist, and Barham, heeding his lawyer's advice, decided not to sue. But he was furious. "They used my name and my results in vain," he says, explaining that while Coke built its case on the superior shape of its bottle, shape is not as important as size. The bigger the bottle, the greater the chance of explosion.

Barham still gets calls from lawyers asking him to testify in exploding bottle cases. He accepts most of them because, he sighs, "somebody has to help." He believes that one solution to exploding bottles is plastic coating, and he has been consultant to a Scarborough company that has developed a coating 15 one-thousandths of an inch thick. It allows for recycling and will double the cost—and the life—of the bottle.

But he would like to get out of the bottle business. "I don't want a new career. This is just a sideline. I'll stop when the industry makes a safe product." He doesn't want another crusade. But he's vulnerable now. "Injuries and callousness would make me angry all over again."

And he can't seem to forget three-year-old Matthew McNair, who has only one eye.

\*   \*   \*

## TURCOTTE v. FORD MOTOR CO.

*United States Court of Appeals, First Circuit, 1974*

McENTEE, Circuit Judge.

Plaintiff, a Rhode Island citizen, filed this . . . suit in the United States District Court for Rhode Island, seeking to recover for the alleged wrongful death of his son. The decedent was a passenger in a 1970 Maverick, manufactured by defendant Ford Motor Company, when the car was struck by another car on the Massachusetts Turnpike near Millbury, Massachusetts, and burst into flames. Decedent died in the fire. The owner of the Maverick was William J. Sullivan of Woonsocket, Rhode Island, who purchased it from Menard Ford Sales, Inc., of South Bellingham, Massachusetts. The driver was Sullivan's son Michael. The operator of the other vehicle was a Massachusetts citizen.

At trial, plaintiff contended that Ford's positioning of the gas tank in the 1970 Maverick in such manner that the tank's top also served as the floor of the trunk constituted a defect in design which caused his son's death by fire. Plaintiff did not argue that the alleged defect caused the collision. Instead, he contended that, upon collision, a properly designed Maverick would not have burst into flames and that his son would otherwise have survived the initial impact. The case went to the jury on the theory of strict liability, and a verdict was returned for plaintiff in the amount of $500,000. The trial court entered judgment for that amount plus $61,315.08 in interest. Ford's motions for new trial and for alteration or amendment of the judgment were both denied. . . .

. . . [T]he trial court [held] that under Rhode Island law automobile manufacturers can be held strictly liable for defects in design which do not cause highway collisions but instead exacerbate injuries therefrom. . . .

We begin our analysis with the leading Rhode Island case of Ritter v. Narragansett Elec. Co. . . . The Supreme Court of Rhode Island there incorporated into state law the doctrine of strict products liability . . .

The *Ritter* court construed this rule as contemplating, "first, that there must be a defect in design or manufacture which makes the product unsafe *for its intended use,* and second that liability does not attach unless the plaintiff was using the product in a way in which *it was intended to be used* when he was injured by it." . . .

Ford argues that since no automobile manufacturer or consumer would rationally intend his car to be involved in a highway collision, the defect in design alleged in the instant case falls outside the scope of the strict liability doctrine as construed in *Ritter.* This pinpoints the crucial issue before us, namely, whether under Rhode Island law the tort concept of "intended use" encompasses foreseeable consequences of normal automobile use, such as collisions, even though such consequences are not literally intended or desired.

Among other jurisdictions there has developed a split in authority on this question, symbolized by the conflicting cases of Evans v. General Motors Corp. (1967) and Larsen v. General Motors (1968). . . . In *Evans,* the Seventh Circuit held that under Indiana law "[T]he intended purpose of an automobile does not include its participation in collisions with other objects, despite the manufacturer's ability to foresee the possibility that such collisions may occur." . . . The court therefore affirmed dismissal of a complaint alleging negligence, breach of implied warranty and strict liability in a fact situation analogous to the case at bar. . . .

However, the Eighth Circuit in *Larsen,* construing Michigan law, rejected the *Evans* position as "much too narrow and unrealistic." . . .

> While automobiles are not made for the purpose of colliding with each other, a frequent and inevitable contingency of normal automobile use will result in collisions and injury-producing impacts. No rational basis exists for limiting recovery to situations where the defect in design or manufacture was the causative factor of the accident, as the accident and the resulting injury, usually caused by the so-called 'second collision' of the passenger with the interior part of the automobile, all are foreseeable.

We agree with the trial court that Rhode Island would adopt the *Larsen* interpretation of "intended use" in construing the doctrine of strict products liability. A literal *Evans*-type interpretation of "intended use" fails to recognize that the phrase was first employed in early products-liability cases such as *Greenman,* supra, merely to illustrate the broader central doctrine of foreseeability. The phrase was not meant to preclude manufacturer responsibility for the probable ancillary consequences of normal use. . . . Instead, a manufacturer "must also be expected to anticipate the environment which is normal for the use of his product and . . . he must anticipate the reasonably foreseeable risks of the use of his product in such an environment." . . . Cf. Raymond v. Riegel Textile Corp., 484 F. 2d 1025 (1st Cir. 1973) (manufacturer held strictly liable where nightgown burst into flames within two seconds of contact with hot grill of electric range). *Larsen* and its progeny have recognized that the "environment" in which cars are used, our nation's crowded, high-speed highways, makes involvement in collisions foreseeable to manufacturers as an inevitable consequence of normal use and thus imposes upon them a duty to guard against needlessly aggravated injuries.

Indeed, the *Ritter* case itself contains a similar construction of the "intended use" concept, although not in an automobile context. In that case, a four-year-old girl opened the drop-type oven door of an electric range and stood upon it so that she could see into a pot on the top of the range. Her weight upon the opened oven door caused the range to topple over upon her and her sister. The action against the manufacturer and the distributor of the range alleged that the range's capacity to tip over when weights equal to that of the child were placed on the oven door constituted a defect in design for which defendants were liable on theories of negligence and strict liability. Obviously, an oven door is not intended to serve as a stepping-stool for children. Yet in its opinion remanding the case for trial on both theories, the Supreme Court of Rhode Island rejected defendants' contention that the child's use of the oven door constituted an "abnormal" or "unintended" use as to which there could be no liability. "[The trial judge] concluded that the jury could find from [the] evidence that [the manufacturer] knew that as a result of the design of the range the danger in the use of the oven door as a shelf was foreseeable and that the jury could have found that it had been negligent in failing to give notice or warning that such a condition would result from such a use of the oven door. We agree."
. . .

In view of the *Ritter* holding on "intended use," it is difficult to see how the Rhode Island courts could reject the similar *Larsen* approach to "intended use" in the automobile context. We are also mindful of the following language from a Vermont decision, Rothberg v. Olenik (1970) . . . which was adopted by the Supreme Court of Rhode Island in Padula v. J. J. Deb-Cin Homes, Inc. . . . (R.I. 1973):

> The law should be based upon current concepts of what is right and just and the judiciary should be alert to the never-ending need for keeping its common law principles abreast with the times. Ancient distinctions which make no sense in today's society and tend to discredit the law should be readily rejected.

Ford has suggested that adoption of the *Larsen* concept of "intended use" in automobile cases will result in its having to produce expensive armored tanks so as to avoid liability for defective design. But this need not be the result. First, plaintiff must still prove that the particular car's design constituted a "defective condition unreasonably dangerous" to the user, and that such defect was the actual and proximate cause of injuries beyond those caused by the collision itself. Ford claims that sympathetic juries will shirk their responsibilities in cases of serious injury and impose liability on the manufacturer no matter what the state of the design or the ferocity of the particular collision. But our review of cases to date shows that juries continue to confound the cynical. For example, both Marshall v. Ford Motor Co. (1971) . . . and Gray v. General Motors Corp. (1970) . . . are cases where juries given *Larsen*-type instructions on "intended use" nevertheless returned verdicts for defendant car manufacturers because they found the particular cars were not defectively designed. Moreover, an arbitrary jury verdict on the defect or causation issues can be rejected by trial or appellate courts as not supported by the evidence.

Second, the defense of assumption of risk remains viable in products liability cases. . . . Thus, where a design is apparent or made known to the automobile purchaser, an action alleging such defect as the cause of injury cannot lie. *Cf.* Burkard v. Short . . . (1971) (rejecting liability for obviously unpadded dashboard). Automobile manufacturers might often relieve themselves of design liability, at least when the purchaser is plaintiff, if they fully informed such purchaser in advance of the relative safety merits and demerits of their cars as compared to other models.*

[We have affirmed] the jury verdict of liability on the part of Ford. We now consider issues concerning the jury's award of $500,000 in damages. . . .

In challenging the size of the verdict, Ford raises three issues . . . (1) Was a projection of decedent's lifetime income properly based on a government publication which encompassed all college graduates, including those who also attend graduate or professional schools? (2) Was consideration of income taxes properly omitted in determining decedent's lifetime expenses? (3) Were future inflation and increases in productivity properly accounted for?

The first issue has little merit. At trial Mark Schupack, an economics professor at Brown University, testified as an expert witness for plaintiff with respect to the probable lifetime earnings and expenses of decedent. Schupack presented the jury with a series of calculations based on varying factual assumptions, first, as to decedent's future education and career, and second, as to future prevailing interest rates. Ford contends it was error for Schupack, when making the factual assumption that decedent would have been a college graduate, to project future earnings based on a Bureau of Census publication which covered all college graduates, including those with postgraduate education. It is clear that decedent stood a good chance of attending and graduating from a four-year college. He had good grades and an outstanding athletic record. Indeed, the most poignant aspect of the case is that decedent was en route with three friends to look over the University of Massachusetts campus at Amherst when the crash and fire which took his life occurred.

Although we have no way of knowing for sure, it is possible that decedent would have gone on beyond college to some form of postgraduate education. But more important, the fact that the census publication relied upon by Schupack included college graduates with postgraduate education does not mean that the resulting income figures were much higher than they would have otherwise been. As Schupack noted at trial, great numbers of persons with graduate degrees, such as teachers, earn less than the average person with only a bachelor's degree. The Rhode Island statute obviously requires a great deal of speculation. It requires the judge and jury

---

*Of course, a purchaser might not be found to have assumed the risk of a known defect if the defect also existed in all other models, so that he had no meaningful choice on the matter. . . . [S]ome states may choose to abolish or greatly limit the defense of assumption of the risk in the purchaser-seller situation, choosing to view injury there as a casualty incident to a profitable business enterprise equipped to distribute the costs of enterprise among its beneficiaries according to principles of insurance.

to take on "the joint role of soothsayer and mathematical analyst in order to foretell what the future held for the deceased." . . . In this context, we cannot find that Schupack's reliance on the census averages for all college graduates was so inconsistent with decedent's reasonable prospects that their admission into evidence constituted an abuse of discretion by the trial court. . . .

However, on the issue of income taxes we feel there was error. To compute decedent's lifetime expenses, as required by the Rhode Island statute, Schupack reduced each annual income figure he projected by one-fourth. This 25 percent reduction was intended to encompass the costs of housing, food, clothing, personal and medical care, tobacco and alcoholic beverages attributable to the husband in a five-person family. Schupack made no further reduction in projected earnings for federal and state income taxes, and Ford contends that this was error. We agree. . . . [The court also held that the calculations accounting for inflation and productivity should be reconsidered.]

\*       \*       \*

## COURTNEY v. AMERICAN OIL CO.

*District Court of Appeals of Florida, Fourth District, 1968*

REED, Judge.

This is a suit by Richard Courtney, a minor child, and by his father, Hubert Courtney, to recover damages for injuries sustained as the result of the alleged negligence of the defendants, The American Oil Company and George E. Doyle. At the conclusion of the plaintiff's case, the trial court directed a verdict for both defendants, and this appeal followed the entry of a final judgment.

[1] The broad question presented is whether or not the evidence was legally sufficient to sustain a verdict for the plaintiffs. If the evidence was susceptible of any reasonable interpretation which would support such a verdict, the direction of a verdict for defendants was error.

[2] This is a dispute in the record as to certain facts, but the version of the evidence most favorable to the plaintiffs is that with which we resolve the question presented. On April 15, 1964, the minor plaintiff, Richard Courtney, accompanied by a playmate, Joe Falco, went to a gasoline station operated by defendant Doyle and owned by defendant American Oil Company. The two boys were approximately ten and one-half years of age. They purchased five cents worth of white gas intended by them for use in a model airplane engine owned by Richard Courtney. The engine was displayed to the defendant Doyle at the time of purchase. The gasoline was placed in an empty oil can by Doyle. The boys proceeded from the station to Richard's home. En route they poured the gasoline out of the can and into a mayonnaise jar. At the time of the purchase, Doyle neither labeled the can

nor warned the boys about the dangers of gasoline. The evidence indicated, however, that both of the boys then knew that gasoline was flammable.

The boys tried to start the motor at Richard's house. When these efforts were unsuccessful, Richard put the motor away and began playing with a rabbit which was in a cage adjacent to his house. While so engaged he smelled gasoline and, upon hearing a clicking noise, he turned and saw Joe Falco pouring the gasoline out of the jar and working a cigarette lighter in its vicinity. At this point the gasoline ignited and burned Richard Courtney.

On the basis of these facts, the trial court concluded that the sale of the gasoline was not the proximate cause of the injury and directed a verdict for the defendants. We affirm on the same ground.

[3, 4] On appeal, the plaintiffs first contend that the trial court erred in not applying the Federal Hazardous Substances Act. . . . In general terms, this act, as it existed at the time of the accident, prohibited the sale in interstate commerce of dangerous substances without a label describing the substance and the hazard to be expected therefrom. Assuming the act was violated, it is an act designed to protect the general public and not a limited class. At most, its violation would constitute negligence, but would not conclude as a matter of law the question of proximate cause.

[5] The concept of proximate cause has at least two functions. One is to require a causal connection between an alleged act of negligence and a result for which damages are sought. The other is to limit the liability of the alleged wrongdoer for the consequences of his negligence. We are concerned with this latter function.

[6, 7] Liability of a negligent actor usually extends only to the reasonably foreseeable consequences of his negligence. Such consequences are defined as those which are of a type that happen so frequently from the commission of the type of act in question that, in the field of human experience, the same type of consequences may be expected again from the same type of act. Such consequences have also been defined as those "which a person by prudent human foresight can be expected to anticipate as likely to result from an act, because they happen so frequently from the commission of such act that in the field of human experience they may be expected to happen again."

[8] The type of act with which we are here involved is the sale of a small quantity of gasoline to minors about ten and one-half years of age for an apparently legitimate purpose, that is, use in a motor. The type of consequence is a personal injury caused by the intentional effort of one of the purchasers to ignite the gasoline on the ground, such act being a total deviation from the original purpose for which the gasoline was bought. Can it be said that the type of consequence which occurred in this case should have been foreseen by the exercise of prudent human foresight as likely to result from the type of act which the defendant Doyle committed? While this is normally a question of fact for the jury, we conclude that the act which brought about the injury—regardless of which version of the testimony is adopted—was so clearly not a foreseeable consequence that the trial court was correct in deciding the issue of proximate cause as a matter of law.

Following the version of the events presented by young Courtney, if Joe

Falco's intentional ignition of the gasoline was not a reasonably foreseeable consequence of the sale, Joe's conduct was an efficient, independent intervening cause which eliminated the defendant's act as the proximate cause of the injury.

Appellee American Oil Company urges that Doyle was an independent contractor. Because of the view we take with respect to the issue of proximate cause, we find unnecessary to treat this contention.

For the foregoing reasons, the final judgment appealed from is hereby affirmed.

\*　　\*　　\*

# THE ATTACK ON NESTLÉ AND FORMULA FEEDING

*[For a number of years, church groups and other organizations concerned with health in Third World countries have attacked Nestlé, a $12-billion Swiss-based corporation, for promoting and distributing baby formula in those countries. The critics of the company argue that in the conditions prevailing there, breast-feeding is, besides its other advantages, safer and more dependable. Mothers cannot, for one thing, take the precautions about sterilization and storage that are easily taken in homes with modern kitchens. The World Health Organization drew up a code, which was to be voted on at its general assembly in May 1981, that would have drastically curtailed the promotion and distribution of the formula. The International Council of Infant Food Industries, whose president, E. W. Saunders, is a vice-president of Nestlé, denounced the code as "unacceptable." A boycott organized against Nestlé continues. Nestlé has endeavored by various means to discredit the boycott. It got some help from an article in* Fortune *accusing the boycotters of being "Marxists marching under the banner of Christ."*

*The information just summarized was drawn chiefly from an article in the Canadian newsweekly* Maclean's Magazine, *February 16, 1981. The news story that follows is an Associated Press report that appeared in the* Montreal Gazette.*]*

### OFFICIALS TO QUIT
### OVER U.S. STANCE
### ON BABY FORMULA

WASHINGTON (AP)—Alleging that one million babies die each year in underdeveloped countries from diseases brought on by bottle feeding, two senior U.S. government officials said yesterday they will resign when the administration of President Ronald Reagan votes against an international code favoring mothers' milk.

*May 19, 1981, p. 15. Reprinted by permission of The Associated Press.

Dr. Stephen Joseph and Eugene Babb, both senior executives of the Agency for International Development (AID), issued their resignation threat during a news conference at the American Public Health Association.

The resignations would make the two men the first top officials to quit over Reagan administration policies. Both went to work for AID during the Jimmy Carter administration.

Joseph, a pediatrician who is the highest ranking health professional at AID, alleged that the administration "has been swayed by the self-interested arguments of the infant formula lobby."

Joseph said that one child in ten born in developing countries dies in infancy, a total of 10 million a year. While precise figures are not available, "the best estimates ascribe up to one million of these infant deaths to diarrhea and under-nutrition associated with artificial formula feeding," he said.

The voluntary code is an attempt to stop advertising and selling tactics designed to convince parents in poor countries that infant formula is critical to child health. It would bar, for example, the practice of sending women dressed as nurses to rural villages—or paying local health workers—to recommend formulas.

Administration officials do not dispute that breast-feeding is preferable, but contend the code represents an unwarranted attempt by the United Nations to regulate how private businesses promote their products.

Meanwhile, a bipartisan group of ten congressmen called on Reagan to personally intervene to reverse the decision to vote against the milk code.

"The United States' vote pits America against every other nation in the World Health Organization," said the congressmen in a letter to Reagan.

"We cannot believe that the U.S. stands for the death of millions of children from hunger and disease."

Several prominent physicians joined Joseph and Babb in deploring the administration plan to cast what is expected to be a solitary vote against the code at the World Health Assembly in Geneva.

At AID, administrator M. Peter McPherson criticized the two men for going public with their opposition. He said they intend to submit their resignations when the vote is cast. "Naturally, I will accept them effective immediately," he said.

At the White House, deputy press secretary Larry Speakes said the U.S. decision to vote against the code resulted from a consensus of several federal agencies that "we did not want to make the World Health Organization an international Federal Trade Commission."

\*     \*     \*

*[The opposition of the United States turned out to be just about as singular as the congressmen had predicted:]*

WHO PRESS

World Health Organization, Division of Public Information . . .
    34th World Health Assembly—Press Release WHA/13, 21 May 1981

INTERNATIONAL CODE ON MARKETING OF
BREASTMILK SUBSTITUTES ADOPTED BY ASSEMBLY

The Thirty-fourth World Health Assembly, meeting in plenary session in Geneva today, endorsed an International Code of Marketing of Breastmilk Substitutes. The vote was 118 in favour, one against with three abstentions on a resolution proposed by the Executive Board of WHO. The resolution adopted the Code as a recommendation to WHO Member States, urging them:

—to give full and unanimous support to the implementation of the recommendations made by the joint WHO/UNICEF Meeting on Infant and Young Child Feeding and of the provisions of the International Code in its entirety;
—to translate the International Code into national legislation, regulations and other suitable measures;
—to involve all concerned social and economic sectors and all other concerned parties in the implementation of the International Code and in the observance of its provisions;
—to monitor the compliance with the Code.

The resolution also requested the Director-General of WHO, Dr. Halfdan Mahler, to report to the Thirty-sixth World Health Assembly, in 1983, on the status of compliance with the implementation of the Code at country, regional and global levels and to make proposals, if necessary, for revisions of the text and for further steps required for its implementation. The resolution stressed that the adoption of and adherence to the Code is a minimum requirement and only one of several important actions required in order to protect healthy practices of infant and young child feeding. WHO was instructed to give all possible support to Member States in the implementation of the Code, particularly through national legislation.

The Assembly's action resulted from its decision in May 1980 at the Thirty-third World Health Assembly, to endorse in their entirety the findings of the joint WHO/UNICEF Meeting on Infant and Young Child Feeding, held in Geneva in October 1979, and to instruct WHO to draw up a draft International Code, in consultation with all interested parties. The Code approved today was the fourth draft and the product of numerous consultations with governments, international and non-governmental organizations, the scientific community and industry.

The Code recognizes that breastfeeding is an unequaled way of providing ideal food for the healthy growth and development of infants. Its aim is to contribute to the safe and adequate nutrition of infants "by the protection and promotion of breastfeeding, and by ensuring the proper use of breast-milk substitutes, when these are necessary, on the basis of adequate information and through appropriate marketing practices."

In scope, the Code applies firstly to breastmilk substitutes including infant formula. It applies to other milk products, foods and beverages, including bottle-fed complementary foods, only *"when marketed or otherwise represented to be suitable, with or without modification, for use as a partial or total replacement of breastmilk."* It also covers the marketing of feeding bottles and tests, products associated with the use of breastmilk substitutes.

The Code calls for the elimination of direct consumer promotion including advertising, gifts and samples and labeling practices which may discourage breastfeeding. It adds that information and education on the feeding of infants should stress the superiority of breastfeeding and should be provided only through the health care system. Products should meet international standards of quality and presentation.

The Code states that governments should take action to give effect to the principles and aim of the Code, as appropriate to their social and legislative framework, including the adoption of national legislation, regulations and other suitable measures.

Manufacturers and distributors of infant food products, non-governmental organizations, professional groups and consumer organizations are called upon to collaborate with governments in both the implementation and monitoring processes.

*   *   *

*Comment:*
_____

## IS IT GOOD BUSINESS FOR FIRMS TO OPPOSE CONSUMER PROTECTION?

The behavior of soft-drink bottlers in the case of the exploding bottles justifies a degree of skepticism about how wholeheartedly firms concern themselves with protecting consumers when they can get away legally with being indifferent. As one might expect, firms are often not eager to be more strictly regulated by new laws, either. Many of them, though not all, have opposed measures of consumer protection. For example, individually and through their trade associations many firms lobbied vigorously against a bill, before Congress for years in the 1970s though finally defeated, which would have set up a "$15 million nonregulatory office of consumer representation to advocate consumer interests before federal agencies and courts." There was likewise strong opposition from business to a $10-million program to award small amounts of "public participation funds" to "citizen groups and small businesses so that they can afford to appear in agency proceedings." (I take both these points from an article by Mark Green, an associate of Ralph Nader, in a book edited by Thornton Bradshaw and David Yogel, *Corporations and Their Critics* [New York, 1981].)

One may well believe that many firms would cheerfully accept the demise of *Consumer Reports* and of similar attempts, public or private, to provide consumers with impartial sources of information. There may be objections to the ways in which consumer research is carried out. The funds for the research may not extend, for example, to buying and inspecting enough samples of a given product to establish statistically reliable results. Or the tests applied to the product may be inappropriate. Yet ought not consumers to have sources of information besides the firms themselves and their advertising agencies? And ought not enlightened businesses, confident that they were producing safe, durable, reliable, and effective products, support the idea of having such sources organized and funded in ways that made sure of supplying appropriate information?

Governments help supply such information by defining grades for apples, meat, insulating material, and other products. Clearly, firms that label their products with higher grades when the products deserve only lower ones act fraudulently and expose themselves to legal action. Governments inspect various kinds of products before they are sold to make sure that occasions for such legal action are minimized. Is this really enough? Should governments do anything more to uphold standards? They commonly do prescribe minimum standards respecting safety and effectiveness and other things. However, the present grounds for doing this consist in part in the fact that consumers cannot be counted on to be fully informed about what they buy, or even to have access to full information. If full information were available to consumers, would it still be a good thing for governments to prescribe minimum standards?

## Paper-Organizing Game:
## How Far Is It Reasonable To Leave Individual
## Consumers To Protect Themselves From Bad Deals?

The object of the game, again, is to put the following questions into a perspicuous order, which will form the overall plan or skeleton for your paper.

1. How far is it sensible to expect individual consumers to inform themselves about the goods that they buy and the terms on which they buy them?

2. Is it in the interest of firms to support efforts by private organizations and by governments to increase consumers' information?

3. What sorts of information are (a) beyond the reach of ordinary consumers, left to themselves, (b) within their reach but troublesome for them to arrive at?

4. Can individual consumers have any discretion about their purchases without running the risk of making mistakes?

5. Will consumers' organizations reach all consumers?

6. Would regulation by the government be needed at all if consumers' organizations existed to supply the public with information?

7. If we tried to protect individual consumers in every way, would we have too many regulations and too many people occupied in enforcing them?

8. Should consumers be protected only from major mistakes?

9. If consumers combine to set up private organizations to increase information, would this take away all responsibility from firms to supply adequate information about their products and their terms?

10. How does it simplify life to minimize the extent to which consumers are misled?

CHAPTER 7

# Further Concerns of Consumers

*Introductory Comment:*

## NONFULFILLMENT OF CONTRACTS; EXORBITANT PRICES; COMBINATIONS IN RESTRAINT OF TRADE

That firms ought to perform contracts once made may seem too obvious to be worth discussing (though it provides a useful reminder and illustration of the triplet principle). There is a less obvious question, which the following case from *Consumer Reports* (1978) suggests, if it doesn't exactly raise, about whether the performance is just as much morally required when no one will know the difference. How many people dig their mothers up, once they've buried them?

## FUNERAL HOME FINED FOR SWITCHING CASKETS*

The disinterment of a Bronx, N.Y., woman nearly seven years after her death revealed a rusted, broken, steel casket rather than the $2,400 copper casket that the family had paid for. The distressed daughter, who was

---

*Copyright 1978 by Consumers Union of United States, Inc., Mount Vernon, NY 10550. Reprinted by permission from *Consumer Reports*, October 1978.

moving the body to a cemetery with better drainage, thought at first that the wrong grave had been unearthed. Later investigation revealed the unhappy truth: the body was indeed her mother's, but the undertaker had placed the body in a cheap substitute for the copper casket.

A complaint to the Bureau of Consumer Frauds and Protection of the New York Attorney General's office resulted in a consent order against Casario Funeral Home Inc., the undertaker for the funeral. The judge ordered reimbursement to the family for the cost of the casket and imposed a $500 fine to cover costs to the State.

Furthermore, the judge required the undertaker to provide an itemized, written statement of costs, as is required by state law, and to comply with the specific demands of customers.

*    *    *

EXORBITANT PRICES

Some contracts between people and firms involve exorbitant prices. They may be invalidated when they do on grounds that the people entered into them under duress or because of deception. They may, as the Arthur Murray case shows, be invalidated on such grounds even when the price is not exorbitant. Mrs. Snevellicci may have been persuaded to take an inordinate number of dance lessons. The studio was evidently ready enough to give her that number of lessons, however, and given the time and skill of the instructors and the costs of maintaining the studio the price per lesson was not necessarily outrageous.

What is to be made of cases in which undeceived customers enter into contracts to pay much more than they need do, given the use that they are going to make of what they buy and the alternatives open to them? Some multi-volume encyclopedias sold for hundreds of dollars are probably not as up-to-date and as efficiently packed with well-selected information as the one-volume *Columbia Encyclopedia,* which can be bought for under $100, occasionally (as an introductory offer from the *Book-of-the-Month Club*) for under $25. Is even the *Britannica,* which is a valuable work, as useful for most of the families that buy it as the *Columbia Encyclopedia* would be, plus a few hundred dollars spent on a dictionary, an atlas, an historical atlas, some history books, and a couple of good popular books on science?

Notwithstanding, encyclopedia firms and their salesmen continue to inveigle many people, who are not aware of this cheaper alternative, into contracting away large parts of their household budgets. In part, this practice may be objected to on the grounds that the customers are in fact being deceived (by being left unaware of the alternatives). Can this objection be entirely separated, however, from the objection that the price of the encyclopedia is exorbitant, in some cases considering the quality, in some cases considering the families' funds?

MONOPOLIES, COMBINATIONS IN RESTRAINT OF TRADE

Clearer instances of exorbitant prices are produced by monopolies. These may be temporary, as when by chance or by astute speculation a merchant finds himself in possession of the only availabe rice in a time of famine. Then, it may be said, a high price is required to match supply and demand, rationing the rice out to the people who are willing to pay most for it. Is that a fair system of rationing, however? And if it is, should the merchant be able to pocket the extraordinary profits? Against prices and profits in cases like these one may oppose the medieval notion of a "just price," conceived of as the customary or normal price. In doing so, however, one is bringing into play questions that strike to the heart of modern business and its rationale— questions, which I am leaving to the end of the book, about the justice of the whole system.

Taking the system as it stands, we find that it relies for the justification of prices on competition. In the long run—normally—prices will be kept as low as they can be, consistent with the costs of producing goods, by the presence of competitors or potential competitors who are ready to bring their prices down near to their costs. Hence it is of special importance— ultimately, moral importance—that competitors not be allowed to combine to suppress competition. Monopolies so formed—combinations in restraint of trade—are specifically forbidden by statute in the United States and Canada. Even before the statutes were adopted, the moral objections to combinations in restraint of trade were expressed in the common law, as the following case makes clear.

# GEORGIA FRUIT EXCHANGE v. D. C. TURNIPSEED

*Court of Appeals of Alabama, 1913*

SOLLIE, Judge.

Action by the Georgia Fruit Exchange against D. C. Turnipseed for breach of contract. Judgment for defendant, and plaintiff appeals. Affirmed.

Count 5 is as follows: "The plaintiff, a foreign corporation, organized under the laws of the state of Georgia, and having its principal place of business in Atlanta in said state, the business of said corporation being that of a fruit and vegetable exchange for handling, distributing, and marketing in American and foreign markets of peaches and other fruits, melons, and vegetables of all descriptions . . . claims of the defendant the sum of $1,000 for breach of an agreement entered into by him with the plaintiff . . . as follows: 'Penrode, Ala., March 10, 1909. In consideration of the benefits I expect to receive in common with all other fruit growers in Georgia by the organization of the Georgia Fruit Exchange, I hereby subscribe for membership and stock therein, and I hereby pledge to the Georgia Fruit Exchange, as follows: First, I agree to make all carload shipments of peaches grown by me during 1909 through the Georgia Fruit Exchange and pay 10 percent of gross sales to cover all commission charges. . . . On orchard and other sales f.o.b. my station in consideration of a protected market and consequent enhanced price, I agree to pay the exchange 5 percent of such gross sales, and I further agree to abide by all the rules and regulations of the board of trustees of said exchange. Second, I hereby subscribe for and I agree to pay for on a basis of 10 percent. Nov. 1, 1908, and 10 percent. monthly thereafter in shares at $10 each of the stock of the Georgia Fruit Exchange aggregating $10. This agreement is not binding until $50,000 of stock is subscribed, and pledges secured covering 60 percent. of the prospective crop for 1909, based on 1908 shipments. D. C. Turnipseed.' And plaintiff avers that prior to the breaching of the said agreement herein set out, $50,000 of stock was subscribed and pledges secured covering 60 percent. of the prospective crop for 1909, based on the 1908 shipments, and plaintiff avers that the said agreement was breached by the defendants in this: That he shipped, to wit, 31 carloads of peaches, grown by him in 1909, which were orchard and other sales made by him f.o.b. his station independent of the Georgia Fruit Exchange, and that 5 percent. of the gross sales of said 31 car loads which he had agreed to pay to plaintiff amounted to $1,000 . . . and that prior to the bringing of this suit the plaintiff demanded that sum from defendant, but he refused to pay. . . .

[1,2] Unlawful agreements—that is, those whose objects are illegal, and to which the courts refuse recognition and enforcement—may be placed in two classes; viz. (1) agreements in violation of positive law, and (2) agreements contrary to public policy. Agreements in violation of positive law are those which are expressly or impliedly prohibited either by some rule of the common law or by some express statutory provision, and which, of course, also necessarily amount to agreements contrary to that part of the public policy expressed in the particular rule or statute violated . . .

[3] Public policy, however, is broader than the mere terms of the Constitution and statutes and embraces their general purpose and spirit. Constitutions are born of the people, and statutes made (including the positive rules of common law adopted) in pursuance thereof emanate, of course, from legislative sources, all designed for the public good; . . . Where they are silent in terms and do not of their own force vitiate contracts detrimental to the public interest or welfare, as may be outlined in, and as is to be determined alone from, a general view of such Constitution and statutes, the courts have supplied in a way the deficiencies of positive law by originating the doctrine of "public policy" and so applying it as to hold void and decline to enforce executory contracts which, though not violating the terms, yet violate the general purpose, spirit, and policy of the law as expressed in the Constitution and statutes. The latter, of course, constitute the standards, changing with the habits, customs, and ideals of the people, by which the courts are to and do determine, in the light of judicial precedents, the public policy of a state or action.

. . . [I]t is therefore perhaps correct to say that public policy is that principle of law which holds that no person can lawfully do that which has a tendency to be injurious to the public or against the public good, as ascertained from and measured by the settled policy of the state or government to be found in its Constitution, laws, and judicial decisions. . . . Where a contract belongs to this class it will be declared void, although in the particular instance no injury to the public may have resulted, and no positive statute be violated. . . .

[4] It is settled that, while agreements in reasonable restraint of trade are valid, yet contracts or agreements in unreasonable restraint of trade are contrary to public policy and void, because they tend to the creation of a monopoly. . . .

[5] A monopoly, as understood at common law, was an exclusive right granted by the crown to one person, or a class of persons, of something which before was of common right, and which enabled the persons who possessed it to exclude others from the defined activities. . . . Without such a grant even then, the obtaining by combined action or individual initiative on the part of private parties of the exclusive power to carry on a certain trade or business, etc., and all attempts to gain control of the market by forestalling, regrating, or engrossing were unlawful and punishable. . . . At a later time, during the reign of James I, there was passed an act of Parliament which by a general sweeping clause demolished all existing monopolies, with certain exceptions, which had been before created by the crown, and declared them also to be contrary to law and void. . . .

[6] Monopolies were deemed odious at common law, not only as being in contravention of common right, but as founded in the destruction of trade by the extinguishment of free and healthy competition. They have, as was said in the old English case of The Monopolies, . . . three inseparable incidents, each detrimental to the public good: (1) The price of the commodity dealt in will be raised, for he who has the sole selling of any commodity may and will make the price as he pleases; (2) the commodity will not be as good and merchantable as before, for the beneficiary regards his private interest, and not that of the commonwealth; (3) it tends to the impoverishment of those that are excluded from or driven out of the business.

Monopolies in their very nature are opposed to the genius and principles of a Republican form of government, and require neither express statutes nor constitutional prohibitions to make them illegal. . . . The inadequacy, however, of common-law remedies and common-law punishments for the purpose of dealing properly with modern trusts and monopolies, which in recent decades have multiplied freely, has led Congress and the Legislature of many of the states to enact drastic statutes against all trusts, pools, and unlawful combinations designed to restrain trade and prevent competition, with a view to the destruction of existing ones and the prevention of future ones by punishing their authors positively as well as still punishing them negatively by denying them the aid of the courts in enforcing their contracts. . . .

There [is now] both a state and national law prohibiting unlawful combinations in restraint of trade—the one law relating to intrastate, the other to interstate, commerce—[and] it is immaterial as to which character of commerce, whether only one or both, is involved in the contract here under consideration; for if the contract is in violation of either law it is void as contravening a positive statute; and, even if it does not go to the extent of being in actual violation of either statute, yet if it tends to create a monopoly by unreasonably restraining trade, it is still void under our law, as at common law, as being against public policy. . . .

[7] The test which is laid down for determining whether a contract is in reasonable or unreasonable restraint of trade is: Does it merely afford a fair protection to the interest of the party in whose favor it is made, without being so large in its operation as to interfere with the interest of the public? . . . Dealing more fully with this latter proposition, it is well said by the United States Circuit Court of Appeals, after reviewing the authorities, speaking through Sanborn, J.: "It clearly appears that when the Anti-Trust Act was passed the rule had been firmly established in the jurisprudence of England and the United States that the validity of contracts restricting competition was to be determined by the reasonableness of the restriction. *If the main purpose or natural and inevitable* effect of a contract was to suppress competition or create a monopoly, it was illegal. If the contract imposed a restriction that was unreasonably injurious to the public, or a restriction that was greater than the interest of the party in whose favor it was imposed demanded, it was illegal. But contracts made for a lawful purpose, which were not unreasonably injurious to the public welfare, and which imposed no heavier restraint upon trade than the interest of the favored party required, had been uniformly sustained, notwithstanding their tendency, to some extent, to check competition. The public welfare was first considered, and the reasonableness of the restriction determined under these rules in the light of all the facts and circumstances of each particular case. . . .

We will undertake an analysis of the contract here presented by dividing it into its component parts as to the things done and the things agreed in it to be done, and consider each separately and then the contract as a whole, to the end of ascertaining if it falls within the prohibited class.

[9] The contract . . . expressly binds the defendant to do certain specific things therein enumerated, to wit: First. To take and pay for one share of stock of the plaintiff corporation of the value of $10, payable 10 per cent. monthly. Second. To make all carload shipments of peaches, grown by defendant, through plaintiff corporation, and pay 10 per cent. of the gross sales thereof as total commission charges for handling and selling same, to be divided, we infer, between plaintiff and the sales broker or commission merchant at the market to which plaintiff might direct defendant to make the shipment, and in such proportion as plaintiff and said broker must agree. Third. To pay plaintiff a commission of 5 per cent. of the gross sales on all orchard and other sales f.o.b. defendant's railroad station, which we construe to mean such a commission on all sales made by defendant to purchasers of the fruit on the trees and all such other sales as were made by defendant, but not through plaintiff, as required in section 2, hereinbefore enumerated. These several promises to plaintiff on defendant's part were conditional, however, and were not to become binding on him unless and until the plaintiff procured further subscriptions to its capital stock, which

with plaintiff's would amount to $50,000 and secured from other fruit growers contracts or pledges, like that of defendant, sufficient with his to amount to a pledge to plaintiff, for purposes of sale, of at least 60 per cent. of the prospective crop for 1909, based on 1908 shipments. . . .

For the share of stock the defendant, as seen, was to pay plaintiff $10, its full value, as stated in the contract, and for plaintiff's services and those of its agents, the commission merchants, in handling and selling the car loads of fruit shipped through plaintiff, the defendant was to pay a total commission of 10 per cent., which apparently is an adequate quid pro quo in return for the service named. What consideration, then, was there moving defendant to agree to pay plaintiff 5 per cent. of the gross sales of all peaches not shipped or sold through plaintiff, and with reference to which disposition plaintiff performed no service, or for which commission he was to give no consideration in return? Could not the defendant ordinarily buy stock in most any corporation, either from the corporation itself or some of its shareholders, by paying its full market value, and without the necessity of promising to give in addition at least 5 per cent. of the gross sales of his crop of peaches forever thereafter; and could not the defendant employ a broker or commission merchant for 10 per cent. commissions to handle and sell all car loads of peaches he might see fit to ship through him, without promising, in addition, to pay such broker or commission merchant a commission of 5 per cent. on all sales of such fruit not made through him, and to do so forever? . . . What was the consideration? We are not left to speculation or doubt, since the contract by its own plain and unambiguous terms informs us. It states (quoting) that "*in consideration of a protected market and consequent enhanced price*," the 5 per cent. commission was promised.

How is the market to be protected and why the enhanced price? It cannot fairly be doubted but what the parties to the contract contemplated that this expected protected market and resultant enhanced price was to come only as a consequence of plaintiff's success in subsequently procuring or securing other peach growers, in such number as with defendant would amount to the producers of at least 60 per cent. of the peach crop, to do as defendant had agreed conditionally to do—become a member of plaintiff corporation by subscribing to its capital stock, and pledge plaintiff the absolute right to handle their fruit crop for a total commission of 10 per cent., and pay 5 per cent. to plaintiff on the gross sales of all fruit they did not let it handle—as a penalty, we infer, for not doing so, and agree to be bound by all the rules and regulations (present and future, we infer) of plaintiff's board of trustees, and that, too, without any limitation of time for the duration of the contracts. Presumably, it was to be a permanent arrangement by all these peach-growing stockholders for the future sale and disposition of their crops, 60 per cent. of the whole, with a view of drawing into the association later the remaining 40 per cent. if possible.

The conclusion cannot be escaped that when plaintiff succeeded in getting said required number of peach growers, inclusive of defendant, each to become a member of its corporation or exchange and to execute a contract like that here under consideration . . . plaintiff thereby became master of the situation, so far as regarded the sale and disposition of at least 60 per cent. of the peach crop of the country, at least, of this section of the country, and would remain such master so long as the parties, defendant and the other required number of growers, kept their contracts with plaintiff to market their crop through it, and to abide by the rules and regulations, not disclosed, of plaintiff's board of directors. . . . It could direct the market to which any shipment was to go, and withhold from any market all shipments, or limit the supply at a particular market, thus forcing up the prices. It is clear that the real design was to stifle and destroy at the various markets competition . . . by allowing plaintiff to divert the crop from the channels of trade in which it would have ordinarily flowed if each grower had been left to act independently and to choose his own market, and to so direct the shipments of these several growers as to avoid competition between them at markets where they before competed.

Looking at the substance and not the form of these several contracts between plaintiff on one side and these 60 per cent. of the peach growers on the other, who thereby became members of plaintiff association, it amounts to nothing more nor less than an agreement or combination between them to place the disposition and sale of their crop each year in the hands of a joint agent, plaintiff, for the purpose of avoiding, as far as possible, competition among themselves, and thereby to raise the price of their products, and with the evident design and intent on their part and that of plaintiff, plainly contemplated in the contract, to get as many other growers into the arrangement as possible; it being both to their interest and to that of plaintiff, whose commissions would thereby be more, to do so. . . .

It is not necessary to the invalidity of the contract here and to the disposition of the present case to decide whether the contract is in violation of the state statute or of the federal statute, or any statute at all. We are not dealing with a criminal prosecution, and need not therefore concern ourselves with the question as to whether the commerce involved in the contract is inter or intra state, or both, or whether the terms of either statute have been violated. It is sufficient, as before seen, to destroy it and all obligations created by it, if it violates the public policy of the state or nation, as declared in judicial decisions predicated upon the principles of the common law obtaining here. . . .

\*     \*     \*

*Comment:*

# DISCRIMINATION AMONG CUSTOMERS

Discrimination, as something firms are morally called upon to avoid, will be treated at length in the next section on relations with employees. However, there have been important instances of firms' discriminating among customers. Firms operating restaurants and other facilities open to the public often used to practice forms of discrimination—like refusing to serve blacks—that, given the nature of their businesses, excluded some citizens from full participation in the basic amenities of social life. Other firms, in businesses that do not fall into that category but which nevertheless supply goods or services that people cannot easily get elsewhere, have been attacked for offering them to certain groups on specially disadvantageous terms, or refusing to supply them altogether. Blacks have complained that banks, for example, "redline"—refuse to lend money for mortgages in specific neighborhoods. The defense that the banks offer is easily imagined; it does not do away with the problem. In the following case, based on a news story in *The Wall Street Journal* (January 26, 1978), the issue is even harder to resolve, in the face of complex arguments on both sides.

# MASSACHUSETTS BANS INSURERS FROM USING SEX, MARITAL STATUS FOR AUTO POLICY*

Under the classifications generally used by insurance companies, unmarried males under 25 (the class with the most accidents, according to the companies) are charged rates several times the rates charged "adults," the class with the fewest accidents. City drivers are charged much higher rates—up to four times more—than their counterparts in rural areas. Critics across the United States have demanded that this system of rates be changed, contending that it discriminates unfairly against various drivers. It would seem to be especially unfair to young urban males with good driving records.

In Massachusetts, the state insurance commissioner announced in January 1977 that the eleven driver classes previously used, which were based on age, sex, and marital status, would be replaced thenceforth with five classes based mainly on driving experience. The new classes were: drivers with three or more years of driving experience; drivers with less than three years of experience who have not taken a driver-training course; a discounted class of such inexperienced drivers with driver-training; a discounted class of drivers over 65 years old; and drivers who use their cars for business. The commissioner also reduced the premiums of city drivers.

Insurance companies viewed the commissioner's action with dismay. One company official said, "He has returned insurance in Massachusetts to the dark ages of a cartel system with essentially uniform rates and a rating plan dictated by a regulator, all of which has been substituted for a competitive rating system which in the view of most industry people was working." Tom Whelton of the Alliance of American Insurers said, "It does make changes in the system contrary to the economic realities of the insurance business. It's an experiment; we feel it's certainly something that shouldn't be looked at as a doctrine until it passes the test of time."

\*     \*     \*

PART THREE

# The Actions of Firms: Firms Dealing with Employees

# CHAPTER 8

# The Right to Be Hired;
# Promoted; Retained

*Introductory Comment:*

## UNEQUAL POWER OPEN TO ABUSES

The chief subject of moral concern in Part Two was deception, as an evil that in many different ways casts a shadow over various transactions: sometimes deliberate deception, sometimes the approximation to deception that occurs when goods do not meet reasonable expectations. With oppression, with which we are now going to be much more continually concerned, the subject of justice inevitably arises; for oppression is flagrant injustice. Oppression is the chief subject of moral concern to be met within the employment relationship; and the subject of justice will share its prominence.

Deception itself could have been treated as a form of injustice. Breaking promises or contracts, a subject that sometimes intersects with deception, sometimes intersects with oppression, and sometimes falls between, invites treatment as injustice even more strongly. Hobbes (1588–1679) thought the not keeping of contracts the prototype of injustice. Justice has to do in one way or another with equality; and we can see how not keeping contracts produces an unjustified inequality—what was agreed on, in a given transaction, as equivalent in value, is not in fact supplied on one side. So if one performs, while the other does not, they end up in unequal positions. In other words—words will serve to show also how deception may be seen as injustice—one side takes advantage of the other.

Both deception and breaking promises, however, at least in clear cases of their being wrong, can be conclusively judged so without bringing up justice or injustice. If there are any moral rules, rules prohibiting deception and prescribing keeping promises are among them, indeed are the most familiar examples; and these rules suffice to characterize the clear cases as wrong. With oppression, matters stand otherwise. One cannot make sense of oppression without looking upon it straightaway as unequal treatment by some one—or some group or organization—in a position to abuse unequal power; and this is to see it as injustice. The inequality that results benefits either some other parties (other employees, or potential employees) or the powerholder (the firm).

Unequal distribution of power might not in all cases be unjust in itself, though questions could be raised about this. I am not, at this point, even going to raise questions about whether the current distribution of power between firms and employees (or potential employees) is unjust. It is certainly very unequal. Even without firms as large as General Electric or General Motors, employers in the past have been much less numerous than the workers dependent on them for employment, and in a much better position to adapt to imperfections of the market: consider, for example, the difficulties that workers have in moving about in search of jobs. Hence a relatively small set of employers have exercised unequal power over a relatively large number of workers. This inequality is greatly heightened, moreover, by the presence of giant firms, on whose decisions about hiring, firing, and promotion tens of thousands of jobs depend. A very small number of people—the top executives of the giant firms—make those decisions, or establish the policies under which they are made. It is no wonder that the public, composed as it is for the most part of people who are employees somewhere or other, has a lot to be concerned about in how this power is exercised.

When the decisions—directly, or by omission—go very badly wrong, oppression sometimes results. The power of the firms is exercised without regard for the vital interests of the employees (or potential employees—I keep adding them, since the chance to be hired is as important as being treated justly once on the job). That implies that oppression interferes with people's happiness or opportunities for happiness.

I shall return to the connection between happiness and justice a little later. For the moment, let it suffice to say that oppression differs from deception (and breaking promises) not only by making reflection about justice inevitable, but also by having a more vivid connection with happiness. People, to be sure, lose something—some means of helping make themselves happy—when they are deceived in transactions or disappointed by broken contracts. Ordinarily, however, the loss involves just one means among many, and is transitory. Oppression, as we conceive it, is more persistent and systematic. Its effects may distort one's whole life.

*[Legislation in the United States and similar legislation in other countries, including Canada, forbids discrimination on grounds of race, color, religion, sex, or national origin. The following case, from Nova Scotia, illustrates the impact of this legislation. Race and sex have been the most common grounds of discrimination at issue. This case involves both, and is doubly typical in that respect. It is typical, too, in its connection with race, in having to do with discrimination against blacks. It is quite untypical, of course, in its connection with sex, in having to do with discrimination against men. Women, we may well believe, have been much more frequently and painfully discriminated against than men.]*

# JOHN CHICK v. THE SARACEN'S HEAD BAR AND GRILL*

*Nova Scotia Board of Inquiry, 1980*

CHAIRMAN GILLIS:

The Saracen's Head Bar and Grill is an attractive country inn located just outside Yarmouth on the western tip of Nova Scotia. It provides lodging for its guests, and also has a dining room and a beverage lounge for use of guests as well as other patrons. Both are popular. Most of the staff at the inn are recruited locally.

On August 15th, 1979, the Grill advertised in the local weekly paper, THE VANGUARD, for "Waitors (sic)/Waitresses and Buspersons . . . temporary and permanent positions . . . and John Chick applied for a job. He is a young man of the Negro race from Yarmouth, and had obtained his teacher's license but had been unable to procure a teaching position at that time, and was working as a bouncer at the Mitre Tavern.

He was hired by The Saracen's Head Bar and Grill to work in the lounge, gave a week's notice to the Mitre Tavern, and began to work at the Grill about August 28th, 1979.

On or about September 5th that year, Tony Humm, the principal share-holder of The Saracen's Head Bar and Grill, advised Chick that he did not wish him to work in the lounge any longer, and Chick ceased work at the Grill that night. Chick now complains that he lost his job because he is black, or because he is male, or both. The first allegation is prohibited by Section 8 of *The Human Rights Act* (S.N.S. 1969, c.11) and the second by Section 11A, "unless there is a bona fide occupational qualification based on sex."

---

*Excerpts from *Canadian Human Rights Reporter*, Vol. I, Decision 30, Pars. 1341–77, September 20, 1980. Copyright 1980 by Canadian Human Rights Reporter, 224 4th Ave. South, Saskatoon, Saskatchewan, 3T7 5M5, and reprinted with its permission. Except for the names of the Chairman and of counsel, names of persons and firms changed throughout.

My duty is to determine whether The Saracen's Head Bar and Grill, through Mr. Humm, breached any of those provisions.

At a hearing in Yarmouth on the 30th of July, evidence was presented by the complainant and by Mr. Humm, as well as a number of employees and former employees of The Saracen's Head Bar and Grill and the manager of the Mitre Tavern. The evidence of Chick and his key witnesses is directly at odds with that of Humm as to critical facts, and unfortunately, the one witness who could have shed some conclusive light on those facts, one Harry Maylie, appeared to be avoiding service of a subpoena and could not be found to testify. With the agreement of both counsel, I undertook to decide this matter on the evidence that was before me, rather than adjourn in hopes of procuring Maylie's evidence.

I must first define Chick's job. The only clear evidence of his terms of employment is his own testimony. He states he was hired by Harry Maylie to work in the lounge. His duties would vary from that of a doorman to that of a bartender to that of a waiter as the requirements of the lounge necessitated. A specific salary was not stated, but he surmised that as a doorman, he would earn $4.00 to $5.00 per hour without tips, and as a waiter, he would expect minimum wage, plus tips, and as a bartender, minimum wage, plus a percentage of tips made by those on the floor. He earned from $30.00 to $50.00 per night in tips on the nights he worked as a waiter, and was expected to pick up bartending as he could learn it while working. . . .

Secondly, I must determine whether he was fired or quit voluntarily or whether it makes any difference to this inquiry. Mr. Humm says that he advised Chick that he preferred females waiting on customers in the lounge and offered him alternate work in the dining room as a waiter. Chick denies that there was any explicit offer as to alternate employment, but that something was said about providing another job. I find that there was some mention made of alternate employment, but in order to determine whether the details are relevant on the main issue, I turn to Section 8 of the *Human Rights Act*. It states: "No person shall refuse to employ or continue to employ or otherwise discriminate against any individual in regard to employment or any term or condition of employment because of the individual's race . . . or colour."

Section 11A of the Act proscribes similar discrimination because of sex.

It would seem therefore that whether Chick was fired or left voluntarily is not relevant to the determination of whether the Act was breached provided his terms or conditions of employment were changed because of his race, color, or sex, and I find that there was such a change in his employment.

Chick's uncontradicted evidence was that he was hired by Harry Maylie to work in the lounge. This was particularly suitable for him as it meant working nights, and would allow his daytime free for substitute teaching work which would be helpful to him in obtaining a full-time teacher's job which was his primary desire. There is no contention on behalf of the Grill that Harry Maylie did not have authority to hire Chick for this job, and since

Maylie did not testify as to terms of employment, I am obliged to accept Chick's evidence and I do so.

## SEXUAL DISCRIMINATION

Regarding the reason Humm gave to Chick for not wanting him to work in the lounge, there is no significant dispute. The words actually used may not be exactly remembered by each party or identical in each's testimony, but it is clear that Humm indicated that it was his policy to have females only waiting on lounge customers. He believed this was good for business with a predominantly male clientele and it also inhibited the clients from becoming disorderly. I accept that he was sincere in this belief.

Humm also indicated in evidence that his policy was to make lounge waitress work available to other staff at the Grill before hiring new employees, as this would give older staff a chance to augment their working hours and accordingly their income. This was supported by Minnie Omer, who testified that she was hired by Humm at the beginning of September, 1979, as a switchboard operater for four (4) nights a week, with a chance to work two (2) or three (3) nights a week as a waitress in the lounge as well.

Mr. Pink argues on behalf of The Saracen's Head Bar and Grill that insofar as the allegation of sexual discrimination is concerned, this amounts to a "bona fide occupational qualification based on sex." He argues a distinction between a "preference" based on sex and a "discrimination" as prohibited by law, and suggests that customary practice in other lounges is a significant factor for this Board to consider in recognizing this distinction.

Miss Garber submits that in order to establish the defense of bona fide occupational qualification provided under Section 11A(1)(d) of the Act, the respondent must lead factual evidence showing the economic loss that would result if he were to hire male waiters.

I have given serious thought to this question and with respect I am unable to agree with either counsel.

To say that the preference of an employer's customers or clients to have either males or females serving them, which preference results in economic differences for the employers, is a bona fide occupational qualification based on sex, would be tantamount to creating a "community standard" test to determine whether discrimination exists. It would be a minor extension of this principle to hold that if most customers in a restaurant held prejudices against blacks or Jews or Scotsmen, the proprietor would be legally entitled to refuse to serve blacks or Jews or Scotsmen. The long history of human rights struggles on this continent and elsewhere can leave no doubt that such an argument is totally without merit.

I cannot believe that in passing the *Human Rights Act*, the Nova Scotia Legislators ever intended that the rights and freedoms so clearly proclaimed in the Preamble and the body of the legislation could be so freely circumvented. The standards are set by the Act, and were intended to be universally applicable throughout the province, regardless of group or community sentiment.

Accordingly, although I have some sympathy of the Grill and Mr. Humm if there is in fact an economic detriment to hiring male waiters, I am obliged to find that Mr. Humm, on behalf of the Grill, breached the provisions of Section 11A of the Act and that the defence provided by Section 11A(1)(d) has not been made out.

### ALLEGATION OF RACIAL DISCRIMINATION

Having so found, it may not be necessary to determine whether there was a breach of Section 8 due to race or color of the complainant, but in order to properly fulfill my appointment, I feel that I should make a finding as to each of the allegations made.

This comes to a determination of the credibility of the witness Phil Pirrip, as opposed to that of Mr. Humm. Pirrip was the assistant manager of the Grill, reporting directly to Harry Maylie. He states emphatically that Humm told him in the presence of Harry Maylie that "he did not want black people working on the floor at the lounge" and ordered him or Maylie to fire Chick. When Pirrip did not do so, he himself was fired by Humm.

Humm flatly denies that such a statement was ever made. He says that the only consideration was that he preferred females as waitresses and that present employees had priority.

Mr. Pink points out that Pirrip's evidence was less than convincing, that his memory dates was awry, that he was a close friend of Chick's and that he was not working out well as an assistant manager. I also caution myself that, having been fired himself, Pirrip could of course be carrying a grudge.

Humm's evidence was clearer in general terms as to dates of employment, since he had the employment records to rely on, but he, like all witnesses, was somewhat vague as to exact dates and days of the week. He was relying on dates of payment in the hotel records.

Having observed both witnesses, and lacking the testimony of Harry Maylie, I am impressed that Pirrip appeared a credible and honest witness who was not in a position to gain anything from his testimony, was not shaken by cross-examination in any material particulars, and readily and freely admitted when he was unsure or could be mistaken regarding his evidence. Humm was perhaps more facile, and if driven to choose, I accept the evidence of Pirrip where it varys [sic] from that of Humm.

Accordingly, I find that the allegation of unlawful discrimination based on race or color has been established as well. In the complainant's case, for the purposes of this hearing, "race" or "color" are synonymous.

### THIRD PARTIES

I would be remiss if I did not make reference to Mr. Pirrip's position. He is not a complainant and had nothing personal to gain at this hearing. His evidence is that Humm ordered him to fire Chick, and when this was not done, he himself was fired by Humm. If Pirrip had done as ordered, he would have kept his job, and in my opinion, would have been safe from legal penalty. Instead, he refused to become a party to a breach of law and has suffered the loss of his job. He may well have a remedy in an action for unlawful dismissal, but it seems strange that the Act carries no remedy for someone in his position, and the Legislature may well wish to consider this as the subject of an appropriate amendment to the Act.

COMPENSATION

Finally I come to the question of how to compensate Mr. Chick for the breaches of the Act that I have determined were made. Section 26A(8) of the *Human Rights Act* states: "A Board of Inquiry may order any party who has contravened this Act to do any act or thing that constitutes full compliance with the Act and to rectify any injury caused to any person or class of persons or to make compensation therefor."

It appears that both parties feel a monetary compensation is the only appropriate one, and I agree that an order of compliance to the Grill would be of little use. Chick now has alternate employment as a teacher, which was his primary wish, and is not really seeking reinstatement. Chick claims that he should be entitled to $1,500.00 for six (6) weeks loss of wages, based on estimate of $250.00 per week for six (6) weeks, plus $500.00 for "pain and suffering" based on the humiliation and embarrassment of losing his job.

The evidence of loss based on the figures provided is not as accurate as it might be. I also question the basis of the claim by Mr. Chick. He was substantially unemployed for a period from the first week of September until the 4th of February, 1980, a term of approximately twenty-two (22) weeks. It would seem to me that compensation by way of damages should follow closely the method of assessment in our Supreme Court. Based on an eight (8)-hour work day, my calculations show that Mr. Chick would have earned more like $275.00 per week if he worked full-time as a waiter, and $200.00 per week as a doorman, but I will accept the sum of $250.00 per week as average wages as accurate. It is noted that he received Unemployment Insurance in the amount of $80.00 per week, and worked one (1) or two (2) days a week at his old job at the Mitre Tavern, which would have earned him approximately $50.00 on an average week, and that he also earned the sum of $50.00 teaching disco dance lessons during the period he was unemployed. It is suggested that these items would go to mitigate damages. . . .

At this point, the face that Mr. Chick was not dismissed from all employment at the Grill becomes significant. In his own words, as well as those of Mr. Humm, he indicated at the time that he was told he would not be working in the lounge that he would quit that day. He was not interested in an alternate position. Humm suggests that the alternate position open would have been one in the dining room. It appears from the evidence that based on the dining room schedule, Chick would have been able to carry on with substitute teaching and that the extra-curricular activities which he claims this employment would have interfered with, would not be a necessary requirement for substituting. The amount that he would have made in the dining room is not clearly spelled out, but I accept that it was something less than was made by most people working in the lounge and, for lack of better information, I fix a figure of $50.00 per week being the differential between what the dining room employees would make and what a lounge waiter would make.

Under the reasoning in *Stead v. Elliott & Caulfield Motors Limited* (1963) 39 D.L.R.(2d) 170, it is clear that in our province, insurance payments are not relevant to damage awards and it is clear that in law, if not in practice, Unemployment Insurance benefits are indeed insurance.

Other benefits that Mr. Chick received for alternate employment would not reduce the amount claimable in damages as he would not have had those available had he been working at alternate employment in the dining room at The Saracen's Head Bar and Grill.

Accordingly, I find that his losses amounted to $50.00 per week for twenty-two (22) weeks or $1,100.00.

As to the humiliation and embarrassment, the incidents complained of all took place in private, or substantially so, and I would hope that the major portion of this humiliation would fall on The Saracen's Head Bar and Grill and not upon Mr. Chick, who had nothing whatsoever to be ashamed of. I therefore fix this compensation at $100.00.

\*   \*   \*

# ARGUMENTS FOR AND AGAINST MANDATORY RETIREMENT
## (U.S. Congress)\*

---

*[In 1978, federal legislation in the United States added age to the grounds on which discrimination is no longer acceptable. In 1977, before the legislation was adopted, the report of a Select Committee of Congress on Aging summed up the arguments for and against mandatory retirement, a practice that at least needs some defending if it is to be reconciled with equal opportunity regardless of age.]*

. . . In hearings on retirement age policies this year, the committee heard from large and small corporations, some of which opposed mandatory retirement. The committee heard from public and private interest groups, labor unions, scholars, legal experts and economists. Finally, it heard from older Americans themselves. While the witnesses differed in phraseology and emphasis, the general arguments pro and con might be summarized in the following lists.

\**The Social and Human Cost of Enforced Idleness*—Report by the Select Comm. on Aging (95th Congress, 1st Session) Aug/77 Comm. Pub. No. 95–91, U.S. Gov. Printing Office.

## A. For Mandatory Retirement

1. Older persons as a group may be less well-suited for some jobs than younger workers because:

    a. Declining physical and mental capacity are found in greater proportion among older persons.

    b. Generally older persons do not learn new skills as easily as younger persons.

    c. Older workers have more inflexibility with regard to work due to work rules, seniority systems and pay scales.

    d. Older workers typically have less education than younger workers.

2. Medical science is not capable of making accurate individual assessments of physical and psychological competencies of employees which would presumably be required if there was no standard mandatory retirement age; or substantial time and money may be required to make such individual determinations of fitness. Also, it is difficult to administer any such individual test of fitness fairly.

3. Mandatory retirement saves face for the older workers no longer capable of performing his or her job adequately, who would otherwise be singled out for forced retirement.

4. Mandatory retirement provides a predictable situation allowing both management and employees to plan ahead.

5. It is sometimes more costly for employers to have an older work force in terms of maintaining various pension, health and life insurance plans.

6. By forcing retirement at an earlier age than a person might otherwise choose, there are more opportunities for younger workers. This may aid in recruiting additions and replacements to the work force and allow infusion of new ideas.

7. Older workers can often retire to social security or other retirement income, making jobs available to younger unemployed workers who do not have other income potential.

## B. Against Mandatory Retirement

1. Mandatory retirement based on age alone is discriminatory against workers. It is contrary to equal employment opportunity. Mandatory retirement laws have been challenged as unconstitutional because of denying individuals equal protection of the law.

2. Chronological age alone is a poor indicator of ability to perform a job. Mandatory retirement at a certain age does not take into consideration actual, differing abilities and capacities. Studies demonstrate that many workers can continue to work effectively beyond age 65, and may be better employees than younger workers because of experience and job commmitment.

3. Mandatory retirement can cause hardships for older persons. For example:

    a. Mandatory retirement often results in loss of role and income for individuals.

    b. Mandatory retirement at a certain age may very well result in a lower retirement benefit under social security if the last years the employee would have worked would have brought higher earnings than earlier years.

c. Mandatory retirement is especially disadvantageous to some women who do not start work until after the children are grown or after being widowed or divorced. Forced retirement limits the work life of these women and reduces their ability to build up significant benefits.

d. Mandatory retirement can cause great economic hardship on a growing number of older workers who have many financial obligations usually considered the province of younger persons, e.g., home mortgages, installment payments on cars, etc. In addition, a rapidly increasing number of older persons ages 60–65 are experiencing the financial responsibility for aged parents or other relatives.

e. Mandatory retirement on the basis of age may well impair the health of many individuals whose job represents a major source of status, creative satisfaction, social relationships, or self-respect.

4. Mandatory retirement causes loss of skills and experience from the work force, resulting in reduced national output (GNP).

5. Forced retirement causes an increased expense to government income maintenance programs such as social security and supplemental security income, as well as to social service programs.

6. The declining birth rate will mean a proportionately smaller labor force supporting a larger retiree population early in the next century. The economics of this situation could be eased by later retirement or elimination of mandatory retirement at any set age.

\*    \*    \*

# ANTHONY VOIGT v. THE MAYPOLE BAKERY\*

[The poignant case that follows illustrates the application of Canadian legislation forbidding discrimination on the ground of age.]

*Nova Scotia Board of Inquiry, 1980*

CHAIRMAN SUTHERLAND:

The issue to be determined is whether the Maypole Bakery in refusing to employ Mr. Anthony Voigt contravened Section 11 B(1) (a) of the Human Rights Act. Section 11 B(1)(a) provides as follows: 11 B(1) "No person or

\*Excerpts from *Canadian Human Rights Reporter*, Vol. I, Decision 24, Pars. 1078–1145, August 20, 1980. Copyright 1980 by Canadian Human Rights Reporter, 224 4th Ave. South, Saskatoon, Saskatchewan, 3T7 5M5. Except for the Chairman and counsel, names of persons and firms changed throughout.

agency included in Section 8, 9, 10 and 11 shall discriminate against an individual because of (a) the age of the individual if the individual has attained the age of forty years and has not attained the age of sixty-five years" . . .

Mr. Voigt, the complainant and first witness, stated that he was sixty years old and that he was a baker. He stated that he was first employed with the Maypole Bakery in 1939 and that he had carried out a number of tasks since his first employment, including progressing from cleaning pots and pans, working in the pastry department, baking bread and baking pastries. He stated that George Pinch, father of Thomas Pinch, Joseph Pinch and Ruth Westlock, was the owner of the company when he was first employed. He stated that George Pinch never complained of his work. He stated that one day in January of 1980, he was working in the Maypole Bakery and Thomas Pinch came to him. His evidence of what occurred is as follows: "I was mixing something, and Mr. Thomas Pinch came to me and he said he had bad news for me, that there would have to be a layoff and it would have to be me, and at that time, I asked him if seniority counted anything, and he didn't say much to that, except he racked his brain trying to figure a solution, but there was none, and I would have to go, and he mentioned that, well I had no more dependants."

He stated that he worked for two more weeks and at the end of two weeks, he ceased to be employed by the Maypole Bakery. He stated that he had worked for the company for forty years and was "kind of shocked" at being laid off, being the longest employee of the Company. He stated that Jarvis Lorry started about the same time but that Lorry was an uncle of the present owners of the Company and that Lorry was now working only three days a week on a part-time basis. He stated that he (Voigt) had no dependants except his wife, that his wife had been working but was not working in January of 1980 because of a back operation. He stated that he thought all of the other employees had dependants except Cissy Jupe. He stated that he had applied for other employment, but as of the date of the hearing, had not obtained a job. He stated that he was receiving unemployment insurance and a compensation pension for loss of fingers on one hand due to an accident some years before.

When asked why he felt he was laid off, he replied: "I can't, I couldn't give a reason, unless it was a difference in age, or—background, or what, I don't know."

When asked about the basis for his complaint, he replied: "Well, yes, I felt if anybody would, that would have to lay off, would lay off their oldest employee, their oldest employees, and keep the younger staff there, because they would be with them longer."

When I asked Mr. Voigt if he could recall any specific reason given by Thomas Pinch for laying him off, he replied: "Well, he told me that it was rough out there, and the business was in serious trouble, or lack of business."

On cross examination by Mr. Kelleher, Mr. Voigt admitted that he had on occasion joked with some of the bakers about retiring but that he had never given notice of his intention to retire. He stated that following his layoff, he went to Manpower, and was told he needed a separation slip. He stated that he filed for unemployment insurance benefits. Mr. Kelleher asked the following question: "When you discussed the matter of receiving those benefits from the Unemployment Insurance Commission, or from Manpower, did they tell you that you would have to file a complaint with the Human Rights Commission, before you received your unemployment insurance?"

Mr. Voigt replied: "No, that was, I think, that was just one . . . of the worker's opinion" (from Manpower).

He could not recall the name of the worker. When asked if when he first went to the Human Rights Commission he told them he was laid off because of his age he replied: "Well, that was determined after that."

When asked who determined that he replied: "Well, by talking to the different ones, they said, at Manpower, the man at Manpower told me that it had to be my age, because there was no other reason, if I didn't miss work in forty (40) years, except for sickness."

On further questioning, he stated that he was never told directly by his employer that he was laid off because of his age but was told that business was slow.

On re-direct examination, he stated that he would have had no objection to doing night work if requested by his employer.

Following re-direct examination, Miss Garber indicated that she would close her case at that point and was prepared to argue the issue of age as being the only factor. Mr. Kelleher moved that the complaint be dismissed for lack of evidence. After hearing arguments from both counsel, I ruled that I was not prepared to dismiss the matter at that time and make a ruling that Mr. Voigt had not been discriminated against. I did so because of the nature of the allegation and the difficulty involved in proving that one has been discriminated against. While the basic onus is on the complainant, I felt that other evidence other than the complainant's should be examined in order to provide a proper hearing for both parties and for that reason, I ruled that I wished to hear Mr. Kelleher's witnesses in defence of the complaint.

Mr. Kelleher called Mr. Thomas Pinch as his first witness. Mr. Pinch stated that he was "a shareholder, President and director of the Maypole Bakery. He stated that he, his brother, Joseph Pinch, and his sister, Ruth Westlock, owned all of the shares of the Maypole Bakery except for a "few preferred shares, or something to that effect, that my mother owns."

His evidence was that a new company of the same name was formed in 1967 when the business was taken over from his father. The employees working in 1967 for his father's company were taken on by the new company, including Mr. Voigt. He stated that he did not regard any of those employees as having seniority in 1967. The new company is broken down into retail and manufacturing. He stated that in retail, six or seven workers are employed and that three or four of those are between 45 and 65 years of age. His sister, Ruth Westlock, and Charlotte Neckett have control over the retail section and that he and his brother, Joseph, control the manufacturing section. He stated that his uncle, Jarvis Lorry, works in the manufacturing section and is 68 years old. About two or three years ago, Mr. Lorry stopped working full time at his own request and now works three days per week. Mr. Lorry carries out a number of functions including checking inventory, ordering, receiving and baking. He stated that Messrs. Tupman, Pott and Gowan, who are bakers, are "swifter" in the work they do than Mr. Voigt. He was asked if he knew how old Mr. Voigt was when he laid him off. He replied: "No, age never came into it at all. I didn't, if age would come into it, I would definitely keep Mr. Voigt, because it would be against our, our good judgement to keep someone with a lot of experience, if he was capable of doing the job."

He said that "As far as I can recall, Mr. Voigt has always been slow," and that he did not notice anything particular in terms of his slowing down as he was getting older. He was asked: "Now he's (Voigt) indicated that he could always do the work that was given to him. What do you have to say about that?"

He replied: "He, he could do the work that was given to him, yes, but someone else could do it in half the time."

He stated that at the time Mr. Voigt was laid off, the company was overstaffed and was having financial difficulties. The fiscal year for the company ends on May 31 each year, and in November of 1979, a financial statement was obtained indicating a loss. He stated that he discussed the overstaffing with his brother and sister and with his brother-in-law, who is the accountant. He stated that between November of 1979 and January 1980, the financial affairs of the company were not improving and that the bakers were, at that time, working about 35 hours per week but were always paid for 42 hours as a matter of company policy. After discussions, it was decided to cut back on the staff. In retail, one full-time girl was laid off.

It was felt that cutbacks in the bakery or manufacturing section were necessary. He stated that if all bakers were cut back in hours, the fear was that they would start looking for other jobs. The financial problems of the company were not discussed with the bakers. He was asked how Mr. Voigt was selected as the one to go. He replied: "We did, a, we figured out from holidays, and things like that, who was the least efficient, who was the easiest person to replace, what would, who would the best people be if we wanted to try to make a go of it, who would we, who could do the most work."

When asked if age at any time played a part in the thought process as to who could be let go, he replied, "Not for a second." He described how he told Mr. Voigt of the company's decision as follows: "I approached Mr. Voigt, in an afternoon, I'm not exactly sure of the date, that we had to make a decision that someone had to go, and I, I was very sorry, it was a hard decision for us to make, because we didn't, we're not used to letting people go. We usually drag them along, as best we could, but I told Tony that we had to make a decision, as we, he was the one that we'd let go, and I said I was sorry. I said I was sorry that it had to be done, but there was nothing I could do about it."

He stated that he did not suggest to Mr. Voigt that it was because he had no dependants, and that he thought Mr. Voigt may have thought that was the reason. He stated that in his opinion, Mr. Voigt could not do the work of Mr. Lorry. He also stated that Mr. Voigt could do some of the work of Mr. Gowan or Mr. Pott but that it would take longer. He stated that if someone other than Mr. Voigt was laid off, a replacement might have to be hired. He stated that if one of the night bakers was laid off, and Mr. Voigt took that job, the work would be done much slower. He stated that he never told Mr. Voigt that he was slow or inefficient and that Mr. Voight did the work that was given him but would take longer than anyone else. He stated that in the bakery, the other bakers did not like to work with Mr. Voigt because he was slow or inefficient, and that since Mr. Voigt left, the work atmosphere in the bakery had improved and "that's working as a better unit, and things are done, being done a lot quicker, and with a lesser amount of staff."

He stated that a major expense was incurred of $13,000–$15,000 for the heating system about the end of 1979, that the company was overdrawn at the bank and that property of one of the shareholders was mortgaged to assist the company. Wages were the biggest expense and business dropped off as a result of cut-backs by Dominion Stores, one of the customers, and a general reduction in sales.

He stated that he had never talked to Mr. Voigt about retiring but that he had heard someone else mention that he might retire. The following questions and answers are relevant:

Q. You're saying that Mr. Voigt's age played no part in your determination to let him go?
A. That would be the worst criteria I'd act on. If age, if, if Mr. Voigt could do his job properly, we would still keep him there, because, if he was experienced, and a good baker, it would be, it would be ridiculous for us to let him go, because of his experience, if he had good experience, and could do the job properly, age would have no bearing on it at all.
Q. Alright. Do you think you said anything to him to give him the suggestion that it was because of his age?
A. None at all.

He stated that there was no plan to hire any full- or part-time bakers to replace Mr. Voigt, and that none of the present staff was working overtime except possibly one or two hours. He stated that the present bakers are now working closer to forty-two hours per week.

On cross examination, he stated that he was reluctant to speak to the employees about the financial situation because he feared they would not "stick with a sinking ship" if they knew of the financial problems. . . . He stated that, "More or less, we have tolerated a lot of employees, rather than let them go, that is one of the mistakes we probably made, for a long time." He stated that he did not think speeding [Mr. Voight] up would help, that he had worked that way as long as he could recall and that he doubted very much if Mr. Voigt would ever change. He stated that his main reason for terminating Mr. Voigt was that he was the least efficient of the bakers and the easiest person to replace. He stated in effect that he had some idea that

Mr. Voigt might want to retire and if that was so, the decision to let him go would be easier, but that he had not discussed retirement with Mr. Voigt. He stated, however, that even if Mr. Voigt was not thinking of retiring, he would be the one to go. He stated that he never never looked at age, that "If Tony could do the job, Tony could do the job. Age had nothing to do with it." He stated that they needed to let someone go who would have an effect on wages. He stated that the company did not have a loss in 1978, but in 1979, expenses increased. He stated that the three shareholders each took out $325.00 per week and that the bakers were paid about $265.00 or $275.00 per week. He stated that in his opinion, a shorter work week was not the answer, that they had to "get rid of a baker, at least one . . . baker, not to put someone on part-time, not the most inefficient baker there."

On re-direct examination, he stated that between May of 1978 and May of 1979, sales increased by $32,000 but the costs of sales increased by about $50,000. He stated that the biggest expense item was salaries and wages. He agreed that the company owed him personally about $15,000, and that his sister was owed approximately $6,000 or $7,000 by the company. He further agreed that the Company's bank overdraft in May of 1979 was approximately $41,000. . . .

Charlotte Neckett was called by Mr. Kelleher. On direct examination, she stated that she was a supervisor with the Maypole Bakery and had been employed for 28 years and worked in the retail section. She agreed that between May of 1979 and January of 1980, the company was having financial problems; and that as a result of this, one full-time girl in the retail section was laid off, and the hours of two part-time girls were cut back and that a driver was laid off. She stated that the cashier was 68 years old and that a Mrs. Dowler employed in the retail department was 65 years old. Mrs. Neckett stated that she (Mrs. Neckett) was the only other person in the retail department over age 45. She stated that those who did less work were cut back in the retail department. She stated that Mr. Voigt had hurt his thumb in 1979 and had been off work for perhaps a month. She said that when he returned to work, he had told her "I wouldn't be here now, I would retire if I could." When asked if she thought he was joking she stated, "At the time, no. I just assumed that he meant that he would like to retire." She agreed with the suggestion that the company has a tendency to "carry people" despite having financial problems. She stated that "They (the company) have more feeling than what they should."

On cross-examination, she stated that she did not inquire as to whether Mr. Voigt was serious about retiring or not. She said that she mentioned Mr. Voigt's comment about retirement to Ruth Westlock a few days after Mr. Voigt had spoken of it. She stated that in the retail section, people were told the truth of the reason for layoffs and that people were laid off because they weren't doing their work. She stated that that was part of the reason for layoffs; but that she did not want to mention the financial situation to anyone in the retail section. . . .

Ruth Westlock was called by Mr. Kelleher and on direct examination confirmed that she was a shareholder, director and an officer of the Maypole

Bakery and that she was a sister of Thomas and Joseph Pinch. She confirmed that the company was formed in 1967, and that she played a part in deciding that someone would be let go in the bakery department. She stated that the decision was long and dragged out going on for about five months prior to January of 1980. She stated that the retail section was first looked at and that one full-time person would be laid off and a part-time girl's hours cut. She stated that at least one and possibly two would have to go in the bakery. When asked why Mr. Voigt was chosen to go over another baker, she replied: "Well, it's hard to say, because his work wasn't up to par really. He could be most, one that could, anyone could take his place, and do what had to be done. It could be, anyone could fill in there, eh."

She denied that age was a reason and stated that when hiring "It doesn't make any difference if they're sixty (60) or seventy (70) years old, we'll always give them a chance." She stated that the 68-year-old cashier was cut back to half-time in the retail section, and that she was not laid off because she is "really an asset to the company" and was trustworthy and a good worker. When asked further about how the decision to lay off Mr. Voigt was arrived at, she replied:

> Well we, we didn't just say, Tony, eh. We studied them all perfectly. Is there anyone that, like okay, one . . . of the other, I mentioned to Tom, and Joe, could one . . . of the bakers that's been here three . . . , or four . . . years, and they said, well there's no way that Tony can take over and do that job, eh. The night baker, there's a lot of that's got to be done quickly, eh. There's the mixing of the doughs, if they're not ready on time, well the rest of the day is really frigged up, eh. If, if certain things aren't out at a certain time, well you lose the sale of that in a day, eh.

She admitted that she never personally worked with Mr. Voigt. The following questions and answers are of interest:

Q. Okay, at the time the decision was made, who was supposed to go to the baker and tell him that?

A. Well there was a big discussion. I said I'm out, because I look after the girls downstairs, that's my department. It's a hard thing to try and fire someone, eh, especially someone like Tony, and we all respect Tony very much, and, as you know, we held on to him as long as we possibly could.

Q. Alright.

A. Because I know Dad would have done the same thing, but when it gets down to the, either losing your business, if you don't start cutting back two (2) or three (3) people, or just keep carrying, and carrying, we carried for two (2) years longer than what we should have, and we've gotten, really, you know, in a mess.

A. Do you know who made the decision, with Tony, who went to see Tony?

A. Who went to speak with Tony?

Q. Yes.

A.  Tommy.
Q.  Did he do it right away, did he, did he . . . ?
A.  No.
Q.  Postpone it, tell us how?
A.  Okay, I let my girls go approximately in November, eh, just after we got the statement back . . .
Q.  Hm mm.
A.  We could look at things financially, well I'm one that's got to go and do it right away, because it keeps bothering me, and bothering me, eh, so I, anyway I said, Tom, now we've done it, now when are you going to go and see Tony, so he says, I'll be there, I'm you know, I'll go to him, and he waited and waited, and I, it was Christmas time coming on, so I said, well we definitely can't leave him go before Christmas, eh, and so, just, so I said, you know, so we waited, and January came, and I said, Tommy, you know, I think it's really time, you have to do it now, and it was hard, he really, that, I think that was one of the hardest decisions Tommy has ever had to do, and, like I say, we don't hire, and fire, people like that. We have most of our staff that's been there for years, and are all treated, whether one's been there forty . . . years, twenty . . . years, or twelve . . . years, they're not, well you're here for sixty (60) years, so, you know, they're all treated the same.

On cross-examination, she confirmed that she had never worked with Mr. Voigt and had never told him that he wasn't doing his work properly. She stated that she had placed a mortgage on her own house in order to provide a loan to the company and that the company was making the mortgage payments.

Mr. Kelleher called Henry Gowan, a baker, who stated that he worked with the Maypole Bakery since 1965 and worked with the new company after its formation in 1967. In 1971, he quit and was away for four months before rejoining the company. He stated that he was a full-time baker and that he knew Mr. Voigt. He stated that he was aware of company problems because of the slowdown in business. He stated that Mr. Voigt worked in the same manner since he knew him. He agreed with the suggestions that Mr. Voigt was laid off because he was not able to "keep pace with what was being requested of the bakers." He also agreed that the other bakers could do the work that Mr. Voigt did. He stated that when Mr. Voigt helped him, the product "wasn't the same product at all."

On cross-examination, he stated that he never heard any of the Pinches complain to Mr. Voigt about his work. He admitted that when Mr. Voigt helped him, he (Gowan) would be criticized by everyone for having poor product. He stated that he sometimes accepted criticism for work done by someone else. He admitted, however, that he never complained to Mr. Voigt about poor product when Mr. Voigt helped him. He stated that he was only working about 32 hours per week at one time and was paid for 42 hours per week.

On re-direct examination, he stated that the bakery was running smoothly now. He stated that Mr. Voigt was sometimes very difficult to work with.

Mr. Kelleher called Jarvis Lorry, who stated that he was a baker and that he started to work for George Pinch in 1939. He stated that he knew the business was in trouble in May of 1979 because he was doing all the buying. He stated that he knew Mr. Voigt and had worked with him. He stated that Mr. Voigt started from scratch in the baking business but that he did not "learn everything." When asked if he would have made the same decision to let Mr. Voigt go, he seemed unsure.

On cross-examination, he stated that Mr. Voigt "couldn't work at every job that's called for the baker." He indicated that he felt Mr. Voigt could not do some of the work some other bakers could do. He admitted, however, that he could not now say whether Mr. Voigt's work was satisfactory or not because he had not worked directly with him recently. He admitted that when he did work with Mr. Voigt, he thought his work was satisfactory but that Mr. Voigt might have slowed down. He stated that it was his (Lorry's) decision to cut back his work to three days per week, that he was too tired to work a whole week and that he wanted more time to himself. He agreed that he was related by marriage to the Pinches . . .

Miss Garber re-called Mr. Voigt. Mr. Voigt stated that his reference to retirement made in any discussion with Ruth Westlock was made in a joking manner and not meant to be taken seriously. He admitted making a comment about retiring to Charlotte Neckett but repeated that it was made "more or less jokingly, not, not being serious about it." He stated that he had no plans to leave the Company prior to his being laid off. His evidence was to the effect that he could do as much as any of the other bakers. He admitted that he made mistakes but in answer to how often he made mistakes, he replied: "Not even twice a month. Yes, I mean, errors are made, but not several times a week, or not even several times a month, not on the same, the same thing."

He implied that he made no more mistakes and likely fewer than other bakers. On the questions of whether he was slower or not than other bakers, he stated that "You can take your time and do things right, or you can hurry things, and just get your work finished, and get out, whether its good, or bad." He stated that he never thought there was any disharmony in the bakery.

On cross-examination, he agreed that business was slow but stated that it was always slow after Christmas. When asked who he would have let go from the list of bakers, he stated that Edward Plummer is not considered a baker, "so the other one would be, would have to be Jack Hopkins," because "he's easy enough to replace, anyone could have done his work." He admitted that Mr. Hopkins was the youngest one in the group and stated that he thought Mr. Hopkins could manage to find work any place else. . . .

Miss Garber called Clara Barley, who stated that she was a human rights officer with the Commission, and that she was employed there prior to and since January 1st of 1980. She stated that she was the officer assigned the complainant. She stated that she had made notes during the investigation and that she had those notes with her. I permitted her to refer to her notes during questioning, and Mr. Kelleher was permitted to see that portion of the notes referred to by her. For the record, Mr. Kelleher objected to all questions put to her by Miss Garber. She stated that Thomas and Joseph Pinch told her that Mr. Voigt was laid off because of financial problems the company was having, and she confirmed that she had made a notation of that at the time the discussions took place with them. Referring to her notes, Clara Barley stated as follows:

> His, his efficiency, his slowness, was not due to that. The duties could be picked up by others. He still might be overstaffed, that was mentioned. He, ahh, okay, to put this in context, at, okay, I'll just go ahead and give you the points, I guess, that would be the best way. That he had to terminate a person with family, or without. He mentioned that Mr. Voigt wished to leave.

Q. Explain that.
A. Yes, okay, if I may explain that. In the initial conversation, I shouldn't say that, in my second conversation with Mr. Pinch, he had said that Mr. Voigt had mentioned to the head cashier that he wished to leave. Now the next time I met with him, with Mr. Pinch, he mentioned that, in addition to mentioning it to the head cashier, Mr. Voigt has also mentioned it to his sister. Those are the major reasons, those are the reasons that I have. . . .

Both Miss Garber and Mr. Kelleher made their closing arguments. Miss Garber argued that discrimination can be found where only one of the factors taken into account is a prohibited factor but not the major factor, only a factor; and I accept that argument. All of the surrounding circumstances must be examined in cases such as these. The thrust of her argument was that the company was having financial problems and someone had to go, but that age was a factor in the minds of the principals of the Company in determining that Mr. Voigt would be laid off rather than one of the other employees. She based this on the fact that only one other employee in the bakery, Jarvis Lorry, was older than Mr. Voigt and that Mr. Lorry was a relative of the Pinches. She pointed out that Mr. Voigt was never given any specific reason other than that the company was having problems and he would have to go. One of the factors argued as playing a part in the decision to let Mr. Voigt go was that he had no dependants; however, the evidence was conflicting as to who suggested that first, that is whether Mr. Voigt or Thomas Pinch brought it up. She argued that it did not seem credible that Mr. Voigt be given one reason at the time he was laid off and that no mention was made of the alleged slowness or inefficiency at that time. She pointed out that Mr. Voigt had not been criticized for the way he did his work. In regard to the evidence relating to whether Mr. Voigt was thinking of retiring, she pointed out that retirement was never discussed with Mr. Voigt by the Pinches and that further, simply by considering that Mr. Voigt might wish to retire, age must be a factor being considered in the minds of the company's owners. She suggested that since allegations were made that Mr. Voigt would not change his work habits, therefore, age again must be a factor in the decision.

Mr. Kelleher, on the other hand, argued that the company was in obvious financial difficulty and that someone had to be laid off. He pointed out that the decision was a very unpleasant one to make and was delayed for some weeks and months, and that Thomas Pinch had dealt with Mr. Voigt in the best way possible in the circumstances. He denied that there was any evidence to suggest that age was a factor and argued that the owners of the company assessed all of the bakers and determined that Mr. Voigt would be the easiest to fill in for since he could not do all of the work of the other bakers and was slow in his work. He further suggested that in an industry such as a bakery where the work is more of an art than a science, it would be unthinkable to lay off a competent, experienced baker. He suggested that in a case such as that, the older a baker was the more experienced he would be and the better quality of the bakery product likely to result. He compared an older, experienced baker to that of a lawyer, doctor or accountant whose skills in his particular field develop with age and experience. In Mr. Voigt's case, he argued that Mr. Voigt did not possess the particular skills that come with experience and that Mr. Voigt could not move into other job areas that were available in the company. He suggested that the company did not have a history of abusing its employees, that to the contrary, some employees had "been carried" and that the company was too soft in its hiring and firing practices. He also pointed out that no one was hired to replace Mr. Voigt after he was laid off. . . .

In the case at hand, before I can find in favour of the complainant I must be satisfied that the evidence before me leads me to the conclusion that it was "more probable than not" that one of the reasons Mr. Voigt was dismissed from his employment was because of his age, contrary to the Act.

In my opinion, age need not be the sole determining factor so long as it was one of the factors in the decision to refuse to continue to employ. . . .

Applying the above test as to the degree of evidence necessary and recognizing that age, even if a minor factor, can support a claim of discrimination, I am not satisfied on the evidence that the Maypole Bakery discriminated against Mr. Voigt because of his age contrary to Section 11B (1)(a) of the Human Rights Act. I find that the company, prior to laying off Mr. Voigt, was in financial difficulty and that some person or persons had to be let go. A review of bakery employees was made. It was concluded that Mr. Voigt's work could be done by other employees and that Mr. Voigt could not perform the duties of other bakery employees. He was told that business was bad and that he had been chosen as the one to be laid off.

While he was not told at that time that part of the reasons for choosing him was because he was considered slow or could not perform all of the functions of other bakers, this fact alone does not lead me to conclude that age was a factor. I accept Mr. Kelleher's argument that the company "carried people" and that that was part of the reason for the financial problems which led the company to be in the financial shape it found itself [sic].

Further, it seems to me highly improbable that in a small bakery such as this, an experienced man would be let go if he could perform all of the functions of a good baker. In such a business, it seems to me that an older and more experienced baker would be highly valuable and beneficial in perfecting the baking art, and such a baker regardless of age would be the last one to be laid off.

If Mr. Voigt had possessed all of the talents of such a baker, the first persons to be looked at would be those who had less experience and skill in determining who would be laid off.

While I have deep sympathy for Mr. Voigt's unfortunate position, the question put to me was whether he was discriminated against because of his age contrary to the Human Rights Act. In the result, I find that he was not.

\* \* \*

## *Proposed Dutch Code on Job Discrimination, with Paper-Organizing Game*

Should other grounds of discrimination besides age be added to the prohibited list? *The Financial Post* reported in 1980 that Dutch authorities were considering a draft code prohibiting job discrimination on any of the following grounds: "Age, sex, civil status, sexual disposition, distinguishing marks or scars, psychiatric history, medical history, nationality, race or color, social or regional background, criminal history, police records, religion, political or any other outlook on life, trade union membership or membership of any other organization, or for being out of work."

In response to this far-reaching suggestion, I supply a Paper-Organizing Game, in three stages, designed to produce a paper on the following topic:

*Select one of the grounds of discrimination in the proposed Dutch code not yet familiar in legislation on human rights and assess the case for including it. The case that is to be assessed should make the most both of justice and of the consideration of decent lives and happiness.*

STAGE ONE
Consider the following argument: "Distinguishing marks and scars should not be grounds for refusing people jobs and promotions, because no matter what marks and scars people have justice requires that they be treated on an equal footing with others, and their chances of decent lives and of happiness will be increased if they get jobs and promotions on an equal footing."
1. Is this true?
2. Can it be true and yet not convincing?
3. Does it need to be amended to bring out what sorts of reasons people might have for treating marks and scars as grounds for discrimination?
   (a) What sorts of jobs might be involved?
   (b) In some of them might not there be good reasons to discriminate?
   (c) In others might there be clearly no good reasons?
   (d) Would not other cases be borderline?

4. Does the argument given need to be amended to show how justice comes to bear against 3(c) or 3(d), perhaps leaving 3(b) as a sphere of exceptions?
   (a) What does justice have to do with equality?
   (b) Does justice override the claims of private property—the employer's right to do as he or she wishes with his or her property?
5. Does the argument need to be amended to show how the consideration of decent lives and happiness comes to bear against 3(c) and 3(d), and yet may leave out 3(b) as a sphere of exceptions?
   (a) Just how are jobs and promotions important to decent lives and happiness?
   (b) If the importance just has to do with desires, how can there be any exceptions for jobs that in fact people with marks and scars desire?

STAGE TWO: PAPER ORGANIZING GAME—JOB DISCRIMINATION
In discussion, form a plan for arranging the following questions and statements—here scrambled—in an order suitable to serve as a model for your paper.

1. Will people count themselves as full members of a society if they are not treated justly?

2. Justice allows—indeed, requires—that people be treated differently when there are relevant differences between them.

3. Even if people are kept alive without jobs, they are likely to live more poorly and their self-respect is undermined along with their sense of participation.

4. Getting the job done and having its benefits as a contribution to people's lives may outweigh heeding the desires of people who cannot perform so well.

5. People's marks and scars do affect their performance in some jobs: for example, models, actors and actresses.

6. People's marks and scars may make other people uneasy. Would jobs as receptionists or as salesclerks be suitable?

7. People cannot live if they do not have jobs and if they must have jobs to have livelihoods.

8. People's marks and scars do not affect their performance in many jobs: for example, machine operators, file-clerks.

9. What does justice require when there are no relevant differences between people?

10. Private property sometimes implies a power to give or refuse employment and promotions. This is necessarily an unequal power, which may be regulated in the interests of justice.

STAGE THREE
Write your own paper, on the model arrived at in Stage Two, but on some ground of discrimination other than marks and scars.

# UNITED STEELWORKERS OF AMERICA, AFL-CIO, v. WEBER ET AL.

*[The cases brought up so far touch on hiring and firing; none has touched on promotion. Perhaps this does not matter, since discrimination with respect to promotion raises much the same issues as discrimination on the other points. Yet it is important to recognize that the objections to discrimination—and the laws against it—cover many different aspects of the employment relationship. Weber, whose case we are about to consider, claimed discrimination with respect to opportunities to be trained in higher skills. The case touches implicitly on wages and promotion also.]*

*Supreme Court of the United States, 1979*

Mr. Justice BRENNAN delivered the opinion of the Court.

Challenged here is the legality of an affirmative action plan—collectively bargained by an employer and a union—that reserves for black employees 50 percent of the openings in an in-plant craft training program until the percentage of black craft workers in the plant is commensurate with the percentage of blacks in the local labor force. The question for decision is whether Congress, in Title VII of the Civil Rights Act of 1964 as amended, . . . left employers and unions in the private sector free to take such race-conscious steps to eliminate manifest racial imbalances in traditionally segregated job categories. We hold that Title VII does not prohibit such race-conscious affirmative action plans.

I

In 1974 petitioner United Steelworkers of America (USWA) and petitioners Kaiser Aluminum & Chemical Corporation (Kaiser) entered into a master collective-bargaining agreement covering terms and conditions of employment at 15 Kaiser plants. The agreement contained, *inter alia*, an affirmative action plan designed to eliminate conspicuous racial imbalances in Kaiser's then almost exclusively white, craft work forces. Black craft hiring goals were set for each Kaiser plant equal to the percentage of blacks in the respective local labor forces. To enable plants to meet these goals, on-the-job training programs were established to teach unskilled production workers—black and white—the skills necessary to become craft workers. The plan reserved for black employees 50 percent of the openings in these newly created in-plant training programs.

[1]This case arose from the operation of the plan at Kaiser's plant in Gramercy, La. Until 1974 Kaiser hired as craft workers for that plant only persons who had had prior craft experience. Because blacks had long been

excluded from craft unions, few were able to present such credentials. As a consequence, prior to 1974 only 1.83 percent (5 out of 273) of the skilled craft workers at the Gramercy plant were black, even though the work force in the Gramercy area was approximately 30 percent black.

Pursuant to the national agreement Kaiser altered its craft hiring practice in the Gramercy plant. Rather than hiring already trained outsiders, Kaiser established a training program to train its production workers to fill craft openings. Selection of craft trainees was made on the basis of seniority, with the proviso that at least 50 percent of the new trainees were to be black until the percentage of black skilled craft workers in the Gramercy plant approximated the percentage of blacks in the local labor force. . . .

During 1974, the first year of the operation of the Kaiser-USWA affirmative action plan, 13 craft trainees were selected from Gramercy's production work force. Of these, seven were black and six white. The most junior black selected into the program had less seniority than several white production workers whose bids for admission were rejected. Thereafter, one of those white production workers, respondent Brian Weber, instituted this class action in the United States District Court for the Eastern District of Louisiana.

The complaint alleged that the filling of craft trainee positions at the Gramercy plant pursuant to the affirmative action program had resulted in junior black employees receiving training in preference to more senior white employees, thus discriminating against respondent and other similarly situated white employees. . . . The District Court . . . entered a judgment in favor of the plaintiff class, and granted a permanent injunction prohibiting Kaiser and the USWA "from denying plaintiffs, Brian F. Weber and all other members of the class, access to on-the-job training programs on the basis of race." . . . A divided panel of the Court of Appeals for the Fifth Circuit affirmed, holding that all employment preferences based upon race, including those preferences incidental to bona fide affirmative action plans, violated Title VII's prohibition against racial discrimination in employment. . . .

## II

We emphasize at the outset the narrowness of our inquiry. Since the Kaiser—USWA plan does not involve state action, this case does not present an alleged violation of the Equal Protection Clause of the Constitution. Further, since the Kaiser-USWA plan was adopted voluntarily, we are not concerned with what Title VII requires or with what a court might order to remedy a past proven violation of the Act. The only question before us is the narrow statutory issue of whether Title VII *forbids* private employers and unions from voluntarily agreeing upon bona fide affirmative action plans that accord racial preferences in the manner and for the purpose provided in the Kaiser-USWA plan. . . .

Respondent argues that Congress intended in Title VII to prohibit all race-conscious affirmative action plans. Respondent's argument rests upon a literal interpretation of §§ 702(a) and (d) of the Act. Those sections make it unlawful to "discriminate . . . because of . . . race" in hiring and in the selection of apprentices for training programs. Since, the argument runs, *McDonald* v. *Sante Fe Trail Trans. Co.,* . . . settled that Title VII forbids discrimination against whites as well as blacks, and since the Kaiser-USWA affirmative action plan operates to discriminate against white employees solely because they are white, it follows that the Kaiser-USWA plan violates Title VII.

[2,3] Respondent's argument is not without force. But it overlooks the significance of the fact that the Kaiser-USWA plan is an affirmative action plan voluntarily adopted by private parties to eliminate traditional patterns of racial segregation. In this context respondent's reliance upon a literal construction of § 703(a) and (d) and upon *McDonald* is misplaced. . . . It is a "familiar rule that a thing may be within the letter of the statute and yet not within the statute, because not within its spirit nor within the intention of its makers." . . . The prohibition against racial discrimination in Title VII must therefore be read against the background of the legislative history of Title VII and the historical context from which the Act arose. . . . Examination of those sources makes clear that an interpretation of the sections that forbade all race-conscious affirmative action would "bring about an end completely at variance with the purpose of the statute" and must be rejected. . . .

[4] Congress's primary concern in enacting the prohibition against racial discrimination in Title VII of the Civil Rights Act of 1964 was with "the plight of the Negro in our economy." . . . Before 1964, blacks were largely relegated to "unskilled and semi-skilled jobs." . . . Because of automation the number of such jobs was rapidly decreasing. . . . As a consequence "the relative position of the Negro worker [was] steadily worsening. In 1947 the non-white unemployment rate was only 64 percent higher than the white rate; in 1962 it was 124 percent higher." . . . Congress considered this a serious social problem. As Senator Clark told the Senate:

> The rate of Negro unemployment has gone up consistently as compared with white unemployment for the past 15 years. This is a social malaise and a social situation which we should not tolerate. That is one of the principal reasons why this bill should pass.

Congress feared that the goals of the Civil Rights Act—the integration of blacks into the mainstream of American society—could not be achieved unless this trend were reversed. And Congress recognized that that would not be possible unless blacks were able to secure jobs "which have a future." . . . As Senator Humphrey explained to the Senate:

> What good does it do a Negro to be able to eat in a fine restaurant if he cannot afford to pay the bill? What good does it do him to be accepted in a hotel that is too expensive for his modest income? How can a Negro child be motivated to take full advantage of integrated educational facilities if he has no hope of getting a job where he can use that education?
> Without a job, one cannot afford public convenience and accommodations. Income from employment may be necessary to further a man's education, or that of his children. If his children have no hope of getting a good job, what will motivate them to take advantage of educational opportunities.

These remarks echoed President Kennedy's original message to Congress upon the introduction of the Civil Rights Act in 1963: "There is little value in a Negro's obtaining the right to be admitted to hotels and restaurants if he has no cash in his pocket and no job." Accordingly, it was clear to Congress that "the crux of the problem [was] to open employment opportunities for Negros in occupations which have been traditionally closed to them," . . . (Sen. Humphrey), and it was to this problem that Title VII's prohibition against racial discrimination in employment was primarily addressed.

It plainly appears from the House Report accompanying the Civil Rights Act that Congress did not intend wholly to prohibit private and voluntary affirmative action efforts as one method of solving this problem. The Report provides:

> No bill can or should lay claim to eliminating all of the causes and conse-quences of racial and other types of discrimination against minorities. There is reason to believe, however, that national leadership provided by the enactment of Federal legislation dealing with the most troublesome problems *will create an atmosphere conducive to voluntary or local resolution of other forms of discrimination.* (Emphasis supplied.)

Given this legislative history, we cannot agree with respondent that Congress intended to prohibit the private sector from taking effective steps to accomplish the goal that Congress designed Title VII to achieve. The very statutory words intended as a spur or catalyst to cause "employers and unions to self-examine and to self-evaluate their employment practices and to endeavor to eliminate, so far as possible, the last vestiges of an unfortu-nate and ignominious page in this country's history," *Albemarle v. Moody*, . . . U.S. . . . S.Ct. . . . (1975), cannot be interpreted as an absolute prohibi-tion against all private, voluntary, race-conscious affirmative action efforts to hasten the elimination of such vestiges. It would be ironic indeed if a law triggered by a Nation's concern over centuries of racial injustice and intended to improve the lot of those who had "been excluded from the American dream for so long," 110 Cong. Rec., at 6552 (remarks of Sen. Humphrey), constituted the first legislative prohibition of all voluntary, private, race-conscious efforts to abolish traditional patterns of racial segre-gation and hierarchy.

Our conclusion is further reinforced by examination of the language and legislative history of § 703(j) of Title VII. Opponents of Title VII raised two related arguments against the bill. First, they argued that the Act would be interpreted to *require* employers with racially imbalanced work forces to grant preferential treatment to racial minorities in order to integrate. Sec-ond, they argued that employers with racially imbalanced work forces would grant preferential treatment to racial minorities, even if not required to do so by the Act. . . . Had Congress meant to prohibit all race-conscious affirmative action, as respondent urges, it easily could have answered both objections by providing that Title VII would not require or permit racially preferential integration efforts. But Congress did not choose such a course. Rather Congress added § 703(j) which addresses only the first objection. The section provides that nothing contained in Title VII "shall be interpreted to *require* any employer . to grant preferential treatment . . . to any group because of the race . . . of such . . . group on account of" a de facto racial imbalance in the employer's work force. The section does *not* state that "nothing in Title VII shall be interpreted to *permit*" voluntary affirmative efforts to correct recial imbalances. The natural inference is that Congress chose not to forbid all voluntary race-conscious affirmative action.

[5] The reasons for this choice are evident from the legislative record. Title VII could not have been enacted into law without substantial support from legislators in both Houses who traditionally resisted federal regulation of private business. Those legislators demanded as a price for their support that "management perogatives and union freedoms . . be left undisturbed to the greatest extent possible." . . Section 703(j) was proposed by Senator Dirksen to allay any fears that the Act might be interpreted in such a way as to upset this compromise. The section was designed to prevent § 703 of Title VII from being interpreted in such a way as to lead to undue "Federal Government interference with private businesses because of some Federal employee's ideas about racial balance or imbalance." . . . Clearly, a prohibition against all voluntary, race-conscious, affirmative action efforts would disserve these ends. Such a prohibition would augment the powers of the Federal Government and diminish traditional management prerogatives while at the same time impeding attainment of the ultimate statutory goals. In view of this legislative history and in view of Congress' desire to avoid undue federal regulation of private businesses, use of the world "require" rather than the phrase "require or permit" in § 703(j) fortifies the conclusion that Congress did not intend to limit traditional business freedom to such a degree as to prohibit all voluntary, race-conscious affirmative action.

[6] We therefore hold that Title VII's prohibition in §§ 703(a) and (d) against racial discrimination does not condemn all private, voluntary, race-conscious affirmative action plans.

## III

[7] We need not today define in detail the line of demarcation between permissible and impermissible affirmative action plans. It suffices to hold that the challenged Kaiser-USWA affirmative action plans falls on the permissible side of the line. The purposes of the plan mirror those of the statute. Both were designed to break down old patterns of racial segregation and hierarchy. Both were structured to "open employment opportunities for Negroes in occupations which have been traditionally closed to them." . . . (Sen. Humphrey).

At the same time the plan does not unnecessarily trammel the interests of the white employees. The plan does not require the discharge of white workers and their replacement with new black hires. . . . Nor does the plan create an absolute bar to the advancement of white employees; half of those trained in the program will be white. Moreover, the plan is a temporary measure; it is not intended to maintain racial balance, but simply to eliminate a manifest racial imbalance. Preferential selection of craft trainees at the Gramercy plant will end as soon as the percentage of black skilled craft workers in the Gramercy plant approximates the percentage of blacks in the local labor force. . . .

We conclude, therefore, that the adoption of the Kaiser-USWA plan for the Gramercy plant falls within the area of discretion left by Title VII to the private sector voluntarily to adopt affirmative action plans designed to eliminate conspicuous racial imbalance in traditionally segregated job categories. Accordingly, the judgment of the Court of Appeals for the Fifth Circuit is

*Reversed.* . . .

Mr. Justice REHNQUIST, with whom THE CHIEF JUSTICE joins, dissenting.

In a very real sense, the Court's opinion is ahead of its time: it could more appropriately have been handed down five years from now, in 1984, a year coinciding with the title of a book from which the Court's opinion borrows, perhaps subconsciously, at least one idea. Orwell describes in his book a governmental official of Oceania, one of the three great world powers, denouncing the current enemy, Eurasia, to an assembled crowd:

> It was almost impossible to listen to him without being first convinced and then maddened. . . . The speech had been proceeding for perhaps twenty minutes when a messenger hurried onto the platform and a scrap of paper was slipped into the speaker's hand. He unrolled and read it without pausing in his speech. Nothing altered in his voice or manner, or in the content of what he was saying, but suddenly the names were different. Without words said, a wave of understanding rippled through the crowd. Oceania was at war with Eastasia! . . . The banners and posters with which the square was decorated were all wrong!
>
> [ [T]he speaker had switched from one line to the other actually in mid-sentence, not only without a pause, but without even breaking the syntax.] G. Orwell, Nineteen Eighty-Four, 182-183 (1940)

Today's decision represents an equally dramatic and equally unremarked switch in this Court's interpretation of Title VII.

The operative sections of Title VII prohibit racial discrimination in employment *simpliciter*. Taken in its normal meaning and as understood by all Members of Congress who spoke to the issue during the legislative debates, . . . this language prohibits a covered employer from considering race when making an employment decision, whether the race be black or white. Several years ago, however, a United States District Court held that "the dismissal of white employees charged with misappropriating company property while not dismissing a similarly charged Negro employee does not raise a claim upon which Title VII relief may be granted." *McDonald v. Santa Fe Trail Transp. Co.,* . . . This Court unanimously reversed, concluding from the "uncontradicted legislative history" that "[T]itle VII prohibits racial discrimination against the white petitioners in this case upon the same standards as would be applicable were they Negroes . . " . . .

We have never waivered in our understanding that Title VII "prohibits *all* racial discrimination in employment, without exception for any particular employees." . . . In *Griggs v. Duke Power Co.,* . . . (1971), our first occasion to interpret Title VII, a unanimous court observed that "[d]iscriminatory preference, for any group, minority or majority, is precisely and only what Congress has proscribed." And in our most recent discussion of the issue, we uttered words seemingly dispositive of this case: "It is clear beyond cavil that the obligation imposed by Title VII is to provide an equal opportunity for *each* applicant regardless of race, without regard to whether members of the applicant's race are already proportionately represented in the work force." *Furnco Construction Corp. v. Waters*, . . . (1978) . . .

Today, however, the Court behaves much like the Orwellian speaker earlier described, as if it had been handed a note indicating that Title VII would lead to a result unacceptable to the Court if interpreted here as it was in our prior decisions. Accordingly, without even a break in syntax, the Court rejects "a literal construction of § 703(a)" in favor of newly discovered "legislative history," which leads it to a conclusion directly contrary to that compelled by the "uncontradicted legislative history" unearthed in *McDonald* and our other prior decisions. Now we are told that the legislative history of Title VII shows that employers are free to discriminate on the basis of race: an employer may, in the Court's words, "trammel the interests of white employees" in favor of black employees in order to eliminate "racial imbalance." . . . Our earlier interpretations of Title VII, like the banners and posters decorating the square in Oceania, were all wrong.

As if this were not enough to make a reasonable observer question this court's adherence to the oft-stated principle that our duty is to construe rather than rewrite legislation, . . . the Court also seizes upon § 703(j) of Title VII as an independent, or at least partially independent, basis for its holding. Totally ignoring the wording of that section, which is obviously addressed to those charged with the responsibility of interpreting the law rather than those who are subject to its proscriptions, and totally ignoring the months of legislative debates preceding the section's introduction and passage, which demonstrate clearly that it was enacted to prevent precisely what occurred in this case, the Court infers from § 703(j) that "Congress chose not to forbid all voluntary race-conscious affirmative action." . . .

Thus, by a *tour de force* reminiscent not of jurists such as Hale, Holmes, and Hughes, but of escape artists such as Houdini, the Court eludes clear statutory language, "uncontradicted" legislative history and uniform precedent in concluding that employers are, after all, permitted to consider race in making employment decisions. It may be that one or more of the principal sponsors of Title VII would have preferred to see a provision allowing preferential treatment of minorities written into the bill. Such a provision, however, would have to have been expressly or impliedly excepted from Title VII's explicit prohibition on all racial discrimination in employment. There is no such exception in the Act. And a reading of the legislative debates concerning Title VII, in which proponents and opponents alike uniformly denounced discrimination in favor of, as well as discrimination against, Negroes, demonstrates clearly that any legislator harboring an unspoken desire for such a provision could not possibly have succeeded in enacting it into law. . .

Were Congress to act today specifically to prohibit the type of racial discrimination suffered by Weber, it would be hard pressed to draft language better tailored to the task than that found in § 703(d) of Title VII:

> It shall be an unlawful employment practice for any employer, labor organization, or joint labor-management committee controlling apprenticeship or other training or retraining, including on-the-job training programs to discriminate against any individual because of his race, color, religion, sex, or national origin in admission to, or employment in, any program established to provide apprenticeship or other training.

Equally suited to the task would be § 703(a)(2), which makes it unlawful for an employer to classify his employees "in any way which would deprive or tend to deprive any individual of employment opportunities or otherwise adversely affect his status as an employee, because of such individual's race, color, religion, sex, or national origin." . . .

Entirely consistent with these two express prohibitions is the language of § 703(j) of Title VII, which provides that the Act is not to be interpreted "to require any employer . . . to grant preferential treatment to any individual or to any individual or to any group because of the race . . of such individual or group" to correct a racial imbalance in the employer's work force. 42 U.S.C. § 2000c-2(j). Seizing on the word "require," the Court infers that Congress must have intended to "permit" this type of racial discrimination. Not only is this reading of § 703(j) outlandish in the light of flat prohibitions of §§ 703(a) and (d), but, as explained Part III, it is totally belied by the Act's legislative history.

Quite simply, Kaiser's racially discriminatory admission quota is flatly prohibited by the plain language of Title VII. This normally dispositive fact, however, gives the Court only momentary pause. An "interpretation" of the statute upholding Weber's claim would, according to the Court, " 'bring about an end completely at variance with the purpose of the statute.' " . . . To support this conclusion, the Court calls upon the "spirit" of the Act, which it divines from passages in Title VII's legislative history indicating that enactment of the statute was prompted by Congress' desire "to open employment opportunities for Negroes in occupations which [had] been traditionally closed to them." . . . But the legislative history invoked by the Court to avoid the plain language of §§ 703(a) and (d) simply misses the point. To be sure, the reality of employment discrimination against Negroes provided the primary impetus for passage of Title VII. But this fact by no means supports the proposition that Congress intended to leave employers free to discriminate against white persons. In most cases, "[l]egislative history . . is more vague than the statute we are called upon to interpret." *United States v. Public Utilities Comm'n*, . . . (Jackson, J., concurring). Here, however, the legislative history of Title VII is as clear the language of §§ 703(a) and (d), and it irrefutably demonstrates that Congress meant precisely what it said in §§ 703(a) and (d)—that *no* racial discrimination in employment is permissible under Title VII, not even preferential treatment of minorities to correct racial imbalance. . . .

Contrary to the Court's analysis, the language of § 703(j) is precisely tailored to the objection voiced time and again by Title VII's opponents. Not once during the 83 days of debate in the Senate did a speaker, proponent or opponent, suggest that the bill would allow employers *voluntarily* to prefer racial minorities over white persons. In light of Title VII's flat prohibition on discrimination "against any individual . . . because of such individual's race," . . . such a contention would have been, in any event, too preposterous to warrant response. Indeed, speakers on both sides of the issue, as the legislative history makes clear, recognized that Title VII would tolerate no *voluntary* racial preference, whether in favor of blacks or whites. The complaint consistently voiced by the opponents was that Title VII, particularly the word "discrimination," would be *interpreted* by federal agencies such as the Equal Employment Opportunity Commission to *require* the correction of racial imbalance through the granting of preferential treatment to minorities. Verbal assurances that Title VII would not require—indeed, would not permit—preferential treatment of blacks having failed, supporters of H.R. 7152 responded by proposing an amendment carefully worded to meet, and put to rest, the opposition's charge. Indeed, unlike §§ 703(a) and (d), which are by their terms directed at entities—*e.g.;* employers, labor unions—whose actions are restricted by Title VII's prohibitions, the language of § 703(j) is specifically directed at entities—federal agencies and courts—charged with the responsibility of interpreting Title VII's provisions.

In light of the background and purpose of §703(j), the irony of invoking the section to justify the result in this case is obvious. The Court's frequent references to the "voluntary" nature of Kaiser's racially discriminatory admission quota bear no relationship to the facts of this case. Kaiser and the Steelworkers acted under pressure from an agency of the Federal Government, the Office of Federal Contract Compliance, which found that minorities were being "underutilized" at Kaiser's plants. . . . That is, Kaiser's work force was racially imbalanced. Bowing to that pressure, Kaiser instituted an admissions quota preferring blacks over whites, thus confirming that the fears of Title VII's opponents were well founded. Today § 703(j), adopted to allay those fears, is invoked by the Court to uphold imposition of a racial quota under the very circumstances that the section was intended to prevent. . . .

Our task in this case, like any case involving the construction of a statute, is to give effect to the intent of Congress. To divine that intent, we traditionally look first to the words of the statute and, if they are unclear, then to the statute's legislative history. Finding the desired result hopelessly foreclosed by these conventional sources, the Court turns to a third source—the "spirit" of the Act. But close examination of what the Court proffers as the spirit of the Act reveals it as the spirit animating the present majority, not the Eighty-eighth Congress. For if the spirit of the act eludes the cold words of the statute itself, it rings out with unmistakable clarity in the words of the elected representatives who made the Act law. It is *equality.* Senator Dirksen, I think, captured that spirit in a speech delivered on the floor of the Senate just moments before the bill was passed:

[T]oday we come to grips finally with a bill that advances the enjoyment of living; but, more than that, it advances the equality of opportunity.

I do not emphasize the word 'equality' standing by itself. It means equality of opportunity in the field of education. It means equality of opportunity in the field of employment. It means equality of opportunity in the field of participation in the affairs of government. . . .

That is it.

Equality of opportunity, if we are going to talk about conscience, is the mass conscience of mankind that speaks in every generation, and it will continue to speak long after we are dead and gone.
110 Cong.Rec. 14510 (1964).

There is perhaps no device more destructive to the notion of equality than the *numerus clausus*—the quota. Whether described as "benign discrimination" or "affirmative action," the racial quota is nonetheless a creator of castes, a two-edged sword that must demean one in order to prefer another. In passing Title VII Congress outlawed *all* racial discrimination, recognizing that no discrimination based on race is benign, that no action disadvantaging a person because of his color is affirmative. With today's holding, the Court introduces into Title VII a tolerance for the very evil that the law was intended to eradicate, without offering even a clue as to what the limits on that tolerance may be. We are told simply that Kaiser's racially discriminatory admission quota "falls on the permissible side of the line." . . . By going not merely *beyond*, but directly *against* Title VII's language and legislative history, the Court has sown the wind. Later courts will face the impossible task of reaping the whirlwind.

*       *       *

# CHAPTER 9

# *Sexual Harassment*

---

*Introductory Comment.*

## THE RANGE AND SIGNIFICANCE OF HARASSMENT

---

Sexual harassment need not be treated as a form of sex discrimination to be both morally and legally objectionable. However, both in the United States and Canada, it has been proceeded against under human rights legislation. So the cases that follow can be looked upon as further illustrations of practices of discrimination. They can also be looked upon as advance installments of matters to come in the next chapter—interference with employees' lives outside business. For in sexual harassment, when it is (as it all too often is) carried to the point of an employer's or a supervisor's demanding sexual favors after work, the power of the employer is intruding into the employee's private life.

Nevertheless, there are reasons to give sexual harassment a chapter of its own. For one thing, a lot of it is not carried to the point of propositioning. A lot of it consists of jokes, pranks, suggestive language, and innuendo, which women (the usual victims) object to as distracting and demeaning. Such harassment may not threaten the victims' jobs (not even all propositioning does that). It may not intrude directly into their lives away from work, either. However, it diminishes the dignity of people's work, and consequently the dignity of their lives as wholes. In all its forms, sexual harassment illustrates, perhaps more vividly than any other issue, the difficulties of reconciling people's aims in life with their having to spend a good part of their lives at work under the power of employers. That is another reason for taking up sexual harassment under a separate heading.

Men and women who meet at work will often be sexually attracted to one another and impelled to make overtures. That is part of what life is about, on the job or off it. Yet sexual harassment is not to be dismissed as a matter of "personal" incidents, unauthorized conduct of one employee with another, arising inevitably from "natural" impulses. Catharine A. MacKinnon, in a vigorously argued passage of her book *Sexual Harassment of Working Women* (New Haven: Yale University Press, 1979, p. 83), cautions:

> Beyond moralizing, the near-universal response of authoritative men—employers and husbands, referees and judges—to women's complaints of sexual harassment is to consider them "personal" incidents, "natural" expressions, or both. Perhaps the purpose, and certainly the effect, of these labels is to remove the events from the social or political arena, hence from scrutiny, criticism, and regulation by legal intervention. To call something personal is to make it too small, too unique, too infinitely varied, and too private to be considered appropriately addressed by law, which is thought to deal in public, social, structural generalities. Similarly, but at the other end of the scale, to call something natural or biological (the two are used interchangeably) is to render it too big, too immutable, too invariant, too universal and, thus, too presocial to be within the law's reach. These terms at once monumentalize and trivialize sexual harassment, simultaneously making change seem impossible, unimportant, and undesirable. Both characterizations, while rationalizing legal noninvolvement, make sexual harassment socially and culturally *permissible* by locating its determinants beyond the social and cultural sphere.

## MONGE v. BEEBE RUBBER COMPANY

*[Here is a case in which objections to sexual harassment are sustained without treating it as sex discrimination. It is (I gather from Catharine MacKinnon's comment on it) too new and unusual to be considered settled law, but that does not detract from its interest, which extends to the general terms of the employment relationship, and simultaneously to illustrating how judges contrive, when they feel the pressure of events, to bring the common law up to date.]*

*Supreme Court of New Hampshire, 1974*

LAMPRON, Justice.

Action . . . to recover damages for an alleged breach of an oral contract of employment. Plaintiff was hired in September 1968 at wages of $1.84 per hour to work on a conversion machine in defendant's factory and was allegedly told that if she worked well she would get better jobs with better pay. Plaintiff claims that she was harassed by her foreman because she refused to go out with him and that his hostility, condoned if not shared by defendant's personnel manager, ultimately resulted in her being fired. Trial by jury resulted in a verdict for the plaintiff in the amount of $2,500. . . .

Plaintiff, before coming to this country in 1964, was a school teacher in Costa Rica. She came to New Hampshire in 1965, and was attending college from 7 to 10 o'clock five nights a week to qualify to teach here. She used the money she earned from her employment with the defendant on the night shift beginning at 11 o'clock for her college expense. She was employed by the defendant in a union shop and joined the union as required after her employment, thereby becoming subject to the seniority and other rules of the union contract. After working without incident on the conversion machine for about three months, she applied to fill an opening on a press machine at higher wages. She testified that her foreman told her that if she wanted the job she would have to be "nice." She got the job at $2.79 per hour and claims that her foreman then asked her to go out with him, which she refused to do because she was married and had three children. After working on the press machine for about three weeks, the machine was shut down and she was put on a degreaser machine at $1.99 per hour. Her overtime was taken away, although no one else's was. She testified that when she told her foreman she needed overtime money he told her she could sweep floors. She agreed to do this and claims the foreman also made her clean the washrooms and ridiculed her.

On July 23, 1969, she ran out of boxes for her machine. When she reported this to the foreman, he told her to make her own, which she claims she could not do while keeping up her production. When she spoke to the union steward about it, the foreman ordered her back to her machine and fired her at 2:00 o'clock in the morning when she refused to comply with his order. After complaining to the union, she was reinstated with a warning.

On Saturday, July 26, she called the personnel manager at his home to tell him that on advice of her lawyer she was calling to say she would not be in on Sunday because of illness. She also called in on Sunday, July 27, to say she would not be able to work because of illness and would enter the hospital the next day. The company's records show her absent with excuse on July 28 through 31.

She testified that when she reported for work at 11:00 p.m. on the night of August 4, the personnel manager was there, although she had never seen him at the plant before at that time of day, and that he asked her "What kind of face I got to come back?" After being at work for two and one-half hours that same night, she was found unconscious in the ladies' room and was taken to the hospital. The company records show her hospitalized for the next four days including August 8. Nothing is shown in these records regarding the next two days but they show her absent on August 11, 12 and 13 without having called in. On August 13, 1969, the personnel manager sent her a letter stating that since she failed to report for work for three consecutive days without notification to the company, she was "deemed a voluntary quit."

There was evidence both from the plaintiff and the foreman that she did in fact call in on Sunday, August 10, to report that she was still sick. There was also evidence that some time after defendant had refused her foreman's advances, the personnel manager had visited her at home about some annoying telephone calls she was receiving. In the course of their conversation, he told her he knew her foreman used his position to force his attentions on the female employees under his authority and he asked her "not to make trouble."

Plaintiff sued for breach of an employment contract for an indefinite period of time. The employer has long ruled the workplace with an iron hand by reason of the prevailing common-law rule that such a hiring is presumed to be at will and terminable at any time by either party. . . . When asked to reexamine the long-standing common-law rule of property based on an ancient feudal system which fostered in a tenancy at will a relationship heavily weighted in favor of the landlord, this court did not hesitate to modify that rule to conform to modern circumstances. . . .

The law governing the relations between employer and employee has similarly evolved over the years to reflect changing legal, social and economic conditions. . . . In this area "[w]e are in the midst of a period in which the pot boils the hardest and in the process of change the fastest." . . . . Although many of these changes have resulted from the activity and influence of labor unions, the courts cannot ignore the new climate prevailing generally in the relationship of employer and employee. . . .

In all employment contracts, whether at will or for a definite term, the employer's interest in running his business as he sees fit must be balanced against the interest of the employee in maintaining his employment, and the public's interest in maintaining a proper balance between the two. . . . We hold that a termination by the employer of a contract of employment at will which is motivated by bad faith or malice or based on retaliation is not the best interest of the economic system or the public good and constitutes a breach of the employment contract. . . . Such a rule affords the employee a certain stability of employment and does not interfere with the employer's normal exercise of his right to discharge, which is necessary to permit him to operate his business efficiently and profitably.

The sole question on appeal is whether there was sufficient evidence to support the jury's finding that defendant, through its agents, acted maliciously in terminating plaintiff's employment. It is the function of the jury to resolve conflicts in the testimony . . . and the law is settled that a jury verdict will not be disturbed on appeal if there is evidence to support it. . . .

The jury could draw the not-so-subtle inference from the evidence before it that the hostility of defendant's foreman and connivance of the personnel manager resulted in the letter of August 13, 1969, and that that letter was in effect a discharge. . . . The foreman's overtures and the capricious firing at 2:00 a.m., the seeming manipulation of job assignments, and the apparent connivance of the personnel manager in this course of events all support the jury's conclusion that the dismissal was maliciously motivated.

In our opinion, however, the verdict includes elements of damage not properly recoverable. The plaintiff lost 20 weeks employment at an average of $70.81 per week. This would account for $1,416.20 of the verdict, leaving $1,083.80 attributable to mental suffering. Such damages are not generally recoverable in a contract action. . . . They could not be found in this case to have resulted from the discharge. Defendant had been having difficulty with her husband and had been receiving annoying telephone calls which upset her. She presented no medical testimony. Although she alleged that her discharge caused her mental suffering, her difficulties all preceded the discharge. We therefore remand the case for a new trial unless the plaintiff consents to a reduction of the verdict by the amount of $1,083.80.

Remanded.

GRIFFITH, J., did not sit; GRIMES, J., dissented; the others concurred.

GRIMES, Justice (dissenting):

In my view, reasonable men could not find for the plaintiff on the evidence in this case even under the new rule of law which the court has fashioned today. The substance of the plaintiff's claim is that she was discharged because she did not accept an invitation of her foreman to go out with him. Although it was denied by the foreman, the jury could find on plaintiff's testimony alone that the invitation was extended. It was a single instance, however, and there is no claim that it was repeated or further pursued. It is not findable that this single refusal was the reason for the termination of plaintiff's employment. There was evidence, and none to the contrary, that it was a shortage of work and her lowest seniority that caused her press machine to be shut down and her loss of overtime. When her machine was shut down, she was given work on a degreasing machine at a higher rate of pay than when she started. When she told the foreman she "needed the money" from the overtime, he offered what from the uncontradicted evidence was the only work available to help her out until her overtime was restored. The only so-called harassment and ridicule claimed amounts to no more than once saying "How do you like my floor boy?" and "My wife wouldn't do that." It is uncontradicted that when she was having trouble with annoying phone calls and needed help, the personnel manager personally went to the police and then to her home to talk with her and her husband; that when she could not pick up her Christmas turkey, the foreman personally delivered two instead of one to her home; and that he also at her request gave her husband, a mechanic, work on his automobile.

Her final termination was in accordance with established company rules and she neither contested the termination nor pursued the grievance procedures under the union contract. She was denied unemployment compensation on the ground that she was a "voluntary quit" and did not appeal that finding.

A finding that this company discharged the plaintiff because she refused her foreman a date eight months before could not reasonably be made and should not be permitted to stand.

Apart from the facts, I cannot subscribe to the broad new unprecedented law laid down in this case. Frampton v. Central Indiana Gas Co., . . . (Ind. 1973), cited for its support was a tort action to recover actual and punitive or exemplary damages for a discharge in retaliation for filing a workmen's compensation claim. The court treated the threat of discharge as a "device" prohibited by the Workmen's Compensation Act to avoid the employer's statutory obligations. The Indiana court stated that it could find no case anywhere to support such an action but held the discharge to be an intentional wrong prohibited by statute and in clear contravention of the public policy. That case, however, is not authority for the court's new contract law. Petermann v. Teamsters Local 396, . . . (Cal. 1959) is also inapposite. There, the court allowed recovery only in order to uphold a public policy against perjury. The protection given by the union contract governing the right to discharge and the grievance procedures therein established remove this plaintiff from that class of employee for which concern is expressed in the law review articles cited by the court. Not a single case has been found which supports the broad rule laid down by the court to support an action for breach of contract in this case. In fact, the law everywhere, uniformly supported by cases is that an employment contract for an indefinite period is one "at will and is terminable at any time by either party" regardless of motive for "good cause, bad cause or no cause" and for "any reason or no reason."

*   *   *

# HEELAN v. JOHNS-MANVILLE CORP.

*[In this important case, sexual harassment is treated as sex discrimination, for reasons set forth in the course of the judgment.]*

*United States District Court, District of Colorado, 1978*

SHERMAN G. FINESILVER, District Judge

In this action under Title VII of the Civil Rights Act of 1964, . . . Mary K. Heelan seeks damages against her former employer, Defendant Johns-Manville Corporation [JM]. She claims that her refusal to have sexual relations with her supervisor, Joseph Consigli, resulted in her employment termination.

Defendant denies any impropriety by Consigli or corporate liability. Defendant contends that plaintiff was terminated for insubordination, lack of application, and general inability to perform at the level required of her position.

We find that JM is guilty of sex discrimination under Title VII, and that the retention of plaintiff's job as a JM project director was conditioned on the acceptance of sexual relations with her supervisor, a company executive.

## FACTS AND CONCLUSIONS

Much of the testimony is conflicting, not only in pivotal areas but in areas of marginal relevance as well. This case is based largely upon the court's view of the credibility of the witnesses, *i.e.* their worthiness of belief.

We have carefully scrutinized all testimony and the circumstances under which each witness has testified, and every matter in evidence which tends to show whether a witness is worthy of belief. For example, we have taken into account each witness' motive and state of mind, strength of memory and demeanor and manner while on the witness stand. We have considered factors which affect the witness' recollection and his or her opportunity to observe and accurately relate to the matters discussed. We have considered whether a witness' testimony has been contradicted, and the bias, prejudice, and interest, if any, of each witness. In addition, we have considered any relation each witness may bear to either side of the case; the manner in which each witness might be affected by a decision in the case; and the extent to which, if at all, each witness is either supported or contradicted by other evidence.

With these factors in mind we find the following as facts and enter our conclusions of law.

I

In 1971, JM, an international corporation, commenced moving its world headquarters from New York to Colorado. The move necessitated temporary offices at Greenwood Plaza near Denver, and ultimately complete construction of a 55 million dollar building and amenities at the Ken Caryl Ranch, Jefferson County, Colorado.

Joseph Consigli of the New York home office, as Director of Facilities Planning, was transferred to Colorado to supervise a team to control and oversee the construction of the Colorado headquarters, obtain temporary office space, and assist relocation of 1500 JM employees and their families to Colorado.

In August 1971, plaintiff was hired by JM as a senior secretary and assigned to Consigli. Her employment with JM continued until May 31, 1974, when she was terminated by Consigli.

The documentary evidence of plaintiff's work performance at JM shows her to be an outstanding employee. All her evaluations rated her consistently excellent. Statements by plaintiff's co-workers also found her to be a good employee and, from their standpoint, no work-related reason existed for her termination. The only person to question plaintiff's competence is her supervisor, and these criticisms do not appear in any of his formal written evaluations, but only in his oral statements and privately maintained notes.

Initially plaintiff's work was typical secretarial work and included assistance in relocation of employees. Her starting salary was $6650 per year. Within a matter of months, plaintiff, under the direction of Consigli, was performing duties best characterized as a facilities planner. Consigli and staff had the responsibility of not only planning the world headquarters but also the interior design of the Greenwood Plaza office. Thus, a major part of her responsibilities involved coordination with the Space Design Group, a New York design firm responsible for the interior work at Greenwood Plaza. Plaintiff's worth was clearly apparent to Consigli and in March 1972 he recommended plaintiff for a "two step" raise, rather than the customary one step advance. The pay recommendation form (Ex. 3) noted that the pay raise was a "special merit increase." Consigli rated plaintiff's work as "excellent" in the following five categories: (1) ability, (2) application, (3) job performance, (4) cooperativeness, and (5) capacity for growth. Because of the unusual two step pay raise Consigli felt constrained to attach a note to the recommendation form indicating his high regard for Mrs. Heelan's excellent employment record.

In November of 1972, plaintiff was promoted at Consigli's recommendation to the position of "associate facilities planner" and her salary increased from $7,500 to $10,000. Her new position carried with it considerable responsibility and attaining the associate position was a major accomplishment. The job description for the associate position provided that it would be filled by a person with a degree, or its equivalent, in architectural design supplemented by courses in business administration and management. Plaintiff had none of these qualifications. Plaintiff's performance in her more responsible position merited a raise in July 1973. The raise came, in part, as a result of her outstanding annual evaluation which was completed on May 23, 1973. The subjective portion of the evaluation indicated that plaintiff performed her duties as JM's "principal contact with design and planning professions and interior contractors . . . very well and exceeded most objectives." Consigli also noted that Mrs. Heelan's "greatest accomplishment and talent" was "[i]n solving problems and adjusting schedules to meet changing job conditions. Her rapport with the design and planning disciplines is a great asset to the company." In the objective portion of the appraisal, Consigli gave plaintiff the highest grades printed on the form.

Soon after the pay raise recommendation, Consigli recommended plaintiff for a JM "A" award. According to a JM President's Bulletin, the "A" award is given to employees

> who, through initiative, ability and wholehearted interest in the Company, perform with unusual merit and show extraordinary accomplishments. . . .
> [¶] Administration of "A" awards requires a high degree of managerial judgment. Selection and approval must be exercised with utmost care. . . .

Plaintiff received her "A" award on June 15, 1973, by letter from the president of JM, Dr. William Goodwin, and a monetary award of $1,000. Another raise to $12,000 followed in November. This raise was the result of a company wide upward adjustment of salary levels and included the following comments: "Mary's application to her work and often on her own initiative, and job performance has been excellent. She has excellent ability and capacity for growth."

In spring of 1973, JM began its construction efforts of the world headquarters at the Ken Caryl Ranch. The Architects' Collaborative [TAC] was selected as the architect; Turner Construction Company [Turner] was the construction manager; and Space Design was chosen to do the interior work. To assist him, Consigli hired Eric Dienstbach as project manager to work with the TAC to coordinate its efforts with the requirements of Turner and JM. Plaintiff, as associate of Facilities Planning, had the responsibility of working with Space Design to coordinate its efforts with the requirement of JM and Turner. In the Fall, plaintiff told Consigli that she felt that although she was doing the same type of work as the department's single project manager, Eric Dienstbach, she was paid less and held the lower title of "associate." Plaintiff claimed that this was a case of sex discrimination. She requested promotion to Project Director. Consigli conferred about plaintiff with his immediate supervisor Francis May, an executive vice president, and Richard Goodwin, then president of JM.

Although Heelan had an excellent performance record, serious reservations were expressed by top management about her attitude which was, at times, stated to be abrasive and arrogant. After several meetings with top management, Consigli recommended plaintiff's promotion to project manager which was approved in February 1974.

## II

Mrs. Heelan articulated specific romantic advances made by Consigli beginning in April 1972, and extending through April 23, 1974, when she was informed of her termination. The sexual advances were occasioned as an integral part of her employment. The initial advances were made in April 1972. Consigli explained that the world headquarters duties would involve substantial travel responsibilities and family sacrifices. Plaintiff indicated her willingness to assume the duties and fulfill travel requirements. During the conversation Consigli put his arm around plaintiff and said that she really did not yet understand the job requirement but that she would in time. Explicit sexual invitations followed in late 1972, and continued on a regular basis through early 1974. All were refused.

In January 1973, Consigli had lunch with Space Design Group's Ronald Phillips. Although they had been discussing business Consigli began to talk about his affection for Mrs. Heelan. Consigli volunteered that he liked plaintiff very much but was not sure that he could have an affair with her as he was married. Phillips was surprised by the conversation and did not respond. Later that month Phillips was again brought into the situation, this time by plaintiff. On January 23, plaintiff, who had not worked with Phillips for over a year, told him that she was distressed about her relationship with Consigli. Plaintiff related that he had offered her an apartment if she would leave her husband and consent to an affair. Phillips apparently told no one about his discussions with Consigli and plaintiff.

During the last few months of her employment Consigli's sexual advances became more frequent, occurring as often as once a week. The final demand came on April 23, 1974. Plaintiff was called into her supervisor's office and told that she was to have an affair or be fired. Plaintiff refused any sexual relations with Consigli and was given notice that May 31, 1974 would be her last day of employment.

The evidence is in conflict as to whether plaintiff was offered another position at JM or extended an offer to return to her former position.

## III

During the months of sexual harassment, plaintiff for the most part kept the matter to herself. On occasion, however, she discussed the matter with Eric Dienstbach, Ronald Phillips, Isabelle Dienstbach, and Francis May. On at least one occasion Consigli mentioned the possibility of an affair to Ronald Phillips.

Although plaintiff repeatedly refused any sexual relationship with Consigli, she did begin an affair with her co-worker, Eric Dienstbach, sometime in September or October. Plaintiff denied the liaison but the evidence contradicts her position. Both Consigli and Isabelle Dienstbach suspected the affair. Consigli asked Mrs. Dienstbach to question her son about the matter. Eric denied having an affair when questioned by his mother. She testified that she did not believe this denial. Of more importance, however, is the fact that during the discussion Eric told his mother that Consigli was pressuring plaintiff to have an affair with him. Mrs. Dienstbach testified that she did not believe this statement either, but nonetheless questioned Consigli. He denied the charge and Mrs. Dienstbach did not pursue the matter. Just when this discussion occurred is in dispute—Eric saying it happened in February or March 1974 while Isabelle recalling the incident to have occurred earlier. Whatever the exact date, this discussion provided notice to top JM management that Consigli might have been making sexual advances toward Mrs. Heelan. It also alerted Consigli to the fact that others knew of those advances. At the earliest, the discussion would have taken place in late 1973 since, according to Eric Dienstbach his affair did not begin until September or October. This time period coincides with the time when, according to Consigli, plaintiff's work product seriously declined.

Some time in December 1973 or January 1974, plaintiff made an appointment to speak with Isabelle Dienstbach. Mrs. Dienstbach had for a long period served as a sounding board for many of the female employees at JM who had work-related problems. At the meeting, plaintiff told Mrs. Dienstbach about Consigli's sexual demands, that they were being made weekly, and that she did not know how to stop the incidents. This meeting was another instance when Isabelle Dienstbach was informed of Consigli's actions. During this period plaintiff again confided in Ronald Phillips of Space Design Group and Eric Dienstbach.

After plaintiff's notice of termination on April 23, she again sought out Isabelle Dienstbach. Plaintiff discussed the termination with her and was told to schedule a meeting with Francis May. Plaintiff met with May at the end of that month. She informed him, as she had informed Isabelle Dienstbach twice before, that Consigli had fired her not because of her work performance but because of her refusal to submit to her supervisor's sexual demands. May suggested that plaintiff discuss the matter with JM's personnel manager. Mrs. Heelan responded that May was the personnel manager's supervisor and that the personnel manager would in all probability not take action unless May ordered it. May agreed and declined to do anything at that time. After the meeting, May telephoned Consigli and asked him about plaintiff's charges. Consigli denied any wrongdoing and the matter was dropped.

CONCLUSIONS OF LAW

The law in this area is of recent vintage. Few trial courts have published pertinent opinions in the Federal Supplement. . . . In addition, only three Courts of Appeals have reviewed this issue. . . .

From these opinions a body of law is developing which, first and most importantly, recognizes that sexual harrassment of female employees is gender-based discrimination which can violate Title VII. . . .

In order to recover on such a claim, however, the plaintiff must allege and establish that submission to the sexual suggestion constituted a term or condition of employment. A cause of action does not arise from an isolated incident or a mere flirtation. These may be more properly characterized as an attempt to establish personal relationships than an endeavor to tie employment to sexual submission. Title VII should not be interpreted as reaching into sexual relationships which may arise during the course of employment, but which do not have a substantial effect on that employment. In general, we would limit Title VII claims in this area, as suggested by one commentator, to "repeated, unwelcome sexual advances" which impact as a term or condition of employment. . .

It is not necessary for a plaintiff to prove a policy or practice of the employer endorsing sexual harassment. . . . To demand that a plaintiff prove a company-directed policy of sexual discrimination is merely to extend a claim for relief with one hand and take it away with the other. In no other area of employment discrimination do the courts require such proof. . . . The employer is responsible for the discriminatory acts of its agents. . . .

Thus, to present a *prima facie* case of sex discrimination by way of sexual harassment, a plaintiff must plead and prove that (1) submission to sexual advances of a supervisor was a term or condition of employment, (2) this fact substantially affected plaintiff's employment, and (3) employees of the opposite sex were not affected in the same way by these actions.

This, however, does not end the inquiry. Under certain circumstances the employer may be relieved from liability. As noted by the court in *Miller v. Bank of America*, supra, where the employer has no knowledge of the discrimination, liability may be avoided if the employer has a policy or history of discouraging sexual harassment of employees by supervisors and the employee has failed to present the matter to a publicized grievance board. If the employer is aware of the situation and rectifies it, the employer may not be held liable for the acts of its agents. . . .

This case can be determined on relatively narrow grounds. It is clear that the repeated sexual demands made on Mrs. Heelan by her supervisor over a two year period developed into a "term or condition" of employment. The facts here do not present a borderline case in which this court must decide whether the acts complained of substantially affected the terms of employment, or were nothing more than a personal flirtation unrelated to plaintiff's job. Here we have the paradigm of the repeated, unwelcome sexual advance. . . .

Nor in this case do we have the problem . . . concerning the liability of the employer for the unknown acts of its supervisor-employee. We have considered and reject JM's argument that plaintiff failed to take advantage of JM's internal grievance procedures. First, the evidence fails to establish the existence of any such procedure and second, during her tenure plaintiff advised top management of her allegations. We find that she did everything within her power to bring her charges to the attention of top management. Here, the employer through its highest officers, knew of the charges of sexual harassment. In JM's organizational scheme Consigli answered to only two people; JM's president William Goodwin and its executive vice president Francis May. May was informed of plaintiff's claims after termination and did nothing more than call the "accused" for verification or denial. More importantly, the administrative assistant to the president had heard charges of impropriety from two sources prior to plaintiff's termination. Her investigation was no more thorough than May's. The depth and scope of these inquiries can hardly satisfy the corporation's obligation under Title VII.

The effect of the Civil Rights Act of 1964, and particularly of Title VII of that Act, has been to impose on employers certain duties which theretofore did not exist. No major employer in this nation can ignore the requirements of equal opportunity in hiring, promotion and general conditions of employment. What little legislative history that exists in the area of sex discrimination has convinced the courts that "Congress intended to strike at the entire spectrum of disparate treatment of men and women resulting from sex stereotypes." . . . This stereotype of the sexually-accommodating secretary is well documented in popular novels, magazine cartoons and the theatre. As we have indicated, Title VII does not concern itself with sexual liaisons among men and women working for the same employer. Title VII does, however, become involved when acceptance of sexual advances is transformed into a condition of continued employment. . . .

Under the facts of this case, the frequent sexual advances by a supervisor do not form the basis of the Title VII violation that we find to exist. Significantly, termination of plaintiff's employment when the advances were rejected is what makes the conduct legally objectionable. Receptivity of repeated sexual advances by a high level supervisor was inescapably a condition of the plaintiff's continued employment. The termination of plaintiff's employment as a retaliatory measure when advances were rejected are [sic] within the purview of Title VII. . . .

Plaintiff is entitled to damages in the form of back pay and lost employments benefits. Appropriate considerations include the difference between the salary plaintiff would have made had she remained in the JM organization and that which she actually made since her departure by way of unemployment compensation, wages, and the like. A determination of the proper amount of damages will be made in a separate order. In addition, plaintiff's attorneys are entitled to an award of reasonable attorneys' fees to be paid by defendant Johns-Manville Corporation.

\*　　\*　　\*

# MARTHA BARDELL AND MINERVA HUNTER v. GEORGE ROUNCEWELL AND THE BLUE LION TAVERN*

*[In this case the charges fail, as they sometimes will. No doubt in many cases where well-founded charges could be laid—perhaps in most—people refrain from laying them to avoid embarrassment or other trouble for themselves.*

*I do not bring the case up because the charges fail, or because it appears to place the burden of proof on the complainant rather than (as in the American case just preceding) on the employer. The issue of which side should bear the burden of proof is worth discussing, but the difference between the American case and the Canadian case on this point may be only apparent. In the American case, the complainant did not have to prove the existence of "a policy or practice of the employer endorsing sexual harassment." In this Canadian case, the complainants have to prove the occurrence of the incidents that they complain of.*

*I bring the case up because the general reasoning clearly recognizes that harassment short of propositioning is objectionable and the case itself gives illustrations (not proven as facts) of such harassment. Some of the remarks allegedly made to Martha Bardell are amusing at first sight, like the purported incident in which Ms. Hunter's behind was slapped. Would such things be so amusing if they happened, not (purportedly) in a restaurant and bar, but in an insurance company office, say, or in a soup cannery? Are they, on second thought, entirely amusing if they happen in a bar?]*

*Ontario Board of Inquiry, 1980*

CHAIRMAN SHIME:

I

In this matter the complainants alleged that the respondent, George Rouncewell, who is an officer and owner of the Blue Lion Tavern, made requests of each of them which they refused and which they believe would not have been made of male employees. In short, they allege that they were sexually harassed and claim that such harassment contravenes the provisions of *The Ontario Human Rights Code* (hereinafter referred to as "The Code"). . . .

*Excerpts from *Canadian Human Rights Reporter*, Vol. I, Decision 32, Pars. 1383–1442, September 20, 1980. Copyright 1980 by Canadian Human Rights Reporter, 224 4th Ave. South, Saskatoon, Saskatchewan, 3T7 5M5. Except for the name of the Chairman, names of persons and firms have been changed throughout.

In my view the purpose of The Code is to establish uniform working conditions for employees and to remove those matters enumerated in Section 4 as relevant considerations in the work place. Consideration of matters such as "race, creed, colour, age, sex, marital status, nationality or place of origin" strikes at what the preamble of The Code refers to "the foundation of freedom, justice and peace", and infringes on the "freedom and equality in dignity and rights" which this province and this society revere as commonly held values and have enshrined those in The Code. Thus, The Code prohibits these values from becoming negative factors in the employment relationship.

Subject to the exception provided in Section 4(6), discrimination based on sex is prohibited by The Code. Thus, the paying of a female person less than a male person for the same job is prohibited, or dismissing an employee on the basis of sex is also prohibited. But what about sexual harassment? Clearly a person who is disadvantaged because of her sex is being discriminated against in her employment when employer conduct denies her financial rewards because of her sex, or exacts some form of sexual compliance to improve or maintain her existing benefits.* *The evil to be remedied is the utilization of economic power or authority so as to restrict a woman's guaranteed and equal access to the work-place, and all of its benefits, free from extraneous pressures having to do with the mere fact that she is a woman.* Where a woman's equal access is denied or when terms and conditions differ when compared to male employees, the woman is being discriminated against.

*The forms of prohibited conduct that, in my view, are discriminatory run the gamut from overt gender based activity, such as coerced intercourse to unsolicited physical contact to persistent propositions to more subtle conduct such as gender based insults and taunting, which may reasonably be perceived to create a negative psychological and emotional work environment. There is no reason why the law, which reaches into the workplace so as to protect the work environment from physical or chemical pollution or extremes of temperature, ought not to protect employees as well from negative, psychological and mental effects where adverse and gender directed conduct emanating from a management hierarchy may reasonably be construed to be a condition of employment.*

The prohibition of such conduct is not without its dangers. One must be cautious that the law not inhibit normal social contact between management and employees or normal discussion between management and employees. It is not abnormal, nor should it be prohibited, activity for a supervisor to become socially involved with an employee. *An invitation to dinner is not an invitation to a complaint. The danger or the evil that is to be avoided is coerced or compelled social contact where the employee's refusal to participate may result in a loss of employment benefits.* Such coercion or compulsion may be overt or subtle but if any feature of employment becomes reasonably dependent on

---

*There is no intention to deal with the implications of bisexual conduct in the circumstances of this case. It is intended to deal with harassment of female employees by a male in authority and the principles equally apply to the harassment of a male employee by a female in authority as well as homosexual exploitation.

reciprocating a social relationship proffered by a member of management, then the overture becomes a condition of employment and may be considered to be discriminatory.

Again, The Code ought not to be seen or perceived as inhibiting free speech. If sex cannot be discussed between supervisor and employee neither can other values such as race, colour or creed, which are contained in The Code, be discussed. Thus, differences of opinion by an employee where sexual matters are discussed may not involve a violation of The Code; *it is only when the language or words may be reasonably construed to form a condition of employment that The Code provides a remedy.* Thus, the frequent and persistent taunting by a supervisor of an employee because of his or her colour is discriminatory activity under The Code and, similarly, *the frequent and persistent taunting of an employee by a supervisor because of his or her sex is discriminatory under The Code.*

However, persistent and frequent conduct is not a condition for an adverse finding under The Code because a single incident of an employee being denied equality of employment because of sex is also prohibited activity.

The next issue to be decided is the extent of liability under The Code. If a foreman or supervisor discriminates because of sex will the company be liable? *The law is quite clear that companies are liable where members of management, no matter what their rank, engage in other forms of discriminatory activity.* Thus, companies have been held liable where lower-ranking members of the management team engage in anti-union activity or discriminate against employees because of race or colour, and the same general law that imposes liability in those cases ought to apply where members of the management team discriminates because of sex. *Thus, I would have no hesitation in finding the corporate respondent liable for a violation of The Code if one of its officers engaged in prohibited conduct and, indeed, the same liability would attach if the violater had a lower rank on the management team. . .*

As a general rule sexual situations do not occur in public. One is often left with only the testimony of the accuser and the accused. How is one to determine the guilt or innocence based on a quick assessment of the proponents in the witness box? It is suggested that the adversary system through the process of examination and cross-examination will lead to the truth. But quite often that is not the case. There is an artificiality to the process which often tends to hide the truth rather than reveal it. The proponents make brief appearances in the witness box. Very often they are examined and cross-examined by lawyers of varying skills. Some witnesses are better than others; often the most consummate liar is the better witness while the truthful person is hesitant and creates a poor impression. *In those circumstances it is equally unjust to deny a remedy to an injured person as to grant a remedy against an innocent person. . .*

## II

The first complaint to be dealt with is that of Ms. Martha Bardell. Ms. Bardell was employed by the Blue Lion Tavern on weekends from the beginning of September in 1977 to mid-October. On November 1, 1977 Ms. Bardell filed a complaint with the Ontario Human Rights Commission alleging sexual harassment by George Rouncewell on October 8 and October 9, 1977 and also October 15 and 16, 1977. These complaints were later amplified in a letter dated September 10, 1979 from counsel for the Commission to counsel for the respondents. There are essentially three incidents about which Ms. Bardell complains. The first involves an incident when Ms. Bardell went to pick up her first pay cheque, the second is concerned with comments that George Rouncewell made to her when she came to work tired and the third incident is concerned with a request by a customer for a drink.

Basically, the evidence and the arguments turned on the question of credibility. Both counsel for the Commission and counsel for the respondents were in general agreement as to the applicable law. The issue of credibility was vigorously contested by the parties. As I have indicated cases involving sex rarely have a host of corroborative witnesses. The two main protagonists in this case are Ms. Bardell and Mr. G. Rouncewell. Ms. Bardell testified that Mr. Rouncewell made comments to her which were sexually harassing and that her refusal to comply with his suggestions brought about her termination. Mr. Rouncewell denied these allegations and maintained that he had at all material times acted with complete propriety.

In this matter the issues of credibility are very difficult; however, after considering all the evidence I found Ms. Bardell's evidence to be less than completely candid.

The first incursion into her credibility concerns her testimony about the impact upon her of the alleged sexual harassment. Ms. Bardell alleged in her complaint and testified that on or about October 18, 1977 when she called to find her hours of work for the following week that she was terminated. Her call followed the alleged incidents of sexual harassment. The willingness to work is of no moment because persons in need of employment may be prepared to endure certain humiliations because of their financial need. Thus, Ms. Bardell's indication that she was prepared to work is only important because of what she says occurred after her discharge.

Ms. Bardell testified that the impact of Mr. Rouncewell's statements were such that she was unable to work for a period of seven months after her termination. She suggests that the trauma of having worked for George Rouncewell was such that she was so deeply and psychologically affected that she was unable to work for such a considerable period of time. I note that Ms. Bardell did not seek medical assistance despite the severity of her alleged trauma.

In my view, her evidence in this regard is inconsistent. On the one hand she was prepared to work at the Blue Lion Tavern, which was the source of her sexual harassment and traumatic state, while on the other hand she was unable to seek employment elsewhere for seven months. Even counsel for the Commission, in his final argument, was hard put to explain Ms. Bardell's failure to seek alternative employment for such a lengthy period or to seek medical assistance even from her family doctor which would have corroborated such a claim.

But that evidence, apart from its inherent weakness, has graver implications. First, it suggests a tendency on her part to exaggerate and, second, it suggests an improper motive by Ms. Bardell in bringing this complaint. I am satisfied, after observing Ms. Bardell in the witness box and considering her demeanour as well as analyzing the evidence that, in all probability, she would not have been incapacitated, for such a lengthy period of time, by the remarks she attributes to Mr. George Rouncewell and that she exaggerated her evidence in order to assist her case.

It is also apparent that if Ms. Bardell's lack of employment for the seven month period resulted from sexual harassment she might be compensated accordingly by bringing this complaint. Thus, the exaggeration of her claim had its financial reward and, by so exaggerating her claim, one is left with the impression that Ms. Bardell's motive in bringing the claim was, in part, improperly motivated. When this evidence is weighed with other evidence it casts considerable doubt on Ms. Bardell's version of events.

Further, on November 1, 1977, after she had been discharged, Ms. Bardell filed a complaint with the Ontario Human Rights Commission. She discussed the complaints with a representative of the Commission, Angela Leath who testified at the hearing. Angela Leath indicated that the complainant, Ms. Bardell, was quite specific about her complaint. Indeed, the complainant specified that the incidents of sexual harassment by George Rouncewell occurred on October 8 and 9, 1977 and October 15 and 16, 1977, approximately two and three weeks prior to the filing of the complaint. It now appears that the incidents could not have happened on those dates because the evidence demonstrates that George Rouncewell and the complainant did not work together on those dates.

It is understandable for someone to make a mistake about dates, and such errors, in some contexts, might be overlooked. However, the complaint was filed only two weeks after the alleged incidents and two weeks after Ms. Bardell was fired. In the light of her own testimony as to the serious impact that the incidents had upon her, Ms. Bardell might be expected to have been more precise in her recollection. She was, as Angela Leath testified, quite specific when she filed the complaints, yet she was wrong and that raises a suggestion that she might not be accurate about the remaining testimony.

In fairness, one of the incidents is alleged to have occurred on October 16, 1977, when George Rouncewell was still at the restaurant and just before he had changed shifts with Walter Rouncewell, but it is clear that the other incidents did not occur on the dates specified. At least one of the alleged incidents, the pay cheque incident, occurred early in September and ought to have been more memorable because it allegedly occurred on the day that Ms. Martha Bardell received her first pay cheque. But Ms. Bardell's testimony about that incident is also lacking.

Angela Leath testified that when she interviewed Martha Bardell, prior to the drafting of the complaint, Ms. Bardell told her that she had been propositioned by George Rouncewell when she had gone to the restaurant to get her first pay cheque. She told Angela Leath that she had her baby with her at the time and that this prompted a conversation that resulted in a proposition. According to Angela Leath she was told by Martha Bardell that she had gone to the restaurant with her baby and George Rouncewell asked her whether it was her baby. He then went on to ask her if she was married and she replied that she was not. There was further conversation about whether Ms. Bardell was on the pill and then Ms. Bardell asserted that George Rouncewell propositioned her.

When the complainant, Ms. Bardell, testified, she gave a somewhat different version concerning the pay cheque incident. Ms. Bardell testified that she had gone to the restaurant with her girlfriend to pick up her pay cheque and George Rouncewell had asked her what she was doing and she replied that she was going out with her girlfriend to the local hotel. She further testified that she and George Rouncewell had some conversation about what she drank and she told him rye and ginger. George Rouncewell apparently replied that drinking rye stimulated him sexually. Some further conversation ensued about the pill and then George Rouncewell is alleged to have propositioned her.

It is apparent that Ms. Bardell's version of the incident given to this inquiry differed from her version of the incident given to Ms. Angela Leath in 1977, just some weeks after the incident is alleged to have occurred. When Angela Leath was cross-examined about the incident she indicated that Martha Bardell had also told her about going to the hotel with her girlfriend but, after reviewing the total evidence, I conclude that there was only one occasion when Ms. Bardell went to pick up her pay cheque and that her version of the incident, as recited to Ms. Leath, differs from and is not consistent with her evidence given at the hearing. At the very least, if only Ms. Leath's testimony is considered, it appears that Ms. Bardell was not consistent in describing the incident to her. Again, one might attribute the inconsistency to the lapse of time between the actual event and the hearing, but when this inconsistency is viewed in the light of the other evidence it tends to affect the credibility of the witness.

The two other incidents relied upon by the complainant arise from comments that were allegedly made to her by sexual propositions. I do not propose to elaborate on these incidents at any length but merely recite them for the purpose of the record. Needless to say they are also denied by George Rouncewell.

The first of these incidents arose when the complainant came into work and told George Rouncewell that she was tired. A brief conversation ensued which Ms. Martha Bardell says concluded by George Rouncewell telling her that the reason she was tired was because she "screwed too much". Ms. Bardell then went to her place in the restaurant to do her work. Again, the date of this incident appears to be incorrect and Ms. Bardell interpreted the remark as a proposition.

The second incident occurred when Ms. Bardell received an order for a drink, referred to as a Sloe Screw. She went to the bar and George Rouncewell asked her what she wanted. When she told him he said he would give her a slow screw and a fast screw if she wanted. Ms. Bardell interpreted this remark as a proposition.

The respondents deny that these conversations occurred and stated that

Ms. Bardell was terminated because of her substandard performance, a suspicion that she was stealing tips from other waitresses, as well as taking money and not ringing up the proceeds of sales into the cash register, and not charging customers whom she knew, the proper amount for what they had ordered.

With respect to her performance Ms. Bardell admitted that she could have been a better waitress, but attributes the lack of performance on her part to being new and to being nervous which resulted from the sexual harassment. She admits to getting orders mixed up and dropping things. However, it is also apparent that, according to her own testimony, fifty percent of the time worked was not with George Rouncewell and from other testimony less than fifty percent of the time worked was not [?] with George Rouncewell, so that there was no reason for her to have been nervous when George Rouncewell was not present.

In addition, there was testimony from other employees that Ms. Bardell was not a willing co-worker and that they were suspicious about their tips. One of the employees testifies that she had customarily received tips from a particular group of customers and that these tips diminished when Ms. Bardell was employed and returned to their former level after Ms. Bardell left.

There is one disturbing piece of evidence concerning a $10.00 bill that Ms. Bardell found under a seat. At the time she saw the $10.00 on the floor there was a customer seated in the booth. Ms. Bardell concluded that the $10.00 could not have fallen from the pocket or wallet of the particular customer, and when the customer left she took the $10.00 bill for herself. In those circumstances it would appear that it might have been more appropriate to have asked the customer whether he had lost any money and the failure to ask the customer reflects on Ms. Bardell's honesty.

In any event, Mr. Walter Rouncewell, the brother of George Rouncewell and an officer of the company who also works in the restaurant, was highly suspicious of Ms. Bardell's performance and was aware of the complaints about her from other employees. On the last night that she worked Ms. Bardell worked with Walter Rouncewell. He became very suspicious about her work and particularly her recording of the proper amount for drinks Ms. Bardell was serving to some customers that she knew. He watched her carefully and concluded that she was not charging them fully for the drinks she was serving them and, based on her total performance, he decided to discharge her. He recorded the drinks she was serving and found that the bill did not correspond with the number or amount of drinks served. According to Ms. Bardell, Mr. Walter Rouncewell spoke to her about the situation that night and she denied it. She also admitted that Mr. Rouncewell was watching her carefully.

Mr. Walter Rouncewell decided to discharge Ms. Bardell and informed his brother, George, who would be on shift when she called in to tell her that she was discharged and to contact Walter Rouncewell if she wanted to discuss it. This is not a case where the employer need establish just cause or that the reason for the employee's discharge was because she acted improperly. There is no allegation of sexual impropriety against Walter Rouncewell and there is nothing in the evidence that connects his decision to terminate Ms. Bardell with the alleged sexual advances of his brother, George Rouncewell. In short, I am unable to conclude, and there is no evidence, Walter Rouncewell fired Ms. Bardell because she refused the propositions of his brother.

I am further satisfied that Walter Rouncewell fired Ms. Bardell because he had reasonable and ample grounds to suspect that her work performance was substandard and that her general conduct as a waitress was inappropriate. I further determine that Mr. Walter Rouncewell was not motivated to discharge Ms. Bardell for any reason that might contravene the provisions of The Code. There is simply no connection between Walter Rouncewell's decision and any matter that might constitute a violation of The Code and Ms. Bardell's complaint cannot succeed on that ground—she was not discharged because she refused to become sexually involved with George Rouncewell.

The only remaining aspect of this case concerns the allegations of sexual harassment during Ms. Bardell's employment and the similar fact evidence called to support those allegations. . . . [including] the evidence of Minerva Hunter, who is also a complainant and after considering the totality of her evidence, I am not satisfied that it should be admitted or given weight in the circumstances of this case. I am concerned that its prejudicial value outweighs its probative value. Based on the general admonitions against receiving similar fact evidence, I am hesitant to accept Ms. Hunter's evidence.

Alternatively, I find that the acts of sexual harassment described by Ms. Hunter differ from those described by Ms. Bardell and do not indicate a pattern. The features, if any, are different with each complainant and do not suggest a particular system or a particular peculiarity. . . . In this case I find nothing unusual in the similar fact evidence tendered that Mr. Rouncewell slapped her rear on different occasions whereas Ms. Bardell does not suggest there was any physical contact of that sort. Ms. Hunter also testified that Mr. Rouncewell invited her out for a couple of drinks and suggested that they go to a hotel room, whereas the approaches made to Ms. Bardell, if they can be interpreted that way, made no mention of going for drinks or going to a hotel room. Indeed, the alleged approaches seem very different in nature and tone and, if anything, demonstrate a lack of consistency of approach. On that basis I am not prepared to find that the alleged sexual overtures made to the two complainants were so unusual, or bore such a striking similarity, that the evidence of each of the complainants should be treated as similar fact evidence having some probative value in the other's complaint.

George Rouncewell also testified on his own behalf. I do not propose to outline his evidence except to note that he denied each of the allegations put forth by Ms. Bardell. While there are some flaws in his testimony, I am not prepared to find, on balance, his testimony to be so unreliable when compared to Ms. Bardell's that I would be prepared to conclude that he made the alleged statements and that he propositioned Ms. Bardell or, alternatively, that the reasonable implications of his remarks in the context of all the evidence was such that sex was a condition of employment.

Moreover, there is an important part of Mr. Rouncewell's evidence which is corroborated by an independent witness, Gus Smorltork. At the time of the alleged incidents, Mr. Smorltork was approximately sixteen years old and worked as a part-time dishwasher at the restaurant. He has no stake in the outcome of these proceedings and his evidence is thus more independent than that of Ms. Bardell or Mr. George Rouncewell. He gave his evidence in a very straightforward manner and without any semblance of guile and, in my view, his evidence weighs heavily in the balance.

Mr. Smorltork witnessed the "sloe screw" incident and completely corroborated the evidence of George Rouncewell that the remarks attributed to him by Ms. Bardell were not made. Also, Mr. Smorltork corroborated the evidence of Walter Rouncewell that he was suspicious of Ms. Bardell's conduct and work performance and buttressed Walter Rouncewell's position in deciding to discharge Ms. Bardell. And, finally, Mr. Smorltork witnessed the situation when Ms. Bardell picked up the $10.00 from the floor and his version of the incident does not enhance Ms. Bardell's credibility.

On balance, where there is a contradiction in testimony, I prefer the evidence of George Rouncewell and I further find that Ms. Bardell's evidence, when viewed alone or in the context of the other evidence, is not sufficiently reliable to found a violation of The Code as alleged by her.

Accordingly, the complaint of Ms. Martha Bardell is dismissed.

### III

The second complaint to be dealt with is that of Ms. Minerva Hunter, who was terminated in mid-October of 1977 after having worked at the Blue Lion Tavern for approximately one month. Ms. Hunter did not file her complaint until March of 1978 and did so only after she was approached by Ms. Angela Leath, who was investigating the complaint of Ms. Martha Bardell.

I place no stock in the fact that Ms. Hunter filed her complaint some considerable time after she was terminated as I infer from the evidence that she may not have been fully aware of her rights.

I do not propose to discuss the principles applicable in this type of situation because they have been discussed in the case of Ms. Martha Bardell which was heard at the same time. Also, the evidence tendered as similar fact evidence has been reviewed in the Bardell case and I have no reason to take a different view of that evidence in this matter

This case also turns on the credibility of the complainant, Ms. Minerva Hunter, and the respondent, Mr. George Rouncewell. Ms. Hunter's complaints are made against Mr. George Rouncewell and it was Mr. George Rouncewell who discharged her. Mr. Walter Rouncewell did not play any relevant part in the employment relationship or in the termination.

Essentially Ms. Hunter's evidence is that Mr. George Rouncewell slapped her rear end on more than one occasion and that this physical contact was unsolicited and undesired. She also claims he made inquiries about her personal life and invited her out to drink with him and to have sexual relations with him.

Ms. Hunter's evidence was basically consistent. There was some evidence that she was motivated to bring this complaint because her financial position was impaired as a result of being terminated and consequently she lost her car.

Mr. George Rouncewell denied all of the allegations and claimed that Ms. Hunter was not a good employee, that she was rough with customers, that she was not neat in appearance and that she did not perform her work at a reasonable standard. He also testified that he felt that she smoked marijuana while at work and that he caught her stealing and it was for all these reasons that he termined her employment.

To some extent some of Mr. Rouncewell's evidence as to Ms. Hunter's work performance is corroborated by other employees, particularly Gus Smorltork, who was the dishwasher.

This particular matter has given me anxious consideration. There are both strengths and weaknesses in the evidence of the complainant and the respondent, George Rouncewell. In my view it would be better to decide this case on the merits but having weighed the pros and cons and the theories of the case put forward in the very able arguments of counsel for the Commission and counsel for the respondent, I am unable to conclude that the position of one side should prevail over the position of the other side. Thus, in the result and after considering the merits of each position, I find that this case falls to be decided on the basis of which side has the onus of proof.

Since, in my view, it is the complainant who must establish that on the balance of probabilities the respondent has acted in a manner that is in violation of The Code, the complaint must be dismissed. I am unable to conclude that the evidence lead [sic] by the complainant goes that far and, accordingly, the complaint of Ms. Minerva Hunter is dismissed.

*   *   *

*Comment:*

# HAPPINESS AND JUSTICE

In the discussion of the cases on sexual harrassment, it may have occurred to you that the persecutor's happiness was at stake in harassment as well as the victim's. In fact we would not weigh the persecutor's happiness equally. If we ask "Why not?" we are immediately led to see that it's not just the happiness of the people involved that we're appealing to when we argue that sexual harassment is wrong and ought to be stopped. It's something like equal opportunities for happiness; or, put in other words, happiness modified by the condition that the opportunities for it shall be justly distributed.

We shall find that the way the consideration of decent lives and happiness operates in the example of sexual harrassment is typical. As a moral consideration, it comes to bear only if certain conditions respecting justice are satisfied: for example, that everyone's happiness be taken into account other things being equal; that if people have unequal power, this power is not abused so that some enjoy happiness at the expense of others; and so forth.

Is there a connection in the other direction? Can justice be invoked without any implication as to decent lives and happiness? We may well hypothesize that in the end it cannot be. For would justice matter to anybody if decent lives and happiness were not at stake? A departure from equality of opportunity, for example, will be deemed unjust (because of the connection in meaning between justice and equality). At the very least, the injustice will be aggravated if (as in the case of sexual harrassment) it affects people's happiness substantially and adversely; and the more happiness is affected, the more the injustice is aggravated. Suppose happiness was not affected at all: injustice involved no more than forestalling someone from placing a paper clip on the left rather than on the right. Then the injustice would be trivial. Now suppose that all cases of injustice were equally trivial. Then it would be difficult to understand how a concept of justice ever developed, much less came to be a matter of such steadily recurring importance. We may in fact hypothesize that it has been developed, and developed in the direction that is familiar to us, because it seemed to assist people generally (even if not every person in every instance) in protecting their opportunities for happiness.

The conclusion to which these arguments tend is that justice and happiness are not independent considerations in ethics; nor is one more fundamental than the other. If either is fundamental, it is so only in the company of the other.

# CHAPTER 10

# Manipulation and Exploitation

*Introductory Comment:*

## FURTHER ABUSES OF POWER

The unequal power of the employer may intrude into employees' private lives in many other ways besides committing or tolerating sexual harrassment. Sometimes the intrusion is unintended, in the sense that it is only incidental to the purposes of the employer in the workplace and is perhaps something the employer does not recognize. A simple but important example is requiring so much effort of employees, perhaps just in the pace of work, perhaps in long hours of overtime, that they cannot see enough of their families or otherwise carry on satisfying private lives. Shift work has much the same effects.

Sometimes the intrusion is intended, but connected, objectionable as it may be in itself, with legitimate purposes of the firm. For example, a firm may insist that its employees vote in a municipal election for bonds to construct a waterworks useful to the firm's operations *(Vulcan Last Co. v. State of Wisconsin,* 1928); or require so far as it can that they support one political party rather than another. Even if the firm is not seeking specific economic benefits from supporting a political party, it may find an employee's political activities embarrassing and fear public retaliation (see *Twentieth Century-Fox Film Corp.* v. *Lardner,* California, 1954, concerning the refusal of a screenwriter to testify before the House Unamerican Activities Committee).

# INTERFERENCE WITH EMPLOYEES' LIVES
# OUTSIDE BUSINESS

Sometimes the intrusion is intended, without even having a firm connection with legitimate purposes of the firm. Henry Ford and his automobile company had a legitimate purpose in having its employees sober and diligent on the job. Could this justify regulating the employees' lives off the job? Edwin T. Layton, Jr., in a paper on "Value Change and the Automobile Industry,"* reminds us:

> In the same year that Ford installed assembly lines throughout his factory (1914), he also instituted the five-dollar day and founded his Sociology Department. The five-dollar day, begun at a time when the standard industrial wage was only half of this, along with the eight-hour day, created a sensation and remains well-known. The Sociology Department is another matter. In its early years, under the direction of an Episcopal clergyman, its agents visited the homes of all Ford's workers, where they investigated every aspect of the worker's lifestyle and morals. They systematically rooted out "any malicious practice derogatory to good physical manhood or moral character." Sinners were not immediately dismissed; they were penalized in wages and encouraged to repent and mend their ways.

In John O'Hara's short story, "Other Women's Households,"† a woman checks the local newspaper to see how many times her activities have been mentioned. Then

> Phyllis [Richardson] glanced about her [living-room], seeing nothing new, and nothing very old that she considered very good. The pictures of her class and Val's class at high school; her own class at the state teachers' college; the high-school football teams that Val had played on; the ship models that had belonged to her own antecedents; the portrait-type photographs of her grandmother and grandfather; the small loving cups that Val had won in the 440 and 220; the furniture she had inherited, and the portable bar, resembling a barrel, which her friends and Val's had chipped together and bought for their wooden anniversary six years ago. Their last good party. She looked at Val and his fat back, hunched over his papers, with a dead cigar in his fat left hand and a thin yellow pencil in his fat right hand. That was a party, all right. At three-thirty everybody had gone home but Bob and Edith Conforth, and Val and Edith went out to the kitchen to get some more ice, and when they came back, Val was wearing Edith's bra and panties and Edith was wearing Val's shorts and shirt. And Phyl and Bob stopped necking long enough to effect the same change.

---

*Read at a conference at the University of Pittsburgh, December 1980. Quoted by permission.

†From *Selected Short Stories of John O'Hara*, by John O'Hara. Copyright 1947 by John O'Hara. Reprinted by permission of Random House, Inc., and Curtis Brown Ltd., London, on behalf of Random House.

Only the four of them were left at the party, but Bob or Edith must have talked, or maybe it was Val, although he always denied he had. Anyhow, it got whispered around. Within a week the men who had left before three-thirty were stopping Phyllis on the street and saying, "Hey, Stingy, why didn't you ask *me* to stay the other night?" and some of the women, including two who had done some heavy necking of their own, stared at Phyllis as though she had burned down the orphanage. Val informed all who asked that the whole thing was exaggerated; he said he had put on Edith's hat and Bob had put on Phyl's hat. That was the story he had given at the bank when Ward Singer spoke to him. Phyl and Val never were sure whether Ward believed them or not. All Ward said was, "O.K., but if that story ever got to Old Lady Booth, your name is mud around here. I'd have to fire you, you know that." Yes, they knew that, all right, and it was what they had chiefly worried about. Old Lady Booth was the bank's principal stockholder. Fear of Old Lady Booth had made it certain that there had been no more parties like that one—hardly any parties at all. Six years of church suppers, ladies' auxiliaries, school activities, Val and his Scout Troop and air-raid-wardening, Phyl and her nurse's aid, Phyl and Val and their blood-donating, watching their step, saving pennies, getting no younger. She looked again at his fat back; you'd think he'd have lost some weight, all the blood he gave.

Later in the story it transpires that Old Lady Booth knew about the party all along. The irony is imperfect: Would the pressure on the Richardsons have been any less if they had known she knew? And the illustration, though it does in fact concern employment by a corporation, is not quite to the point about oppressive demands by firms. Old Lady Booth treats the corporation as her own property and its employees as her employees. Nevertheless, the question arises: Is it acceptable that firms should interfere in any way with their employees' lives outside business, however scandalous those lives might be?

## RIVALRY AND CULTIVATED RIVALRY

Firms use their power to affect employees' lives in questionable ways when employees are on the job, too, with demands that spring (unlike sexual harassment) out of legitimate purposes of the firms, though the demands are pressed too far. The broad term for what is objected to here is *exploitation*, which covers not only features of employees' lives and activities while they are on the job but also the pay that they get from being on the job, carrying on their jobs under the conditions offered them.

I am about to distinguish several forms of exploitation and supply materials illustrating some of them. Before I do, I note under the present heading an issue that does not seem to fit easily under "exploitation." One could make it fit by argument, but it does not yet have a familiar place there. Nor is it easy to find cases to illustrate it, partly because it is not an issue that lends itself to litigation. I have not found a good case to present.

The issue is nonetheless real and important. One might put it this way: Is employment by a firm in which employees compete to stay on and to be promoted compatible with the employees' being genuine friends with one another? To the degree that it is not, then people are being compelled to sacrifice at work, in respect to other people who would otherwise be very close to them, one of the great good things of life. Some workers refuse to make the sacrifice, renouncing any pretension to advancement to make sure of continued friendship with their workmates. This attitude has been ascribed to British miners; indeed, it has been frequently remarked upon as an aspect of working-class feeling in Britain.

The issue is one of degree. Firms vary a good deal in internal pressure of competition. They are not the only institutions that generate a considerable amount of pressure. Considerable pressure is often found in officer corps of the armed forces; in university faculties; in sports, music, and the theater. Moreover, the pressure in those other institutions is as often as it is in firms an effect of deliberate policy, aimed at bringing the most proficient people to the top. This seems admirable; certainly, if the standards invoked are relevant ones and they are impartially applied, there are powerful arguments for thinking it so. (We can nevertheless recall some points from Knight's discussion that tell in the other direction.) Moreover, people can adapt themselves even to quite vigorous competition. Partly, no doubt, because they themselves accept it as having an admirable purpose and can often rise above their own disappointments to make a detached, objective view of the results, they often contrive to be friends with their rivals, and even to stay friends with superiors who have stopped them from rising and with past rivals who have been promoted above them.

There are several strains on such friendships, however, strains illustrated in several vignettes in Earl Shorris's "Scenes from Corporate Life" (*Harper's Magazine*, March 1980) and at greater length in many novels. Moreover, in some firms internal competition is evidently carried to an extreme. A story in *Newsweek* (8 June 1981)* draws a sharp contrast between two firms in "Silicon Valley"—the center, in California, of the American semiconductor industry. One, Fairchild Camera and Instrument Corporation, is said to have "flourished in the early years under a highly centralized management that pitted employee against employee in ferocious competition." The other, Hewlett-Packard, had "a tradition of paternalism, hiring with meticulous care, generously sharing profits, and imbuing its employees with the Zenlike precepts of the company philosophy, 'H-P way'." "H-P's managers decided early that they would not run a hire-and-fire operation. When semiconductor orders slumped in 1970, everyone in the company took a 10 per cent cut in work and pay, and no one was laid off." Hewlett-Packard has also been remarkable for offering employees' flexible work schedules "tailored to [their] individual needs." Its virtues have evidently paid off (though that is not the only consideration, certainly not the chief moral one). While

Fairchild has lost many of its best employees, Hewlett-Packard has established "a record of high productivity and top-quality products [that] is the envy" of competitors.

## EXPLOITATION: INTENSIFICATION OF WORK

Marx and other critics of capitalism are not ready to accept there being any income to property; so for them, if property-holders are getting income in the form of interest, profits, or rent, workers' wages must be less than they should be, and in that sense the workers are being exploited. I shall put off discussing this issue, which touches on the justice of the business system as a whole, until the very end of the book. Here we continue to consider variations in respect to justice and other subjects of moral concern that can be judged to be such—for good or ill—assuming the current system. Exploitation with respect to wages can still be charged, if some workers are getting lower pay than other workers in comparable situations; and, as we shall see, there are forms of exploitation with respect to wages that do not consist simply of getting abnormally low pay. I count as exploitation undue intensification of work, where the pay may continue to be normal, as compared with the pay elsewhere, but people are being compelled to put forth more effort in each hour's and each day's work. Putting people to work in dangerous conditions, or even in conditions that are just physically uncomfortable, also raises an issue about exploitation. When any premiums paid in wages as danger pay have been allowed for, along with public provisions for medical care and compensation in the event of disability, are the employing firms bearing the extra costs of accidents and injuries, or are the costs being shifted to the workers, in effect lowering their pay below normal rates?

Women planting potatoes, or a man mowing a hayfield with a scythe, may have to work hard for long hours, but they have a chance to vary their movements as it suits them to do so, to pause now and then, at least briefly, at intervals of their own choosing. People tending machines do not have this freedom. They have to conform, in the rhythm of their work, to the speed of the machines and to the inexorable regularity with which the machine operates. If the machines that people must tend are continually supplanted by machines that operate faster, with less and less scope for variation in guidance, working with them, though it may demand less physical strength, becomes more and more arduous in other ways. More concentrated attention may be required; or the physical effort put forward has to conform in timing and otherwise to a more rigid pattern.

Even when the machines remain the same, time-and-motion studies may lead to the prescription of a rigid pattern, certified scientifically as the one best way of doing the job. It is true that from the time of pioneers in such studies (Frederick W. Taylor [1856–1915]; Frank B. Gilbreth [1868–1924]; and

Lillian Gilbreth [1878–1972]) industrial engineers might sincerely claim to be doing no more than show how with the same physical effort, more smoothly and comfortably organized, workers could produce more. Workers themselves, however, have often found the requirement of conformity to the prescribed patterns oppressive.

Is it morally acceptable for firms to intensify work in detail? Do any moral objections subside if workers are given a share (as they very commonly are) in the increased productivity that results from having more advanced machines and more systematic ways of tending them? These moral questions also arise about the larger patterns in which work is organized. Is the common practice of requiring workers to be on the job at a time fixed for everybody (or for everybody on a given shift), and not to leave before another time fixed for everybody, entirely acceptable? It is not, as it turns out, something that is to be taken for granted, any more than the number of hours elasping between the fixed times—the length of the working day—is to be taken for granted.

*[The following brief selection from a book published by the International Labour Office gives some indication of the range of issues that come up about the timing of work, and of their interconnections.]*

# D. MARIĆ, "NEW TRENDS AND ATTITUDES [TOWARD THE TIMING OF WORK]"*

SIGNIFICANCE OF THE TIME FACTOR

The problem of working hours has until recently always been seen in purely quantitative terms. The aim has been to reduce the total time spent at work: (a) directly, by setting standard hours and overtime limits per day and week, and (b) indirectly, by prescribing spells of free time of varying length over longer periods of up to a year, in the form of public holidays and vacation leave.

While this approach is still useful in concrete cases, it is no longer adequate for present-day conditions. Modern developments have made it necessary to consider the qualitative aspects of the pattern of working hours, in the light of new thinking on the subject. What are needed now are ways of working less hours, differently and better, so as to achieve— without detriment to production and productivity—a balance between work, rest and leisure that meets the needs of the individual and of the community. This has involved analysis of working conditions and of the physical, economic and social environment of work, and the results have brought a new awareness of the importance of the time factor.

---

*Excerpts from *Adapting Working Hours to Modern Needs* by D. Marić, 1977, pp. 1–5. Copyright 1977, International Labour Organisation, Geneva. Reprinted by permission of the International Labour Office.

Since industrialization began, the individual has increasingly been forced to surrender control of his time and, as a result, working time has had to be quantified in order to set a fair price for it. We now see that this cannot be done in monetary terms alone. The well-worn saying that "time is money" has fallen out of use, since it considers only what an individual earns—but not what he sacrifices—by working for a given time.

This brings us to a further question: what does a worker's pay really represent? Whether the criterion is muscular, mental or nervous effort, skill or know-how, the remuneration is always the result of multiplying the physical or mental qualifications by a time coefficient: time spent working, time devoted to vocational training or time lost at work—this last element representing a loss of "living time". Looked at in this way, remuneration clearly embodies an element of compensation for loss of time. The time dimension is now an inherent part of an individual's conditions of work and the main factor in the constantly rising social cost.

As a result, people are beginning to be conscious of how their time is spent, and to want to exercise choice in using it as profitably, agreeably and sensibly as possible.

For those living today, time means something radically different from time in the olden days. Work was then spread over the hours of daylight, without a set timetable. The human time-pattern corresponded to the alternations in nature and to human psychological and biological needs.

All this has been changed by industrialisation. Our way of life today follows a job and production engineering model that favours productivity at the expense of the natural needs and deeper motivations of the individual. We are reaching a point where the pattern of working hours ceases to correspond to human physiological and biological rhythms, since machines can function regardless of the natural divisions of time. Time is becoming a scarce and therefore more costly factor and is divided up into ever-smaller segments. As Pierre Naville puts it, it is now the prize in a bitter conflict between working for somebody else and working for oneself and the whole community.*

Two other factors have contributed to the startling increase in the value of the time factor. It is one of the parameters in measuring productivity, and we are only too aware of the priority given to this in modern industrial societies. At the same time, many kinds of work are unpleasant and the price for time spent on them is accordingly increasing. The price may be paid in cash or, when a given level of prosperity is attained, in the form of extra time off. As Grossin has pointed out, the reason why workers hand over control of their working days is that they want fuller enjoyment of their non-working time, which is for them a period of "de-alienation."

REORGANISING THE USE OF TIME

Technological progress, the development of large-scale production, and division of labour with the specialisation and assembly-line methods to

---

*[Footnotes omitted here and hereafter.]

which it leads, have impoverished the worker's relationship to his work. The work process is often broken down into simple and constantly repeated operations so that the worker has no real feeling of contributing to the final product or result. Work is consequently unsatisfying and there are increasing signs of discontent. Fatigue now tends to be nervous rather than physical as formerly, and may disturb the individual's psychosomatic health, emotional life, and powers of attention and thought. The whole process is one of increasing alienation, attributable to two main causes: dissatisfaction with the actual tasks involved in the job, which give no scope for self-fulfilment, and dissatisfaction with extraneous factors, such as the physical conditions, supervision, the state of labour relations, etc.

Now, employee alienation represents labour's share of the social cost of a given activity. In some cases it is shown by passive resistance: lateness, absenteeism, high labour turnover and inattentiveness; in others, by aggressive behaviour such as deliberate waste, threats, violence or quarrelsomeness in daily work.

In spite of the changed working environment and social climate, there is still a rigid pattern of working hours that leaves practically no scope for individual choice. Rationalisation of individual and group behaviour has gone so far that it almost entirely eliminates spontaneity, initiative and imagination. The individual has in many cases ceased to have any influence on the timing and schedules of the work process. Yet these are among the main variables as regards his job and working conditions. This explains the strong reaction aiming at the removal of all avoidable constraints and at less standardised and more personal patterns of behaviour.

There is justifiable pressure to get rid of outdated or harmful forms and methods of work, and this has been partly responsible for the gradual introduction of new ways of organising work taking account, among other things, of progress in the behavioural sciences. Many believe that a revolution in attitudes to work is taking place and that it can only lead to a completely new framework for work.

The question that most are asking concerns the direction of change in conditions of work, i.e. new patterns of working time, improved pay systems, wider application of ergonomics, new and more imaginative ways or organising work, increased protection of the physical and social environment. Out of these various alternatives, it does seem that a loosening of the constraints so as to allow some degree of freedom to organise one's own working time is one of the best means of reducing the feeling of being a slave to one's work and improving the quality of working life. . . .

NEW PATTERNS OF WORKING TIME

In industry, the new approach has been reflected, in some cases, in the scheduling, staggering and co-ordination of working hours, and in other cases, in a more or less free pattern over the day, week, year or even over the individual's working life. Some of the new arrangements apply to groups of workers; others are based on a choice freely made by individuals. They have been adopted for various reasons, some deriving from sociology and the psychology of human needs, and others from economic necessity or simple recognition that adjustments have to be made in every type of society.

The real significance of the new arrangements comes out most clearly if they are viewed as ways of making work more worth while and improving the quality of living, in a strategy for humanising the individual's working life.

The new approaches can be considered according to units of time—
1. As regards the working day, they may consist of—
   (a) compressed working day [e.g. by shortening the lunch break];
   (b) staggering of the set hours;
   (c) individual choice between alternative timetables offered by management;
   (d) flexible working hours subject to certain conditions and limits.
2. The working week may be compressed into 5, 4½, 4 or even 3 days.
3. As regards the working year, efforts are made to stagger annual holidays.
4. As regards the individual's whole working life, the new approach regards the age for starting work and the age of retirement as flexible, and allows for substantial amounts of recurrent education during working life as a means of achieving greater social equality and as a catalyst in the improvement of the social environment.

\* \* \*

## Comment:

# DANGEROUS OR PHYSICALLY UNCOMFORTABLE WORK

The triplet principle, one might expect, would sort out most of the cases relating to issues about the timing of work within a rather narrow range, from being somewhat objectionable to being somewhat laudable. In other words, most of the variation is not dramatic; even when objections (or the reverse) are called for, one perhaps has to strain a little to make an issue of them. It is not so with dangerous work. Here the issues are so dramatic and exciting that there may be some difficulty in preserving enough detachment to work one's way through the many serious complications of resolving them.

# BOTTLING BEER*

*[Asked to bring in a case or cases illustrating dangerous work, a student, William Lahey, in one of my classes on ethics in business brought in this report of his observations during a summer job in a local brewery.]*

The process of pasteurizing the draft into ale or beer involves heating the bottles in a machine called a pasteurizer. The bottles are heated to approximately 140° F for thirty minutes. This creates a very volatile liquid which explodes quite frequently. When the bottles leave the pasteurizer they behave like small bombs until they cool off. Under normal conditions a very light tap would result in the bottle exploding, throwing glass through the air.

From the time the bottles leave the pasteurizer until they are put in cases the bottles explode quite frequently. On the average a bottle explodes every five minutes. Employees are cut almost every day as a result of exploding bottles. During peak production periods at least one employee per week will lose time on the job because of lacerations resulting from exploding bottles.

Many safety measures have been taken to prevent lost time and accidents due to exploding beer bottles. Safety glasses are issued to every employee. Gloves, protective clothing, and face masks are issued on request. Protective glass barriers are put up around machines working with bottles to prevent exploding bottles from striking the employees. Accidents most often occur when an employee must handle the bottles because of a breakdown in a machine or on a line which transports the bottles around the plant.

Workers and management should react by following all of the safety procedures set down, but the plant employees don't always follow the rules of safety. There may be occasions when hands and arms are exposed because of lack of safety wear and an accident is the result. Safety wear is not worn all of the time because of the lack of mobility and the fact that it is very uncomfortable, and some jobs require a certain amount of mobility.

\* \* \*

*The text by William Lahey is printed with his permission.

# POWDER-ACTUATED TOOLS

*[This case and the three following it ("Hair Hazards," "Pressure and Spray Guns," and "Accident at Laboratory Tube Furnace") are all taken from Safety Perspective (1972),\* a magazine published by the Department of Labour, Canada.]*

An electrician's helper was injured when shot in the chest by a two and a quarter-inch threaded fastening stud fired from a powder-operated gun. The stud was propelled with such force that it penetrated his body, puncturing his left lung.

The electrician and his helper, on an electrical wiring renovation job, were installing a ¾-inch conduit. The electrician was working from a 10-foot high stepladder and his helper, 3 feet away, was on a fixed catwalk approximately 6 feet above floor level. The helper was holding one end of the conduit to the ceiling while the electrician was attaching the other end to a concrete column. The ceiling was 15 feet in height.

A powder-actuated stud driver, powered by a .22 calibre cartridge, was used to drive studs into the concrete.

The electrician had fired two shots with no apparent problem. As he snapped the breech closed the gun fired and the stud struck his helper in the chest.

The electrician dropped the gun and jumped over to the catwalk to assist the injured man who was nearly knocked off the walk by the impact. He was lowered to the ground, a dressing was applied, and he was removed by ambulance to the local hospital emergency ward.

The normal method for loading and firing this tool is to insert the fastening stud into the front end of the barrel. The breech mechanism is opened and the cartridge is inserted. The breech is then closed and locked by rotating the centre of the breech housing a quarter turn to the right. As a safety measure a spall, or adapter guard, must be engaged and depressed approximately one inch against a firm object before the tool can be fired.

It was found on examination that the handle of the tool was cracked. The firing pin was jammed in a forward position, protruding approximately ¹⁄₃₂ of an inch beyond the firing pin plate, and the firing pin plate was badly pitted from incorrect firing. In this instance, the cartridge that fired the shot had its rim flattened to a razor thin edge. The tool would fire without the breech being locked. The adapter guard was heavily damaged from previous ricochets and the barrel attachment portion cracked and damaged. The spall guard also was damaged from previous ricochets.

The tool was test-loaded with a cartridge but no drive stud. Six attempts were made to fire it by snapping the breech closed and not pulling the

---

\*Vol. 1, no. 1. The selections are reprinted by permission of Labour Canada.

trigger or depressing the guard plate. Two of the six attempts were successful.

On the strength of this test, the tool was condemned by the Canada Department of Labour Regional Safety Officer, and recommendations were made that this type of tool should be kept in working condition at all times and be regularly inspected.

\*     \*     \*

## HAIR HAZARDS

For both sexes, longer hair styles are in. Socially acceptable, long hair adorns the heads of many—from office boy to executive.

However, as the following accidents illustrate, long hair can be a potential hazard to watch for.

Tests in a laboratory involved the use of beakers and small fractional horsepower motor stirrers. When a female technician bent down to read a pipette, her hair was caught in the revolving shaft of an adjacent stirrer, and a small patch was pulled out.

The stirrer motors, rated at 1/10 hp and with 10-inch shafts, could easily be stopped by hand. The girl's hair was not particularly long, but the work area was congested and the stirrers were too closely spaced for safety.

A young man operating a vertical drill press, rotating at 200 rpm, leaned forward to watch the progress of his job. His hair was caught by the unguarded drill spindle. Despite his instant response to the sensation of his hair being entangled, the operator, in pulling himself free, damaged the scalp on the crown of his head. The resulting bald patch can be hidden only by a hairpiece.

It should be noted that even low horsepower motor shafts can inflict injury and where shafts are exposed they should be guarded to prevent contact with long hair or loose clothing.

\*     \*     \*

## PRESSURE AND SPRAY GUNS

Several articles have been written on injuries caused by high-pressure gases and liquids being forced through the skin. This hazard was again brought to light recently when an axle-packager received an injection of rust preventive in the first finger of his right hand.

As the axles are prepared for shipment they are placed on a layout table and sprayed with rust preventive. This is done with a spray gun operated at a pressure of 40 pounds per square inch. The gun clogged while the axle-packager was spraying and he wiped his right forefinger over the tip. At that instant the gun discharged and the man received an injection of rust preventive in the finger. The finger had to be amputated.

Supervisors have the responsibility to point out to employees the hazards of gases, liquids, and semi-solids (such as grease) under pressure by:

Making it clear that serious injuries can result if these substances penetrate the skin.

Stressing that a gun, or other applicator, should never be pointed toward any part of the body, and that pressure should be removed from the line, or hose, before any repair work is attempted.

\*      \*      \*

# ACCIDENT AT LABORATORY TUBE FURNACE

A research scientist working on a project in a laboratory was attempting to move a glass capsule in a tube furnace with a pair of tongs. The capsule, which was under pressure from the contained vapours, exploded, sending glass into one of his eyes. So severe was the injury that the scientist lost the sight of the eye.

The front of the furnace was 18 inches square, with a tubular oven an inch and a half in diameter, 14 inches long, and closed with a removable plug.

The glass capsule was about one inch in length and approximately 5/16 of an inch in diameter. The compounds to be tested were placed in the capsule, the ends were sealed and the capsule was placed in the oven.

Capsules may remain in an oven for days, depending on the circumstances of the tests. The temperature is raised to the required heat and held during the period of test, in this case, at 1000°F.

The supervisor's report of the accident states, "The worker only intended to change the position of a capsule in the furnace and neglected to wear his face shield. He picked up the metal tongs, removed the furnace plug and began to move the capsules; one of them exploded."

A Department of Labour Safety Officer who visited the laboratory to investigate the accident was informed that the scientist normally wore his face shield, in fact he was noted for cautioning technicians always to wear a face shield when working at the ovens.

The face shield that should have been worn was lying on a bench in front of the ovens. The tongs used, were normal laboratory tongs of the scissor-action type. They had been lengthened to reach to the back of the oven and were awkward, cumbersome and difficult to use in a confined space.

Discussion with the injured man, after he returned from the hospital, revealed that he had changed the position of one capsule, then reached further into the furnace to bring another capsule forward. Concentrating on the second capsule, and trying to see into a small dark area, he did not notice that the tongs had gripped the first capsule and were dragging it toward the front of the furnace.

The recommendations made at the laboratory—to post a warning notice to wear face shields and to reaffirm instructions to all staff to wear face guards at all times when working with furnaces—were reviewed by the Safety Officer and rejected as being only a partial safeguard. He reasoned that a safeguard that relied on the human element for its effectiveness would be effective only if the staff were on their toes the whole time. It would not safeguard the worker during a moment of aberration, to which even the most precise worker is subject.

The Safety Officer's application of the principles of ergonomics led to:

The design of a tool that would operate with the hand in a natural position;

Elimination of the scissor action to avoid tangential point contact on a smooth cylindrical surface;

The gripping portion of the tongs being designed to enclose the capsule;

A guard being placed on the tongs to minimize the risk of the operator being struck by flying fragments.

A rough sketch of the proposed tool was drawn up by the Safety Officer and the idea discussed with the head of the laboratories who arranged for his technical services staff to make a pair of tongs, observing the principles described. To improve visibility and to eliminate the sighting problem in the dark furnace, a light was added with a pre-focused bulb positioned to beam the light at the pick-up point.

The tongs have been in use for some months and have improved and eased the operation considerably; furthermore, the chance of anyone coming to harm because of a capsule exploding has been virtually eliminated.

A combination of job study, know-how and application of a technical remedy has produced a safe system of work. That's what accident prevention is all about.

It is fitting that the last word should come from the man who lost his eye. When asked if the new tongs were satisfactory he said, "Thank you, yes. They will certainly prevent anyone else losing an eye in the same circumstances and they are so much easier to use. Why do we have to have a major injury to produce something which, with hindsight, is an obvious need?"

\*      \*      \*

## UNSAFE ACTS: WHO IS RESPONSIBLE?

*[The following passage comes from another article in the same issue of Safety Perspective.\* The article is attributed to W. A. Martin.]*

It is assumed by many employers that victims of industrial accidents are, to some degree, responsible for their own misfortunes and that more often than not the principal cause of the accident was an unsafe act.

\*Vol. 1, no. 1. Reprinted by permission of Labour Canada.

In a particular accident, the unsafe act may have been a flagrant disregard of a well-known safety rule or gross indifference to good safety practice, while in another accident it may have resulted from insufficient knowledge of the safety rules, a lack of skill or a failure to recognize a hazard in time to avoid an accident.

The last mentioned unsafe act is of particular interest because in a surprisingly large number of cases an unsafe act is attributed to insufficient employee knowledge or skill or to some other employee deficiency. To too many accidents reports convey the impression that unsafe acts are largely beyond the control of the employer and therefore are attributed to "employee carelessness."

But such a diagnosis will not lead to the implementation of appropriate preventive measures because only the symptoms and not the causes of the problem have been noted.

If the pupil has insufficient knowledge of the rules, to what extent has the teaching been deficient? If his skills are below an acceptable level, was the training appropriate? What measures were in effect to test the adequacy of the pupil's knowledge and skill? The answers to these and similar questions often will lead to the conclusion that the unsafe act and the so-called employee carelessness did not begin with the employee but were, in fact, the unsafe conditions or deficiencies of his employment for which the employer is responsible.

If an employee trips over a loose tile, a broken step or a misplaced object, can it properly be claimed that he should have recognized the hazard and taken appropriate action to avoid it? Surely it is not reasonable to expect an employee to notice every potential hazard in time to avoid it, and the seriousness of the unsafe condition should not later be diluted by the assertion that a marginal but contributing factor to the accident was an unsafe act. If an employee has exercised reasonable care, he cannot fairly be charged with acting unsafely. In the instance just cited, the employee fell victim to a man-trap.

Where the dangers of certain work hazards cannot be completely eliminating, it is often possible to bring them within acceptable limits of risk by ensuring that every employee exposed to them is fully warned with respect to their nature and is trained in the precautions and preventive measures necessary to avoid them. To accomplish this, suitable education and training programs must be implemented to ensure that the requisite knowledge and skills are acquired by the employee.

Only those hazards that are constant as to location and degree are easily controllable through human response. For the rest there are so many variables that the average employee cannot be expected to cope with them all. It may then be asked, "To what extent is an inappropriate response, due to insufficient knowledge and skill, an employee deficiency?"

From the employer's point of view the less effort and attention an employee must give in order to avoid danger the more effort and attention he can give to the productive and quality aspects of his work. It is, therefore, in the employer's best interests to reduce the risk of accidents to the lowest level that is reasonably practicable of achievement. This being the case, why are there employers who still accept accidents as an inevitable part of work and who are so quick to conclude that accidents are the result of employee carelessness? The answer must lie in their inability to appreciate the difficulty the average person experiences in responding safely to an unexpected hazard and in their failure to provide the amount and quality of education and training required to ensure reliable and safe reactions to known hazards.

Although the injured employee is as often the innocent victim as he is the cause of his own misfortune, it will readily be conceded that, except for certain natural conditions such as weather, an unsafe condition is usually the result of an unsafe act—the supervisor failed to ensure that the employee was properly trained and instructed in the safe conduct of his work, the designer overlooked the need for a guard on a machine, the planning engineer did not make sufficient allowances in a new production schedule for easy compliance with safety requirements, the manager underestimated the cost of maintenance and repairs in his annual budget thereby creating unsafe conditions, or the tradesman failed to clean up an oil spill promptly and by such negligence unconsciously set a trap for a fellow employee.

\*    \*    \*

# ACCIDENT CAUSATION\*

Some work accidents occur because the employee is given inadequate warning of danger, has insufficient control over the circumstances which may lead to an accident, or is a victim of a booby trap.

Other accidents occur because of an employee's indifferent attitude to safety, acts of gross carelessness, inattention or lack of judgment.

The first category embraces those accidents which are entirely the responsibility of management. They are caused by conditions wholly outside the control of the employee. They result, among other things, from faulty or inadequate design, or hazardous substances and unsafe processes, the hazards of which have not been properly or fully explained to the employee, or which have not been neutralized by appropriate safety measures.

The second category includes those accidents within the power of the employee to avoid—accidents which occur in circumstances and conditions that may be unusual but in which the hazard can be readily recognized and avoided by proper attention to the job in hand, by observance of safety rules and by proper concern for safety.

Management must provide safe conditions for the average person doing his job with reasonable care, and must convince all employees that it is

---

\*Taken from Section 4 of *Planning for Safety,* a safety manual issued by the Department of Labour, Canada. Reprinted by permission of Labour Canada.

genuinely determined and sincere about safety by providing as safe a working environment as is reasonably practicable, by ensuring that employees are fully familiar with the hazards of their work and are properly trained to take all necessary precautions. It also has a responsibility to the work force to remove or otherwise discipline those who are habitually unsafe.

The employee for his part has an obligation to learn the safe way of doing his job and being alert to its hazards, to observe work rules and to generally adopt an attitude and habits favourable to accident prevention.

Approximately 80 per cent of all accidents are caused by errors of judgment, lack of care or attention to the task in hand, and other similar unsafe acts or by a combination of unsafe acts and unsafe conditions. An accident, therefore, is a clear pointer to a breakdown in management control, and a challenge to the ability to manage. It is no part of a supervisor's role to be perpetually surprised by accidents. He should know what is going on and what to expect—and the duty of prevention rests squarely on him.

In most enterprises rather more than 60 per cent of all employment injuries occur in the following categories: manual handling of goods and materials (25 per cent); falls of persons (15 per cent); persons striking against objects (8 per cent); persons struck by falling objects (8 per cent) and persons using hand tools (7 per cent).

Experience shows that, expect for minor fluctuations, this pattern remains substantially unaltered. There is a temptation, therefore, to regard these categories as the irreducible hard core. The problems they pose cannot be solved with the same degree of permanence possible when it is a question of fitting a guard to a machine, or providing a safe electrical installation. On the contrary, the hazards that contribute to the accidents are often recurrent, and their elimination requires not only rigid competent supervision of the methods of work and the organization necessary to ensure that rules are obeyed, but also a substantial degree of co-operation from employees.

But to anyone wishing to make rapid inroads into a poor safety performance, systematic study of these five categories will probably pay good dividends. Some of the remedial measures which have been found to be of help in eliminating these types of accidents are the enforcement of tidiness and good housekeeping, the study and planning of the movement of materials, the substitution wherever possible of mechanical and automatic handling devices for manual handling, the isolation of men from machines, the wider use of personal protective equipment, the training of new employees and the retraining of older ones where necessary.

It is axiomatic that tidiness and housekeeping are indispensable to good safety and no time should be spared in clearing up the work place or even the whole plant if that is required.

Where manual handling must continue to be done, there is often a need for more thorough instruction in the principles of lifting and handling; these are frequently not understood, and failure to appreciate them may easily result in injury, even though the load being handled is, in theory, well within the capacity of the individual concerned.

*   *   *

## Comment:

# CUMULATIVE HAZARDS

Accidents are by no means the whole story of dangerous work. Death and severe impairment to health can also result from breathing in injurious materials—dust, asbestos particles, poisonous chemicals—the effects of which show up only after a number of years; or from steady exposure to physical shocks that the human body cannot cope with adequately.

Some of these cumulative hazards are very gruesome. The hazard of working with asbestos is an example. Years, even decades, after working for only a little time with asbestos in some form, people may come down with asbestosis, "an irreversible lung disease that makes the victim highly susceptible to pneumonia and bronchitis." Working continually with asbestos increases the risk. Asbestos workers who smoke, taking on one hazard on top of another, have an incidence of lung cancer ninety-two times higher than the incidence for smokers in other industries. Besides the 7 percent who contract asbestosis, 7 to 10 percent suffer in time from mesothelioma, "a fatal and otherwise very rare form of cancer affecting the lining of the chest and abdominal cavity." (Quotations and statistics taken from a story in *Newsweek*, 8 May 1978.)*

*[Noise and vibration, the cumulative hazards described in the materials below, do not have such gruesome results. How often and in what circumstances it is really urgent to do something about them is therefore more open to dispute. Do the issues disappear when the hazard comes down to being little more than physical discomfort.]*

# PROTECTION OF WORKERS AGAINST NOISE AND VIBRATION IN THE WORKING ENVIRONMENT [excerpts]

---

(1) NOISE*

Noise may be the cause of various types of injury, disorders, annoyance and disturbance. The effects of noise may be physiological, mental and pathological; a distinction is made between the effects on hearing, the effects on other organs of perception and the general effects.

*Effects on the auditory system:*

(a) Masking

Noise of greater intensity may, in certain conditions, mask less intense noises and make them less readily audible, i.e., reduce the subjective intensity. The former are called masking noises and the latter masked noises.

The masking effect may have certain advantages but it may also have severe consequences when it renders less audible or completely inaudible sounds or noise which, in other circumstances, would give warning of an imminent danger against which the subject should seek protection.

(b) Interference with spatial localisation of sound

The presence of intense sound or noise may reduce the capability of localising a sound source in space. In particular, it may become difficult to perceive the movement of the sound source. This may have serious consequences since the closeness of danger may no longer be correctly perceived.

(c) Pain

High levels of sound and noise become difficult to bear and subsequently intolerable; at even higher levels (about 130 dB), auditory sensation is replaced by pain.

(d) Auditory sensation

Auditory sensation does not occur immediately even if the establishment of the sound or noise that produces it is virtually instantaneous; it develops progressively. Some 100 to 200 ms may be required before the maximum level is attained; in the same way when the noise or sound disappears, the auditory sensation terminates only after a short period of time.

If one measures the time between the onset of sound emission and a predetermined voluntary motor response, one encounters what is called the

---

*Excerpts from *Protection of Workers Against Noise and Vibration in the Working Environment*, 1977, pp. 61–65. Copyright 1977, International Labour Organisation, Geneva. Reprinted by permission of the International Labour Office.

"reaction time". This is relatively long and varies in length depending on the circumstances and a variety of factors such as the sound intensity and the subject and his or her physical and mental status. Even with perfectly healthy and well trained individuals, the reaction time may be between 100 and 400 ms. An increase in the length of the reaction time increases the accident hazard.

(e) Auditory fatigue

Auditory fatigue results in a reduction of auditory sensitivity—progressive rise in the perception threshold as the duration of noise exposure is increased. The greater the auditory fatigue, the more intense must the noise be to be perceived. Recovery from this fatigue is always complete.

The appearance of auditory fatigue depends not only on the duration but also the intensity of the noise exposure. Noise which is very intense but of a relatively short duration may, for example, cause auditory fatigue equal to that produced by a significantly less intense noise but for which the exposure time is longer.

Auditory fatigue occurs only if the sound or noise level is sufficiently intense (at least 60 or 70 dB); below this level, exposure may be very prolonged without ever causing auditory fatigue.

(f) Pathological effect on hearing

The deleterious effect of noise on hearing is essentially one of permanent hearing loss, also caled auditory trauma. This is the result of lesions to the ear caused by very intense noise.

Acoustic trauma is characterised by irreversible hearing loss in a frequency band of varying width. In the majority of cases and, in particular, in hearing damage due to industrial noise, the frequency band affected is centered around 4 000 Hz.

Noise-induced hearing loss does not progress after exposure to the noisy environment is terminated. Consequently, it is only necessary to remove from a noisy environment anybody in whom the onset of permanent hearing damage has been detected, in order to prevent any further aggravation.

*Effects on other organs of perception:*
Exposure to very high noise levels may often disturb the sense of balance and give the impression of "walking in space". Sufficiently high noise levels may also cause vertigo and nausea.

*Psychological effects:*
The psychological effects of noise consist basically of various feelings of discomfort caused by noise. They may occur as malaise and a feeling of discomfort which may extend even to well characterised mental or neurological disorders. Noise may also be the cause of discomfort due to the impairment of speech communication and speech intelligibility and may also reduce intellectual or psychomotor performance.

(a) General psychological disorders

General psychological disorders are widely encountered but, unfortunately, they are usually ill defined and vary from person to person. The cause-and-effect relationship between noise and the observed disorders is not always easy to establish.

They vary widely in type and degree, ranging from malaise to neurological or psychiatric disorders. The malaise may be a feeling of distress, discomfort, annoyance or surprise.

(b) Interference with intellectual and psychomotor performance

The effects that noise may have on intellectual and psychomotor performance are seen in particular by the greater difficulty subjects experience in a noisy environment when carrying out intellectual operations or tasks which require concentration or special psychomotor ability.

*General somatic effects:*

A distinction is made between two types of physiological reaction to noise: the first is a startle reflex (alarm or stress reaction) as soon as the noise appears; the second is that which develops when exposure to the sound is prolonged.

*Protection of workers against noise . . . :*

Prolonged exposure to intense noise leads to fatigue, lassitude sometimes accompanied by general debility. This may be followed by the development of various disorders such as giddiness, fainting, headaches, migraine, loss of appetite, loss of weight and anaemia, depending on the case.

(2) VIBRATION

The physiological and pathological effects of vibration transmitted to the human body may be grouped in the following four categories:

(1) *Very low-frequency vibration (lower than 1 Hz).* Responsible for the motion sickness which has as its symptoms nausea and vomiting; this sickness is due to the action of changes in acceleration on the labyrinth of the internal ear.

(2) *Low-frequency whole-body vibration (between 1 and 20 Hz).* Gives rise to a wide range of pathological phenomena including lumbago, sciatica in the lumbar region, neckache, hernia and twinges in the intervertebral discs; these manifestations may occur after a period of exposure in persons who were initially in good health.

(3) *Low-frequency vibration (between 10 and 20 Hz) transmitted to the hands and arms.* Leads to high biomechanical and muscular strain as a consequence of resonance.

(4) *Higher frequency vibration (above 20 Hz).* May produce the following pathological effects:

(a) vibration in the 20-30 Hz range applied to upper limbs is the cause of osseous or articular lesions in the hands, wrists, forearms and upper arms;

(b) vibration in the 40-300 Hz range produces vascular manifestations; these may be attributed to local disturbance of the nervous system controlling vasomotor action;

(c) vibration in the 500-1 000 Hz range may cause sensory and trophic manifestations giving a burning or numb sensation.

(3) REGULATIONS FOR THE PREVENTION OF RISKS DUE TO NOISE
AND VIBRATION*

The question of noise and vibration is touched on in several ILO Conventions and Recommendations, and has been discussed at various meetings and in publications prepared by the Occupational Safety and Health Branch or by the CIS.

Recommendation No. 97 (1953), concerning the Protection of the Health of Workers in Places of Employment, lays down that "measures" should be taken "to eliminate or reduce as far as possible noise and vibration which constitute a danger to the health of workers" (Article 2(h)).

Convention and Recommendation Nos. 120 (1963) concerning Hygiene in Commerce and Offices also deal with noise and vibration. The Recommendation, more especially, provides:

"Particular attention should be paid:

(a) to the substantial reduction of noise and vibrations caused by machinery and sound-producing equipment and devices;
(b) to the enclosure or isolation of sources of noise or vibrations which cannot be reduced;
(c) to the reduction of intensity and duration of sound emissions, including musical emissions; and
(d) to the provision of sound-insulating equipment, where appropriate, to keep the noise of workshops, lifts, conveyors or the street away from offices."

Should such action not be enough "to eliminate harmful effects adequately", then:

"(a) workers should be supplied with suitable ear protectors when they are exposed to sound emissions likely to produce harmful effects;
(b) workers exposed to sound emissions and vibrations likely to produce harmful effects should be granted regular breaks included in the working hours in premises free of such sound emissions and vibrations;
(c) systems of work distribution or rotation of jobs should be applied where necessary."

*Excerpts from *Noise and Vibration in the Working Environment*, 1976, pp. 111–112. Copyright 1976, International Labour Organisation, Geneva. Reprinted by permission of the International Labour Office.

## STRESS

Dangerous work is not just a problem for blue-collar workers. Offices, it is true, are much more likely to be quiet and well-ventilated than factories. Major accidents and most sorts of cumulative hazards are usually absent. Yet even in offices as physically comfortable as designers can make them, people may suffer from stress to a degree that leads to nervous breakdowns, or to early deaths. Stress can occur on the factory floor too, in addition to all the other hazards there. Its occurrence in the office and the executive suite is more ironic, besetting people who have freed themselves from the other hazards and to some extent impose this hazard upon themselves by undertaking too much work.

An article in a publication addressed to people in business,* after citing several cases of nervous breakdowns, quotes a downtown Toronto physician as saying that relatively few people have breakdowns. "Far more frequently," he says, "I'll see a guy who was sitting at his desk and suddenly finds himself vomiting blood. Or someone who begins hyperventilating, shows rapid heart rate and loses consciousness. Or maybe he's suffering from low blood sugar, or has a coronary." The article goes on to quote a physician who practices in the suburbs. "The very word 'business' makes Dr. Storey wince. He's seen its leveling effect on countless patients over the past 25 years. 'There's no room for failure in the business world,' he contends. 'There's not even a little room for failure, and that's what I hate about it. Just as soon as you stop winning, you're out. Or transferred. There's no leeway, no *give*.' "

An industrial psychologist cited in the article "waves aside" the 20 percent of cases that he concedes are "brought on by . . . struggling with too big a workload." Eighty percent of stress, according to this psychologist, is "change-oriented" and "comes from the inability of some people to shift gears" when the demands of their work change.

*Clarke Wallace, "Why Everything Goes Wrong," *The Financial Post Magazine,* May 1980, p. 2. Reprinted with Clarke Wallace's permission and the permission of *The Financial Post.*

*Comment:*

# THE MORAL CLAIMS OF
# HEALTH AND SAFETY

There will, I hope, be less appearance of there being disproportionately many materials under the heading of dangerous work and certain other headings (like sexual harassment) if one reflects that they are topics especially apt to engender far-ranging discussions of general moral ideas. Dangerous work could hardly be more fertile in this regard. What could be more important morally than preserving people's lives and health and enabling them to lead, in health and safety, decent sorts of lives—if you like, lives with decent chances of happiness? This consideration, as I have already intimated, appears somewhere at the bottom of every serious conception of ethics: In the Ten Commandments ("Thou shalt not kill"); in Kant's prescription never to treat other people as mere means, but to make respect for their lives an end of one's own; in the utilitarian principle that the end to aim at in every choice is the happiest possible life for everybody affected.

How far does the consideration go? "Enabling people to lead lives with decent chances of happiness" suggests that one should help people as much as possible in this connection, compatible, one might say, with retaining a decent chance of happiness for oneself. On the other hand, the consideration might be taken negatively, as going no further than to require standing out of other people's way and refraining from doing them harm. If we count omitting to provide opportunities as harm, the distinction may break down. Let us be ready to do whatever may be required to keep the distinction up, so that we can see how far a limited, even grudging acceptance of the consideration will take us.

In fact, it will take us quite far. Suppose the following scheme for dealing with health and safety at work is proposed: Workers are to be given full information about the dangers of the jobs offered them and it will be left to them to choose whether to take the jobs and run those dangers. The negative conception of the consideration of decent lives and happiness suffices to demonstrate that in a society like ours the scheme is not a morally acceptable one.

Most people in our society, as we have continually had to keep in mind, must look for employment and most (taking them one by one) have no alternative to accepting the working conditions offered by a small set of employers—perhaps one employer in the vicinity. Assume that everyone in the society is agreed that at least negatively conceived the consideration of decent lives and happiness is to be given full effect. Assume also that employers and employees have together complete responsibility for health and safety and only the employers can afford substantial expenses in this connection. But if the workers have no alternative means of obtaining a livelihood, they will have to take the jobs no matter what the dangers, and without being able to demand premium pay to offset them.

The employers may then well do less than they could (even without much affecting their profits) to provide safer conditions. They will in fact be harming the workers, not just by omitting to provide them with opportunities for increased happiness (in recreation, for example) but by imposing dangers upon them. Therefore, the scheme proposed is morally unacceptable, being inconsistent with the consideration of decent lives and happiness. Moreover, if it is unacceptable—impermissible—for employers to behave as they do under the scheme, they have a moral obligation, arising from the consideration, to behave otherwise, which amounts to having a moral obligation to provide safer conditions.

Is this argument just fancy idealism? That it or something like it has had some impact on actual policy may be inferred from reflecting on the list of motives that we might compile to explain why employers do in fact spend money on measures of safety. This list would include self-interested motives of various sorts: improving productivity (by lowering turnover in the work force); avoiding bad publicity; conforming to a legal obligation. We might add that if there is more competition in the market for labor than assumed above, so that some premium has to be paid for dangerous work, a firm might save on wages what it spent on safety. We need not go on to list motives that are not self-interested (though they often have, I think, an important place among the motives of employers) to see how this list betokens acceptance in the surrounding society of something like the argument outlined above.

For, let us ask, why is there a legal obligation? Laws requiring employers to provide safe conditions would not be on the books if society was satisfied that the scheme of full information would suffice. Is support for the laws by many people who do not themselves have dangerous work likely to be just self-interested?

Let us ask, too, why would publicity about unsafe conditions be bad? Once the legal obligation is imposed, of course, an employers may be reproached for breaking the law. Is it plausible that this is the whole story?

Something like the argument to a moral obligation not only helps explain why there is a legal obligation; it explains why employers are reproached so vehemently for unsafe conditions. The law in question is not just a technical commercial regulation. It is something that makes it easier for competing firms to heed an important moral obligation; and to be, if they wish, humane.

Some difficult problems remain. One of them is, How far are measures of health and safety to be carried?

A further problem is, Given that employers are to bear some part of those expenditures, how much are they to bear? What measures are they to pay for? In other words, how are the costs and the responsibility to be divided between the employers and employees (and between the government and consumers as well)?

If we have got this far, we will be ready to question, besides the scheme of relying on full information, any scheme that relies on private charitable contributions as the sole supplementary measure. Such contributions have played a significant part, for example, in creating and maintaining lifeboat stations around the coast of Britain; but whether they would suffice over the whole range of health and safety considerations is doubtful. The moral appeals that elicit charitable contributions are still relevant. If the appeals are to inspire public policy and legislation, however, they may have to meet a more stringent test than simply moving enough people, one by one, to amass a substantial sum of contributions. They will have to meet the test of public debate; and if this debate is balanced, systematic, and fair in the respects that adequate moral discussion demands, the appeals will have to rest on considerations capable of winning reasoned assent from every participant and everyone affected by the issues.

I pointed out earlier in this book how the test of public debate, so conceived, helps explain why justice and the consideration of happiness are so prominent in ethics. We need not assume that people are steadily more attached to these considerations than to their own self-interest. It is not the elevation of people's feelings, when people are left to themselves, that is decisive, but the circumstances compelling them to behave one way rather than another. In a public debate aimed at reaching a social decision, no one can expect to get any more attention to his or her self-interest than he or she is prepared to give to the interests of other people. Hence once an issue is taken up in public debate, it comes under conditions that will be demanded for the fairness and balance of the debate itself. Those conditions require the issue to be resolved by considerations, like justice and happiness for all, that go beyond self-interest.

How far do those considerations go toward deciding just how much is to be spent on safety, and who is to spend it? Quite far, in fact. The problem may be made easier by the presence of a natural point of inflection, beyond which the benefits gained from expenditures on health and safety drop off sharply. If such a limit is not present, however, or it is some distance away from present expenditures, it seems reasonable to aim at trying to reduce rates of mortality and disease in industries where they are high (lumbering, mining, fishing) to the rates prevailing in industries where they are low (retail trade, banking). Doing so would answer to justice, by equalizing rates for the people concerned; and answer to the consideration of decent lives and happiness, by equalizing the rates downward, so that people lived longer and more comfortably.

Would we go all the way to equalization in one step? Probably not. There might be different natural points of inflection in different industries. We would have to consider, if some industries were going to remain more dangerous, what would be a just basis for assigning people to those industries. There will also be other claims on resources—for example, current needs for food, clothing, shelter, heat.

Balancing safety against other claims, suppose we decide how much should be done in the current year toward equalizing rates of morality and disease. Who is to bear the costs? We may distinguish four groups each of which would have some responsibility: employers; employees; the public (acting through government); consumers. Even without arriving at an exact division of costs, we can advance toward making one by identifying some decision points. For example, we cannot expect employees to protect themselves when the machines that they work with require more care than tired human beings can be expected to give toward the end of shifts. Here protective devices will have to be installed on the machines. Who is to pay for them? Both employers and employers might be just getting by, so that if the employers paid for the devices without shifting the costs to the consumers they would go bankrupt and if the employees paid for the devices they would not have enough income left to cover minimum needs. (Notice how quickly and closely relevant the consideration of lives and happiness becomes.)

If the employers cannot shift the costs, then the public must decide whether it is worthwhile keeping the industry going; if it is, a subsidy would be in order. A subsidy might cost less than the costs of medical care and unemployment through disability that the public would have to bear if the industry operated without the protective devices; and cost less than the costs of unemployment and social dislocation if the industry was shut down.

Will not the public also be moved by fellow-feeling for its fellow-citizens employed in the industry? It is hard to believe that the public provisions for medical care, unemployment insurance, and welfare payments already in force do not reflect a substantial amount of concern for justice (some people are more vulnerable to economic distress than others) and happiness (no one is to be allowed to fall below some minimum standard for decent lives). People may not steadily put these considerations ahead of self-interest; but they feel them sometimes, strongly enough in appropriate circumstances to act upon them.

## HOW FIRMS TREAT SAFETY AND COMPENSATION

Some firms are prepared to go to a lot of trouble to promote their employees' health and safety. Irving S. Shapiro, the chairman of the board of Du Pont, cites with some pride a *Wall Street Journal* article (28 June 1976) entitled "Hunt for Hazards: Protecting the Health of Du Pont Employees Is a Costly Proposition." In the article it said, "Concern about safety and health takes on a slightly manic air at Du Pont." Shapiro says, "Our policy is that *all* accidents and illness from exposure to known hazards can be prevented. Every supervisor . . . learns quickly that Du Pont is not prepared to accept any predictable level of injury or illness in any manufacturing unit; he or she learns that the supervisor's job is to see to it that employees do not get hurt"

(Shapiro, "Occupational Health and Safety," in Thornton Bradshaw and David Vogel, eds., *Corporations and Their Critics* [New York, 1981], pp. 211–216, at p. 211). Du Pont, according to Shapiro, insists on periodic medical examinations of its employees and keeps epidemiological records. Since 1935, it has maintained a large laboratory continually inquiring into health hazards relevant to its operations—the Haskell Laboratory for Toxicology and Industrial Medicine, with a staff of about two hundred.

Another firm that in such matters can claim a position on the clearly right side of the triplet principle is Anaconda, a subsidiary of the Atlantic Richfield Company. At its copper smelter in Montana, Anaconda was one of the first companies in the industry to try to measure the danger posed by arsenic in the concentrates smelted. It has led the industry in introducing engineering-control systems that reduce hazards. It supplies good respirators and makes sure they stay in effective condition. Since 1970 the smelter has had a joint labor-management safety and health committee that takes part in inspections, investigations, and precautionary planning. The company gives workers access to their own medical records, which are not available at the smelters of some other companies. Workers at Anaconda may refuse unsafe or unhealthy work without losing their jobs and they are the only workers in the industry who do not risk losing pay if they are reassigned for reasons of health.

INFORM, the national nonprofit research organization founded and directed by Joanne Underwood, compiled this information about Anaconda (Underwood, "Land Development and Working Conditions," in Bradshaw and Vogel, pp. 173–185). It has the opposite story to tell (in the same article) about Newmount Mining Corporation and the smelter that it runs in Arizona. There, very unusual in the industry, no workers' safety and health committee exists. "Workers are not allowed to participate in investigating accidents, nor are management's findings on accidents made available to them, although the smelter has more than six times the industry average rate of recordable injuries and illnesses." Workers at the Newmount smelter do not have the right to refuse unsafe work. Workers cannot see their medical records or the data that the company has in hand about health hazards. Even Anaconda does not make this data available. Giving workers full information may not suffice as a scheme for coping with the problem of dangerous work; yet it evidently outruns current business practice even so.

Evidently Newmount comes out on the other side of the triplet principle, among the clear cases of being wrong. Besides being right or wrong in internal safety programs, firms may be right or wrong in their behavior about compensating employees; and they may be right or wrong in welcoming or opposing government regulations on both subjects. How firms deal with governments is a topic assigned a heading of its own, later in the book. We may nevertheless go along for a moment with the natural tendency of issues about health and safety to develop into issues about government regulations.

In connection with compensation, for example, not only do firms often oppose giving compensation to particular workers; in doing so they are simultaneously trying to induce less generous policies in government agencies. According to a story in *Maclean's Magazine* (19 May 1980, pp. 45 ff.), "Some of the most bitter worker-industry confrontations take place over compensation claims, with grisly debates about whether a dying man's cancer is or is not the result of his work."* At stake for industry are the amounts of its contributions to compensation funds. In Ontario, the premiums paid by firms went up from $263 million in 1974 to $539 million four years later. James Findlay, the executive vice-president of the Industrial Accident Prevention Association of Ontario, an employers' organization, is cited as denouncing these costs as "obscene." "In an effort to reduce them, industry recently has been fighting compensation claims even more vigorously than it did in the past." The health and safety coordinator for the United Steelworkers claimed, "Industry has begun to appeal disability awards even after they have gone through the regular appeal stage. We never had any of these appeals before, and now we've had five in the past six months." Findlay, it is said, commented, "Sure, companies have made appeals. Companies are getting sharper. That decreases costs."

*Maclean's* states, "Unions were quick to react . . . when it was reported that an occupational health consultant had advised a group of employers meeting in Hamilton . . . to frustrate compensation claims they felt were invalid" by leaving out the social insurance number. "Then it won't go into the computers." The consultant now says that "he was only trying to improve communications between industry and the [compensation] board, since leaving out information on the form makes it more likely board officials will phone the employer. This gives the company an opportunity—in addition to the space allotted on the form—to raise its objections to the claim."

In one case, a company opposed compensation for an employee of 35 years' standing who died "after developing a larynx cancer that forced doctors to remove his voice box. 'He couldn't even talk his last year,' recalls his wife, Ivy. In ruling against a widow's pension, the board argued that it was not clear [the dead man's] cancer was caused by his work since he'd spent *only six years* working near one of the most hazardous parts of the asbestos grinding plant, although the open-concept design allowed dust to circulate freely throughout the plant (board rules stipulate a minimum of 10 years' 'proven' exposure)."

"Industry's counter-attack isn't confined to compensation," *Maclean's* asserts. "Perhaps even more significant, in the long run, is its push for less government control over dangerous substances in the workplace. Industry lobbied Ontario hard for less provincial regulation when the province was drawing up its new health and safety bill. . . . In briefs to the government, both employers' associations and individual firms argued against giving government inspectors too much power and replacing provincial 'guide-

*Copyright Linda McQuaig; drawn on with her permission and with the permission of *Maclean's Magazine*.

lines' with legally binding standards. In fact, by and large, industry would like a free hand to regulate itself."

Just how far firms (and their associations) have been justified or unjustified in their activities cannot be determined here, any more than it can on other subjects, on the basis of one story in a popular magazine. The story does, however, give a number of vivid clues as to what sorts of good and evil are to be looked for, including possible assignments of responsibility.

*Comment:*

# ABNORMALLY LOW WAGES AND BENEFITS

Whether or not some people are to derive income from other sources, it is generally accepted that justice requires, for people who do depend on wages, equal pay for equal work. The question immediately arises, when differences in wages are observed, whether the differences are consistent with this requirement. If they are not, are the firms employing the lower-paid workers exploiting them in some especially unjustifiable way?

## REASONS FOR WAGE DIFFERENCES (ILO)*

What are the main reasons for wage differences, and especially for their persistence, which frequently continues year after year? Here a distinction must be drawn between differences which are fair and those which are unfair. It will generally be accepted as fair that workers who are skilled should be paid higher wages than semi-skilled and unskilled workers, though the question of how much more they should get is difficult to decide. Usually they have gone through courses of apprenticeship or other training to become skilled, and may have earned very little during the years of training in order to obtain higher wages later on. It is fair that workers doing heavy work under unpleasant and dangerous conditions should receive more than similar workers in light industries where conditions are

---

*Excerpt from *Wages: A Workers' Education Manual*, 1968, pp. 134–138. Copyright 1968, International Labour Organisation, Geneva. Reprinted by permission of the International Labour Office.

pleasant and safe. Coal miners working underground in dirt and danger should reasonably be paid more than workers requiring similar energy and skill in agreeable surface conditions.

Yet economic and other factors may prevent workers doing unpleasant or dangerous work from receiving wages which are fair in relation to other manual workers. Coal miners should be high in the wage scale. In the United Kingdom, for example, from the middle 1920s and in the 1930s, as a result of the rapid increase in the use of oil, the more economic use of fuel, and other developments, the demand for coal fell so much that the industry suffered severe unemployment and wages were reduced to low levels in comparison with other industries. Not until the size of the industry and the number of miners had come down to a competitive level with other fuels and general industry prosperity had been restored did coal mine wages rise again to a more appropriate level in the scale. In the same inter-war years the experience of coal miners in other European countries was similar to that in the United Kingdom.

In more general terms wages in different industries are generally affected by the prosperity or depression of each industry. . . . If the demand for the products of an industry is high, employers want more workers and, especially if skilled workers are scarce, will compete to get them by offering higher wages and other advantages. Therefore wages in such industries rise above the general average. The opposite is true in depressed industries which suffer from a capacity to produce far more goods than can be sold in the market.

There are some economic advantages in wages in prosperous industries being somewhat higher than the general average and in depressed industries somewhat below it. If the prosperity or depression is likely to be long and represents a permanent change in the quantities of products that the community wants to buy, the difference in wages will cause workers to move from depressed to prosperous industries or, perhaps more important, will cause newcomers to the labour force to enter chiefly the prosperous and not the depressed industries, and wages in them will sooner or late tend towards greater equality as a proper economic balance is restored. Yet in a period when industries are out of balance the wage differences should, as far as possible, be prevented from being unduly wide. If a wide gap develops the principle of equal pay for equal work becomes seriously violated. Workers in the depressed industries may do work requiring the same skill, energy and ability as demanded of those in the prosperous industries and yet be kept at substantially lower standards of living. This inevitably causes discontent.

The question must also be raised whether highly prosperous companies—for example diamond, brewery or tobacco firms—should, because their profits and capacity to pay are so much greater, pay wages much higher than the textile, clothing or furniture industries.

Some wage differences are due partly to the strength or weakness of trade unions. In occupations and industries with strong trade unions their bargaining power may enable them to raise wages above those in industries where trade unionism is weak. Workers in other industries who, because of trade union weakness or depression, are unable to win higher money wages find that their standards of living lag behind rising prices and are worse off because of inflation. It could be urged that such workers should form equally strong trade unions to protect their standards of living. But, as is well known from experience in many countries, the formation of strong trade unions is often difficult in some occupations.

Custom or tradition is also a factor which may cause wage differentials to persist over long periods. In many countries, and particularly in those that are developing, the wages of agricultural workers and the standards of living of self-employed peasants are usually much lower than those of industrial workers in the cities. This is partly because rural people are accustomed to life in the villages and cling to any land which they own. They are often ignorant of the higher wages they could earn in the towns or of the conditions of factory employment. Also, especially in heavily over-populated agricultural countries, the vast number of workers in the rural areas keeps wages down, and they suffer from underemployment because few opportunities are available for working in industry. However, these opportunities increase as industrial developments are undertaken; with better transport and communication the rural populations know more about wages, working conditions and living standards; and, especially among the younger men, the exodus to the towns increases. This tends gradually to narrow the gap between rural and urban wages, as also does the development of more efficient methods on the farms.

Wages, of course, are not the only sort of personal income. In strict economic terms, wages are the reward for labour, which in turn may be defined as human effort of any kind employed to meet an economic demand. Thus, the effort most of us put into a game of football is not labour, but the effort of a professional footballer is, and he receives wages in return. The greater part of the earnings of a small shopkeeper, who does all his own work, are wages in the strict sense. So are the fees of lawyers and doctors, the stipends of clergymen, authors' royalties, the salaries of presidents and prime ministers and the incomes of working farmers. A burglar's takings are not wages, though he may work quite hard to obtain them, because he is hardly meeting an economic demand. The crops grown by subsistence farmers may be regarded, economically, as a form of wages in kind.

The other forms of income, in the strict economic sense, are (*a*) rents, being payment for the use of land and premises, and (*b*) interest, being payment for the use of capital. Most economists would add profit, being the reward for enterprise in bringing labour, land and capital into productive employment. Others would argue that profit is a variable form of interest, the reward for supplying capital; others, again, that it is theoretically a form of wages, inasmuch as enterprise is in fact a form of work.

\*    \*    \*

# THE UNEQUAL WAGES OF WOMEN (ILO)*

---

*[The fact that women are typically paid less than men for the same work, or for comparable work, poses the questions about justice and exploitation for one particular subset of workers; but it is a very large subset, for which the questions take on a large magnitude.]*

Some jobs are done almost exclusively by men because they are unsuitable for women. Work involving heavy physical toil or strain is usually, but not always, done by men—underground mining, quarrying, heavy iron and steel work, dock labour, shipping and fishing trawler work. Heavy farm work is usually undertaken by men, while women do the lighter jobs. In the textile industry some jobs are done only by men, others only by women; and there are certain textile occupations in which both men and women are employed. The same is true of the clothing industry. In many countries women are employed mainly, though not exclusively, on shorthand and typing, but the practice varies from country to country. Cooking, waiting at table and certain other kinds of domestic work are done by either men or women, though mainly by women. In some professions which are open to both men and women, for example law and medicine, the men greatly outnumber the women; and even if both are paid at the same rates the men's earnings are higher and their promotions more rapid.

To an increasing extent, however, many former distinctions between men's and women's jobs are breaking down as a result of technological changes in methods of work, including automation and other labour-saving devices. There are still wide differences in the numbers of men and women in different sectors of the economy, and also what is considered to be women's work differs from country to country and from period to period. For example, at one time engineering [making and repairing machines] was almost exclusively a man's job, but now much light engineering is done by women. Substantial progress has been made in recent years in increasing better-paid employment opportunities for women. Indeed, the number of jobs open to women and the size of the overlap area are growing because of the greater use of mechanical methods that reduce the amount of physical effort required.

The largest proportion of women are still employed on lower-paid, less-skilled jobs and in consequence their average earnings are considerably less than those of men. Such differences can be reduced by the better education and vocational training of girls and women so as to raise their qualifications. The efficiency of women at work can be raised in this way. Because many women do not undertake paid work for some years when their children are young they lack experience, seniority and length of service relatively to men

---

*Excerpt from *Wages: A Workers' Education Manual*, 1968, pp. 112–117. Copyright 1968, International Labour Organisation, Geneva. Reprinted by permission of the International Labour Office.

and this tends to result in lower wages for them. Greater provision of day nurseries to take care of their young children during working hours could reduce the length of time women remain away from paid employment, while more retraining courses would help more quickly to restore their efficiency when they return to work as their children grow older.

Most countries prohibit the employment of women on work regarded as unsuitable for them, for example underground mining, and restrict their employment in various ways, such as by prohibiting or regulating night work and overtime work by them. Thus stricter limitations may be put on the amount of overtime worked by women than on that worked by men. Even where employment of women is not limited by legislation the preferences of employers for employing men in many occupations and the opposition sometimes shown by male workers to working with women reduce the occupational range and the employment opportunities of women, no matter how strongly one may disapprove of such attitudes.

An important factor affecting women's wages is that most of them expect to marry. Many employers, and some governments, are reluctant to provide expensive courses of apprenticeship or other training which would qualify women for skilled and other highly paid work. Most of them, therefore, go into semi-skilled or unskilled work, which they can quickly learn in a few weeks or months. This is one of the main reasons why the average wages of women are considerably below those of men, which include the wages of a much higher proportion of skilled workers. Problems arise for women who try to combine home duties with paid employment. In many industries women's wages average only about two-thirds to three-quarters of men's wages. This does not necessarily indicate a violation of the principle of equal remuneration for work of equal value but may be due to the fact that many more men than women are doing skilled work, for which higher wages are paid. The fact that women may have been denied opportunities of acquiring these better paid skills is, of course, itself unfair. They may be entitled to equal pay for equal work but cannot perform equal tasks because they have not been trained to do so, possibly through no choice of their own. This is not strictly a wages issue, however. It is a question of equality of opportunity.

A main difficulty in applying the principle of equal remuneration for work of equal value is that of defining "work of equal value". The simplest case is where men and women are doing the same kind of work: for example weaving identical qualities of cloth on the same kind of looms in the same working conditions. If women and men produce equal quantities of equal quality, then their pay should be equal. . . .

The application of the methods of job analysis and evaluation by classifying different jobs into grades or categories can help to establish fair relations between men's and women's wages, because such methods direct attention to the requirements of the job, irrespective of whether it is done by men or women. Wage differentials should be based only on the qualities required for each job, such as education, training, skill, experience, responsibilities and efficiency, and not on sex. Thus, wage rates for the same job should be equal for men and women, even though the earnings of workers on piece-rates will differ, some men earning more than some women, but the more efficient women earning more than the less efficient men. Where different rates are fixed for different jobs they should be determined solely by differences in the qualities required for each job. If this is done, discrimination based on prejudices and custom can be avoided. Between people with equal qualifications and ability there should be no pay differentials.

The main demands for equal pay are made in respect of jobs where the kind of work, including the grading of the workers, is the same or very similar. Where, for example, men and women teachers or civil servants have the same qualifications and experience, strong demands are made for equal pay. Yet often differences of 10 or 15 percent are found in favour of men. This is partly because employers believe, usually without evidence, that on the average men workers are worth more than women workers.

In some occupations the output of women is lower because they are not as strong as men. Absentee rates, especially from sickness, are somewhat higher among women than men, and this is sometimes given as a reason for paying them at lower rates than men. Turnover is also greater among women. Restrictions on their work due to special protective legislation are another factor. A much larger proportion of men have dependents to maintain, and this results in a tendency to work harder, especially when on piece-work, in order to earn more. Married men with families are often keen to work overtime. On the other hand, many women and girls are not entirely dependent on their earnings. Married women who work often regard their earnings as a supplement to the family income. Because married men have responsibility for family maintenance they are likely to be more determined, through their trade unions, to struggle for good wages than are women workers, many of whom have few or no dependants to support and are therefore willing to acquiesce in lower wages. Also, women are less inclined to join and actively participate in trade unions. Their bargaining position is therefore often weaker than that of men.

It is because of the weaker bargaining position of women that some of the earliest laws for fixing minimum wages were either limited in their scope to women and young persons or applied in industries where large numbers of women were employed, often at sweated wages involving severe privation and misery. Some States, in the interests of social welfare, undertook the regulation of the wages of women in industry to prevent their exploitation.

The spread of education and training among girls is opening up new careers for women and enabling them to enter more skilled and better-paid occupations. So long as the education and training of girls are inferior to those of boys, their opportunities of employment on equal terms in the better-paid jobs will be restricted. It must, however, be recognised that some girls are reluctant to prepare for careers involving long training. . . .

The principle of equal remuneration to men and women alike for work of equal value is socially just as well as economically sound. Employers try, in every circumstance, to get work done efficiently at the lowest cost. The removal of prejudices and traditions against the employment of women would enable demand and supply to determine both the occupations in which the efficiency of women equals or exceeds that of men and the proportions in which men and women can be employed with the greatest efficiency in diffeent industries. In occupations where women can hold their own and do equal work with men the interaction of demand and supply will strengthen the trend for equal pay.

The principle of equal remuneration for work of equal value can assist women in their struggle to remove irrational prejudices which restrict their employment. Application of the principle can also be of value to men by removing the danger that, in some occupations, they may lose their jobs to women because of wage undercutting. On the other hand, especially in countries with heavy unemployment, the possibility must be recognised that the adoption of equal remuneration for work of equal value might reduce employment opportunities for women.

*   *   *

# EXPLOITATION IN FORMS AND METHODS OF PAYMENT (ILO)*

In addition to the need for wages to be fixed at reasonable standards it is essential that the workers shall receive regularly what is due to them. Yet unscrupulous employers have evaded their responsibilities and it has become necessary to protect workers against abuses. Such measures are also of value to good employers, who [again] would otherwise suffer from wage undercutting by competitors paying less than the rates fixed.

ABUSES OF PAYMENTS IN KIND

One of the earliest abuses was under the system by which a substantial part of the wage was paid in kind. If only a small part of the wage was in cash, workers had little freedom to buy in the markets the goods they wished to have. The goods supplied in kind might be of poor quality and little worth. This was particularly true of perishable foods. In suitable circumstances there is no objection and even some advantage if employers buy foods and other goods of adequate quality and then distribute them to the workers at wholesale cost or even at subsidised prices. Workers should, however, be protected against having to accept poor goods as part of their wage or being required to buy such commodities at company stores managed by the employer for his own profit.

Some workers were paid partly in goods they produced; for example coal miners would receive several tons of coal a year, and farm labourers might be paid partly in potatoes or other produce. These various forms of payment became known as "truck" and were so extensively abused that many countries passed truck Acts to regulate or even prohibit payments in

*Excerpt from *Wages: A Workers' Education Manual*, 1968, pp. 120–123. Copyright 1968, International Labor Organisation, Geneva. Reprinted by permission of the International Labour Office.

kind. Some of the Acts require employers to pay the whole wage in cash. Others provide for strictly regulated payment of a limited part of the wage in kind, so defined that the workers receive proper value or even benefit from such payments; the provision of good meals in factory canteens at favourable prices is an example.

In many of the developing countries the custom of paying a substantial part of the wages in kind is still a serious problem. In most African countries, for example, the people live traditionally in small villages, in houses of their own construction, cultivating the nearby family or tribal land. The development of industry and of plantation agriculture, requiring the services of relatively large labour forces, brought a shortage of housing, among other things. It became the practice for the employer to provide accommodation, rations and in some countries clothing and medical care— in fact, the basic requirements of existence. In the circumstances of the time little else could be done. Colonial legislatures passed laws which laid down certain minimum requirements of nutrition, housing space, ventilation and the like. This was a sound policy, given the situation, although the standards were sometimes very low. To make the situation more difficult, many of the workers were and still are immigrant labourers, who have trekked in from remote parts and are willing, if not content, to put up with bad conditions for a short time while earning something to take back some day to their families.

This problem will not be solved until the workers are able to live settled lives with their families in homes of their own, and buy food and clothing to their own taste in shops where they have some freedom of choice; in other words, until they receive their wages in cash and not partly in kind. Meanwhile, the houses and the shops are not there and cannot be provided overnight. The policy of trade unions in these circumstances is to campaign for the necessary social changes, and in the meantime to press constantly for improvements of the minimum standards required by law.

Of course, it should be recognised that some "fringe" benefits are really a sophisticated form of wages in kind. So are dinners enjoyed by company directors at the firm's expense. The meal vouchers issued to clerical staffs in cities like London, for use in nearby restaurants, are a similar payment. It would obviously be absurd to lay down as an unbreakable rule that employers must pay everything in cash and absolutely nothing at all in kind. The important thing is that wages should be paid in such a way that the worker can choose his own way of life. That means that for most purposes he should have the cash and spend it personally as he thinks best for himself and his family.

WAGE DEDUCTIONS FOR DEFECTIVE WORK

Another kind of abuse is making deductions from workers' wages because of defects in the products of their work, damage to the machines, or loss of the tools they use. Arbitrary deductions of large amounts decided by the employer or his managers can be most unfair to the workers and substantially reduce their wages. They may even be charged for defects or damage that were not their fault. Such deductions or fines are now often regulated by collective agreements, which usually prohibit them or limit them to quite small nominal amounts—for example 5 per cent of the weekly wage—and leave the employers free legally to discharge workers whose consistent carelessness results in defective output or damage. In the hotel and restaurant industry, for example, breakages of crockery due to a worker's carelessness may, under some agreements, be charged to the worker, but often the amount deducted from his wages is limited to a small percentage of the value of the articles broken.

Fines for breaches of discipline are prohibited in some countries by collective agreements. Where fines are permitted they are often subject to strict regulation, with limits to their amount and provision for workers to appeal against the penalties to a joint committee.

GUARANTEED MINIMUM WAGES

Piece-workers may be guaranteed minimum time-wages by collective agreements and wage boards' orders. As the earnings of such workers depend on their output anything that interrupts their work reduces their output and therefore their earnings. A weaver who completes his week's work without interruption, for example, may earn $36. If, however, his work is interrupted for considerable periods through no fault of his own his output will be greatly reduced and his earnings may be only $24. Such interruptions may be caused by a defective machine that breaks down, or he may be kept waiting for a supply of yarn. It would be unfair that he should suffer because of faults of the management. In order to protect him against serious reductions in his earnings he may be guaranteed a minimum wage of, say, $30 a week. Such guarantees also have the effect of stimulating employers of piece-workers to ensure that interruptions of work are reduced to a minimum so that they will not have to pay wages for workers' idle time.

Some occupations are liable to uncertainties about the amount of work to be done and yet it may be important to have workers available for work. Agreements may provide that building workers who report for work shall be paid wages for half a day or a day, even though bad weather may prevent outside work being done. Similar arrangements are made at various ports for dock workers.

Some industries (for example motor-car and clothing manufacture) are seasonal and each year there are slack periods when some workers are laid off and others work short time. At other seasons the industry is busy and overtime is worked. The question has, therefore, been considered whether arrangements can be made for a guaranteed annual wage.

Such a scheme has been adopted by agreements in the motor-car industry in the United States. A minimum annual wage is guaranteed in the sense that if a worker's earnings during the year, together with any unemployment insurance benefits he receives, are less than the amount guaranteed, the company will pay the difference.

*   *   *

# CHAPTER 11

# *Unionization, Trustworthiness, and Participation*

*Introductory Comment:*

## THE GOOD AND BAD IN UNIONS

The formation of unions can be treated as an effort by workers to protect themselves, in all the connections that we have been surveying, against the unequal power of firms and its abuse. Unionization can also be regarded as a device enabling workers to participate in decisions that affect them—not only decisions about amounts and methods of pay, negotiated in collective bargaining, but also decisions about individual worker's grievances and the sorts of decisions that joint labor-management committees on health and safety take up.

Unions are more effective on some of these matters than on others. Labor economists tend to doubt whether unions have done much to raise prevailing wage rates in the long run. On the other hand, unions may often have been effective in raising the rates paid by a given firm to the rates prevailing generally in the industry. They have also had a good deal of success in establishing grievance procedures, and this may be their major accomplishment, enough in itself to make them worthwhile in the eyes of their members (see Neil Chamberlain, "The Corporation and the Trade Union," in Edward S. Mason, ed., *The Corporation in Modern Society* [Cambridge, Mass., 1966], pp. 122–140).

Even when unions are effective in advancing workers' interests, democratic in organization, and fortunate enough to have enlightened and incorruptible leaders, firms may have some reservations about whether unions are good things. They may not be good things for the firms if they push up costs that the firms cannot easily pass on; or good things for the public, if the costs are passed on (then they may be combining with the firms in exploiting a monopoly position). It is not a foregone conclusion that the firms are morally wrong to resist the rise in costs portended by unionization, even when the resistance is wholly self-interested.

Moreover, the best of unions may have some bad effects: They may start up an adversary relationship where none was felt to exist before; destroy existing bonds of trust between workers and management; impair the loyalty of workers to the firm and its purposes. Firms would, if they were allowed, sometimes cite these considerations without being sincere about them; or be sincere, but blind to the discrepancy between their views of relations with their employees and the employees' views. Nevertheless, given the variation in firms and circumstances, it is hard to believe that the considerations do not sometimes have genuine force.

Moreover, there is the unpleasant fact that some workers never willingly go along with unionization and yet may be forced sooner or later to pay dues (or some contribution to union expenses in lieu of dues). Unions restrict liberties in other ways. For example, workers who do not want to go on strike may feel they have to vote to authorize one, or else disastrously weaken their union's position in bargaining. Firms are sometimes, because of these considerations, in a position to claim that in resisting unions they are acting to protect liberties of their employees.

They are, as it happens, restricted in giving effects to these claims. Laws protecting workers' rights to organize and bargain collectively forbid the use by firms of certain tactics that might prevent unionization. Under some laws, firms have been prohibited from freely putting the case against unionization to their employees, even when in the circumstances, it is a good case. Understandably, management has found these restrictions hard to bear when they have been confronted by the best of unions. How much more frustrating must the situation be when the unions are not the best. Some unions are, regrettably, very far from being democratically run; and some of them are corrupt, in the worst instances being led by mobsters and their associates. What firms may be required to do or refrain from doing in the face of unionization is a subject on which right and wrong can properly be determined only after taking into full account the variation between unions as well as the variation between firms.

# THE AFL-CIO CASE
# FOR HAVING UNIONS*

WHY UNIONS?

Ever walk into your local chain department store and ask to see the president? Or into your local telephone office and ask for an appointment with the chairman of the board?

Or maybe you are a high school student or one of the millions of college students in America. How many times have you talked with the principal or president of the college or university? For that matter, how many times have you personally talked to your professor in that large auditorium-packed lecture course, "Humanities 1," or something similar?

Now suppose you are out in the world working for a living as an engineer or technician or administrative and clerical worker in an aerospace, electronics, or insurance firm. Or in one of the big companies in the basic industries such as steel, auto, or food processing. Or as a skilled building trades worker. You need a day off to move to a new home, or to look after things at home because your spouse is ill. Or maybe you unexpectedly come down with sickness. Do you call your supervisor or department head and ask for time off? What if the supervisor says "No?" What do you do then? Go to the chairman of the board?

Or maybe you've been a loyal, productive worker for the past year or two. You know the company is doing well and making money. So you want a raise and figure you're worth more than you're earning. Do you ask your boss? What if the boss says "No" or offers a few pennies?

What do you do then?

Or assume you've been a loyal dedicated employee for 17 years. You've got a husband or wife, kids in high school hoping to go to college, equity in the house and stature in the community. You are over 40 but retirement is a long way off yet. Then one day your company is merged with or acquired by another one. New management moves in and decides you're through. They want younger employees; it's new company policy. Or they want more efficient production and are installing some new automated equipment that eliminates the need for your job—and you.

What do you do then and who do you talk to about finding a new job or taking another job in the same company through job retraining? How are you going to pull up roots in your community?

In each of these cases, what can you as an individual do to protect yourself and your livelihood? Who has the final word if you disagree with your employer's decision?

---

*Excerpts from a pamphlet, *Why Unions,* published by the American Federation of Labor and Congress of Industrial Organizations, 1980. Reprinted by permission.

Now consider that there are millions of other wages and salary earners, just like you, working for a living in organizations or firms that are apt to be very large, fluid and impersonal.

Some people say you can't fight city hall or buck the boss. In a democracy this isn't true. You can. And this is what unions are for. To establish industrial democracy in our private enterprise and corporate-oriented economy. To represent the individual's interest when the company's interest conflicts with it or fails, even, to consider it. To represent the public or government employee as he seeks to apply industrial democracy to his job and working conditions.

Look at it this way. Without collective bargaining, the individual employee has no voice, but is subject to every arbitrary decision the employer makes. Some minimum legal standards excepted, the employer sets hours of work, level of wages and salaries. He determines job assignments, production quotas, and when promotions are involved, he can reward his favorites and ignore qualified workers of longer service. He can lay off or fire whomever he chooses—for any reason or even for no reason. He can manipulate the organization chart and demote or shunt aside.

He can, in fact, be a dictator, answerable to no one but himself. Neither democracy nor human dignity has any place in this scheme of things.

In a nation, the benevolent dictator, trying to look out for the best interests of his subjects, is no substitute for democratically structured employee organizations and collective bargaining.

Where there is collective bargaining in industry, the individual worker has a voice and is not subject to arbitrary decisions. That worker shares with other employees and with the employer the responsibility for establishing orderly procedures for determining wages, hours of work, rates of production, promotion and layoff policies, and just penalties for the violation of necessary work rules.

As part of a union, you have the strength that comes from numbers and, through your union, the ability to hire able staff people—negotiators, lawyers, research specialists, and others who are skilled in the arts of collective bargaining.

Only as part of a group do you have the economic strength that permits bargaining with the employer on a basis approaching equality.

You may not find all the answers to your job problems by becoming a union member. But you will be free to present your problems and have them considered. This is the function of shop and department stewards, grievance committees and business agents. If you don't like the job they're doing, you have an opportunity to do something about it. They're not appointed. They're elected—by you and your fellow employees. The same goes for the other union officers. They're democratically elected and the members do the nominating.

The policies and conduct of the union are determined by its constitution and by-laws and these, too, are subject to amendment and change by the membership.

WHAT UNIONS WANT

. . . Collective bargaining is a rational, democratic and peaceful way to resolve conflict. In recent years, some 150,000 collective bargaining agreements have been made. Only two percent of them were affected by strikes. So in 98 percent of all cases, collective bargaining was successful. Not a bad record.

Back around the turn of the century, things were different. There were not very many unions then, and those that existed had a tough time of it. Employer resistance to collective bargaining was fierce and many times violent. There was no National Labor Relations Act then to give workers the right to organize and to promote collective bargaining. But workers persisted and the fledgling unions survived. Collective bargaining became the accepted way of regulating employer-employee disputes.

It took a lot of nerve for employees to stand up for their rights in those days. There were no job safety standards, paid vacations, sick leaves or retirement plans. Hiring and firing, promotion and layoff policies were under the exclusive control of employers.

But they did it, and today we are enjoying the results. You can't put a price tag on the human dignity individual workers feel when they stand up for their rights, either.

It hasn't changed today. Every time the union-negotiated contract expires, the members have to assess the situation again. They look at their wages and compare them with current price levels; look at company profits; determine if pensions, health and medical care plans are adequate. These are the quantitative factors that go into wages and salaries at collective bargaining time.

There are qualitative factors, too. Things like work rules, work speeds, occupational safety and health, time off for vacations and holidays, and promotion policies.

Put them all together and you have a package of wages, benefits, and work rules that become the subject of contract negotiations. Employers—large or small—don't just hand out this package. The employees have to stick together, send their elected representatives into the negotiating room with employers or their representatives, and through a process of fact finding, discussion, argument and debate, make an agreement on just what the package will contain. Then the membership has to ratify or reject it.

We call it collective bargaining, and it has played a vital part in lifting the living standards of the American worker to the highest level in the world.

Think about this next time you hear a company official say, "Here's what we give our employees." Even if that company doesn't have a union or the employees he is talking about aren't part of the union in the firm, do you really think they would give these wages and benefits if there were no unions? Maybe. But it isn't likely unless a pattern of union-won gains is in existence.

But even then, the employee has no voice in matters affecting the job. Where's the dignity in that system? Or security?

ABOUT STRIKES

Unions negotiate for agreements—not strikes. No union wants a strike. Strikes develop only when both sides—labor and management—can in no other way reach an agreement.

To a union member, a strike means sacrifice for himself and his family. And he will not vote to go on a strike unless the issues involved are so great they are worth the sacrifice.

Remember, strikes are not called or ordered by union leaders. They are voted by the union membership—to take strike action or not to take it—and the majority rules.

We've already said 98 percent of all contracts negotiated result in agreements achieved without a strike. In fact, the work time lost because of strikes in recent years has been less than three days for every four work years. The common cold causes more lost time than strikes.

But strikes are controversial and controversy makes news. This, no doubt, is why many people think strikes are the rule rather than the exception.

Management can trigger a strike simply by refusing to bargain or to yield on a point of contention. But the union has to take the first overt action and the strike is the first visible sign of dispute. This probably accounts for the public blaming unions for strikes in many cases.

But the right to strike—or right to withhold one's labor in unison and agreement with fellow workers—is paramount to maintaining democracy. In totalitarian countries the right to strike is prohibited along with all other freedoms. Put in proper perspective, then, the right to strike is a matter of freedom, and a democracy cannot function without freedom.

\* \* \*

# A UNION AT J.P. STEVENS: ANATOMY OF A SEVENTEEN-YEAR STRUGGLE*

1963: The first union card is signed at J. P. Stevens, the world's second largest textile company. No one knew it would be 17 years before Stevens employees got their first union contract—but they knew it wouldn't be easy, because 100 union supporters were immediately fired after those first cards were signed. 1963 was the 150th year of Stevens, which started in New England but began moving South as early as 1946, making the major move of buying the Roanoke Rapids plant in 1956. That was already a milestone year in southern textile history because Roger Milliken shut down the Darlington Manufacturing Co. in Darlington, S.C., that year to show workers that unions would not be tolerated at textile mills. And 1963 was

*From the AFL-CIO *American Federationist*, December 1980, pp. 5–6. Reprinted by permission.

the year the Textile Workers Union (TWUA) selected Stevens as an organizing target because workers had worse working conditions and more union sympathies than other plants. The AFL-CIO Industrial Union Department pledges its resources to the campaign.

1964: TWUA charges Stevens with labor law violations before NLRB, including discharges for union activity, but also spying on union meetings, threatened discharges for union activity, and offering bribes for remaining anti-union.

1964–1967: Violations continue. Union supporters' jobs are downgraded and even relatives of union supporters are harassed and intimidated.

1967: Supreme Court orders reinstatement of 71 Stevens workers fired for union support. Stevens fires workers who testified in the case.

1969: Union is declared the bargaining agent at Stevens's Statesboro, Ga., plant, after NLRB sets aside a 1968 election.

1972: U.S. 2nd Circuit Court of Appeals holds Stevens in contempt for refusing to obey previous order enjoining it to stop violations.

"Our system of justice cannot survive if litigants are seized with the notion that they can ignore the lawful orders of a court simply because they disagree with them," the court said. Court also rules that organizers can have access to company bulletin boards in Roanoke Rapids and make speeches in plants.

1973: Crystal Lee Jordan, whose experiences became the basis for the movie "Norma Rae," and several other workers are fired for union activities during an organizing drive at Stevens's Roanoke Rapids, N.C., plants. In Wallace, N.C., where there are two Stevens plants, organizers discover Stevens is "bugging" their motel rooms. Two company officials indicted by federal grand jury; Stevens pays union $50,000 in settlement of suit.

. . . By the end of this year, Stevens has paid more than $1 million in backpay and other settlements ordered by the NLRB and federal courts.

1974: On Aug. 28, a majority of the 3,500 workers in Roanoke Rapids votes union. Contract negotiations will drag on for 6½ years as Stevens refuses to discuss essentials like wages, seniority or arbitration.

1975: Stevens closes its Statesboro plant to avoid bargaining with the union.

1976: ACTWU is formed with the merger of TWUA with the Amalgamated Clothing Workers of America (ACWA). At the merger convention AFL-CIO President George Meany calls Stevens the "nation's No. 1 labor law violator." AFL-CIO mounts a nationwide boycott of Stevens consumer products to bring "this outlaw company" to the bargaining table.

1977: In March a coalition of labor, church and civil rights groups attends Stevens stockholders meeting at corporate headquarters in New York. A number of Stevens workers are also present to challenge company policies, the first action in the union's "corporate campaign."

In August the 2nd U.S. Court of Appeals again finds Stevens in contempt for continued violations of court directives. It orders the company to give union organizers access to all 63 Stevens plants in North and South Carolina and to educate its supervisors on the organizers' rights.

Also in August, congressional hearings on labor law reform take place at Roanoke Rapids Civic Center, where Lewis Harrell tells the poignant story of what it means to be the victim of "brown lung," a disease some textile company officials say doesn't exist.

1978: Boycott of Stevens consumer products gathers momentum. Support is pledged by student groups, city councils, women's groups and religious organizations throughout the United States and trade union movements from Japan, Israel and Australia endorse boycott. Stevens asks the union to discuss a possible settlement. Talks are held in 1978 and 1979, but don't really get going until 1980. . . . The Rev. Joseph Williams and Crystal Lee Jordan are re-instated to their jobs in Roanoke Rapids by Supreme Court order upholding an earlier court decision. Lewis Harrell dies of bysinossis.

Stevens Board Chairman James Finley resigns from board of Manufacturers Hanover after a union campaign to expose the bank's ties to the Stevens company. David Mitchell, head of Avon products, resigns from Stevens board. Later, R. Manning Brown, head of New York Life Insurance, resigns from Stevens board and Finley resigns from New York Life.

1979: Congressional leaders, retiree groups and community action councils pledge not to buy Stevens consumer products. . . . Release of the film "Norma Rae," by 20th Century Fox gives public at large awareness of the Stevens struggle. . . . Workers vote for the union at Stevens plants in High Point, N.C., and Allendale, S.C. . . . Court orders Stevens to bargain in Wallace, N.C. . . .

In Milledgeville, Ga., evidence is uncovered of J. P. Stevens's 2½-year involvement in campaign of illegal surveillance of union organizers and its own workers—including wiretapping. The union takes Stevens to court in a $11.9 million civil rights suit.

Roanoke Rapids workers mark fifth anniversary of union election victory. . . . Company denies to its Roanoke Rapids workers the wage increases paid in other plants.

1980: Six southern Roman Catholic Bishops endorse the Stevens campaign, saying that a union contract would be "an effective way of ensuring human dignity in the workplace." . . . 351 safety and health violations are discovered in Stevens's South Carolina plants. . . . 100 Stevens Workers meet for leadership training classes in Spartanburg. . . . NLRB orders five illegally discharged workers reinstated in Stuart, Va. . . . The 4th U.S. Circuit Court says June 11 that Stevens has been bargaining in bad faith at Roanoke Rapids and, for second year, Stevens withholds wage increase from Roanoke Rapids workers while paying it in other plants.

Hundreds of trade unionists protest Sperry Corporation links with Stevens at Sperry stockholders meeting. . . . Whitney Stevens becomes chairman of the board and meets with ACTWU officials to negotiate a settlement to the long, costly campaign. . . . Oct. 19, settlement is agreed to and signed by company and ACTWU in New York. Contracts are ratified in 10 plants—and there is a union at J. P. Stevens.

\*     \*     \*

# THE UNION TELLS STEVENS WORKERS, "YOUR BEST PROTECTION: THE UNION CONTRACT"*

*[During the struggle at the Stevens mills, the Amalgamated Clothing and Textile Workers Union produced a pamphlet aimed at unorganized workers. I am reproducing it at full length (without the pictures of some of the people involved), because it does so much, within the compass of a single selection, to teach one of the chief lessons of this book. The topics of moral concern are relatively few and familiar, but the ways in which each topic turns up in the real world are various, subtle, and unexpected.*

*Here we are concerned with what on the part of workers is felt to be oppression. I think that even people who have had some experience in factory work would not be able to give anything like a complete list of the connections in which workers may find the actions and policies of their employers oppressive. Would the list even be sure to include all the headings in the following pamphlet? Might not "Transfers" be overlooked, or "Job Security" (as something distinct from "Discipline"), or even "Work-loads"? Yet these are all matters in which, as the pamphlet makes clear, workers have a great deal at stake. Moreover, even a list that did contain all these headings could not anticipate in concrete detail the variety of ways in which the headings are continually being illustrated in the real world.*

*The pamphlet gives us only a sample. It is a sample from the past, before Stevens agreed to unionization. Even in respect to the past, the sample may not be fair to the Stevens company. The company might take a different view of the cases that the union cites; and the company might contend that even if they occurred, they were not, as the union claims, typical.*

*I cannot resolve such a dispute here; and I do not bring the cases forward as indictments of the company. Well-founded or not, they illustrate the sorts of things that the union expected the workers to find oppressive. If we agree about the sorts of things, then the sample of cases in the pamphlet gives us a substantial start toward appreciating the sorts of concrete details to be looked for in instances of oppression.]*

As a report on J. P. Stevens in 1978, we present a handful of Stevens workers whose experiences were typical. Stevens workers know them:

—Workers who were hurt on the job because the company didn't fix safety hazards until after the accident happened.

—Older workers who didn't get a job because the company hired someone younger off the street.

---

*From a pamphlet prepared by the Amalgamated Clothing and Textile Workers Union during the campaign to organize J. P. Stevens. Reprinted with permission.

—People who were fired the first time they broke one of the new rules, when a warning would have been sufficient.

—Workers who had their rates cut or their workloads increased.

This past year at J. P. Stevens, it was business as usual. Unnecessary accidents. Unfair disciplinary action. Undeserved firings. Speed-ups. Stretchouts. Rate cuts. Favoritism.

"Maybe so," you say, "but what could the union do about it?"

In this report, we also assembled a handful of union members to tell you what our union—the Amalgamated Clothing and Textile Workers Union (ACTWU)—did about these kinds of conditions in Southern textile mills this year.

Many of the things that happened to Stevens workers happened to workers in other mills. At Stevens, there was nothing you could do. The company's word was law. But at ACTWU mills, workers could and did change what their company did because they had the protection of a union contract.

A union contract is like any other agreement. It's worked out and signed by both parties—the company and the union—and sets out exactly what can and can't be done. If the company breaks the rules, the union has the power to see the wrong corrected.

In this report, we talk about only a few of the many items covered in typical ACTWU contracts in the Southern textile industry. Seniority. Transfers. Job security. Health and safety. Workloads. Warnings and firings.

We present Stevens workers and what happened to them. For each example, we also present a similar situation in one of our organized plants— and exactly what the union did to see that justice was done.

A union contract is the best protection you have.

WORKLOADS: AT J. P. STEVENS

"A fair day's work for a fair day's pay" is one thing. But there's nothing fair about having your piece rates cut or your workload increased so that you have to do more work to make the same (or less) money. That's "more work for less pay" and there's plenty of *that* at J. P. Stevens.

Take W. A. "Daulk" Cooper. His already heavy workload was almost doubled—just like that—with no increase in pay. It was like it or leave it after 46 years.

Some workers can't keep up with excessive new workloads or changed job conditions. When Stevens worker Joanne Hovis couldn't meet new workloads, she was forced onto a less desirable job.

Without a union contract, J. P. Stevens can speed you up or stretch you out any time it wants. Your only choice is "like it or leave."

W. A. "Daulk" Cooper, Head Fixer at Stevens' Dunean plant, is at an age where he can't afford to be laid off by J. P. Stevens—he can't compete with younger men and women for jobs at other companies. So Mr. Cooper is worried about having to cope with a heavier workload—without a union "grievance procedure" by which he could protest the new standard:

There used to be two of us to fix on the new looms, and now there's just me. They gave me a warp man to help me with lifting, but that's not like having two fixers. Really, they've just about doubled up on my job.

There hasn't been anything said about extra money. It'll all be the same price. I've worked here for 46 years, and I'm not as stout as I used to be. The doctors have taken half my left lung out. So it's not going to be easy.

W. A. "Daulk" Cooper
*Dunean Plant, J. P. Stevens*
*Greenville, South Carolina*
Head Fixer

ACTWU local unions can challenge increased workloads. When Local 2337 loom fixers found their workload had been increased, they had a say in deciding how much work they could handle. Joe Daniels, elected local union President at Fabrics America, helped the fixers with their grievance:

The company started a preventive maintenance program in the weave shop. The men were told they would have to upgrade three looms per day while trouble shooting and getting the flags down. Nobody thought it was humanly possible. A lot of pressure was put on the men to upgrade the three looms—so much pressure that they were afraid they would lose their jobs. So we filed a grievance and got the company to agree the fixers would only upgrade one loom per day.

Joe Daniels
*Local President, ACTWU Local 2337*
*Bama Mills, Fabrics America*
*Enterprise, Alabama*
Weave Shop, Overhauler

Joanne Hovis had no trouble doing her own "wash test" job at J. P. Stevens' Rock Hill, S. C. mill. But when her bossman added duties which she hadn't previously been required to perform, Joanne Hovis couldn't challenge the newly enforced job description. Her only alternative was to give up the "wash test" job on a regular shift and take a job in the cloth room with a twelve-hour and Sunday schedule:

I had been a wash test operator in the finishing department on a regular 8-hour shift for over a year. One day the boss asked me to help run the sanforizer helper's job. The sanforizer helper has to pull 1000 pound rolls from the finishing machine to the sanforizer. I had suffered a heart attack and couldn't do the job. He said they'd have to get someone on the wash test job that could. They told me, "You'll just have to go to another job."

As it turned out, my replacement wasn't required to help on the sanforizer helper after all. I had always suspected my boss had hard feelings toward me, but there wasn't anything I could do about it.

Joanne Hovis
*Industrial Plant, J. P. Stevens*
*Rock Hill, South Carolina*
Cloth Inspector

When the back tenders at Rock Hill Printing & Finishing found they had to lift more than they could handle, they didn't have to choose between breaking their backs or going to another shift. Franklin D. Armour, jack room worker and shop committee member, explains how he dealt with the problem as an ACTWU Local 710 shop steward:

> The cloth we used to have was light. Then they started running fireguard cloth—fireproof cloth they use for kids' pajamas and housecoats—and it's real heavy. The rolls weigh about 1100 pounds. The back tender on the print machine said he couldn't handle 'em by himself and asked me to talk to the foreman about it—I was shop steward then. When nothing was done, I put in a grievance, saying lifting that much was a hazard to the guy's health. After that they put up chain hoists for the guys that ran fireguard.

> Franklin D. Armour
> *ACTWU Local 710*
> *Rock Hill Printing and Finishing,*
> *M. Lowenstein & Sons*
> *Rock Hill, South Carolina*
> Jack Room Worker

*With an ACTWU contract:* If you are an ACTWU member, you can deal with workload problems just like these:

—By getting management to reduce your workload if it's unrealistic. Company changes in workloads are subject to the grievance procedure. And many ACTWU contracts require that employers tell the union about changes in workloads, machinery, or equipment before they are put into effect.

—By negotiating a new rate when your work assignment or job responsibilities are increased.

—By calling in an ACTWU industrial engineer to time study your job and set a fair rate.

—By arranging an acceptable transfer when you can't keep up with or tolerate changed job conditions.

Piece-workers for non-union textile firms like J. P. Stevens often complain that the company increases their quotas to offset wage increases—and their take-home pay is no different after the pay raise than it was before. The workload clauses of ACTWU contracts are designed to prevent such "stretch-outs."

DISCIPLINE—WARNINGS AND FIRINGS: AT J. P. STEVENS

J. P. Stevens worker Debra Ware was fired for breaking a minor company rule.

For thousands of J. P. Stevens workers, their rights as American citizens are left behind at the plant gate every day they go to work. Once inside, the company alone acts as prosecutor, judge and jury. In fact, if a supervisor accuses a Stevens employee, chances are he'll be judged guilty without a chance to prove his innocence or appeal his punishment.

There was nothing to stop J. P. Stevens from firing "open end spinner" Debra Ware for a technical rule violation—even though it was her first offense and she had received no previous warnings:

> A few weeks after the company put in new rules, I was out sick. When I went back to work, I was fired. They said I had only called in sick once, instead of calling in every one of the three days I was out.
>
> I don't feel that it's right. If it's your first time doing something, they could have said, well, Debra, you know if you stay out for three days without calling in each day you're fired. They could have given me a warning and they could have let me keep my job. But they just said I was discharged and they had to go by their rules.

> Debra Ware
> *Appleton Plant, J. P. Stevens*
> *Anderson, South Carolina*
> Open End Spinner

In a union plant, the form of discipline a company uses must match the offense. A first offense for a minor violation merits only a verbal warning. When it comes to discipline for absenteeism at ACTWU Local 1840 in Opelika, Alabama, procedures the company must follow are actually spelled out in the contract:

> I was out sick for a couple of days. I went to the bossman and handed him my doctor's statement. He said he was instructed to write me up for excessive absence. It was only the third or fourth occasion where I'd missed work. According to our contract, you're allowed to stay out for six occasions without getting written up. And every 6 months your record is cleared.
>
> I filed a grievance. About a week later the company told me that the writeup would be cleared.

> Ronnie Clark
> *ACTWU Local 1840*
> *Opelika Manufacturing*
> *Opelika, Alabama*
> Spinning Room Fixer

With no union contract, Stevens doesn't have to respect rules of fairness. In fact, no one can make J. P. Stevens abide by their own work rules, as yarn storage operator Ronald Wright recently discovered. And when Wright was fired, he had no one to take his side:

> They brought in a new supervisor, and he ordered me to do my job different from the way I was doing it. I told him that I was doing my job like I had always been told to do it. I showed him I was doing my job just like it was posted on the company bulletin board. He had a deputy sheriff escort me out of the plant.
>
> The next day I was called to the personnel office and fired by three company officials. When I tried to explain my side of it they just broke up their gathering and walked away.

The way I look at it, they make the rules, but they don't abide by them. When the employee brings the rules to their attention, they try to twist it up so they come out on top. When I tried to tell my side of it, they wouldn't listen.

> Ronald Wright
> *Tifton Woolen Mills, J. P. Stevens*
> *Tifton, Georgia*
> Yarn Storage Operator

At Canton Textile Mills, where workers have a union, both the company and workers must abide by rules spelled out in the contract. And when a worker is fired, the union provides that worker with a representative to defend him and present his side of the story. Spinner Sarah Hillhouse:

The boss had been onto me all the time about my cleaning. I had done part of it, but my job was running bad. He said I'd have to do all of it. So I said I'd do what I could. He said if I couldn't do my job I'd have to go home.

I told Charles Gearing, the local union Vice President, about it and he went right to work on it. We filed a grievance as soon as we could. I turned it over to the union and we settled at the fifth step of our grievance procedure. I settled for my job back and my seniority. And since then, my boss has been just great. He's treated me real nice.

> Sarah Hillhouse
> *ACTWU Local 1604*
> *Canton Textile Mills*
> *Canton, Georgia*
> Spinner

*With an ACTWU Contract:* Thousands of textile workers have found that only a union contract can give them the same rights in the plant as they enjoy in the outside world as American citizens. To ensure these rights, ACTWU contracts provide for:

—the right of all workers to representation at any disciplinary hearing, if they want it—by their elected shop steward, or, if it proves necessary, by a union officer or full-time ACTWU staff member.

—the right to be assumed innocent in disciplinary hearings until the company can produce actual proof of guilt.

—the right to equal treatment. In a union plant, the company can't single out a worker for discipline, while others enjoy freedom from discipline for the same behavior. And a company's discipline must fit the offense. Union workers can't be fired for a minor violation of the rules.

—the right to demand that company rules be reasonable. Under most ACTWU contracts management notifies the union of changes in the rules and discusses them with the union before putting them into effect.

—the right to have special or unusual situations considered, when a company disciplines workers for offenses due to circumstances beyond their control.

TRANSFERS: AT J. P. STEVENS

Whenever Danny Washington is transferred to a lower-paying job he gets lower pay. Whenever Romeo Holloway is transferred to a lower-paying job he gets his regular higher job rate.

Danny Washington has no way of stopping his company from putting him on that lower-paying job as often and for as long as it likes—no matter how much he loses. Romeo Holloway must give his company permission before he can be transferred from his regular job for more than two weeks.

Why the difference? Danny Washington works for J. P. Stevens, where the company's word is law. Romeo Holloway, like thousands of other southern textile workers, is a union member and has the rights and protections of an ACTWU contract.

When a worker is absent, any textile mill must find someone else to fill that job and keep the department running. But who should be picked (especially if it's an unpopular job)? How much should he be paid? How long can the transfer last? These questions are vital to thousands of J. P. Stevens workers like Danny Washington, who lost money from frequent and arbitrary transfers, or like Jeannie Mae Sievers, who lost her regular job to a much less senior employee when she helped the company out of a bind.

Without a union contract, J. P. Stevens can transfer whomever they want, whenever they want, for as long as they want, even if it seriously hurts that worker's earnings. Stevens gave half of "drawing tender" Danny Washington's job to a less senior man, who worked as a can hauler, and gave half of the can hauler's job to Washington:

> I'd been working on production (piece rate) as a drawing tender. After 4½ years I'd gotten to be fairly good at it. Then one day the company told me I'd have to work every other week as a can hauler on straight time.
>
> It cut my pay $30 every other week. I'm not a can hauler, I'm a drawing tender. When I work as a can hauler, I make what I did in 1975, and I can't make it on that.
>
> I complained and it did no good. Four and a half years down the drain for nothing.
>
> > Danny Washington
> > *Pamplico Plant, J. P. Stevens*
> > *Pamplico, South Carolina*
> > Drawing Tender

Romeo Holloway works under an ACTWU contract at Opelika Manufacturing which, like most contracts, spells out rules for job transfers. Those rules protect workers from pay cuts resulting from transfers:

> I had bid on a weaver's job and had the seniority to get it. But the week I was supposed to start, they didn't have enough work for me. So I was temporarily transferred back to my old job, at my old rate.
>
> Right there the company broke our contract. So when my paycheck came up $34 short, I went to talk to my supervisor. But I didn't stop at that.
>
> I went to see Billy Tankersley, the local union President. It only took about 30

minutes to straighten it out. That same day I got my money. The company might not have liked it, but they had to pay me.

> Romeo Holloway
> *ACTWU Local 1840*
> *Opelika Manufacturing*
> *Opelika, Alabama*
> Weaver

J. P. Stevens unicone winder Jeannie Mae Sievers was temporarily transferred, even though she had more seniority than others in her department. When it came time to return to her old job, she found she had no right to claim it:

> I was training a trainee on my machine and a girl went out on sick leave. They asked me to take her job temporarily. When the girl came back, they told me that I would not go back on my old job, because they were giving it to the trainee. All my years of service didn't mean a thing. The new winder I went on was a machine on which I could not make quota. The only justice I got was when the trainee got married a couple months later. Then they gave me my old job back.

> Jeannie Mae Sievers
> *West Boylston Plant, J. P. Stevens*
> *Montgomery, Alabama*
> Unicone Winder

A union contract puts a stop to arbitrary transfers. In a union plant like Fabrics America in Enterprise, Alabama, the most senior person is last to transfer. To "Tie-in-man" John Boswell, most important is the right to have a say when it comes to temporary transfer:

> Before the union came in they could move you and place you anywhere they wanted. You had no say-so at all. We stopped that when we voted the union in last year.
> Before we organized, I used to go back and forth from the tie-in machine to the slasher room. They would just come up and say, we need you in the slasher room and you'd have to go. Now they have to come up and ask if I want to go, because as long as your own job is running, you have a right to say no. That's in our contract and it's a lot better. I never did like nobody just coming up and saying you got to do something. I like having a say.

> John Boswell
> *Shop Steward, ACTWU Local 2337*
> *Bama Mills, Fabrics America*
> *Enterprise, Alabama*
> Tie-In Man

*With an ACTWU contract.* ACTWU contracts protect each employee from unfair transfers or loss of pay. Here's how:

—By limiting the length of time the company can transfer any one worker.
—By limiting the company's ability to transfer arbitrarily. Most contracts do

this by seniority: the most senior qualified worker will be last to transfer.
—By protecting earnings on a transfer. Most contracts say the company
must pay whichever rate is higher: your regular rate, or the rate of the job
you are transferred to. In the case of piece rate workers, most ACTWU
contracts guarantee the continuation of previous average earnings in
cases of transfers for the company's convenience.
—By making sure that your old job is there for you after you have finished a
temporary transfer.

HEALTH AND SAFETY: AT J. P. STEVENS

After J. P. Stevens fixer Larry Bush was injured on the job, he reported the
safety hazard. But Stevens did nothing and Bush was injured a second time.

Stevens worker Tommy Catoe told Stevens the guard on his machine was
broken. But they didn't fix it until Catoe was seriously injured.

Too often, J. P. Stevens doesn't care about a safety hazard until there is a
serious accident, until it is too late. Thousands of textile workers have had to
learn the hard way that only a union contract can ensure them the job
protection they deserve. Without a union contract, a worker's choice is too
often between risking an injury, like Tommy Catoe, or risking discharge for
refusing to work in unsafe conditions. And that's no choice at all.

In a Stevens plant there is no way of forcing the company to correct a
safety hazard before a serious accident happens. Or so it must seem to
slasher tender Tommy Catoe:

> Five months ago the guard on my machine broke. I reported it to the company,
> and they told me they'd fix it. But they never did. Finally I got my hand jerked
> into the rollers up to the wrist. The doctors can't even tell me how much
> damage there is, or how long I'll be out of work. But the day after I got hurt,
> Stevens fixed the machines.
>
> > Tommy Catoe
> > *Industrial Plant, J. P. Stevens*
> > *Rock Hill, South Carolina*
> > Slasher Tender

At Cranston Print Works, the ACTWU contract provides for a safety
committee made up of union members and management. Both active and
efficient, the committee is on the lookout for safety hazards and tries to
prevent accidents from happening. One member of this safety committee is
David Dunbar, a "jack man" in the print department:

> The guys in my department spotted a cracked pulley on one of the print
> machines. These pulleys are about two feet across. We were afraid it would just
> disintegrate and hit whoever was in the line of fire. The safety committee called
> an on-the-spot meeting with management. We were firm in our position—that
> the company should shut the machine down until it was fixed. The company

agreed, and now they have a procedure to test the pulleys for hairline cracks. So the problem is pretty much under control.

> David Dunbar
> *Shop Steward, ACTWU Local 1355*
> *Cranston Print Works*
> *Fletcher, North Carolina*
> Jack Man, Print Department

How quickly did J. P. Stevens provide the proper safety devices when loom fixer Larry Bush mangled his hand in the machinery he was working? They didn't fix it at all:

I've been in two serious accidents in the last year. I was working on a loom when it cut on accidentally and messed up my hand pretty bad. The machines should have had guards on the switches so that won't happen. But I work on 90 looms, and only 20 of them have this kind of guard. Anyway, I reported it to the company safety officers, and they said guards should be put on. But they never were. That's how come I had a second accident. The guards were never put on and the same thing happened again. The doctors had to fuse the joint in my left thumb.

> Larry Bush
> *Republic Plants, J. P. Stevens*
> *Great Falls, South Carolina*
> Loom Fixer

Members of ACTWU Local 1933 have worked out a way to correct safety problems promptly at Schlegel Tennessee Corporation. Local union President Ted McKee, a plant electrician, explains how the union and the company came to an agreement:

Jerry Matlock, a line operator, had to take temperature readings manually on the curing ovens, which are usually about 400 degrees F. This meant he had to open some doors and stand right over all this heat and fumes to do it. He thought this was unsafe, so he refused to do it. The second time he refused he got a three-day suspension. So we filed a grievance. As a result of this case, we got the company to agree that they will meet with us on a health and safety grievance within 48 hours. They also agreed to install specially made long-stem thermometers, so temperature readings can be taken at a greater distance from the heat and fumes. And, of course, Jerry's record was cleared.

> Ted McKee
> *Local President, ACTWU Local 1933*
> *Schlegel Tennessee Corporation*
> *Maryville, Tennessee*
> Electrician

*With an ACTWU Contract:* ACTWU believes that every textile worker has the right to safe working conditions. That is why ACTWU employs full-time experts on industrial health and safety to help union members with inplant problems. And that is why ACTWU members insist on contracts which make that right a reality:

—By requiring the company to provide working conditions that are as healthy and safe as possible.

—By giving members the right to file grievances to correct safety problems.

—By establishing and training safety committees of union members in each plant to spot safety hazards and get the company to correct them before accidents occur.

—By utilizing the union's legal rights to get information about dangerous chemicals, accident records and progress reports on company attempts to correct safety and health violations.

The textile industry is a dangerous place to work. New technology is creating new and more complicated hazards. The record shows that without a union contract textile workers cannot choose between safe and unsafe conditions. Only with a union contract can textile workers protect themselves.

### JOB SECURITY: AT J. P. STEVENS

Randy Beck really needed his job at J. P. Stevens. Although he was only a high school student, he brought home the family paycheck. He never suspected that when he returned from personal leave to study for exams, there would be no job for him.

Even Stevens workers who are out as a result of company-caused injuries never know if a job awaits them upon their return.

Luck. That's what it amounts to at J. P. Stevens. If you're lucky, you'll have a job when you return from a leave of absence. Regardless of what company rules J. P. Stevens puts in writing, there's no way to force them to play by the rules without a union contract.

Although Stevens' company policy states a worker will have a job when he returns from a leave of absence, there was really no way creeler trainee Randy Beck could force Stevens to reinstate him after a leave:

> I'm a senior in high school and I was working second shift. I asked for a leave of absence 'cause I wanted to catch up on my school work. The personnel manager said, OK, he'd give me one. When I went back they said I didn't have a job, that there wasn't any place in the mill they could put me. I asked if I was fired or what and they said that as far as they could see, I'd quit. They say they'll have a job for you when you get back from a leave, but if they don't want to give you one, they don't.

Randy Beck
*Dunean Plant, J. P. Stevens*
*Greenville, South Carolina*
Creeler Trainee

The guarantee of a job after a leave of absence is something many union workers take for granted. ACTWU Local 903 member Dot Knight, who works at Arrow Shirt in Cedartown, Georgia, speaks from experience:

> I applied for personal illness leave and I was out for two months. And when I came back, I had the same machine, the same job, the same job seniority as the day I left. If you're out on leave you hold your own machine for six months. If someone's been using your machine, they immediately give it back to you when you come back to work. I guess it's just something I expect because it's spelled out in our contract.
>
> > Dot Knight
> > *ACTWU Local 903*
> > *Arrow Shirt*
> > *Cedartown, Georgia*
> > Sewing Machine Operator

At J. P. Stevens, new employees are often placed on dangerous jobs without the training to allow them to run the jobs safely. Raymond Allen had been on the job two weeks when a supervisor told him to clean the picker machines. Allen told the supervisor he didn't know anything about cleaning, but the supervisor told him to *"do the best he could."*

> I said I'd turn them off to clean them, but he said to clean them first, then turn them off. I started blowing the pickers, the air hose hit something, I lost control of the hose and my hand fell into the machine.
>
> I started screaming for help to get my hand out, but it was 30 minutes before someone heard me. It took 45 minutes to get my hand out. My hand was completely broken and the nerves in my hand and wrist were torn out.
>
> For eight months, I called or went to the plant about every week asking for a lighter job I could do with my disability. I even said I'd sweep. They just gave me a runaround and said they'd let me know. They never have given me a job since.
>
> > Raymond Allen
> > *Watts Plant, J. P. Stevens*
> > *Laurens, South Carolina*
> > Picker Tender

Pauline Ray, a labeling machine operator at the Levi-Strauss plant in Valdosta, Georgia, was also hurt in the plant, and was no longer able to do her regular job. But the ACTWU contract at her plant gives employees who are unable to do their regular job for health reasons the right to bid down to a lower job:

> I almost cut my finger off, and they thought for about a week they were going to have to amputate it. But luckily, I didn't lose it. And the doctor wouldn't let me go back to the job I'd been hurt on because I couldn't perform on that job.
>
> According to our contract, if you can't do your job for health reasons, the company has to let you bid to a lighter job. So when the doctor called and told

them I could go back in to work if they would find me a lighter job, they said come in in the morning, we'll see what we can do for you. And the second day after that, I was back at work on a lighter job. If we hadn't had a union contract, I'd have been at home without a job.

> Pauline Ray
> *Trustee, ACTWU Local 714*
> *Levi-Strauss*
> *Valdosta, Georgia*
> Sewing Machine Operator

*With an ACTWU contract:* ACTWU believes that textile workers deserve more than wages in return for the goods they produce, the hours they work and the profits they make for their employers. They deserve job security. When personal or emergency matters call them away from work, they deserve to know there will be a job waiting for them when they return.

ACTWU contracts ensure these job rights, by providing:

—That workers can take a leave of absence for personal illness, pregnancy, death in the family, jury duty, military service, or other valid reasons.
—That workers' seniority rights will be protected while out on leave. And many ACTWU contracts guarantee that workers will return to their old jobs or jobs of equal pay and status when they get back.
—That leaves of absence will be granted according to the rules spelled out in the contract. It's no longer just up to the boss.

The union acts when that job security is threatened—by filing a grievance, or by negotiating an acceptable solution with management. ACTWU local unions often make sure companies find suitable work for injured or disabled employees who can no longer work their old jobs.

\*　　\*　　\*

*[Two advertisements upholding against unions the "right to work" follow, to be followed in turn by a reply from the union side.]*

## BABIES, STRIKES AND COMPULSORY UNIONISM DON'T MIX\*

Marlene Swanson, R.N., is a dedicated nurse who takes care of newborn babies, many of them premature, most of them black and Hispanic, and all of them in need, at a community hospital outside Providence, Rhode Island.

When an illegal strike was called, Marlene refused to join it. She crossed the picket line and reported to work because, as she says, "Nurses take the

\*An ad as it appeared in the 26 June 1980 *New York Review of Books.* Reprinted with the permission of the National Right to Work Legal Defense Foundation, Inc.

Hippocratic oath too, like doctors. I felt a moral responsibility to those infants."

Angry union officials immediately retaliated. Marlene, along with the other nurses at the hospital, had been forced to join the union to keep her job. This compulsory union membership, union officials claimed, made all nurses subject to fine for any disobedience of their decisions.

They charged Marlene Swanson with violating union by-laws, held a sham "trial," and fined her $250 for taking care of her infant patients during the strike. When Marlene appealed the fine to the union membership, they increased it to $300!

An undaunted Marlene refused to pay the fine, and the union took her to court. At first, she didn't know where to turn for the legal help she urgently needed. After all, she was just one member against the entire Rhode Island State Nurses Association.

Then she remembered reading about William F. Buckley, Jr.'s legal battle against a union, and called his office. She was referred to the National Right to Work Legal Defense Foundation, which agreed to provide counsel.

A defense was prepared and presented so effectively that the union suggested the case could be settled out of court if Marlene would give the fine to charity. She flatly refused "because a lot of other nurses were watching to see what happened to me. I could not admit I was guilty of anything."

A judge of the Rhode Island Superior Court emphatically agreed, handing down a directed verdict against the union and for Marlene Swanson. Judge Clifford J. Cawley ruled that state public policy was quite clear that strikes by nurses were illegal, and that it is the "zenith of asininity" to fine anyone for failure to take part in an illegal strike.

The importance of Marlene's victory became quickly apparent. When another illegal strike occurred at the hospital, not just one, but 18 nurses crossed the picket line, putting their patients first and their union second.

Marlene Swanson was fortunate. She received experienced legal help in a case that lasted nearly two years. She would not have won and established an important principle—that nurses cannot be compelled to participate in an illegal strike—without that expert legal assistance.

The National Right to Work Legal Defense Foundation is helping everyone it can—currently in more than 100 cases involving illegal union political spending, violations of academic and political freedom, union violence, and other abuses of basic employee rights.

If you'd like to help people like Marlene Swanson, we'd like to hear from you.

The National Right to Work Legal Defense Foundation, 8001 Braddock Road, Springfield, Virginia 22160

\*     \*     \*

## JOB DISCRIMINATION . . .
## IT STILL EXISTS*

Paul Robertson is not a member of a persecuted minority. But he has experienced blatant discrimination all the same because he has chosen not to join a union.

Paul Robertson is a working man, a skilled licensed electrician with more than 20 years experience. He found out the hard way how a big company and a big union can discriminate on the job.

Paul was hired by the Bechtel Power Corporation to work on their Jim Bridger Power Plant project in the Rock Springs, Wyoming area. Only three months later, he was fired, supposedly because of a reduction in force.

But during the week preceding his discharge, Bechtel hired at least 19 union electricians referred by the local union and retained at least 65 unlicensed electricians.

A determined Paul Robertson filed unfair labor practice charges against the company and the union.

An administrative law judge ruled and was upheld by the full National Labor Relations Board that the union and the employer had indeed discriminated. The judge ordered that Robertson and seven other electricians be given the back pay they would have earned if they had been treated fairly.

The NLRB later reversed part of its decision, but Paul Robertson did not give up. With the help of the National Right to Work Legal Defense Foundation, he appealed the Board's decision to the U.S. Court of Appeals, arguing that hiring hall favoritism is discriminatory and unlawful.

Paul Robertson was fortunate. He found experienced legal help—all important because the case dragged on for nearly four years in the courts and the union still refuses to obey the NLRB's backpay order.

The National Right to Work Legal Defense Foundation is helping everyone it can—currently in more than 75 cases involving academic and political freedom, protection from union violence, and other fundamental rights. But it would like to do even more.

If you'd like to help workers like Paul Robertson write:

The National Right to Work Legal Defense Foundation, 8316 Arlington Boulevard, Suite 500, Fairfax, Virginia 22038.

\*     \*     \*

---

*Reprinted with the permission of the National Right to Work Legal Defense Foundation, Inc.

# NORMAN HILL, "THE DOUBLE-SPEAK OF RIGHT-TO-WORK"*

. . . If we briefly examine the history of the 1947 Taft-Hartley Act, whose Section 14(b) makes right-to-work laws possible, we can see clearly that its supporters hid their true intentions behind a dense smoke screen of ingenious, but insincere, rhetoric. For the most part, the business groups that organized and financed the drive to weaken the National Labor Relations Act described their movements as one of reform and liberty. No American, they argued, should be compelled to join any organization, whether it be a church, political party, or union. Such compulsion, they claimed, was un-American and a dangerous affront to liberty. Businesses have a strong, vested interest in crippling the labor movmeent, and frame the issue of right-to-work as a matter of personal liberty vs. slavery. They depicted themselves as the champions of the little guy against the union colossus, defending the rights of the weak. Having won the crucial public relations battle, business easily won the war. . . .

Trade unionists, business leaders, politicians, and academics also knew what Taft-Hartley was intended for. In the mid-1960s, for instance, an article appeared in a magazine called "Personnel Management," a journal read by thousands of labor relations specialists on the management side of the bargaining table. The authors were amazingly blunt: "The real issue in the right-to-work battle is collective bargaining power," they said. "Amidst all the conflicting arguments is the hidden, basic issue of union security and its ultimate relationship to collective bargaining power. This is the bread and butter issue that separates labor and management, namely, union strength." . . .

If you listen to right-to-work proponents, or if you read the literature of the National Right-to-Work Committee, you might think that unions exercise enormous powers over their members. "Union bosses," to use the rhetoric of the anti-labor forces, supposedly control the votes of the workers, exact tribute in the form of high dues, and decide who will work and who will spend time in the unemployment line. Many of the right-to-work supporters are well versed in the intricacies of our labor laws, so they know better. They know the truth, but they choose the excessive rhetoric as a smokescreen.

What exactly does union membership entail? In reality, it requires nothing

*The AFL-CIO American Federationist*, October 1980, pp. 13–15. Reprinted with permission.

more than the payment of dues. Union members, contrary to what you may have heard, cannot be forced to vote for union-endorsed candidates; they cannot be compelled to contribute money to political campaigns; they cannot be required to boycott selected products or stores; they cannot be forced even to attend union meetings; they cannot ever be forced to strike. . . .

Unions that endorse candidates for federal office are prohibited by law from making political contributions from union funds derived from dues, initiation fees, or agency shop fees. This prohibition is strictly enforced and violators risk heavy penalties. Unions that decide to make political contributions to such candidates must rely exclusively on funds donated voluntarily by rank-and-file members. Anyone, therefore, who claims that the union shop somehow forces people to act against their conscience in political matters is deliberately obscuring this part of the law.

Second to that slurring of the distinction betwen union treasury money and voluntary political contributions by members, perhaps the worst distortion peddled by the rights-to-work proponents involves how a union security clause gets into a contract. It can get there only through management agreement to such a clause via the free give-and-take of collective bargaining. In short, a national ban on the union security clause wouldn't involve any tinkering with law at all—either federal law through the Taft-Hartley Act or through the state compulsory open shop laws Taft-Hartley makes possible. All it would take is a nation-wide consensus among employers not to bargain a union security clause in their contracts. The truth—and the National Right-to-Work Committee knows this but would never admit it—is that a great number of employers have absolutely no interest in such a bargaining posture, because a guaranteed labor force through the union contract is much to their liking, especially in industries, like construction and maritime, where the union provides the employer with workers of exceptional skills because of apprenticeship and other training programs.

What the right-to-work forces also aren't telling on their topic is that some employers feel, as former secretary of Labor John Dunlop expressed it, that "a good contract with a good union is good business." That employer, who wants the more stable, more productive workforce under written terms of a legal contract, can bargain a union security clause in Illinois, then be forbidden to do so at his other plant across the border in Iowa. For that employer, the Iowa state law represents a form of "compulsion," but it's not the type of compulsion the right-to-work forces are likely to tell you about.

What they call compulsion—and what they want to tell you about—involves the millions of workers, who, they say, are forced to join unions against their will. But the truth is the exact opposite of this assertion. No one in the United States is now compelled to join or remain in a union. While union shop agreements which are bargained voluntarily by employers and unions require that workers pay dues after 30 or more days on the job, no one is forced to work in a union shop. And as any business leader will gladly tell you these days, the proportion of enterprises organized by unions is around 30 percent, which means, of courses, that a worker who wants to work in an open shop has many employers and occupations to choose from.

But even if unions organized every shop in the country, the worker who is opposed to union membership still has two other options. First, he could file a decertification petition with the National Labor Relations Board which would then be required to hold an election to determine whether the workers still wanted union representation.

If, however, decertification seems to be too drastic for most workers, a dissident employee can file for a deauthorization election. In this type of election, workers are not asked to keep or to dump the union. They are asked whether they want to continue a union shop. Again, this is not an excessively complex proceeding and it requires no special skills or knowledge on the part of anti-union employees.

*    *    *

*Comment:*

## LOYALTY TO THE FIRM AND TRUSTWORTHINESS

Firms may lose something in the loyalty of their employees when unionization comes in. The employees may be less enthusiastic in performing their jobs, and less ready to put forward extra effort in crises; in the confrontations of collective bargaining, the employees will act in opposition to the aims of the firms. Yet good relations can be restored; in time at least, employees may become as enthusiastic and as helpful after unionization as they ever were before it. Whether they do or not, there is a minimum of loyalty that emloyees owe to firms throughout employment, and even afterward. It is a minimum made up of duties to refrain from taking bribes, from divulging information, from converting to their own use assets of the firm, including secrets about its methods and products. Other duties should perhaps be added: Is there not a duty to refrain from sabotage? Can it be excusably waived even during confrontations? Waived if the firms do not play by civilized rules, and the confrontations degenerate into warfare?

Taking bribes does not seem to be a useful tactic in confrontations; perhaps on that account alone it never seems excusable to do harm to an employing firm in this way. But when is it a bribe, and when is harm being done? Purchasing agents commonly accept gifts from salesmen eager to do business with them. They do not think of themselves as taking bribes. A case of Gewürztraminer at Christmas, even a case of Gewürztraminer every Christmas, is not going to persuade them to buy turbines from Unified

Conglomerate rather than from Horizontally Integrated. They will hear out the arguments for each.

Would we find this defense equally plausible if the Christmas gift were a three-week vacation in Rio, accompanied by the Playmate of the Year, all expenses paid? Is it entirely conclusive when it's only the wine that is in question? Suppose that Horizontally Integrated, which makes excellent turbines, is not willing to come through with the Gewürztraminer any more than with the trip to Rio.

I do not mean to be priggish: A lot of things to which there are strictly speaking objections can be excused under accepted practice, as doing more good in promoting friendly relations (useful to the firm in crises) than it does harm in twisting critical decisions. Part of the problem is to find solutions that are not priggish.

Accepting a bribe for divulging information that it is best for the firm to withhold from competitors is such outright disloyalty that it can be condemned without a hint of priggishness. May not a firm justly, without oppression, demand even more, that its employees should not lightly divulge confidential information to anyone unauthorized to have it? Industrial spies evidently come in all shapes and forms. Similarly, it is not just walking off with one of the firm's drill-presses to set up in business for oneself, which is theft, that is objectionable. It is also making use of assets like secret information, which employees come to know because they are inevitably entrusted with the assets in the course of employment.

# EXTRIN FOODS v. LEIGHTON ET AL.

*Supreme Court of New York (Kings County), 1952*

HART, Justice.

Plaintiff here seeks an injunction restraining defendants from manufacturing and distributing certain flavoring products with the use of alleged secret formulae and processes claimed to be plaintiff's property, and from aiding any one in the manufacture and distribution of these products. The prayer for relief requests that defendants be also enjoined from imitating plaintiff's "seal, script, layout, trade names, claims or simulations thereof." Plaintiff as incidental relief seeks an accounting of profits and to recover damages.

The Court finds the facts established by the proof as follows:

Plaintiff corporation was organized in 1942 as successor to a partnership created in 1938 and known as Extrin Laboratories. The partners were individuals named Kugelman, Fontana and Sweet. Kugelman had developed formulae and processes for synthetizing a butter flavor to be imparted primarily to baked goods and confectioneries. These formulae and processes were assigned by the partnership to plaintiff. Defendant Ciconte had been hired by plaintiff in 1943 as an errand boy and general helper. He eventually became the production manager. Defendant Leighton was hired as a chemist in 1946 to establish a laboratory for plaintiff. His duties included the mixing of the flavoring ingredients, improving existing products and the development of new ones. Under the practice existing in the plaintiff organization the flavoring ingredients were prepared by the chemist in a part of the buildling separate from the production room where they finally were blended with other ingredients into the finished product.

The original Extrin product was in the form of a powder. Prior to Leighton's employment Kugelman had prepared a formula of the ingredients for the butter flavor in paste form which bears the trade mark "Extrin-AA."

One of the most important assignments given to Leighton by plaintiff was the development of a product containing the butter flavor in the form of a free flowing fluid. As the result of many months' experimentation and research by Leighton under the supervision of and with the assistance of Kugelman a formulation of an emulsion was developed. The process of manufacture was established in the production room by Leighton and Kugelman with the assistance of Fontana and defendant Ciconte. The resulting product became known as Extrin's "Creme Royale."

Basically the "Creme Royale" and the paste "Extrin-AA" in regard to the flavoring elements are the same with respect to their ingredients which vary quantitatively in the paste and the emulsion. The ingredients required to establish the flavor were blended together by the chemist pursuant to the formula developed by Kugelman and is referred to as the "K Special." The chief difference between the paste and emulsion is the medium by which the flavor is carried. Defendant Leighton helped to a great extent, after exhaustive experiments at plaintiff's expense to develop the emulsion. He claims that he also improved the "K Special." He prepared for plaintiff a Madeira flavor under the trade name of "Revelex." Ciconte was given the formulae for the blending of each product but not the "K Special." It therefore appears that Ciconte and Leighton thus in their respective capacities learned and knew the ingredients and the quantities and methods of production of each of plaintiff's products, including the flavoring elements.

In 1949 or 1950 the original founders of plaintiff corporation fell out among themselves. Litigation ensued. As a result Fontana and Kugelman sold their interests and Sweet alone remained. Fontana went into business as Nutrin Laboratories.

On September 18, 1950, defendants Leighton and Ciconte left plaintiff's employ and became associated with Nutrin. Within a month thereafter they became sole stockholders and directors of Nutrin Foods, Inc., and Fontana severed his connection with the corporation. In the interim, within a few weeks after terminating their employment with plaintiff, defendants were producing competitive products. Defendant Leighton, when he terminated his employment with plaintiff, appropriated about one hundred fifty cards which showed the results of various baking tests. Though at first denying that he had misappropriated them, they were subsequently returned to plaintiff through defendant's counsel. At the time of the commencement of business by defendant, Nutrin Foods, Inc., simulated plaintiff's trade mark and labeling. After the instant action was commenced, so as to avoid the charge of imitation of plaintiff's trade mark and label, defendants changed theirs. The defendant corporation was reorganized and the name changed to Nutrol Laboratories, Inc. . . .

The preponderating evidence satisfies the Court that the defendants' emulsion is substantially the same as plaintiff's "Creme Royale." Defendants concede that the ingredients of their product are substantially the same as plaintiff's, though they claim that the products themselves were different since the flavoring ingredients differ. Defendants claim their product is dissimilar since their flavoring is based on butter derivatives (esters and organic acids purchased commercially) whereas plaintiff's main flavoring ingredients is diaceytil. A chemical analysis by a competent chemist establishes that the products are substantially identical chemically and in taste, odor, appearance and consistency. From the Court's own observation the products are substantially identical as to color, odor and consistency. Plaintiff established upon the trial that Ciconte, as president of defendant corporation, shortly after the commencement of business, wrote to a former salesman of plaintiff, offering him employment and representing that defendants manufactured the same product. Two of plaintiff's customers testified (and were not contradicted) that Leighton, in soliciting their business, told them that he had been Extrin's former chemist and was manufacturing exactly the same products as Extrin. All of the foregoing satisfies the Court that with regard to the "Creme Royale," defendants' emulsion is substantially identical. With respect to the paste, however, plaintiff failed to prove the similarity of their products or their ingredients. . . .

As between the parties, are the formulae and processes secret? If so were they unlawfully appropriated by defendants?

[1] In resolving this issue the Court is first required to define the term "secret" as applied to a formula. The term "trade secret" is defined in the Restatement of Torts, § 757, p. 5, as follows:

> b. *Definition of a trade secret.* A trade secret may consist of any formula, pattern, device or compilation of information which is used in one's business, and which gives him an opportunity to obtain an advantage over competitors who do not know or use it. It may be a formula for a chemical compound, a process of manufacturing, treating or preserving materials, a pattern for a machine or other device, or a list of customers. *** A trade secret is a process or device for continuous use in the operation of the business. Generally it relates to the production of goods, as, for example, a machine or formula for the production of an article. . . .

[2] The mere fact that the constituent ingredients of plaintiff's product are on its label does not preclude the existence of secret formulae. As expressed by plaintiff's expert:

> The Witness: I would call both of them or either of them a product resulting from a secret formula for the reason that while ingredients are declared on the

label, the proportions in which they are present and the method of compounding the product is not revealed either on the label or is it revealed in any standard or any definition which applies to such products.

The Court: In other words, among chemists a formula is still secret even though the component parts are known if the method of preparation is not known and may only be ascertained as a result of experimentation; is that correct?

The Witness: That is correct.

[3] Nor is it of great moment that plaintiff's formula can be revealed after examination of its labels, experimentation and analysis by a competent chemist. . . .

[4] Even though the contract of hiring contained no express covenant, the individual defendants by an implied agreement bound themselves not to disclose, reveal or appropriate secret processes or formulae. . . .

[5] In an action such as this, to enjoin the use of a formula claimed to be a secret, communicated in confidence, the important issue of fact is not whether it is new or could have been discovered by defendants by fair means but whether the parties dealt at arm's length and whether their negotiations were of such character as to put defendants in a position whereby they are bound to respect the information given to them by plaintiff and not to use it for their own benefit. . . .

> It may well be that if defendant had never been in a confidential relationship with the plaintiff, upon the plaintiff's publication to the world of its wrap, the defendant might rightfully have purchased the same. Not by any action of plaintiff, but by its own violation of confidence, it has deprived itself of that opportunity, which is open to the rest of the world. It cannot obtain in confidence the details of an alleged invention, of the process for making the same, and of the machine by which it is made, and proceed to make the product by that or similar process, or by equivalent or similar machine or methods before the plaintiff makes its publication to the world, and then assert that it is a member of the public to whom the publication has been made. A court of equity cannot approve such breach of confidence.*

[6] Applying the foregoing principles of equity to the action at bar, the Court is satisfied that as between the parties the individual defendants were informed in confidence of the formulae for the emulsion and its flavoring ingredients known as "K Special," both of which were used in the preparation of plaintiff's "Creme Royale," and that defendants appropriated them to their own use. . . .

The Court finds that the formula for the "Creme Royale" was a trade secret within the meaning of § 757 of the Restatement and the authorities above cited, and preserved as such by plaintiff. Defendants were aware of its secret character. These findings apply also to the flavoring formula known as "K Special." As heretofore noted, though "K Special" is used in both the paste and the emulsion, there is no proof in the record that

---

*[Allen-Qualley Co. v. Shellmar Products Co.]

defendants' paste product is the same as plaintiff's or that defendants employed the "K Special" in the Nutrol paste. Likewise this proof is lacking with respect to the other competitive products of the parties.

*    *    *

## Comment:

# PARTICIPATION

---

Unionization, looked upon as an effort by workers to participate in important decisions about their work, may, even in the best of unions, represent a very limited gain in this respect for any individual worker. As one member of a large organization he or she cannot ordinarily expect to count for much in shaping union policies. The organization may steadily favor the interests of most of its members, but an individual member does not have much more control over it than over the firm.

Moreover, unions (especially in North America) have largely confined themselves to issues about pay, hours of work, safety, fringe benefits, and grievances about work assignments, promotion, and dismissal. These are all important matters, on which (in the clear cases of being wrong) oppressive conduct on the part of firms needs to be opposed. They do not, however, by any means exhaust the aspects of work about which workers might with justification wish to have a say.

Those other aspects come into view if one shifts the perspective for viewing work from protecting people against abuses of power to enabling them to have as much enjoyment out of work as possible—under our present assumptions, we might say, as much enjoyment as is compatible with the firms' earning at least a normal rate of profit. It is a striking fact that this second perspective is relatively so unfamiliar that it may be felt to be irrelevant. Why should work be fun? Or, at least, what basis in ethics is there for arguing that it should be?

The basis is not hard to find. People spend a lot of time at work—the best part of their lives, if we consider time at work as a proportion of that part of their waking time in which their powers are fullest and most alert. Is it compatible with their having the happiest lives possible that their work should be less interesting and enjoyable than it could be? Or than they could make it for themselves if they had more chance to say how it was to be done?

More is at stake here than the purpose of the participation. The purpose, accomplished, would be work organized so as to be more interesting and enjoyable. However, just being able to pursue this purpose through participation would give employees a reassuringly enlarged sense of being in control of their own lives—a larger sense of personal freedom. The freedom will be larger, and sensed as larger, moreover, if it is exercised not just in casting one vote among thousands or tens of thousands in a union, but face-to-face with the half-dozen workmates with whom one is given the responsibility of organizing a significant part of a production process.

## Paper-Organizing Game: Happiness and Justice
### In The Relations of Firms and Employees

The object of the game, as before, is to put the following questions into perspicuous order, which will form the overall plan or skeleton for your paper.

1. How much variety is there in the possible abuses of power over employees?

2. Why is it important, on grounds both of happiness and justice, to check abuses of power affecting employees' lives at work?

3. Is employees' participation in the design and conduct of their jobs consistent with greater overall efficiency?

4. Would the present distribution of property be unquestionably just if it did result entirely from honest efforts in the past? Is it just for some people to be—regardless of their own efforts—under the power of others?

5. Will some abuses of power—some forms of oppression—affect the happiness of employees' lives outside of work?

6. If employees are able to participate in the design and conduct of their jobs, as well as in determining whether they'll be employed and how much they'll be paid, will not the distribution of power have been made more just?

7. Is the present distribution of property, including the property held by firms, entirely the result of honest efforts in the past?

8. Should we be content from a moral point of view to check abuses of power that affect employees' happiness outside of work?

9. Will it suffice to check abuses of power affecting employees' lives at work to have firms make the tasks that they set as congenial as they see fit to make them?

10. Does not the concentration of property in the hands of firms give them power over employees that might lead to multiple abuses?

# ARRANGEMENTS FOR WORKERS' PARTICIPATION (ILO)*

I. INSTITUTIONAL ARRANGEMENTS FOR PARTICIPATION
OF WORKERS' REPRESENTATIVES IN DECISIONS

*1. Workers' management of undertakings and related systems.* From a conceptual viewpoint, workers' management of undertakings or self-management represents the most far-reaching degree of association of workers in decisions concerning them.

Probably the best known example of this type of workers' participation is the Yugoslav system of self-management which has been the subject of a large number of studies and publications and has some twenty years' experience. Under the Yugoslav system, the workforce of the undertaking exercises the principal functions of management through the self-management organs, the organisation and powers of which have been established since the sixties by the statute or internal regulations of the undertaking, namely, the workers' assembly and the workers' council. The latter is elected by secret ballot by the personnel from among its members, usually for a term of two years, at the end of which its members are not immediately eligible for re-election, in order to ensure rotation of membership. The workers' council enjoys wide powers in the field of management in general; for example, it adopts the internal regulations (including those concerning distribution of income), development plans and other programmes of the undertaking, supervises their implementation, decides on investments and approves the balance sheet. Every four years, it elects the director of the undertaking, whom it is also empowered to dismiss, and it generally sets up a management board and a supervisory committee, as well as a whole series of specialised committees to which are delegated advisory or decision-making powers in specific fields (for example, recruitment and dismissal of certain categories of employees, grievances, planning, financial and commercial affairs, etc.). Important matters such as mergers or the conversion of the undertaking may be, in general, submitted to a referendum of the personnel, but in practice, decisions on these matters are usually taken by the workers' assembly.

This system of self-management, introduced in 1950 after a period of highly centralised management and planning, was extended after 1953 to so-called non-economic activities (education, administration, health and social security services, etc.). Since 1971, a great many efforts have been made to carry out a thorough renovation of the system and to remedy

*Excerpts from *Workers' Participation in Decisions Within Undertakings* (1976), pp. 3–31. Copyright 1981, International Labour Office.

certain difficulties to which even the highest authorities in the country have drawn attention.

In this perspective, a Workers' Self-Management Congress, organised by the trade unions, was held in Sarajevo in May 1971, which adopted almost thirty important resolutions. Among the twenty-one constitutional amendments adopted the following month by the Federal Assembly, those which dealt directly with self-management of undertakings gave constitutional sanction to the recommendations of this Congress relating among other things to the policy of distribution of income and to the total application of the principle of direct self-management by the workers in the basic work units, in order to avoid a situation where the workers participated less and less directly in self-management. These principles have been incorporated in the new Federal Constitution of Yugoslavia promulgated at the beginning of 1974. Thus, at the present time, while on the one hand the autonomy of undertakings has been reinforced, on the other hand self-management is being decentralised through the operation of self-management organs at two, or, in the case of large enterprises, three different levels, namely, at the level of undertaking as a whole, at the level of its economic units (plants or establishments) and at the level of its work units (shops or departments, etc.). The shop-floor assemblies, which constitute the basic self-management organs, are empowered, for example, to adopt production plans and works rules for the unit, as well as deciding upon the distribution of income among the workers, taking account of the principles of distribution established by the workers' council and of the legal minimum. They may also delegate certain of their functions to the executive committee elected by their members. . . .

*2. Participation of workers' representatives in management organs.* For varying lengths of time, in a large number of countries, and by virtue in most cases of a legal obligation, workers' representatives have been included in management organs in the public sector as a whole or in certain nationalised undertakings, or again in the railways, national airways, or various public services such as posts and telecommunications, gas, water and electricity services, etc. . . .

These workers' representatives may be directly nominated by the trade unions, or by the government on the proposal of the trade unions, or elected by the personnel. Their number and influence vary a great deal from one country to another and from one undertaking to another, by reason of the functions entrusted to them by law or in practice, and because of their standard of education and training for this role.

In the private sector, the system which has pushed workers' representation to the furthest degree is that of co-determination applied in the Federal Republic of Germany since the beginning of the fifties. This system has been the object of numerous studies and has attracted special attention in many countries. By an Act of 1951, equal representation of workers was established on the supervisory boards of large iron and steel and mining undertakings. These boards generally include five workers' representatives (one worker and one salaried employee nominated by the works council from among members of the personnel of the undertaking, and three representatives nominated by the trade union organisations, one of whom must come from outside the undertaking and the said organisations), five representatives of the shareholders, and an eleventh member nominated by mutual agreement. In addition, one of the members of the directorate or management board (appointed by the supervisory board) namely, the "labour director" who is generally responsible for personnel questions and social affairs, may only be nominated or dismissed in agreement with the majority of the workers' members of that board.

Under an Act of 1952, the workers' representation on the supervisory boards of companies which do not belong to the above industries is only one-third of the total membership. For some time and with increasing insistence in recent years, the German Confederation of Trade Unions has been demanding equal representation of workers on the supervisory boards of companies in sectors other than iron and steel and mining, at least for undertakings of a certain size or with a certain financial turnover. This demand has met with strong opposition on the part of the German Employers' Confederation, which has seen in it, among other things, an attack on property rights as well as a threat to the market economy, to the autonomy of the parties in collective bargaining and to the efficiency of management. The present coalition government of the Social Democratic and Liberal Parties has reached agreement on the principles of new legislation on this subject, which is in preparation.

In several other Western European countries, legislation has been drafted or adopted during the past few years with a view to introducing workers' representation in management organs of private undertakings, or to reinforcing existing representation, but in most cases workers have only been granted a minority representation as compared to that of share-holders. . . .

3. *Works councils, works committees, joint consultation bodies and similar institutions for workers' representation.* Works councils or works committees, or again joint consultation bodies, remain by far the commonest form of machinery for workers' participation in decisions within undertakings in both industrialised and developing countries. . . .

. . . In Austria, the Federal Republic of Germany and the Netherlands, the trend has been towards extension of the information to be given to the works councils concerning the economic and financial situation of the undertaking to include forecasts such as investment programmes, plans for rationalisation and the introduction of new methods or processes, the reduction of production and changes in the structure of the undertaking (closing down or transfer, in whole or in part, mergers, etc.), thus including generally forecasts which may entail substantial changes in the employment situation or pattern and working conditions. In most cases, this right to information is henceforth accompanied by the right to consultation at the planning stage; the employer is generally obliged to indicate the measures he intends to take to avoid or lessen any unfavourable consequences for the workers, and the works council is empowered, for its part, to discuss these forecasts and proposals and to suggest other solutions.

In Belgium, where a Royal Decree of 27 November 1973 issued regulations concerning the economic and financial information to be supplied to works councils, under the terms of national agreements concluded some years ago, the head of the undertaking is obliged, on request from the workers' delegates, to inform the works council of the rules in operation concerning personnel policy, applying in particular to recruitment, selection, transfers and promotion. The works council is empowered to determine, on a proposal by the head of undertaking or the workers' delegates, the general criteria to be followed in case of redundancy or re-employment resulting from economic or technical circumstances.

In France, the works committees play an increased role in the participation of the personnel in profits, which was instituted by an Ordinance of 1967. In addition, under the terms of a national agreement of 1969 on job security, they must be consulted when collective dismissals are envisaged for economic reasons. The Act concerning continuous vocational training, adopted in 1971, also makes their consultation compulsory on a certain number of points relating to such training. Finally, an Act of December 1973 entrusted to them new attributions in the field of conditions of work and provided that a specialised committee be set up for this purpose in enterprises with 300 or more employees.

As regards the right of co-decision, in the Netherlands, an Act of 1971, which replaced that of 1950 concerning works councils requires not only consultation with these organs but their consent before any decision may be taken relating in particular to the establishment or change of work schedules or holiday arrangements and any safety or hygiene measures. An Act adopted in January 1972, in the Federal Republic of Germany, extended the already substantial list of questions on which decisions must be taken jointly by the employers and the works councils, including, among other matters, the determination of standards of piecework and incentive payments. Co-decision is also obligatory henceforth for directives concerning the selection of personnel in connection with recruitment, transfers or changes of grade. . . .

4. *Participation through trade union action.* . . . Collective bargaining at the level of the undertaking, in so far as it is tending to broaden the scope of subject matter with which it deals and in this way to replace unilateral management decisions by decisions negotiated with the trade unions, is thus becoming an increasingly important means of participation. In many countries, in fact, collective bargaining is the only means of participation in decisions, or the most efficient means.

Among the industrialised countries where this type of participation in decisions within undertakings is most widespread mention may be made of Canada, the United States, Japan and the United Kingdom. In the United States, where the trade unions continue to oppose on principle the repre-

sentation of workers in management organs, collective agreements, negotiated generally at the level of the undertaking, but also sometimes at the
plant level, are the main form of participation. These negotiations have in
fact reached a point over the years where they cover most decisions affecting
employment and working conditions. The same is true in Canada and to a
significant degree Japan. In the United Kingdom, the trade union delegates
elected at the shop-floor level (shop stewards), of whom there were estimated to be some 300,000 in 1971, i.e. an average of one for every 50 or 60
unionised workers, whereas, at the same period, there were only some
3,000 full-time trade union officials, have for a certain number of years
played an increasingly important role, while their committees enjoy a high
degree of autonomy in collective bargaining. Some trade union leaders hold
the view that everything occurring in the undertaking which workers wish
to discuss should be subject to collective bargaining. . . .

II. ARRANGEMENTS FOR ASSOCIATING WORKERS WITH THE
DETERMINATION OF WORK ORGANISATION AT THE
SHOP-FLOOR LEVEL

*1. New concepts of work organisation.* The systems described above are those
in which workers participate in decisions within undertakings through
representatives. While conceptually, of course, under these systems,
workers as a collectivity as well as individually are the direct or indirect
beneficiaries of, and participants in, the decision-making process, such
workers' participation schemes through collective bargaining, consultation
or workers' representation on management bodies do not by themselves
normally affect directly the participation of workers in the organisation of
work at the shop-floor level. Decisions concerning the choice of equipment,
method of work, manning and job design generally remain within the realm
of management prerogatives. Although some input of workers' ideas and
experience may go into management decisions on these matters through the
use of suggestion schemes, or by informal, direct consultation of workers
and their shop-floor representatives by supervisors, at various levels, as to
the best way of doing a job, in general, hierarchical structures of authority in
enterprises have effectively precluded the direct involvement of shop-floor
workers in decisions affecting the organisation of work, even where
formalised consultation or participation of workers takes place at higher
levels.

This absence of direct participation in decisions of immediate concern to
them in their daily work is held to be one of the major ingredients of the
dissatisfaction which is being increasingly manifested in various ways
among industrial and other types of workers. With increasing exposure to a
consumptionist society and rising educational levels, workers' aspirations
also rise for a more satisfying work experience, including more control over
the organisation of their work, better knowledge of its end results, greater
freedom of movement, more chance for self-development and promotion,

wider scope for the exercise of initiative and the use of their intellectual capacity and acquired skills. Younger workers, in particular, are impatient with the limited scope of many jobs in factory and office, the monotony of assembly-line types of activity and the constraints of authoritarian methods of supervision. The high rate of absenteeism and labour turnover, a general decline of interest in work and increase of indifference and apathy leading to carelessness and a lowering of standards of quality, which are common phenomena today in enterprises throughout the world, are widely attributed to the hiatus between the aspirations of workers and the realities of jobs as they are organised in many cases, and to the increasingly felt cleavage between workplace and life outside the factory or office. . . .

For decades, social scientists and other observers have denounced the excessive fragmentation and simplification of machine-paced tasks which characterise the scientific organisation of work popularised by Taylor, pointing out the meaningless nature of such jobs to workers and the sense of powerlessness they engender. A few experiments—in particular those carried out by Hyacinthe Dubreuil in the Bat'a shoe company in the thirties—demonstrated that workers organised in co-operative groups could take an active part in a wide range of decisions directly concerning their jobs without disrupting the flow of production, and, indeed, with salutary results on productivity and on worker attitudes within the plant. Such views have gradually gained a wider currency, under the influence of developments in management theory in recent years which stressed the effectiveness of a less authoritarian and more "participative" management style, and studies of worker motivation. Trade union pressures for better conditions in the workplace and a more human organisation of industrial work, and, in some countries, government interest in promoting systems of workers' participation in decisions, have also contributed to a widespread reconsideration of accepted forms of work organisation. The flattening out of the structure of authority in undertakings by the delegation of decision-making power to the shop-floor level is thus beginning to appear as a complementary trend to the promotion of worker participation through representatives.

At the present time, a great deal of experimentation is taking place in an effort to adjust the social and technical systems of production to more livable patterns of work, allowing the workers a greater span of decision-making power on the shop-floor. However modest may be the practical achievements so far, in terms of their over-all impact on the workforce in the plant or the industry concerned, some of these experiments do appear to represent a new vision of the workplace for the future. But breaking as they do into traditional patterns of management structure, work organisation and labour-management relations, they often raise difficulties of implementation and are nowhere accepted without question or opposition. . . .

Very often, the more direct association of workers with the organisation of their work is being introduced within the context of a broader movement towards the improvement of the whole working environment and physical conditions of work, which involves changes in many aspects of the workplace situation. Some of the following types of innovations are found in many of the present experiments:

—Changes in the technology or the mechanics of the production process. For example, the reorganisation of assembly-line conveyor-belt systems so that work can be performed on a stationary object, the product can be moved at the will of the worker or automatically placed so as to facilitate work in a more natural and less tiring position; the shortening of assembly lines and their arrangement so that the product is visible at all times to the operators; the introduction of automatic devices to handle repetitive or dangerous operations.

—Changes in the physical environment of the workplace. For example, improvements in plant layout allowing for more spacious and better lighted work areas, better ventilation and noise control and general plant housekeeping; grouping of operations in order to create a more intimate atmosphere; more efficient arrangements for the supply of material and parts, by the constitution of "buffer stocks" which allow workers greater flexibility in the pace of work.

—Changes in the design of jobs. For example, the enlargement of the scope of operators' jobs to include some preparatory and maintenance operations as well as quality control; the rotation of workers between different operations on assembly lines or in continuous-flow processes; the lengthening of the work cycle in production, sometimes to the extent that one worker can complete a whole series of operations or even build an entire unit; rotation of workers between preassembly operations and work on the assembly line.

—Organisation of work in autonomous groups. For example, the setting up of production groups, the size of which may range from three to forty workers in different circumstances, with responsibility for one production assignment which constitutes a homogeneous unit; such groups usually have varying degrees of freedom to organize the work and the interchange of jobs among workers within the group, to plan breaks and to take or propose other decisions concerning the work within the limits of an assigned production goal or schedule.

—Changes in the conditions of work. For example, new systems of wage calculation and payment, including group incentives, to take account of changing job structures; more flexible time schedules and individualised pace of work.

—Changes in the methods and contents of training, to broaden the range of skills of workers, increase the flexibility of the workforce and improve use of human resources.

Many of the above types of changes, which are designed to combat the monotony and fatigue of repetitive jobs, result in an enlargement of workers' power of decision-making at the level of the execution of work, for example, in the arrangement of job rotation and break schedules within a work group, increased authority to call for supplies, to reject defective products, to make needed repairs and even sometimes in personnel matters such as the replacement of absent workers or the selection of new members of the group. In a few instances, the authority of the group has been extended to the planning of production schedules over a certain period of time, even as long as three months in advance. Many decisions formerly taken by supervisors concerning job assignments and work methods now form part of the operators' daily responsibilities. Relations with supervisors are thus altered; the latter assume functions of a more technical, advisory nature, providing assistance in the solution of shop-floor problems and generally acting in a supportive rather than a managerial role. First line supervisors may even be dispensed with almost entirely, being replaced by a team leader chosen by the members of the work group in a number of experiments. Similarly, the inspection staff may be released for more conceptual tasks, such as the development of standards, where routine decisions regarding quality control are largely delegated to the operators themselves. . . .

*2. Promotion of worker participation in the organisation of work: Different approaches and motivating factors.* The association of the workers concerned in decisions relating to their job may be seen as instrumental—as a means of creating a sense of personal involvement of workers in the aims of the undertaking, of making work more meaningful, of increasing individual satisfaction in work by enhancing responsibility and interest in the job; as a means of improving employees' performance, of achieving higher levels of productivity; as a means of forestalling potential grievances and employee-management conflict. Participation at this level may, on the other hand, be considered as an end in itself—a system which embodies respect for human values and the dignity of the individual or as a just sharing of power in the enterprise in recognition of the workers' essential contribution to its functioning. . . .

Taken even in its most limited sense, the job enrichment approach provides greater scope for workers' participation in day-to-day decisions immediately affecting their work. It tends to introduce more flexible methods of control, less direct supervision, increased communication between workers and supervisors and an improved flow of information to employees at the shop-floor level, including data relevant to the execution of their jobs (production charts and schedules) and information concerning their own performance. Job enrichment techniques, such as the rotation of tasks, the broadening of qualifications and responsibilities of workers, and the enhancement of the intrinsic interest of the job, form an essential element of many more broadly-conceived experiments in work reorganisation. The fact remains nonetheless that the introduction of such changes alone often represents a change in management style rather than a modication of the structure of authority in the enterprise. Employee participation in preparing the introduction of changes in work organisation has in some instances simply taken the form of answering questionnaires designed to locate the sources of dissatisfaction and to suggest possible avenues of improvement. Advance information or consultation of workers concerned is, in fact, expressly discouraged by the job enrichment theorists from the fear that this might confuse the issues at stake and raise false expectations. It is also thought by some that giving employees a sense of participation will not produce any lasting benefits; moreover, such procedures are felt to conflict with management's rights and to be ineffective and disruptive in practice. The hierarchical structure thus remains intact, the level of decision-making accessible to workers being limited to matters immediately related to their tasks.

Much more profound changes in the distribution of decision-making power are envisaged by the socio-technical systems theory, an approach developed several decades ago by a group of researchers of the Tavistock Institute of Human Relations in the United Kingdom. Their studies stemmed from the notion of the "joint optimisation" of the social and technical systems within an enterprise—each being designed in relation to the other to serve the best interests of worker satisfaction and technical efficiency. Great emphasis was laid on the value of workers' sharing responsibility for decisions concerning their jobs through the organisation of work in groups or teams, in order to allow maximum scope for individual development, while, at the same time, the technical systems are adapted to the human needs of operators as well as to organisational requirements. . . .

. . . Norway was the first country to pioneer in this field, a decade ago, by undertaking a series of experiments carried out with the advice and assistance of researchers from the Tavistock Institute, and within the framework of a programme to promote industrial democracy which was developed jointly by the central employers' and workers' organisations. In one of the plants selected for the trials, engaged in the manufacture of electric radiators, the tasks of production, supervision, planning, maintenance and handling of goods, which were formerly fragmented and assigned to specialised workers, have been regrouped and entrusted to autonomous teams composed of from fifteen to forty workers. Each group elects annually its own leader, who is responsible for co-ordination with other groups and for contacts with management where necessary. The group leaders and the local plant management form a committee competent to take decisions on production planning, financial management and all aspects of the plant's development. Within the groups, workers decide among themselves the distribution of jobs and are trained to be interchangeable. The autonomy of the groups extends to the planning of production schedules—initially for a four weeks' period, but later, at the request of the groups, a planning period of three months was introduced. Another experiment of this type was carried out by the Norsk Hydro Company in a new plant in Porsgrunn, producing chemical fertilizer. Work in that plant has been organised in five teams of twelve workers each, each team being composed of three work groups of four workers each who are trained to carry out all the operations in one particular area of the work, including maintenance and cleaning of work areas as well as quality control. A special "action committee" composed of an outside researcher, the plant manager, representatives of the local union, of the supervisors and of the personnel department, met weekly to watch and guide the experiment in the early stages; later this work was taken over by the "department committees" which had been set up throughout Norwegian industry under an agreement concluded between the central unions and employers' organisations in 1967. . . .

In Sweden, a parallel impulse for such experiments has come from the national employers' organisation, which has been active in stimulating the search for new work systems among its members with a view of promoting job satisfaction and higher productivity. It is noteworthy that the motivating factors mentioned above—the need to rationalise production in a competitive market, difficulties of recruitment and higher labour turnover, absenteeism and other symptoms of worker alienation—are urgent problems in these countries as elsewhere, impelling managements to seek solutions in a reorganisation of the workplace. The theories and techniques of job enrichment and the restructuring of work in autonomous groups have had a wide influence. But the particular labour relations system in these countries, characterised by a long tradition of joint co-operation at the national level, has provided a framework for a co-operative approach to innovations at the workplace level. Thus, even where the initiative for changes has come from the management, the trade unions as well as the workers themselves have been directly involved, and the systems developed have sought to introduce a very large degree of worker autonomy in the execution of work and participation in the planning process.

In the SAAB and Volvo automobile companies, for example, a policy has been followed for a number of years of encouraging plant managements to develop ways of putting into effect certain principles of worker participation in the organisation of work. This has resulted in a variety of innovations; for example, in the SAAB-Scania works in Södertalje, producing truck chassis and engines, the management worked closely with representatives of all the unions as well as technical specialists in a "reference group" set up to define objectives for experiments and to select areas for trials; work groups, including operators, were then established in the selected areas to make suggestions for changes in present systems of work; eventually, the assembly work was organised in production groups composed of operators representing the various trades involved. These groups were given complete responsibility for organising and carrying out an entire operation, under the general supervision of development groups responsible for preparing production plans and objectives. Another experiment carried out in a plant producing SAAB 99 engines involved the redesign of the assembly line to allow workers to build an entire engine at their own pace, within an over-all production goal; this design was developed by a project group which drew on the experience of operators, supervisors and other personnel. Many plants in the Volvo company have also introduced systems of group production which involve the rotation of workers between a number of different work stations on the assembly line or the formation of a small team of workers responsible for one work assignment which they organise independently. Such changes have in every case been planned in consultation with union representatives as well as the operators concerned. At present, two new plants are being built on designs worked out by project groups in which unions and operating personnel take part, and which incorporate many of the new concepts and techniques developed during previous experiments to provide for group work and greater worker autonomy.

\*      \*      \*

# CHAPTER 12

# *Closing Down, Shifting Operations, Fleeing to the South*

*Introductory Comment:*

## AN INTRACTABLE PROBLEM?

The all-too-familiar, all-too-painful theme that figures in this chapter is generally rendered, as Robert Howard's article illustrates, in lamentations directed at the firms making decisions to close down plants and shift capital or operations (or both) elsewhere. The people and the towns left behind are obviously, palpably hurt. Firms and stockholders may gain; but, one wonders, might not they have been content to gain a bit less and to have avoided sacrificing the livelihoods of so many? Sometimes, as in the demise of the New England textile industry, whole regions suffer. One thinks of bloodless financial manipulations on the one side taking an unfortunate precedence over the vitality of a region and of a way of life, on the other. It would seem that this theme will strain the triplet principle by making it hard to find unobjectionable examples.

However, if there is a strain here on the triplet principle, it works, contrary to first impressions, as much against finding examples of clear evils, wrongly done, as against finding clear examples of good things, or at least unobjectionable things, rightly done, or at least done with no blame attaching. There is, to be sure, no want of pain and unpleasantness—bad things; but these are mixed, perhaps everywhere we turn on this issue, with good things. Moreover, even if there were net losses all around from the decisions to cease operations, it would be difficult to fix unambiguous responsibility on the firms. They do not cease operations gratuitously; their hand is forced.

The damage that is done is damage done as a result of the firms responding to signals in the market. Will the market undo the damage? In the real world, the market can hardly be expected to operate so quickly as to offset all the costs borne by the people and towns left behind. They will lose wages and tax revenues for a time; have to go to the expense of moving, retraining, attracting (if they can) new industry. The market may in fact offset their costs, if it ever does, only with the delay of a generation. Many of the workers laid off will be too old to qualify for retraining and too old to get comparable employment elsewhere. Many of them, with other family members still at work, will find it impractical to move elsewhere themselves, especially when they are not sure of finding work even if they do. Whatever new industry does come in may come in only years later and offer only employment of an entirely different character, as has happened with the replacement of older industries in New England by high-technology light industry.

Meanwhile, the market leaves the firms that move out little choice. Certainly they can sometimes give the workers who will be left behind a chance to help lower costs. They can also sometimes do various things to mitigate the damage: phase out operations slowly or assist in making facilities available for new industry. Yet they must meet the competition that the market brings forward. They cannot, under competition, pay higher wages than other firms for the same amount of work; and in this respect they are forced to drive hard bargains with unions at their present plants— forced, perhaps, to ask for more concessions than the unions, under various pressures themselves, can give them. It is true that often the competition is not in fact so relentless that the firms on the point of moving have no margin to operate on. Their profits may be quite comfortable. But will the profits continue comfortable if the firms do not keep their costs as low as other firms do? Moreover, even if they enjoy comfortable profits with no prospect of close competition, their stockholders will expect them to seize any opportunities of making profits larger still, due allowance being made for the danger of risking the long-run interests of the firm in some cases. Are the stockholders being greedy? Not necessarily: they, too, may have other people's interests to look after. In any case, they are acting according to the rules of rationality in the market when they seek to invest their money where it will give them the greatest return.

Critics of capitalism would no doubt declare that a planned economy would achieve a higher degree of rationality in this connection, as in others. This claim carries us outside the business system and hence outside the scope of this book. I shall not examine the claim seriously. I might point out that in this connection at least it has appearances against it. One can easily, of course, outline in words the possibility of having the authorities in a planned economy phase in innovations and distribute them and their costs and benefits, geographically as well as temporally, so that noone in the economy suffers a significant loss even for a moment, and everyone gets a comparable share of the benefits. In practice, the authorities would face great difficulties about identifying the costs and benefits actually felt by the people affected. Moreover, the authorities would be under political pressure to maintain the status quo, in the older plants and industries, indeed under pressure to maintain it, regardless of efficiency, alongside the innovations, which would generate political pressure, too. The innovations thus hampered would not all be trivial matters of fashion and taste either: in the General Tire case below, the new radial tires are said to be both safer and more durable.

## ROBERT HOWARD, "RUNAWAY PLANTS"*

The day after President Carter's well-publicized visit to Clinton, Massachusetts, in March 1977, Colonial Press—the town's biggest employer—announced the closing of its printing and binding factory. At its height, Colonial had employed 1750 people, but after mergers which placed the company into the hands of first one, then another conglomerate, the work force was pared to 800. Sheller-Globe, a Toledo-based automobile parts firm, had obtained Colonial almost by mistake; it happened to be one of the subsidiaries of the Victorine Corporation acquired by Sheller-Globe. With neither the interest nor the expertise to maintain the high-quality work for which Colonial was known, the corporation finally decided to shift its investment elsewhere. After refusing to sell the factory to Clinton workers, the owners auctioned off the plant machinery and shut down.

The story of Colonial Press illustrates one facet of a twin economic phenomenon known as the "runaway corporation" and the "runaway plant." Some businesses, like Sheller-Globe, close subsidiaries in order to free capital for investment elsewhere. Others transfer entire industrial operations from one state to another (or from the United States to a foreign country) in search of a more profitable business climate. In either case, the result is economic dislocation for the workers and communities left behind.

Runaway businesses are a growing issue on the left. United Auto Workers president Douglas Fraser said recently, "Moving a plant without regard to the people laid off or the communities affected is unacceptable social conduct in a democracy and should be ended." Labor unions and public interest organizations are beginning to focus attention on the social costs that runaways leave in their wake. In states throughout the north central and northeast regions, citizens' groups have proposed legislation to put a tether on the runaways. The complex problems of economic dislocation

*From *The New Republic*, 26 May 1979. Reprinted by permission of *The New Republic*, © 1979 The New Republic, Inc.

present a promising opportunity to a labor movement desperately in need of new ideas and new political vision.

The conceptual problem is determining which plant closings are inevitable or justified and which ones constitute truly antisocial behavior. Such distinctions are not always easy to establish. International competition forces the rationalization of work and the search for lower labor costs. The cancelation of a government defense contract or new environmental regulations can contribute to the closing of certain plants. Sometimes simple obsolescence does a factory in. Statistics on plant closings are scarce (the federal government doesn't keep any), and those that do exist are notoriously uninformative.

Whatever the cause, economic dislocation has become very serious in some parts of the country. While manufacturing employment in the United States dropped by 3 percent between 1967 and 1976, the decrease in the northeast and north central regions was 13 percent, representing nearly 1.5 million jobs. Plant relocations alone accounted for the loss of 30,000 jobs in Michigan between 1970 and 1974. Of the 1.5 million manufacturing jobs in Ohio in 1969, over 150,000 have been lost in the past ten years.

The growing movement of investment capital abroad (from 5 percent of total invested capital in 1950 to nearly 10 percent in 1972) has severely contracted the domestic job market. Cornell economists Robert Frank and Richard Freeman place the net job loss between 1966 and 1973 at 1.06 million, with 735,000 in manufacturing alone. This trend also affects the jobs that remain behind. The fewer jobs to go around, the stiffer the competition among regions of the country for them. Investment moves to areas offering the best combination of low wages, docile unions, and tax subsidies. Regions of the country compete to supply these things.

This high mobility of capital is primarily a function of its concentration. The growth of national and multinational conglomerates has exacerbated economic dislocation. Small family firms tend to be rooted in communities with ties to the local population and local financial institutions; subsidiaries of conglomerates have no such ties. As in the case of Colonial Press, absentee decision-makers are more apt to shift their operation far away. Corporations scout the countryside for healthy small businesses, ripe for take-over. But when conglomerates impose normal corporate mechanisms on these small plants—a higher profit rate and more rigid management systems—they suddenly become "unprofitable." After going on an acquisition binge in New England in the 1960s, one conglomerate required a 25 percent pretax rate of return on investment from its subsidiaries in an industry where the average profit rate was only 8 percent. Subsequent closings accounted for about 4000 lost jobs. "There are a lot of anecdotal cases," said Bennett Harrison, an MIT economist who heads a Harvard-MIT research project on corporate acquisition. "We're trying to see how generalized it is."

The corporate world believes the fuss over runaways is a false issue. The American Enterprise Institute has a new pamphlet called "Restrictions on Business Mobility." Its author, Clemson University economist Richard

McKenzie, claims that any effort to regulate runaways is "a solution to a nonexistent problem." The cornerstone of McKenzie's argument is data, compiled by two MIT professors, comparing rates of industrial growth and decline in the "northern industrial tier" and the "sunbelt." Using Dun and Bradstreet code numbers which identify firms by location from year to year, they concluded that a mere 1.5 percent of employment losses in the north were due to the "out-migration" of businesses or runaway plants. But the Dun and Bradstreet coding system drastically understates relocations. Often a move from one state to another is accompanied by a change in the legal name of a firm. The disappearance of the old code number is registered as a closing rather than "out-migration." Moreover, the data McKenzie uses cover only four years, 1969–72. Most relocations result from a phased closing of old plants and phased expansion of new ones. Therefore, employment patterns he explains by "contraction of firms" in the north (44.7 percent) and "expansion of firms" in the south (64.3 percent) probably conceal many "runaways in progress." Finally, the Dun and Bradstreet system only considers domestic movement of business. The effects of relocation abroad go wholly unrecorded.

McKenzie's theoretical approach underestimates the problem of dislocation because he only considers the actual physical relocation of a plant. In this framework, firms like Colonial Press—victims of runaway corporate capital—are written off as business failures. The real issue is not so much business mobility as capital mobility.

For McKenzie and other corporate spokesmen, the migration of capital is a natural by-product of market forces. Their buzz-word is the "dynamic" economy whose invisible hand produces an ever new and more efficient equilibrium with free choice and lower prices for all. This free-market idyll neglects a central issue in the runaway debate: government subsidies to relocating businesses. The federal government and the states actually encourage runaways. Runaway plants are eligible for the same federal tax incentives as any brand new industrial operation; but in the case of runaways no new jobs are added to the economy. Say corporation A wants to move its ball-bearing factory from Michigan to Alabama. Beside the obvious advantages to the corporation of a new plant, lower wages, and most likely a nonunionized work force, the tax code provides many inducements. Operating losses incurred as the old plant is phased out can be written off against profits elsewhere. Meanwhile, all that brand new equipment purchased for the new plant receives an investment tax credit and is eligible for accelerated depreciation. Tax programs that ostensibly encourage good things like corporate investment and job creation end up contributing to economic dislocation as well.

Federal tax breaks even subsidize businesses that move abroad. Multinationals take deductions to relocate in a foreign country, pay no U.S. taxes as long as their profits remain abroad, then take another deduction (foreign tax credits) when these profits are repatriated. Special tariff regulations encourage American companies to export certain stages of production of goods meant for the American market.

Competition between the states forces them to give tax breaks to runaways too. Most evidence suggests that these breaks are self-defeating. Ohio has sliced its corporate taxes to the bone, but the jobs keep leaving. The only real accomplishment has been to create a climate of fear among workers and communities, as businesses use the threat of relocation to get new breaks or silence collective bargaining demands.

In some states, however, a movement is taking shape to address the multiple problems that runaways create. It has drawn wide support from labor unions and community groups. Legislation to discourage unnecessary plant closings is either before state houses or on the drawing board in Ohio, New Jersey, Massachusetts, Michigan, and five other states.

The Ohio Public Interest Campaign (OPIC) has written a "runaway plants bill" which has become the model for most of these initiatives. It has three essential provisions: advance notification at least two years before any closing of a factory employing over 100 people (an "economic impact statement" detailing the effects of the closing on employment must be submitted within 90 days of the announcement); severance pay to each laid-off worker equaling one week of full salary for every year at the firm; and the payment into a "Community Assistance Fund" of a sum equal to 10 percent of the total annual wages of all employees who lose their jobs. The state government would administer the fund to combat the effects of dislocation.

The purpose of runaway plants bills is not to deny corporations the freedom to move their operations. Rather, the point is to make corporations bear the genuine social cost of their relocations and—more important—factor these costs into their calculations when deciding whether to move or close a factory. Right now, the cost of runaway plants is paid entirely by the people who are left behind. Besides losing their jobs, workers often lose pension and health benefits precisely when they need them the most. And communities are trapped between a shrinking tax base and increased social welfare payments to the newly unemployed. Most serious are the social costs that accompany factory closings: urban blight, social disruption, and the underutilization of local resources.

The corporate opposition has consistently misrepresented the proposed laws as a concerted attack on the prerogatives of investors. The Ohio Manufacturers Association has branded the OPIC legislation the "Industrial Ransom Bill." And there is even a dark hint at the gulag in the *Wall Street Journal's* overblown comparison between the bill and the "education tax" levied on emigrating Soviet Jews.

Most of the fireworks have occurred on the local level, but it is clear that any effort to move beyond defensive measures to the actual control of dislocation must be national in scope. A state-by-state approach puts those states which pass a runaway plants bill at a disadvantage in the competition with their neighbors. To avoid this would require federal legislation more comprehensive in scope and universal in application.

Certain unions are trying to make economic dislocation a national issue. Last summer, representatives from the UAW, Machinists and Steelworkers visited Britain, West Germany and Sweden, all of which have laws for managing dislocation. In each of these countries, workers are protected from the effects of dislocation by transfer benefits and retraining programs. In addition public institutions actually direct investment to minimize unemployment in depressed regions and industries. The Swedish Labor Market Board, composed of representatives from business, labor and government, directs a special tax-free fund of "investment reserves" for job creation in those areas that need it the most. American unionists point out that European societies—and the American subsidiaries that have been profitably investing in them—have been living with dislocation controls for years. They argue that such public institutions are best suited for planning the necessary restructuring of traditional American industries, such as steel and textiles.

The federal equivalent to the OPIC bill is the National Employment Priorities Act, first introduced by Michigan congressman William Ford in 1974. It has the usual provisions for advance notice and transfer benefits. It still does not prevent any particular relocation, but it does address the issue of investment decisions in a way the state proposals do not. A "National Employment Relocation Administration" in the Labor Department would determine the "economic justification" of disputed closings and could cut off tax benefits to businesses found to have arbitrarily closed their operations. Economic justification is a crucial concept; unfortunately the Ford bill leaves it wholly undefined. To identify precisely what economic justification means would be to engage the real issue behind the entire runaway debate: the degree to which the general concerns of a public community can impinge on the particular activity and decisions of private corporations.

Even its supporters concede that the Ford bill has no chance of passing soon. But this need not mean that the movement to curb the runaways will collapse before it gets off the ground. The Ford bill and its state cousins may be most important as a vehicle for labor's rethinking of its role in American politics. Already some labor leaders see economic dislocation as a tangle of problems touching economic planning, international trade policy, defense spending, tax law, and environmental and health and safety regulation. "There are no real remedies until we're prepared to take on two fundamental tenets of the economic system," said Dick Greenwood, aide to Machinist president William Winpisinger, "management's investment prerogatives and proprietary rights to information."

Such language is certainly not designed to win congressional votes. But given labor's disarray, a more immediate task may be defining those new directions that promise to revitalize the unions as a political force. The costs of economic dislocation will continue to be borne unequally by workers and their communities unless American unions move toward a more aggressive political unionism on the Western European model. But before selling that to the lawmakers, it will have to be sold in places like Clinton, Massachusetts.

*       *       *

# WILL CHAMPION SPARK PLUG KEEP ITS PLANTS IN TOLEDO GOING?

*[Howard suggests in his article that "businesses use the threat of relocation to get new breaks or silence collective bargaining demands." It would not be wonderful if they did. On the other hand, may not firms sometimes have genuine problems with costs at existing plants, and their workers sometimes be in a position to solve those problems, or at least reduce the dimensions of them? In that case, the workers would have grounds for wanting the firms to discuss what could be done about the problems, besides closing down the existing plants. The letter that follows\* enumerates the points of agreement reached in discussions between Champion Spark Plug Company and the United Auto Workers local in its Toledo plants. The Toledo Blade reported, April 7, 1982, that when the union members were asked to ratify the modifications that the agreement implies in their existing contract, the members voted 848 to 418 against ratification.]*

Champion Spark Plug Company
P.O. Box 910
Toledo, Ohio, U.S.A., 43661
Telephone: 419-535-2567
March 29, 1982

Mr. Thomas Hall
Chairman, Champion Unit
Local 12, UAW

Dear Mr. Hall:

During our recent discussions regarding the productivity problems at the Toledo manufacturing facilities it was agreed that there were numerous contributing factors. Such items as too many work classifications, poor quality, high training costs, inaccurate time keeping, distribution of work among production employees and between the production and skilled groups, poor work habits and job performance, etc., were stressed by the Company as the major contributors.

The Company has advised the Union that new initiatives must be made to correct these as well as other problem areas if the existing Toledo manufacturing facilities are to endure.

To that end, therefore, the Company and Union have agreed to the following items for implementation:

1. Day-rated employees shall be required to work at 100% day-work pace for the entire work shift.
2. All waste of time or materials is prohibited.

\*Reprinted with the permission of Champion Spark Plug Company.

3. Excessive lunch or break time (personal time) is prohibited. To properly regulate such time a warning bell will be sounded to signal for break periods, lunch and wash-up before quit.

4. Each employee shall have the primary responsibility for the quality of work he produces. Gauges and inspection tools will be provided for use in the work area, and employees will be trained to perform any inspection functions necessary to monitor their work. Incentive standards shall be adjusted as required to provide the time for employees to perform inspection requirements.

5. Each employee shall have the primary responsibility for the cleanliness of their work place, tools, equipment, and machinery and will be expected to fully cooperate in programs designed to reduce upkeep and housekeeping costs.

6. The "Detail" classification will be eliminated.

7. The in-plant transportation function will be consolidated and assigned to Department #23 at the respective plants.

8. The general plant housekeeping function at the Upton Plant will be consolidated and assigned to Department #29.

9. A new Job Classification (Category) Program will be implemented for the purposes of job bidding, job elimination, layoff and recall, daily job assignments, and determining manpower needs. Copies of the program are on file in the Industrial Relations Department and the Union Office for reference purposes. Specific job bidding, job elimination and layoff and recall programs are assigned hereto as Attachments #1, #2 and #3 respectively.

10. Guidelines for distribution of work between skilled trades and production employees have been developed and are attached hereto as Attachment #4. The objective of these guidelines is to permit the Company further use of its semi-skilled production workers in the performance of tasks heretofore assigned to skilled trades personnel.

11. Overtime will be assigned as specified in Attachment #5 hereto.

12. The departmental seniority system will be revised in accordance with Attachment #6 hereto.

13. The proper downtime or off-standard rate of pay for an incentive employee is hereby reaffirmed as base rate.

14. The "buddy system" for lunches, break periods and personal time shall be implemented wherever feasible.

15. The Company will institute an employee cross-training program to give employees within a category (see Item #9 above) the opportunity to enhance their job related skills. Additionally the Company will establish an employee self-development training program which will offer employees the opportunity to enhance their skills in such areas as shop math, blueprint reading, etc.

It is agreed that the objective of these corrective measures is an overall increase in productivity by at least 15% (without adversely affecting the quality of the product, housekeeping, maintenance of the facilities or equipment, etc.) and the parties shall work together earnestly to assure the achievement of that objective.

Very truly yours,
CHAMPION SPARK PLUG COMPANY
Franklin D. Snyder
Director of Industrial Relations

\*     \*     \*

# PASSENGER TIRE MANUFACTURE
# BECOMES EXTINCT IN AKRON

*[Sometimes unions and union members go to considerable lengths to help firms stay in existing facilities. Yet the efforts may be in vain. The facilities— even the products made in the facilities—may be obsolete, and renovating the facilities may not be an attractive investment for the firm. The following materials—a press release plus two excerpts from the magazine that General Tire circulates among its employees\*—give a poignant account of just such a case.]*

FROM: Jack Marshall, Director
Public Relations & Advertising
The General Tire & Rubber Company
Akron, Ohio 44329
Telephone: 216 798-5192

FOR IMMEDIATE RELEASE

### GENERAL TIRE TO CLOSE AKRON PLANT

Akron, OH, March 1 [1982]—The General Tire & Rubber Company announced today it will close its tire manufacturing plant in Akron this year. The announcement was made by M. G. O'Neil, Chairman and President.

"This is the most difficult and painful announcement I have ever made," O'Neil said. "I say this because of the cooperative effort made by the URW Local 9 leadership, its members and our management team to keep this plant operating."

"When we announced in 1979 the possibility of building a new plant to replace our obsolete Akron facility, we thought it would eventually be done. Since that time, overcapacity within the industry has forced the closing of 14 tire operations by other rubber companies. If we could proceed with a new plant, we would. However, it is not feasible to build a new one from the ground up when our factories are operating at less than capacity," O'Neil said.

In 1979, General Tire's workers agreed to a 36¢-an-hour reduction in pay

*All reprinted with the permission of The General Tire & Rubber Company.

to be deducted from future wage increases with the proviso that a new tire operation would be constructed in the Akron area. These funds, amounting to almost $2,000,000, will be distributed to the men and women according to the hours they worked since that agreement was finalized three years ago.

Some jobs—banbury mixing, janitorial, power house operation and some mechanical work—will be maintained at the present site, employing approximately 185 people. There are 1,018 hourly and 247 salaried employees currently working. In addition, there are 421 workers on layoff.

As General's first tire plant, the Akron facility began operation in 1915.

"Most of the production is bias-type tires," O'Neil said, "and the demand for these has been greatly reduced by the growing use of radials."

"In a different era, time would have taken care of industry capacity problems. The natural growth in the marketplace for tires would have quickly offset plant underutilization. Today, however, there has been a substantial reduction in the overall unit tire market. The technological changes that led to the development of long-wearing radials, the high cost of fuel with the consequent reduction in average miles driven and the impact of imports, all played a role in the decline in demand for U.S.-produced tires. As a result, future growth in the tire industry will be much slower than in the past," he said.

The Company has estimated that the closing costs will be between $40,000,000 and $50,000,000 pre-tax which will be charged against 1982 earnings.

*[Two comments follow from the company magazine, Generally Speaking, March 24, 1982.]*

A CHANGING INDUSTRY

When the Akron plant ceases production, it will become the 26th tire-manufacturing facility to shut down since 1970. What's caused these upheavals and disruptions? How could an industry that only ten short years ago was stable, predictable and reliable, with an impressive 6 percent annual growth, be experiencing this type of shakeout?

If one word were to characterize the Rubber Industry in the last decade it would be change. Change in technology; change in product mix; change in marketing; and change in manufacturers.

To a large extent the Industry's problems can be traced to the radial tire. Radials are safer, withstand heavier loads, offer improved cornering and faster braking. Furthermore, since they have less rolling resistance, they provide better gas mileage—up to 10 percent more per gallon and can double the life of bias-ply tires.

In the late '60s the radial appeared on the American scene as the giant retailer, Sears, introduced it as its top-of-the-line tire. Consumer acceptance was gradual. But something was added to the equation in 1973—the Arab oil embargo. American drivers were faced with skyrocketing fuel prices. They began to demand fuel-efficient cars and tires. The radial, a safe gas-saving tire, was an ideal solution. Radial sales accelerated further when Detroit, faced with meeting strict government mandated miles-per-gallon regulations, turned to the fuel-saving tire.

The Tire Industry invested billions of dollars in new building machinery, new production processes and new plants. General Tire spent over one billion dollars during this period, most of the money going for new equipment, expansion, and of course, building our newest radial tire plant in Mt. Vernon, Ill.

The radial tire was not like the hula hoop—it was here to stay. It had caught the American motorist's fancy and its effect on the Industry and marketplace has been devastating. No other technological change has created such a dramatic impact on the Industry.

How great of an impact? In 1972, radials accounted for less than 5 percent of autos made in this country. Last year for the first time ever, all American-made automobiles were equipped with radials.

Radial technology has not stopped with the passenger tire market. It logically moved into the truck tire field and by 1985 is expected to account for nearly 55% of the marketplace. And forecasts indicate this penetration will continue upward.

Other factors entered the picture. Rising imports captured a larger and larger share of the domestic car market. Domestic sales plummeted and with it original equipment shipments.

In 1978, a record automobile sales year, 11.3 million cars were sold. Imports garnered an 18 percent share. In 1980, the import figure was nearly 27 percent. That translates into 2.4 million autos and at five tires per car over 12 million tire units lost to the domestic industry. The magnitude of this can be seen when you realize that this figure represents approximately one-third of the tire shipments to Detroit that year.

The radial's growing popularity caused excess capacity problems. This kept inventories bulging. Prices were slashed in an effort to move tires. The marketplace became a consumer's paradise and a seller's nightmare. The cost/price squeeze kept profit margins low. Layoffs and plant closings became inevitable. Those whose financial resources were limited struggled to survive.

None of the domestic companies were spared. All have reduced work forces and closed plants. During the remainder of this decade changes the radial has wrought will continue to be felt.

There's no doubt the Industry we once knew is gone. But the shakeouts and changes will make the Industry stronger, profitable and better able to serve its customers.

## CLOSING BRINGS LONG-RANGE EFFECTS

The closing of the Akron plant will have long-range effects not only on the people who work there, but on the City of Akron, the state and area merchants.

Approximately 1,018 hourly and 247 salaried employees currently working will be idled by the closing. Presently there are 421 workers on layoff and 485 are eligible for immediate pension.

Their total payroll, of which a large portion reaches area businesses through sales of goods and services, added up to $37.3 million in 1981 and a projected $35 million in 1982.

City and state government will be affected too. City tax withheld from employees was almost $650,000 in 1981; state tax withheld was $686,018 that same year.

The area's utility companies will also feel the loss of revenues—charges for gas, water, electric and telephone ran $5.6 million last year.

\*     \*     \*

# PART FOUR

# The Actions of Firms: Firms Dealing with Stockholders and with Other Firms

# CHAPTER 13

# *Dealing with Stockholders*

---

*Introductory Comment:*

STOCKHOLDERS
IN GILBERT AND SULLIVAN
AND LATER

---

Beside consumers and employees, there is a third set of people whom firms, when they are (as they now typically are) incorporated businesses, may treat rightly or wrongly: their stockholders. With incorporation a firm obtains simultaneously a charter to operate on certain lines (or in certain regions) and the privilege of limited liability, signified in Britain and Canada by appending "Ltd" to the name of the firm. In the United States the appendix is used to suggest that special prestige and luxury attach to a firm and its products; but all that it means, in the countries where it is at home, is that the liability of the stockholders for debts or damages incurred by the firm is limited to the amounts of their shares in it. When the stockholders were in fact entrepreneurs carrying on business under the name of the firm, this limitation seemed an evasion of responsibility. Individual owners and partners had no such privilege; when they piled up debts in business, their personal fortunes were at risk in meeting them.

As late as 1893, the feeling that limited liability was morally suspect was strong enough to be a sounding board for mockery. In the last of the Gilbert and Sullivan operettas, *Utopia Limited*, first produced in that year, Goldbury, a company promoter, proposes to the King of Utopia that he incorporate his country:

> Utopia's much too big for one small head—
> I'd float it as a Company Limited

The King replies,

> A Company Limited? What may that be?
> The term, I rather think, is new to me.

Goldbury, with the chorus, is moved to answer in song:

> Some seven men form an Association
>    (If possible, all Peers and Baronets),
> They start off with a public declaration
>    To what extent they mean to pay their debts.
> That's called their Capital: if they are wary
>    They will not quote it at a sum immense.
> The figure's immaterial—it may vary
>    From eighteen million down to eighteenpence.
>       *I* should put it rather low;
>       The good sense of doing so
>    Will be evident at once to any debtor.
>       When it's left to you to say
>       What amount you mean to pay,
>    Why, the lower you can put it at, the better.
> CHORUS. When it's left to you to say, etc.
> They then proceed to trade with all who'll trust 'em,
>    Quite irrespective of their capital
> (It's shady, but it's sanctified by custom);
>    Bank, Railway, Loan, or Panama Canal.
> You can't embark on trading too tremendous—
>    It's strictly fair, and based on common sense—
> If you succeed, your profits are stupendous—
>    And if you fail, pop goes your eighteenpence.
>       Make the money-spinner spin!
>       For you only stand to win,
>    And you'll never with dishonesty be twitted,
>       For nobody can know,
>       To a milion or so,
>    To what extent your capital's committed!
> CHORUS: No, nobody can know, etc.
> If you come to grief, and creditors are craving
>    (For nothing that is planned by mortal head
> Is certain in this Vale of Sorrow—saving
>    That one's Liability is Limited).—
> Do you suppose that signifies perdition?
>    If so you're but a monetary dunce—
> You merely file a Winding-Up Petition,
>    And start another Company at once!
>       Though a Rothschild you may be
>       In your own capacity,
>    As a Company you've come to utter sorrow—
>       But the Liquidators say,
>       'Never mind—you needn't pay,'

So you start another Company to-morrow!
CHORUS. But the Liquidators say, etc.

In many firms today, and in most large firms, stockholders are not entrepreneurs active in the firms' business. The legal theory is still that they control the firm and can turn out the officers of the firm, who manage it on their behalf, whenever they please. The theory is now more fiction than fact, however. In a typical firm, there are many stockholders, none of whom own more than a very small fraction of the outstanding stock. None of them are in a position either to rally enough support among other stockholders to challenge the officers' control of the firm. The officers are in fact a self-recruited and self-perpetuating elite.

They are subject to certain checks: if consumers do not like their products, the profits of the firm suffer, and the salaries and perquisites that the officers have decided upon for themselves may be jeopardized (though often the benefits go on, unaffected, even during declines in business). The firm must heed numerous government regulations, and the officers must see to its doing so. They are also concerned to maintain the financial reputation of the firm. In this regard at least they pay some attention to the interests of the stockholders, since if a lot of stockholders, dissatisfied with management and with their returns from the firm, sell out, the price of the stock will go down and the firm will have difficulty raising money.

Yet, by and large, the officers managing the firm make the decisions. They appoint the directors, though they arrange for the formality of having the appointments ratified by the stockholders (generally through obtaining proxies from them). They appoint themselves, though they arrange for the formality of having the appointments ratified by the directors.

Given this picture, the joke about limited liability fades away. The stockholders are not allied with the firm against the world. The firm—that is to say, the firm as controlled by its management—has a relation to its stockholders that in part is something like the relation it has to consumers, since it originates in transactions. It is also in part like the relation it has to its employees, since it involves unequal power. It may fall at odds with the stockholders in both these connections.

## FISCHER v. KLETZ

---

[The following case has to do with the obligation of a firm and its auditors to provide full and accurate information about its financial condition to its stockholders. The immediate issue is the auditors' obligation to inform the investing public; but the firm's obligation underlies this obligation, and what part of the investing public could be more concerned with knowing the condition of the firm than the stockholders? Without the relevant information, how are they to judge whether they should keep the stock that they bought from the firm (or from somebody in a chain of transactions that began with a transaction involving the firm as a party) or sell it? How can *they determine whether they should be satisfied or dissatisfied with the way that the firm is being run?]*

*United States District Court for the Southern District of New York, 1967*

TYLER, District Judge. . . .

Sometime early in 1964, [Peat, Marwick, Mitchell & Co. ("PMM")] acting as an independent public accountant, undertook the job of auditing the financial statements that Yale Express System, Inc. ("Yale"), a national transportation concern, intended to include in the annual report to its stockholders for the year ending December 31st 1963. On March 31, 1964, PMM certified the figures contained in these statements. On or about April 9, the annual report containing the certification was issued to the stockholders of Yale. Subsequently, on or about June 29, 1964, a Form 10-K Report, containing the same financial statements as the annual report, was filed with the SEC as required by that agency's rules and regulations.

At an unspecified date "early in 1964," probably shortly after the completion of the audit, Yale engaged PMM to conduct so-called "special studies" of Yale's past and current income and expenses. In the course of this special assignment, sometime presumably before the end of 1964,* PMM discovered that the figures in the annual report were substantially false and misleading.

Not until May 5, 1965, however, when the results of the special studies were released, did PMM disclose this finding to the exchanges on which Yale securities were traded, to the SEC or to the public at large.

Plaintiffs attack PMM for its silence and inaction after its employees discovered, during the special studies, that the audited and certified figures in the financial statements reflecting Yale's 1963 performance were grossly inaccurate. They contend that inasmuch as PMM knew that its audit and certificate would be relied upon by the investing public, the accounting firm had a duty to alert the public in some way that the audited and certified statements were materially false and inaccurate. PMM counters that there is no common law or statutory basis for imposing such a duty on it as a public accounting firm retained by the officers and directors of Yale.

[1, 2] Strict analysis leads to the conclusion that PMM is attacked in the complaint because it wore two hats in conducting its business relations with Yale during the period in question. PMM audited and certified the financial statements in the 1963 annual report and Form 10-K as a statutory "independent public accountant" whose responsibility

> is not only to the client who pays his fee, but also to investors, creditors and others who may rely on the financial statements which he certifies. * * * The public accountant must report fairly on the facts as he finds them whether

---

*There is a factual dispute here. PMM maintains that the falsity of the figures was discovered after the filing of the required 10-K report with the SEC on June 29, 1964; plaintiffs contend that the discovery was made before this filing.

favorable or unfavorable to his client. His duty is to safeguard the public interest, not that of his client. (In the Matter of Touche, Niven, Bailey & Smart, 37 S.E.C. 629, 670-671 (1957)) (footnotes omitted)

Following the certification, PMM switched its role to that of an accountant employed by Yale to undertake special studies which were necessitated by business demands rather than by statutory or regulatory requirements. In this sense, it can be seen that during the special studies PMM was a "dependent public accountant" whose primary obligations, under normal circumstances, were to its client and not the public.

[3] It was, of course, during the conduct of the special studies that the inaccuracies in the audited and certified statements were discovered. The time of this discovery makes the questions here involved difficult and unique. On the basis of the Commission's *Touche, Niven* opinion, an accountant has a duty to the investing public to certify only those statements which he deems accurate. This duty is not directly involved here, however, for the inaccuracies were discovered after the certification had been made and the 1963 annual report had been released. PMM maintains, therefore, that any duty to the investing public terminated once it certified the relevant financial statements. Plaintiffs, of course, contend to the contrary. Thus, the serious question arises as to whether or not an obligation correlative to but conceptually different from the duty to audit and to certify with reasonable care and professional competence arose as a result of the circumstance that PMM knew that investors were relying upon its certification of the financial statements in Yale's annual report. . . .

Plaintiffs' claim is grounded in the common law of deceit, albeit an unusual type in that most cases of deceit involve an affirmative misrepresentation by the defendant. Here, however, plaintiffs attack PMM's nondisclosure or silence.

It is Dean Prosser's view that, in contrast with the issues raised when an affirmative misrepresentation is involved, "a much more difficult problem arises as to whether mere silence, or a passive failure to disclose facts of which the defendant has knowledge, can serve as the foundation of a deceit action." Prosser, Torts 533 (2d ed. 1955). The law in this area is in a state of flux due to the inroads being made into the old doctrine of *caveat emptor*. Although the prevailing rule still seems to be that there is no liability for tacit nondisclosure, Dean Prosser adds the following important qualification: "to this general rule, if such it be, the courts have developed a number of exceptions, some of which are as yet very ill-defined, and have no very definite boundaries." Id. at 534. One of these exceptions is that

one who has made a statement and subsequently acquires new information which makes it untrue or misleading, must disclose such information to any one whom he knows to be still acting on the basis of the original statement. (Ibid.)

Section 551 of the First Restatement of Torts, which is couched in the specific terms of "a business transaction", is in substantial agreement with Dean Prosser. The Restatement position in Section 551(1) is that one who fails to disclose to another a thing which he knows may justifiably induce the other to act or refrain from acting in a business transaction is subject to the same liability to the other as though he had represented the nonexistence of the matter which he has failed to disclose, if, but only if, he is under a duty to the other to exercise reasonable care to disclose the matter in question.

Section 551(2) lists the instances when the requisite duty to disclose arises. For present purposes, the following portion from that subsection is important:

One party to a business transaction is under a duty to exercise reasonable care to disclose to the other before the transaction is consummated * * * (b) any subsequently acquired information which he recognizes as making untrue or misleading a previous representation which when made was true or believed to be so.

[4] Generally speaking, I can see no reason why this duty to disclose should not be imposed upon an accounting firm which makes a representation it knows will be relied upon by investors. To be sure, certification of a financial statement does not create a formal business relationship between the accountant who certifies and the individual who relies upon the certificate for investment purposes. The act of certification, however, is similar in its effect to a representation made in a business transaction: both supply information which is naturally and justifiably relied upon by individuals for decisional purposes. Viewed in this context of the impact of nondisclosure on the injured party, it is difficult to conceive that a distinction between accountants and parties to a business transaction is warranted. The elements of "good faith and common honesty" which govern the businessman presumably should also apply to the statutory "independent public accountant".

PMM, of course, disputes the imposition of a duty to disclose and, for its purposes, properly emphasizes that the Restatement speaks in terms of "a business transaction" to which the alleged tort-feasor is a party and in which he has a definite pecuniary interest. Indeed, the cases discussed and cited heretofore involve instances where both plaintiff and defendant are economically affected by the defendant's nondisclosure.

PMM contends that the duty imposed on a party to a business transaction to disclose that a prior representation is false and misleading is "in no way pertinent to the standard of responsibility applicable to the independent auditor" . . . and that the obligation to disclose is contingent upon the presence of the opportunity for the accrual of personal gain to the nondisclosure party as a result of the nondisclosure.

The parties and the SEC have not supplied, nor has the court found, any cases which analyze the issue raised by this contention within a factual framework involving nondisclosure of information which makes a prior representation false. As the ensuing discussion will show, however, this does not mean that plaintiffs' cause of action for deceit must be dismissed at this stage of this litigation, nor does it preclude a rational analysis of the issue raised by defendant.

[5] In cases involving affirmative misrepresentations, it is now the settled rule that a misrepresenter can be held liable, regardless of his interest in the transaction. . . .

[6] In my view, accepting the pertinent allegations of the complaint to be true, PMM must be regarded as bound at this preliminary stage of the litigation by this rule of law. Though concededly "disinterested" in the sense that it achieved no advantage by its silence, PMM is charged in the complaint for losses realized by plaintiffs as a result of its nondisclosure. This is sufficient, at least in the pleading sense, under the cases discussed, save for one remaining problem—whether or not plaintiffs must plead and ultimately prove intent by PMM to deceive by its silence. . . .

[8] Liability in a case of nondisclosure is based upon the breach of a duty imposed by the demands of "good faith and common honesty." . . . The imposition of the duty creates an objective standard against which to measure a defendant's actions and leaves no room for an analysis of the subjective considerations inherent in the area of intent. . . .

[9, 10] In light of the foregoing discussion, I find no sound reasons to justify barring plaintiffs from the opportunity to prove a common-law action of deceit against PMM. . . . The common law has long required that a person who has made a representation must correct that representation if it becomes false and if he knows people are relying on it. This duty to disclose is imposed regardless of the interest of defendant in the representation and subsequent nondisclosure. Plaintiffs have sufficiently alleged the elements of nondisclosure on the part of this "disinterested" defendant. Accordingly, they must be given an opportunity to prove those allegations. . . .

\*     \*     \*

# LEWIS ET AL. v. McGRAW-HILL

*[If management cuts or eliminates dividends, stockholders can always sell out, though they will not usually get any compensation by doing this for what they may feel was an unreasonable decision on the part of management. Their interests and the interests of management may be opposed on this point, but they are powerless to have the decision changed. The opposition is even more striking and unambiguous sometimes when management resists a takeover bid. The stockholders might make more than they could either by holding on to their stock or by selling it at the ordinary price in the market. Management, however, may face losing jobs and privileges. As things stand, the only direct and sweeping challenges to their self-perpetuation in control that the officers of many firms have to fear as a group arise in this way.*

*In the following case, outraged stockholders failed in a lawsuit brought under a federal law in the United States, though the court points out that suits under state laws might fare differently. At the very least, the case makes it clear that a genuine issue about whether the firm treated the stockholders wrongly arises, whether it is provided for in the law or not.]*

*United States Court of Appeals, Second Circuit, 1980*

Before KAUFMAN, Chief Judge, MESSKILL, Circuit Judge, and BRIEANT, District Judge.

PER CURIAM:

[1] The instant action is a consolidation of five similar lawsuits brought on behalf of McGraw-Hill, Inc. stockholders, alleging that McGraw-Hill and its directors made false statements of material facts in response to two proposals of the American Express Company for the acquisition of substantial amounts of McGraw-Hill stock. The issue before us is whether shareholders may maintain a cause of action for damages under the Williams Act, 15 U.S.C. § 78n(e), where they concede that no tender offer has been made to them. We conclude that they may not.

I

On January 8, 1979, American Express proposed to McGraw-Hill what plaintiff describes as a "friendly business combination" of the two companies through payment by American Express of $34 in cash for each McGraw-Hill share. Alternatively, American Express indicated its willingness to acquire 49% of McGraw-Hill's shares for cash or a combination of cash and securities. McGraw-Hill common stock was trading at $26 per share immediately prior to the announcement. On January 15, 1979, Mc-

Graw-Hill announced that its Board of Directors had rejected the proposal and made public a letter to American Express characterizing the offer as "reckless," "illegal," and "improper." The following day, American Express filed Schedule 14D-1 with the Securities and Exchange Commission concerning its intention to make a cash tender offer for any and all of McGraw-Hill's stock.

The proposed offer was never made, however, for on January 29, American Express retracted its earlier announcement, and in its place submitted a new proposal to the McGraw-Hill board. This offer, at a price of $40 per share, would not become effective unless McGraw-Hill's incumbent management agreed not to oppose it by "propaganda, lobbying, or litigation." The offer was rejected by the McGraw-Hill board two days later, and expired, by its own terms, on March 1.

Plaintiffs' consolidated, amended complaint charges that:

> Defendants announced publicly that the tender offer price of $40 per share was inadequate, although they knew that the price . . . was fair. . . .
>
> Defendants, in resisting the AMEXCO [American Express Company] tender offer [sic], challenged the integrity and honesty of AMEXCO (by indicating that AMEXCO had illegally complied with the Arab boycott), publicly challenged the legality of the tender offer (by indicating that the federal Bank Holding Company [Act] may preclude the tender offer), and publicly stated that the tender offer somehow threatened freedom of expression under the First Amendment of the Constitution (by stating that since the McGraw-Hill [sic] was engaged in publishing, its independence would be smothered by a large financial institution such as AMEXCO).

These statements, as well as McGraw-Hill's characterization of the initial proposal as "reckless," "illegal," and "improper," are alleged to be false, as evidenced by the fact that, some months earlier, McGraw-Hill had advised American Express that it considered it to be a proper and desirable merger partner.

Plaintiffs concede that no tender offer ever took place—that no McGraw-Hill shareholder was ever in a position to offer his shares to American Express at a stated price. The $34 proposal was withdrawn before it became effective, and was replaced with a $40 proposal that could have ripened into an offer only upon the acquiescence of the McGraw-Hill board. Nonetheless, plaintiffs claim, "had defendants provided . . . shareholders and the public with complete and truthful information about AMEXCO and its proposed tender offer (*i.e.* that $40 per share was a fair price, and that AMEXCO was a company with which defendants themselves had wanted to merge), the AMEXCO tender offer would have been consummated." Accordingly, they each seek damages from the company and its directors for the difference between the $40 proposed tender price, and the $25 price to which the stock returned after the expiration of the American Express proposal.

Judge Motley dismissed the consolidated amended complaint . . . noting that "plaintiffs fail to allege that McGraw-Hill stockholders, or anyone else for that matter, in fact relied upon the alleged misrepresentations or omissions. While plaintiffs do allege deception on the part of defendants, plaintiffs do not allege that anyone was deceived or that anyone acted in reliance upon the alleged deception to their detriment." Having found plaintiffs' federal claim critically insufficient, the district court dismissed plaintiffs' pendent state claims for want of jurisdiction.

## II

[2] The complaint was properly dismissed. Section 14(e) of the Williams Act . . . has as its "sole purpose" the "protection of investors who are confronted with a tender offer." . . . It is designed "to ensure that [investors] will not be required to respond [to a tender offer] without adequate information." . . . Accordingly, one element of a cause of action under § 14(e) is a showing "that there was misrepresentation upon which the target corporation shareholders *relied*." . . . In the instant case, the target's shareholders simply could not have relied upon McGraw-Hill's statements, whether true or false, since they were never given an opportunity to tender their shares.

[3] Plaintiffs do not contest this indisputable fact, but rather rest upon cases holding that reliance may sometimes be presumed from a showing of materiality. . . . These cases, however, in presuming reliance, did not abolish it as an element of the cause of action. Rather, they held that in cases in which reliance is possible, and even likely, but is unduly burdensome to prove, the resulting doubt would be resolved in favor of the class the statute was designed to protect. . . .

We therefore presume reliance only "where it is logical" to do so. . . . Here, where no reliance was possible under any imaginable set of facts, such a presumption would be illogical in the extreme.

We note in closing that our holding today does not place statements made on the eve of a tender offer by target or tendering companies wholly outside the scope of the Williams Act. On the contrary, where the offer ultimately becomes effective, and reliance can be demonstrated or presumed, such statements may well be made "in connection with a tender offer" as required by § 14(e). Otherwise, either party would be free to disseminate misinformation up to the effective date of the tender offer, thus defeating in substantial part the very purpose of the Act—informed decisionmaking by shareholders. Injunctive relief, moreover, may be available to restrain or correct misleading statements made during the period preceding a tender offer where it appears that such an offer is likely, and that reliance upon the statements at issue is probable under the circumstances. . . . Finally, we must bear in mind that many of the wrongs alleged in this complaint may be recast as state law claims for breach of the fiduciary duties owed to shareholders by directors. . . . Indeed, we note that several plaintiffs have commenced state court actions arising out of the abortive transactions at issue here. In this case, however, since American Express never made its proposed offer to the shareholders of McGraw-Hill, plaintiffs cannot state a cause of action for alleged misstatements under the Williams Act.

\* \* \*

# CHAPTER **14**

# *Dealing with Other Firms*

## LIMITS TO BARGAINING

Firms often number among their customers other firms as well as individual consumers. Some firms, indeed, have only such customers. The same problems about right and wrong arise as arise for transactions with individual consumers and for the use of unequal power in driving hard bargains with them. I shall not bring those problems up again here. Here we shall consider instead firms dealing with other firms, or acting upon other firms, when the other firms are cast in the roles of suppliers, agents, and rivals. Again, we have problems that have to do with transactions; a lot of them have to do, when things go wrong, with suppliers or agents being cheated one way or another of what is due them. The problem that I wish to focus on, however, as being most distinctive and most prominent in these connections are problems about the use of unequal power. To what limits is it permissible to press hard bargaining with suppliers and agents? When does competition become, not just vigorous, but vicious?

Firms that can drive especially hard bargains are firms that have powers—whether of monopoly, on the selling side, or of its equivalent (technically, "monopsony") on the buying side—imperfectly checked by competition. Whether or not they have in some sense earned the powers by being especially efficient and innovative, they are still powers that have to be used with care.

# BARGAINING WITH SUPPLIERS: FEARS ABOUT THE HUDSON'S BAY COMPANY*

*[Other things being equal, firms naturally seek to pay lower prices rather than higher ones for what they buy. If it is workers' time and effort that firms are buying, the result may be low wages, sometimes wages too low to live on, or at least to live on decently. It is not only workers that suffer from such hard bargains, however. Those that suffer may be other firms, which survive only by supplying the firms that have the advantage in bargaining.*

*The main target of complaints and apprehensions in the following two letters is the Hudson's Bay Company, the oldest firm, I think, still operating whose chief field of operations is in North America. Its charter dates from 1670. Still active in the fur trade and in other ventures in the Canadian North, "the Bay" is nowadays also important among Canadian department stores. One letter is addressed to the Prime Minister of Canada; the other, to the Minister for Consumer and Corporate Affairs (a Privy Councillor— "P.C."—like Trudeau and like him a Member of Parliament.)]*

Canadian Apparel Manufacturers Institute
Institut Canadien des Manufacturiers du Vêtement
Directeur Exécutif
Executive Director
Peter Clark
141 Laurier Avenue West, Suite 804
Ottawa, Canada K1P 5J3
Tel: (613) 238-7743
Telex 053-3702

June 30, 1980
The Right Honourable Pierre E. Trudeau
Prime Minister
House of Commons
Room 309-S
Ottawa, Ontario

Dear Mr. Trudeau:
Canadian manufacturers of wearing apparel are becoming very concerned about the over-concentration of buying power among the major retail chain and department stores. I am enclosing copies of correspondence dealing with demands for special cash discounts by Woolco and a volume rebate arrangement based on the combined purchasing power of the Bay and the Robert Simpson company. There are over 2000 apparel manufacturers in Canada. They cannot dominate the market. The major retail stores on the

---

*The two letters that follow are reproduced by permission of the Prime Minister of Canada, the Minister of Consumer and Corporate Affairs, and Mr. Peter Clark.

other hand enjoy a considerable amount of marketing power. Few apparel manufacturers can exist without serving one or more of the major stores. It is extremely difficult, especially for smaller manufacturers, to refuse demands for special treatment and discounts. However, under the Combines Investigations Act manufacturers are required to treat all customers on a non-discriminatory basis. Discounts must be offered under the same terms and conditions to all accounts. Apparel industry margins are not large enough to absorb the costs of these special deals. Apparel manufacturers must increase their prices to maintain normal profit levels. These increases are quickly passed along to the consumer. At the same time, as prices increase, fewer units are sold and manufacturers are forced to lay off staff.

We need broad markets for our products. The Director of Research under the Combines Investigation Act noted in his report for the year ended March 31, 1979, "While there was understandable anxiety particularly from those in the garment industry about the reduction of alternative markets for suppliers should the merger (Bay-Simpsons) take place, the evidence was considered insufficient to demonstrate detriment to this sector beyond a reasonable doubt, particularly if Simpsons-Sears buying operations were separated from those of the Bay and Simpsons". The report goes on to note that the merger involving only the Bay and Simpsons covered about 35 per cent of sales by full service department stores in Canada. This, we submit, is a very substantial share for one entity. In addition the Bay also controls Zellers Ltd. and Fields Stores—who are also heavily involved in retailing wearing apparel, making their power in that sector quite considerable. We submit that recent mergers in the retail sector have significantly intensified the oligopolistic situation prevalent among retail buyers of wearing apparel. This overconcentration, in our view, inhibits competition, and should be examined for its restrictive trade practices implications. I have been instructed to seek your assistance and intercession in this matter.

Yours truly,

Peter Clark

/lm

Encl.

Canadian Apparel Manufacturers Institute
Institut Canadien des Manufacturiers du Vêtement
Directeur Exécutif
Executive Director
Peter Clark
141 Laurier Avenue West, Suite 804
Ottawa, Canada K1P 5J3
Tel: (613) 238-7743
Telex 053-3702

January 26, 1981
The Honourable André Ouellet, P.C. M.P.
House of Commons
Room 309-S
Parliament Buildings
Ottawa, Ontario

Dear Mr. Ouellet:

Thank you for your following up so energetically on our concerns about concentration of buying power among major retail chain and department stores. It is unfortunate that existing Combines legislation is weak.

We feel though that the proposal by the Hudson's Bay Company to take over full ownership of Zeller's Limited poses such serious dangers to our numbers that it should be stopped. We predicted to your Department that if the Bay was permitted to buy Simpsons they would use their combined clout in a way which would disadvantage small suppliers. We were right. They make no secret of their intention to use their massive marketing power to the maximum benefit of their shareholders. But who else benefits?

I believe there are some very important questions which should, indeed must be answered, before the public interest implications, or lack of them, of the proposed merger can be properly assessed.

For example:

Zeller's now undersells the Bay on many branded or identical items. We did a survey of the Bay and Zeller's in Ottawa to determine just how much difference there was between their prices. The results are in Annex 1. The Bay must certainly find competition from Zeller's, backed up with excellent television advertising, to be very uncomfortable. Would the Bay, with 100% control of Zeller's, be prepared to permit Zeller's merchandisers to undercut them to this extent?

Would Zeller's be permitted to run an independent merchandising policy? They must now in order to protect the interests of their minority shareholders. If the central buying direction were to come from the Bay for all divisions there would be a reduction in variety and in competition. What does this do for the Canadian consumer who demands a wide variety of consumer goods?

Zeller's now buys from many small suppliers. There are, we understand, more than 2000 and perhaps as many as 3000 companies in this small supplier category. A large number of these sell only to discount stores, some are very heavily dependent on Zeller's. Many will not be able to cope with the Bay's buying structure which is biased in favour of larger suppliers. Those who sell to other discount chains such as Woolco and K-Mart are not likely to be welcomed by the Bay whose mark-up structure is much higher. Do the benefits to Bay shareholders of gobbling up yet another competitor outweigh these disadvantages?

The Bay has a very large direct import program and it is getting bigger. If Zellers were to be forced to join in this program, it would become even more disruptive to Canadian apparel manufacturers who have increasingly become relegated to the status of residual suppliers to the giant retailers. . . .

We understand that the combined volume rebates which will be sought by the Bay will be retained at the corporate level to improve the bottom line, rather than being passed on to the individual stores to enable them to reduce prices. How does this benefit the consumer?

There are a number of areas in Canada where the Bay and Zeller's are the only two retailers in the market. Our research suggests that the following communities are among those in this situation [:] Fort MacMurray, Alberta and Lloydminster, Saskatchewan. How will the proposed merger help the residents of communities such as these? . . .

I will be recommending to my Board of Directors that they formally request you to initiate an inquiry under section 7(1) of the Combines Investigation Act into the concentration of buying power among major retailers. This meeting will be held early in February. Obviously my members are reluctant to sign the petition required by the legislation because they fear victimization by their giant customers. It would greatly facilitate matters if you could initiate an inquiry on your own authority. We also request that you order a moratorium on further takeovers or mergers in the retail sector while the inquiry is in progress.

Thank you for your help and understanding in the past. We would be pleased to co-operate with you in any way we can to try to resolve this growing problem.

Yours truly,

Peter Clark

PC/ls

cc. Mr. John Bulloch

    Canadian Federation of Independent Business

\*     \*     \*

## ANNEX 1

|  | Zeller's | The Bay |
|---|---|---|
| GWG Scrubbies Jeans | $19.88 | $25.95* |
| Levi Strauss Jeans | $19.99 | $31.95 |
| Sweet Baby Jane Blouse (very closely similar but not identical) | $19.99 | $31.95 |
| Philips 12 cup coffee maker | $49.77 | $69.99 |
| GE Automatic Kettle | $29.99 | $44.90 |

*$19.99 on sale, reduced from a claimed regular price of $25.95.
Source: Personal visits to stores located in downtown Ottawa.

# BARGAINING WITH AGENTS: GULF OIL
# AND ITS DEALERS

In its issue of February 24, 1979, *The Nation*, an American magazine not friendly to big business, carried a story by James Gannon, "How Gulf Dealt Its Dealers Out."* It described what appears from the story to have been a ruthless policy in California and neighboring states of eliminating individual dealers in traditional full-service gasoline stations. Gulf preferred to shift to self-service stations operated by its own employees. The dealers who were eliminated were portrayed as individual persons (or as husband and wife teams). I expect a number of them had incorporated their businesses. Whether they did or not, the effects on them of being eliminated would have been the same. Being incorporated would not have saved the agents' positions.

Their position, while they continued to have the position, was this:

> "Typically, the company owns the land (or holds it on a long-term master lease), and builds and equips the station. The dealer takes a short-term lease (usually one to three years) with an agreement to sell products supplied by his company. As landlord and supplier, the company holds two powerful strings. . . . Often it adds a third, that of creditor, by which the stranglehold can be further tightened."

According to Gannon, since the OPEC countries raised the price of oil, Gulf has become more concerned with retail profits and has become determined to cut back its "overbuilt, inefficient dealer system." It deliberately marshalled "its powers as supplier and creditor in creating the conditions that made it difficult, more often impossible, for dealers to stay in business. When that failed . . . it brought in the landlord power to administer the *coup de grâce.*"

One technique for exerting pressure appears to have involved a change in policy respecting deliveries of gasolines. "Before 1974, gasoline delivered to the station and stored underground was still owned by Gulf. Technically, the dealer never owned it until it passed through the pump, and never paid for it until afterward. The only advance cash was a small good-faith deposit, perhaps $1,000 a load." Under the new policy, the dealer had to pay for gasoline on delivery, "plus a deposit" evidently equal to the cost of each load. "A dealer with two storage tanks holding about $8,000 worth of gasoline each thus paid $16,000 for the gasoline and $16,000 in deposits; a $2,000 'good-faith' deposit was turned into a $32,000 investment." Furthermore, the gasoline was measured on leaving the refinery, when its volume

---

*The extracts given here from the story are reprinted by permission of *The Nation*. Copyright 1979 *The Nation* Magazine, The Nation Associates, Inc.

was significantly larger than when it reached the station, and it had to be paid for according to that measure.

Rex Kerr was a dealer in Buellton. "I would get the stuff in writing from Gulf" he is quoted as saying, "telling me to lower my prices, to increase my hours. In the meantime, they were raising my prices right along." Gannon comments, "If Gulf was suggesting something, Kerr never took the hint. So the company had to be blunt." He quotes Kerr further:

> Two Gulf representatives came to my station . . . and told me they wanted the station back. They wanted to make it a self-service. How fast could I get out? I was in a state of shock. I said, 'I don't know. It would take some time.' So they says, 'Well, as quick as you can, we'd like for you to pack up your stuff and get out.'
>
> . . . I asked if they could buy back some of this stuff, like some of my tires, batteries and accessories, and the gasoline in the ground I owned. And they said, 'No, it would be best if you took all that with you.' And I said, 'Well, what about the gas? How am I going to get it out?'—and, you know, four or five thousands gallons of gas. They said, 'Well, you'll have to get some barrels and fill them up and take them out'—you know, get the gasoline out of there if you want it—'if not, just leave it.'

Gannon reports that Gulf denies ever having pressured a dealer to leave a station.

## UNFAIR COMPETITION WITH RIVALS: BERKEY PHOTO, INC. v. EASTMAN KODAK CO.

*[If there is too little competition on one side or the other of the market—the demand side or the supply side—advantages appear that enable some firms to deal harshly with their suppliers or with their customers (or with both). Firms also acquire advantages over their rivals, and may treat them so harshly as to evoke objections about there being too much competition— "ruthless" or "cutthroat" competition. The excerpts that follow, from a Memorandum by the Court on posttrial motions, shows in arresting detail how a firm may exploit its advantages over rivals.]*

*United States District Court for the Southern District of New York, 1978*

FRANKEL, District Judge.
Defendant has moved . . . for judgment notwithstanding the jury's verdicts. . .

### 110 CAMERAS

The largest single item of damages awarded by the jury was for Berkey's lost profits, $15,250,000, resulting from Kodak's unlawful monopolization and attempt to monopolize the amateur camera market. The predominant part of the evidence supporting this claim dealt with the introduction of the 110 camera line as part of a system of interdependent photographic products, without prior disclosure to competing camera manufacturers of the information about the new Kodacolor II film format that would have enabled these other manufacturers to enter the market at about the same time as, and compete on the merits with, Kodak's initial line of 110 cameras.

For the most part, defendant's contentions on this score, as it observes, retrace ground plowed earlier in denying defendant's motion for summary judgment and formulating the charge to the jury. This reflects a superficially bemusing situation: that despite the length of the trial, the basic historical facts on this, as on many aspects of the case, are not in significant dispute. Without recounting these facts in detail, we may note that the jury undoubtedly found that defendant resolved some years before the 110 introduction to introduce the new camera and film, made to work with each other, and designed to displace with overwhelming suddenness huge segments of the market for 126 cameras. Defendant's responsible executives determined that the simultaneity of these introductions was to be the key weapon against competitors, brushing aside technical objections that the new film was unsatisfactory, inferior to the predecessor Kodacolor X in vital respects, and requiring further research and development to become a satisfactory product. The paramount strategy and goal were thus to use the film monopoly—Kodak's power in a field where its market share consistently exceeded 80%—as a lever for suddenly swelling defendant's power in the camera market, achieving there at least a temporary total monopoly of a vital new segment to be created by the system introduction. Some "responsible persons" within Kodak urged unsuccessfully that predisclosure concerning the new film format be given to camera competitors (as well as photofinishers and photofinishing equipment makers) so that they would not suffer in one blow the instant obsolescence of inventories and work in progress and the inability to compete at all with their cameras in the terrain of the newly announced system. The 110 announcement came substantially as a surprise, following some minimal predisclosures, for a price, two or three months earlier. And these events, it is worth mentioning, followed hard after a magicube coup in June of 1970, when Kodak gained a similar advantage of surprise and temporary exclusivity from what the jury found, and the court entirely agrees, was an unlawful combination in restraint of trade with Sylvania.

Without dwelling further on the facts of a huge record leading to the jury's award, the court refers briefly to some recurrent arguments defendant has pressed on this subject and sketches the reasons why they have been, and are once again, rejected.

1. *The claim of immunity* per se *for product introductions*

[1] Throughout the case, defendant has urged, and it urges once more, that a company's introduction of a new product—though the company be a huge one like Kodak with monopoly power in a mosaic of interconnected

markets, and though the introduction be designed deliberately to employ monopoly power in one market to create or enhance such power in another—must "as a matter of law" be immune from attack under the antitrust laws. If this is sound law, defendant should indeed be relieved of the verdict with respect to 110 camera damages. The court remains persuaded, however, that there is no such enclave for "product introductions," and that the mode, purpose, and impact of product introductions may, as in this case, play central parts in findings of unlawful monopolization and attempts to monopolize, no less than other, ordinarily lawful and "normal" business activities like leasing rather than selling machinery, *United States v. United Shoe Machinery Co.*, (1953, 1954) . . . [and] the creation of useful resources for added productive capacity, *United States v. Aluminum Co. of America* (1945) . .

Before *United Shoe* and *Alcoa*, arguments similar to Kodak's could have been mounted with respect to the practices of defendants there involved—leasing, building capacity, etc. Indeed, they were made. Thus, in the *United States Shoe* case, seeking reversal of Judge Wyzanski's historic ruling, the appellant company accepted the restrictions the *Alcoa* case had placed upon it as a dominant firm but assailed bitterly the notion that leasing of machinery could be the basis for a judgment against it. United Shoe complained of being condemned for its decision merely "to continue a business policy which it found in existence at its birth." It noted that this was "the policy of its more important American competitors," that it was among United's familiar practices "which are traditional, natural and normal," and that allowing such practices to be outlawed after years of use would subject every dominant company to the threat of unpredictable, retrospective, destructive judgments by judges and juries. That plea was unavailing; leasing practices were held subject to scrutiny and capable of being proscribed in a proper case as exclusionary techniques in the hands of a company with monopoly power. Kodak accepts that, as it must, but would draw the line now at product introductions. To reject that position does not mean, of course, that Kodak's product innovation techniques are *ipso facto* to be denounced. It means merely that they were open to informed inspection in this case, in the setting of all the circumstances of Kodak's power and practices, and that the jury could well have found (as the court would have found) anti-competitive uses by Kodak of its monopoly power in the manner and timing of its product system introductions.

[2] There are few mechanical rules to take the place of informed judgment in the enforcement of the antitrust laws. . . . [T]he task usually is to weigh "all of the circumstances of a case" to determine whether a company has engaged in unlawfully anticompetitive practices. . . . The ultimate judgment . . . must commonly rest "upon demonstrable economic effect rather than . . . upon formalistic line drawing." . . So, here, the jury was commissioned and instructed to appraise all the facts and circumstances and decide whether the manner, timing, and effects of the 110 introduction amounted to the anticompetitive employment of monopoly power not merely "to gain a competitive advantage" . . . but to attempt unlawfully to monopolize, and

to monopolize, another market. The court is compelled to conclude that the record and the law wholly justified the verdict in this aspect against Kodak. . . .

Defendant is not helped by protesting that under the law applied in this case "all product announcements by companies with large market positions are at risk without any legal standards to guide the businessman as to when and how and under what circumstances to bring out new products to market." It is at least a little demure for defendant to describe itself as a mere company with a "large market position." Kodak is, as the jury found and its counsel early observed, a "giant," with a nearly unique agglomeration of enormous powers over adjoining markets in a huge industry. Thus, the problem does not arise here in a way that ought to be of desperate concern to some uncertain class of "companies with large market positions. . . ." Overlooking that it has been found on compelling evidence to be a monopolist in an array of markets, Kodak also overlooks that monopolies are not darlings of the antitrust laws. Whatever supposed uncertainties inhere in the standards applied in this case—and it must be conceded surely that there are some—these standards would appear to be, if anything, more lenient toward Kodak than the stringent rule of *Alcoa,* allowing a monopolist to avoid illegality only if it could show that the disfavored position of power had been "thrust upon" it as a result of its superior business acumen or skill in the relevant market. Far from approaching a showing to satisfy that standard, the evidence reveals a monopolist in one market (film) engineering that power to thrust itself into a monopoly position in a second market (cameras). The result was a world away from being "economically inevitable," *United Shoe* . . . , it was plainly avoidable, and the means Kodak chose to employ were plainly to be shunned.

Kodak's complaint at root is that it faces liability for conduct which other business firms, lacking monopoly power, engage in regularly with impunity. Even if the factual premise were to be credited, the short answer is that the antitrust laws do not permit willful maintenance of monopoly power by conduct that might for a company without such power be deemed "honestly industrial." *Alcoa* . . . *United Shoe* . . . The present case illustrates the now settled rule that "[t]here are kinds of acts which would be lawful in the absence of monopoly but, because of their tendency to foreclose competitors from access to markets or customers or some other inherently anticompetitive tendency, are unlawful . . . if done by a monopolist . . . [*Sargent-Welch Scientific Co. v. Ventron* (1977).]

### 2. Predisclosure

[3] Plaintiff's theory on the camera monopoly claim included the contention that if defendant had given them advance information about the size and other pertinent qualities of the new Kodacolor II film, other camera manufacturers, including plaintiff, could have geared up to be ready to compete on the merits with Kodak in offering cameras suitable for use with the new film. Treating this aspect of the claim, the court cautioned the jury

that a company normally has a perfect right to keep its secrets, winning competitive advantages by launching new and better products in its own way and in its own time. Undertaking, however, to apply the teachings of the authorities on section 2 of the Sherman Act, the court went on to instruct that Kodak's monopoly power in film, if it was found to disable competitors who could not offer cameras comparable to Kodak's, might lead the judges of the facts to decide that the failure to give camera makers the necessary predisclosure concerning film should in all the circumstances be deemed anticompetitive. These instructions applied to a record on which the jury could readily have found among other things: (1) that Kodak timed the 110 system to cope with the inroads its competition was making in the 126 camera market, not as a result of the pace of design evolution; (2) that the simultaneous offering of a new color print film was a use of the firm monopoly to gain a competitive jump, not a genuine improvement or benefit to consumers; (3) that the anticompetitive purpose and effect of the introduction could be inferred from evidence that the new products were inferior in important respects, including, notably, the "red eye" problems, which Kodak took pains to conceal, beginning with the carefully planned lighting arrangements at the gala press conference called to launch the new system; and (4) that the highly publicized new Kodacolor II was restricted for a critical interval of time to the 110 format, for which only Kodak could supply cameras, for that anticompetitive purpose alone, not because of any technological or legitimately commercial concerns counseling this timetable.

Without disputing the foregoing facts and others from which the jury could have found the 110 introduction a scheme contrived almost wholly to crush competitors, and scarcely or not at all to compete by serving consumers better, defendant preserves its position that failure to predisclose could not as a matter of law go before the jury as a possibly material factor. The argument, characteristically robust and uncompromising, is that "the law," according to Kodak, "leaves to Kodak, acting in its own commercial interest, the decision when and how to bring its products to market."

[4] That extends the line Kodak has sought to have drawn throughout the case. The court adheres to the view that defendant is in error. Again, the court perceives the principles of the Sherman Act and the pertinent precedents as demanding a frequently subtle, inevitably comprehensive appraisal of actions by a company like Kodak wielding enormous monopoly power. Given such power, we were reminded not long ago, it becomes an essential question whether the evidence shows "the willful acquisition or maintenance of that power as distinguished from growth or development as a consequence of a superior product, business acumen, or historic accident." *United States v. Grinnell Corp.* . . . (1966). Here, then, plaintiff was entitled to have the triers of fact consider whether, in the total setting portrayed by a long record, an inference of "willful acquisition or maintenance" might be promoted or strengthened by the deliberate decision to keep secret the plan to use the combination of monopoly powers so that camera makers would be blocked for a substantial time from competing at all for the custom of

amateurs who would want the "remarkable new" Kodacolor II film and would be forced to deal with Kodak alone as the purveyor of "the film that was made for the camera that was made for the film."

### 3. *Business decisions and product quality*

[5] On legal reasoning essentially like that affecting predisclosure, the court continues to reject defendant's thesis that the jury should not have been permitted to appraise "business judgments" as to whether a new product is adequate and when to introduce it. As we approach the Sherman Act's centennial, it seems extraordinary to suggest that conduct questioned under that broad enactment may be shielded from scrutiny because it results from "business judgments." This was not so for the decision to lease rather than sell in *United Shoe* or for the countless business decisions that have been evaluated, whether to condemn or absolve, in antitrust cases. It seems equally clear that there is no legal shield covering questions of product quality. Turning no farther back than the quotation just above from *Grinnell*, we see it was a material question in the present case, as in others, whether Kodak's accession of increased monopoly power through the 110 system could be attributed to a "superior product." The jury was properly permitted, the court reaffirms, if not required, to appraise the 110 system for this purpose: to think whether the new film was somehow superior, and to evaluate in that light the new camera as well—whether *it* was "superior," or whether, perhaps, the ultimately decisive thing about the camera was its being designed to be protected in the market from any direct comparisons or competition of any kind.

The jury was cautioned at some length that it did not sit to second-guess business judgments as such, and that the quality of Kodak's products was not a concern in the case for its own sake. The only question in this quarter given to the triers of fact was the possibly difficult, but seemingly appropriate one of determining if the relative character of the products in question might cast light on whether the securing of monopoly power in the camera market was a natural and innocent business development or the kind of willful acquisition condemned by *Grinnell* and other cases. . .

The court records that the verdict for lost profits on 110 cameras will be sustained.

### KODACOLOR II PHOTOFINISHING DAMAGES

The jury found, on unquestionably sufficient evidence, that defendant had used its film monopoly—itself unlawfully mantained, as the jury also found—to injure plaintiff as a photofinisher. Under the court's charge, it was essential to this finding that the jury condemned "Kodak's mode of introducing the 110 system without predisclosure to photofinishers. . . . [as] exclusionary or anticompetitive conduct unlawfully affecting Berkey and other competing photofinishers . . ." That determination emerged from circumstances that included a pattern of dealing with photofinishers by which Kodak kept these enterprises relatively small, numerous, dependent upon Kodak, subject to shocks and shifts of their business resulting from sudden changes in Kodak's film operations, and almost inevitably inferior to, and less informed than, Kodak's own Color Print and Processing organization ("CP & P").

Without disputing the factual basis for this finding of liability, and the award of $55,700 in damages for this, defendant argues two grounds of law for setting aside this portion of the verdict:

(1) That the failure to predisclose, notwithstanding the circumstances in which it was shown, could not in law be a basis for liability.

(2) That the finding of illegality cannot stand in the face of the jury's findings that Kodak has neither monopolized nor attempted to monopolize the photofinishing market.

[7] The legal issue as to predisclosure, though its factual cast is different, is largely the same in this connection as in the dispute about 110 cameras. Like the camera manufacturers, photofinishers lived under the shadow, and at the mercy, of Kodak's omnipotent film monopoly. Like defendant's camera manufacturing division, its processing organization was secretly informed, and specially prepared, to process the new film promptly after its arrival on the market. Other finishers were left to scramble to catch up; were offered only equipment markedly inferior to CP & P's;* continued to be kept ignorant of technical facts and developments needed for maximally effective performance of the finishing service; were barred from competing while CP & P enjoyed a temporary monopoly; and had to watch helplessly as CP & P's reputation for preeminence was enhanced, not only by being first and best informed, but also by being needed for some time to process the other finishers' Kodacolor II orders and by being enabled to employ this opportunity to stuff these competitors' return envelopes to customers with Kodak CP & P advertising literature. Once more, the general proposition that predisclosure of new products is not required is subject to modification, as the jury found, when it is tested by circumstances of market power like Kodak's, capable of paralyzing impacts upon adjoining sectors of the economy. . . .

## THE MAGICUBE AWARD

The jury awarded a total of $1,747,300 on Berkey's claims of lost profits in 1970 and 1971 resulting from the joint development program between Kodak and Sylvania culminating in the simultaneous introduction in June 1970 of Sylvania's magicube and Kodak's cameras, unique for at least the time being, constructed to employ the magicube. The award is attacked both on the ground that there could be no liability as a matter of law and on the further ground that the evidence was insufficient to sustain the damage

---

*There were some light, and illuminating, moments at the trial when a Kodak technician went through a series of fumblings and contretemps attempting to demonstrate in the lighted courtroom a Kodak processing machine sold to independent photofinishers for employment in total darkness.

award. The latter contention is sustained to the extent that the court now finds no sufficient evidence on which the jury, answering question 5 on damages, should have been permitted to make its award for the year 1971 in the amount of $1,417,330. The prior award of $330,000 on this branch of the case, for 1970, is left to stand.

[10] As for liability, under both section 1 and section 2 of the Sherman Act, plaintiff defends on several theories. Without reviewing them all, the court notes a central core of scarcely disputed facts upon which the jury must have found, and the court itself would surely have found, a restraint to be denounced under the rule of reason and a form of exclusionary conduct supporting the finding of liability under section 2. It is hardly crucial, though it is much discussed by defendant, whether and to what extent Kodak and Sylvania were potential competitors. The heart of the matter, to summarize very briefly the compelling evidence on this subject, begins with Kodak's commanding position of monopoly power over key components of the amateur photographic industry—the cameras (to use the proposed flash devices), film, and color print paper. It was that dominant position, the jury could have found, that brought Sylvania to Kodak, ready to share its secrets and, under Kodak's pressure, to withhold them from Kodak's competitors in the manufacture of cameras. The jury could scarcely have failed to find, from the documentary and other evidence, that Kodak employed its power to pressure Sylvania and postpone the latter's explicit desire to furnish information concerning the flash device to other camera makers so that they might be less far behind—or, as Kodak effectively meant to avoid, abreast of Kodak—when the race to sell cameras fitted for the magicube began. Sylvania's yearning to be more forthcoming was heightened by its prior flashcube experience and the bitterness of Kodak's competitors when a similar regime of secrecy was enforced with respect to that earlier device. Kodak's insistence was effective. Sylvania's responses to inquiries from equipment manufacturers were carefully limited, thus helping defendant further to entrench its monopoly position by coming forth first, and remaining alone in the field for crucial months, in the sale of magicube cameras.

Adding to this central core of sharply and deliberately restrictive behavior in its combination with Sylvania, Kodak extracted patent rights in Sylvania inventions broader than Sylvania wished to give, and more effective as obstacles to other camera manufacturers.

If there is no exact case in point, there are apt analogies to teach that exclusionary arrangements in concert may be found unlawful restraints of trade without regard to Kodak's insistent premise that the parties acting in combination must be found to have been in a relationship of "horizontal" competition.

Even if the precedents were less persuasive, it is not good antitrust doctrine to demand cases squarely in point as preconditions for applying the basic principles under a rule of reason. . . . In sum, the court adheres to the premises of the charge to the jury in sustaining the finding of liability for the Sylvania-Kodak secret combination relating to magicubes.

*   *   *

*[The memorandum goes on to discuss further changes, also persuasive to the jury and to the court, of excessive prices for film, color print paper, and photofinishing equipment. The objections to this behavior are sufficiently illustrated by the charges set forth in the preceding excerpts.]*

## Comment:

# MULTIPLE APPROACHES TO EXCESSES OF COMPETITION

When we are perplexed about the moral judgment of a practice in business, the perplexity often arises as much or more from not knowing exactly how the practice is to be understood as from not knowing what general moral ideas to invoke. Perplexity about just when the price was set was one aspect of the mixed nuts case. A similar perplexity, on a much larger scale, with many more complications, arises about the lengths to which firms may carry competition with each other. Besides the sorts of things charged against Kodak, we can think of others. Imagine, for example, a shoe store that encouraged friends and relatives of its staff to pack a rival shoe store and occupy the salesclerks' time there fruitlessly. Or imagine—an example in which what is legal and what is moral pull apart—a firm announcing that it is going to cease giving rebates to substantial customers. Other firms in the industry may follow suit. Then they discover that, secretly, the first firm has continued rebating all along.

How are we to understand such practices? If an analogy with warfare (sometimes invoked in discussions of business) held, then the trickery involved in these practices would clearly be excusable; indeed so would the use of force—for example, sending a gang of roughnecks to wreck the rival firm's premises. Even so, not all uses of force and fraud would be excused: For example, it is not excusable to fire upon a hospital ship; or to disguise as a hospital ship an armed cruiser; and the rules of war exclude (or attempt to exclude) many other things, too, like killing opponents who have surrendered on stipulated terms. The analogy with warfare does not really hold, however: Force and trickery at least of the more flagrant sorts are prohibited by law.

Are firms left morally free to use the sorts of force and trickery that are not prohibited by law? Here one might resort to an analogy with sport. In some sports (football, hockey), force (within defined limits) is permitted and expected, as is trickery. No one condemns a football team for duping the opposing team into expecting a pass rather than a run through the center of the line. Even in sports where no force is allowed (footraces, tennis), players are permitted to deceive their opponents about the strategies that are being followed and the moves to expect. If every firm, like every player in a well-defined sport, understood just what range of practices to expect, including trickery, then some objections to the practices mentioned would fall away. There would at least be nothing dishonorable about the practices. They would not only fit within the rules of the game; they would be anticipated by them. The trickery involved would not invite condemnation as underhanded.

Yet the practices might be objected to on other grounds. Do they not tend to reduce the social product? It seems especially clear in the shoe store case that resources which could be used in other connections, where people's needs or wants go unsupplied, are being used to obstruct the production and distribution of shoes. The proper business of the shoe stores is to supply the public with shoes. The practice mentioned interferes with that business and (since it takes resources away from other uses) imposes on the public a double loss.

Theoretically, we might (returning to the analogy with sport) allow for the entertainment value obtained by the players in the rival firms and by the public. The public, however, is not consulted; it may well prefer to have an efficient supply of shoes and to make its own choices of entertainment elsewhere. The players, for their part, may find the entertainment less considerable than the risks. In sport, the rules aim at limiting the damage so that the players can go on to further games. Ideally, if they lose today, they can hope to win tomorrow. In business, the survival of the players is at stake. The shoe store that is being packed with pseudo-customers, and the firms that have naively given up rebating, may be ruined. That fact pushes us back to the analogy with the war, this time not a ground for excusing the practices, but as a ground for abolishing or regulating it.

Risks of ruin also operate against our being able to endorse, unreservedly, competitive practices even when these do promote efficiency. A supermarket chain can compel its suppliers to give rebates that are not available to corner stores. If, as a consequence, the supermarkets charge lower prices—passing the rebate along—consumers enjoy some of the economies of large-scale production and distribution. Some corner stores, unable to reduce their prices, may have to go out of business. Economics teaches us that they have been inefficient and that we must expect competition to eliminate inefficient firms. Yet do not the owners of the corner stores deserve some sympathy? Can we contemplate their ruin with equanimity?

We need do no more than mention the danger that we run of having monopolistic firms emerging from the ruin of small firms by present sacrifices of competition. The point that I want to make, however, is that we are all attached to some degree to the aim of having a civilized society in which everybody has some protection in status and way of life. Competition, even when it results in greater efficiency, disregards any such protection.

If we go back to the practices first mentioned (the fake rebating, the packed shoe store), we can see that this aim of having a civilized society tells against those practices, too. Firms may be rivals; but when they are also members (legal persons) of the same society, they owe each other a minimum of respect, forebearance, and even (on occasion) mutual assistance. We may think of them as moral agents themselves. Even if we do not, we must consider that they are staffed by moral agents who as members of the same society cannot show full respect for each other if they do not restrain the firms that they belong to from excesses in competition.

# PART FIVE

# The Actions of Firms: Cumulative Impact of Firms' Activities

CHAPTER **15**

# *The Effect of Advertising on Culture*

*Introductory Comment:*

## AGGREGATIVE AND CUMULATIVE EFFECTS

One beer can in the woods does not present much of a problem. Any active and conscientious nature-lover can pick it up and carry it away in her knapsack. Hundreds of beer cans, all along the woodland path on both sides as far as the eye reaches, lay down a challenge to social policy too big for one person to handle casually. It is an aggregative effect of many people's activities. If one imagines its being brought about all at once—by supplying hundreds of people with one can of beer each, which is consumed at the same time, then thrown away—the effect is aggregative without being cumulative. More likely, in any real instance, it will be cumulative—a load on the environment built up over time, from half-a-dozen people's beer cans one day and half-a-dozen's the next, day after day. For the most part, when they demand attention, both sorts of effects can be expected to come hand in hand; and I shall treat them as doing so.

Hand in hand, they constitute a third major subject of moral concern to place beside deception and oppression. It is not an entirely independent subject: The evils involved in deception are aggravated when deception is practiced all around and time after time. Distrust becomes generalized and deepens. The evils of oppression likewise include aggregative and cumulative effects: greater numbers of people resentful and alienated; resentment and alienation deeper and more intractable as time goes on. However, aggregation and cumulation may create a problem that, as with the beer cans, is hardly present with a single instance, even if the instance itself is harmful. A nonsmoker's happiness may be diminished enough to notice if just one person smokes in his presence; but the effect is transitory, and no permanent injury has been done him. It is a different matter if he is compelled to spend his waking hours in crowded places where lots of people are smoking; and he may, of course, suffer the effects along with a number of other nonsmokers.

Often, a single instance is only vanishingly harmful or not harmful at all. Mayor Jimmy Walker of New York used to hold that no girl was ever ruined by a book. Like most academics and intellectuals, I despise most of the programs run on TV, and I shall present some arguments for thinking that TV has pernicious aggregative and cumulative effects. Even I, however, would concede that no one's mind and morals were ever ruined by looking at a single program. One car in the village, carefully driven, won't hurt anybody, and certainly does not create a pollution problem. One aerosol can of deodorant poses no threat to the ozone layer, even if the can is in use four or five times a day. Aggregate these things, however, and repeat them over time, perhaps in ever larger quantities, and you have dangers and actual injuries to people's happiness as great as anything that could be created by deception and oppression, and hence ethical problems as big as any that are faced in business.

[*Advertising, gone wrong, may injure culture through the aggregative and cumulative effect of deception. We have already considered deception at some length, and had, I think, chance enough to discern what these effects would be. So here I shall bring up matters other than deception—other ways, some of them subtle (though subtler in single instances than in the aggregate), in which advertising may do harm. The harm may be redoubled by the use of television as the medium of advertising, and so its full extent cannot be judged until, later, we take up the impact of TV itself. The printed word and picture—and the radio'd word—suffice, however, to indicate that the effects, for good or ill, are probably far-reaching.*]

## ABSURDITIES: COLA WARS

In a story* carried in its issue of April 26, 1979, *The Wall Street Journal* reported that the big soft-drink firms were preparing, after "disappointing volume growth" in the previous year, for a period of intense competition. Though many observers (including executives of the firms in question)

*Excerpts printed by permission of *The Wall Street Journal,* © Dow Jones & Company, Inc. 1979. All Rights Reserved.

attributed the slowdown to "a sharp rise in soft-drink prices," the firms will rely mainly upon advertising expenditures to win increased business. "To send consumers such messages as 'Coke adds life' and 'Have a Pepsi day,' they are expected to spend about $200 million."

The Pepsi-Cola company has evidently become more modest in its communication. From claiming a whole "Pepsi generation," which it did for several years running, it has descended to offering people one by one a day at a time. Aren't all the slogans absurd, however? Drinking one cola rather than another can hardly make that much difference to one's life, even for a day. Can having any cola drink at all?

One may assume that people recognize as much, if they pause to think about the slogans at all. Moreover, in reaction to the barrage of such slogans with which the public is afflicted, most people probably simply tune out.

Can they tune out entirely, however? Isn't something taken away from the claims of having a good meal with stimulating friends, of reading *Emma* or *Bleak House*, of playing two sets of tennis with a well-matched opponent, by the suggestion that having a drink of Coca-Cola or of Pepsi-Cola can add as much to one's life? How can people keep in proper perspective sensible judgments about what is important to life if those judgments are continually diminished, relatively, or drowned out, by the absurd judgments conveyed by advertising? It's not just the advertising of soft-drink firms, omnipresent though their advertising may be, that has to be considered. The messages about soft drinks form just one stream in the flood of messages of the same sort.

Tuning out is itself a disturbing effect. We may approve of it as a measure of self-defense. Doesn't it imply, however, a failure of interest and trust in the system of communications? And doesn't that add to the difficulties of communicating truths that are important to the community and to the people who make it up? One might wonder whether the astonishing indifference with which millions of people have shrugged off warnings about the dangers of cigarettes does not illustrate tuning out, and result from its having become a habit.

It is instructive to compare the slogans with what any cola company might truthfully claim: "Many people obtain a modest pleasure from drinking cola pop like ours from time to time. You might, too." (It's true that my students tell me that if this is the sort of advertising I'd produce, they'd never hire me to do their advertising.)

## MISPLACED FOLKSINESS

The sociologist Robert K. Merton has reported, after reflecting on the results of a survey of people representative of the public for mass media in the United States:

> On every side, they feel themselves the objects of manipulation. They see themselves as the target for ingenious methods of control, through advertising

which cajoles, promises, terrorizes; through propagandas that . . . guide the unwitting audience into opinions which may or may not coincide with the best interests of themselves or their affiliates; through cumulatively subtle methods of salesmanship which may simulate values common to both salesman and client for private and self-interested motives. In place of a sense of *Gemein-schaft*—genuine community of values—there intrudes *pseudo-Gemeinschaft*—the feigning of personal concern with the other fellow in order to manipulate him the better. Best sellers provide popular instruction in the arts of pseudo-Gemeinschaft: "how to influence people through the pretense of friendship." . . . As one informant phrased it, "In my own business I can see how a lot of people in their business deals will make some kind of gesture of friendliness, sincerity and so forth, most of which is phony." [Merton, *Mass Persuasion* (New York, 1946), pp. 142–143]

What in this connection are we to make of Betty Crocker? General Mills makes sure that this ageless fictional character—widely known to women in the United States and Canada—is continually before the public. Her picture or her signature, both fictions, figure everywhere on its packages or in its advertising. It is Betty Crocker who, going along with the fiction, one supposes is at work day after day in the experimental kitchens of General Mills at Minneapolis, producing recipes for use in North American homes and maintaining the nutritional standards of General Mills' products. Those kitchens really exist; and, of course, this sort of personification is practiced by other firms, too. Yet will not this device, multiplied on every side, tend to make people somewhat confused about who cares for their interests and in what way? And even somewhat confused about who's real and who's not?

## FOUR FULL-PAGE, FULL-COLOR ADS SOBERLY DESCRIBED

[Three of the following ads seem to me to have a novel twist, which makes them arresting and amusing. The one that is not novel is clever too—not so distinctively clever, but carefully studied in ways that invite close inspection. Clever as ads may be, often individually amusing as well, what happens when people are flooded with them every day?]

1. On a California beach, a motorcycle, painted like the sidecar attached to it in a mottled camouflage pattern, is at rest. A strong-featured young man with thick black hair and a thick black mustache is sitting astride it, with one foot on the ground. He is dressed in washed-out blue denim pants and shirt and a red-quilted flak jacket. A helmet rests on the leg that does not reach to the ground. Standing beside the sidecar is a smallish young woman with long blonde hair curling around her face. She is wearing a red T-shirt and dark blue denim "cut-offs"—cut off very short. She has an attractive figure and a more than passable face. At the moment, she is regarding the young man with intense interest. The young man is lighting a long cigarette. In the lower righthand corner of the page, a package of

Camel filter cigarettes is shown, with three cigarettes protruding and bearing the legend, "Famous Camel Quality!" At the lower left, in a small box, one may read, "Warning: The Surgeon General Has Determined That Cigarette Smoking Is Dangerous to Your Health." Above it, in much larger type, is the main printed message of the ad: "Satisfaction, Camel Filters style. Some men taste it all: Rich warm flavor. Smooth even taste. Solid satisfaction. Only from the Camel Filters blend of Turkish and domestic tobaccos."

2. A mother and three children are gathered at the foot of the stairs in a house spacious enough and elegant enough in decorations and furnishings to belong to an exceptionally prosperous doctor or lawyer or top executive. A handsome little boy of about seven is farthest in the background. He is standing four or five steps up the stairs, with both hands on the left railing, which descends in a sweeping curve from the second story, and his body turned away; but his head is turned so that he can look to the right of the picture. Sitting on the second step is a girl of twelve or thirteen, attractive but touchingly gawky. She has on a T-shirt, very short denim shorts, knee-high pink socks with blue tops, a pair of lace-up, full-shoe roller skates. She is also wearing kneepads, at which she is staring, waiting for the incident pictured to be over. Standing just to the left of her, the mother, like the little boy, is looking to the right. She, a trim blonde with medium-short hair, in her late thirties, is dressed in a light-blue checked blouse with long sleeves and a Copen-blue skirt. The central part in the incident is being played by the third child, a girl of eleven, who is quite plain, with heavy glasses; she has on, besides a red T-shirt, a one-piece dark-blue denim costume ending in mid-length shorts. On her knees, she has, like her sister, kneepads, and evidently she has just taken off her own roller skates, which appear in the lower right corner of the picture. Behind her on the floor is a fluffy cat, reddish-brown and white, who is reposing beneath a mahogany eighteenth-century-style chest of drawers. The chest serves as a stand for a gold-colored Princess phone, a slender vase of flowers, and a photograph in a gold frame. The little boy and the mother are looking at this girl, who is speaking into the handset of the phone. The mother, who is holding an open shoebox filled with tan tissue paper, is looking, with a deprecating half smile, at the girl's feet, which are adorned with high-heeled white shoes perhaps somewhat too big for her. The girl is purportedly saying into the phone, "Mom said it was from my fairy godmother. I thought, 'Could it be?' Oh yes! I love 'em. I've been begging for heels just forever. Yes. Yes. They fit. They're just like the ones I wanted. Oh, Mom told you, didn't she? They'll really go with my new dress for the dance. I feel like Cinderella already! Thanks, Aunt Connie." The Bell System, from which the ad stems, comments, "Though family and friends move far apart, you can continue to grow together. Just reach out and walk back into each other's lives." Then, in type four times as large, "Reach out and touch someone."

3. Occupying the whole space of the page is the face and part of the enormous white beard of a man who has a long white moustache as well, and white bushy eyebrows. A bit of his white hair is shown, too. He is

wearing wire-rimmed round spectacles, which have slid down his nose; and, looking directly out from the picture, he has a benign but intent expression. Superimposed on his beard, at the bottom center, is the picture of a bottle of whiskey, with light shining through the amber liquid, and beside it both a dark blue velvet bag, trimmed in gold, and a dark blue and gold box, showing the name of the whiskey and its trademark. Above the whiskey and its luxurious packaging runs the message: "Can you look this man straight in the eye and honestly say you deserve Crown Royal?"

4. We are looking from the other side of the East River, north of the Brooklyn Bridge, at lower Manhattan, in which (some liberties having been taken with their actual geographical position) have been placed several landmark New York skyscrapers, including the Chrysler Building, the Empire State Building, and the World Trade Center. It is early evening, just after sunset, and these buildings are lit up from top to bottom, as are the square, less distinctive high-rise office blocks that line the river. There are lights strung along the cables of the bridge, too, and lights marching across it at deck level. In the distance, to the left, the Statue of Liberty is clearly visible, draped in green bronze and holding a flaming torch. At the lower left, by a brick parapet overlooking the bridge, stands a man in the khaki shirt and shorts and pitch helmet of an African explorer—or of a British district commissioner in the old days of the Colonial Service. He is peering through binoculars at a huge white structure that is standing next to the Empire State building on the downriver, Statue of Liberty side. The structure is much larger in bulk than the Empire State, though the radio-mast on top of the latter building rises a bit higher. It is a white, gold-capped bottle, which glows like a huge light bulb against the purplish sky. There is no printed text in the ad, except for the two labels on the bottle. One, a crescent label just below the neck, reads "London Dry, since/depuis 1857"; the other, a diamond-shaped label on the near face of the bottle, says, "GILBEY's London Dry GIN."

*Comment:*

# THE MISAPPROPRIATION OF OUR WORLD BY ADVERTISING

One might feel some distaste for having beautiful people and beautiful scenery associated in advertisements with miscellaneous products, some of them trivial, some, vulgar necessities. However, is this distaste perhaps just superrefined aestheticism, which most people would not take seriously? Does it in any case have any significant moral implications?

We shall find that it does, if we pursue the following line of argument.

Consider first some extreme cases—more extreme than anything attempted in the advertisements so far considered—the first fact, the second fiction:

1. In a TV commercial, a beautiful woman is shown writhing in orgasmic ecstasy; the associated message is that Dingo's toilet paper is wonderfully soft.

2. A radio commercial sets a jingle about beer—or toothpaste—to the music of the "Ode to Joy" in the last movement of Beethoven's Ninth Symphony.

One might think that doing the latter is irreverent; but that is not quite to the point, since a reverential attitude toward art is often misguided. The "Ode to Joy," like other great works, can withstand a good deal of irreverent parody, from which we all might derive a good deal of fun. So we might—and do—from jokes about orgasms.

The point is that in the commercials, some features of our world that offer important opportunities for enjoyment and happiness have been appropriated by other people for irrelevant purposes, in ways that interfere with our being able to make up our minds about these features by ourselves and enjoy them in suitable ways.

Jokes and parodies may interfere, too, but when they are good they are relevant to the features in question. They offer us, in compensation for the interference, some new light on the features, for example, light as regards what to take seriously about them, what not. The associations with toilet paper, beer, and toothpaste tell us nothing about female beauty, orgasms, or the "Ode to Joy."

Furthermore, we cannot easily evade them. It is by our own choice that we take up jokes or parodies produced outside advertising. As things stand, with some exceptions in countries like Britain and Canada with extensive public broadcasting systems, we cannot get information or entertainment from radio, TV, or the magazines without running into advertisements. Moreover, we repeatedly run into the same advertisements. The damage done is repeated so often that it may begin to affect our central perception of the features appropriated, so that we no longer find the "Ode to Joy" exciting and peak sexual experiences no longer make their full impact on our lives.

Thus advertising of the sort in question here jeopardizes people's chances of happiness. The moral dimension of the distaste that some people feel—and all might feel, on reflection—is now visible. We need not describe it in terms of happiness alone, moreover. I favor a cautious use of the concept of rights, thinking that it is used most convincingly when it attaches (as with the right to vote) to definite familiar rules. Does not the concept of rights have a convincing use here, however, even though the rights would be very general ones? It seems natural to maintain that the advertisers have no right to mess up the only world that people have to live in; and that people generally have a right not to have opportunities valuable to them taken away without deliberation and consent.

The present point is quite distinct from the objection that associating certain products with beautiful people and glamorous locales misleads people into thinking that they will find themselves with beautiful people in glamorous locales if they drink or smoke the products thus advertised. It is distinct from the subtler objection that people will be encouraged to buy and use these products to demonstrate to themselves that they, too, are beautiful and glamorous (compare Arthur A. Leff, *Swindling and Selling* [New York, 1976], p. 167). It is distinct, finally, from the objection that associating a product with a fictive person (piecrust mix with Betty Crocker) gives a false personal touch to the advertiser's operations, misleading people into thinking that the advertiser somehow cares as a friend would for them and their welfare.

All these objections do, however, relate to people's happiness. In the first case, people are misled about where to look for happiness, and they are misled to much the same effect in the second case, where they again orient themselves in life in accordance with the ads and imitate the purchases of the people pictured there. In the third, they are misled into not guarding themselves and their happiness carefully enough. They should be placing no more (though indeed no less) confidence in General Mills's products than the products themselves warrant, taking into account comparative merits demonstrated in actual use, and General Mills's system of quality control. Might Betty Crocker be taken to symbolize General Mills' good reputation and the trust that it deserves? Perhaps. However, the reputation and trust should not be founded on the success with with General Mills personalizes its image; and competition with other firms in personalized images may confuse people about what matters to them in the firms' activity. A firm might gain an edge in personalized image and yet have worse products or higher prices.

## CONFUSION ABOUT THE ENVIRONMENT: TESTIMONY BY AN AD MAN*

*[Advertising is not only presumptuous when it misappropriates parts of our world. According to one rather untypical advertising man (from whom we shall hear again as a dedicated enemy of television), it is actively subverting efforts to develop sensible policies about protecting the environment. We wind up this discussion of advertising by anticipating further discussion under the two succeeding headings of the impact of business and industry on the environment.*

*In March, April, and May 1970, a select subcommittee on education of the United States House of Representatives held hearings on the bill that became the Environmental Education Act of 1970. Congressman Brademas was chairman of the subcommittee. The following passage is extracted from*

*As reprinted by the Social Science Education Consortium, Inc., and The ERIC Clearing House for Social Studies/Social Sciences Education in *The Environmental Problem* (Boulder, Colo., 1971), pp. 160, 161–163.

*the minutes of the subcommittee for the twelfth day of hearings, 1 May 1970.]*

INTRODUCTION OF JERRY MANDER, DIRECTOR, FRIENDS OF THE EARTH

Mr. Brademas. Our next witness is Mr. Jerry Mander, president of Freeman, Mander & Gossage Advertising. . . .

Mr. Mander. I would like to put forth the proposition that the way people behave and what they believe in today's America is at least as influenced by advertising impressions as by what they are taught in schools. This is especially true, of course, of people who do not have much of an education with which to put advertising into a context but it is also true of most of us— of all of us.

There is no way of avoiding ads today; they are everywhere, and they influence us concerning life styles, status, standards of taste and behaviour, and whatever is new. They are, like it or not, the place where we gain many of our perceptions about the world, whether positive or negative. None of this might seem pertinent, but let me point out that, God save us, advertising men have discovered ecology.

At first, I thought it was a good thing that hundreds of ads began to appear from all kinds of companies, soul-searching about their own products and stating all the wonderful things they were doing to save the environment.

But as my late partner, Howard Gossage, was fond of pointing out, advertising people have an inordinate fascination with "image." They assume that by seeing a certain way, the world will come flocking around tearing at their clothes. Gossage preferred the word "identity" to "image"— having to do with the way one really is—which made him a lonely man in the advertising business.

Well, at one time, the difference may not have been all that important except for the psychic good health of advertising people. But at this point in history, the way I perceive it right now, the difference may be more like life and death, and may foredoom any other educational effort that's made.

With the sudden, immense outpouring of words from business and industry concerning all the wonderful things they were doing, technologically-wise, to solve the pollution problem—most of these words being expressed in ads—it's worth having looked closely at what's being said and, of course, it's all image and no identity.

Most of the industry still sees pollution and environment questions as more of a public relations and advertising problem—in other words, an image problem—than they do anything fundamental about the way they are doing business.

Shell Oil Company, for example, recently ran a four-ad series showing:

1. how they saved the lives of a lot of fish by not polluting things as much as they had been;
2. how they are feeding starving millions by producing more and better

pesticides (which on the other hand are killing the fish they just saved);

3. how they overcame a lovely little Connecticut town's fears that their new gas station would prove a blight because it would replace a number of lovely trees, by showing the townspeople that the station would itself be a lovely gas station; and

4. came out against littering.

I'm sure that the president of that company feels he is a conservationist for this position because until recently it was unusual for an oil company to even mention pollution or ugliness. I would not be surprised if he became the industry's spokesman on protecting the environment.

Now that there is public good will in conservation, now that it's a hot topic, it's "good business to think of the environmental implications of industrial action", as a major chemical company executive recently suggested.

Another example: a recent copy of *The New York Times* carried a Pan American Airways ad which announced the "latest breakthrough" in relieving airport congestion. I was ready to be told they had reduced their total number of flights, or scrapped the Boeing 747, or canceled their SST orders.

But it turned out that what they had done was to build a second terminal at Kennedy Airport in New York, so they could handle up to twice as many passengers with less congestion inside. Getting the planes onto the ground without bumping each other is another matter and getting into New York City from the airport, somehow, was somebody else's problem. They were doing their bit.

POWER COMPANIES' ADVERTISING VERSUS RESEARCH

And we've all seen more than our share of power company ads. Usually they bring us one of four urgent messages:

1. Use more electricity.

2. The folks at your neighborhood power company are working overtime to develop new and creative means for winning the war on pollution.

3. We need more powerplants to fill our growing needs—atomic ones, and they're safe as apple pie. (Southern California Edison, by the way, actually had the gall to blandly state in an ad two months ago that nuclear powerplants cause no pollution at all. They simply ignored thermal pollution and radiation.)

4. They need a rate raise to finance the research and the new construction.

I had thought I had already reached the pinnacle of my own shame and disgust concerning utility advertising—what they are doing advertising at all if they are a public utility—when I came across an old *Congressional Record* by chance and found in it a speech by Senator Metcalf which somehow has gone unnoticed by the press and by conservationists. Listen to this:

Senator Metcalf pointed out that during 1969, public utilities spent nearly $300 million on advertising, more than eight times what they spend on research—all the while proclaiming in the ads how much antipollution research is going on. Metcalf also pointed out that about a fourth of all power companies in this country actually did no research at all, while spending millions in advertising to talk about research and to sell us all on using more electrical power at the same time as they tell us there's a power shortage.

If advertising dollars are going to be spent on utilities, one would think—considering this so-called power shortage which makes introduction of polluting nuclear plants "inevitable" in the words of *Newsweek*—that the ads would be appeals to use less power.

I am prepared to make the case that this $300 million in advertising spent by the power companies—which by the way is about a third of the entire federal antipollution budget in Mr. Nixon's budget message—combined with the millions from oil companies, chemical companies, auto companies, industrial associations, the newly burgeoning antipollution industries, and so on—about a billion dollars altogether this year, I would guess, much of it talking about how everything's going to be all right, just don't you worry, industry is taking care of things—is actually producing a net loss in this so-called war on pollution.

It's called "co-optation" in other circles and I believe, fairly certainly, that it's operative here, perhaps not deliberately but in effect.

INFORMATION POLLUTION

I fear that all the recent government rhetoric, magnified by industrial assurances, might have the net effect of encouraging a society already dazzled by technology to be further assured that technology is solving the problem—people want so much to be assured—and so it's back to the television set.

Perhaps even worse than the fact that the ads are misleading, or even lying in many instances, is the fact that they divert the reader from a more central understanding about what's really going on. That technological society is beginning to reach its limits, and expansionism is going to end, and endless consumption is going to end, and we're all of us going to begin adopting techniques of societies who live on islands and for whom a finite system is given.

The ads are even destroying the word "ecology" and perhaps all understanding of the concept with it.

A few weeks ago, P.G.&E. ran a headline advocating a "balance between ecology and energy."

But ecology is not a thing that is balanced against anything else. The word describes a science of the interrelatedness of everything. Energy is a detail which only man has decided to make a fuss over. That is what must be remembered and it is getting increasingly hard to do so with this immense outpouring of diversionary, false, and deadening information.

While industry is spending a billion dollars putting out this stuff as nearly as I can determine, conservation organizations are spending roughly $200,000 to attempt to offset it and to accomplish other urgent educational messages concerning one issue or another. That is, roughly two hundredths of one percent of the industrial budget. That much money to educate people to what the industrial ads are leaving out, or saying falsely, or to educate people so that they'll not be lulled into false security.

This is an educational struggle which is taking place right now, today, and without some kind of immense outpouring of counterinformation from conservation groups, I am very much afraid that the ecology fad will be even shorter than anticipated. People will relax and think everything's all right. We will have lost their attention.

## FUNDS TO COMBAT INFORMATION POLLUTION

If you agree with me that there is an educational impact to advertising which is direct and immediate, and considering industry's behavior, critical, I would ask you to include provision in the bill to finance conservation organizations in their efforts to use advertising in the following three educational ways:

1. Fairness doctrine advertising. Friends of the Earth, in concert with other groups, has begun proceedings to apply the results of fairness doctrine case against cigarette advertising, to advertising of polluting industries. If we succeed, as I believe we will, all radio and television stations will be required to provide a conservation organization with time in which they may present a counter message to an ad.

If an automobile company runs a one minute spot advertising its new model, Friends of the Earth could indicate what the implications of the annual style change are, or talk about the pollution from cars, or the raw material that went into building it, or the problem of disposing of it, and the roads needed to run it on.

When a Standard Oil ad appears for its F-310, calling it "the greatest automative advance in history" we will be able to put it in perspective by showing that it represents only a five-percent pollution improvement, leaving 95 percent to go. And talking about oil spills, and so on.

But even with free air time, and free agency work—there are dozens of ad agencies willing to do it—still, hundreds of thousands of dollars are needed to actually film and produce such spots, and we don't have the money.

2. General educational advertising. As I stated earlier, with respect to the bill as written, the idea here is to speak of basic solutions and basic understanding of environmental problems; to speak of consumption patterns and life styles and waste; to create an understanding in the general public which could help make it less susceptible to glamour appeals; and to attempt to put out of fashion the importance of "newer, faster, bigger" and "more, more, more."

The attempt here would be to develop a real understanding of ecology—a basic acquaintance with the fact that man is just one small part of the natural system with no greater rights than any other growing thing in it, and no rights whatever to intrude in the natural order of things.

As understanding of what it means to live on an island. We would like to see industrial innovations considered guilty until proven innocent, instead of vice versa.

3. The third area of desperately needed advertising funds is the issue-oriented advertising.

When a timber supply act hits Congress, or an Alaska pipeline lobby, someone has got to speak out for the wilderness that has no voice of its own, and if it is to succeed—as the anti–Grand Canyon dam campaign proved it could, for the Sierra Club—it must be done with the same modern tools used by industry to tell everyone everything is going to be all right.

Right now, any conservation organization which does take an ad runs the risk of having done to it what happened to the Sierra Club—losing its tax-deductible status. So, at the moment, even with money, organizations are effectively prevented from stating an alternative point of view.

\*      \*      \*

CHAPTER **16**

# *The Character of Products, Compared with Alternatives*

*Introductory Comment:*

## THE CUMULATIVE IMPACT OF MULTIPLYING PRODUCTS

Alarming aggregative and cumulative effects can come either from products themselves or from the technologies used to produce them. These matters are hard to separate neatly. Sometimes, to be sure, the distinction is clear enough. Cigarettes are products with harmful effects, including aggregative and cumulative effects suffered by nonsmokers; but I do not suppose that the technology of producing them is especially worrisome in its effects. Paper towels, by contrast, are harmless products, but the technology of producing them can create a spectacular amount of pollution. In many cases, however, the product and the technology both have effects that demand moral attention. Automobiles and jet airplanes, for example, pose various sorts of danger to health and to the environment; and so do the technologies used to produce them, beginning with the mining of metal ores and the smelting to which the ores are subjected.

There are further interconnections. I shall bring up TV as a product, the TV set, whose use by large numbers of people over substantial stretches of time raises problems. However, doesn't TV also invite being considered a technology of communication? Automobiles, similarly, together with the highways that they run upon, constitute a technology of transportation. All the same, I shall treat them, too, chiefly as raising problems as products. Large jet passenger airplanes I would assign for discussion under technology. One can think of them as involving products—so many one-passenger trips between various localities—but the products are intangible, the planes are means of producing them, and the planes remain in the hands of the producers.

Again, I intend the topic of products to embrace the topic of packages. Both can have important aggregative and cumulative effects. This time, however, I am not assuming that products and packages of the kinds to be discussed are given, except for certain features susceptibe of being better or worse. One alternative to having cars or TV sets or cigarettes of the kinds present on the market is in each case to have nothing of the kind at all—no cars, no TV sets, no cigarettes. At any rate, this is a discussable alternative: I do not mean to suggest that critics of these things (like me) should have the power to prohibit them unilaterally.

## A: Effects of Products on Public Health

*[Products affect public health through affecting the environment; but it is useful to separate the impact on public health. Objections on grounds of health are not controversial in the ways objections springing from environmental considerations often are. One can hardly attempt to dismiss them as merely aesthetic; and they are not class-biased—the poor have as much at stake in health as people free enough from daily cares to be concerned with the environment.]*

### TOO MANY CIGARETTES

*Time Magazine*, in its issue of 7 April 1980, had a short item that began by recalling, "Nonsmokers have been fighting for years to get smoking banned from public places. They argue that the habit subjects non-smokers to unpleasant odors and eye irritation. Smokers have countered that as long as they are not hurting anyone except themselves they have a right to do as they please."*

The reply seems to miss the point. Are the unpleasant odors and the eye irritation, if they are real effects, not hurtful?

In any case, *Time* goes on to say, "That report has not been undermined by researchers at the University of California at San Diego who found that long-term exposure to cigarette smoke causes measurable lung damage in people who do not smoke . . . Nonsmokers who did not work in smoky

*Excerpts from "Tobacco Wars." Copyright 1980 Time Inc. All rights reserved. Reprinted by permission from *Time*.

environments came out best on tests of the lungs' ability to hold air and expel it . . . But nonsmokers who had worked for more than 20 years in smoke-filled areas had scores similar to those of light smokers."

## TOO MANY AUTOMOBILES

Many people enjoy driving a car. Others enjoy at least the convenience of being able to make journeys entirely of their own timing, which may take them to places otherwise hardly accessible; and enjoy the door-to-door comfort of the journeys, which anyone waiting on a street corner for a bus on a cold rainy day can vividly appreciate. All these things are gains in respect to happiness, and through reduced stress, for health; being able to stay off rainy street corners is no doubt a gain for health against respiratory diseases. There are other good things that have been brought about by automobiles. Some I shall mention later, when I bring up the impact of automobiles on the environment. I shall not bring up their impact on culture, though there is much to be said, both for automobiles and against them, there, too. So I might just mention here the important gain for social democracy that widespread private ownership of automobiles has realized. Working-class people, limited generations ago to one-day excursions to a handful of resorts, can now move about the country as freely as the rich can.

No wonder people set such store by car-ownership—so much store that democratic governments have not dared to do anything to check its multiplication. Yet there have been—there continue to be—important adverse effects on public health from the multiplication of automobiles. In the United States, as many people may be killed and injured (some horribly) in automobile accidents in any current peacetime year as were once killed or injured under the American flag in a savage year of war. It is true that people forget about the accidents—real and frequent ones—to which past forms of transportation, including horse-drawn carriages, were liable. As a function of the number of miles traveled per capita per annum, accidents with the automobile may not look so bad compared with accidents caused by runaway horses. Still, they look bad enough, indeed, looked at without habitual discounting, they look stupendous.

Equally obvious, and accepted with equally astonishing equanimity, is the air pollution created by masses of automobiles. Everyone has heard of the smog in Los Angeles: a mass of reddish brown junk that visibly overlays the city from early June on, with the radio reporting every day how far the air remains breathable. During a "first-stage alert," old people and other people with delicate lungs are urged to remain indoors; during a "second-stage" one, schools are closed and people generally are advised not to go outdoors except on essential business. With a "third-stage alert"—which has not yet, I believe, occurred—won't it be best for everyone to leave for Nevada? (But if people go to Nevada by car, won't they take the smog with them?)

Congestion by itself endangers health. What the automobile takes away from stress on the one hand, surely it more than doubles on the other. Driving in rush-hour traffic—when the "rush" slows everyone down, often to a standstill—is a terrible burden on the psyche. Millions of people have little choice but to spend a couple of hours a day—an hour on the way to work, an hour to back—under just this burden. There are subtler effects as well. For example, the congestion creates confusion for pedestrians, and so much noise that people cannot carry on conversations on the sidewalks in normal tones of voice.

Congestion, without much more massive roadworks than yet seen, seems bound to increase. In Great Britain, a small, crowded island, there were fewer than 5 million vehicles in 1952, about half of them private cars; in 1962, there were 6 1/2 million cars, 10 1/2 million vehicles all told. The prospect, which British officials considered had to be allowed for, since it could not be staved off by a democratic government, was that the number of vehicles might rise over 40 million by the year 2010. At that figure, the number would reach a saturation level, though only in the sense that with that number, every family in the country would have as many cars as it wanted by American standards, and vehicles would multiply thereafter only as population increased. Long before 2010 will not Britain, which with "clean-air" legislation has just about eliminated the old coal-fired fogs that it was once notorious for, have American standards of smog to cope with, too? It is not just a Los Angeles standard: the same junk is in the air over Denver and Boston.

## B: Effects of Products upon the Environment

*[Leaving aesthetic considerations to be brought up regarding the environment only after separating out public health problems, I said that such considerations were more controversial. I do not think they are hopelessly controversial. Controversial or not, they cannot be dismissed as unimportant. Our chances for expanding happiness depend on having a favorable physical environment. This connection suffices to make the impact of products upon the environment, when it is substantial, a matter of moral importance.]*

### TOO MUCH GARBAGE: TESTIMONY FOR THE UNIFORMED SANITATIONMEN*

*[Congressman Brademas was in the chair at the beginning of the eighth day of the hearings on the Environmental Education Act of 1970, in New York City, 11 April 1970.]*

*Excerpted from the minutes of the hearings as reprinted by the Social Science Education Consortium, Inc. and The ERIC Clearing House for Social Studies/Social Science Education in *The Environmental Problem* (Boulder, Colo., 1971), pp. 108–110.

INTRODUCTION OF JOHN DeLURY, PRESIDENT, THE UNIFORMED
SANITATIONMEN'S ASSOCIATION

Mr. Brademas. Our first witness this morning is Mr. John DeLury, president
of the Sanitationmen's Association. I will call on Mr. Scheuer at this point.

Mr. Scheuer. I want to thank Mr. DeLury for coming here today. Mr.
DeLury is one of the men in New York City who have perhaps critical
responsibility for our urban environment, how the city looks and feels, and
how it relates to the individual.

He is a man of enormous responsibility. He is a man who works under
tremendous pressure for the thousands of men whom he represents in the
top policymaking activities in which he is engaged. I think it is an indication
of his civic concern and tremendous involvement as a civic leader in every
aspect of the welfare of New York City that he has chosen to come out here
today.

So I want to thank him and welcome him and also thank the very
impressive group of delegates from his union whom he has brought along
to share the privilege of listening to him this morning.

So thank you very much, Mr. DeLury, for coming.

Mr. DeLury. Thank you for your kind words, Jim.

Mr. Chairman, on behalf of the 10,500 members of the Uniformed
Sanitationmen's Association, I strongly support H.R. 14753, and urge its
immediate adoption.

It seems as if America is waking up to the damage being done everywhere—to the air, water, and soil. I hope that this new interest will be
sustained—that it will not be a passing fad for the students, the media, and
politicians. I am disturbed by the effort to find scapegoats, one-shot cures,
and sure-shot gimmicks. But that won't clean up our physical environment.
It will only add to the pollution in the air.

The faddists can always find another fad, but we sanitation men, the
practical ecologists of the city streets, must stay with the almost impossible
job of striving to keep the capital city of the world clean.

I have endorsed H.R. 14753 because it points to a crying need—the need
to educate people—and because it provides the money to educate in this
specific area.

THE URBAN PRIORITY

I have endorsed H.R. 14753 on the assumption that money for the required
educational programs will be available in the first instance to the cities of our
country.

The cities are where the people are.

The cities are where the air pollution is.

The cities are where the congestion, slums, rats, vermin, dirt and decay
are.

New York City, the city I know best, cannot now cope with the pollution
of its streets and its garbage problem, in spite of its budgetary allocation.

Yes, additional funds for additional manpower and equipment are clearly necessary. And yet without an educated citizenry more money won't buy the needed results.

Our city is a polluted city. And pollution of our streets is a lasting impression with which visitors leave. Is this inevitable? Is it a necessary byproduct of our size, density and congestion? Almost eight million human beings live here. They occupy 742,582 residential dwellings. Daily they are joined by another two million people coming from the suburban bedrooms around the city to make their living here. Two million automobiles find their way into Manhattan each day.

This population living, working, and consuming here, generates more than 10,000 tons of garbage a day. They abandon 60,000 cars on our streets which they no longer want. Our 6,000 miles of streets are, for many, their litter baskets and garbage cans.

How does the city cope? What does the administration do to prevent the people from choking on their own swill and being asphyxiated by the gas fumes of their own cars?

$353 million is the cost. That's the current annual budget for the Environmental Protection Administration. More than half that amount goes for sanitation services. That makes possible the daily employment of 14,000 people, of whom 10,500 are sanitationmen. They are the men who go into the 6,000 miles of streets. They are the men who go to the doors of each of the 742,582 dwellings. They are the ones who collect the 10,000 tons of garbage a day and they clean the 12,000 curb-miles in the city.

They use 3,047 trucks of all types. The cost of this equipment is $60 million.

They dispose of this waste in eight huge incinerators, four landfills, and eight marine stations, using cranes, bulldozers, 40-yard trucks, conveyors, barges, and tugs whose costs exceed $30 million.

That's the city's effort. In addition, another 2,500 tons of garbage, waste, and construction debris collected privately are disposed of by the city each day.

The end is not in sight. Each year sees an escalation in waste generation of nine percent. And this is the situation throughout the country. A leading business magazine recently estimated the cost of waste removal to be $5 billion a year nationally, with a cost increase of 20 percent a year.

(*Forbes* magazine, Jan. 15, 1970, page 18.)

ANTI-LITTER EDUCATION

Yes—more money is needed from all sources—local, state, and federal. More capital equipment is required, but in addition, the people have a role; they can and have to help. H.R. 14753 can provide the means of educating people so they will help.

People, not some impersonal corporation, are the street litterers. People abandon their cars and scatter garbage on the city streets. If this pollution can be curbed at the source, then our city will be cleaner and the nation's cities will be cleaner.

Education must begin in the schools with the kids. The adults must be reached through television, radio, and the press. There must be booklets, clean-up drives, stay-clean drives. No one-shot gimmicks, but sustained effort and constant education are needed.

H.R. 14753 can mark the beginning of this education and re-education until finally we develop pride of neighborhood and we see dignity in cleanliness.

One final thought. This type of education is also needed with those who supply our daily needs. Much has already been written about the responsibilities of the utility companies and the oil companies. I need not develop this point further. But our newspapers, a primary source of education, are ironically enough in the forefront of those who tax our public resources.

Take our Sunday papers in New York as an instance. The table which follows shows the cost of removing only two Sunday papers—the *Times* and the *News*. That costs the city a staggering $13,260,000—or 7.8 percent of our total sanitation budget.

I am not suggesting that the *Times* and *News* not publish Sunday editions. That would be like saying religion has to go. I am suggesting that those who contribute to the burdens should pay the costs, at least in part.

Mr. Chairman, there are no total answers. We must seek and find partial ones. Your bill is a partial answer with profound consequences. That's why I urge its passage.

If there is anything we can do, to insure that end, it will be done. [Applause.]

WHEN GARBAGE BECAME IMPORTANT

Mr. Brademas. Thank you, Mr. DeLury, for a most useful statement. I am particularly impressed by your characterization of the sanitationmen as the practical ecologists of the city streets. It is a very telling phrase.

Let me ask you this question. What can you tell us about what kind of efforts are made in the city of New York to provide education in your elementary and secondary schools about pollution control, natural resources conservation and environmental problems, generally?

Mr. DeLury. Nothing at the present time. About six years ago, we had in the Department of Sanitation a unit of professional sanitationmen and officers to go into the school and talk to the children. That has been eliminated. We had motion pictures to show the children in the schools. That's all gone by the board. Nothing is being done.

Garbage was not important in this town, Mr. Chairman, until we had a strike in February 1968 and then all of a sudden everyone realized the impact of garbage on the community and from that time they have been getting to realize that sanitation is a primary function of the Department of Sanitation.

It may amaze you. Ten years ago we had 6,000 men who went out into the streets manually to sweep and clean the streets. We have less than 400. Included in that 400 are those who operate the power broom.

Now a power mechanical broom in New York City is like me needing an additional head. You can't get to the curb to clean it because New York City is the largest garage in the world, parking on both sides of the street, double parking and triple parking. We can't clean it with mechanical equipment.

What we actually need—and I have been saying this again and again—is for men to be out mechanically with the broom and with that pushwagon we have to get in and clean it.

And another thing we used to do that we no longer do: Where it's a lot of heavy debris that you can't get in and sweep it out, we used to hand-flush it—come with a hose and flush under it and force it out so we could get that. All of these things have disappeared.

Mr. Scheuer. You can do the hand-flush under the parked cars?

Mr. DeLury. Yes, sir.

Mr. Brademas. I would hope, Mr. DeLury, at least in the light of the extraordinary amount of money that must be spent in a great city like this—that must be spent for removal of garbage and refuse—that at least in time one of the great values in the kind of environmental education program that we contemplate in this bill would be that you would reduce the cost to the city of collecting the garbage, because you would, as you have already suggested, educate the citizenry to practices that would be far less demanding on the city's resources.

## GARBAGE DISPOSAL: HOW AND WHERE?

Mr. DeLury. Mr. Chairman, it must get more expensive. Although it is not within the scope of this subcommittee, our major problem is our union says three years—the city says five years—you are in a congressional district here—in San Francisco, Philadelphia, a year and a half or two years.

Where are we going to put it in five years?

I hear you saying, 10, 20, 30 years ahead. We don't have the time.

Where are we going to put it, assuming we can collect it in the street, all the garbage that's vomited out? Where are we going to take it? Put it to sea?

Mr. Reid. If the chairman would yield.

Mr. DeLury. Westchester has a problem, too, Mr. Congressman.

Mr. Reid. A kind of serious one. I wanted to ask you about two specific suggestions ecologists are very interested in. One is [about] the recycling and utilization of certain material after processing, such as is being done in Israel.

The other question I wanted to ask you is: What are the possibilities of compacting garbage with the new techniques? I gather you have even got a home compacting unit at this point. I don't know the cost.

Mr. DeLury. I don't know the cost either. They have tried it throughout the world. The only place where I know they do anything with it is in Japan and they construct homes with the packages.

I know that part of your Department of Health, Education, and Welfare—I have met with them and they were suggesting that they compact it, take it out into the middle of the ocean and drop it.

But we are thinking of a total picture and thinking in time, and I am going with you, 10, 20, 30, 40, and 50 years. The ocean is fillable.

There is only way to destroy garbage and that's by proper incineration with high B.t.u. unit of heat that will completely dispose of it at 3,200°, 3,300°, 3,400° of heat.

All of these gimmicks I have heard since I have had the honor of representing this union, even to making wood alcohol out of the garbage, even to taking paper back and reclaiming paper, reprocessing paper. It all failed, it all fell by the roadside.

Take all the abandoned cars. I am talking about 60,000 cars we took off the roads, off the streets of New York City last year, and the next year it will be 80,000.

Mr. Reid. What suggestions do you have Mr. DeLury—because I think you made a very thoughtful statement here—to answer your own question of where do we put it? What new techniques were brought in which would be helpful?

Mr. DeLury. Modern incinerators such as they have in Scotland. I believe they have a plant in Germany, and this is only one way.

Mr. Reid. This is the high temperature?

Mr. DeLury. Right.

ANTI-INCINERATION PRESSURES

Now, you have a major problem there. There isn't a politician in New York City that is going to stand up to the pressures that's brought upon him by his local constituency when they say, "Let's put a site here."

Jim, up in Hunts Point when they wanted to put a marine disposal unit there or incinerator, the community rebelled.

Where are we going to put it? They will not allow it in any part of their areas and, politically people being as they are—and I can't blame them for it—they have to be re-elected and they are not going to fly in the face of their local constituents.

This problem must be handled by Washington, the federal government, because it is harder to get out a man that's elected by 50 states than a man that's elected in a local election like New York City, White Plains, or Westchester.

Mr. Reid. Of the amount of garbage you mentioned that you collect— 10,000 tons plus the 2,000 collected privately—how much of that is incinerated and how much of it has to be placed in some form of landfill or taken out to the ocean?

Mr. DeLury. Six thousand tons per day goes into the incinerator of which 2,000 to 2,500 reverts back to what we call residue, the unburnable, and [is] taken to landfills or waterfront disposal places and taken out and dumped.

Sixty percent that's collected goes to the incinerator, of which 35 percent or more then reverts back to the landfills and the waterfront disposal places. . . .

Mr. Brademas. Thank you very much, Mr. DeLury, for your support.

\*    \*    \*

## TOO MANY AUTOMOBILES (AGAIN)

The adverse aesthetic effects of masses of automobiles on the environment have inevitably already been suggested. When that blanket of smog becomes visible over Los Angeles, not only does the air smell worse to people living under it. People (millions of people) living on the plains to the south can no longer see anything of the snow-capped mountains behind Los Angeles except their peaks. The rest is covered by the smog.

There are some good effects on the environment that must be credited to the automobile. Streets and roads, which, especially in the country, used to be mostly dirt tracks, very dusty when they were not impassable bogs of mud, are now, built to accommodate automobiles, much smoother and cleaner. Moreover, they permit comfortable access to country scenes that could not easily be visited in former days. In that respect, automobiles and roads have made the good things in the environment more available.

On the other hand, those same roads have eaten up a good deal of land in the country, as well as overwhelmed some urban neighbourhoods and pedestrian amenities downtown. More land—some of it, as in southern Ontario, prime arable land in a country with little such land to spare—has been built over for miles and miles by the sprawling suburban developments that the automobile and the network of good roads have made possible. (By contrast, suburbs built up in the railroad age tended to cluster within walking distance of the stations.) Finally, one might mention the effects on the environment of having to supply automobiles with petroleum products. The recurrent spills from oil tankers run aground and from oil wells drilled at sea are instances.

## TOO MANY AEROSOL CANS

Aerosol cans, when they are produced and after use discarded in great numbers, present in common with a great many other products of modern industry a problem about disposal. Where is all the junk to be put, especially when it does not rapidly decay through biological processes? Otherwise, it would seem a matter of indifference whether people buy shaving cream or deodorants or dessert topping in an aerosol can or not. Except for one startling aggregative and cumulative effect: the tiny amounts of the gas propellant (Freon) released into the atmosphere from single cans may build up with widespread use into enough gas, scientists have feared, to begin disintegrating the ozone layer that shields the earth from the full impact of the sun and its ultra-violet rays. The scientists' apprehension may, of course, have been exaggerated; but if there is any risk to the ozone layer at all, would it be entirely reassuring, and a license for business as usual, to be told that it is just a small risk (say, one in one hundred)? The apprehension has been responded to by changing to other gases for propellants; in the United States, Freon has been banned from such use since 1979. Evidently it has been feasible to do this without much raising the costs of aerosol packaging, though the substituted propellants have their own drawbacks (flammability, for one thing). What would the manufacturers of aerosols have done if the only alternative to risky propellants had been prohibitively expensive?

## C: Effects of Products on Culture

*[TV is the most obvious, spectacular, and impressive example of a product that is capable of changing both the way people live and what they think about. Again, good effects must be balanced against bad ones. Consider, for example, how much better watching even a trivial drama may be for someone—a shut-in, for example, without the habit of reading—who would otherwise be gaping vacantly at space. Moreover, not all of the dramas are trivial. Besides a number of great plays, operas, concerts, and ballet performances, there are some good programs about science and current events; and the news and sports coverage has advantages unique to the medium, though the news coverage in particular is often superficial. It is hardly fair to judge TV by the soap operas, the quiz shows, and the Saturday morning cartoons.*

*I shall begin with critical views of TV, however, and move on to the description of an alternative to commercial TV networks that might make the best of the medium. Then I shall bring forward some generalized criticisms of the consumer culture that commercial TV fosters and preys upon.]*

### FOUR ARGUMENTS FOR THE ELIMINATION OF TELEVISION*

---

*[You will have to look up the impassioned book with this title (New York, 1978) by Jerry Mander, a somewhat eccentric advertising man, to see how he elaborates the four arguments. I give them here as he offers them before he begins elaborating.]*

ARGUMENT ONE: THE MEDIATION OF EXPERIENCE

As humans have moved into totally artificial environments, our direct contact with and knowledge of the planet has been snapped. Disconnected, like astronauts floating in space, we cannot know up from down or truth from fiction. Conditions are appropriate for the implantation of arbitrary realities.

Television is one recent example of this, a serious one, since it greatly accelerates [aggravates?] the problem.

### ARGUMENT TWO: THE COLONIZATION OF EXPERIENCE

It is no accident that television has been dominated by a handful of corporate powers. Neither is it coincidental that television has been used to re-create human beings into a new form that matches the artificial, commercial environment. A conspiracy of technological and economic factors made this inevitable and continue to.

### ARGUMENT THREE: EFFECTS OF TELEVISION ON THE HUMAN BEING

Television technology produces neurophysiological responses in the people who watch it. It may create illness, it certainly produces confusion and submission to external imagery. Taken together, the effects amount to conditioning for automatic control.

### ARGUMENT FOUR: THE INHERENT BIASES OF TELEVISION

Along with the venality of its controllers, the technology of television predetermines the boundaries of its content. Some information can be conveyed completely, some partially, some not at all. The most effective telecommunications are the gross, simplified linear messages and programs which conveniently fit the purposes of the medium's commercial controllers. Television's highest potential is advertising. This cannot be changed. The bias is inherent in the technology.

Some of these arguments are more extravagant than others; and some parts of each argument may well seem exaggerated. A sensible response to the arguments should be to try to state for each of them an entirely sober, rigorously defensible revised version. On some points—for example, the suggestion that television causes neurological illness—only experts would be able to carry this project through. Yet most of the points that Mander brings up can be discussed on the basis of general knoweldge by people familar with TV.

It helps, on one of these points—the assertion that television has created a new form of human being—to know that Mander has in mind making our personalities "competitive, aggressive, mentally fast, charming and manipulative. These qualities succeed in today's world and offer survival and some measure of satisfaction within the cycle of work-consume, work-consume, work-consume" (p. 123). However, advertising, at its most potent with TV, "intervenes between people and their needs, *separates* them from direct fulfillment and urges them to believe that satisfaction can be obtained only through commodities" (p. 127).

Without specifically laying blame on TV, a more cautious writer takes much the same view:

It is at least arguable that the continual, almost continuous, propagation of messages the point of which is that a given product will bring about some complex and lasting life joy, or cancel some central despair, has what one might call a *cognitive* opportunity cost. It may eventually block, for many people, the very perception of alternative possibilities, such as that many kinds of salvation don't come from outside, or if they do, don't come from things, or if they do come from things, don't come from marketable or marketed things. . . . Thus there may be in this country (and increasingly in the world) a systematic misattribution of power among the various alternative modes of cause and vocabularies of effect. It may begin to appear to many people that happiness comes, and comes only, from things you can buy. [Moreover, modern advertising may be] modifying people to fit goods, rather than the other way around. By 'casting' the goods as having a certain causative relationship to highly desirable self-identities of people, to the extent that the people accept the alleged causation they themselves are altercast as people who are indeed causally manipulated by goods in just such a way. [Arthur A. Leff, *Swindling and Selling* (New York, 1976), pp. 172–173]

# A BRITISH VIEW OF TV: THE PILKINGTON REPORT*

*[In 1960, a committee on broadcasting appointed by the British government and chaired by Sir Harry Pilkington discussed TV from a point of view familiar with TV and radio carried on by a public authority rather than under commercial auspices. The committee made the following assertions in its report.]*

"By its nature, broadcasting must be in a constant and sensitive relationship with the moral condition of society. Broadcasters are, and must be, involved; this gives them a responsibility they cannot evade. (p. 15)

"It seems to us that 'to give the public what it wants' is a misleading phrase: misleading because as commonly used it has the appearance of an appeal to democratic principle but the appearance is deceptive. It is in fact patronising and arrogant, in that it claims to know what the public is, but defines it as no more than the mass audience; and in that it claims to know what it wants, but limits its choice to the average of experience. In this sense we reject it utterly. If there is a sense in which it should be used, it is this: what the public wants and what it has the right to get is the freedom to choose from the widest possible range of programme matter. Anything less than that is deprivation.

"The alternative is often presented as this: that the broadcaster should 'give the public what he thinks is good for it.' This philosophy, too, we reject as patronising and arrogant. But it . . . is not the only alternative. . . . There is an area of possibility between the two; and it is within this area that the choice lies. The broadcasting authorities have certainly a duty to keep sensitively aware of the public's tastes and attitudes as they now are and in all their variety; and to care about them. But if they do more than that, this is not to give the public 'what someone thinks is good for it.' It is to respect the public's right to choose from the widest possible range of subject matter and

*As excerpted by Robert J. Blakely, *The People's Instrument* (Washington, D.C., 1971), pp. 12–13. Reprinted here by permission of Her Majesty's Stationery Office.

so to enlarge worthwhile experience. Because, in principle, the possible range of subject matter is inexhaustible, all of it can never be presented, nor can the public know what the range is. So, the broadcaster must explore it, and choose from it first. This might be called 'giving a lead': but it is not the lead of the autocratic or arrogant. It is the proper exercise of responsibility by public authorities duly constituted as trustees for the public interest." (p. 117–18)

"Television has been called a mirror of society: but the metaphor, though striking, wholly misses the major issue of the responsibility of the . . . broadcasting authorities. For, if we consider the first aspect of this responsibility, what is the mirror to relfect? Is it to reflect the best or the worst in us? One cannot escape the question by saying that it must do both; one must ask then whether it is to present the best and the worst with complete indifference and without comment. And if the answer is that such passivity is unthinkable, that in showing the best and the worst television must show them for what they are, then an active choice has been made. This is not only to show the best in our society but to show also the worst so that it will be recognized for what it is. That this choice must be made emphasises the main flaw in the comparison. Television does not, and cannot, merely reflect the moral standards of society. It must affect them either by changing or by reinforcing them." (p. 19)

## MICHEL BOSQUET, "THE COMMODITY CULTURE: IS PROSPERITY AND ILLUSION?"*

*[André Gorz (Michel Bosquet), a French writer of the Left, directly challenges the notion that people are better off with more goods to consume.]*

Greater consumption—that is, access to greater quantities of consumer goods—does not necessarily mean an improvement. It can mean simply that one now has to pay for what used to be free, or that one has to pay more (in real money) to compensate for a general deterioration of the environment. Are city-dwellers living better because they 'consume' an increasing quantity of public and private transport in daily commuting between their places of work and their increasingly remote dormitory suburbs? Are they living better because they now buy linen every five or six years to replace what in earlier times would have lasted a generation or more? Because they buy more so-called mineral water as the taste of tap water grows nastier? Because they burn more fuel to heat their cheaply insulated modern housing? Are they less poor because instead of frequenting the corner cafe and the local cinema—both dying institutions—they

---

*From Michel Bosquet, *Capitalism in Crisis and Everyday Life,* translation by John Howe, (Hassocks, Sussex, 1977), pp. 167–68. Copyright 1977. Reprinted by permission of Harvester Press Ltd. and Humanities Press Inc., New Jersey 07716.

spend their money on TV sets and cars through which they can seek imaginary, solitary escape from their concrete desert? . . .

I know, I know. Household equipment has been democratised. Labour-saving devices are not the elite luxuries they were forty years ago. The same thing applies to consumption of meat, canned food, cars, holidays. . . . Does it follow that manual workers, say, are less poor now than they used to be? Ask the older workers. They will tell you that during their paid fortnight in 1936 a husband and wife could go on a cycling holiday, eat and sleep in a hotel for the two weeks and return home with money in hand. To pay for their present-day motoring holiday, the couple have to work and save; there is no time for cooking or shopping so they have to have a fridge, canned food, quick grilled meals, and they have to work overtime to pay for it all. Is this a better life? Is this the better 'quality of life' brought by labour-saving devices?

> Letter from a woman reader of *France Nouvelle:* Primarily it's a question of leisure, of time for living . . . when we struggle for a working day of five or six hours, electric gadgets can be consigned to the museum. . . . There's nothing difficult about a family wash for four people if you get home at 4 p.m. every day. And what's so terrible about eight plates and the pots and pans, when everyone in the family takes his turn at washing up?

Some people will still argue that the fact that today's workers possess luxury consumer goods once available only to the bourgeoisie means that they are 'less poor'. This is the moment to ask: less poor than whom? Indians? Poor Algerians? The workers of half a century ago? The comparison is wholly abstract: poverty is not an objective, measurable datum like destitution or undernourishment. It resides in *difference*, inequality, the impossibility of reaching what society defines as 'good', exclusion from the dominant mode of life—that of the most prosperous 20 percent of the population, who set the tone for everyone with privileged, ostentatious consumption. In a society where everyone is poor, there are no poor. What makes one poor is having, and being, little by the standards of the so-ciocultural norm which shapes and stimulates our desires.

In Peru, the poor walk barefoot. In China, they do not own bicycles. In France, the poor cannot raise credit for a car. In the 1930s you were poor if you could not afford a wireless; in the sixties if you had to do without TV; now the seventies are here people without *colour* TV feel a bit shabby.

\*   \*   \*

*Comment:*

# ITEM-BY-ITEM CONTROL FOR THE PROTECTION OF CULTURE

Bosquet attributes the harmful effects that he describes to the capitalistic system and argues that they cannot be avoided without undoing the system. Is this entirely clear? Can't we imagine how without changing the fundamental arrangements of the system we could still control, item by item, this product or that, when it poses a grave danger to culture? Could we not, continuing under capitalism, have had the blessings of TV and the automobile without the drawbacks?

We can certainly imagine how things could have been different. TV, on the Public Broadcasting Network in the United States, under the BBC and to a lesser extent under CBC—the Canadian Broadcasting Corporation—is free of advertising for junk food and free of other aggravations of the evils of printed advertising. It is relatively free, too, of junk programs. Were TV wholly uncommercial, it could reduce the amount of programming to the time that could actually be filled with good programs or to a time per week consistent with robust family lives and friendships—whichever time was shorter. Conceivably, except for an hour of news and information every day and one or two hours of educational programs, it could normally be shut down during the week and broadcast six hours on Saturday and six on Sunday.

As for the automobile, suppose that automobiles were generally available to private citizens, except for farmers, only on a rental basis for a limit of forty days a year per household; and there were no long-distance trucks. Our cities, in ease of use by pedestrians and cyclists and public-transit passengers, would be a great deal more congenial; and most of the other troubles caused by automobile would be dramatically reduced.

Were the advantages of these imagined policies not to be appreciated beforehand? Hindsight, of course, is more accurate than foresight; and no one could have predicted exactly what the consequences of commercialized TV and free (indeed, subsidized) proliferation of the automobile would have been. However, it was possible at least by the 1920s and the 1930s to estimate from projected increases in car-ownership the dimensions of the dangers. Some such estimates were actually in circulation, for example, for writers like Lewis Mumford. The dangers posed by TV were perhaps subtler and harder to predict; but some apprehension of the dangers may be presumed to have been at the bottom of the original decision in Britain to assign broadcasting to a public corporation.

Even with reasonable predictions before them, it is true that politicians work within a short-term horizon, established first by their desire to be re-elected five, four, or even two years hence (sometimes less than a year) and second by the indifference of the public to remote events. The politicians' record is not a good one. Even in Britain, the success of the policy of broadcasting through the BBC has been undermined by the introduction of commercial TV and commercial radio, which tend to operate on the same low level as their counterparts in the United States and Canada. Moreover, Britain—with even more to lose, in a small country packed with irreplaceable historical relics—has had no more success than other countries in controlling the automobile.

Yet the problem of mobilizing political support for sensible long-turn precautions is not insoluble. What is required are short-term efforts by people taking a long view; and there are such people—some in the bureaucracy, some in universities, some in journalism. Politicians could (if they wished) cite predictions by these people in appealing to the long-run interests of members of the public, which extend in their own persons maybe twenty-five years ahead and through their children and grandchildren fifty or more. Establishing highly visible agencies to develop long-term policies is a practical short-term policy. We probably cannot deal in a morally adequate way with the claims even of the nearest future generations without such agencies.

What are the moral lessons for business? Mainly, perhaps, that people in business should not stand in the way of government planning in this connection and should be prepared to forego some opportunities for short-term private profits. Inevitably, some of the planning will be too restrictive, suppressing opportunities that would have turned out harmless; but—in revenge, comme l'on dit en français—equally inevitably, some of the planning will be too lax, and allow opportunities that turn out disastrous. The firms that profit from these opportunities may then be excused, provided that they did not knowingly subvert effective planning. Unfortunately, some very substantial profits are at stake.

CHAPTER **17**

# The Character of Technology

*Introductory Comment:*

## NO PROBLEMS TOO BIG FOR
## MITIGATING SCHEMES

The problems that we have taken up about the aggregative and cumulative effects of advertising and of various sorts of products soar out of the hands of individual people in business, as well as of individual students and professors. One despairs of trying to grasp them. What can one do about them anyway? This reaction is natural and understandable; yet I think that it should be overcome. We can organize to do something about the problems; we have organizations already in being that are capable of doing something about them. Even individually, as citizens and as participants in the world of business, we can do something helpful. We can support the adoption of enlightened policies; we can refrain from subverting, before their adoption and afterwards, the aims that enlightened policies would pursue.

Something can be done by individuals even about the yet more grandiose problems that we are now going to survey, arising from the aggregative and cumulative effects of the technology with which the products of modern industry are manufactured. One problem is the depletion to the point of exhaustion or extermination of natural resources. Surely individual firms—and individual persons who have some influence on the decisions of those firms or some responsibility for giving them effect—can do something about such things. They can introduce what I shall call "mitigating schemes." If the specific resource at stake were (genuine) white pine, *Pinus strobus*, these schemes might range from furniture companies finding substitutes for white pine in uses where its distinctive qualities are less important to lumber companies cutting down stands of white pine no faster than the stands can be regenerated. The price system might add to the attractions of these schemes (for example, by driving up the price of white pine as the wood becomes scarcer, though left to itself the price system might not raise the price high enough to preserve the resource). The schemes would not be practical for any firm if they were not consistent with making profits. Nevertheless, some willingness to forego certain short-run profits for less certain profits in the long-run may be required, and if it is forthcoming, represent a moral contribution.

It is a moral contribution even if one cannot easily say what the limits of moral obligation are in these connections. The effects of present technology are felt the world over; and they will be felt by future generations. Received moralities have not (except in some counsels of perfection) given much attention to obligations extending to the whole of the world population or to people in generations yet unborn. Even here, however, refraining from doing irreparable harm is one thing; assisting others to be as well off as ourselves is another. The first can be an effective basis for moral appeals when the latter far outruns what we are prepared to do. Difficulties of reaching agreement on the latter project should not be used to justify indifference or procrastination in the former one.

I shall present issues that arise about the aggregative and cumulative effects of technology in four connections: culture; the environment; world resources; and public health. The third is the only one in which the worldwide scope of the issues is referred to in a heading; but it is to be understood that the others, too, all have world dimensions. In all four connections the issues have obvious implications for future generations.

## A: Effects of Technology on Culture

This topic is an intricate and far-reaching one, but I have so much material to present elsewhere that I shall confine myself here to quoting the following short passage from Robert L. Heilbroner's *An Inquiry into the Human Prospect.** It conveys, without mentioning the complex assemblies of machines to whose inexorable operation our social life is subordinated, how the machines shape our society and our lives.

> [I]ndustrial civilization achieves its economic success by imposing common values on both its capitalist and socialist variants. There is the value of the self-evident importance of efficiency, with its tendency to subordinate the optimum human scale of things to the optimum technical scale. There is the value of the need to "tame" the environment, with its consequence of an unthinking pillage of nature. There is the value of the priority of production itself, visible in the

*New York: W. W. Norton & Company, Inc., 1974, p. 77. Reprinted by permission of W. W. Norton & Company, Inc.

care both systems lavish on technical virtuosity and the indifference with which both look upon the aesthetic aspects of life. All these values manifest themselves throughout bourgeois and "socialist" styles of life, both lived by the clock, organized by the factory or office, obsessed with material achievements, attuned to highly quantitative modes of thought—in a word, by styles of life that, in contrast with non-industrial civilizations, seem dazzlingly rich in every dimension except that of the cultivation of the human person. The malaise that I believe flickers within our consciousness thus seems to afflict industrial socialist as well as capitalist societies, because it is a malady ultimately rooted in the "imperatives" of a common mode of production.

## B: Effects of Technology on the Environment

*[The materials regarding world resources and public health will have to do with the environment, too, inevitably. It seems useful, however, to show how the issues build up from matters of aesthetic concern and domestic national policy to questions about depriving people abroad of the means of a good life, even of an adequate one; and build up, too, on another line, into hair-raising dangers to health.]*

### NATURAL BEAUTY THREATENED BY ELECTRIC POWER*

---

*[We dip again into the congressional hearings on the Environmental Education Act of 1970.*

*Sive's article, originally published in the Journal published by the Division of Higher Education, United Church Board for Homeland Ministries, vol. 8, no. 4 (January–February 1970), was included in its entirety in the committee's minutes. I quote just part of it.]*

INTRODUCTION OF DAVID SIVE, ATTORNEY, SIERRA CLUB

Mr. Brademas. The Chair recognizes Congressman Scheuer to present our next witness.

Mr. Scheuer. It is a great pleasure for me to recognize perhaps the nation's most distinguished environmental lawyer, David Sive. I want particularly to welcome Walter and Teddy Sive who have accompanied their dad and constitute, I know, his real brain trust.

I would ask for your unanimous consent for an article by Mr. Sive, entitled "The Law and the Land" to be printed in its entirety before his oral testimony.

---

*Excerpted from the minutes of the hearings as reprinted by the Social Science Education Consortium, Inc., and the ERIC Clearing House for Social Studies/Social Science Education in *The Environmental Problem* (Boulder, Colo., 1971), pp. 110–115.

Mr. Brademas. Without objection, it will be included. (The article mentioned above follows:)* . . .

[NOVELTY OF ISSUES]

What are the problems of the conservationists in court other than the basic inequality of financial resources? One is the sheer novelty of some of the issues to be tried before the courts or administrative agencies. In an increasing number of cases, starting with that of the proposed Consolidated Edison power plant at Storm King Mountain (the Scenic Hudson case), the issue is beauty versus utility. The two must be weighed under a legal formula provided by a statute or a court ruling which provides that the protection of natural beauty is to be given due consideration.

In the Scenic Hudson case, the basic statutory formula is in the Federal Power Act governing the grant or denial of the application which requires that the project:

> "be such as in the judgment of the commission will be best adapted to a comprehensive plan for improving or developing a waterway or waterways for the use or benefit of interstate or foreign commerce, for the improvement and utilization of water power development, and for other beneficial public uses, including recreational purposes.

The place of beauty in a "comprehensive plan" was stated in a now-historical sentence in the opinion of the Court of Appeals which reversed the original grant of a license to construct the Storm King Project. After pointing out the errors of the Commission in its granting the license to Consolidated Edison, and requiring new proceedings in order to receive additional evidence, the Court described the fundamental questions which the renewed hearings were to examine. They must, it said:

> include as a basic concern the preservation of natural beauty and of national historic shrines, keeping in mind that, in our affluent society, the cost of a project is only one of several factors to be considered.

The intervenors opposed to the Project, primarily the Scenic Hudson Preservation Conference and the Sierra Club, relied upon this statement of principle of the beginning of the adoption of a different philosophy in our developing law of natural resources. Thoreau phrased it this way a century ago:

> Most of the luxuries and many of the so-called comforts of life, are not only not indispensable, but positive hindrances to the elevation of mankind.

While the society of Thoreau was not "affluent," ours certainly is, at least in that by applying to our social and economic organization some small fraction of the intelligence we apply to going to the moon, we can provide every person with all the necessities and some of the comforts of life.

---

*Excerpts from the article are reprinted here by permission of *Journal of Current Issues*, New York. [D.B.]

Beyond those necessities and "necessary" comforts, we must take a choice of goals, and perhaps the choice should at least sometimes be to elevate, rather than fatten, mankind. Scenic Hudson and the Sierra Club have interpreted the mandate of the Court of Appeals to require a sophisticated analysis of the nature and degrees of scenic beauty. Their position has been that scenic beauty can be objectively analyzed, and degrees of beauty stated.

ANALYZING DEGREE OF BEAUTY

Both Scenic Hudson and the Sierra Club did analyze the degree of beauty. They produced testimony of several experts on scenic beauty, including Professor Charles W. Eliot, II, of Harvard; Charles Callison, Exeuctive Vice President of the National Audubon Society; Professor Vincent Scully (History of Art), of Yale; and David Brower, Executive Director of the Sierra Club. All of them testified that Storm King and the Hudson at Storm King were not simply places of scenic beauty, but the supreme river scenery in eastern United States.

Mr. Callison called the Hudson at Storm King "the most beautiful stretch of river scenery in the United States." Professor Scully's description was perhaps the most lyrical. He described Storm King Mountain as follows:

> It rises like a brown bear out of the river, a dome of living granite, swelling with animal power. It is not picturesque in the softer sense of the word but awesome, a primitive bodiment of the energies of the earth. It makes the character of wild nature physically visible in monumental form. As such it strongly reminds me of some of the natural formations which mark sacred sites in Greece and signal the presence of the Gods. . . .

Each of the several experts classified the Hudson at Storm King as equal in scenic beauty and magnificance to many of our national parks.

The beauty of the mountain and the surrounding area has not been seriously disputed by the Company, although Con Edison has not accepted the conservationists' analysis of degrees of scenic beauty. The Company's principal point has been that the project would not mar the beauty of the mountain, because from most angles at most seasons of the year it would not be seen. The issue of the precise visibility of the project works was the subject of many hundreds of pages of conflicting testimony.

The claims of Scenic Hudson and the Sierra Club, that the construction of the project and of the attendant facilities would seriously damage the value of the mountain and the surrounding area as objects of natural beauty, are not based solely, however, upon the degree of visibility of the project works. They have raised an issue of the effect of the project upon the integrity of the mountain itself. This point, the "integrity of the mountain," was made in the testimony of another of the Sierra Club witnesses, Richard Pough. His point, essentially, was that the ultimate value of scenic beauty is its impression on and in the minds of the persons who perceive it.

Even though much of the project works may be camouflaged by paint, plantings, artificially roughened rock, and other devices, if those who perceive the mountain and the surrounding area understand that the mountain is subordinated to the project, the end result is appreciation and admiration of engineering works, and not of the works of the Creator of the mountain.

The point is summarized in the following extract from the Sierra Club's principal brief:

> It is the character and 'integrity of the Mountain' and the surrounding areas that must be borne in mind in determining the extent to which the Project, and all that goes with it, will mar the natural beauty of Storm King and its environment. If its meaning is changed, in the eyes of those who behold it, its supreme value as a preserver and embodiment of the spirit of . . . New York . . . . to a whole nation, particularly the vast millions in its greatest metropolitan area, is forever lost. In that event, no combination of orders of this Commission, funds of the Applicant, and skill of its eminent landscape architects, can be any more successful in putting the earth rocks and trees of Storm King back together again, than were 'all the king's horses and all the king's men' in the case of Humpty Dumpty. Painting concrete green cannot deceive its beholders into believing that it is the handkerchief of the Lord, or, if it can, this Commission should not, in the absence of some overwhelming economic necessity, direct such deception.

In increasing numbers of cases under the same or similar statutory and court criteria as in Storm King, courts will have to balance cost against beauty, to determine what really contributes to "the elevation of mankind." . . .

It is an interesting irony of history that in the Thirties and early Forties— the New Deal period—the persons and groups fighting for broad reviewability of administrative decisions were primarily right of center. They looked to the court to stem the tides of social and economic reform being effected by the National Labor Relations Board, the Securities and Exchange Commission, and other New Deal agencies. "Big government" was evil to those on the right; it was salvation to those on the left.

In large part, the struggles of the conservationists and environmentalists are now struggles against big government. Virtually every important project that would appropriate for a special use any resource which the conservationists seek to preserve, by representing what they hope is a large majority just awakening from silence, involves approval or actual construction by a government agency. Unless some mechanism exists for review by an agency of government whose orientation and training is general, conservationists feel that literally every river, mountain, plain, and city will be appropriated by the Federal Power Commission, the Army Corps of Engineers, the Atomic Energy Commission, or some other administrative agency whose purposes and *raison d'être* are parochial.

The Army Engineers' conviction that dams solve all problems—in modern times, if not in the days of Noah's troubles—has been documented. The Federal Power Commission's world is that of power. More kilowatts are, to them, synonymous with progress; and to oppose progress as defined by utility companies is to oppose the principles upon which our nation was founded.

Mr. Scheuer. Dave, it is a pleasure and a joy to have you here today. . . .

Mr. Sive. Turning to the problem of environmental education, I can go to as recently as 35 minutes ago where I passed along, coming here, Sickle-town Road in Rockland County, and there is the root of our environmental problem.

Here is a road that goes through a still unspoiled area of Rockland County in which I live. It would be the most lovely lane, lovely place for any person to live and take a walk along the land.

But what is it? It is a garbage dump—garbage dumped by individuals, by the town of Orangetown, by various persons who don't want to pay what we have to pay in Rockland County, to a private purveyor of garbage.

It is dumped, and we are not going to get to the root of our environmental problem by simply forcing more duties on people or court cases or other ways in which I would try to use my lawyer's arts.

We must change the ways people look at the land and the manner in which they live.

We must somehow convince people that roadsides and campgrounds and city streets are to be treated as their own living rooms, and this can only be done through educational programs of the nature of those which I think can come out of this legislation.

Now just to give you a few examples of the limitations of law and the imposition of duties. I think they are particularly important in connection with the key problem we have, which I think was alluded to by the gentleman that preceded me.

That is the basic problem as to whether we gear our national force and energy and our whole civilization toward simply a multiplication of goods and services, toward increasing the gross national product; and the most fundamental educational and political job we have in the environment is to direct ourselves toward something different from the simple multiplication of goods. It may seem as though this is what all of us conservationists say and perhaps a somewhat hackneyed and trite observation, but in this all that I do is go back to one of the gods and one of the founders of our environmental movement whom many of us are going back to for many other lessons these days, and that is Thoreau.

### THE RESPONSIBILITY OF PEOPLE TO THE LAND

Now if I may be somewhat romantic, let us say I would certainly believe that the function of your committee as well as that perhaps of all congressional committees is to promote the elevation of mankind, and I think we have now begun to learn that the elevation of mankind is not simply promoted by increasing the number of physical luxuries and the so-called comforts of life, and that indeed some of them may be positive hindrances to this elevation.

And this again can only be accomplished by educational programs which turn the minds of men and women and children to have a certain ethic and a certain feeling about land and resources and a certain reaction to the beauty of land.

And here perhaps one other observation which may seem somewhat basic and, again, somewhat romantic, I would like to make, now that we are concentrating a great deal on national goals and national aims, and we are also concentrating on the environment.

Well, I have long believed that there is a very definite relationship between what is within the land in terms of its resources and its natural beauty and the duty and responsibility of people who are in that land. And if our nation is one which is blessed with the greatest of resources and the greatest of natural wonders and the greatest areas of natural beauty, from the place where I once tried to lead Mr. Scheuer in late April in the center of the Adirondack wilderness to the Grand Canyon and the Smokey and Cascade Mountains, then certainly we have I think some higher duty to fashion some kind of ethic, some kind of principle by which we treat this land with these resources and combine that with the technical advancement and technical knowledge we have.

That is what I think this environment bill must do. It must change the minds and attitudes of people and, until we do that, much of what we may accomplish through laws and court decisions may be of little avail. Because it doesn't really do many of us much good to, let us say, save the face of Storm King Mountain, which is the object of a tremendous legal and litigation effort, and then right along the roadside at the base of Storm King Mountain simply look at the beer cans and the discarded garbage of that town. . . .

CONSUMER PRODUCTS VS. IRREPLACEABLE RESOURCES

Mr. Scheuer. Mr. Sive, I want to thank you for your marvelous testimony. I am only going to ask one question.

You gave us a very beautiful and moving quote from Thoreau. What do you think, as a leader in perhaps the environmental consumer movement, ought to be our education attack or political grass-roots attack on the kind of galloping GNP and consumerism you mentioned?

How do we convince the average housewife that when she buys an electric hair dryer or electric toothbrush, an electric carving knife—all of which I think would fit in with Thoreau's definition—that she is inevitably contributing to environmental pollution, since apparently there is no way of producing electric power, either through the fossil fuels, coal, oil, gas, or through atomic energy, that doesn't have a polluting fallout?

How do we convince the American family to perhaps abandon the idea of the third car and to use mass transportation?

How do we convince them to give up some of these cherished comforts and conveniences and do things in order to achieve the greater good, perhaps a greater level of total satisfactions of which they may not be consciously aware now?

Mr. Sive. Well, that really gives me the floor to make one suggestion which I have stated in several places and maybe is in part an answer to your question.

I think that one of the really needed things in this whole environmental movement, and the problem of gearing our production to our elevation, is a study by a body—and it may very well be the university groups and others who would be funded by this legislation—which would run through every consumer product we have and try to figure out how much does that take out of irreplaceable resources, how much does it consume and how much hardened product which cannot be put back into the earth and water does it take away and how much does it contribute toward what we ultimately seek.

Just to give an example, you mentioned electric appliances. I would say many electrical appliances even the greatest wilderness advocates use and want, and it may well be with the proper siting we can have most of the electricity we want and not irrevocably damage the environment.

But let us take aluminum soft drink cans. Is there any difference in the world toward our elevation or even our comfort between something that can be disposable and can be turned back into the earth and an aluminum can?

None.

Take the vast amount of paper we use. I think somehow we can cut down, maybe by changing our laws to restrict and discourage junk mail. What social progress we would achieve by that alone, getting rid of some of the mail and saving several thousand acres of pine forest.

If we can go through each and every product we use, from a toenail clipper to a box of Kleenex, and try to inventory those, then I think we can begin to convince people that you are not really going to lose much. . . .

THE ENVIRONMENTAL MOVEMENT AND THE POOR

There is one other problem related to this—a very basic one again—which troubles me very much and which may well be again the subject of study by groups that would be funded by this act, and that is the relationship of the environmental movement to the ghetto, to the inner city, to the groups of the population who have not achieved the affluence which enables us to turn to other things.

Mr. Scheuer. May I add, I want you to answer this question having in mind that some of us liberal congressmen have been criticized for our concern about the environment. We have been accused of copping out of the improved education struggle, improved civil rights struggle, improved urban life struggle.

How do we answer this? How do we convince the black and Puerto Rican Americans that they have as much a concern in this limited planet, this spaceship, as we do and that it isn't a cop-out but rather that it goes to the heart and core of their problem? . . .

Mr. Sive. There are two answers. One is a theory of mine which still has to be studied but still is a theory, that if we take the total of our sum of goods and services and we more equitably distribute them and we lop off a bit like the aluminum beer cans along the road which contribute nothing toward anybody's elevation, then I think there is sufficient to distribute to those who have not shared in the affluence.

I am convinced of that, although I am not an economist, and I would like people to study that.

Second, I think it is correct that generally speaking those groups of the population who have been fortunate enough, by simple historical accident, to perhaps have gone beyond the problem of getting out of the ghetto—and I can say here I would just go back one or two generations in my own family history—it is only physically and I think figuratively when you solve that problem of the day-to-day necessities, that you can turn to matters such as the environment and the preservation of natural beauty.

If that is so, then all the more valuable and necessary and urgent is the saving of this for those who have not yet done that, because if, as I am confident, within not too long a time there can be this greater justice in the distribution of goods and if 10, 20, or 30 years from now the Grand Canyon or the Adirondacks or Storm King Mountain—if that is then gone, then those who will only share in the affluence a few years from now if we really devote ourselves to it will never know it, and that, I think, would be the ultimate tragedy.

I think that is one of the answers to this problem of relating the environmental matters to groups of the population who still don't share as much as they should in our society's affluence. . . .

Mr. Brademas. You have been most helpful in your commentary and statement. Thank you very much.

Mr. Sive. Thank you very much, sir.

## CONSOLIDATED EDISON REPLIES*

---

*[Electric power plants are instances of technology. The power that they produce and that people consume bit by bit is a product. Once again we are dealing simultaneously with the aggregative and cumulative effects of products and of the technology of producing them. In this case, the picture is further complicated by the presence of other products—electrical appliances—whose more frequent and widespread use (in the past strongly promoted by firms in the power industry) implies greater consumption of power and hence greater impact upon the environment.]*

---

*Excerpted from the minutes of the hearings as reprinted by the Social Science Education Consortium, Inc., and The ERIC Clearing House for Social Studies/Social Science Education in *The Environmental Problem* (Boulder, Colo., 1971), pp. 143–148.

INTRODUCTION OF JOHN T. CONWAY, EXECUTIVE ASSISTANT TO
CHAIRMAN OF THE BOARD, CONSOLIDATED EDISON COMPANY OF
NEW YORK, INC.

Mr. Scheuer. We are very happy to have you here, Mr. John T. Conway, executive assistant to the chairman of the board of Consolidated Edison of New York.

Mr. Conway. Thank you, Mr. Chairman.

For the record I am John Conway, executive [assistant] to the chairman of the board of Con Edison, and former executive director of the Joint Committee on Atomic Energy, and if it please the committee I request that my statement and attachment be introduced into the record as if read.

Mr. Scheuer. There being no objection, so ordered. It will be introduced in the record at this point.

Mr. Conway. Yes, I thank you.

(Mr. Conway's prepared statement follows:)

STATEMENT OF JOHN T. CONWAY, EXECUTIVE ASSISTANT TO
CHAIRMAN OF THE BOARD, CONSOLIDATED EDISON COMPANY OF
NEW YORK, INC.

On behalf of Con Edison, I wish to say that we are in favor of this bill and its objectives. We agree with the statement of Congressman Scheuer that "many of our environmental problems are the results of ignorance" and believe it is desirable that the United States Commissioner of Education be authorized to establish educational programs to encourage understanding of policies and support of activities designed to enhance environmental quality and maintain ecological bonds, which is the stated purpose of H.R. 14753. . . .

As the electric utility company privileged to serve this area, Con Edison feels a heavy responsibility to meet the needs of the nine million persons residing within the 625 square mile area it services, at the lowest cost possible with a minimum impact on the environment. We are required by law to meet the demands for electricity placed upon us; demands which currently are growing at approximately 375,000 kilowatts per year.

Under present technology and technology foreseeable in the future, there is no way of producing large amounts of electricity required by modern society without some effect on the environment. It is important, however, that the adverse effects be kept to a minimum and Con Edison is dedicated to that objective. However, the problem of pollution is not only a problem of electric generation any more than it is solely a problem of any specific industry. In the final analysis, it is an individual problem since each of us in one way or another causes pollution of one sort or another. It is imperative if we are to be successful in cleaning up our environment that every individual in his daily life conscientiously conducts his activities in such a way as to cause a minimum impairment to the environment. If proper environmental education is made available to all Americans beginning at the primary school level and continuing on through secondary and higher learning, a major step forward will be made in securing the necessary cooperation of all citizens.

Con Edison has undertaken a program to inform the public of environmental actions it has taken in helping to improve the environment in the New York City area. . . .

We recognize, however, that a much broader educational program is necessary covering not only the electric utility industry, but all industry and all individuals. This type of educational program with the objectives set forth in H.R. 14753 cannot be accomplished by industry alone, but must get down into the very fabric of our educational system.

If we are to successfully solve the ever-increasing pollution problem brought on by modern society, there is no question but that we must all have an increasing awareness of our environment and man's ability to live in that environment. There would appear to be no question but that we should begin at the primary school level and carry through into the universities, an educational program to help teach our youth how best to live on this earth. H.R. 14753 would be a major step in that direction. . . .

Mr. Conway. I would like to make some additional personal comments in support of your bill.

In connection with my present occupation and my former employment, I have had the opportunity on a number of occasions to visit universities and other schools around the country and I have been impressed by the interest of the students and their desire to take an active part in trying to improve their environment, and to understand their environment.

I am also impressed and somewhat disheartened by what I feel to be the ignorance I find among the students, and this even includes students in engineering schools, of the knowledge of ecology and some of the other sciences that go into the making up of the overall study of ecology. Therefore it would seem to me highly desirable that some attempt be made to help educate these students who are so interested and who do so desire to make a contribution in this field. . . .

I think there has been a tendency over the years to put federal money into more advanced fields of knowledge which benefit a very small segment of the student body. A bill like this, I think, would assist on a much broader base of helping to advance the educational qualifications of the students in our country. That's one additional reason I would like for this bill to pass.

Mr. Scheuer, I am prepared to respond to any questions you may have on the basis of that statement and the statement I submitted for the record.

ADVERTISING BY POWER COMPANIES

Mr. Scheuer. John, I appreciate your testimony very much. I want to state for the record that Mr. Conway for a number of years was executive director of the Joint Committee on Atomic Energy and, as such, he is a highly professional and highly skilled Capitol Hill hand. Therefore I take your words very, very seriously.

Mr. Conway. Thank you, sir.

Mr. Scheuer. And I appreciate your support, John.

Mr. Conway. Thank you, sir.

Mr. Scheuer. . . . I would like to ask you just one or two simple questions about the policy of utilities in general of stimulating demand for their product.

. . . [Y]ou say, very rightfully, under present technology and technology forseeable in the future there is no way of producing large amounts of electricity required by modern society without some effect on the environment.

Mr. Conway. That's correct.

Mr. Scheuer. What you are saying is in effect what a number of us have been saying, that there is no known technology that we can produce electric power either by the fossil fuels or by atomic energy that doesn't have some negative environmental impact.

Mr. Conway. That's correct.

Mr. Scheuer. Now this being true, is it in the public interest for utilities as a group to engage in institutional advertising with taxpayers' dollars, since they are tax deductible, encouraging more use of electricity, encouraging the electric toothbrush, the hair drier and meatcutter and all nonessential gadgetries in which we are submerging ourselves?

Mr. Conway. Yes, let me answer as I see it, from the point of view of my company and how we handle advertisement.

Number one, we do advertise. We do not spend, however, more money on advertisement than we do on research, which in other sections of the country apparently is the case. An electric utility company, and I believe justifiably, can spend money on advertisement to the benefit of the consumer and I will give you the example of Con Edison.

Con Edison reaches its so-called peak—peak demand on its services—in the summertime somewhere between the hours of 3:00 and 4:30 in the late afternoon. Last year, for example, in the worst day we had in the summer, we had a demand put upon us which was the highest in the history of our company, in the neighborhood of 7.3 million kilowatts of power demand. By seven or eight o'clock that evening and into the night the demand fell off to less than one half of that.

We find that the demand upon us is growing at about 375,000 kilowatts per year. We must put in new capacity to meet that peakload. In some parts of the country they have a heavy industrial base—aluminum production, for example—which continues 24 hours a day. We do not have an industrial baseload in this area. Therefore we have a heavy investment in capital equipment to meet the peak demand which lasts only a few hours each day. When I talk about capital equipment, I talk about $200 or $300 million investment for a facility. That facility must be paid for during the life of it; it must be amortized. The consumer in the final analysis pays for the cost of that particular facility.

ADVERTISING TO ENCOURAGE NON-PEAK LOAD USE OF POWER

Now if we can get our night load up a little closer to our peak, and if we can get our winter load up a little closer to our peak—try to even it out—then the unit cost of the power becomes less. Otherwise the electricity that's being used during that short period of time must carry the brunt, if you will, in paying for the whole plant.

We advertise electric heating, because that helps bring up our winter load. But we also believe that if the homes are not heated by electricity, they must be heated by something else. They have to be heated, for example, by oil.

Mr. Scheuer. A fossil fuel of some sort.

Mr. Conway. Some fossil fuel and, if you take individual burners per house, the actual amount of heat energy that's being obtained—the B.t.u. per pound of fuel burned—will be less than if you can do it all in a large efficient boiler. It is more efficient to do it in a single boiler. So we think we can justify going to electric heat insofar as the overall environmental impact on the area is concerned. We believe it is helping the problems of the environment.

Similarly in lighting. We had an advertising program to "light a light, stop a thief." We entered into that advertising campaign on the request of the city. This was an idea that originated with the city and from all reports it did help in cutting down on crime. Again, this is off-peak load. As long as our peakloads are in the summer, you will not see our company advertising for air conditioning.

Now that is our answer—justification if you will—for advertising our product.

Mr. Scheuer. How can you urge the selective and pinpoint use of additional electricity to coincide to your off-peak hours? Aren't you simply encouraging the use of more electricity, sort of scattershot across the 24 hours, which in effect is going to require you to increase your plant, increase the environmental fallout?

Mr. Conway. If you listen to advertising specialists—and I am not one—and our sales force, they claim to be very effective in how they can pinpoint a particular pattern. To pinpoint, we give special rates on electric heating, to make it economically worthwhile for the individual party or individual consumer to purchase equipment to use electricity during a given period of time.

So that's one way you can offer electricity and pinpoint for getting off-peak loads.

ADVERTISING TO DISCOURAGE OVER-CONSUMPTION
OF ELECTRICAL POWER

I have been asked several times when I am out on the campus, "Shouldn't you be advertising for people to cut back on their use of power and telling people not to use air conditioning?" Well, by law electric utility companies are required to meet the demands put upon them and there's no question of the demand going up; we are doubling it nationally every ten years; somewhere, sometime we have to stop that geometric progression. Maybe the time is either here or getting close.

In answer, however, I think it would be the height of arrogance for a utility to tell consumers that they should not be using any more of their product, "that this is as much power as we are going to produce and we are going to stop at this level and you have to work out some way of apportioning its use." That decision I think has to be made by the citizens themselves, operating through the legislature, operating through the body politic. But it is something I don't believe should be put upon the utilities, because I think it would be arrogant for them to assume that responsibility.

Mr. Scheuer. You are sort of kicking a dead horse. I am not saying utilities should tell people not to buy electric toothbrushes, but they should cease and desist urging them to buy an electric toothbrush, and they might have sort of Smokey the Bear kind of advertising saying, "You know, additional electricity costs us in dollar terms and in social terms and think about it. Do you really need it?" Obviously you can't tell people you are not going to deliver the power. But it seems to be you are putting the worst possible face on it.

Mr. Conway. Right. I have been taking it to the extreme.

Mr. Scheuer. *Reductio ad absurdum.*

Mr. Conway. Yes.

Mr. Scheuer. How about some institutional advertising telling people what you say . . . , that there is no foreseeable technology where electricity will not produce negative environmental fallout and just saying, "Go easy."

The liquor companies say it. They say, "If you drive, don't drink; if you drink, don't drive." And they are saying to people, in effect, under certain conditions desist from using our product.

Mr. Conway. Right. I have two comments. Con Edison does not participate in institutional advertising since Charles Luce took over.

Mr. Scheuer. Right. It could even be humorous, like, "Look what this is going to do to us. Stop, look, and listen."

Mr. Conway. Mr. Congressman, there are some in the company who have advocated a policy along this line. In my mind, for example, I question the use of electric windows in a car. It is easier for me to turn a handle around. It is much more efficient for me [indicating].

Mr. Scheuer. Now wait a minute, John. Off the record.

(Discussion off the record.)


ELECTRIC TOOTHBRUSHES AND OTHER THINGS

Mr. Scheuer. Could you list some of the items you would consider sort of nonessential in the larger uses of electricity?

Mr. Conway. In my own mind the electric toothbrush—which I don't use personally, but my dentist tells me I ought to use them—but I would prefer in this New York area there would be a cutback in the use of air conditioning in the summertime.

372 The Actions of Firms: Cumulative Impact of Firms' Activities

However, I find it very difficult to go out and tell somebody who has to stay in this city during the summer and can't go up to the Catskills or Adirondacks, or anywhere else, that he can't have this type of comfort. I would like to see less use of it in the summer because that's when we have our problems in our particular area.

But in the case of, as I say, electric heating or lights, we feel we can justify it. I find that lighting by electricity, for example, helps the students in their reading. We are warned constantly by doctors and eye experts that students should have better lighting when they are reading.

Mr. Scheuer. We are all agreed on that. But how about the nonessential uses, the electric hairbrush or the electric meatcutter?

Mr. Conway. No, I would not think that's an essential use. I don't have it in my house. On the other hand, it is argued by those who are advocating the use of this, usually they are the manufacturers of a particular product, that it is essential for the housewife.

If you took the incremental additional use of electricity that these would cause, it would be fairly *de minimus*. However, the use of electricity has been going up at fairly rapid rate, much faster than population.

Mr. Scheuer. What's the component? Is it industrial, homes, air conditioning?

Mr. Conway. In our particular area here it's air conditioning, basically.

NATIONAL ZONING

Mr. Scheuer. If you had total power over decision-making, what national powers would you advocate, at least to slow down the rate of increase, policies that would be consistent with our democratic way of life?

Mr. Conway. That's a tough one and I can't know whether I could come up with a solution—

Mr. Scheuer. Education policies and regulatory policies.

Mr. Conway. Yes. The point is, I say I wouldn't be able to come up with a solution I believe that would meet or receive the acceptance of everyone.

I think there is no question in the matter that we have got to find solutions starting in the regional areas first, because I think it's easier to work on that basis. But I think in a final analysis we will have to come to a national basis for making decisions. How we wish to grow in those areas, what type of power facilities we are going to place and where we are going to place them.

It means setting up a regulatory procedure in which we have to put in one body the capability of analyzing the pros and cons as to one form of fuel versus another, one site versus another and—

Mr. Scheuer. One form of energy, don't you mean, versus another rather than fuel?

Mr. Conway. Right. I have to get energy, and from energy I have to decide how I'm going to get that energy and which fuel to use.

We are going to have to decide as to our streams, which streams, which rivers we want to save for recreation, for fishing, for what kind of fishing, for commerce; we have to be selective on this because we cannot use all of our facilities, all of our assets for every purpose.

We do this constantly on a zoning basis in the cities. In the cities as they get more crowded we start zoning and then the counties begin to zone. We are at the point in the national area and no question, we are moving into the international area. We have to do what the large cities and small cities do—zone, not only in the use of land but also in the use of fuels and the use of energy.

## RESERVATIONS ABOUT DISCOURAGING
## INCREASED POWER CONSUMPTION

Mr. Scheuer. Are there any national policies, either educational policies or regulatory policies, that would dampen somewhat the increase in the rate at which we are consuming power?

Mr. Conway. Well, let me say this. It concerns and I think it should concern us, the demands upon the use of electric power.

I see on the other hand some of the things that go with the inability to have power and problems inherent in lack of electricity. For example, in parts of India, in parts of Pakistan and even some of the remote areas of Russia—I spent three weeks in the remote Siberian areas of Russia—

Mr. Scheuer. When did you do that, John?

Mr. Conway. I did this about a year and a half ago when there were some hearings in Novosibirsk on fusion; they had scientists from all over the world and Dr. Gerard Tape headed up the U.S. delegation and invited me to accompany him—at the time I was still on the Joint Committee. When you see in some of these remote areas the problems they have of not having enough energy and the effect on the people who have to work—I have seen in India when they were building the Tarapur nuclear reactor women were making the equivalent of one and two cents a day carrying rock on their head to move rock out of the area. You see these people [who are] hardly more than beasts of burden.

Mr. Scheuer. You seem, John, again to have a real talent for going with unerring instinct to *reductio ad absurdum.* We have the Women's Liberation Movement in this country that would prevent that kind of limitation to electric power.

Mr. Conway. Recently, I was at Columbia Law School debating this question with some conservationists. We were in a beautiful room like this, well lighted, air conditioned, with no windows. Years ago it was different. We went during the summer, to try to make up time after World War II in the old Columbia Law building.

Mr. Scheuer. You find they didn't have an elevator.

Mr. Conway. That didn't bother me, because I was in better shape than I am now but the windows had to be left open because of the hot, heavy August days of New York and we had no air conditioning. The dirt and noise came in.

Which would I prefer? No question which is more pleasant for a student. Is it essential to study with air conditioning and in a quiet well lit building at Columbia Law School? Maybe some of us would have been better lawyers if we had the same. I don't know.

But I personally do not believe we are at that stage in the U.S. today where we have to stop additional uses of electricity, because I still believe and I say this without having the available facts, that the alternatives are less desirable.

Now we are getting, we have to get to the point where we can't keep doubling our electric production every ten years. FPC chairman John Nassikas, in his testimony in Congress, stated we are going to have to build an additional one billion kilowatts installed capacity by 1990. We will have power plants all over the place and no place for you and me to stand if the United States continues indefinitely to double its demand every ten years.

We have to level off at some place. What that point is I don't know. I don't think we are at it in this country as yet. We may be coming very close. . . .

When I was in school studying I was basically a mechanical engineer, but I did have to take courses in electrical and civil engineering, but we had no courses in the field of ecology.

If anyone had used the word, I don't think I would have understood what it was. We had no attention directed along that line. In fact engineers in the early days gave little or no attention to what we would today call beautification.

Mr. Scheuer. Of course, the word *ecology* has nothing to do with beautification. Essentially it comes from the Greek, "oikos," which means the house we live in. It's the housekeeping concept and its sphere is our home.

Mr. Conway. We have seen, at least in the electric utility field the last ten, twenty years, an evolution in the education of engineers and technicians. We try to have them be more than just technical experts or to approach problems just solely from a technical point of view.

We began to recognize the need for powerplants to blend into the area and to be more pleasing to the eye. We now take into consideration esthetics and that's been an educational process.

We are now at the stage and already past the stage where environmental considerations have to be taught and understood. We should start at the primary school level. . .

When you get down to it, the proper study of ecology is really a moral question. At school and even at home the children should be taught ethics and morality and, as the student moves along, by the time he goes into law or any professional field, he has been taught over the years standards of ethics, which really is how you live with your neighbor. Really, when you get down to it I would suggest that in the final analysis that is what it is—it is ethics and morality.

Mr. Scheuer. "How do you conserve your house?" as the Greeks put it.

Mr. Conway. Very good.

Mr. Scheuer. Well, how do we get that into the engineering schools?

Mr. Conway. I was an engineer as an undergraduate but I left it right after I graduated from school. So I have been more of a lawyer than I have an engineer. But in defense of engineers, my experience has been that once they get the idea, an engineer or a scientist is more adaptable to this way of thinking than others. In C. P. Snow's concept of two cultures, I find it's easier for the technical man to cross the bridge and pick up the other side and he's usually willing to do this.

I am concerned a great deal I think on the other side of it, the liberal arts student and the lawyer—their inability to cross the other way and understand the technical scientific field. We really have to have both sides understand the other.

I think we can teach engineers and I think they are learning, they have been learning. But on the other hand I find that many of those who are well motivated—and I have said this up at Columbia Law School—the lawyer who wants to get in there and wants to correct things too often is ignorant. He says, "I want to stop thermal pollution of the water, this is wrong and we have to stop it." We may recommend and we may draft laws that can and will eliminate or prevent the thermal pollution of the water. But it may cause wrong effects, unintentional effects if we really don't understand the technical, scientific facts of life.

In my limited experience in this field, I find it has been more difficult for me to get the nontechnical man to understand the technical facts than vice versa.

\*     \*     \*

# PROSPECTS FOR ENVIRONMENTAL POLICIES IN RICH COUNTRIES (OECD)\*

*[The following synopsis of prospects for policies to protect the environment is taken from a publication of the OECD—the members of which are mostly very prosperous countries like the United States, Canada, countries in Western Europe, and Japan.]*

PROSPECTS FOR ENVIRONMENTAL POLICIES

[A] major challenge in the 1980s will be to find the right balance between quantitative and qualitative growth and the choice will be influenced by the following considerations:

i)    the demand for basic human needs, food, shelter, clothing, etc. are being increasingly met in the majority of OECD countries;

ii)   consequently the environmental side-effects of quantitative economic growth are perceived as having more pervasive consequences on the welfare of the individual.

[T]wo types of implications emerge for environmental policy making. One is the efficiency of environmental policies, which could be improved through the increasing use of economic incentives in addition to regulations. More recent innovations in this field include the emission offset market which would require firms to obtain emission reductions from other firms in a region before adding to it.

The second is the need to measure the magnitude of the benefits to be gained from environmental measures.

Some estimates of national benefits and costs of pollution abatement have been calculated but they have not been developed to the point at which it is possible to locate the expenditure level which equate incremental benefits and cost. The available national studies, however, suggest that total benefits are well in excess of total costs of pollution abatement.* It is likely that, in most countries, incremental costs and benefits will be equated only at a higher environmental quality than has yet been achieved. Recent estimates suggest that, whereas pollution abatement expenditures in Member countries amount to 1–2 percent of GDP, pollution damages range between 3 and 5 percent of GDP. Although the benefit figures are rough estimates, they suggest that, in economic terms, the present situation entails a welfare loss and that pollution abatement expenditures should be increased.

The continued strong support for environmental improvements is notable, given the difficulties of measuring and quantifying the benefits of quality improvements. The costs of achieving environmental improvement are visible and, indeed, recorded in both national income accounts and estimates of economic productivity changes. Although it is widely acknowledged that GDP has its limits as a welfare indicator and that maximising GDP does not maximise welfare, this fact is rarely taken into account in policy discussions.

It should be emphasized that while relativities might change, the basic justification for pollution control programmes remains the same in good times and bad, when prices go up or down, when unemployment is high or low: a high quality and low-pollution environment improves the welfare of and is valued by citizens. Air pollution is a hazard to health, property and crops. Water pollution entails health, recreational and aesthetic damages. Noise becomes an omnipresent nuisance affecting health and welfare of a growing proportion of populations. Pollution control expenditures are justified by the benefits they produce, even if these benefits are difficult to state in monetary terms.

The benefits of pollution control are difficult to measure because the output, a high quality environment, cannot be bought and sold in markets. As a result, indirect measurement techniques must be employed. Such techniques are inevitably approximate and controversial. But progress has

---

*a) A recent U.S. study calculated that benefits from a 60% reduction in air pollution of $SO_2$ and particulates would result in a $43 billion (1978 prices) worth of annual benefits from reduced mortality and morbidity.

b) The latest data for 1977 estimate that cost of incremental pollution abatement expenditures for air at $12.2 billion. Sources: Unpublished Report of Contractors to the Environmental Agency, U.S. "Methods Development for Assessing Trade-Offs in Environmental Management" 1978 and The Ninth Annual Report of the Council on Environmental Quality.

been made during the last decade. There are official and private estimates of health damages from air and water pollution and on the impact of noise. There are now also many estimates of recreational damages caused by water pollution. Because air and water pollution abatement have some characteristics of luxury goods, available evidence suggests that the benefits of a high quality environment rise rapidly as income and leisure time increase.

In addition to the benefits listed earlier in this section it should be emphasized that the welfare gains yielded by pollution controls also produce indirect and long-term economic benefits: savings in health expenditures, improved labour productivity in a less-polluted and quieter environment, improved productivity of land if crops are not damaged by air pollution, and so on. A high quality environment can appropriately be viewed as both an intermediate good which contributes to production and a final good demanded in itself. And, finally, environmental programmers can be used to create both economic demands and employment in a slack economy. In Japan, for instance, the production of pollution control equipment reached 693.9 billion yen in 1976, as compared to 34.1 billion yen in 1966. By 1976, the number of employees in industries manufacturing pollution control equipment and facilities reached 50,000. In the U.S., markets for pollution control equipment and products in 1977 totalled roughly $1.8 billion and are projected to grow to a level of $3.5 billion by 1983.

A further indirect benefit from environmental policies has been termed "technology stimulation", i.e., environmental policies have induced innovations in production processes. Indeed, regulation perhaps more than anything else, has forced firms to engage in wholesale rethinking of their production processes and products. Often this shocks them out of a rather inflexible production system and thereby provides the catalyst which is necessary for innovation to occur. This is most likely to occur in mature and highly concentrated industries where the pattern of innovation is characterized more by process changes than by new products and where market conditions pose few challenges to the status quo.

Such "technology stimulation" has been documented in the U.S. When the initial requirements of the Clean Air and Water Acts began to take effect, many industrial firms reevaluated their entire production system in terms of product recovery and waste minimization. The process review led many firms to adopt innovations that led to significant economic benefits, including energy savings.

In Japan also the setting of stringent standards led to rapid technological innovations in comparison to other countries. When PCBs were banned, substitute products were developed at low additional cost. When strict standards on automobile emissions were set, several ways of meeting them were found and, in contradiction to the extravagant cost estimates which had been associated with these standards, no significant increases were recorded. The Japanese experience in the field of pollution abatement lends support to the idea that to a large extent it is not technology that constrains policy choices but policy choices constrain technology.

In Norway stringent air pollution control measures triggered technological innovations in the production of ferrosilicons by forcing a change from open to closed furnace operations. This resulted in energy savings, better working conditions and reduced air pollution. The savings in the cost of production varied between 8–12 percent per unit of production improving the profitability of the operation.

Examples of enterprises that actually decreased production costs as a result of pollution abatement measures are given in a study prepared by the French Ministry of the Environment. Cost reduction is achieved through two main mechanisms: the necessity to re-think and re-design production processes leads to technological improvements, and the discovery that some previously unrecovered pollutants have economic value ($SO_2$ contains sulphur, and the dust emitted by a cement factory consists largely of cement).

Public satisfaction with the environmental achievements is evidenced by the continuing strong demand for environmental improvements, and, in particular, opposition to major new sources of environmental disruption. For example, in the United States, recent opinion surveys indicate that environmental quality is an important concern, and ranks at about the same level as concern with health and education. In 1977, 47 percent of the people surveyed believed that insufficient financial resources were allocated to environmental improvements. Another survey in 1978 in the U.S. showed that the public wants both more energy and environmental protection, however, 47 percent of those interviewed preferred environmental protection while only 31 percent preferred energy. Environmental concerns such as clean air and clean water rank as high or higher than other basic concerns to Canadians, such as quality of food, housing, education and social services. More than half of Canadians expressed the view that they would pay higher taxes if they felt the money was going to anti-pollution measures and more than three-quarters said they would pay more for some products on the same basis. Similarly, in France, surveys show that environmental degradation is perceived as one of the most important problems. However, where the goal of environmental protection is compared with other socio-economic objectives (such as unemployment and inflation) public support for environmental improvement is somewhat less strong. In France, pollution control and nature conservancy ranked just behind employment but before inflation in 1976.

*       *       *

*Comment:*

# EFFECTS OF TECHNOLOGY ON
# WORLD RESOURCES

Some of the problems about exhausting resources are pretty clearly problems posed in terms of national interests disregarding—or even opposing—the interests of other countries. For example, Americans who wanted the United States to be as strong a world power as it had been, even Americans who just wanted it to be as secure from external threat, might have wondered about the wisdom of using up domestic supplies of petroleum at such a rate that in the mid-seventies the United States suddenly changed from being substantially self-sufficient in oil to having to depend on imported oil for the major part of its supplies.

People in other countries, of course, might not feel the problem so acutely; they might not wish American power to be unfettered. For them the American problem about national security intersects with problems about offsetting American power, or about keeping their balance in the face of it. Nor will people in other countries accept it that the national security of the United States is the prime consideration in allocating world resources, whether of oil or of anything else.

They will be even less inclined to agree that Americans are entitled to use up a lion's share of any of those resources, maybe exhausting some of them before other countries have begun to use anything like a comparable amount. Americans—or Canadians—might, it is true, claim that it was their business what they did with resources within their own boundaries. If they used up their white pine forests, and were prepared to suffer the consequences, what grounds could there be for objections from other countries? But suppose there is no close substitute for the resource, and it is vitally needed the world over. Would the happenstance of its being found mainly or exclusively within the boundaries of one country entitle people in that country to use it up at any rate that they pleased, and as frivolously as they wished? Imagine that Florida and California were the sole sources of Vitamin C.

The so-called advanced countries in fact do something more questionable than use up resources on their own territory. They have arranged, one way or another, to use up a disproportionate share of the resources found in other countries, too. Someone has pointed out that every child born in the United States or Canada adds, given the standard of living that he or she may expect, a burden upon world resources dozens of times greater than any child born in the poorer countries. Moreover, the discrepancy has been growing as the technology—the technology of consumption as well as the technology of production—expands in the richer countries.

# UN REPORT ON IRRATIONAL AND WASTEFUL USE OF NATURAL RESOURCES*

*[The following passages are taken from a report of 23 January 1976 prepared by the Executive Director of the United Nations Environment Programme for the meeting in Nairobi, March and April 1976, of the Governing Council of the Programme.]*

IRRATIONALITY AND WASTEFULNESS

The outcomes, in terms of policies, programmes or projects of decisions relating to the use of natural resources are "rational" if they make use of known resources in the best possible known ways to further the aims which a given society has set itself, taking account of all effects known to follow from the choice. A distinction should be made between "irrational use", in which existing knowledge is not acted upon, and "non-rational use", which is the result of defective or incomplete knowledge. Thus *rationality* implies the adjustment of behaviour to a perceived human purpose. While the nature of this purpose is not in itself subject to criteria of rationality (encompassing, as it must, moral or spiritual values), it includes the satisfaction of basic human needs and the handing down to successive generations of at least the same opportunities for fulfillment of their purposes as have been enjoyed by those which preceded them.

"Wastefulness" is probably best regarded as the particular form of irrationality in which a given level of fulfillment of human purposes is achieved with the use of *more* resources than necessary. In any case, the *composition* of resources used may entail "waste" in the sense that some resources are used to excess while others are under-utilized. Finally, resources may be "wasted" in support of profligate life styles for some while others lack the resources for even basic subsistence. While the first form of irrationality wastes resources, this last wastes opportunities for human satisfaction.

Private firms, transnational corporations and States are all capable of irrational action. If the overriding purpose and the criteria for judging actions derived from it can be clearly defined, the *global* rationality of resource use could be improved: (a) by inducing all decision-making units to rely more extensively on the approved criteria, or (b) by shifting the power of choice to those units which do.

Rationality, as defined here, must not be confused with "commercial rationality" in the sense of maximum profitability *in terms of market costs and prices:* these may not reflect the "true" burdens and benefits accruing to

*Excerpts from *Environmental Impact of Irrational and Wasteful Use of Resources,* a United Nations publication (UNEP/GC/79) of 1976, pp. 2–12 and 15–18. Reprinted by permission of the United Nations Environment Programme, Nairobi, Kenya.

society from the activities involved. At both the national and the international level, the aim should be to achieve broader social needs rather than the private demands of those who have the purchasing and political power to own and control resources. The rationality of actions must be tested in terms of *socially* meaningful prices, costs, and interest-rates, which aim to take account of all effects, including the environmental effects which ordinary market criteria tend to neglect. . . .

### THE INTERACTION OF MAN AND PLANET

The earth's biosphere consists of: (a) the *atmosphere*, comprising the ozone shield, oxygen, nitrogen and carbon dioxide; (b) the *hydrosphere*, and its composition of rivers, lakes, underground water and the oceans; (c) the *soil cover* of the earth's terrestrial area; and (d) the *vitasphere*, i.e. so-called "living matter" of the earth. The four components are in constant interaction with each other, and changes in one component will inevitably lead to changes in the others.

Human activity directed at the satisfaction of material wants has inevitably become a part of these interactions and affected the evolution of the biosphere. Until recently, however, man has not been guided by a knowledge of the complex changes in the biosphere which his activities have initiated, or even by a consciousness of the need for rational planning of his activities in relation to its components. As understanding of these effects and this need has improved, man's earlier non-rational attitude to the biosphere has become increasingly irrational, in that it ignores the knowledge that continuation of current trends in both industry and agriculture implies growing environmental degradation, depletion and pollution, and consequent feedback effects on human welfare and opportunities for improvement.

However, more "rational" management of human activity and the biosphere, aimed at improving the quality of human life and simultaneously conserving the quality of the planetary environment, is still possible. The feasibility of this option depends on (a) the improvement and diffusion of knowledge about the interaction between environmental effects and quality of life and (b) the strengthening of political will and social awareness so that both public and private decisions are duly influenced by man's growing environmental knowledge.

### THE NATURE OF ENVIRONMENTAL CONTAMINATION

Some "resource-encroachment" effects which may be identified as flowing from recent patterns of economic activity are:

(a) A steady reduction of areas of biologically active soils in favour of the construction of towns, ports, roads, mines, factories, etc. This process absorbs perhaps 7–8 million hectares of arable land every year;

(b) Soil erosion and compression (by heavy vehicles), which provoke degradation of the soil, reinforce its vulnerability to droughts, and may induce climatic changes;

(c) Growing contamination of soils, waters and bioproducts obtained from them with toxic compounds.

The knowledge which will be required in order to understand man's impact on his environment and to improve the basis for his decisions affecting it must be developed through intensive research on environmental effects and extensive monitoring of the environment itself. As these activities develop, perhaps man will perceive more clearly than he now does the ecosystem in which he plays an ever more active role and will begin to shape his activities toward a more rational pattern of use of the world's natural resources.

Knowledge of the physical effects of man's activities on his environment must in turn lead to a substantial modification in the existing pattern of human activities. In addition to knowledge from the natural sciences, improved knowledge is needed from the social sciences about how the present complex of human activities evolved and how those patterns of behaviour might be modified in the future.

THE SOCIAL PATTERN OF MAN'S INTERVENTION

Four principal human factors have made important interacting contributions to the present state of environmental affairs. The first is the growing power to inflict damage on the environment that has resulted from the combination of population growth and rising *per capita* incomes, together with technological advances which have increased man's ability to divert resources to his own purposes. These three factors interact with each other, but are also capable of acting separately: in cases where population growth has subsided, the drive for higher material standards of living has tended to maintain environmental pressures.

Power alone, however, will not corrupt the environment. It is the way in which man has chosen, through both private and public decisions, to use that power that has been detrimental. The principal hope for improvement must therefore lie in modifying the information and the criteria employed in the process of those decisions and in reconciling conflicts among them.

The lack of awareness of the impact of man's decisions and activities on his environment and the quality of the habitat in which present and succeeding generations must live has led to life styles which are more environmentally threatening than they might otherwise have been. It has also led producers to select production technologies with little regard for environmental consequences and social cost, and these choices, in turn, have reinforced the tendency to use up the world's resources rapidly and wastefully as judged by the environmental criteria now coming to light.

Technology, the principal instrument for man's management of the biosphere, is conditioned by the social, economic and political milieu in which it is generated, as well as by the constraints of nature. It is developed by society in response to perceived needs and can be shaped to reflect a greater (or lesser) concern for the rational and non-wasteful utilization of natural resources. The factors that influence the choice of technology are also critical. Invariably, there are several ways of producing goods or exploiting resources, and the effect on the environment is an inevitable consequence of the particular choice of technology that is made. If environmental consequences can be firmly established among the criteria governing the choice of technologies, the rationality of resource use must improve.

The environmental impact of present patterns of resource use has also been intensified by the tendency toward concentration of wealth, income and resource control. The resulting inequalities have in many cases become essentially self-perpetuating. The consequence has been to shift the composition of global output toward those patterns favoured by the wealthy, be they nations, groups or individuals, which are more heavily weighted than the patterns of the poor with luxury items and products based on exhaustible resources. Global output is thus more wasteful of resources than it would be if resources and incomes were more equitably distributed. The duality between rich and poor has, with industrialization and modern means of communication, taken on the character of competing ecosystems, and has become international in scope. . . .

### LIFE STYLES AND THE ENVIRONMENT

It is those who control budgets, whether of households, public or private enterprises, or Governments, who determine the uses made of the world's resources, and it is through change in their preferences and the factors which influence their attitudes that these uses can be modified. There are life styles at every level of income which are wasteful of resources. This also implies, however, an opportunity to modify wasteful life styles in environmentally beneficial ways. The behaviour of households and their expenditure patterns are influenced by the information they have about the private and social benefits and consequences of the specific goods and services they consider for purchase.

The "technologies" available for shaping and influencing preferences directly are not often applied with either social or environmental objectives in mind. Yet commercial organizations have used such means widely and with substantial effect. Similar tools may be equally effective in modifying life styles in ways favourable to the environment and the conservation of exhaustible resources. Improved means for disseminating information and enhancing understanding about the environmental effects of alternative life styles should therefore be actively sought and widely and vigourously utilized. At the same time, more effective controls over the dissemination of false or misleading information should be implemented.

The advocacy of such tools—and indeed of price controls and income transfers—to modify life styles suggests a knowledge of environmentally desirable directions of change which may in fact be far from incomplete. In any event, the obvious cases of decay or damage, can and must be managed with more direct techniques, for example the total prohibition of the use of DDT by some countries. The aggregate environmental effect of smaller finite changes in life styles is more difficult to assess. A modified input-output approach which relates classes of goods and services (including leisure) to the kinds of resources used and environmental costs entailed directly and indirectly in their production might advance knowledge and provide at least rough guidelines for the improved assessment of alternative life styles. In this context, both the rate and form of material growth and their future consequences for the environment must be the object of assessment.

Much of the world's expenditure is controlled through institutional and governmental budgets. Their "life styles", too, are not immune to improvement through increased understanding about the environmental costs and consequences of alternative policies and programmes. Constraints have been placed on atomic testing and the build-up of military systems. More effective constraints may follow as environment-contaminating and resource-exhausting effects are more fully comprehended.

PRICES AND SOCIAL COSTS

Prices and the quantitative rationing of goods and services have frequently been used as social tools for altering the structure of expenditures, although their use to repair or prevent environmental decay is still not widespread. Prices have the obvious effect on choices that a higher price discourages use and a lower price stimulates consumption. Market prices typically reflect only those costs and benefits which accrue directly to the price-setting authority, whether public or private. If the costs of environmental damage are excluded from price-setting calculations, resource use will be stimulated despite its social cost.

The problem is to ensure that all social costs and benefits are entered into the price-setting calculus, whether the agency responsible is public or private. Stating the problem and finding an explicit solution for it in specific cases are, unfortunately, two very different things. Converting social effects into explicit monetary terms is usually a hazardous and controversial undertaking. Moreover, the consideration of social costs and benefits in the making of policy decisions, say on soil erosion and land reforestation, will not necessarily prevent environmental decay unless those who cause or prevent the damage are explicitly penalized or rewarded for their actions.

It is not, of course, only the configuration of final goods prices that matters but also the prices of the intermediate products and the primary resources which enter into their production. To adjust prices for social costs and benefits along the entire production chain would be an enormously complex task. Nevertheless, it may be possible to make adjustments which shift prices in clearly desirable directions, for example, by ensuring that firms bear the costs of preventing or repairing the environmental damage which can be directly attributed to their activities.

Price adjustments of these kinds should not, however, be regarded as substitutes for direct efforts to modify preferences and income distribution in environmentally favourable ways. Raising the cost of luxury items may reduce consumption, but residual differences in life styles may yet be obviously inequitable and wasteful. Decision-making at all levels therefore needs to be more adequately informed by scientific information and analysis, accompanied by improved understanding of the criteria for judging environmental effect, whether local or global.

INCOME DISTRIBUTION AND RESOURCE USE

An important determinant of the composition of the final bill of goods, and hence of the life style or styles in a country, is inequality in the distribution of purchasing power. If the gross domestic product of a country was evenly distributed, the production system would be oriented towards meeting the needs of the ordinary people, subject, of course, to resource constraints. When on the other hand the distribution is highly skewed, there is a natural tendency for producers to accord higher priority to the needs of those with higher purchasing power.

A good example is the tendency in most countries to direct more scarce resources to the building of luxury flats than to the far more urgent social needs of providing shelter for the dwellers of slums, shanty towns, and pavements. Another, particularly blatant in some developing countries, is the allocation of large amounts of scarce foreign exchange and energy resources to private transport which is highly valued as a status-symbol by the rich, while neglecting the development of a public transport system which requires substantially fewer resources per consumer. The present pattern of industrial growth is itself a product of inequality in the international distribution of purchasing power. In such conditions, the task of promoting the co-operative efforts and the community spirit required to further common ends, such as the improvement of the environment, becomes even more difficult than it need be.

The expenditure patterns of the higher income groups also divert large amounts of resources to the support of their life styles. Large amounts of energy, for example, are devoted to the production and operation of cars and air conditioners, and oil-based agricultural inputs such as fertilizers, pesticides, tractors and diesel pumps are by and large the preserve of the richer farmers. Land is often preempted for large farms and gardened estates while the poor are both landless and homeless.

The social abuse of resources is not, however, restricted to the rich; the poor at the other end of the spectrum are often forced into living patterns which are environmentally destructive. Inequality in the distribution of land-holdings often forces those at the margin to use their limited land so intensively as to cause soil erosion and deforestation. The establishment of squatter colonies in central business districts of large cities is another example of environmental decay caused by those at the lower end of the income scale who are deprived of shelter and arable land in the village. Thus environmental damage and the wasteful use of resources might be diminished at both ends of the income scale if inequalities in income distribution could be reduced. . . .

DISPARITY BETWEEN RICH AND POOR COUNTRIES

No less important is the growing disparity in the standards of living between rich and poor countries, and its impact on the global pattern of resource use. Through their superior purchasing power, the rich countries have succeeded in consuming an overwhelmingly large proportion of the aggregate world production of natural resources, while many of the countries of origin of those resources have been left with little for their own domestic use and/or have been paid very low prices for their exports.

Consumption levels are very high not only in the rich countries. Similar resource-wasteful habits, made possible by imports, are quickly acquired by the elite in the poor countries, making it difficult to generate a high rate of saving or to channel internal investment towards capital goods with high multiplier effects on employment and income.

Just as the large and widening differences in economic opportunities between city and country within a country cause urban migration, similarly, a large proportion of international migratory movements is a response to the large and widening disparity between the living standards of the rich and poor countries. To the extent that such migration relieves population pressures on land and other resources in the latter and improves their resource utilization, it is to be welcomed. Unfortunately, restrictions in many developed countries are a major obstacle to migration as a means for achieving a more even global distribution of population over land and other resources. Such laws favour those with incomes and education, and the migration of skilled manpower from the poor countries involves a heavy social cost for them in terms of the resources required to develop those skills.

CONFLICTS OF INTEREST IN RESOURCE USE

The unequal distribution of resource location and production gives rise to various types of conflict of interest between countries, for example over the right to use particular resources. Conflicts over the use of rivers which pass through or between several countries, or over the territorial limits of a country, for the purpose of defining the fishing rights in the sea or exploring the seabed, are quite common, and often lead to excessive utilization of resources to forestall competitors. International agencies can play a vital role in resolving such conflicts, and in providing machineries for adjudication in cases of dispute regarding the interpretation and implementation of agreements.

A second type of conflict arises between the *producers* and the *consumers* of a particular resource. Whereas the rich industrialized nations with a high propensity to consume would prefer an unrestricted flow of oil to the world market, the interests of many of the leading oil-producing countries demand a conservationist approach in order both to maintain its price and to limit the rate of depletion. Such conflicts of interest are not easy to resolve internationally through formal rules and procedures, given the unqualified sovereign right of Governments over the resources contained within their national boundaries. On the other hand, considering the need to ensure rational use of natural resources from a global viewpoint, and also to avoid international conflict which might lead to war, embargo and various other wasteful activities, it is imperative to take into account global ecological interests in formulating national policies for both production and consumption.

A third type of conflict arises over the prices at which resources are bought and sold. Whereas a large proportion of the world's natural resources are *located* in the poor countries, their *production* and *use* are controlled by demand in the rich countries, and by the institutions through which world trade in most goods and services takes place. The existing structure of world trade leads to unequal exchange; the prices of resources sold by the poor countries are low and declining compared with the prices of manufactured goods sold by the rich countries. While low resource prices encourage excessive use in rich countries, the countries of origin benefit little from the possession of resources, in terms either of revenues or of their use in the domestic economy.

THE PRESENT MEANS OF RESOURCE MANAGEMENT

The management of the world's natural resources is the result of a bargaining process at many levels in which the main actors are:

(a) The Governments and domestic enterprises of nations—often found in two groups, the rich (net users of resources) and the poor (net suppliers of resources)

(b) The multinational corporations, which often represent the interests of the developed nations, but are increasingly assuming an independent status in resource negotiations

(c) Multinational commodity organizations of Governments, such as OPEC.

1. *The transnational corporation.* Transnational corporations operate in many countries of the world through a large network of subsidiaries, affiliates and associates. They control much of the world's trade in natural resources. In a very real sense, they have been *the* institutions of resource management, responsible for fixing prices of both final and intermediate products at different levels of the production process, for determining how much to produce from and sell to which countries, and for research and development to find new and cheaper ways of producing goods and develop new products and uses from a particular resource.

The transnational corporation is typically interested in maximizing its total profits. It may, therefore, deplete mineral resources rapidly in one country because they are high-grade, easily transportable or under threat of nationalization, while holding similar resources in another country as reserves; it may only extract resources at the source, exporting them (possibly at fictitious transfer prices) for further processing in its own plants abroad; and it may ignore environmental and other social costs that do not enter into its calculations of private profit. The decisions about resource management which transnational corporations find natural must be tempered by other forces if the global public interest is to be well served.

The most obvious counterbalancing force is the Governments of the producing and consuming nations in which transnational corporations operate. Unfortunately, the corporations can often play one Government against another, as a consumer against a producer or one resource source against another, or bargain technology and knowledge for access to resources, often on terms favourable to themselves. In these ways, the corporations may gain preferential tax treatment, duty rebates on imported goods, and freedom from pollution controls and measures to protect the environment.

Governments, and particularly those of poor countries, may find themselves too weak to bargain effectively or to uphold principles which depend on co-ordinated and concerted efforts of Governments for their effectiveness. Thus higher tax rates, requirements for in-country processing of resources, and pollution controls imposed by one country alone may simply destroy its own hopes for immediate development as the corporation affected takes its business to less far-sighted nations.

2. *Commodity organizations.* A recent development of considerable significance is the foundation of organizations of Governments owning a particular resource (e.g. OPEC for oil, CIPEC for copper, and similar organizations for countries exporting tin, bauxite, or iron ore). These act as a counterbalance to the multinational firms in the world market, and have succeeded in negotiating better prices and improved conservationist measures, in enlarging the participation of the host Governments in the production process, and in ensuring better utilization of the country's natural resources within the national economy. However, the degree of success achieved by these organizations varies with the natural resource. In the case of oil, which is exhaustible, and where the large exporting countries are geographically and culturally close, OPEC has succeeded over the past five years in displacing the multinational firms in control over production, distribution and prices and has been able to bring the development of the oil industry in individual countries closer to their respective environmental and developmental needs. In contrast, in the case of copper, which can be recycled, and whose leading exporting countries are spread over the whole world, such a transformation of the production-ownership structure has not yet been accomplished.

Attempts have also been made in recent years to bring together major consumers of a particular resource (e.g. oil), mainly in order to improve their bargaining position *vis à vis* the countries producing that resource. So far, for a variety of political and economic reasons, such attempts have not been successful. However, a useful objective for such organizations could be to find ways of regulating excessive consumption of depleting resources and narrowing the gap in consumption standards between their members and the rest of the world.

3. *The control of resources within a country.* No less important than the international control of natural resources in relation to environment is the relationship between the two *within* a country. The issue of disparity among regions within a country in terms of resource use is analagous to the disparity among countries discussed above. In the case of very poor countries, part of the explanation lies in their pattern of development during the colonial period when physical space and the accompanying infrastructure were organized to facilitate export and import; lines of transport and communication therefore tended to inhibit integration of the national space and instead facilitate its integration with the outside world. Part of the explanation for the disparity also lies in differences in their factor endowments and in the differences among regions in terms of their influences on the policy-makers in the country.

Where the developed regions also happen to be those with high resource endowments, this encourages wasteful consumption in them, and the gap between them and the other regions. Where the natural resources are produced in backward regions and consumption takes place in developed regions, the situation is not dissimilar to that existing between a rich oil-consuming country and a backward oil-producing country. A major policy issue in both cases is where to locate the processing industries, which create jobs and increase income but also pollute the environment.

A second issue arises with respect to the ownership and control of natural resources within a country. As already noted, many of these resources, particularly mines and plantations, are owned by large multinational enterprises. In several countries there are also private firms owned by the nationals of the country, but these are usually small in scale and poor in skills and resources, and are usually run without any regard for the conservationist and safety practices prescribed by national legislation. Because of their overrriding concern with profit generation, they are badly placed to orient their activities towards social needs and the minimization of environmentally harmful effects. Indeed, these enterprises, like the multinationals and perhaps more so, are often in the forefront of those interests which resist stringent environmental regulation by Governments.

In theory, public enterprises should be in a better position to take social and environmental considerations into account. However, how well they perform this task will depend on the way in which social and governmental objectives are defined, and also on the degree of consciousness among politicians, officials and managers of public enterprises of the long-term and indirect effects of resource use on the environment and on the biosphere in general. Governments which seek to emulate the "development path" of today's rich countries may end up with similar patterns of resource use of environmental impact.

\*   \*   \*

# SCIENTIFIC FINDINGS ABOUT ACID RAIN

*[The technology of the advanced countries may not only use up resources, both their own and other countries', at an alarming rate. It may directly, through polluting the sea or the atmosphere, impose on other countries waste products that damage the resources there. These aggregative and cumulative effects sometimes occur uncomfortably close to home, as the protests that the government of Canada and the province of Ontario have made about acid rain show. Joining in the protests have been—a hopeful sign for Canada—the governments of the northeastern states, which have been affected by the same damage.*

*The following passage\* is excerpted from the Second Report (November 1980) of the United States–Canada Research Consultation Group on the Long-Range Transport of Air Pollutants. The Group includes officials of the United States Environmental Protection Agency and of Environment Canada, along with experts from other bodies.]*

### EFFECTS ON ECOSYSTEMS

Results of research on acid rain effects in many locations show that both long-term and short-term consequences for soils, vegetation, wildlife and aquatic resources can be studied adequately only in an ecosystem context. Specifically, all of the following must be considered:
—*Changes in rain chemistry* caused by passage through canopy and litter layers;
—*Effects of altered soil solution chemistry* (including potential fertilizer effects) on uptake of chemicals by plants;
—*Effects on soil biological processes* such as decomposition, nitrogen fixation, nitrification, sulphur oxidation/reduction etc.;
—*Effects on weathering and mobilization of materials* into surface and ground water; and
—*Role of sulfate absorption* by the soil in controlling the chemistry of the soil solution and of the base flow to streams and lakes.
Understanding these relationships requires a detailed knowledge of the processes by which soils and ecosystems respond to acidic inputs, as well as the measurable effects. The following sections, therefore, explore these processes and related effects on groundwater, terrestrial and aquatic ecosystems.

---

\*Reprinted by permission of Environment Canada.

*Understanding the mechanisms of effects.* Because of differences observed in the type and magnitude of effect from a given level of acidic input, research is being focused on all aspects of the mediation of H+ inputs during passage through forest canopies and various soil layers (Morrison, 1980). Results reported by Cronan and Schofield (1979) show considerable increase in the cation content, as well as in H+ and $SO_4^{2-}$, in through-fall precipitation compared with above-canopy concentrations. In the soil, these inputs cause comparatively high concentrations of dissolved aluminium and other potentially toxic ions, leading to similar elevated concentrations in surface and ground water. The phenomenon appears to result from moderate increases in soil cation leaching, and represents an important biogeochemical linkage between terrestrial and aquatic environments exposed to acid precipitation. Transport of this aluminium and other ions to acidified lakes ultimately results in the gross disturbance of normal ionic balances, with consequent degradation of fish habitat.

To address the research implications and potential toxicities of ionic substitutions and place them in a context to determine governmental regulatory needs and options, several major research programs are being developed. In one, coordinated through the US EPA laboratory in Duluth, Minnesota, effects on groundwater, terrestrial systems, and aquatic systems are treated as a consequence of ionic mobilizations from the atmosphere to the affected resource. Effects from $Al^{3+}$ toxicity are integrally linked to effects from H+ concentrations and from Ca and Mg stripping. The goal of the Duluth program is to use understanding of the response processes shown here, in a background of soil and watered characterizations for the Great Lakes States, to define a "tolerance" for H+ additions and a basis for establishing possible regulatory standards.

Another topic which requires research is the elucidation of the chemistry of the components of acid rain which affect soils. In this regard, nitrogen forms may enter into acidifying reactions in soil, such as nitrification of ammonium, or may have essentially neutralizing effects, as is the case when nitrate is lost through denitrification or plant uptake (Coote *et al.*, 1980). The reactions of the various constituents of acid rain with soil components call for appreciable study, especially in the case of very acid but nutrient-poor podzolic soils that support so much of the eastern North American forest vegetation.

*Effects on crops and forests.* Direct effects of acidic precipitation have been observed by comparing the relative sensitivity of crops to simulated acidic precipitation. The results showed that of 35 crop varieties examined, the foliage of 31 was injured at pH 3.0, 28 at pH 3.5 and 5 at pH 4.0. At pH 3.0, the foliar injury to spinach, swiss chard and tomatoes was severe enough to affect marketability, extending also to root crops such as radish and beets where such crops are marketed with leaves attached.

Tests showed that yield was reduced for five crops (radish, beet, carrot, mustard green and broccoli); stimulated for seven crops (tomato, green pepper, strawberry, alfalfa, orchard grass and timothy); and ambiguously affected for two crops (potato and ryegrass). For fifteen crops, yields were not statistically significantly affected.

Effects on yields were not generally correlated with foliar injury but grouping crops revealed major differences. Only the yields of dicotyledons (plants with two seed leaves) were reduced. Radish, beet and carrot were the most adversely affected, followed by the leaf crops (mustard, green spinach, chard, lettuce and tobacco); then the cole crops (cabbage, broccoli and cauliflower); and finally the tuber crop (potato). In contrast, legumes (green pea, alfalfa and red clover), and fruit crops (tomato, pepper and strawberry) were more frequently stimulated by acidic preparation, and some monocotyledenous (plants with one seed leaf) forage crops (the grasses) were more productive (Lee *et al.*, 1980).

Air pollutants may also directly affect plants. For example, gaseous $SO_2$ impacts directly on plant cells causing chronic internal acidification and may act synergistically with other airborne pollutants. High $SO_2$ concentrations usually occur near sources and the transboundary and long-range implications of these effects are not well understood. Improved monitoring data are required from rural areas. Fruit, vegetables, white beans and soybeans are among the sensitive and valuable crops.

The direct effects of a range of air pollutant and other stresses upon the foliar tissues of numerous forest vegetation species have been described and illustrated in a comprehensive symptomology manual (Malhotra and Blauel, 1980), while two attempts have been made to rank the relative sensitivity of the vegetation of extensive geographical areas. One of these focuses on the forest vegetation of eastern Canada (Robitaille, 1980) and the other on the agricultural crops of Ontario (Malvern *et al.*, 1980). In the southern areas of Quebec, for example, sugar maple/yellow birch forests which also include beech, paper birch, balsam fir and white pine appear to be highly sensitive. To the north lie less sensitive areas dominated by balsam fir associated with yellow and paper birches or by black spruce. The sensitivity rises again in the far north due to the extensive areas of lichens within the open black spruce stands. The situation for forest vegetation in Quebec somewhat resembles that for agricultural crops in Ontario in that the more sensitive and valuable vegetation appears to occupy the areas more heavily impinged by acid rain.

Although the direct effects of acidic precipitation upon agricultural and tree tissues are in need of considerable elucidation in the light of the particular pollutant mixtures being deposited, a recent critical review underlies the considerable cause for concern that is felt for the nutrient-poor soils that support eastern North American forests (Rennie, 1980). Much existing indirect data suggest acid loading will sooner or later lead to a reduction in site productivity that would be very costly in socioeconomic terms and not feasible to remedy. Investigations are proceeding to quantify in the field, greenhouse and laboratory the rate of degradation that can be expected and to estimate the degree of reduction in pollutant depositions necessary to preserve environmental values.

*Effects on aquatic ecosystems.* The effects of acid precipitation on aquatic ecosystems were presented in the first RCG report in terms of loss of buffering capacity, decreasing pH and associated biosystem damage and evidence of collapse of sensitive fish populations. Research efforts have been directed towards further quantification of the extent of acidification of the aquatic regime, quantification of geochemical processes regulating acidification and definition of processes relating to biosystem response.

A recent analysis of Ontario Fisheries Information System data base (1980) has produced some preliminary but significant results. In the region of Ontario covered by the inventory, there may already be as many as 2,000 to 4,000 lakes (mostly less than 10 hectares in size) that are acidified to a point where most desirable fish communities cannot be sustained. The analysis also shows that a large proportion of the Province's brook trout, lake trout and smallmouth bass resource lives in lakes that are apparently highly sensitive to acid stress and that are currently receiving very high acid loads. Since the acidification rate of sensitive lakes appears to be related to lake size, small shallow lakes respond to changes in precipitation acidity more quickly than large deep ones, and since fish associations such as brook trout only, bass only, and brook trout with bass, tend to occur in smaller lakes, these communities are in most immediate danger. However, lake-trout-containing lakes, although larger and deeper, are also sensitive to acid stress and thus a greater loss of lake trout fish population is possible but only over a longer time period for given present acid loadings. This Ontario situation is expected to exist in the other sensitive regions of eastern Canada and work is continuing to try to assess the extent of the potential loss of inland fishery resources in all regions due to acidific precipitation.

Evidence of acidification of rivers in the coastal areas of Nova Scotia was shown in the first RCG report. Additional study of the Tusket and Medway Rivers (Thompson and Bennett, 1980) has shown a pronounced correlation and dynamic response between the stream acidity and excess sulphate load. This research appears to indicate a rapid response of the stream pH to changes in sulphate loading which would indicate rather rapid recovery if loadings were to be reduced. Such rapid response of basins with longer residence times could not be expected nor would recovery to a suitable acidity imply recovery of the damaged biosystem.

The influence of acidification of the Nova Scotia rivers on the native Atlantic Salmon is not well documented but recent records indicate serious loss to the fisheries. During 1980 only five native salmon returned to the Tusket (Peterson, 1980). Similar losses are typical of other rivers where pH has decreased to less than 5. Rivers having pH greater than 5.4 appear to support normal salmon spawning. . . .

As food availability is frequently a limiting resource for many species of wildfowl, studies are being initiated to determine the effects of acid lake biosystem losses on the higher orders of the food chain. The diet of the Common Loon (*Gavia immer*) is roughly 80% fish, the remainder being made up on crustaceans, molluscs, leeches and aquatic insects. This would lead to a possible destruction of loon habitat if fish populations declined due to acidification. Studies in New York indicate that loon productivity has remained high but nesting densities have declined in the Adirondack region (Trivelpiece *et al.*, 1979). Other wildlife communities may also suffer losses due to acidification. . . .

*     *     *

# THE PROVINCE OF ONTARIO APPEALS TO THE UNITED STATES ENVIRONMENTAL PROTECTION AGENCY*

*[In March 1981, the Ministry of the Environment of the province of Ontario, in a report on acid rain, intervened with the United States Environmental Protection Agency to oppose relaxation by the EPA of clean air standards. In part the Ontario report read as follows.]*

It is the objective of the Ontario government to reduce acid deposition as far as possible. To this end, Ontario is protecting its environment and that of its neighbours by reducing its own $SO_2$ emissions, as well as pressing for a reduction from sources in neighbouring provinces and states.

### 8.3 INTERIM ACTIVITIES

Ontario has enforced in the past, is currently enforcing and will continue to enforce vigorously its existing regulations. Additionally, Ontario has proceeded with an aggressive program to identify major emission sources which contribute to acid deposition. This program is expanding, updating, and refining the scientific and engineering data base. As these results become available, Ontario is issuing and enforcing new regulations which will further reduce $SO_2$ emissions.

On the international front, Ontario is undertaking five actions.

First, the Ontario government is participating wholeheartedly in the Canada-United States Working Groups on acid deposition. These scientific groups are laying the foundation for the urgently needed air quality agreement with our American neighbours.

Second, Ontario is pressing the U.S. government to enforce vigorously its existing $SO_2$ emission standards, as set out in the various State Implementation Plans. This submission comprises one part of this activity.

Third, we are urging adequate evaluation of the cumulative effects of any proposed SIP revisions on Ontario and other provinces.

---

*Excerpts from the submission of 12 March 1981 (expanded 27 March 1981) by the Ministry of the Environment, province of Ontario, to the United States Environmental Protection Agency. Reprinted by permission of the Ministry.

Fourth, the government of Ontario is opposing any actions by the U.S. and State governments which relax the existing SIP requirements.

Fifth, Ontario seeks to participate in any U.S. proceedings which could effect, as a result of long range transport, our environmental quality.

Ontario is undertaking these five actions because its leadership in reducing acid deposition within its jurisdiction will be of little consequence unless other jurisdictions follow this lead, due to the nature of the problem, that is, the transboundary exchange of pollutants between Canada and the United States. Canada receives two to four times the amount of $SO_x$ from the U.S. that it sends to the U.S., and the $NO_x$ exchange is 11 times greater from the United States to Canada.

A review of emission trends from U.S. sources over the past forty years clarifies and substantiates this statement. First and foremost, $SO_2$ emissions have increased by about forty percent. Although $SO_2$ emissions have decreased from most economic sectors during this period, the electric utility sector's emissions increased by more than a factor of six during this same period. Second, the increase in $SO_2$ emissions from this one sector occurred concurrently with a substantial increase (by approximately a factor of five) in the stack height for utility sources. Third, $SO_2$ emissions from coal burning changed from a wintertime peak to a more level rate throughout the year, with a small peak in the summer emission rate. Fourth, the precursor emissions for photochemical oxidants increased markedly during this time. In the earlier parts of this century, photochemical smog was hardly recognizable as a problem. Now, however, photochemically-produced oxidants frequently blanket the continental Northeast during the summer months. Fifth, total $NO_x$ emissions approximately quadrupled during this period.

These trends suggest a situation in which the atmosphere has become chemically more reactive. Simultaneously, greater quantities of acid-forming precursors are being added to the atmosphere. Further, a substantially greater quantity of these emissions is now injected high into the mixed layer where the emissions and their reaction products have much longer residence times as they travel to areas remote from their points of origin.

In Ontario, there is firm scientific evidence that if these omissions of sulphur dioxide *continue*, or *increase*, the resultant acidic pollutants are threatening to kill aquatic life in thousands of Ontario lakes and waterways within the brief span of another 10 to 20 years. Serious concern also exists that damage to terrestrial life forms may also occur, and that man-made structures will be impacted.

With the substantial increase in the use of coal as a source of energy in the United States, and the projected increases in $SO_2$ and $NO_x$ emissions in the U.S. between now and the year 2000, controls to reduce existing U.S. utility emissions are vital to the protection of Ontario's environment and that of Eastern Canada. The United States $SO_2$ emissions from power utilities are estimated at 18.6 million metric tons annually, accounting for roughly two-thirds of total $SO_2$ emissions—compared with *total* $SO_2$ power utility emissions in Canada of 700,000 metric tons annually.

In summary, because transboundary pollution is of critical concern to Ontario and Canada's eastern provinces, there is an immediate need to reduce the emissions of these serious pollutants from *existing* U.S. power plants as well as the hundreds of *new* plants which are expected to be built in the United States during the next two decades.

\*   \*   \*

# THE CANADIAN EMBASSY TAKES UP ACID RAIN WITH THE STATE DEPARTMENT\*

NO. 286

The Embassy of Canada presents its compliments to the Department of State and has the honour to refer to the current review by Congress of the Clean Air Act.

The Embassy understands the Administration is now formulating its position on this matter. It accordingly takes this opportunity to draw the Administration's attention to the bilateral implications associated with review and reauthorization of the Act which are of concern to Canada. It also requests that these implications be given careful consideration before the Administration comes to a determination.

In essence, the Canadian Government is concerned that revisions to the Act not impede ongoing Canada/United States efforts to address transboundary air pollution. It is also concerned that the Act provide to the United States Government the tools necessary to deal effectively with this growing problem.

For both Canada and the United States, effective domestic federal legislation is an essential counterpart to the implementation of the 1980 Memorandum of Intent. This committed both countries to negotiate a transboundary air pollution agreement, and to take significant interim measures, including the development of domestic control policies and the legislation support to give effect to them. The Canadian Government welcomed the assurances from President Reagan when he visited Ottawa in March 1981 that these negotiations would proceed, and that the United States wished to work cooperatively to understand and control air pollution crossing the international border.

Amendments last year to Canada's Clean Air Act provided the necessary legislative and administrative capacity at the federal level in Canada to control transboundary air pollution. In the Canadian Government's view, revised United States legislation should likewise both be capable of support-

---

\*The statement that follows is reprinted by permission of the Secretary of State for External Affairs, Canada.

ing effective control measures, and ensure federal capacity to implement the eventual air quality agreement.

Scientific understanding of long range air pollution, in particular acid precipitation, and awareness of their socio-economic impacts have developed rapidly since the clean air laws of both countries were written. As a result, it is now timely, and consistent with our mutual obligations, that federal governments develop and utilize measures for controlling transboundary air pollution, and for dealing effectively with the interjurisdictional inequities to which it gives rise.

As the National Commission on Air Quality determined, existing measures under the Clean Air Act are not adequate to deal with long range transport problems, such as acid rain. Canada therefore endorses the Commission's recommendations for stronger measures to control transboundary pollutant transport.

Studies already completed in both countries substantiate the Commission's consensus that enough is now known about the problem of acid deposition to warrant significant emission reductions. Ongoing research programs in both countries should assist by refining understanding of the problem and improving the means to control it; such research should not however be used as a reason for delay in beginning to take reasonable and effective control action. Appropriate provision in the revised Act of measures that facilitate implementation of such reductions should parallel development of a bilateral agreement.

The Embassy notes also that a variety of actions have been taken or proposed whose cumulative impact may be to increase the northward flow of pollutants. In the view of the Government of Canada, proposals that bring about an increase in long range pollutant transport and accelerated acid precipitation would be inconsistent with existing United States commitments to work with Canada to achieve significant pollutant loading reductions.

Moreover, possible related programmes such as conversion of power plants to coal without adequate environmental safeguards would also have the potential of worsening the problem, and would appear to run counter to the thrust of the NCAQ's concern that current sulphur dioxide emission levels not be increased.

The Government of Canada notes the conclusion of the National Air Quality Commission that existing controls under the Clean Air Act do not directly address long range transport, and its recommendation that significant reduction be made in the current level of $SO_2$ emissions in the eastern United States by 1990. The Embassy commends this recommendation, and the Commission's further recommendations that consideration be given to adopting a phased program requiring interim reductions by 1985; the enactment of a moratorium on the relaxation of sulphur dioxide emission limits in State Implementation Plans; and measures to prevent sulphur dioxide emission increases arising from coal conversion.

The Embassy is also aware of proposals for regulatory reform and decentralization of government control of air pollution. The Canadian

Government considers such decentralization must be accompanied by a corresponding provision of capacity at the federal level to control interjurisdictional pollutant transport, including the discharge of international responsibilities.

It has been a tradition of long standing that the United States and Canada seek to consult in advance on proposed policies or actions that may have significant transboundary impact. The Government of Canada therefore requests that no decisions on Administration proposals for modifying the Clean Air Act with a potential for worsening transboundary air pollution be taken without prior consultations. The Government of Canada further requests that the serious bilateral implications of such actions be carefully considered.

The Embassy of Canada avails itself of this opportunity to renew to the Department of State the assurances of its highest consideration.

Washington, D.C.

June 19, 1981

## THE IMPACT OF TECHNOLOGY ON PUBLIC HEALTH: HORROR STORIES ABOUT CHEMICAL WASTES

Acid rain has a devastating effect upon the health of fish and plants. Through its effect upon the soil, if in no other way, it threatens the health of human beings, who depend for food on what the soil produces. Technology has already had worse effects upon public health in other connections. Most striking of all, perhaps, have been the dangers posed by the disposal of hazardous chemical wastes. This problem, too, overlaps national boundaries. It has been felt (in both directions) in the Great Lakes and on other parts of the boundary between Canada and the United States.

In a long article carried in the issue of 22 September 1980, *Time* magazine reported that Julius Richmond, the Surgeon General of the United States, had "declared that throughout the 1980's the nation will 'confront a series of environmental emergencies' posed by toxic chemicals." According to *Time*, "The EPA estimates that the U.S. is generating more than 77 billion lbs. of hazardous chemical wastes a year and that only 10% are being handled in a safe manner. At least half of the wastes, says Gary N. Dietrich, an EPA official, 'are just being dumped indiscriminately.' " *Time* added, in a later passage, "All too many waste handlers have merely tossed the refuse into leaky burial pits, or carted it off to municipal dumps to mix with household garbage, or paid farmers small fees to let them hide 55 gal. drums on unused land, often by dark of night. Some haulers have pumped liquid wastes into tank trucks and driven down rural roads with the pet cocks open, releasing the chemicals into ditches."

Having dumps operating in broad daylight does not cure matters; and it is not clear that concentrating the wastes is an advantage. *Time* describes a spectacular instance of such a dump.*

ELIZABETH, N.J.

On a small peninsula between New Jersey and Staten Island, the charred remains of what had been a collection of about 50,000 drums, some stacked four high, adjoin a brick-and-steel building once owned by the now bankrupt Chemical Control Corp. The containers had been left to rot for nearly a decade. Many of the drums had never been properly labeled; others were so seared by the explosive fire in April that neither the manufacturer nor the nature of the chemicals they contain can be determined from outside markings. Some barrels are leaking unidentified chemicals into the ground. Unknown wastes seep into an adjacent stream called the Arthur Kill and eventually ooze into the Hudson River. A huge tank holds a fluid laced with 4,000 parts per million of PCB, a chemical that has been linked to birth defects and nervous disorders. Explains George Weiss, coordinator of the cleanup from New Jersey's department of environmental protection: "No one knows what to do with that. No one even knows if we can touch it."

Wearing a respirator and a suit like an astronaut's to seal out fumes, the operator of a front-loader cautiously picks up one drum at a time. He is well aware of the fate of a bulldozer driver who hit a container of flammable phosphorus at a landfill in nearby Edison, N.J.: the man was incinerated so quickly that he died with his hand on his gearshift. State officials have identified a horrific arsenal of chemicals at the site, including two containers of nitroglycerine; two canisters of a chemical similar in effect to mustard gas; barrels full of biological agents; cylinders of phosgene and pyrophoric gases, which are so volatile they ignite when exposed to air; wastes contaminated by lead, mercury and arsenic; plus a variety of solvents, pesticides, plasticizers, including dangerous vinyl chloride and even picric acid, which has more explosive power than TNT.

Toxic wastes are trucked to New Jersey's single licensed toxic-waste incinerator in Logan Township, where the chemicals are burned at more than 5,000°F. After months of work, an 80-man crew has removed all but 700 drums from the site. Once the barrels are all gone, metal detectors and aerial photography will be used to uncover evidence of any additional buried wastes. The contaminated topsoil must be hauled away. Probing for possible poisoning of the underlying water will come later.

How was the mess created? Chemical Control Corp. had signed contracts with some of the state's chemical companies and factories to dispose of their wastes. The company was supposed to solidify nontoxic materials for safe burial in landfills and detoxify the poisonous chemicals for similar disposal. Instead, the corporation just stacked the drums out back. Reacting to the

---

*The passages that follow, from the issue of September 22, 1980, are copyright 1980 Time Inc. All rights reserved. Reprinted by permission from *Time*.

fears of Elizabeth residents, state officials seized the site in March 1978 and began the slow cleanup. The companies, whose barrels were clearly labeled, included the 3M Co. and Union Carbide; the firms had no legal obligation to retrieve their drums but promptly did so when notified by the state.

"We don't have any choice but cleaning this place up," says Jerry English, a lawyer who heads New Jersey's department of environmental protection. "We simply cannot allow a situation like this to continue." Wearing a white vinyl coverall over her fashionable suit, yellow plastic bootees over her high-heeled shoes, a respirator and protective gloves, English recently climbed on a rooftop and looked out over the sea of barrels. She broke into a wry laugh, grandly swept an arm toward the rubble and declared, "Some day, my son, this will all be yours."

*[The effects of dumping chemicals upon the aquifers that carry under-ground water supplies is especially worrisome. Time devoted a special boxed feature to this subject:]*

DEEP CONCERN: GROUND WATER

At the very top of the environmental scientists' list of concerns about pollution damage is something that most Americans probably believe to be safely beyond the reach of contamination: ground water. This is water that lies buried from a few feet to half mile or more beneath the land's surface in stretches of permeable rock, sand and gravel known as aquifers. In the U.S. there is five times as much water in such subterranean reservoirs as flows through all its surface lakes, streams and rivers in a year. While most ground water is believed to remain pure, concern is rising because it is one of nature's greatest nonrenewable resources. Unlike surface water or the air, ground water is all but impossible to purify once it has become chemically polluted.

Ground water is not exposed to the natural purification systems that recycle and cleanse surface water; there is no sunlight, for example, to evaporate it and thereby remove salts and other minerals and chemicals. Nor can ground water be counted upon to clean itself as it moves through the earth, for it scarcely "flows" at all. Says Eckardt C. Beck, the EPA's assistant administrator for water and waste management: "Ground water can take a human lifetime just to traverse a mile. Once it becomes polluted, the contamination can last for decades."

In the past, ground water was kept pure because the soil at the earth's surface could be counted on to act as a filtration system, a kind of geological "kidney" that would scrub out bacteria and other insoluble contaminants placed on or in the ground before they could seep down to the water table, the ground water's upper limit. But this filtration system does not reliably screen out the waste chemicals that now leach into the soil from a variety of sources, including cropland that has been sprayed with pesticides, and industrial dumps like the pools into which liquid chemicals are placed so that the water they contain will evaporate.

The EPA has located 181,000 such "lagoons" at industrial or municipal waste disposal sites around the country. In a study of 8,200 of them, the agency found that 72% were just holes in the ground, not lined with concrete or other materials to prevent the chemicals from leaching into the soil; 700 of these unlined lagoons were within a mile of wells tapping ground water.

Bacterial wastes, such as the effluent from the nation's estimated 16.6 million residential septic tanks and cesspools, can be filtered fairly simply out of drinking water. But chemical contaminants are another matter. Says EPA Administrator Douglas Costle: "We are not even sure if, not to mention how, chemical contaminants can be removed. It takes sophisticated testing just to determine if there are chemicals present at all."

The most serious cases of ground-water pollution confirmed so far have been in the Northeast states, where the problem is largely the result of surface dumping of industrial wastes, and in California from agricultural chemicals. But awareness of the vulnerability of ground water is still so new that EPA officials do not really know how far the fouling of the aquifers has spread. Says Costle: "We cannot even begin to say how much of our drinking water, actual or potential, may have been contaminated. We are going to be doing a lot of detective work."

\*    \*    \*

# PART SIX

# The Actions of Firms: Firms Dealing with Governments

CHAPTER **18**

# Regulation and the Costs of Regulation

*Introductory Comment:*

## LAISSEZ-FAIRE AND GOOD BEHAVIOR

According to Adam Smith (1723-90), businesses and governments were to have as little to do with one another as possible, not because he thought freedom from government regulation was a basic moral ideal, but because he thought competition was the only really effective way of checking tendencies on the part of businesses to aggrandize themselves at the expense of the public. Regulations by government were comparatively ineffective; worse, if governments had much to do with businesses, they would begin to play favorites. The main aim of Smith's argument, in application to policy, was to get governments to stop playing favorites.

This aim has never been achieved. Governments never stopped playing favorites even when the approximation to laissez-faire was greatest. Consider how the railroads of the United States and Canada were built, with huge donations of wealth by the governments. Consider how they were run, once built. At times in the late nineteenth century, the members of the New York State legislature were in the pay of the railroads, in proportions large enough to assure favor for the interests of the railroads, or at least of the railroads that paid best.

Contemporary governments have receded very far from laissez-faire. They regulate business more or less closely in a thousand different connections. They make large purchases from private industry. (Indeed, even in former days, they made purchases big enough to be matters of importance to many eager firms). Firms have a lot to win or lose from government in both connections. It is no wonder that they busy themselves trying to safeguard their interests in the face of regulation and trying to advance them in the way of increasing sales to government. Much that they do on these lines is legitimate enough, even when the business in question is the sale of arms. On the other hand, it is clear that firms often go too far in winning favor, wrongly subverting the responsibility of the government to protect the interests of other parties—the public interest.

I have frequently mentioned the triplet principle. In accordance with it, I have presented some cases—some of them at length—in which firms have clearly been doing things that are not wrong at all. Illustrating the principle, these cases have done something to balance the cases in which we have found firms doing things that are highly questionable. The balance, I expect, has not been sufficiently redressed to avoid giving the impression overall that firms are bent more often than not on doing wrong and need to be checked. The selection of cases has been affected by something like the newsworthiness that brings forward in the papers so much scandal and leaves so little space for stories about things going along all right. My local newspaper once printed a story headlined "No More False Fire Alarms Than Usual"; but my local newspaper is notorious for not having much sense about what makes news.

Nevertheless, when we allow for the bias of newsworthiness, and recognize that most firms most of the time are behaving reasonably well, we may infer that in part their behavior is an effect of present regulations. We are also left with some behavior that present regulations do not prevent. Should it be checked by further regulations? That is all too easy a response. It disregards the possibility that it might be better to have increased competition. It also disregards the possibility that even where we cannot rely on increased competition to control behavior, further regulations may do more harm than good. Regulations don't come without drawbacks; and some sorts of regulations have more drawbacks than others. These matters are explored in an essay, which I now bring forward, by the Princeton economist William J. Baumol; they can be explored further in the paper-organizing game that follows. Baumol's essay also gives a penetrating treatment of the much discussed general topic of the social responsibility of business.

# WILLIAM J. BAUMOL, "BUSINESS RESPONSIBILITY AND ECONOMIC BEHAVIOR"*

Under pressure from many sides, corporate managements have been quick to assert their agreement in principle to the proposition that the firm should concern itself with the ills of society, particularly as those ills have begun to seem increasingly threatening. After all, the modern firm has shown itself to be one of the most efficient economic instruments in history. Since the beginning of the industrial revolution it has increased real per capita incomes perhaps twenty-fold, incredible though that may seem. It has doubled and redoubled and redoubled again the energy placed at the service of mankind, and has achieved an increasing productivity of human labor which is astonishing both in its magnitude and its persistence. With such a record, what other institution can be better adapted to deal with the difficult economic problems that underlie so many of our social issues?

I will argue that this line of reasoning is fundamentally valid, but not if interpreted and implemented in the obvious manner which generally seems to be proposed by both business and its critics. The proposal seems to be that industry should exhibit a massive outburst of altruism, modifying its goals to include in addition to the earning of profits, improvement of the environment, the training of the unskilled, and much more. As John Diebold has put the matter in a recent address: "[There is the danger that] . . . business as 'good corporate citizen' [will] start to view itself, or be viewed by others, as an all-purpose institution that should right all social wrongs. (If you added together the rhetoric in this field you wouldn't fall far short of business being called upon to do just this!)."[1]

I will argue that any such undertaking is undesirable even if it were achievable. Moreover I will give reasons why it cannot be expected to work—why the task undertaken on such a basis is likely to be managed badly. Tokenism is the natural product of such a process. Indeed, not only is business likely to prove inefficient as a voluntary healer of the ills of society, but the attempt to play such a role may well have adverse effects on its efficiency in the fields where it now operates and in which its abilities have been demonstrated so strikingly.

I will argue that the primary job of business is to make money for its

*M. Anshen, ed., *Managing the Socially Responsible Corporation* (New York: Macmillan, 1974). Reprinted with permission of the Macmillan Publishing Co., Inc., and the Trustees of Columbia Univerity. Copyright © 1974 by The Trustees of Columbia University in the City of New York.

1. "The Social Responsibility of Business," address at the conference on "An Economic Society for Man," June 21, 1972.

stockholders. This does not mean that the best way to do everything is as it is done now. On the contrary, society has every reason to ask business to be much more careful in its use of the environment, to do much more to protect the interests of consumers, etc. But we neither should nor can rely on "voluntarism" for the purpose.

If we want business to behave differently from the way it does today we must change the rules of the game so that the behavior we desire becomes more profitable than the activity patterns we want to modify. If pollution is made expensive enough, we will be treated quickly to a spectacular display of business efficiency in reducing emission rates. If the production of unsafe products is made sufficiently costly, one can be confident of a remarkable acceleration in the flow of innovations making for greater safety. Business will then do the things it knows how to do best and society will be the beneficiary.

Under the terms of such an approach, is there no role for "business responsibility"? Is the firm simply to pursue profits and no more? That is not quite enough. Responsibility on the part of business, from this viewpoint, has two requirements: (1) when appropriate changes in the rules are proposed by the duly constituted representatives of the community, responsible management must refrain from efforts to sabotage this undertaking; (2) business should cooperate in the design of these rules to assure their effectiveness in achieving their purpose and to make certain that their provisions interfere as little as possible with the efficient working of the economy. But, by and large, these are just the things businessmen have, in effect, refused to do.

### DANGERS OF VOLUNTEER "SOCIAL RESPONSIBILITY"

The notion that firms should by themselves pursue the objectives of society is, in fact, a rather frightening proposition. Corporate management holds in its hands enormous financial resources. Voluntarism suggests, or rather demands, that management use these resources to influence the social and political course of events. But who is to determine in what way these events ought to be influenced? Who is to select these goals? If it is management itself, the power of interference with our lives and the lives of others that management is asked to assume is surely intolerable. The threat to effective democracy should be clear enough.

The point is made most clearly by recent demands that business firms exercise responsibility in their investments abroad, meaning specifically that firms should abstain from investment in countries whose governments draw the disapproval of the person who happens to advocate such a course. The firm may be asked to eschew investment in countries that repress or persecute particular ethnic groups, or whose governments trample civil liberties, or are aggressive militarily, or simply oppose United States foreign policy with sufficient vigor. I do not want to argue here either the efficacy or the desirability of boycotts. Nor do I wish to defend the countries which have been attacked by critics of corporate policies on overseas investment. I, too, am repelled by some of their governments. In sum, I am not arguing for isolation or for the ignoring of oppression. Rather, I deplore the notion that American business should attempt to arrogate to itself the determination of our foreign policy.

It may or may not make sense to boycott some particular foreign government. But I do not want a business management to decide what government should be boycotted. And certainly I do not want management to use the capital I have entrusted to it to impose its notions of international morality upon the world.

Again, in Diebold's words,

> I personally believe [the choice of social goals] is the job of the politician working in a democratic political process. The businessman as businessman should not be making essentially social decisions. The businessman should be the tool who responds to market demand by making what society shows it wants. Do not make him more mighty than that.

An increase in corporate power is probably the last thing that those who call for greater "corporate responsibility" would want. Yet that, paradoxically, is precisely where some of their prescriptions lead.

### TOKEN ACTIVITIES

Predictably, there has been a considerable gap between business' glowing accounts of its own accomplishments and the actual magnitude of its achievements. Newspapers report many cases in which their public relations men have run far ahead of what companies have actually accomplished. *Newsweek* reported the case of a company with the

> . . . only industrial mill in the U.S. to have been the subject of separate air and water pollution abatement hearings before Federal authorities whose advertising asserted 'it cost us a bundle but the Clearwater River still runs clear' . . . [W]hat [the firm] neglected to mention was that the picture [in the advertisement] had been snapped some 50 miles upstream from the . . . plant [where] it dumps up to 40 tons of suspended organic wastes into Clearwater and nearby Snake River every day.[2]

After citing several other such cases, the article goes on to report some more routine examples.

> Even without bending the facts, companies may inflate their ecological contributions with half-truths. FMC Corp. recently took out double-page spreads in national publications to boast of its participation in the $3.8 million Santee, Calif., water-reclamation project, which converts sewage into water fit for swimming and boating. Conveniently omitted was the fact that FMC did no more than sell the project some $76,000 worth of pumps and equipment. Nor was there any mention of the company's inorganic-chemical plant in West Virginia which daily dumps more than 500,000 pounds of wastes, mostly toxic, into a nearby river, according to the Federal Power Commission.

2. *Newsweek*, December 28, 1970, pp. 49–51.

Similarly, Union Carbide began an ad boosting its efforts to reduce auto pollution with the observation that 'Driving through this beautiful land of ours, you can get all choked up.' To the residents of the Kanawha Valley in West Virginia this is hardly news. So much smoke billows from the chimneys of Union Carbide's main ferroalloy plant there—28,000 tons of particulates a year—that a nearby Roman Catholic church had to encase an outdoor statue of St. Anthony in a fiber glass case to protect it from corrosion.

The conclusion to be drawn from this and the many other illustrations that can be cited is not that businessmen are particularly dishonest. Having associated with many businessmen over the years, I have come away with the impression that their personal integrity, their good will, and their distress at injustice does not differ notably from those of other groups. Of course, the honesty and the degree of concern with social issues will vary from one businessman to another, as it does elsewhere.[3] But even with the best intentions, given the rules of the game as they are today, there is little the individual businessman can do.

It is the prime virtue of the competitive process that it leaves little up to the good will of individual managements. The firm that is inefficient or that does not provide the public with the products it wants is given short shrift by the market mechanism. It is a merciless process which has no pity for the weak, ineffectual businessman. The chiseller who undercuts an inefficient concern is the consumers' best friend, though he is anathema to the firms that long for the quiet life and its permissive mediocrity.

But that same competitive process which prevents laziness or incompetence also precludes voluntarism on any significant scale. The businessman who chooses voluntarily to spend till it hurts on the environment, on the training of the handicapped, or in support of higher education is likely to find that he, too, is vulnerable to the chiseller without social conscience who, by avoiding such outlays, can supply his outputs more cheaply.

In the words of Edward L. Rogers, general counsel of the Environmental Defense Fund, "If I were a company president right now, I wouldn't do any more than I had to on the pollution front, because that would hurt my company more than its competitors."[4]

The invisible hand does not work by inducing business firms to pursue the goals of society as a matter of conscience and good will. Rather, when the rules are designed properly it gives management no other option. Adam Smith was acutely aware of this. The famous invisible hand passage is often quoted, but, for some reason, the two critical sentences that conclude the paragraph are often omitted: "I have never known much good done by merchants who affected to trade for the public good. It is an affectation,

---

3. Note that consumers' records of voluntary compliance in these areas are no better than those of business firms. It is easy to document cases in which there has been a response that is less than spectacular to voluntary programs for recycling of solid wastes, for the increased use of car pools, or for installation of inexpensive emission control kits in automobiles.

4. *Newsweek*, December 28, 1970, p. 51.

indeed, not very common among merchants and very few words need be employed in dissuading them from it."

## USE OF THE PRICE MECHANISM

Economists have long argued that when faced with mounting social problems one should not abandon the profit system or undermine its workings. Rather, if one is really serious about the social goals that are being urged upon business, one should use that powerful economic instrument, the price mechanism, to help attain them.

For example, it has been suggested that the reason industry (like others) has been so free in using the atmosphere as a dumping ground for its gaseous wastes in that clean air is a valuable resource available for use by anyone at a price far below its cost to society. Imagine what would happen if, say, coal or cloth or some other such resource were supplied free to anyone who wanted to use it, in any desired quantity and with no accounting for its manner of utilization. The resulting wastes and inefficiencies are all too easy to envision. But that is precisely what is encouraged when society, by virtue of long tradition, makes available on precisely those terms the use of its water, its air, and its other resources that are held in common.

Economists have, therefore, suggested that an appropriate remedial measure is to levy an adequate charge for the use of such resources. If made costly enough, their use will rapidly become more sparing and less inefficient.

There are many virtues to such a program which need not be gone into in any detail. Any such system of charges (e.g., a tax of x dollars per gallon on the discharge of certain types of effluents into waterways) is as automatic as any tax collection process. It does not involve the uncertainties of detection of violations and of the subsequent judicial process. It does not rely on the vigor of enforcement agencies, which seems so often to wane rapidly with the passage of time. It offers its largest rewards in the form of decreased taxes to the firms that are most efficient in reducing emissions. It thereby makes use of the full force of the market mechanism as an instrument of efficiency. It may be added that these are not all the virtues that can be claimed for such an arrangement. From the point of view of the businessman himself there is a great deal to be said for it.

First, it is a natural extension of the profit system, which he should welcome as a means to strengthen its workings and its social acceptability in the long run.

Second, it protects him from the notion that he is engaged in criminal activity when in the course of his productive operations wastes are unavoidably generated. By making him pay the full social costs of his activities, including all of the resources he utilizes in his operations, it becomes clear that he is engaged in a normal and commendable productive process, rather than the antisocial activity of which he is all too easily suspected under current arrangements.

Third, such a set of rules protects him against undercutting by competitors when he does behave in a manner consistent with social objectives—there is no room created for undercutting by the chiseller when everyone is subject to similar costs imposed for the protection of society.[5]

Finally, and this should in the long run be most important of all to the businessman, the proposal avoids completely the imposition of direct controls by the government. A management is not told how to run its business—whether to install taller smokestacks or to recycle or to adopt a higher-grade fuel. Rather, emissions are made highly unprofitable and the businessman is invited to decide for himself the most effective ways of reducing them or of eliminating them altogether. There need be no acceleration in the process of erosion of the freedom of enterprise. Changes in prices of inputs are a normal business phenomenon. Fuel can be expected to grow more expensive as its scarcity increases, and other inputs grow cheaper as innovation improves their productive technology, but neither of these changes undercuts the prerogatives of management. Similarly, the imposition of a charge corresponding to the social costs of the use of environmental resources does not interfere with the managerial decision process. It merely changes the structure of the economy's rewards to the company, increasing the profitability of the behavior desired by the community.

CHANGES IN RULES

This proposal is not, in itself, my central point. Rather, it illustrates what I mean by a change in the rules of the game. Many other types of changes in rules are possible.

The type most frequently talked about is direct controls: for example, quotas assigned to firms or to municipal treatment plants, specifying maximum quantities of emissions and standards of purity which they must meet before they can be discharged into waterways. All sorts of things can be specified by direct controls. They can require the installation of specified types of devices which limit the emissions of automobiles; they can make mandatory the use of various safety devices. The range and variety of such regulations should be obvious enough.

Besides such direct controls, whose enforcement is left to government agencies, other changes in rules are also possible. For example, legislation authorizing legal suits by interested private citizens has often been advocated. Something intermediate between direct controls and the fiscal methods described above is represented by the construction of treatment facilities by governmental agencies, whose costs polluters are then required to bear.

The essential point is that all of these procedures involve changes in the rules themselves. The firm is not expected to do anything as a pure act of

5. Of course, if such a rule applies only in a small geographic area, it does not protect the firm from the competition of suppliers located elsewhere. But this argues that such rules should cover as large a geographic area as possible, not that they should be avoided.

benevolence. Rather, it is faced with a new set of conditions under which it and its competitors must operate, and they must adapt themselves as effectively as they can. The two most important characteristics of such changes in the rules, as far as we are concerned, are that there is nothing voluntary about following them, and that it applies equally to all competitors. In this way, it frees management from pressures to undertake a role in the policy-making process which it has no reason to want and which society has every reason to fear. Moreover, it protects the firm from attacks by those who stand ready to undercut it at the first opportunity, an opportunity which would be opened were the firm to bow to social pressures for the voluntary pursuit of its social responsibilities.

THE RESPONSE OF BUSINESS

With such potential advantages to the firm, to the free enterprise system, and to society, one might have expected that at least a substantial segment of the business community would have welcomed such changes in the rules with open arms. After all, does not that constitute a true acceptance by business of its social responsibility, through an arrangement that elicits desirable behavior from everyone and avoids the ineffectiveness and inequities of voluntarism?

But nothing of the sort has in fact occurred. Only recently have there appeared a few breaks in the solid opposition of the business community, when one automobile manufacturer (Ford) and one gasoline distributor (Mobil) joined those who question the desirability of the Highway Trust Fund as currently constituted. However, such defections are still very much a rarity.

Let me illustrate the point. When I first undertook the preparation of this paper it seemed appropriate to see what might be suggested by the newspapers. For the next twelve days I searched the *New York Times* for relevant materials and encountered not a single example of industry support for anything that could be interpreted as a change in the rules designed to strengthen the protection of the public's interests. But I did find a profusion of pertinent cases in which industry took the opposite position. These are summarized in the following excerpts:[6]

*Example 1. Consumer Protection*
   Legislation to create a consumer protection agency which would represent consumers before federal courts and regulatory agencies died on the Senate floor, a victim of a filibuster. The bill, regarded as the most important consumer measure of the present Congress, commanded majority support in the Senate; but it ran into intensive opposition from industry.[7]

6. I do not mean to suggest that this is a random sample, i.e., that this represents the number of such stories one would encounter in a representative two weeks. The period that happened to be chosen encompassed the adjournment of Congress and so the number of pieces of legislation whose fate was settled was unusually high.
   7. J. W. Finney, *New York Times*, October 8, 1972, Sect. 4, p. 1.

*Example 2. Regulation of Phosphate Utilization*

Administration officials reported today that Governor Cahill will push next month for final legislative approval of a controversial measure that would give New Jersey the power to ban phosphates from detergents and other cleaning agents. . . . State officials reported that the Senate's Republican leadership now favors the measure, which died last year in committee at the hands of the detergent industry and organized labor interests in the Legislature.[8]

*Example 3. Control of Strip-Mining*

Legislation to provide for regulation of the strip-mining of coal and the conservation and reclamation of strip-mining areas was passed by the House today and sent to the Senate. The vote was 265 to 75.

The House measure would give the Interior Department authority to issue cease-and-desist orders against any surface-mining of coal when the health and safety of the public or employees is involved; to designate certain areas as unsuitable for strip-mining if lasting injury would be caused to the environment; and to issue and revoke permits for strip-mining.

Six months after enactment, no coal strip-mining could be conducted without a permit. Except for reclamation plans, any permit application would have to have the written consent of the owner of the surface of the land.

Carl E. Bagge, president of the National Coal Association, representing coal operators, said the bill was a punitive, unrealistic measure which would reduce the nation's production of coal by 25 percent almost overnight.

Mr. Bagge assailed the bill as an "arbitrary, simplistic solution" to a complex problem. He urged the Senate to reject it, contending that it was too late in the session to amend the House bill to one that was satisfactory.[9]

*Example 4. Safety of Drug Products*

In an effort to persuade the House to narrow the legal remedies in a pending product safety bill, Thomas G. Corcoran, a Washington lawyer who represents major drug interests, pointed out that the bill could overburden the Federal courts with new cases. The drug industry was leading the fight against the bill, which is now nearing enactment.[10]

*Example 5. Inspection for Disease-Carrying Pets*

When the polyethylene bag was invented, the tropical fish industry ballooned. Its bubble may burst, pet supply wholesalers say, because of a proposed Federal law affecting fish imports, modeled after other regulations restricting the sale of turtles and banning the import of certain birds to prevent communicable disease.

"We recognize the need for inspection and regulation", says Richard Kyllo of Saddle River, vice president of the newly organized Tropical Fish Institute of America. "But the new codes were enacted in a state of panic. They are so loosely worded that they leave an open road to any kind of interpretation."

New Jersey is among many states that recently passes restrictions on selling turtles unless they were found free of salmonella, a bacteria that causes intestinal disease. The regulations were a reaction to the death in 1969 of a 9-year-old turtle owner in Connecticut.[11]

---

8. R. Sullivan, *New York Times*, October 11, 1972, p. 1.
9. *New York Times*, October 12, 1972, p. 1.
10. F. P. Graham, *New York Times*, October 14, 1972, p. 1.
11. J. Marks, *New York Times*, October 15, 1972, p. 96.

*Example 6. Information on Restaurant Sanitation*

The New Jersey Public Health Council tonight ordered all restaurants in the state to post the results of their state sanitary inspection reports conspicuously near their entrance, in an effort to open heretofore confidential inspection files to public scrutiny.

"We have kept intact our promise to provide consumer health protection unequaled anywhere in the country," Dr. Cowan said.

As a result, the restaurant industry, which bitterly opposed the open posting of inspection reports at a public hearing here last month, is expected to contest the council's order in the courts.[12]

*Example 7. Water Pollution Control*

The Senate and House of Representatives overrode today President Nixon's veto of the Federal Water Pollution Control Act of 1972, which thus becomes law and authorizes $24.6 billion over three years to clean up the nation's lakes and rivers. During nearly two years of Congressional deliberation on the bill, the White House had supported industry's opposition to many of its provisions, particularly the goal of no discharges of industrial pollutants by 1985 and the setting of limitations on effluents for classes for industry.[13]

Other illustrations are easy enough to provide. The billboard industry, the manufacturers of plastics, of tetraethyl lead, and many others have all played the same game. The outcries have become familiar: proposed regulations are "punitive," "unworkable" "staggeringly expensive," and even "ruinous." Said a representative of the pet fish industry (in the October 15 article just cited): "if [the bill as it now stands] passes, I'll be completely wiped out and so will the industry."

But we rarely hear of industry representatives who volunteer drafts of alternative regulations which really prove to be effective. Certainly I have never heard of an industry representative arguing that a proposed piece of legislation is not sufficiently strong!

RESPONSIBILITY AND VOLUNTARISM

We can only conclude that business still has a long way to go before it will have succeeded in a program of effective cooperation with the duly constituted authorities, the only bodies that do have any authorization to decide on social goals. Of course, the fault has not been entirely that of the businessman, but the illustrative cases of the preceding section suggest to me that so far he has done remarkably little to try to make such a process work, and that he as often effectively served as an accomplice to the undermining of any workable measures for the treatment of a number of the more pressing social ills.

I am aware that there is an element of inconsistency in my position. On the one hand I have argued that business should have no truck with voluntarism which, at best, offers the illusion of effective activity and, at worst, poses a threat to the democratic process. Yet at the same time I am

12. R. Sullivan, *New York Times,* October 17, 1972, p. 1.
13. E. W. Kenworthy, *New York Times,* October 18, 1972, p. 26.

urging businessmen to cooperate voluntarily in the design and implementation of effective legislative measures as the appropriate medium of social responsibility. However, though both processes call for voluntary acts on the part of managements, the two differ completely in their potential consequences.

The adoption of new rules differs in two fundamental respects from a regime of pure voluntarism. First, it involves no takeover by business management of powers of decision that belong more properly to others— government retains the final authority on matters of social policy. Second, because what is involved is a change in rules that applies equally to everyone, there is no reason why a well-designed action of the variety under discussion need turn out to be ineffective. For the market mechanism, instead of undermining such a program, certainly need not interfere with it, and in some cases will actually serve to implement it. With competitors all subject to the same regulations, competitive pressures will not forestall the program, and if the structure of rewards and penalties is so modified in the process as to make failure to cooperate highly unprofitable, then the profit motive becomes the automatic force behind this program.

Thus, in my view, the true social responsibilities of business can be met only by a new spirit which may be called "meta-voluntarism"—systematic cooperation in the design and implementation of measures which are basically involuntary.

Let me not be misunderstood. I am not suggesting that all companies call in their lobbyists and turn their instructions about by a full 180 degrees. Such a goal is neither particularly attractive nor achievable. It would surely be unreasonable to expect the representatives of industry to spearhead a drive to impose the costs of public interest programs on themselves. And I am not particularly attracted by political activity on the part of corporations, no matter what it may happen to favor.

Rather, I am suggesting that, once the issue has been raised, and once it seems clear that some sort of government action is about to be undertaken, the time is ripe for constructive participation by the business sector. That is the time for voluntary cooperation in the design of more effective changes in the rules drawn up so that they are not unnecessarily burdensome to anyone. By concerning itself with the last of these matters, business will still look after its own interests as well as those of the general public, but then it will do so in a manner that is fundamentally constructive and that can help to lighten the clouds of suspicion that now hang over the business community.

\*     \*     \*

## Paper-Organizing Game
### on Regulation

Again, the game is played by rearranging the pieces—the questions given below, xeroxed from the book—so that they come up in due order in a firmly organized argument.

Consider Some Specific Failing of Firms On A Matter Discussed Under Previous Headings. Is Regulation the Only Way of Dealing With the Failing? Discuss the Advantages and Disadvantages of Regulation.

1. What are the costs of regulation (and of any alternatives to it)?

2. Will the vexations and costs of regulations diminish once people are used to them?

3. Will measures that cost little to uphold be effective?

4. Is not regulation by the government sometimes unavoidable? When?

5. If we regard regulation as involving a rule explicitly adopted by some organization together with provisions for enforcement, will we not still have to distinguish between regulation by private associations and regulation by the government?

6. One way of dealing with the failing would be moral training. Ideally, people with such training would refrain because of conscientious scruples. Would that be regulation?

7. Regulation by the government might consist of prescriptive standards (for example, for emissions) or of taxes (including license fees) and subsidies. Would the latter approach require little administration? What are its advantages?

8. How might consumer support be mobilized for firms that undertake to remove or minimize the failing?

9. Regulation might mean just having a moral rule. Is that the meaning to adopt here?

10. Would using a combination of devices reduce the overall costs of the measures taken? How?

# CHAPTER 19

# *Connivance with Political Corruption and Political Oppression*

---

*Introductory Comment:*

## POLITICAL CORRUPTION

---

V. O. Key, commenting on his fellow political scientists, once said that a professor, "for whom 25 dollars is a lot of money," is not in an ideal position to appreciate the significance that is attached to much more valuable considerations by politicians who accept gifts or by donors who offer them. Philosophers, who are not better paid than political scientists and whose preoccupations are typically even more unworldly, must be in an even worse position. I bring up the subject of political corruption with some diffidence. One can moralize about it narrowly and rigidly, like progressive WASPs denouncing the political machines (run by Irish-Americans and other non-WASPs) of American cities at the turn of the century. One may be blind to the main point: those machines provided the less securely comfortable segments of the city population with services that the WASPs did not need and were not prepared to have "reform" governments give: orientation for immigrants to a strange environment; intercession with government; jobs; coal during hard winters; and baskets of food.

Similarly, relations between firms and government that, strictly judged, amount to political corruption may in some cases enable both firms and government to serve the public better than they could if, say, some vexatious regulations were adhered to. It has been suggested, moreover, drawing a lesson from the corruption in eighteenth-century England and in nineteenth-century America, during the industrialization of those countries, that corruption facilitates beneficial economic developments which traditional elites, formally opposing them, would otherwise block. As a path to development alternative to revolutionary terror, corruption is worth considering.

On the other hand, surely there is some basis for moral uneasiness about corruption. There may be no way, as things stand, to have issues fully examined in public and decided on their merits by people authorized to decide them. If there is a system for doing this, however, does not corruption subvert it? And if there is not, should one not be created? The experience of Britain and the United States indicates that corruption in one period is not necessarily an insuperable obstacle to having a comparatively honest government in a later one. Life is so complicated that we have to allow for the possibility that, far from being an obstacle, it was some help. Yet one way that corruption might be unhelpful—not only worse than an honest system that was equally responsive, in more justifiable ways, but an evil active twice over—would be to frustrate efforts to bring about a better system. Corruption may be intolerable currently, too. It has a tendency to go too far and commit outrages upon public policy. What keeps it from going too far, at least in part, is the process of exposure and condemnation to which moral judgments are indispensable. Looked at in this light, those judgments cannot be written off as merely unworldly and priggish.

Politicians do not need the help of firms to be corrupt. From time to time, they are caught helping themselves directly to government funds, or otherwise abusing for their own purposes the privileges of their offices. They take payroll kickbacks from members of their staff. They no doubt manipulate their expense accounts. They put their mistresses on their official payrolls; worse, they put mistresses there who are not qualified to do the jobs; even worse, they put mistresses there who actively cause trouble with their colleagues. They support legislation, like bills granting reserve officers handsome pensions, that pays off financially for themselves. Not every politician does any of these things; probably the proportion doing them is no more than one has to allow for in human beings generally; but at times and places such corruption has even become systematic, all without the help of business. It has been alleged that there were special categories of jobs in the Illinois public service for the girlfriends of state legislators.*

It is firms that corrupt politicians look to for major killings, however. Firms have the free-floating, easily laundered money to make big donations. The Abscam investigation, in which the FBI set up a number of congressmen and at least one senator to do favors for what seemed to be an Arab investor, showed how receptive some politicians are to such dona-

---

*I owe several of the examples just given to conversations with Lewis A. Dexter, who also insisted helpfully that I take a balanced view of political corruption.

tions. However, stakes as high as they were (or seemed to be) in Abscam are perhaps too dramatic. With them matters have become too unambiguous to provoke much discussion. The first two items to follow concern much smaller matters and require carefully balanced judgments.

# STATE v. PRYBIL

*Supreme Court of Iowa, 1973*

McCORMICK, J.

The State appeals trial court's judgment acquitting defendant Ralph Prybil, a member of the Johnson County board of supervisors, of receiving gratuities from contractors in connection with county business transactions in violation of Code § 741.1. We reverse but do not remand since defendant has been in jeopardy. . . .

Code § 741.1 provides:

"It shall be unlawful for any agent, representative, or employee, officer or any agent of a private corporation, or a public officer, acting in behalf of a principal in any business transaction, to receive, for his own use, directly or indirectly, any gift, commission, discount, bonus, or gratuity connected with, relating to, or growing out of such business transaction; and it shall be likewise unlawful for any person, whether acting in his own behalf or in behalf of any copartnership, association, or corporation, to offer, promise, or give directly or indirectly any such gift, commission, discount, bonus, or gratuity . . .

The offense is an indictable misdemeanor, punishable by a fine of not less than $25 nor more than $500, or by county jail imprisonment for not more than one year, or by both such fine and imprisonment. . . .

Defendant was alleged to have violated the statute by receiving meals, books, and convention hotel expense from contractors in connection with county purchases of equipment, material and services. He entered a not guilty plea, waived jury trial . . . and was tried by the court.

The State introduced evidence relating to five separate transactions, three with the Herman M. Brown Company, one with Wheeler Lumber, Bridge and Supply Company, and one with the L.L. Pelling Company. Expense vouchers submitted by salesmen for the Brown and Wheeler companies indicated the companies paid for lunches at which purchases were discussed with the board of supervisors. On one occasion, two days after the Wheeler company sold the county a pole shed, its salesman entertained the board at a Des Moines supper club. A month later he sold them an enclosure fence for the county yard. The State contended defendant's proportionate share of these meals constituted unlawful gifts to him under § 741.1.

Records of the Pelling Company showed expenses of $21.53 in payment of December 11, 1969, convention hotel expense for defendant and his wife, and $20.95 on December 22, 1969, for a gift of books to defendant. In a series of transactions between September 11, 1969, and January 19, 1970, the company did more than $10,000 worth of road and equipment repair for the country.

Trial court held the State failed to carry its burden of proof and acquitted defendant. The court also interpreted § 741.1 differently than the State believed it should. The State alleges trial court erred in (1) limiting the terms "gift[s], commission, discount, bonus or gratuity" to kickbacks, (2) requiring proof such kickbacks were made as specific inducement for a particular sale or as a reward for a particular purchase, and (3) finding the State's evidence insufficient to establish defendant's guilt.

I. We have not previously interpreted § 741.1. Familiar principles of statutory construction are applicable. The goal is to ascertain legislative intent in order, if possible, to give it effect. Words are given their ordinary meaning in law. Other pertinent statutes must be considered. Effect is to be given to the entire statute. Its terms are not to be changed under the guise of construction. . . . In searching for legislative intent, we consider the objects sought to be accomplished as well as the language used and place a reasonable construction on the statute which will best effect its purpose. . .

Code § 741.1 was enacted in 1907. . . . It was entitled "AN ACT to prohibit the corrupt influencing of agents, representatives, employees, officers of a private corporation, or public officers acting in behalf of a principal in any business transaction and provide a penalty therefor."

The statute thus reaches private as well as public employees. In its relationship to private employees it is a commercial bribery statute. As to public employees it fits in the scheme of statutes prohibiting public officer corruption. The purpose of statutes like § 741.1 has frequently been discussed. New York prohibited commercial bribery in § 439 of its Penal Law of 1909 . . . . In People v. Davis (1915), the [New York] court held the purpose of § 439 was to prohibit agents from considering their own personal welfare by making contracts favorable to themselves rather than their employers. The court said "secret commissions are to be condemned because they prompt a servant to betray his master, and thus prejudice the master's interests in consideration of pay received from others." . . . and also, "[a] bonus or commission, secretly given is nothing short of a bribe to betray one's employer,". . .

Under a statute similar to ours the Connecticut court in State v. Aldridge . . . (1964) said, "It is the intention of this statute to prohibit a person who has the authority to make contracts or transact business on behalf of a public or private corporation from accepting any payment, commission, or compensation or gratuity of any kind from the person with whom he makes the contract or transacts business." . . .

In its application to public officers § 741.1 resembles 18 U.S.C. §§ 201(f) and (g), lesser offenses in the hierarchy of federal officer corruption defined in 18 U.S.C. § 201. Section 201(f) prescribes punishment for one who, "otherwise than as provided by law for the proper discharge of official duty, directly or indirectly gives, offers, or promises anything of value to any public official . . . for or because of any official act performed or to be performed by such public official . . ." Section 201(g) makes punishable the receiving of such benefit by the public official. The scope and purpose of these prohibitions has been defined:

"The awarding of gifts thus related to an employee's official acts is an evil in itself, even though the donor does not corruptly intend to influence the employee's official acts, because it tends, subtly or otherwise, to bring about preferential treatment by Government officials or employees, consciously or unconsciously, for those who give gifts as distinguished from those who do not. . . . The iniquity of the procuring of public officials, be it intentional or unintentional, is so fatally destructive to good government that a statute designed to remove the temptation for a public official to give preferment to one member of the public over another, by prohibiting all gifts 'for or because of any official act', is a reasonable and proper means of insuring the integrity, fairness and impartiality of the administration of the law." United States v. Irwin (1965) . . .

[1] We believe the plain language of § 741.1 and its relationship to [other sections of the] Code, prohibiting other kinds of official corruption, demonstrate the legislature intended it to have the same scope, purpose, and effect as 18 U.S.C. §§ 201(f) and (g).

Trial court relied upon Dukehart-Hughes Tractor & Equipment Co. v. United States, . . (1965), in giving it a much more limited effect. That case was an action by a contractor for a tax refund after disallowance by the Internal Revenue Service of deductions for expense of entertainment of Iowa public officials. In granting the refund the court held the entertainment did not violate Iowa public policy manifested in § 741.1. The court decided the statute is aimed at kickbacks, does not necessarily bar entertainment of or gifts to agents of potential customers, refers to bounties paid in connection with a particular transaction, and uses the enumeration "gift, commision, discount, bonus, or gratuity" as an elaboration of types of kickbacks. A dissent argues the statute is not limited to kickbacks and bars gratuities related to multiple as well as single business transactions. We find the dissent accords with our view of the statute.

[2, 3] The statute does not use the word "kickback," and there is nothing in its language, context, or purpose to justify substituting that word for the words that are used. In its normal meaning, a kickback is the "payment of money or property to an individual for causing his employer . . . or principal to buy from, to use the services of, or to deal otherwise with, the person making the payment." Ballentine's Law Dictionary (Third Ed. 1969). Limiting the bounties enumerated in § 741.1 to kickbacks would have the effect of reading the terms "gift," "gratuity" and "bonus" out of the statute. Also, by prohibiting only payments to reward corrupt influence, the Dukehart-Hughes majority interpretation contradicts the statutory language which broadly enjoins benefits "connected with, relating to, or growing out" of any business transaction. The statute does not require proof the transaction is corrupt, only that the transaction is the reason for the payment. If it is, the payment is corrupt but not necessarily the transaction.

"It is not necessary for the Government to show that the gift caused or prompted or in any way affected the happening of the official act or had anything to do with its nature or the manner or means by which it was performed." United States v. Irwin . . .

The prohibition of § 741.1 is not limited to kickbacks. Trial court erred in holding it is.

[4, 5] II. We also disagree with trial court's conclusion that the statute requires the State to single out one of what may be a series of business transactions as connected to a single unlawful payment. Unless otherwise specified, the use of the singular in a statute includes the plural. § 4.1(3), The Code. The statute thus bars corrupt influence as to "any business transactions" as well as to "any business transaction." The word "any," which is used seven times in § 741.1, is employed to enlarge rather than limit the terms modified. It means "every" and "all,"not "one." . . .

Under trial court's reasoning, based upon Dukehart-Hughes, it would become proportionately more difficult to prove guilt as the number of transactions with the donor increased. If a gift followed one purchase and preceded another, the State would be charged by that view with proving its connection with one to the exclusion of the other. The gift may in fact have been a reward for the first purchase and an inducement for the second. We believe the statute plainly permits a jury to convict in such circumstances if it finds the gift was related to both transactions or either of them.

Similarly, when there is a series of purchases, the State meets its burden as well by showing the gift was connected with the series of transactions as it would be singling out one of them. It is as great a wrong under the statute for a public officer to enter a series of transactions in relation to a single gratuity as it would be for him to enter a single transaction in relation to the same gratuity. The same is true as to gratuities received by reason of a series of completed transactions. . . .

Trial court erred in holding the term "business transaction" as used in the statute is restricted in singular meaning.

III. In its third assignment of error the State asks us to apply the correct interpretation of § 741.1 to the evidence in this case and hold trial court erred in acquitting defendant. This we decline to do. "A pronouncement from us on the fact situation in one case rarely serves any good purpose in determination of future cases. Such appeals by the State are useless. While the matter of sufficiency or insufficiency of the evidence is a question of law this court will refuse to review the record where it will benefit no one." State v. Wardenburg, . . . (1968).

There is however one question of law raised in this assignment of error which can be decided. That is whether §741.1 is violated by a contractor's payment of the expense of an ordinary business luncheon with a public officer at which a past or future transaction is discussed.

[6] We do not believe such payment is a prohibited gift or grauity. The statute is directed toward conduct by its nature calculated to undermine an employer's relationship of trust with his employee. To be corrupt the influence must involve the transfer of something of value for the employee's

own private use. At an ordinary business luncheon the employee is on his employer's business and not in any substantial sense receiving an inducement to breach his trust. He would frequently prefer to be somewhere else. The motivating factor for the occasion is the employer's business and not the private interest of the employee.

Apart from our interpretation of legislative intent in § 741.1, there is additional authority for recognizing this distinction. This kind of occasion was an early exception to common law bribery. 3 Coke, Institutes, 145 (1648). It is also an exception to the analogous federal statute, 18 U.S.C. § 201, . . . , recognized in Executive Order 11222, establishing "Standards of Ethical Conduct for Governmental Officers and Employees," . . . Federal employees are expressly permitted to accept "food and refreshments available in the ordinary course of a luncheon or dinner or other meeting or on inspection tours where an employee may properly be in attendance." We believe the same conduct is permitted under § 741.1.

[7] But free dinner and drinks at a supper club in celebration of a large purchase by the county, if proven, would not be in the same category. Similarly, a gift of books or payment of convention hotel expense would ordinarily be no different under the statute than an outright payment in cash to the public officer for his own use and, if related to a business transaction, would constitute prohibited corrupt influence. . . .

\* \* \*

# BRIBERY ABROAD

In 1977, after a great flap about bribes paid by American firms to promote sales abroad, in which huge amounts of money said to have been laid out by Lockheed Corporation in Japan was the most spectacular illustration, Congress enacted a law prescribing stiff fines and jail sentences for such practices. Many people think the law is quite unrealistic. Rival firms from other countries competing for the same business operate under no such restraints. In many countries where bribes make a difference to getting the business, it is claimed that bribery is "a way of life." In those countries government officials, for instance, are expected to make up for low salaries by taking bribes as perquisites of their offices. It is accepted that they will be the same means provide for retirement and safeguard themselves against dismissal. Bribes thus function as a sort of tax levied on the firms that use government services, and they are held to be essentially harmless. What the officials do in return for the bribes is just what they are supposed to do anyway—carry out their jobs.

A U.S. Senate report, commenting on the antibribery law, offers some room for distinguishing between serious sorts of bribery, which the law aims to stop, and sorts that the law passes over. According to the report, "payments for expediting shipments through customs, placing a transatlantic telephone call, securing required permits, or obtaining adequate police protection"—illegal though they may be in the United States—do not violate the statute when they occur abroad.* Some firms have found this distinction enough to go on. *Business Week,* in a story published 3 September 1979, said,

> Honolulu-based Castle & Cooke Inc., the diversified food company, is one of the few American companies willing to detail its facilitating payments. "You've got a banana boat that comes in at two or three in the morning with its perishable cargo," says a spokesman. "Every hour means something, so you must get a customs official out of bed. You are not going to be very successful unless you make it worth his while to come down."**

Other firms do not believe that the distinction can be carried out in practice. To be on the safe side of the anti-bribery law, they are banning so-called "facilitating payments" as well as more serious bribes.

> "You can't guarantee compliance," explains [Hewlett-Packard]. "That's why we have put everything off limits rather than run the risk of somebody not understanding the distinction in the law."
> The president of a U.S. chemical company in Brazil agrees. "If what you are trying to do is legal—like getting a legitimate shipment out of a warehouse—I might be willing to make expediting payments myself," he says. "But how do you delegate that authority to 200 or 300 people in the company without risking abuses? It is so much easier to prohibit everything and be completely sure."

By such a policy, of course, American firms can forestall moral objections to the practices; they abandon the practices. Other firms, however, will not; and won't they get the business that American virtue has made unattainable for American firms? *Business Week,* winding up its story, noted,

> Europeans and Japanese businessmen generally regard such stringent regulations with wry amusement. Those who noticed were even more tickled on August 12 when Senator William Proxmire (D-Wis.) urged President Carter to convene an international conference to "outlaw corporate bribery," contending that "informed public opinion all over the world will stand behind" such a move.

One feels that something could be said in Senator Proxmire's defense. Is it entirely ridiculous to try to form a common front against bribery? And may not even small "facilitating payments" be better done away with, in favor of the practices that the so-called advanced countries prefer for themselves? Could such payments—little bribes—be done away with, without a common front?

The problem created by big bribes may be no different in kind, even though more spectacular when an instance of it comes to light. When they are paid systematically in the poorer countries they are bound to raise questions about their helping to perpetuate the poverty. *The Wall Street Journal* reported 9 April 1975 that United Brands, a multinational corpora-

---

*Report of United States Senate Committee on Banking.

**This and the two succeeding quotations reprinted from the September 3, 1979, issue of *Business Week* by special permission, © 1979 by McGraw-Hill, Inc., New York, N.Y. 10020. All rights reserved.

tion dealing in foods, had admitted paying $1.25 million in 1974 to obtain a reduction of the export tax levied by Honduras on bananas. The payment was made to "an official of the Republic of Honduras." According to *The Wall Street Journal*, "United Brands said that it was part of the original understanding with the Honduran official that an additional payment of $1,250,000 would be made. Although the company declined to identify the official, sources close to the investigation [by the United States Securities Exchange Commission] say that the payments were to Gen. Oswaldo Lopez, the president of the Central American nation." Presumably, United Brands was going to pay considerably less in export tax to the Republic of Honduras than it was paying in bribes; and the revenues of the Republic were going to be reduced by the amount of the lost taxes.*

*Comment:*

## OPPRESSIVE REGIMES

It is bad enough if bribes the size of those that United Brands paid in Honduras help maintain regimes that are corrupt, and ineffective besides. The regimes that firms have to deal with abroad are all too often not just corrupt; they are oppressive. Some, like the present regime in South Africa, may be oppressive without being especially corrupt; but corruption and oppression often go hand in hand. However this may be, any relationship of mutual benefit to a foreign firm and an oppressive regime is open to objection as contributing to the continuance of the regime, with whatever amounts of terror and torture it practices.

Selling the regime arms is objectionable. Doesn't it remain objectionable if the regime could get arms elsewhere? Maybe even selling it (or businesses operating under it) cement or locomotives or filing cabinets is objectionable, too. So may be just operating a branch plant that produces something harmless—baking powder, let us say—and does not, in the treatment of its workers or any other way, participate directly in any of the oppressive practices carried on by the regime or sanctioned by it. There are, of course, arguments on the other side: the branch, by providing some workers with decent jobs and the population with a useful product of high standard, does something to offset and alleviate the hardships of oppression.

What is to be said of operating in ways that themselves illustrate oppressive practices? Practicing racial discrimination among workers when the regime upholds such discrimination is one instance. Another, less straightforward, is offered by the involvement of the Coca-Cola Company in

---

*Paraphrased in part and in part reprinted by permission of *The Wall Street Journal*, © Dow Jones & Company, Inc. 1979. All Rights Reserved.

Guatemala, where the regime is notoriously oppressive and vigorously opposes attempts by farmers and workers to organize and better their condition.

## COCA-COLA IN GUATEMALA

*[Coca-Cola does not have a branch plant in Guatemala. Its link there was with a franchised bottler.]*

In the course of the events reported below by Robert Morris, a group of Coca-Cola stockholders representing religious organizations and coordinated by the Interfaith Center on Corporate Responsibility introduced the following resolution* for consideration at the annual general meeting of the company in 1980.

> Whereas, the August 1979 Amnesty International, Nobel Peace Prize winner, "confirmed at first hand reports of intimidation, threats and murder of trade union organizers in the Coca-Cola [franchise] bottling plant Embotelladora Guatemalteca";
>
> Whereas, in 1979 report "Human Rights in Guatemala" of the International Commission of Jurists states" . . . members of the Coca-Cola Union were subjected to various kinds of threats, both in and outside the plant . . . by the plant's own security forces, which included a number of former military officers";
>
> Whereas, in a letter to President Carter urging implementation of his human rights policy, Congressman Pease of Ohio wrote, "The most disturbing reports and allegations pertain to egregious labor abuses in the operations of a Coca-Cola franchise bottler in Guatemala . . . for more than four years the workers at the Coca-Cola Embotelladora Guatemalteca franchise . . . have been subjected to an unmercifully ruthless campaign of intimidation and terror . . .;
>
> Whereas, over the last several years Coca-Cola's share of the cola market in Guatemala has declined significantly due in part to the fact that this violence has, we believe, resulted in a boycott of Coca-Cola products;
>
> Resolved, that shareholders request the Board of Directors to develop and make public by September 1980, Company policy required of all subsidiaries and future franchises requiring their observance of their employees' basic human rights. This policy will permit, where management deems advisable, termination of franchise agreements with bottlers consistently violating Company policy.

In support of this proposal the stockholders stated:

> Church shareholders have received numerous reports of extreme violations of human rights linked to anti-union activity at our franchise bottling plant in Guatemala. There have been numerous armed attacks on and two assassinations of union leaders in the last two years.
>
> Coca-Cola has been studying for four years what, in our opinion, is an international scandal for four years.

*Reprinted with the permission of Interfaith Center on Corporate Responsibility.

In South Africa, Coca-Cola has not even signed Sullivan's minimum principles of fair employment.

Although Coca-Cola is not directly responsible for abusive labor practices of independent franchises, such practices damage our Company's reputation and long-term profitability. Since franchise agreements already stipulate certain requirements (e.g., quality control, trademark use), we believe that the policy suggested here would not unduly intrude in franchisee affairs.

### Coca-Cola management commented in response:

The Board of Directors favors a vote AGAINST this proposal.

A proposal submitted last year by five of these stockholders to develop a code of minimum labor standards to be required of the Company's independent bottlers was defeated by over 98% of the shares voted.

As to the violence to employees of Embotelladora Guatemalteca, S.A., an independently-owned and operated company, the Company conducted an investigation which failed to uncover first hand evidence as to the persons responsible for such acts. The duly constituted legal authorities in Guatemala have not brought charges against any person with respect to the acts of violence. The Company is concerned about the violence to employees and management of the independent bottler and continues to review the situation closely.

As to the proposal that the Company develop a policy requiring all future independent franchisees to observe the basic human rights of their employees, the proposal is in our opinion unworkable and would constitute an improper and unnecessary intrusion into the business affairs of the independent bottlers.

The above stockholder proposal concerns itself with complex relationships between independent bottlers who purchase soft drink syrup and concentrate from the Company and the employees of these independent bottlers. The proposal would require the inclusion of a code of basic human rights in agreements with independent bottlers regulating certain relationships between the independent bottler and its employees. Overall, the independent bottlers, we believe, are among the leaders in employer-employee relations throughout the world. This proposal, in our opinion, would be considered by most of the Company's independent bottlers to be an improper and unnecessary intrusion by the Company into their business affairs.

The proposal does not identify what is intended to be included in the proposed policy on basic human rights for employees of independent bottlers. However, such a policy in our opinion would be too vague and indefinite to be effectively applied in specific situations.

Furthermore the laws of most countries protect employees' basic human rights. Thus, in those countries, such a policy would serve no purpose. If adopted, the proposal makes the Company a party to controversies between independent bottlers and their employees. This will only add, in our opinion, to the complexity of the situation and will not facilitate a prompt resolution of the differences between the independent bottlers and their employees.

The inclusion of such a proposal in agreements with independent bottlers increases the possibility of the Company being liable for acts or omissions of the independent bottlers. The inclusion of a policy of basic human rights in the contracts may be found by the courts to make the independent bottler an agent of the Company and thereby make the Company liable for taxes, negligence and other obligations of the independent bottler over which the Company has, in fact, no control.

The inclusion of the policy in contracts with the independent bottling companies requires the agreement of the independent bottlers. This may mean that the Company, in order to obtain their consent to the inclusion of the policy, may have to give concessions to the independent bottlers which may be of greater importance to the stockholders.

We believe that these complex contractual issues should be left to the management to decide whether and when to request them. There are no simple solutions to the resolution of industrial controversies or other employer-employee relationships. In our opinion, the clause suggested by the stockholders will only aggravate most situations by interjecting an additional party to the complex employer-employee relationships.

We believe that good employer-employee relationships are the result of the combined sincere efforts of the employer and its employees. Such relationships must be based upon mutual respect and trust. Any requirement that all independent bottlers be subject to the proposed policy of basic human rights with respect to their employees, in our opinion, will cause the parties to look to the Company for solutions to their problems rather than to work out the problems themselves. We believe that over the long run, the proposal will weaken the good relationships which have been developed rather than build better relationships in those few instances where there is alleged to be a problem.

The Company and its subsidiaries have long observed employees' basic human rights. Therefore the stockholder proposal has no applicability to the Company and its subsidiaries.

The Board of Directors favors a vote AGAINST the stockholders' proposal. Proxies solicited by the Board of Directors will be so voted unless stockholders specify in their proxy a contrary choice.

The shift of the franchise to another bottler later in 1980 was preceded, not only by pressure from some stockholders, but (as Robert Morris notes) by pressure from unions. Coca-Cola products were boycotted in a number of countries. In Sweden there was not only an effective boycott; unions stopped Coca-Cola production at Pripps Brewery, the Swedish licensee (*Business Week*, November 24, 1980).

## ROBERT MORRIS, "COCA-COLA AND HUMAN RIGHTS IN GUATEMALA"*

As they crossed a busy street in downtown Guatemala City last April, union leader Marlon Mendizabal told a U.S. church representative, "If I am still alive in October, I would like to study abroad." After a few steps, he paused, thinking of what he had just said, and remarked, "Can you imagine that? What a thing for a 22-year-old guy to be saying." Unfortunately Mendizabal's premonition turned out to be all too real. On May 27th at 4:30 P.M. he was cut down in a hail of machine gun fire as he waited at a bus

*Excerpts from an article in *ICCR Brief* November 1980. Copyright 1980 by the Interfaith Center on Corporate Responsibility. Reprinted with its permission and the author's.

stop near his work place, the Coca-Cola franchise bottler, Embotelladora Guatemalteca.

Mendizabal was the third secretary general of the bottler's union to be assassinated in the eighteen month period from December 1978 to May 1980. During that period, three other members of the union's executive committee were also murdered, two of those three were brutally tortured. Four additional union workers have "disappeared", and are presumed dead. Guatemalan workers clearly attribute the human rights abuses at the bottler to a systematic, coordinated union-breaking campaign orchestrated by the Coca-Cola plant's management and the Guatemalan police. . . .

On August 11, 1975 the present union was organized with the specific purpose of enabling the workers to improve their wage rate ($2.08-$2.50 per day). Union resources cite that, at the time, some workers who had had fifteen to twenty years experience with the company were earning only $2.85 per day. Resistance from management was swift. One attempt to destroy the union occurred in March of 1976, when the bottler's management fired 154 employees and brought in non-union workers. Protesting union workers assembled outside the plant and managers called the crack riot squad of the Guatemalan police to dislodge the workers. Several workers were hospitalized from injuries related to this incident. Soon after, the Guatemalan labour courts ordered the bottler to rehire the 154 workers.

Harassment against the union members mounted steadily. On February 10, 1977 two workers, Angel Villeda and Oscar Humberto Sarti, filed a legal affidavit stating that plant manager Ricardo Mejicanos threatened them with death, if they did not quit the union. Less than three weeks later both men were machine-gunned by unidentified gunmen but fortunately survived the attack. On the following day the union's legal advisors, Martha and Enrique Torres, had their car run off a highway and were seriously injured. On other occasions the two lawyers had received death threats in the form of intimidating phone calls. Enrique saw his name appear on no less than five death lists which appeared in Guatemala City and were sent to Guatemalan newspapers by the so-called Secret Anticommunist Army.

An agreement with management was reached in February of 1978 and a collective pact was signed. At that time 94 percent of the workers at the bottler had joined the union. This achievement, however, did not end the labor violence. In 1978, threats against union workers by plant managers began again. As Israel Marquez, the union's secretary general, drove up to his home on the evening of October 15, 1978, the windows of his car exploded in a burst of machinegun fire. Prior to the assassination attempt, Marquez had been death warned by plant managers on several occasions.

Soon after the attack on Marquez, union sources reported that there was a meeting between the Guatemalan Police Chief German Chupina, the bottler management and several members of a rival management-supported union, during which the police chief allegedly stated that "the union would be destroyed within six months." The well respected *Latin American Political Report* (London) has indicated that Police Chief Chupina has been directly linked to death squad activities.

On December 12, 1978 Pedro Quevedo, the union's financial secretary and former secretary general was shot and killed while making deliveries. Although the police denied complicity in the Quevedo murder, union sources reported that police involvement was evident when the unit of military police guarding the plant was reinforced with additional men, several hours before Quevedo's murder. After this, one death list of the Secret Anticommunist Army included the names of the union's entire executive committee and advisory council. Threatening notes were also sent to workers' houses. Union leaders stated the only source for the correct home addresses of the workers was the bottler's office. By this time three army lieutenants were working for the plant in the positions of personnel director, warehouse director and security director.

On January 23, 1979, the union placed an ad in the newspaper *Nuevo Diario* which detailed a chronology of violent actions that had been taken against the workers. The following day Manuel Moscoso Zaldana, a man who had rented Israel Marquez' house, was machinegunned and killed as he left the union leader's house. Guatemalan press reports indicate that Zaldana was probably confused with Marquez. Once again, several hours before the murder, the plant guard was reinforced this time to twenty men. After a third attempt on his life, Marquez was asked by the union's executive committee to go into exile. In January 1979 he sought asylum in the Venezuelan Embassy with his wife and child and a month later fled to Costa Rica.

On April 5, 1979, while on his delivery route, like Pedro Quevedo, Manual Lopez Balam was assassinated—beaten with an iron tube and his throat cut from ear to ear. Several months later Balam's wife told a U.S. church representative that her husband was repeatedly threatened before his assassination and that plant manager Lieutenant Rodas had verbally threatened him three times the week of his death, including once on the day he was killed. As Manuel went out to his truck, Rodas said to him, "Don't you know what happens to those who don't know how to cooperate?" Two weeks after the assassination of Balam, 22-year-old Marlon Mendizabal assumed the position as the new secretary general of the bottler's union and immediately received threats from plant managers. According to union sources he was shown a list of all his closest relatives and their respective addresses and taunted, "Don't be foolish, resign your post. Can't you see, we have the names of all your loved ones? . . . Remember, torture is extremely painful. . . ." Pressure in the form of threats and surveillance against the union continued unabated throughout the remainder of 1979.

On several occasions the CNT issued press releases describing specific death threats which various plant managers directed at union workers. Two of these press releases described threats from army Lieutenant Rodas, the plant's chief of industrial relations. On May 31, 1979 Rodas warned the union's executive committee that their movements and actions were under constant surveillance by various police agencies. On July 3, 1979 he gave death warnings to the union's entire executive committee. By now the percentage of unionized workers at the plant had dropped to less than 50 percent from a high of 94 percent in early 1978. The union's leadership learned to travel in small groups and sleep in different houses.

Coke union leaders Arnulfo Gomez and Ricardo Garcia were kidnapped on May 1, 1980. Their torture ridden bodies were later discovered several miles outside of Guatemala City. The sadistic details of their murders were later described to a U.S. church representative by Coke unionists—Gomez's lips were cut with razor blades, his tongue was cut off and placed in the breast pocket of his shirt, many of his teeth were broken, he had been severely beaten in the stomach and back and there was one gun shot wound at the base of his nose, from a bullet that was fired at close range. Garcia was also tortured.

On May 14th Efrain Zamora the leader of the management created employees association was murdered in the midst of rumors that he wanted to resign from the association just prior to his death. On May 27, 1980 the Coke union's secretary general, Marlon Mendizabal, was gunned down. Within a month, in what seemed a bid to win popular support, the Rebel Armed Forces, a leftist guerrilla group murdered plant manager Rodas. (Another guerrilla group had claimed responsibility for an attack on plant manager Riege during the summer of 1979.) The next day the Guatemalan police responded with yet another murder of a Coke unionist. Edgar Rene Aldana was assassinated by gunmen on the plant grounds in view of police guarding the plant. The same day, two more Coca-Cola union leaders were kidnapped by police along with twenty-five other Guatemalan labor leaders.

In a protest action demanding the return of the missing twenty-seven labor leaders, a strike began at the Coke plant. In response, on July 1, 1980 approximately eighty heavily armed riot police were called to the plant and began to beat the striking workers. During this attack two more Coke unionists were abducted. As a result of the violence of May and June 1980 and the simultaneous condemnation and pressure from international unions in thirty different countries, the parent Coca-Cola Company agreed to change the ownership and management of the Guatemalan bottler.

Although Coca-Cola executives may well understand the differences between a subsidiary and franchise business relationship, most Guatemalans do not. Coca-Cola's reluctance to take action against its franchise until it met international boycott sanctions has certainly not enhanced the image of American business in Guatemala. As one U.S. official in Guatemala recently noted, "Coca-Cola is the classic ugly American for many in Guatemala and this is damaging all U.S. investors here." One U.S. investor summed up the bottler's dismal image by stating "Coca-Cola is becoming a leading brand name of oppression here. . . . And believe me they've got heavy competition for that market."

Though undoubtedly the most notorious, the Coca-Cola Company is not the only American firm whose workers have experienced anti-union violence. Three members of the Ray-O-Vac battery factory union were tortured and killed this year. Other U.S. firms that have experienced labor problems include U.S. Steel, Del Monte, Kellogg, Bank of America, Singer and Phillip

Morris. In addition several of the forty-three union leaders who "disappeared" work for American firms.

How is it that such human rights violations can continue unchecked? Part of the answer lies in the subtle, if not outright, endorsement of the Guatemalan military's tactics by the American business community. For instance, a lengthy article on Central America that appeared in *Forbes* was most apologetic for the Guatemalan generals, noting that most of the victims of Guatemalan's violence were "leftists" and added that Amnesty International statistics were probably exaggerated.

The American Chamber of Commerce in Guatemala City has been quite enthusiastic in its support for Guatemala's military leaders. In February of 1980 Chamber President Tom Mooney wrote to the U.S. Ambassador that:

> The government of Guatemala, despite its numerous faults is better than most governments in the world in terms of the very human rights grounds on which it is so severely attacked and is infinitely better in these same terms than would be a government formed by those who are determined to overthrow it.

In a *National Public Radio* program on Guatemala, Mr. Mooney stated that, in his opinion, the Guatemalan government has made a "very strong effort to support legitimate union movements." The Chamber's petition for resumption of U.S. military aid to Guatemala, made during Congressional hearings in April of 1980, is indicative of the extensive support that U.S. business gives to the present regime. But perhaps the most chilling indication of the American Chamber of Commerce's support for current regime in Guatemala came in a speech by its president, Mooney, to corporation leaders in New York City when he stated:

> The State Department opposes the use of violence as a weapon to subdue the leftist oriented groups which seek to depose Guatemala's government. It is, above all, opposed to non-official exercise of violence; spokesmen for the Department of State feel that privately controlled and financed "death squads" only serve to incite the people against the established order and motive them to support the communists.
>
> There is another point of view that contends that the only feasible way to stop communism is to destroy it quickly. Argentina and Chile are demonstrated as nations which used this approach with considerable effectiveness and have gone on to become Latin America's most stable and successful countries. In spite of the fact that they do not enjoy U.S. support on human rights grounds . . .

\* \* \*

# BUSINESS STUDENTS PLAY
# GAMES WITH CHILE

In the Third Annual Canadian Intercollegiate Business Competition, held at Queen's University in January 1981, teams of students from business schools at universities across Canada engaged in debate ("Resolved, Canada's national symbol should be the ostrich"). They vied in amassing computer-simulated profits (the team from the University of Calgary built up a $20 million equity "from scratch" in seven years). They also took part in a "case study competition," which dealt with the decision faced by a Canadian firm (Noranda) about investing some $400 million in the Andocollo copper mines in Chile. Should the investment be made or shouldn't it?

According to *The Financial Post*, which sponsored the affair at Queen's and reported on it in its issue of 31 January 1981,* "Four schools said no; two said yes. Of the ones that recommended rejection, three made the decision on economic grounds alone. Simon Fraser University stipulated that even if there were good economic reasons for going in, Noranda should refuse to do so on moral grounds alone—no Canadian company, it said, should be seen investing in a country that denies its citizens basic rights.

"Western [the University of Western Ontario], which rejected the investment on economic grounds (low future demand for copper would mean low prices for commodity), disagreed with this. A successful operation, it said, would benefit Chileans (as well as the government) by providing more jobs and a stronger economy.

"The University of British Columbia, which determined that long-term prospects for copper were sufficiently bright to go ahead with the project, took an even more aggressive posture. If the pressure groups (churches, political activists) are so dead set against Noranda investing in Chile, it asked, then why doesn't Noranda prepare an estimate of what it stands to gain by investing in Chile and then ask these groups or the Canadian government if they're willing to pick up the tab.

"If they are, we'll stay out of Chile. If not, we'll go in, is the way UBC's Bruce Stuart put it."

*Story Copyright 1981 *The Financial Post* and quoted with its permission.

# CHAPTER 20

# *The Arms Business*

*Introductory Comment:*

## IS BUSINESS JUST TO SERVE GOVERNMENT POLICY?

A firm might be reproached for making even one weapon, if it had no use (like a hand grenade, say) except to kill people and was likely to fall into the hands of someone who would use it irresponsibly. So manufacturing arms does not create only the sorts of problems that come with aggregative and cumulative effects. Moreover, even massive arms production is sometimes, in the view of most conscientious people, clearly permissible, even laudable. Is it morally outrageous for a country to equip millions of soldiers if it has to defend itself against the likes of Hitler's Germany? Pacifists would have to say yes, and they can point to the frequent abuse by governments of the notion of legitimate defence; they can also argue that arming to ward off menaces like Hitler increases the likelihood of having to ward them off by arms. Yet they have to acknowledge that most conscientious people do not share their fundamental conviction that arming and using arms is evil in all circumstances.

One reason that they have in fairness to acknowledge this is that they will find themselves allied with many conscientious nonpacifists about the production and use of certain arms. Many people who approve of a country's arming in defense do not approve of the use of napalm or dumdum bullets or nerve gas. They will be allied with pacifists also in denouncing certain uses of weapons—dropping antipersonnel fragmentation bombs on civilian populations, for example. What are firms to do in the face of objections from conscientious people allied against them and governments on points like these?

One thing that they can do, and have done, is pass the buck to the governments. The management of Dow Chemical, attacked during the Vietnam War for supplying American forces with napalm, responded by saying that it was not for them to decide what the government of the United States required for military purposes. Was this a conscientious position, or an evasion of responsibility?

The same response, conscientious or not, could hardly be used by a firm that sells weapons to all comers. As things go, firms can usually invoke conformity to government policy for arms exports, too: they sell only to comers that it suits their governments to have armed. Moreover, if some countries have got arms, perhaps from other sources, other countries near them can argue that they need weapons, too, as means of legitimate defence.

Under the triplet principle—modified to exclude strict pacifist convictions—conscientious people may expect to find not only some transactions sanctioned as permissible, even laudable, by these arguments, but also some cases of arms buildups that can be morally approved, too. Yet, in the end, and taking an overall view, can it be a good thing to have the tanks and cannon and fighter-planes at the command of small countries in the Middle East, Asia, Africa, and Latin America multiplied? The arms are used to carry on wars—or warlike expeditions—that less well-armed countries might have hesitated to engage in. Or they are used to repress domestic opponents of oppressive regimes.

Proliferating arms among the importing countries amounts to enabling them to carry on an arms race. The firms in the exporting countries and their governments have helped to foster such races. Nor have the governments taken all the initiative, though the governments of the United States and of France—to name just two—have actively promoted the export of arms. The governments have not taken all the initiative in the arms race in which the great powers are involved. Firms manufacturing arms actively seek (sometimes with the support of their unionized workers) to have the governments give them more business. They even have the expenses of these efforts paid for them. *Time* Magazine, in its issue of 22 June 1981, cites a report by the Council on Economic Priorities, "a liberal research group," on "the Iron Triangle," composed of firms in the arms industry, arms procurement agencies, and Congress. *Time* commented that the report shows that "the Washington offices of the defense contractors charge a good part of their expenses to the Defense Department through contracts they are working on. The practice is perfectly legal, but it amounts to spending taxpayers' money to influence the government to spend more of the taxpayers' money."

Excerpts from the CEP's own summary of its report follow.

# THE IRON TRIANGLE*

The U.S. defense budget, which now accounts for roughly one quarter of all Federal spending, will rise rapidly in the 1980s. This rise stems in part from the intimate relationship between the public and private sectors of the defense community and the extraordinary pressures it allows defense contractors to exert on Government.

Over the years, the defense industry has become an active participant in policy-making. People, power, and money move freely among three centers—the Congressional, the Executive (DoD), and private industry—creating a community of shared interests and assumptions which defends itself against outsiders.

### THE CEP STUDY

In order to examine the Government relations practices of defense contracting firms in this iron triangle, CEP selected a sample of eight firms. All are highly significant Department of Defense (DoD) contractors and all dependent on DoD contracting for over 25 percent of their sales in the years 1970-1979. Boeing, General Dynamics, Grumman, Lockheed, McDonnell Douglas, Northrop, Rockwell International, and United Technologies together received 25 percent of all DoD contracts, 36 percent of all NASA contracts, and over 37 percent of all DoD contracts for research and development in the 1970s. The scale of dependency on Government contracting runs from Grumman's high of 82 percent of corporate sales (in the 1970s) to Boeing's low of 31 percent.

Having selected the companies, we gathered a wide range of available data on corporate Government relations practices, using company disclosures and a variety of Federal and local resources. Each company is profiled in the study and the profile data were sent to each of the eight firms for review. Three firms did not reply: General Dynamics, McDonnell Douglas and Rockwell. Two companies—Boeing and United Technologies—provided a small amount of public information. Two others—Northrop and Lockheed—responded with threatening letters. One, Grumman, provided a fair reading of the profile and some additional data.

### RESEARCH AND DEVELOPMENT

Contractor Government relations begin at the research and development stage. R & D is at the heart of the Iron Triangle. Long before members of Congress or the general public become aware of weapons development and changes in strategic policies, new weapons and missions are being defined

*Reprinted by permission of the Council on Economic Priorities, New York.

by DoD and specialists in the industry. Even the Congressional committees given the specific responsibility of watching over defense Research and Development are forced into a subsidiary and ineffective role.

The Iron Triangle serves the purposes of contractors who design weapons for sales to the Government. Well aware of the importance of early access, the defense industry uses virtually all tools of Government relations to ensure an early, close and sustained intimacy with DoD and NASA. Contractors frequently take the initiative themselves in defining future weapons needs. Through advisory committees, trade associations and, especially, the transfer of R & D personnel, contractors have early access to information on R & D planning and an opportunity to play a role in defining future weapons systems long before Congress or the public are aware of these decisions. Once a major system exists, momentum is created in the company, the DoD and Congress to continue to fund it through production.

POLITICAL ACTION COMMITTEES

Defense contractors, like other corporations, have taken quick advantage of the possibilities created by the 1974 Federal Elections Campaign Act to create Political Action Committees (PACs). Like other aerospace contractors, the eight companies in our study each created PACs between April 1976 and February 1978. These eight PACs spent over $2 million by 1980. According to Federal Elections Commission (FEC) data, $1.2 million of that sum took the form of Federal-level campaign contributions (from 1977 to 1978). Of the top 10 U.S. corporations in gross PAC receipts (1977–1978), Grumman ranked ninth ($171,434) and Boeing tenth ($165,155). Of gross disbursements (covering all spending—Federal, state, and local candidates; party committees and other), Grumman ranked eighth among all U.S. companies ($156,435), General Dynamics ninth ($155,956), and Boeing tenth ($135,377). Of the top 10 in contributions to Federal candidates, United Technologies ranked ninth ($198,725).

Among the eight companies in our study, General Dynamics had the largest PAC in gross disbursements (from its inception to mid-1978), nearly $510,000, followed by Grumman—$391,000—United Technologies— $342,000, and Boeing—$260,000. We also examined the Federal-level campaign contributions of the eight firms (combining contributions to candidates with those to campaign committees), and ranked the companies by amount.

PAC contribution patterns indicated a strategy of directing a sizeable proportion of contractor campaign contributions to candidates for Congress who either represented districts and states where the company had plant locations, or who were members of committees in the Congress which considered legislation and appropriations of importance to the company. Grumman contributed the largest amount to candidates from key geographic locations ($81,540), though McDonnell Douglas contributed the highest proportion (54.14 percent). Other company PACs ranged between 12 and 39 percent of contributions to candidates from key geographic areas.

Grumman, again, contributed the highest amount to members of the key

House and Senate committees—$129,350, while McDonnell Douglas was again highest in proportion—60.37 percent. The general range for the other companies in this category was higher than that for key geographic areas—from 29 to 48 percent.

## WASHINGTON OPERATIONS

A contractor's Washington office staff follows issues and seeks to shape legislation, procurement and appropriation decisions as they move constantly between the Executive and the Congressional side of the Iron Triangle. It also plays a critical role in planning a company's overall political strategy.

Washington office staffers can become so central to the flow of information that they become the medium for communications between the other two sides of the Iron Triangle. According to one Pentagon source, "The best thing about corporate lobbyists is that they pass on to us a lot of stuff that they've learned on Capitol Hill. It's usually the quickest way for us to find out what's happening up there."

Available data on lobbying is woefully incomplete because the Legislative Reorganization Act of 1946, which covers lobbying, is inadequate. Much of the Washington activity of the eight companies in CEP's study is, accordingly, undisclosed.

The eight companies in the CEP study, however, have each maintained a substantial Washington operation for some years. Rockwell International has the largest staff with 85 employees, roughly 40 of whom work on defense issues. Other companies that undertook significant Washington efforts included, as follows in decreasing order of size and staff: United Technologies, Boeing, Northrop, General Dynamics, McDonnell Douglas.

All eight office directors play an active role in coordinating, directing and carrying out information gathering and advisory activities, but only two, Boeing's Russell Light and Grumman's Gordon Ochenrider, are registered lobbyists.

On the basis of preliminary Defense Contract Audit Agency reports, released by the Defense Department to Common Cause in January 1981, we found that the Washington offices of the five companies in our study which were audited—Boeing, General Dynamics, Grumman, Lockheed and Rockwell International—spent nearly $16.8 million between 1974 and 1975 for their Government relations activities, over $15.8 million of which was initially charged to contracts.

Both the preliminary and the final versions of these audits indicate that a substantial portion of these expenditures were for lobbying activities that sought to influence legislation and appropriations in Congress. In the opinion of DCAA some of these expenditures were not "unallowable costs" against contracts.

## TRANSFER OF PERSONNEL

A flow of personnel—uniformed and civilian—links the Executive with the industry side of the Iron Triangle. Defense contractors regularly hire DoD civilian employees and retiring military officers, who bring a wealth of professional experience and useful contacts to the company. The Defense Department hires personnel from the companies, providing the Government with skilled executives.

To the insider, this intimacy seems to foster technical and political knowledge that smooths the contracting process, ensuring a more efficient defense of national security and the public good. To the outsider, however, it suggests a closed community in which the private and Government interests converge.

In this study, we have examined the employee transfer reports for eight companies which hired 1,672 former military and civilian employees of DoD and NASA. During this same period between 1970 and 1979, 270 company employees, who moved to DoD and NASA, filed reports. In short, the flow of personnel has continued unabated, bringing the Executive and the industrial sides of the Iron Triangle ever closer.

Boeing ranked highest in total transfers for the decade—(398), followed by Northrop (360) and Lockheed (321). General Dynamics, McDonnell Douglas and Rockwell had over 200 transfers with DoD each, while Grumman and United Technologies both had under 100. While such number of transfers may provide a rough indication of the closeness of the relationship of the corporation with the Federal Government, it may also indicate that some companies urge their employees to comply with the reporting requirement more strongly than others.

In terms of civilian transfers, particularly from DoD, a slightly different pattern emerges. Northrop hired the largest number (50), while Rockwell was the source of the largest number of civilian employees hired by DoD during the decade (47).

Our review of transfers focused on the category of "appearances of potential conflict of interest." We noted transferees who worked in similar areas of policy-making and weapons systems on one side of the Iron Triangle before moving to a similar area on the other side. We reviewed these cases carefully, since disclosed data varies enormously and a person's responsibilities on either side are not always clear. Moreover, we did not assume that these transferees were insensitive to the conflict issues. Many of them may well have taken strict measures to ensure that they had no involvement with their former employer. Our review showed that 122 transferees had job descriptions which suggested an appearance of potential conflicts of interest.

PENETRATING THE IRON TRIANGLE

Though defense procurement and national security policy are of crucial importance to all Americans, decisions on defense policy and weapons procurement rest almost entirely in the hands of experts who are isolated from outsiders and alternative perspectives. The advantages of having such a concentration of expertise are offset by the way the closed nature of the policy process works to narrow views and to reinforce shared expectations that another generation of weapons is both desirable and necessary, whatever the cost. Are there practical ways to pry open the Iron Triangle of defense policy and weapons procurement, to enhance public awareness of policy alternatives, to effectively restrain Government relations activities, and to broaden public involvement in the policy process itself? We offer several suggestions:

—Broaden disclosure requirements for defense contracting, research and development data and local impact of defense contracts and subcontracts. Enforce transfer of personnel reporting requirements. Disclose corporate interests in work that Federal advisory committees consider, and board member ties with Government.

—Revise the definition of lobbying to cover a broader range of individuals and groups seeking to influence policy or legislation.

—Broaden disclosure requirements for Political Action Committees to cover all categories of PAC spending, rather than merely the contributions to Federal candidates presently regulated.

—Reform personnel transfer (Conflict of Interest) legislation to clarify the "arms length" between contractor and Government. Prohibit defense contractors from passing on their lobbying costs to the taxpayer.

—Consider lower ceilings on PAC contributions to Congressional candidates. Undertake a careful study of Federal funding for Congressional election campaigns.

—Encourage direct public participation in the military policy-making process through closer Congressional scrutiny of the Defense Department and public membership on Federal advisory committees to DoD and NASA.

\*　　\*　　\*

# PART SEVEN

# Ethics in Business Compared with Ethics in the Professions

# CHAPTER 21

# Ethics in Business and in the Professions

---

*Introductory Comment:*

## IS BUSINESS AS MUCH A PROFESSION AS LAW, MEDICINE, ENGINEERING, UNIVERSITY TEACHING AND RESEARCH?

---

Business could be compared with any of the professions mentioned in the heading above. I doubt whether either in standards of competence or in standards of moral conduct, people in business would come out worse in comparison with professionals in any of those fields. In some connections, they may even come out better: more scrupulous about keeping their word; franker in describing the efficacy of their services; less secretive about unpleasant responsibilities; less insistent on having their own way.

It is true, one takes a certain liberty in treating business as a profession. It is characteristic of a profession that for every given jurisdiction in which it operates there is a recognized corporate body composed of the members of the profession, which prescribes and enforces standards of professional learning that have to be met before people are admitted to the profession. Characteristically, the same body prescribes and enforces standards of professional conduct that have to be met as long as people continue in the profession.

University teaching does not fit this model very neatly. There are standards of learning and of conduct, but they are for the most part enforced university by university, and enforced there as much by administrators acting for the teachers' employers as by fellow teachers. Even engineering does not quite fit. Societies of engineers publish standards of conduct, but they do not, I believe, enforce them systematically any more than national associations of university teachers enforce the standards that they too publish (though in both cases, the standards can be invoked to justify enforcement by other bodies). The standard model of a profession fits medicine and the law best, and it is from those fields that the model is derived.

One might well think, however, that to treat only medicine and law as professions is to use the term *profession* too narrowly. If the term is used more broadly, to take in engineering and university teaching (and the clergy, in a country with many churches and sects), it becomes difficult to deny it application to business, too. Some people in business enter it and rise with little or no education; they learn on the job. But so did doctors and lawyers in the past; Abraham Lincoln became a lawyer by working under a lawyer already established. To some extent, lawyers and doctors still get part of their training by apprenticeship, lawyers (in Canada) as "articled clerks" and doctors as interns and residents. Moreover, it is becoming an increasingly common expectation, commonly justified, that people in business will share the body of specialized learning acquired in the course of taking a bachelor's degree in business administration or an M.B.A. Members of one profession that fits the standard model quite well—accountancy—are specifically trained to be occupied with business matters, and this profession is the source of many business executives (many of whom are drawn from the legal and engineering professions if they do not start as accountants).

Even in respect to standards of moral conduct—codes of ethics—business is not so different from law and medicine. Observers have been far from satisfied that the legal and medical societies do an effective job of enforcing their codes. Some codes have been drawn up by people in business (consider the code, set forth earlier in this book, of direct mail merchants), and they may be as well enforced as the codes for lawyers and doctors. Those codes are in some respects relaxing. Lawyers are now permitted to advertise their fees and engage in open price competition. Hospitals in the United States are running vigorous advertising campaigns to attract more patients. There are some known differences of fees among doctors, and patients take some account of the differences; so price competition isn't entirely absent even there.

Business could be compared with any of the professions. I shall, however, confine myself here to presenting material about lawyers. Except for accountants, they are more involved in business than people in the other professions. No wonder then that what is morally troubling about what lawyers do is often something morally troubling about business. The two fields intersect and mirror each other. We have some new points about business to discover in considering how lawyers let themselves be used by business; for that is, of course, the same thing as considering how business uses lawyers.

# PHILIP SHUCHMAN, "LAWYERS, TRUTH, AND THE SERVICE OF BUSINESS"*

*[This selection on the law consists of excerpts, amounting to the major part of an article, "Relations between Lawyers," by a professor of law at the University of Connecticut. It originated as a paper contributed to a conference that reviewed the Code of Professional Responsibility of the American Bar Association.]*

A verdict is neither true nor untrue. It is an authoritative statement of the outcome of a trial to decide who shall obtain or be denied some particular remedy sought. Indeed, an appeal may not be taken by reason of the verdict being incorrect or "untrue." I think it is most prudent to assume that the American trial, conducted by advocates in an adversary system, is only incidentally a search for truth. The American trial includes factors which are obtained in the pursuit of other social aims and goals, which are too often antithetical to those of truth-seeking and truth-finding.

This position has the distinct advantage of making my premise explicit—that lawyers do not deceive in their professional roles. I address my comments to relations between lawyers; but, as lawyers represent clients, in some situations a lawyer's relations may extend to another lawyer's clients.

Most of the relations relevant to my purposes take two forms:

(1) A transaction such as a sale or formation of a business firm or business situation. I will assume that more than one person (and this includes business firms) is represented.

(2) A claim made by a person or firm which, in some way, to some extent, is contested by another person. This contesting may go as far as an informal counterclaim. Both parties would be represented by lawyers whose primary purpose and most common activity would be to reach a negotiated settlement on terms most advantageous to their respective clients.

These two types of activity constitute the bulk of most lawyers' gainful employment. It appears that most civil claims are abandoned (although the data seem hard to come by and there is some disagreement), because the cost in time, money and aggravation is not worth the possible recovery. Consider too that, not only are most pressed claims settled without instituting a lawsuit, but that most civil lawsuits are settled without a trial. For the whole set of actual civil cases (those claims resulting in lawsuits), well over nine-tenths are terminated by a negotiated settlement.

So, we add a third activity:

(3) Representation in lawsuits, nearly all of which will be settled by negotiation between lawyers and never tried. Obviously, this would

*From *Ethics and Advocacy* (Washington, 1978), pp. 75–97, with omissions of most of the footnotes and of other material. Reprinted by permission of the publisher, The Roscoe Pound–American Trial Lawyers Foundation.

include pretrial discovery and the remote possibility of an actual trial—an eventuality taken into account by the lawyers and, variously, by the claimants and litigants.

For all three of these activities I will pose much the same questions: Can a statement made (or not made) by a lawyer be fairly called a lie, given the social situation in which it is stated? Does the Code of Professional Responsibility (CPR) cover such situations and, if so, with what strictures or admonitions? What sanctions, if any, can be imposed and, by whom and in regard to what sorts of statements? . . .

Deceit in daily life involves an inherent stigma. It is entirely appropriate for one to demand a reason for lying, while no one, except in extraordinary circumstances, would ask why a person is telling the truth. This does not apply to litigation. We observe that lawyers are not sworn before a judge or jury. The judge will not direct jurors to attend to what the lawyer has said, but rather to attend to the witnesses and exhibits. The lawyer realizes that his audience is justified in not taking him seriously as regards the truth of his statement.

Pleadings* might very well be the utterance of lies. A lawyer often has no basis for believing the assertions in his pleadings; he states them in writing with the very formal intention that others shall be led to believe he has proof. Such pleadings are not dishonest, if only because the inherent credibility of lawyers' pleadings is, to a professional audience, almost nonexistent. A lawyer is aware that his audience does not rely upon his statements. (Perhaps some lay persons do, but only because they haven't been socialized.) No judge tells a jury to read what the pleadings say; rather, he directs it to assay the evidence ruled admissible and presented to it.

The most conspicuous feature of nearly all pleadings—complaint and answer—is that they do not inform too much or too well. Because of past problems with complex pleadings, the forms of action legacy, most states and the federal courts now operate with simple statements which, it is generally accepted, do not provide adequate information regarding the specific contentions of the parties. The pleadings are too vague and too general. Most lawyers think or act as though they think the less specific information provided in the complaint, the better. There are good reasons for their belief, most having to do with the adversary system. Answers to the complaints are equally uninformative. Also, for reasons of economy and efficiency, it is rare that a lawyer will do more in preparing a pleading than make appropriate minor changes of name, place, and other details on a form. In fact, most pleadings are taken from form books or forms in the lawyer's files. Judge Pollock goes beyond the truism that these variations on past forms are uninformative regarding the case:

> When [the lawyers] get a case, for security, they reach for forms which relate to the subject matter. For obvious reasons, these forms contain alternatives for

---

*[Pleadings are specific forms of legal claims. In a suit for damages, for example, the lawyers for the plaintiff might plead breach of contract; negligence; failure in professional duty; etc. Which of these pleadings would be pressed if the case came to trial would depend on the evidence that the lawyers could then get before the court. D.B.]

liability, and counsel use most of them in traditional pretrial contentions in order to insure that they will have at least one contention for the evidence that they will be able to adduce at the trial. This is a set-up made to order for false issues.

These are properly-termed allegations, even when the pleadings do state, deny or controvert facts. There does not have to be the slightest assurance of their truth. There are very few civil cases in which a lawyer is censured because, in retrospect, some statements in his pleadings ought to have appeared incredible to any reasonable observer at the time they were written.

Also, all pleadings must, in some way or other, be cast in syllogistic form. "The major premise is the rule of law involved which even if it could be succinctly and unambiguously stated is never explicitly stated. . . ." The minor premise consists of the facts which the pleader claims bring his case within the operation of the rule of law embodied in the major premise.

In some cases of complaint and answer, the syllogistic form may be stretched to the point of gross distortion, for lawyers can and do make inconsistent, mutually exclusive claims and allegations. Once more, given the nature of the process, there are good reasons for this. During pleadings, the lawyers do not know what they can later "prove," what might persuade, or what a judge or jury might believe. Hence, rather than lose any possibility, the prudent lawyer will plead all manners of things and, certainly, any and all possibilities. The failure to allege a basis for relief in the pleadings can sometimes foreclose that possibility at trial or on appeal.

Because of some apparently egregious problems with the very technical niceties of pleadings from early on through the nineteenth century (and, indeed, until quite recently), we now use other mechanisms for preliminary revelation of facts and past events. (We now rely much more—almost entirely it is thought—on pretrial discovery and the pretrial conference for knowledge of the specifics.) The pleadings are supposed to state the facts upon which a claim is based and which show that the person is entitled to relief (usually money, rarely some other form of remedy). Although "[t]he signature of an attorney constitutes a certification by him . . . that to the best of his knowledge, information and belief there is good ground to support [the pleading]," this applies only to the extremes and is difficult to controvert in the usual case. Only at the very boundary conditions of overt and explicit dishonesty can the lawyer be held responsible.

When a client relates possible facts which might support a civil claim or defense, the lawyer is not obliged to do any more unless "it is obvious" there is no merit to the claim. In fact, the lawyer is better protected from later civil suits and the ethics committees by not conducting any investigation, thus insulating himself from knowledge that might cause ethical problems under Federal Rule 11 or DR 7-102 (A)(1).

As matters are now, nothing more than questioning of the client is required in most cases to discharge the lawyer's ethical responsibilities. The prudent lawyer is apt to carefully question his client anyway, especially if his fee is contingent on recovery. Even in contingent fee situations, lawyers by no means undertake any other investigation. Also, when the lawyer's billing is not contingent, there is little incentive for his doing more than listening and internally probing his client's case. . . . *

In many situations which can be identified as routine, similar and repetitive, Federal Rule 11 and its state law equivalents should impose upon the lawyer some duty of investigation, a burden which may vary greatly, depending upon such factors as the type of claim, the client, and the likely impact on the other parties. Such an investigation should, I think, also be a function of the expense and financial means of the client and, perhaps, of the other parties.

For example, I have no compunctions in requiring more investigation when a large business firm or governmental agency is the client and an ordinary individual or small business firm is the other party. Such clients should have a greater burden to justify the lawyer's belief in the truth of the factual allegations of the complaint or answer. There is now virtually no such burden and there are only rare sanctions for filing what amounts to a pleading which may be unsupported to the point of being captious. Some pleadings, perhaps many, are true only in the sense that it is true that Tom Sawyer ran away from home. . . .

In those lawsuits where the cost of the initial investigation is shifted from the plaintiff to the defendant who can easily obtain discovery, there need not be a problem. The cost of getting the information is usually then shifted back to the plaintiff, easily and inexpensively, by means of written form interrogatories. But in the following examples those costs cannot be so shifted, because the mere starting of the lawsuit imposes a burden on the defendant which is a substantial harm to him. The cost of retaining counsel and having him endeavor to shift the cost of reasonable investigation back to the plaintiff is too great as regards to both the amount in controversy and his own means. The defendant is compelled to settle or even be better off defaulting than litigating. These actions, moreover—typically by business firm financers against consumers—make up the largest number of civil actions in most state courts of general jurisdiction. Another example is of certain civil actions in the federal bankruptcy courts, now occurring some ten to fifteen thousand times a year, with more such actions threatened and not brought because they are settled.

A lawyer who transgresses even slightly and technically regarding his client or his relations with other lawyers (vide, *Grove* v. *State Bar)* is often—and often with notoriety—sanctioned by his peers and by the courts. Indeed, we have created for clients a remarkable catalogue of responsibilities and have even seen to a variety of conventional insurance plans and security funds to indemnify the individual client. However, an entire and sizable group of lawyers habitually acts in a manner which they know to be

---

*[At this point, Professor Schuchman shifts from showing that as things stand lawyers are not expected to make sure of the truth of their representations, including their pleadings, to arguing for a change in practices and expectations that would imply a more sensitive concern for truth. D.B.]

prejudicial to large groups of individuals—hundreds of thousands of persons a year—and nothing is done. The reason is that our Code of Professional Responsibility relegates such behavior to ethical nonreality.

We contend that the interests of society are best served by the individually-based, one-on-one adversary system. There is little empirical support for this nostrum, and there is plenty of contrary evidence in the examples of typical and common lawsuits I have mentioned involving the large, or merely larger, business firm against the natural individual of ordinary means. This behavior may—more than the singleminded defense of the client's interest—influence the public who think ill of lawyers. They experience this sort of thing more often and are hurt by such actions more often.

I agree with Professor Freedman that the lawyer should represent his client with zeal and not be influenced by his own moral judgments of his client or his client's cause.* His examples—those actual cases and hypothetical situations illustrative of that ongoing debate—are relatively unusual lawsuits if only because they went to trial. Also, most are lawsuits in the accepted literary sense, with full representation of the parties at trial; many went through appellate review and became reported cases. Professor Freedman's examples are the sports, the occasional dramatic situations of actual litigation, with a complete record of the proceedings and the scrutiny of an appellate review, to say nothing of newspaper and law journal commentary.

The examples I suggest are different and, by comparison, mundane and uninteresting. There is little drama in the routine collection cases that make up most of the civil litigation in most state courts of general jurisdiction. Each of these examples, however, occurs tens of thousands of times a year. Although the amounts of money at issue are small and the defendant's freedom is not at hazard, these are the only experiences with lawyers and the legal system that most people have in their lifetimes. For example, they find that, although they may have borrowed money in Austin, Texas where they reside and made their payments in Austin, the lawsuit is brought in Amarillo, nearly five hundred miles distant. This practice was and, to a fair extent, still is lawful in many states. What of the lawyers who, by glancing at the files, know that this is what they are doing? They zealously represent their clients by taking advantage of the venue laws to create defaults. In this setting, that singlemindedness of purpose seems less attractive. I believe it is wicked for the lawyers representing Montgomery Ward to zealously represent their client by suing consumer debtors a thousand miles or more from their residences. It is not an adequate excuse to reply that the legislatures or the courts should change these laws. Those lawyers who start collection actions in courts at great distances from the defendant's residence are not acting unethically within the meaning of the CPR. If the lawyer failed to take advantage of the venue laws and the contractual provisions of the loan contract, he would be considered derelict in his duties to his client.

*M. Freedman, *Lawyers' Ethics in an Adversary System* (1975), ch. 2.

Lawyers are aware of these great inequities and unfairnesses amounting to oppression through manipulation of the legal system. They tend to become cynical and accepting. This related aspect of lawyers' ethics may be seen in another example—a practice that is rarely contested: lawyers' passive acceptance of petty theft from their clients and other parties. Deputy sheriffs and private process servers, in states where those functionaries are paid on a piece-work basis, so to speak, commonly overcharge, especially in matters such as divorce and landlord-tenant proceedings. Often the defendant is not represented and the judgment entered includes the unlawful charges. Sometimes the client pays. It isn't that the lawyer has, in any direct sense at least, gotten a piece of the action (that extra and unlawful five or ten dollars), but that he has permitted the other party or his client to bear that cost without protest and without advising anyone. In the long run, the lawyer has indirectly benefitted. The sheriff or other process server is grateful and in the normal exchange relationship will bestow favors on the lawyer. He will reciprocate by making prompt or difficult service without an extra charge. In some states the relations between lawyers and those who serve civil process are so close as to prejudice the lawyer-client relationship, although only in little ways and for small sums.

In many civil cases, such as consumer credit contract cases, there is a high incidence of default judgments. We do not ask whether the complaint is true or whether the lawyer has any basis for believing its factual allegations other than that the information was provided to him by his client. Although the complaint may be entirely true, no investigation is made. The allegations of fact and law are "true" for purposes of the default judgment. I expect that many lawyers who do collection work for banks, financers, retail installment sellers, credit card firms and other commercial clients know nothing about the truth or bona fides of the complaints they file. Some employee gives them the requisite information on a printed form. This is often all the lawyer knows, if he can be said to know that much. I think this is true of full-time lawyer employees and outside counsel.

Deficiency judgment proceedings are but one of a whole panopoly of such civil actions. There is nothing complicated about most of them. I assert that, in many of these similar and repetitive civil actions, the lawyers do know that the pleadings are false.

Consider another example. A few years back we conducted a study of personal bankrupts. There were mostly semiskilled blue and white collar workers of lower middle class income. Many had borrowed from banks and business firms engaged in consumer lending and were required by these experienced lenders to sign a form listing all other loans and obligations. The major purpose of the lenders in this ceremonial was that, if a borrower sought to have his debt discharged in bankruptcy, they would have a good archival evidentiary basis to claim reliance and have their debt excepted from the bankruptcy discharge by reasons of the bankrupt's fraud within the meaning of § 17a(2) of the Bankruptcy Act. The lawyers engaged in this work know full well that there is little reliance on these forms and that credit reports and, especially, past experience are the determining factors in most consumer loans. However, our data showed that almost a fifth of all personal bankrupts were sued in the state courts on the basis of such a misrepresentation in writing upon which the lender claimed to have relied.

I have little doubt that even a slightly experienced attorney, with knowledge of the consumer lending business and faced with the frequency of such actions, would be aware that most (nearly all, in my opinion) are staged occurrences. Yet the lawyers continue to file the actions, most of which are settled, and the lawyers know that also, because to the bankrupts they are not worth the cost of litigating.

I put to you that reasonable inquiry and probing would have revealed to the lawyers that most of these actions were fictional; that no loan manager is deceived that often by the same devices and by the same group of ill-educated but obviously very shrewd felons. (By my estimates, at that time some 35,000 to 40,000 such actions a year were started in the nation.)

I incline to requiring more of the lawyer in such civil actions, assuming the usual disparity of means. If the lawyers are burdened with some measure of truth-telling requirement, there may be fewer mistakes and less unlawful behavior by their clients. It is worth an experiment with careful monitoring and analysis of the results in a set of cases. . . .

More than a quarter of all lawyers are salaried employees of business firms and government. About 40 percent of all lawyers are solo practitioners as compared to about 60 percent in 1948. About half of the nonsalaried lawyers fall into the category I have called LL's (little lawyers), individual practitioners and small firms (some in name only, merely cost-sharing arrangements) of two or three lawyers. The trend towards lawyers as salaried employees and into the BLF's (big law firms) has continued and there are fewer independent lawyers in the sense that many commentators discuss in their examples.

The lawyers who specialize, especially in the lucrative work, are predominantly in the BLF's. There has been a large increase in the number of salaried lawyers employed by large business firms as house counsel and in government. The BLF's get larger and there are fewer LL's. There is a greater disparity of income and status between BLF lawyers and the LL's.

These changes in occupational setting are of such a degree that the profession now may be different in kind than it was two or three decades back. Certainly the full-time employment of so many lawyers by business firms and governments raises questions which go to the very core of the lawyer-client relationship as it is regulated by the CPR and the various rules of practice and procedure. There are many more young lawyers today than ever before who have never been employed as independent practitioners in the traditional sense. They have never practiced in the manner that most of us have. Their only experience as lawyers has been as full-time employees of a single client. It is immediately obvious that a different kind of autonomy is involved today.

Other changes have become commonplace. We need ask what it means when we say that "a client (who need not be a litigant) acted on the advice of counsel" when the lawyer was the full-time employee of the client. How far does the lawyer-client privilege extend and regarding what activities, when the "client" has dozens of lawyer-employees and thousands of other employees? Ought all those lawyers and all those employees be able to assume the rights and privileges that go with the lawyer's work-product and the confidentiality of the lawyer-client relationship?

Consider the recent example of Covington & Burling refusing to submit documents for inspection sought under the Foreign Agents Registration Act on the ground that "the Act should be interpreted [as subject to] the lawyer-client privilege. . . . " The client was the Republic of Guinea. That law firm was in the fortunate position of having other such clients—South Africa, Cambodia, Pakistan, Czechoslovakia, Iran and Poland. . . .

These formerly extreme situations are now more common as business firms grow larger and the income and employment prospects of law students who would become LL's worsen. That the federal and state governments can assert the lawyer-client privilege in these cases strikes some educated laymen as bizarre, rightfully so, I think. Even prosecutors who withhold or suppress evidence favorable to the defendant in a criminal action are virtually immune from sanctions in what is the worst perversion of our system of justice.

There are occasional cases in which severe sanctions are imposed, but they appear to be unusual and extreme. One recent example is the falsification and destruction of evidence by an employee of the federal government. When this was discovered by the defendant business firm during depositions (itself an unlikely occurrence), the court ordered the government's case dismissed. The court stated that the government is held to a high standard of conduct in civil litigation, and willful failure to meet this high standard of conduct justifies dismissal. The opinion does not inform us whether the government's lawyers (our lawyers) might, by reasonable investigation, have had knowledge of this dereliction or reason for disbelieving their pleadings. We may be assured that, short of their outright knowing deception, nothing much would happen to our government's lawyers. The result is, of course, that we the people pay the price, not the lawyers engaged in such conduct.

The recent revelations that a laywer defending Kodak falsely claimed that certain documents were destroyed and that he had lied about it in an affidavit illustrates only an extreme case. More prudent lawyers would have finessed the oath, seen to the destruction of the documents or, in a more advantageous situation, have avoided or prevented the creation of such documents.

But these are the large business firms at their usual work. They can, on the whole, protect themselves. If Kodak had been against a smaller business firm or if this were not an antitrust case (where there are treble damages and court-awarded counsel fees) which can be worth the time and direct expense of the lawyers, it is nearly certain that the proceedings would not have progressed far enough for us to know of such matters.

Lawyers are part of a professional community with long-accepted and distinct conventions that are at odds—even in conflict—with most of society. Young lawyers and even law students are quickly socialized into a setting which includes a fiercely adversarial posture supported by the nearly absolute privileges of confidences given and not to be revealed even under the most difficult circumstances. These include related matters such as the work-product immunity, where what the lawyer has done for this client's cause in the form of research, investigation and tactically advantageous moves of many kinds is also privileged information. Ordinarily, none of these need be revealed. . . .

Quite apart from considerations such as the stratified bar, sharply differentiated by social status, type of legal work, and by income and the source of income, we may ask what premises apply to any such normative analysis of the CPR. What are the ontological commitments of a system of legal ethics? What sorts of things and processes are presupposed by the discussants?

These I have put earlier as two questions which I answered in the negative: Is the civil trial a truth-seeking process? Are lawyers' statements such as can be characterized as deceptions?

What can be taught regarding legal ethics? I take it that virtue cannot be taught. Gilbert Ryle's colloquy is illustrative:

Q. Don't you know the difference between right and wrong?

A. Well, I did know it once but I have forgotten.

The answer is unacceptable, presumably because charity, kindness, fairness, tolerance and a courageous concern for justice cannot be taught. Indeed, we speak of these as a person's characteristics or qualities. We do not speak of persons knowledgeable in virtue.

If I ask about your Latin or geometry, it seems entirely appropriate for you to respond that you once knew that verb or that theorem, but you have now forgotten. But then we know what to do about that. A regular study or review is the usual and acceptable response.

To the extent that virtue can be taught, the process involves the students' understanding and acceptance of examples of good behavior. These we provide by positing hypotheticals and, by pointing to some persons or particular activities as models. Above all, we "sensitize" our students to what might be questionable behavior. We teach them what kinds of situations might pose problems in legal ethics. We advise them how to avoid falling into the clutches of the ethics committees. This is but another version of Holmes' "bad man" theory; it teaches them the necessary minimum conformity to the CPR and to avoid transgressions which might get a lawyer into trouble. But unless we identify conformity with the CPR with good behavior, we may have taught prudence but not morality. I am not prepared to say (and which of you can prove) that the CPR mandates good and even desirable behavior for most lawyers or litigants, or that the results on the whole are better than they would be with a different CPR. Or none at all.

I take it that we should teach and are to the largest extent engaged in teaching our students (who become your young associates) how to win more cases than they would without our training. To teach people how to win (or avoid losing), irrespective of the substantive morality of their victories, is, at best, neither good nor bad. However, if most of what we teach our students is how to win, that does not seem to me an activity of which moral persons necessarily should be proud.

There is one sense, however, in which legal ethics is a subject of knowledge and can be taught. First, we must agree on what are good and bad results, or postulate them. Then we must investigate whether the CPR in its present form tends, on the whole, to bring about more or less of these results (assuming there are no side effects) than some other CPR or, perhaps no CPR at all. It is possible that some of us could agree on what are good and bad results of a particular form of CPR and agree that we would be bound by those rules. Other groups could agree on different CPR's. Then the laity could be informed and prospective clients could choose a lawyer whose CPR (whose ethics) they prefer. Or, it might be that, as suggested, there should be varying CPR's for different types of claims or different clients. Perhaps governments as governments and large business firms as governments should be subject to CPR's more stringent regarding probity, the use of expensive and dilatory devices and so forth.

It does not seem to me at all self-evident that there must, or should be a single mandatory CPR for all lawyers. Perhaps we should try more of an open market in legal ethics. I suspect that we now have a greater range of accepted behavior than is comprehended by the CPR. But as we do not know (because we do not systematically investigate), we discuss our mostly *a priori* and relatively uninformed notions of legal ethics.

We can avoid some of the problems attendant upon searching for rules of ethical behavior applicable to all lawyers in all types of legal work. A better approach is that of Karl Popper's piecemeal social technology.* We should start with benchmark information on little problems within some limited areas of common activity. The impacts of the discrete changes we make can then be assayed and the effects of any failure will not be so great.

\*    \*    \*

## TWO CASES IN WHICH YOU MIGHT BE INVOLVED, ACTING FOR A FIRM

*[Most of the discussion that the preceding cases about activities of firms will have provoked took, one might expect, a view of firms in which they—or the people responsible for deciding upon their policies and actions—figured as third parties, candidates for external judgment by the people using this book. Nevertheless, from time to time the questions may have crossed every reader's mind, "Just what could I do about any of these things if I were an employee of the firm? What could I do if I were just one middle manager among many? What could I do even if I were the chief executive officer, considering that even so I would be answerable to the rest of top*

---

*See P. Winch, "Popper and the Scientific Method in the Social Sciences," in P. Schilpp, ed., II. *The Philosophy of Karl Popper* (1974), pp. 889, 890.

*management, if not to the stockholders?" In the following two invented cases, you are asked to face these questions. Not having been a business executive, you will probably not be able to draw, as you were able in previous invented cases (with the possible exception of the ones about stockholders), on your own experience. One may hope that even so, if you make an effort to think of all the dimensions of the job and the pressures that it involves, you will be able to imagine quite concretely what it would be like to be such an executive.]*

SKID ROW PROFITS

You are the chief executive of a wine producing firm, which is small enough, with its stock held tightly enough, to be effectively controlled by a half-dozen stockholders who have quickly jettisoned past chief executives when profits were not so high as they hoped for. You are in your fifties. You have three children midway in their university studies. You do not believe that you could straightaway, or perhaps ever, find another job that would pay you half as much. You have always known that the firm gets most of its profits from selling cheap sherry and cheap port to winos in skid row districts and to more clandestine alcoholics elsewhere—old women, for example, living in poverty behind drawn blinds. At the moment, moreover, you understand that whatever competitive advantage your firm has over other wine producers consists in the following that the firm has as the longest-established and best-known source of cheap sherry and cheap port. Now the sales manager comes to you with his latest analysis of the market. It shows that your firm is losing ground to rival firms in other products, though it is gaining ground in sales of sherry and port. Your sales here can be expected to increase anyway, as the incidence of alcoholism in your society increases, which it apparently is, given the substantial increases reported in per capita consumption of alcohol. Your firm's established name, its advertising, and its sales force have combined to enable it to gain overall a relatively higher share of the increased sales by the industry. Do you have any reason to be uncomfortable in your conscience? What can you do about it if you do?

GETTING ALONG WITH THE GOOD OLE BOYS

*[An approach that you may have found helpful in the last case was to ask, What can I do that will do most to improve matters? Resigning is not likely to be the answer; but neither is doing business as usual and taking no risks yourself. In some cases—the last one may have been an instance—it is easier to find something useful to do—some mitigating scheme—than in others. The following case is harder.]*

You are the regional sales manager for a firm that makes bulldozers and other heavy construction equipment. Sixty-five percent of your sales go to municipal and county highway departments; the rest to private contractors, who themselves do most of their business with governments. The region is one in which a traditional political culture prevails much more than it does in most parts of the country. Road building—public construction generally—is looked upon as the chief field for distributing political patronage; it is at any rate the field in which more people get political favors than any other. Moreover, even though equipment is bought by the government agencies only after bids are called for and compared, in almost all cases the chosen firms have paid "gratuities" to various government officials, elected and appointed. (The firms not chosen were ready to pay "gratuities," too; some may have paid them. Perhaps they did not pay enough or pay the right people; perhaps they just have to wait their turn.) Purchasing agents for the private contractors have the same expectations. Your firm does not want to have any scandals, and you know that it might disown you if you got involved in too many scandals or in really spectacular ones. On the other hand, it is ready to supply you with enough funds to keep the firm in good standing with the good ole boys with whom you have to deal.

# PART EIGHT

# The Issues Reviewed and a Look at Larger Issues

# CHAPTER 22

# *Putting Things Together*

*Introductory Comment:*

## TIME TO LOOK BACK

Although there is a chapter yet to come, the time has come to look back upon the discussion that this book was designed to promote. In that discussion, the system of business—a market economy with private firms, imperfectly competitive but competitive nonetheless—has been taken as given. In the next and final chapter, I shall remove that assumption and bring forward for consideration some criticisms of the system as a whole. That chapter, however, will be in the nature of a postscript, and the consideration given to the matters that it takes up will be brief.

Our task, trying to put things together and to make as much sense as possible of them, lies chiefly and centrally with the matters that we have already discussed, under the assumption prevailing when we discussed them. However, I can be brief here, too, partly because I have already given, as we went along, a number of clues as to what findings might be reached and how the findings might be put together. Moreover, though I shall now press on a bit further toward establishing findings and reaching a settled, organized view of them, I shall again be leaving plenty of room for options and discretion in elaborating what I say.

## REVIEW OF ETHICAL THEORY

The moral judgments that have been evoked in the preceding chapters could all be thought of, whether they were about specific goods and evils, about general forms of good or evil (like truth telling or deception), about different moralities suitable for different circumstances, or about fundamental moral principles, as expressing shared intuitions about what is right and wrong. Once we begin thinking of these judgments as falling into a structure or hierarchy in which some are more general than others, moreover, our intuitions have the prospect of benefiting from certain strengths of organized thought; we can see possibilities of deducing less general judgments from more general ones. I shall return in a moment to the structure of ethics, but I shall begin the review of ethical theory farther back than we ever got before, on the other side of any of our intuitions, and outside the structure of ethics. From beginning to end, I present the review in the form of an outline—an outline of questions, in which my own view will be pretty clear from the way I steer the discussion, but which nevertheless indicates by its form that elaboration by you, even amendment, is called for.

1. If we are asked, "Is it true that a good life involves a chance to do some of the things that one enjoys doing?" or "Is it true that one ought to keep one's promises?" would we hesitate to answer yes?
    a. Yet, however natural it is to use "true" as a way of signifying our endorsement of what is expressed in such judgments, do truth and falsity work in the normal way with them?
        (i) One reason for doubt lies in the fact that we can easily imagine a commandment substituted at least for judgments of the second sort: "Thou shalt keep thy promises without fail." Would it make sense to speak of a commandment as true or false? Or we might imagine a rule substituted: "Henceforth everyone shall keep his promises." When we lay down a rule, do we do so because it's true?
        (ii) A second reason for doubt lies in the fact that some of the moral rules which people uphold differ dramatically from culture to culture, and even within our own culture (though this may be a respect in which it is unusual). What are some instances of differences between cultures? Of differences within our culture?
        (iii) A third reason for doubt is that there is some difficulty in seeing what fundamental criterion or principle we might look to to resolve these differences. A natural suggestion is that only those rules should be accepted that help people who observe them to lead a good life. But do not people disagree about what is a good life?
    b. In the face of these doubts, does our natural inclination to endorse moral judgments by saying "true" seem anything more than unreflective habit, by which we simply demonstrate that we've had the moral training customary in our culture and that as a consequence we've adopted (at least in form) its outlook?
2. Yet can we refer to the customary training and the prevailing views of our culture without implying that there is in fact a large measure of agreement on at least some of these matters? How many people in our culture hold that it's not part of the good life to have a chance to do some

of the things that one enjoys doing? Or that one ought not to keep one's promises?

a. Perhaps, if we could find some fundamental principle behind the matters which there is general agreement, we could use it to sort out the matters on which there is not. Might there not be some traps to watch out for here, however?

b. We can distinguish between unreflective morality (accepting some moral judgments just because they are traditional and familiar) and critical ethics. Taking up critical ethics, we might ask, Might not people be got to agree sufficiently on what a good life involves to allow us to settle on some rules? Or if they could not agree about a good life, might they not at least agree on some rules that would enable them to realize various conceptions of it?

    (i) The sort of agreement that we would want would be agreement that was forthcoming under special circumstances. Wouldn't we demand free, unbiased, and informed agreement? How could we accept without question agreement by people as they are, with privileges and vested interests to protect in some cases, and with some possibilities of being intimidated in others?

    (ii) The agents entering such an agreement might be expected to have some concern to protect their chances for a good life. Hence, to carry out a reconstruction of morality by discovering what rules could be derived from such an agreement would bring together the considerations of consent and happiness. How does consent relate to justice, which was earlier held to be always joined with happiness when this is a moral consideration? How does consent relate to publicity?

    (iii) It would be quite disconcerting to carry out such a reconstruction and find it wholly at odds with our present moral beliefs. Suppose, however, that where there is now general agreement in moral judgments (see 2(a) above), the reconstruction carried out by critical ethics leads in most cases to the same judgments—to the same rules, when it is general judgments that are in question. Do we then have some way of rebutting the charge that our moral judgments simply reflect the prejudices of our particular culture?

c. Suppose it is said that nevertheless any of us can choose not to accept the judgments so sustained; for any of us might in fact repudiate all interest in advancing other people's plans for a good life and renounce all help from others in advancing his or her own plan (if there is one). Does admitting this undermine ethics irreparably? Compare admitting that someone who liked mysteries and gambling might take no interest in scientific bases for predictions.

3. Does reconstructing ethics on the basis described have the advantage that it opens up the possibility of enlarging the body of people affected to include people from other cultures?

a. The degree to which the reconstruction relies on agreement reached in circumstances specially assumed to forestall certain objections will remind those familiar with current ethical theory of "contractarianism" or "social contract theory." Is the reconstruction really committed to that approach as opposed to utilitarianism (reliance on the Greatest Happiness Principle)?

   (i) Doesn't happiness figure prominently and essentially in the reconstruction?

   (ii) Implicit in the reconstruction, moreover, are notions of what people need to have chances of a good life and hence of what they will require before giving their consent. Would not exploring these topics give a view of ethics as founded on natural laws about the opportunities open to the human species?

   [I might perhaps interpolate the comment that I for one think it is impossible to give a convincing comprehensive account of ethics (received or critical) without giving full credit to each of the three organizing ideas, agreement, happiness, natural conditions.]

   b. Social contract theory, as it is currently expounded, characteristically tries to demonstrate that the reconstructed ethics will emerge from an agreement among agents who are rational and indifferent to the interests of other parties to the agreement. Will such agents extend the benefits of their agreement to human beings who cannot offer a substantial benefit in return? Is the agreement referred to in the reconstruction sketched above subject to any limitation in this respect, following from the narrowness of the agents' concerns? Can we not in fact assume that the agents there are moved by compassion as well as by interest?

4. Have we, with the reconstruction, provided grounds justifying the use of "true" and "false" for moral judgments? Consider in turn particular judgments putting single cases under appropriate moral rules; judgments expressing general rules; judgments favoring different moralities for different circumstances; a judgment expressing a fundamental criterion or princple that critical ethics relies on in making the reconstruction.

5. What does the reconstruction imply about the costs of being moral?

   a. Does it not imply, on the one hand, that waiving external dangers that may require extraordinary sacrifices, everyone will get something like as much chance of a good life as everyone else if the rules are obeyed?

   b. Can it be expected to guarantee, on the other hand, that anyone will make more money by obeying the rules than by not obeying? In this connection, the Bible takes us a long way toward the right general answer: "Greed is a disgrace to a man; better be a poor man than a liar." (*Proverbs*, xix, v. 22).

# CRITICAL THINKING AT TWO LEVELS

In the passage just preceding, I have not set forth much more about critical ethics than enough to acquaint the reader with its existence and with some of the themes treated in it. This was enough, even so, to make intelligible the contrast that I drew between it and "unreflective morality"—that is to say, "accepting some moral judgments just because they are traditional and familiar." The contrast, moreover, is an important one. It signifies that reflective people must be prepared not only to rise, sooner or later, to considering arguments in critical ethics, but also to give some of those arguments more weight than customary judgments in cases of conflict, and revise their customary judgments accordingly.

I would not, however, want the importance and significance attached to the distinction of critical ethics from unreflective morality to overshadow the importance of awakening people to moral issues in the first place, even when those issues are going to be judged by applying traditional and familiar terms. Indeed, the chief purpose of this book has been to bring about such an awakening. As I said in the preface, the book has offered an opportunity to "gain practice in asking moral questions"; and, with such practice, to become "habituated to asking questions about actions now too often taken for granted." "Good and evil in business take many different forms." Many of these forms, it by now should have become abundantly clear, are not commonly recognized as inviting the moral judgments that they in fact call for.

Moving from taking actions and policies for granted to being awake to their moral significance, even in traditional and familiar terms, is itself a move from a relatively "unreflective" condition to "critical" thinking. I want to claim that it is a big advance. How much is gained by it, however, if on a second, higher level of critical thinking—where critical ethics operates— arguments are going to come up that may require revising familiar and traditional moral judgments? Isn't there an unsettling prospect that every- thing supposedly achieved by the advance in critical thinking on the first level will be undone when critical thinking on the second level is taken up?

I think the little that I have said about critical ethics has been enough to accomplish the further task of showing that this prospect is not a real one. For what I have said has made it clear that critical ethics will reaffirm the moral significance of deception, oppression, adverse aggregative and cumu- lative effects, justice, happiness, and public agreement. Deception and oppression are not going to be discovered to be good things, or their opposites, evil ones. Moreover, we may anticipate that most of the specific actions and policies now firmly judged to be deceptive or oppressive are going to continue to be judged so after critical ethics has done its work. If they were not, so much change would occur in the concepts of deception and oppression that we would no longer be able to be sure of the findings of critical ethics. The task of critical ethics is to refine morality, not destroy it. What would its findings have to do with morality if they upset most of our firm judgments about forms of good and evil?

The revisions that critical ethics can justify requiring are going to apply with most conviction, and hence with greatest likelihood, to in-between cases. The closer a case is to being one that under the triplet principle is firmly recognized as good, or firmly recognized as evil, the less likely it is to suffer revision. This will be true, I think, both of cases recognized as such before the awakening on the first level of critical thinking occurs, and of cases recognized and judged, like many of the cases brought forward in this book, only after people have advanced beyond taking the actions or policies in them for granted. For I suppose that some of the latter cases, too, will, once they are looked at critically, be seen to invite firm moral judgments. They will have firm analogies with cases recognized previously. In other, in-between cases, the moral judgments arrived at will have to be accepted as tentative. More than the others, they will have to wait on findings in critical ethics; hence, more than the others, they will incite work at that level. Their being tentative is as it should be; even so, it is something accomplished that the judgments upon them are the best that we can reach by careful thinking at the first level.

Critical ethics will not only have significant places for the moral terms that have been key ones in the discussion which this book has intended to promote. It will have, we may expect, places for them connected in at least the ways postulated in the framework for ethical discussion continually used in the book. Happiness, for example, will not, according to the findings of critical ethics, be something to seek apart from justice; and critical ethics will imply that justice would hardly be of any importance if it did nothing to promote happiness. Thus, with reasonable confidence we can return to that framework, and to the three subjects of moral concern that we meet with immediately in it—deception, oppression (or, more broadly, abuses of power), and adverse aggregative and cumulative effects—to review what we might hope to have accomplished, mainly on the first level of critical thinking, in the course of working through this book.

## THREE LEADING SUBJECTS OF MORAL CONCERN IN BUSINESS

Many of the moral issues that we have discussed arise about transactions (or contracts, which may be regarded as features of some sorts of transactions). Transactions invite, immediately, applications of notions of justice. The consideration of happiness and opportunities to lead decent sorts of lives, though it is sometimes easily visible in the background of transactions, comes in only indirectly, as an ultimate reason for attaching importance to justice.

Why do things go morally wrong with transactions? How do injustices occur in them? Things go wrong partly, we have found, because people are not agreed in their conception of procedures. When and how is the price set on the mixed nuts? Is competition so much like sport that deception of certain sorts is allowed, even encouraged, under the rules of the game? Even if the second question is answered yes, we might well expect to find considerable disagreement as to which sorts of deception are allowed. These are matters that people in business can act to clear up. The people running supermarket chains, for example, can announce that the price at which they offer goods is the price on the sticker, or the price given at the shelf location, or whichever of these is lower. Where it is clear that a practice (like putting big price-signs on end-of-counter displays as if they were displays of "specials," when it is the regular price that is being asked) is effective only when it misleads the public, firms can abandon the practice. They may be asked to assume some responsibility, moreover, to see whether the public is being misled, for example, by conducting appropriate survey research.

One might think of traders' morality as a code applicable even before procedures are settled upon. Then, though force and failure to hold to contracts would be ruled out, it would be up to everyone to look out for himself or herself even respecting confusion or deception in procedures. It seems more sensible, however, to leave the choice of codes—different "moralities" for different kinds of transactions—until after the procedures are settled upon. However, this choice, too, should be one that all participants are aware of. It should, in other words, be a public choice and one that can be publicly defended.

For some kinds of transactions—where the participants have equal bargaining power, for example, and (as a feature of equal bargaining power) equal resources in information; or where the costs of supplying more information exceed what is at stake in the transactions—traders' morality may no doubt be chosen, and along with it rules forbidding those sorts of deception that are to count as outright fraud. It will then define the demands of justice for those transactions in a way consistent with doing the utmost to satisfy the consideration of happiness and decent lives. In regard to most kinds of transactions, however, will not the tendency of moral argument be to favor adopting something more like neighbors' morality?

The attention and solicitude (sometimes, unselfish solicitude) of neighbors' morality can no doubt not be fully realized very often. It requires closer acquaintance and in other ways requires more time and other resources than most transactions can admit of. Still, an approach to neighbors' morality that we might call "the morality of possible friends" could prevail widely in business. Under this morality, people in business would do nothing, in designing and manufacturing their products in the first place, and in selling them in the second, that would tell against future friendly relations with customers. In particular, they would refrain from making false or misleading suggestions about the character of their products; they would indeed make available, early enough to count fully, all the information that the customer needed to know to understand that character.

Satisfying a publicity condition of this sort would not quite amount to satisfying the condition of being able to present a full public defense of the product. It would, however, encourage people to make changes in the product so that it, as well as all aspects of the transaction, could be fully known and publicly defended. Moreover, if the procedures under which the transaction takes place and the morality governing transactions of that kind are both fixed, it will generally be quite clear what is morally required of parties to the transaction. Unless the information concerned is, by general agreement on something like traders' morality, something that one is not required to disclose, no party to the transaction should do anything or hide anything the disclosure of which would give other parties to the transaction grounds for objecting to it.

The things that I have alluded to so far as going wrong with transactions have all been instances of deception. If injustice is done in these instances, the injustice is done through deception; if it is avoided, it is because no one as watchful as he or she should have been and was would be misled, or because everything important has been revealed. In cases sorted out by the triplet principle as not merely clearly all right, but laudable and good, pains will have been taken to match the customers' needs and preferences as closely as possible.

Not all the things that go wrong with transactions are covered by deception, however. A second subject of moral concern that crops up with transactions—though not only there—has to do with unequal power. I brought it up earlier, time and again, with the term *oppression*, which may be said, roughly, to keep company with unequal power when the power is abused. Only roughly, however. The abuses of power in transactions— monopolistically extortionate prices, excessively hard bargains with a firm's agents or suppliers, cutthroat competition—are not all happily called oppression, though sometimes when they are not, instance by instance, one may properly call the arrangements under which the instances occur oppressive. People are not oppressed by a firm's charging them monopolistic prices for diamonds, or even for asphalt shingles. A firm that in a given instance gives a farmer or a fisherman the lowest price that it can get away with is not oppressing him. On the other hand, arrangements that put farmers or fishermen at the mercy year after year of a few packing firms will be oppressive, if the firms show no mercy.

The term *oppression* is more at home with the abuses of power that occur not in transactions, but in the employment relationship. However, this is because the employment relationship is usually enduring and because people depend on it for their livelihoods. Moreover, the employment relationship can be thought of both as beginning in a transaction and as being carried on by the transaction being continually renewed as employees sell their services. Where in fact (as in dock labor and certain sorts of construction work) the relationship lapses every day, with rehiring the next, an oppressive relationship is manifested in a series of transactions. It may also be manifested in a series of transactions with agents or with suppliers, even when these are not bound to a firm by enduring contracts.

Publicity is not the same cure for oppression that it is for deception. By itself it undoes deception, giving agents who would otherwise have been deceived into consenting a chance to spurn transactional overtures. People who are oppressed sometimes do not realize that they are; they need consciousness-raising. Very commonly, however, they already are aware of the oppression. Whether they are or not, they may, even when the facts have been publicized, still have no option but to consent to high prices or low wages, dangerous work or sexual harassment. Yet publicity is at least a step toward remedying the oppression, because, besides whatever it does to encourage the people oppressed to help themselves, it prepares the larger society for action against the oppression. That action will be motivated and justified by, among other things, the consideration that people ought not to be subjected to arrangements which they would not consent to, were they free to choose (having some alternative way of meeting their needs) and fully informed. Oppression immediately evokes the concept of justice and justice brings with it all the fundamental ideas of ethics about agreement on happy and decent lives for everybody.

Publicity is at least the beginning of useful moral guidance in the third grand category of issues arising about business—the category in which the aggregative and cumulative effects of business operations are the subject of moral concern. These issues sometimes, as in political corruption, involve transactions that could not stand the light of day; or, sometimes, they involve actions that could not stand that light either—actions suppressing information about dangers to environment, or actions subverting attempts to assess such dangers impartially and reduce them. Moreover, the contrast between different moralities bears upon issues of aggregative effects, too. Traders' morality may be expected, so far as it is practiced in relevant connections (for example, in deciding what products to put onto the market and what to reveal about their character), to be less concerned with aggregative and cumulative effects than some approach to neighbors' morality. Excessively widespread practice of traders' morality is itself likely to have an adverse effect on culture, undermining mutual trust among citizens and other features of a civilized society. On the other hand, sometimes it is possible to use market processes, even processes governed by traders' morality, as the means for dealing with aggregative effects. Selling licenses at prices proportioned to the pollution permitted, or to the resources used up (taking into account long-run demand), are instances.

However, to deal fully with the issues raised by aggregative and cumulative effects it does not suffice to rely on the sort of guidance suited to transactions. We have to consider directly how the aggregative and cumulative effects impinge on the prospects for happiness and decent lives and then concert upon a social policy to control these effects. Here the problems may seem intractable, even for governments; and so grandiose that individual people in business cannot expect to have any impact in helping with remedies, and so little or no responsibility to help.

At most, would not the responsibility be limited to voting, in one's capacity as a citizen, for politicians who seem to be addressing themselves effectively to the problems? But there are, besides, duties to refrain from subverting public efforts to deal with the problem. Firms in an industry that is endangering the environment can do a great deal, which they ought not to do, to block such efforts.

Moreover, there is often a good deal that they—and the people with managerial responsibilities in them—can do by acting on their own to mitigate the aggregative and cumulative effects. They can invent and install antipollution devices; or develop styles of advertising that anticipating reasoned, fully informed decisions on the part of their customers, do not contribute to cumulatively undermining reason and culture. Some headway can be made even with the most intractable problems by adopting mitigating schemes. A convincing example can be produced for operations in poorer countries laboring under corrupt and oppressive regimes. A firm might argue that it was at least defensible to continue operations even under a bad regime. Whether or not the argument was convincing, the firm would put itself in a better moral position by making sure it paid good wages, offered good working conditions, and gave substantial parts of its profits to international charitable organizations working in the same country and to international organizations trying to find ways of improving the position of such countries in the international economy. Of course, the more comprehensive a mitigating scheme is, the better, other things being equal; the more costly it will be, too, and the more difficult for any person in business to carry his or her firm along with it. But that is no excuse for not making at least a modest effort to improve on the present situation.

Where are we to look for the motivation to do all these good things? Sometimes—indeed very often—the conduct required will be in the long-run interest of the firms involved and of everyone else. We should look upon that coincidence, however, perhaps more as something that happily makes upright and public-spirited conduct less strained than it otherwise would be, instead of relying on it as the principal source of motivation. Should we not rather rely on conscientiousness, self-respect, and fellow feeling—all motivations that can be fostered by enlightened upbringing, civilized education, and civilized practices? Among those practices are the practices that we end up recommending for business anyway; the more they prevail, the easier they will be to keep up, since they will foster the very motivations that sustain them.

CHAPTER **23**

# Moral Questions About the Business System as a Whole

*Introductory Comment:*

## WHY RAISE SUCH QUESTIONS?

Criticisms of the whole system of business as it is conducted today have come up already, or been implied, in some of the materials brought forward for discussion: for example, in Marx's objections to exchange; in Knight's critique of competition; in Bosquet's picture of irrational consumption. These criticisms have not, however, heretofore been the focus of attention. The selections from Marx and Knight were included to demonstrate that there were moral issues to raise about business even in the absence of forms of organization—firms—that are now characteristically present. The selection from Bosquet was intended to illustrate in a general way the adverse impact that business might have upon reason and culture when it is carried on unmindful of that impact. The possibility was left open that without fundamental modifications in the system business might be adapted to reduce such effects—just as it can be adapted to reduce physical pollution.

This is not the place to press criticisms of the whole system and this is not the book to do it in. The book has been addressed throughout to people who assume that business and capitalism are better than alternative systems, or who are at least willing to adopt the assumption that they are acceptable and consider how people and firms might act for better or worse within the system.

The assumption that capitalism is at least acceptable, even preferable, to alternative systems seems to me a reasonable one. Various horrors have been committed by the only alternative systems currently practiced on a large scale. Personal and political liberties continue to suffer abridgement under those systems (in China, for example, as well as in the Soviet Union). The fact that capitalism has been compatible in practice, as thoroughgoing attempts at socialist planning so far have not, with a good deal of political and personal freedom is impressive enough to offset a lot of particular failings.

I think that it has a good claim to remaining impressive even in the eyes of people who are acquainted with criticisms exposing—or purporting to expose—the fundamental failings of capitalism. For these failings turn out to be, in considerable measure, failings also of the alternative systems currently practiced. The basically authoritarian character of firms is paralleled in the organization of industry under noncapitalist auspices, and so (I suspect) is the disproportionate influence of the elite figures who are the chief executives of industry here. The distribution of income is unequal in the alternative systems—in some systems, in some connections, more unequal than it is under capitalism; and privileged people are able to pass on some part of their privileges to their children. The alternative systems offer a much smaller proportion of their populations chances of achieving personal autonomy—control over one's life. Here and there, at times, the alternative systems may have succeeded in fostering a spirit of mutual aid among people enthusiastically participating in them; but it is doubtful whether over time that spirit has been any more prevalent there than in the capitalistic democracies. Being commanded to do things by an authoritarian regime may be quite as withering to the spirit of mutual aid as being incited to do them for personal gain.

Why then do I bring up criticisms of the business system on these points at all, even by way of a postscript? Part of the answer is that the criticisms indicate further respects in which the system can be improved even on the assumption that it is to be retained. My chief reason, however, is that they prevent people who understand them from treating business or capitalism as morally sacrosanct. It is reasonable, given the alternatives, to support capitalism, especially if one is ready to improve its performance in all the matters that we have discussed. It is not reasonable to treat it as the embodiment of all moral virtues; and not reasonable, either, to view any of its features as prescribed by fundamental moral intuitions.

Even so characteristic a feature as the inheritance of private property is not essential to it, and its elimination is not something that it is immoral to contemplate. On the contrary, some advocates of capitalism have thought that the system would work better without inheritance. Private property in the means of production is essential, but might be limited in various ways without moral offense (it is already). It is not immoral to try to live without it, though outside very small communities doing so may be difficult to arrange for, compatibly with various other desired conditions.

Judge Learned Hand once said, "The spirit of liberty is the spirit that is not sure it is entirely right." The morally enlightened view of business, I think, is the view that is not sure business is entirely ideal. Let us consider briefly some fundamental criticisms of business as a whole.

## FIRMS: UNDEMOCRATIC ORGANIZATIONS IN A DEMOCRATIC SOCIETY

To recall some points from discussion earlier in the book, business leaders—the top executives of firms—are undemocratically selected, and within their firms they exercise authority for which they are not answerable democratically to any internal electorate. Stockholders are too unequal in the votes that they cast to form a democratic electorate. In the typical large firm they do not exercise substantial control anyway. Workers, through their unions, can sometimes oppose internal checks to executives' power; but they have left management plenty of authoritarian prerogatives—for example, in dealing with nonunion employees.

Outside the firm, business leaders exercise great influence in politics in two ways. As C. E. Lindblom points out in *Politics and Markets* (New York, 1977, part 5), they can in effect often veto policies that they hold to be adverse to business. Politicians want business to be prosperous and they are very wary about obstructing it. Business leaders also play an important part in the selection of politicians, not only through contributing to campaign funds. In both connections, the leaders of business have much more influence than rank-and-file citizens.

One may wonder whether, given their experience exercising power without democratic checks within their firms, business leaders will be entirely democratic in exercising power outside. Will they interfere so much with the process of arriving at laws that the laws cannot in the end be said to be democratically arrived at? If the laws are democratically arrived at, will business leaders respect them once they are on the books or try to subvert them?

One way of getting perspective on these questions is to recognize that even executives elected by democratic organizations might act, representing those organizations, to subvert broader democratic processes; so might executives appointed from outside by public authorities themselves answerable to the general electorate. For it is inevitable that the leaders of other organizations, as well as leaders in business firms, will identify their aims with the special interests of their organizations.

Another way of getting perspective is to recognize that executives vary a great deal in their commitment to democracy, as they do, for that matter, in personal cultivation. Some have deliberately used their power to promote democratic policies, not only loyally conforming to the law, but going beyond it. For example, they have not only made sure that their firms abided by antidiscrimination laws; they have had branches set up in regions with great unemployment among disadvantaged minorities and steered purchases toward suppliers run by people from minority groups. Similarly, some business leaders and some firms have intelligently and effectively promoted programs in the arts.

These are the sorts of good things that are cited as evidence of "social responsibility" on the part of business. There are, nevertheless, various reasons to be uneasy about this notion—reasons that many business leaders share. All told, considered as a portion of the firms' budgets, the expenditures do not amount to much (though, shrewdly directed, they may sometimes make dramatic strategic differences). They may not make up for the diversion, brought about by the practices of business as a whole, of production and consumption from more important purposes to less important ones: clean, quiet, well-organized cities, for example, rather than a proliferation of drive-in movies and fast-food outlets.

We may ask with Baumol, Where do the leaders and the firms get the authority to carry out projects in "social responsibility" anyway? (We are of course not talking about responsibly abiding by the law.) In many cases, stockholders in the firms would rather have the money coming to them in increased dividends; and in theory it is their money. A broader objection arises from just the lack of any democratic origin and answerability in the powers that the leaders are here exercising in what is after all the sphere of public policy. Democratically answerable officials might not, on occasion, do a better job, or even a job half so good; but what they do may be expected to be done after somewhat more systematic consultation of the public's view of the public interest.

Thus, even when business leaders undertake, in a public-spirited way, to do good, their power is difficult to reconcile with democracy. It is also far from being the case that they are always trying to promote the public interest.

## UNEQUAL DISTRIBUTION OF INCOME AND PROPERTY

The difficulty about the unequal power of business leaders is aggravated by the fact that it reflects a very unequal distribution of income and property. "Reflects,": it does not exactly match. Nevertheless, in a loose way, the interests of business leaders coincide with the interests of the richest and most comfortable stratum of the population—with the stratum in which are concentrated the very small proportion of the population that owns shares in business.

Even when honestly obtained by highly useful effort on the part of the people who actually own this property—which is far from being the case for all of it—property in large amounts is a means of political power that as such is not justified by the justifications for acquiring property. People with money, and firms with money, acting in alliance with them, can afford to take leading parts in politics, or to give substantial support to people who do. One consequence is that democratic governments, even democratic socialist governments, treat concentrations of property tenderly. Taxes on inheritances are often halfhearted (in Canada they have even disappeared); taxes on incomes often, as in the United States, leave so many loopholes that some very rich people with very large incomes have managed year after year to pay no income tax at all. Hence, politicians come and go, but the concentrations of property persist, in the same families; and generation after generation, the owners continue to persuade governments that they warrant favorable treatment.

Yet the arguments against great inequalities are very powerful. Democracy is subverted even if the propertied use their power to do no more than evade searching public debate about their holdings. There is always the danger (unhappily realized in some former democracies like Chile) of more thoroughgoing subversion. The spectacle of enormous fortunes obtained through inheritance or by questionable financial maneuvers is bound to undermine people's sense of justice, and with it their incentive to contribute usefully to society. How can it even appear just that some must work hard at tasks essential to meeting people's needs, while others do no useful work at all, or actually disrupt economic life? What grounds can there be for justifying the present limitation to the rewards given the people doing useful work, when the others are rewarded at all, and in fact (in many cases) rewarded abundantly?

## FAILURE TO MEET EVERYBODY'S NEEDS AND RESTRICTED OPPORTUNITIES FOR PERSONAL AUTONOMY

Business as a whole, in capitalist countries, may claim that the persisting inequalities of property and income do not matter as much as the fact that the system has succeeded in meeting the basic needs of everybody in the population. It is true that people officially classified as poor in countries like the United States and Canada have, in great numbers, a standard of living, reckoned in material goods, that even relatively prosperous people a couple of generations ago did not attain to—and do not attain to even now in less favored countries. Certainly, the system is capable of meeting the needs for food, shelter, clothing, medical care for everybody in the population; and to the extent that it actually does so, inequalities of property and income are less offensive.

However, not everybody's needs are in fact taken care of. There are, even in the United States and Canada, instances of desperate poverty: among the elderly; among Indians; among migrant farmworkers. Moreover, does the system not cost the people whose material needs it does meet something in respect to other needs? Some authors argue that the inequalities of property and income function to create appetites for increased consumption: "The arrival on the market of a new product and its purchase by the rich *deprive* the poor until such times they too can acquire it. . . . There exists a social class dynamic which works for the manufacturers, whose outcome is nil in terms of improving well-being and which explains at least in part the impetus for economic growth" (Jacques Attali and Marc Guillaume, *L'Antiéconomique*, Paris, 1974, cited by Bosquet in the book I drew on earlier, p. 353 above). The "deprivation" is felt deprivation—a feeling of pressure that not only makes life restless and uncomfortable but also diverts people's attention and energy from other matters—from other needs, including the need for a good deal of autonomy if they are to make as much of their lives and talents as they could.

Imagine how it might be otherwise. Imagine everybody's having useful, absorbing work for (say) thirty hours a week, with most of the rest of waking time divided between sport and art and inquiry, all of these things overlapping into intelligent entertainment. The distribution of time among these activities would vary from person to person, according to choices arrived at experimentally. The activities themselves would take different forms for different people: for some, "art" would be poetry; for others, cookery or tinkering with motors. The activities and the distribution of time would change as life proceeded; so might the work. How much they would change would depend again upon people's own choices.

Only if people were roughly equal, not just in hours and conditions of work but also in the income available to them for expenditure on the activities of leisure, would they have the same opportunities for personal autonomy under such a scheme. Suppose they did. Then, both in respect to equality in meeting needs and in respect to opportunities for personal autonomy the scheme just outlined offers a standard for assessing the performance of the business system as a whole. It is a standard that the system seems very far from fulfilling. Yet it is far from clear, in spite of the poor performance in this respect, too, of current large-scale alternative systems, that no system could be devised for meeting the standard. Moreover, in the "dynamic" of inequality, and in other respects, the business system seems to be continually, characteristically distorting the lives of its participants so that they do not make the most of whatever approximation to the standard some at least of them might enjoy.

## OBSTRUCTION OF MUTUAL AID

The term *personal autonomy* unfortunately suggests that everybody is to solve the problems of life on his or her own. Yet many of the activities of leisure, like work for most people, would be carried on jointly with other people. Inevitably, when the activities are joint ones, people help each other. Yet does it not make all the difference to people's happiness—to their satisfaction in life—in what spirit this help is offered and received?

In principle, people working under the business system are expected to offer the help only so long as it is profitable to furnish it. Rival merchants are not in business to help each other at all; if they do, it is only for so long as they are not sacrificing competitive advantages. Do they help their customers? Simmel's point about competitors seeking to discover and meet the customers' desires does not disappear when the competitors are large firms dealing ultimately with millions of customers. Even when these firms compete vigorously, however, they deal with classes of customers and with desires averaged and standardized—and to some degree shaped to suit the firms' purposes. When they do not compete vigorously, they simply watch to make sure that the other firms do not seize competitive advantages over them; and meanwhile they collect profits without worrying too much whether their services to the public could be improved—the help that they furnish increased.

Individual employees are expected to act in much the same way—to help fellow employees in a common task only so long as doing so is consistent with seizing every opportunity to advance themselves. Even unionization, though it may come in with a demonstration of solidarity, becomes not a way of helping one's fellow workers but a device for increasing one's own economic advantage—a coalition of entirely self-interested agents. That is not what Prince Kropotkin (1842–1921), a prototype at once of benevolence and anarchism, had in mind in stressing the inclination of the human heart to "mutual aid."

The activities of leisure, under the business system, are infected by the same competitiveness and all-engrossing self-interest. Consumption is competitive. People signify their achievements to others and to themselves by consuming more and consuming more expensively. They must capture, of course, the attention of other people if their self-display is to be successful. They do not intend any helpfulness by the display, however. They may well spend less time than they would under other arrangements, in a different culture, on the joint activities that call for teamwork; and in the time that they do spend, whether it is in lovemaking or sports or theatrical performances, it is their own satisfaction that preoccupies them, or their chances of moving upward and onward in careers ever more flattering to the ego.

The business system does not succeed in deforming everybody's character and outlook in these ways, on or off the job; nor is it the only system to be found among human cultures that has such effects. The Indians of the Pacific Northwest devoted themselves even more extravagantly, in their potlatches, to competitive consumption. Most people, on the job as well as off it, find some time and energy to act in the spirit of mutual aid. Business can be practiced—it is practiced, by some people—with humanity, generosity, and a continuing delight in being useful to other people. But are such people swimming against the current, or in pools and eddies out of the mainstream? Does business as a whole flow in the opposite direction?

# Suggestions for Further Reading

Essays by philosophers on ethics in business have been only sparingly represented in the present book. *Just Business*, a collection edited by Tom Regan, which Random House, New York, will be publishing in 1983, will consist of nothing but such essays. A fair number of essays by philosophers, mixed with case-material, can also be found in two pioneer textbooks both published in 1979 (Prentice-Hall, Englewood Cliffs, N.J.): Tom L. Beauchamp and Norman E. Bowie, eds., *Ethical Theory and Business*, and Thomas Donaldson and Patricia H. Werhane, eds., *Ethical Issues in Business*. Taken together, these three collections contain a substantial proportion of what philosophers in our time have so far written with specific application to business. However, two recently founded journals, *Business and Professional Ethics* and the *Journal of Business Ethics*, promise to redouble philosophical output in this field, and one may hope that they will greatly increase the variety of cases and topics treated from a philosophical standpoint.

For reflections within the world of business itself on ethics, and many specific illustrations, the lively collection edited by Thornton Bradshaw and David Vogel, *Corporations and Their Critics* (New York: McGraw-Hill, 1981) may be recommended; I have drawn on it several times in the present book. I have also drawn upon Arthur A. Leff's *Swindling and Selling* (New York: Free Press, 1976). Leff, a professor of law, gives a rich, subtle, and highly original account of social phenomena that are at the same time familiar and perplexing.

There are innumerable books offering rationales of business and the market economy; and as many, or more, offering criticisms, more or less sweeping. For an instructive and amusing account of how businessmen themselves justify the system, see Francis X. Sutton, et al., *The American Business Creed* (Cambridge: Harvard University Press, 1956). Accounts of the modern corporation and its effects on society and social life can be found in Edward S. Mason, ed., *The Corporation in Modern Society* (Cambridge: Harvard University Press, 1966) and in James S. Coleman, *Power and the Structure of Society* (New York: W. W. Norton, 1974). Both are books, again, that I have drawn upon in the present one. Coleman is particularly instructive on the difficulties that people and corporations have in intercourse with each other. On the chances of personal success in business, specifically of making a spectacular lot of money, Lester C. Thurow has some penetrating things to say in *Generating Inequality* (New York: Basic Books, 1975), as he does on jobs and the distribution of income generally. Disillusioned reactions to the overall success of business in continually stimulating and expanding consumption can be found in the eloquent title essay of Randall Jarrell's *A Sad Heart at the Supermarket* (New York: Atheneum, 1962) and in Jeremy Seabrook's study of contemporary popular culture in Britain—*What Went Wrong?* (New York: Pantheon, 1979).

The works of ethical theory—what I have called "critical ethics"—nearest in concerns and views to those invoked in the present book include the following: Kurt Baier, *The Moral Point of View,* abridged edition (New York: Random House, 1965); Bernard Gert, *The Moral Rules,* Torchbook edition (New York: Harcourt, Brace & Row, 1973); and G. J. Warnock, *The Object of Morality* (London: Methuen, 1971). John Rawls's *A Theory of Justice* (Cambridge: Harvard University Press, 1971) may daunt readers on their first coming to it by its mass and density; but readers who follow Rawls's own advice (pp. viii–ix) about how to get to the heart of his teaching can quickly acquire a working command of it both as a means of assessing business and other social institutions and as a contractarian view of the foundations of ethical theory. I myself think that the discussion of utilitarianism by many current philosophers, including Rawls, is perverse, and obstructive both to appreciating its historical significance and its present promise. Utilitarianism is best appreciated, as a phenomenon in the history of thought, in John Stuart Mill's brief book of that name (originally printed in London 1863), its most persuasive expression. A present-day account, which shows how utilitarianism has been practically effective, and promises to continue to be, can be found in the latter half of the book that I joined C. E. Lindblom in writing, *A Strategy of Decision: Policy Evaluation as a Social Process* (New York: Free Press, 1963). For Kant's contribution to ethical theory, a contribution usually—I think wrongly—held to be opposed to utilitarianism, it is best, again, to go back to the original texts. But I suggest that these writings, more than any of the others that I have mentioned, call for being studied in courses on philosophy, with the help of an instructor.

—D.B.

# Acknowledgments

Students in my class on ethics in business at Dalhousie University in three successive years helped me collect cases for this book and in discussion helped me gain some perspective on the cases. Deborah K. Smith, one of the most proficient, and certainly one of the most articulate and stimulating, students in the 1979–80 class, after her graduation acted as a research assistant collecting cases for me. Her searches in the libraries at Dalhousie were continued by Barbara Blakley and Elizabeth M. Haldane, students in the faculty of law, and by Anne E. Anderson, later a student in the 1981–82 class. Dorothy Long, a librarian at the law library, kindly advised us on how to go about the search. Walter J. Chute, of the Dalhousie chemistry department, gave me some useful advice about aerosol sprays. I owe one of the cases that I have included to Nicholas Katsepontes of the 1979–80 class, and other cases that survived all the rounds of selection, to members of the 1980–81 class: besides William M. Lahey (credited in the text with the report on bottling beer), Douglas V. Ettinger, Philip MacDonnell, Mark O'Connor, and Carmen Ann Stewart. This list may not be complete; I am chagrined to say that I did not keep sufficiently systematic records to know and I would like to hear from anybody whom I have omitted. All the members of the 1980–81 class deserve thanks for their enterprise throughout the year in collecting cases. The cases that I did not in the end include or allude to helped form my thinking about the subject; and the same is true, with appropriate thanks, for several excellent cases supplied by members of the 1979–80 class. My son-in-law, Nicholas Portman, gave me, from the point of view of an advanced student of commerce, some helpful comments on parts of the text; his wife, my daughter Elizabeth, gave me some examples of legal pleadings. Margaret Odell organized the typing and collation of the book, and herself did most of the typing; in the final stages of preparation, a substantial amount of the typing was contributed by Leslie Adamson. A number of people at Rowman & Allanheld have put friendly encouragement, expert advice, and hard work into this book. I do not know the names of all of them, but I must particularly mention Marshall Cohen (general editor of the Philosophy and Society Series), Jim Feather, Sally Held, and Janet Johnston. Sally Held persuaded me to adopt the present division into parts and chapters. I am very grateful to have had the advantages of the skill and interest rising to enthusiasm of all these people, named and unnamed.

D. B.

# *Index*